Improving

Statistical Reasoning

Theoretical Models and Practical Implications

Improving

Statistical Reasoning

Theoretical Models and Practical Implications

Peter Sedlmeier
University of Paderborn

LEA LAWRENCE ERLBAUM ASSOCIATES, PUBLISHERS
1999   Mahwah, New Jersey   London

Lawrence Erlbaum Associates, Inc., Publishers
10 Industrial Avenue
Mahwah, NJ 07430

Cover design by Kathryn Houghtaling Lacey

Library of Congress Cataloging-in-Publication Data

Sedlmeier, Peter.
Improving statistical reasoning : theoretical models and practical impli-cations / Peter Sedlmeier.
        p. cm.
Includes bibliographical references and index.
ISBN 0-8058-3282-3 (c : alk. paper)
1. Mathematical statistics. I. Title.
QA276.12.S424   1999
519.5—dc21   98-35642
                                                        CIP

10 9 8 7 6 5 4 3 2 1

Contents

Preface

Statistical literacy, the art of drawing reasonable inferences from an abundance of numbers provided daily by the media, is indispensable for an educated citizenship, as are reading and writing. Unlike reading and writing, however, sound statistical reasoning is rarely taught, and if it has been taught, it was with little success. This book presents and discusses new empirical and theoretical results about the topic of everyday statistical reasoning, that is, how people think and act on probabilistic information. It focuses on how processes of statistical reasoning work in detail and how training programs can exploit natural cognitive capabilities to improve statistical reasoning.

To date, the majority of researchers in the field of judgment and decision making still hold the opinion that in their statistical reasoning, people do not follow laws of probability theory but instead apply rules of thumb or *heuristics* that often lead to judgmental errors called *cognitive biases* or *cognitive illusions*. This opinion has been widely popularized and, indeed, is considered by many to be common knowledge. This *heuristics-and-biases* view holds that like visual illusions, cognitive illusions cannot be overridden by conscious effort or formal training. This book demonstrates and explains why both assertions, that people are generally bad at statistical reasoning and that they cannot be trained effectively, are wrong.

That statistical reasoning can in principle be improved has already been shown. However, to date, the training effects obtained were only modest in size and were not stable over time. This book shows that training procedures that rely on empirical and theoretical results from evolutionary psychology (e.g., the dependence of reasoning on the kind of external representation used) and that take into account findings from instructional theory (e.g., the necessity of learning by doing), lead to considerably greater and lasting success than found in previous training regimens.

Finally, a new perspective in statistical reasoning is offered in the form of an *associationist model*. The model is motivated by the fact that the current approaches to statistical reasoning have the weakness of not specifying the processes behind statistical judgments. In particular, none of these approaches explains how the mind acquires knowledge about relative frequencies and probabilities. Such a learning mechanism is the core of the associationist model. The model is able to simulate every type of statistical reasoning dealt with in the book. It bridges statistical reasoning and associative learning and may serve as a basis for further theoretical developments relating to the question of how people reason statistically.

In addition to the theoretically relevant results outlined above, the findings of several training studies have implications for the construction of effective tutors for statistical reasoning. Such tutors can be used to enrich statistics courses at the university level as well as in schools, and if appropriately tailored, in training regimens for specific groups of professionals who have to make decisions on the basis of statistical information (e.g., physicians). These practical implications are derived from the research approach taken in this book, namely using computer tutors to test different theories of statistical reasoning.

The book begins with an introduction to empirical and theoretical results in the field of statistical reasoning. Chapter 1 explains several basic models from probability theory that have been used to construct tests of statistical reasoning, and reviews studies examining how people solve them. Tasks dealing with conjunctive and conditional probabilities, Bayesian inference, and the impact of sample size are considered. Significance testing (along with some common misinterpretations of its result) is discussed as an example of a procedure that incorporates several of the basic models. (The continued emphasis on significance testing is criticized in Appendix C). The results of previous studies are interpreted in the light of four different theoretical approaches to statistical reasoning in chapter 2. These include the *pragmatic-implications* approach (e.g., Hilton, 1995), the *heuristics-and-biases* approach (e.g., Tversky & Kahneman, 1974), the *abstract-rules* approach (e.g., Nisbett, 1993), and the *adaptive-algorithms* approach (e.g., Cosmides & Tooby, 1996). Based on each of the approaches, predictions are then derived as to whether and how training in statistical reasoning should work. These predictions allow for the theoretical approaches to be tested against each other. The strategy of comparing the success of training regimens designed according to different theoretical approaches has apparently never before been employed to discriminate among theories. A post hoc analysis of the results of previous training studies is used to perform a preliminary evaluation of the approaches in chapter 3. The adaptive-algorithms approach cannot be evaluated at this stage because there are no prior studies with training procedures derived from this approach. The training effects found in these studies favor the abstract-rules approach, but are disappointingly small overall. Chapter 4 argues that the only modest success of previous training studies is at least partly attributable to their failure to incorporate two features, which according to instructional theory should facilitate training: learning by doing and flexible training materials (e.g., realized in a well-designed computer interface). Moreover, the importance of representational format in comparing the abstract-rules and adaptive-reasoning approaches is stressed.

Chapters 5 to 10 examine the differential effectiveness of training programs developed according to the different theoretical approaches.[1] Chapter 5 compares training on conjunctive probabilities based on the abstract-rules approach to training derived from the adaptive-algorithms approach. The effects of both regimens are very high and no difference is found due to a ceiling effect. Two training regimens on conditional probabilities, which are more complex and difficult to reason about than are conjunctive probabilities, are used to compare the two approaches in the same way in chapter 6. For conditional-probability tasks, the adaptive-algorithms approach yields better results than the abstract-rules approach, especially in the long term. Chapters 7 and 8 compare different versions of abstract-rules and adaptive-algorithms training programs on Bayesian inference. The difference in training effectiveness for Bayesian inference tasks is even more pronounced than that for conditional probability tasks, which suggests that the advantage of the adaptive-algorithms training over the abstract-rules training increases as tasks become more difficult. In chapter 8, an alternative explanation for the superiority of the adaptive-algorithms training, namely its use of graphical displays, is ruled out. Training on sample-size tasks based on the pragmatic-implications approach is put to the test in chapter 9. The beneficial effect is comparable to that of prior training procedures on sample-size tasks. Because the training dictated by the pragmatic-implications approach consists solely of linguistic disambiguation, these results indicate that some of the difficulties people had solving statistical tasks in previously published studies may have been mistakenly attributed to lack of ability. In chapter 10, a dynamic frequency representation called the virtual urn is introduced and its effectiveness in training people to solve conjunctive- and conditional-probability tasks, Bayesian tasks, and sample-size tasks is explored. Training with the virtual urn led to such high spontaneous solution rates that the virtual urn seems ideally suited for use in training people to solve notoriously difficult sample-size tasks. The usefulness of such a training program is explored in chapter 11 and it is shown to yield convincing results.

Chapter 12 summarizes the training results reported in the previous chapters and draws practical and theoretical implications. On the practical side, recommendations for the construction of effective statistical tutoring systems are given. On the theoretical side, it is argued that the results are most consistent with the adaptive-algorithms approach. However, because none of the approaches is very precise and none explains how the mind learns about relative frequencies or probabilities, a more precise and comprehensive model of statistical reasoning is called for. Chapter 13 lays the groundwork for a model of statistical reasoning based on associative learning and spells out the empirical and theoretical

---

[1] Several of the chapters draw on papers that are currently submitted for publication: Chapters 5 and 6 include portions from Sedlmeier (1998a), and chapters 7 and 8 contain parts of Sedlmeier and Gigerenzer (1998).

constraints on such a model. The model, *PASS* (*P*robability *ASS*ociator), is fully specified in chapter 14. Tests of PASS confirm that it is able to model all of the basic phenomena of statistical reasoning reported in the book. Finally, chapter 15 relates PASS to the four theoretical approaches and recommends it as a starting point for building a comprehensive computational theory of statistical reasoning. The chapter also briefly discusses social implications of the present results.

This book has greatly benefited from the help of many people. Tilmann Betsch, Hartmut Blank, Valerie M. Chase, Berna Eden, Jeanne Enders, Klaus Fiedler, Jens-Jörg Koch, Ralph Hertwig, Jürgen Locher, Frank Renkewitz, Michael Waldmann, and Manfred Wettler read several chapters each, some of them even the whole manuscript. Heartfelt thanks to them all for their very useful comments. Thanks also to Brad Pasanek and Detlef Köhlers for their help in the data collection. I acknowledge Gerd Gigerenzer's impact on my work with gratitude. I spent many fruitful years working with him, first as a student and then as an assistant and collaborator, so it is no wonder that traces of his thinking can be found throughout the book. I am also particularly grateful to Manfred Wettler, who generously provided me with everything I needed, material and otherwise, including long discussions about associative learning and other interesting topics, to complete this book. Financial support by the Alexander-von-Humboldt foundation and the German Science foundation (DFG) is greatfully acknowledged. Last but not least, I would like to thank Valerie M. Chase and Anita Todd for helping me to transform my German English into real English, and the staff of Lawrence Erlbaum Associates for their professional assistance during all stages of the editorial process.

1

Statistical Reasoning: How Good Are We?

SUMMARY: An influential line of research about *judgment under uncertainty*, the process of making judgments in uncertain conditions, suggests that people cannot avoid making reasoning fallacies. Because it has been claimed that these fallacies might have severe consequences for people in daily life, this research has attracted much attention outside of the field. This chapter reviews the evidence. Research about statistical reasoning commonly starts with a normative model against which people's answers are evaluated and with a text problem that corresponds to this model. The three models most often used in this research are equations or inequalities that describe conjunctive probabilities, conditional probabilities, and Bayesian inference. A fourth model refers to the impact of sample size. Representative research relating to these four models is described in this chapter. Moreover, common misunderstandings in the interpretation of the results of significance tests, which rely on conditional probability judgments, and whose results are highly sensitive to sample size, are addressed. Although there is an abundance of research demonstrating so-called reasoning fallacies, thorough analysis affords a more complex picture of human reasoning.

Statistical reasoning, sometimes called judgment under uncertainty, has received a great deal of attention in academic circles and in the media since Kahneman and Tversky's seminal work on the subject in the early 1970s (e.g., Tversky & Kahneman, 1974). What is the reason for this unusually strong interest in psychological research results? Perhaps the interest is because the conclusions drawn have been serious: Human minds "are not built (for whatever reason) to work by the rules of probability" (Gould, 1992, p. 469). Instead, we poor "saps" and "suckers" often "stumble along ill-chosen shortcuts to reach bad conclusions" (McCormick, 1987, p. 24). In more scientific terms, people apply heuristics that lead them to biases or cognitive illusions that might have severe consequences for judgments and decisions (e.g., Arkes & Hammond, 1986; Kahneman, Slovic, & Tversky, 1982). The problem is viewed as a general one: "Quite without distinction, politicians, generals, surgeons, and economists as much as vendors of salami and ditchdiggers are all, without being aware of it, and even when they are in the best of humors and while exercising their professions, subject to a myriad of such illusions" (Piattelli-Palmarini, 1994, p. x).

How do we know when people's judgments are indeed in error? In much research in this area, there is assumed to be only one correct way to solve a problem, which is derived from logic, probability theory, or statistics (e.g., Kahneman & Tversky, 1982). Usually, researchers have a model in mind according to which they construct a task. This model is normative because it specifies the correct answer. If participants' answers do not conform to this model, the participants are assumed to have committed reasoning errors. A model can be as simple as the rule that the occurrence of a conjunction of two events is at most as likely as the occurrence of one of the events.

Before this book more closely examines these models and their corresponding tasks, let us return to the sweeping conclusion that we are all poor probabilists—can this be right? This conclusion is certainly wrong in its generality. Christensen-Szalanski and Beach (1984) reviewed a large body of studies about decision making, judgment, and problem solving in the period between 1972 and 1981, in which the performance of participants was compared to some normative model derived from probability theory. They found that about 44% of all studies reported results that reflected positively on human reasoning. These studies, however, were only cited 4.7 times on average in the sampled period, whereas those that put human reasoning in a bad light were cited an average of 27.8 times in the same period. Lopes (1991) attributes this citation bias to the rhetoric associated with the heuristics-and-biases literature and to secondary gains to authors outside psychology (e.g., sociology, political science, law, economics, business, and anthropology) who evoke interest and attention by relating bias problems to substantive issues in their own fields. Indeed, it appears to be more interesting to demonstrate errors than good judgment, which might be obvious or uninteresting. Imagine giving friends or students some tasks to solve and finding that all are able to solve them easily. This result would probably not provoke a lively discussion. However, if people give solutions that they later accept (or do not accept) as wrong, interest in the topic is likely to be high.

Let us assume (until the end of this chapter) that there is only one normative *model*, meaning rule or principle, for the solution to every task described in the following section, against which people's solutions can be compared. In this book, we will consider the four models which are probably the most commonly used in the literature about judgment under uncertainty. They specify how conjunctive and conditional probabilities should be treated, how probabilities should be revised given new information (Bayesian inference), and how the size of a sample should influence one's confidence in the mean or proportion of that sample. This chapter discusses text problems that elicit both poor and good solutions according to each model.[1]

CONJUNCTIVE PROBABILITIES

Consider two events: You receive a rise in salary (A) and you fall in love (B). The probability that both events occur, that is, that you receive a rise in salary and fall in love (A & B) in a given period, cannot exceed the probability of either event during the same period. More formally,

$$p(A \& B) \leq p(A)$$
and
$$p(A \& B) \leq p(B).$$

This model is often referred to as the *conjunction rule*. Ample research, stimulated by an article by Tversky and Kahneman (1983), has shown that people reliably often disobey the conjunction rule, a violation typically referred to as the *conjunction fallacy*. The best known example of a *conjunction task* is the Linda task (Tversky & Kahneman, 1983). In its simplest form, it reads:

> Linda is 31 years old, single, outspoken, and very bright. She majored in philosophy. As a student, she was deeply concerned with issues of discrimination and social justice, and also participated in anti-nuclear demonstrations.
> Please indicate which of the two following statements is more likely:
> Linda is a bank teller.
> Linda is a bank teller and is active in the feminist movement. (p. 299)

The probability of a conjunctive event (e.g., being a bank teller and in the feminist movement) is commonly judged by a vast majority of participants to be more likely than the probability of a component event (e.g., bank teller), which is a violation of the conjunction rule.

Frequency Format Versus Probability Format

Now let us change the question slightly without changing the description of Linda:

> Imagine women who fit the description of Linda.
> How many of these women are bank tellers?
> How many of these women are bank tellers and active in the feminist movement?

---

[1]This will not be a comprehensive overview of the results obtained in studies on statistical reasoning. However, the examples given can be regarded as a representative sample.

In about 80% to 90% of all cases, participants now adhere to the conjunction rule, as compared to the 10% to 30% usually observed for the first version (Fiedler, 1988; Hertwig, 1995; Tversky & Kahneman, 1983). Even children are able to solve conjunction tasks if the problem information is given in terms of frequencies. Inhelder and Piaget (1959/1964) used pictures showing objects (e.g., yellow primulas and primulas of other colors) that could be brought into inclusion relations (e.g., yellow primulas are included in primulas, which in turn are included in flowers). Most 8-year-olds recognized that conjunctive sets (e.g., flowers that are both yellow and primulas) cannot be more numerous than component sets (e.g., primulas). Why do the results differ when tasks are formulated in terms of frequencies versus probabilities? There are at least two explanations for this effect. One rests on the difference between natural language and the language of probability. For instance, in natural language, many intended meanings are not stated explicitly, but can be easily inferred from the context. In an everyday conversation, and in the context of Linda's personality description, the statement "Linda is a bank teller" can be understood as "Linda is a bank teller but not a feminist." This inference may be blocked by a frequency formulation (see chapter 2). The other explanation for this startling effect rests on the observation that over millennia, the human mind was exposed to raw frequencies and not to single-event probabilities. Therefore, evolution tuned cognitive algorithms to *frequency formats*, wherein numerical information is expressed in terms of frequencies (as in the second version of the Linda task), and not to *probability formats,* wherein numerical information is expressed in the form of single-event probabilities or percentages (as in the first version of the Linda task). These explanations are discussed in more detail in the next chapter.

Other Influential Factors

Researchers have examined several other differences in task formulation that are hypothesized to influence the solution of conjunctive probability tasks. None of the factors examined to date has produced an effect as large as the frequency–probability distinction. For instance, Thüring and Jungermann (1990) varied the perceived strength of the causal relation between the two components of a conjunctive event to examine the hypothesis that the strength of the causal link determines the extent of bias in the probability judgment. In their tasks, two diseases (K1 and K2) were either causally related (e.g., K1 causes K2 as a side effect) or not. The strength of the causal link did not influence adherence to the conjunction rule. Similarly, Yates and Carlson (1986) found that it apparently does not make a difference whether two events involve a common process (e.g., Linda looks up and Linda scratches her ear) or distinct processes (e.g., Linda looks up and the girl next door scratches her ear).

In summary, people appear to easily solve conjunction tasks formulated in terms of frequencies, but often do not follow the conjunction rule when the representational format is probabilities or percentages. Conjunction tasks have been examined in a great number of studies (for an overview see Hertwig, 1995; Hertwig & Chase, 1998), but surprisingly, the design of these tasks has not changed since Tversky and Kahneman introduced it in 1983. Next, we will deal with conditional-probability tasks, which, in contrast, are less well examined.

CONDITIONAL PROBABILITIES

Conditional-probability tasks can be tricky. Try to solve the following one (Bar-Hillel & Falk, 1982):

> THREE CARDS
> Three cards are in a hat. One is red on both sides, denoted RR. One is white on both sides, denoted WW. One is red on one side and white on the other, denoted RW. We draw one card blindly and put it on the table. It shows a *Red* face *up*, denoted R_u. What is the probability that the hidden side is also red? (p. 119)

If you came up with a probability of 1/2, you opted with the majority of the students in Bar-Hillel and Falk's study (1982). One way to come to that solution might be as follows: The card cannot be WW, so there remain two possibilities, RR and RW. Because the card is randomly drawn, the chances that it is either of these two cards is 1/2. By now you might sense that this solution is not quite right.

Before we discuss the solution to the three-card task, let us introduce the model for reasoning about conditional probabilities and illustrate it with a less difficult example. This model is more complex than the conjunction rule because it contains that rule as a part. A conditional probability can be obtained by dividing a conjunctive probability by the appropriate component probability. More formally:

$$p(A \mid B) = p(A \& B) / p(B)$$
$$\text{and}$$
$$p(B \mid A) = p(A \& B) / p(A).$$

Let us illustrate that model with an easy task (Pollatsek, Well, Konold, Hardiman, & Cobb, 1987):

> FEVER AND SICKNESS
> In which prediction would you have the greatest confidence?
> (a) Predicting that a person who has a fever is sick.
> (b) Predicting that a person who is sick has a fever.
> (c) Equal confidence in both predictions. (p. 258)

Let A denote that a person is sick and B that this same person has a fever. Now (a) can be expressed as $p(A \mid B)$, the probability of a person being sick if she has fever. The calculations for the conditional probabilities corresponding to (a) and (b) only differ in whether $p(A \& B)$, the probability of the conjunctive event (sick and has fever) has to be divided by $p(A)$, the probability of sickness or $p(B)$, the probability of fever. It seems reasonable to assume that the probability that a person has a fever is smaller than the probability that the person is sick. Therefore, (a) is more probable than (b) (because division by a small number gives a larger result than division by a large number).

One might think: "What do I need this lengthy explanation for? I knew the solution right away." The advantage of this model is that it also helps one in solving more difficult tasks. Let us return to the three-card task. What do we have to calculate? We need $p(RR \mid R_u)$, the probability that we got the card that is red on both sides if it is red on the side facing up. To begin with, what is the probability of R_u, that is, the probability that the side facing up is red? Here, this probability is 1 because we know it with certainty. Therefore, the conjunctive probability $p(RR \& R_u)$ is equal to the sought-for conditional probability, which is 2/3. Why? Because in two out of three cases, a randomly drawn red face belongs to an RR card and in one of the three cases the red face belongs to an RW card. For further discussion and more difficult examples, consult Bar-Hillel and Falk (1982) or Tversky and Kahneman (1977).

Anecdotal evidence (e.g., Dawes, 1988) suggests that people also experience problems with everyday conditional-probability tasks that include more contextual information than the three-card problem, and which require free responses. The Bavarian police task (Sedlmeier, 1993, original in German) is such a free-response task and is based on a real occurrence:

> BAVARIAN POLICE
> Some years ago, the Bavarian police concluded in a statistical survey that 60% of heroin addicts had smoked marijuana before they became heroin addicted. The Bavarian secretary of state regarded this as proof that marijuana is an entrance drug. If somebody smokes marijuana, he argued, he or she will later on end up (with a probability of about 60%) being a heroin addict.
> What do you think about this conclusion—is the Bavarian secretary of state right? (Why or why not?) (pp. 129-130).

What conditional probability can the secretary of state extract from the statistics? He is provided with $p(\text{marijuana} \mid \text{heroin})$, the probability of having smoked marijuana, given heroin addiction. However, he needs $p(\text{heroin} \mid \text{marijuana})$, the probability of heroin addiction given prior smoking of marijuana. Given the very discrepant *base rates* of the two events, that is, the large difference between $p(\text{marijuana})$ and $p(\text{heroin})$, his conclusion is not warranted. One immediately recognizes the error in his reasoning if one imagines replacing $p(\text{marijuana} \mid \text{heroin})$, the conditional probability given in the task, by the even higher

p(chocolate I heroin), the probability of chocolate consumption given heroin addiction. Although all heroin addicts have probably consumed chocolate, that is, p(chocolate I heroin) = 1, the Bavarian secretary would never have claimed that chocolate is an entrance drug to heroin.

Compared to the many studies about conjunctive-probability tasks, conditional-probability tasks have not been studied very systematically. In his review of research about probability and statistics, Shaughnessy concluded: "Although there has been a lot written about misconceptions of conditional probabilities, there is almost no actual empirical research reported on students' beliefs and intuitions that deals specifically with conditional probabilities" (1992, p. 474). In the few studies that have been completed, there are wide variations in the solution rates found. For instance, whereas the fever and sickness task described previously was solved correctly by 87% of Pollatsek et al.'s (1987) participants, performance on formally equivalent tasks used in the same study ranged from this value down to about 25%. It is not clear yet what accounts for this huge variability. Conditional-probability tasks, especially in the short format used in the fever and sickness task, seem to be prone to misunderstandings (Pollatsek et al., 1987). They also seem to be influenced by whether one event is regarded as the cause of the other. Consider the following task (Tversky & Kahneman, 1982):

> In a survey of high-school seniors in a city, the height of boys was compared to the height of their fathers. In which prediction would you have greater confidence?
> (a) The prediction of the father's height from the son's height.
> (b) The prediction of the son's height from the father's height.
> (-) Equal confidence. (p. 119)

If one assumes the distribution of heights to be the same in successive generations, then one should have equal confidence in both predictions, which 46% of participants did have in Tversky and Kahneman's (1982) study. But 41% still chose (b) because, according to Tversky and Kahneman, they saw a causal connection from father's to son's height, but not the reverse.

In summary, we are presented with a mixed picture. Regarding the large effects of frequency format in the conjunction tasks, one might expect similar effects for conditional-probability tasks. However, the relevant studies have not yet been completed. Most people cannot solve brain teasers dealing with conditional probabilities. In other tasks, the solution rates seem to depend on both the context and the wording. For more richly formulated tasks, anecdotal evidence indicates that people do indeed have difficulty solving conditional-probability tasks when their performances are evaluated against the normative model (see also paragraph about the ritual of significance testing below).

Next, we will consider a special kind of conditional-probability task, so-called *probability-revision* or *Bayesian* tasks, in which a prior probability is revised in light of new information. This kind of task has been extensively studied.

BAYESIAN INFERENCE

One of the best known Bayesian tasks is the mammography task (adapted from Casscells, Schoenberger, & Grayboys, 1978; Eddy, 1982).[2]

> MAMMOGRAPHY
> A reporter for a women's monthly magazine would like to write an article about breast cancer. As a part of her research, she focuses on mammography as an indicator of breast cancer. She wonders what it really means if a woman tests positive for breast cancer during her routine mammography examination. She has the following data:
> The probability that a woman who undergoes a mammography will have breast cancer is 1%.
> If a woman undergoing a mammography has breast cancer, the probability that she will test positive is 80%.
> If a woman undergoing a mammography does not have breast cancer, the probability that she will test positive is 10%.
> What is the probability that a woman who has undergone a mammography actually has breast cancer, if she tests positive?

How can we figure out that probability? We must revise the a priori probability that a woman who undergoes a mammography has breast cancer, p(cancer), which according to the text is 1% or $p=.01$, in light of the new information that the test was positive. That is, we are looking for the conditional probability

---

[2]Probably the best known Bayesian task for which a solution has been publicly discussed for several years now originated from a game show on American television (*Let's Make a Deal*) and is widely known as the Monty Hall problem, named after the host (for a collection of Internet sites that discuss the task and possible solutions, consult this address: *http://math.rice.edu/~ddonovan/montyurl.html*). A version of the task is as follows: A contestant in the show is faced with three doors. She knows that behind one door there is a desirable prize (e.g., a fancy car) and behind the other two there are undesirable items (e.g., a goat). The contestant picks a door and Monty Hall says, "I will now reveal to you what is behind one of the other doors." One door is opened and there is a goat behind it (Monty only opens doors with a goat behind them). Then Monty says "Would you like to change your door selection?" (e.g., Krantz 1997). This task can be solved by applying Bayes' theorem (see the above Internet sites, or von Randow, 1992, for a thorough discussion, including some problematic issues) but a more straightforward solution that illustrates the value of good external representations is as follows: There are six possibilities of how two goats (G1 and G2) and a car (C) can be distributed behind the three doors. Behind Doors 1, 2, and 3, respectively, there can be (G1, G2, C), (G2, G1, C), (G1, C, G2), (G2, C, G1), (C, G1, G2), and (C, G2, G1). Now assume for simplicity that the contestant always selects Door 3 (the same argument holds for any door). In the first two of the six possible distributions (i.e., when the car is behind Door 3), switching is not to the contestant's advantage, but in the four remaining cases it is clearly advantageous to switch because one goat is behind Door 3 and the other door that covers a goat is identified by Monty Hall. Therefore, switching is advantageous in four of six possible cases, or, in other words, the (a posteriori) probability of picking the right door after switching is 2/3 and thus higher than the a priori probability of picking the right door without switching, which is 1/3.

p(cancer | positive). The probability of a positive result given breast cancer, p(positive | cancer), is 80% or $p=.8$, and the probability of a positive result given no breast cancer, p(positive | no cancer), is 10% or $p=.1$. Bayes' theorem provides a model for solving this task. A simple version looks like this:[3]

$$p(A \mid B) = \frac{p(A)p(B \mid A)}{p(A)p(B \mid A) + p(\neg A)p(B \mid \neg A)}$$

Now let A stand for cancer and B for positive and we obtain:

p(cancer | positive) = 0.01 x 0.80 / (0.01 x 0.80 + 0.99 x 0.10) = 0.075.

The vast majority of people presented with this (and similar) tasks vastly overestimated the probability that the woman who tested positive actually had breast cancer (e.g., Casscells et al., 1978; Cosmides & Tooby, 1996; Gigerenzer & Hoffrage, 1995). In a study by Eddy (1982), for instance, 95 out of 100 physicians given numerical information nearly identical to this estimated the probability p(cancer | positive) to be 70% to 80%, which is about 10 times the Bayesian solution of 7.5%. A recent study in which physicians had to solve Bayesian tasks involving medical diagnoses revealed similar results (Gigerenzer, 1996a; Hoffrage & Gigerenzer, 1998). Participants seem to ignore the vast difference in base rates, that is, the difference between the number of women who do and do

---

[3]There is no mystery involved in deriving Bayes' formula, which is apparently not named after its inventor, like many other famous scientific insights (see Stigler, 1983). The starting point for the derivation is the definition of conditional probabilities:

$$p(A \mid B) = p(A \& B) / p(B) \tag{1}$$

and

$$p(B \mid A) = p(A \& B) / p(A). \tag{2}$$

Dividing Equation 1 by Equation 2 results in

$$p(A \mid B) / p(B \mid A) = p(A) / p(B) \tag{3}$$

and if we solve for $p(A \mid B)$ we obtain

$$p(A \mid B) = \frac{p(A)p(B \mid A)}{p(B)}. \tag{4}$$

This does not look exactly like the same formula. However, $p(B)$ can be divided into that part which it holds in common with $p(A)$: $p(A)p(B \mid A)$ and that which it does not ($\neg$) hold in common: $p(\neg A)p(B \mid \neg A)$. Splitting up $p(B)$ into these two components finally results in the above form of Bayes' theorem:

$$p(A \mid B) = \frac{p(A)p(B \mid A)}{p(A)p(B \mid A) + p(\neg A)p(B \mid \neg A)}. \tag{5}$$

not have breast cancer, apparently committing what has been termed the *base-rate fallacy* (e.g., Bar-Hillel, 1983).

Frequency Format Versus Probability Format

Remember the effect of replacing the probability format with a frequency format in conjunction tasks? A similar manipulation has been made in Bayesian tasks. Gigerenzer and Hoffrage (1995) presented one group of participants with 20 Bayesian tasks in a probability format, that is, with all numerical information stated in percentages as in the mammography task. On average, only 16% of their solutions coincided with the Bayesian solution. Another group received the same tasks in a frequency format. Here is a frequency version of the mammography task (adapted from Gigerenzer & Hoffrage, 1995, p. 688):

> MAMMOGRAPHY: FREQUENCY FORMAT
> A reporter for a women's monthly magazine intends to write an article about breast cancer. As a part of her research, she looks into mammography tests, which are used to diagnose breast cancer. She is interested in the question of what it means if a woman tests positive for breast cancer. She finds the following data:
> 10 out of every 1,000 women who undergo a mammography have breast cancer.
> 8 out of every 10 women with breast cancer who undergo a mammography will test positive.
> 99 out of every 990 women who do not have breast cancer will test positive.

This frequency format yielded a solution rate about three times higher than the probability format. Cosmides and Tooby (1996) conducted a series of studies in which they gradually changed the presentation of the mammography task from a pure probability format to a pure frequency format enhanced by a pictorial grid representation in which every woman was represented by a square in a grid. Solution rates covaried with degree of format change, reaching a high of 92% correct answers in the enhanced frequency format compared to 12% in the pure probability format. Similar results were obtained by Betsch, Biel, Eddelbüttel, and Mock (1998).

Random Sampling

Bayes' theorem assumes that data used in the calculation are randomly sampled. If this were not the case, for instance, if the probability of breast cancer were calculated from women over 45 but was used to calculate p(cancer | positive) for women of all ages, the formula would give misleading results. Random sampling is usually tacitly assumed in probability tasks, but sometimes it is also explicitly mentioned, as in the following task (Kahneman & Tversky, 1973):

ENGINEER-LAWYER

A panel of psychologists have interviewed and administered personality tests to 30 engineers and 70 lawyers, all successful in their respective fields. On the basis of this information, thumbnail descriptions of the 30 engineers and 70 lawyers have been written. You will find on your forms five descriptions, chosen at random from the 100 available descriptions. For each description, please indicate your probability that the person described is an engineer, on a scale from 1 to 100.

The same task has been performed by a panel of experts, who were highly accurate in assigning probabilities to the various descriptions. You will be paid a bonus to the extent that your estimates come close to those of the expert panel. (p. 241)

In Kahneman and Tversky's (1973) study, there were two groups of participants, one of which was given this text. The base rates, that is, the percentages of engineers and lawyers, were reversed for the second group of participants. One of the personality descriptions was the following:

DICK

Dick is a 30-year-old man. He is married with no children. A man of high ability and high motivations, he promises to be quite successful in his field. He is well liked by his colleagues. (p. 242)

The description of Dick was thought to be totally uninformative with respect to whether he was an engineer or a lawyer. In fact, the median judged probability of Dick being an engineer was 50% in both groups. Participants apparently seemed to completely neglect the base rates and only appreciated that the personality description was uninformative. Gigerenzer, Hell, and Blank (1988) replicated this finding in one condition and added a condition in which the randomness of the description sampling was observable. In this condition the experimenter showed each participant 10 sheets of paper. On one side, 3 (or 7, depending on the base-rate condition) of the 10 sheets were marked with an E for engineer and 7 (or 3) were marked with an L for lawyer. The personality description appeared on the other side of each sheet, which the participant could not see. The experimenter then folded the sheets, put them into an empty urn and shook the urn. The participant drew one sheet and gave it (still folded) to the experimenter, who read the description aloud (without showing the marked side of the sheet). After the drawing, the participant was asked to judge the probability that the man described was an engineer. This procedure was repeated with several urns. Unbeknownst to the participants, all descriptions in each urn were identical. In this condition, participants' judgments corresponded much more closely to the Bayesian solution; that is, the base rates were taken into account to a much greater extent than if random sampling had only been mentioned in the text rather than physically demonstrated (see Appendix A for the normative Bayesian solution).

Other Influential Factors

In a recent review of studies about Bayesian inference, J. J. Koehler (1996) identified several factors that directed participants' attention to base rates. Apart from manipulations that evoke a frequentist representation (e.g., directly experiencing base rates), participants' estimates were influenced by whether they considered the base rates to be relevant and reliable. For instance, when the description clearly referred to a lawyer in the engineer–lawyer task (see above), Ginossar and Trope (1980) found that base rates were given less weight than when the description was less diagnostic of a lawyer or engineer and therefore less relevant. A later study of theirs (Ginossar & Trope, 1987, Exp. 5) also illustrates the impact of source reliability. Participants were told that the personality descriptions were written either by a group of trained psychologists, a student, or a palm reader. Base rates influenced probability judgments, depending upon who was believed to be the source of information: least when the group of psychologists, more when the student, and most when the palm reader was viewed as the source.

Before Heuristics And Biases: Conservatism Reigned

Research about whether people reason according to Bayes' theorem started long before researchers thought about heuristics and biases, in the year 1962, according to Edwards (1982). A typical pre-heuristics-and-biases task read like this:

> BOOKBAG AND POKER CHIPS
> This bookbag contains 1,000 poker chips. I started out with two such bags, one containing 700 red and 300 blue chips, the other containing 300 red and 700 blue. I flipped a fair coin to determine which one to use. Thus, if your opinions are like mine, your probability at the moment that this is the predominantly red bookbag is 0.5. Now, you sample, randomly, with replacement after each chip. In 12 samples, you get 8 reds and 4 blues. Now, on the basis of everything you know, what is the probability that this is the predominantly red bag? Clearly it is higher than 0.5. (p. 361)

Initially, Edwards and his collaborators had not tested "simple" tasks such as the bookbag-and-poker-chips task, but tested tasks containing many possible observations (e.g., different numbers of samples) and hypotheses (e.g., more than two urns). Their main result was, however, always the same. Participants did take account of both base rates and new information, although the impact of the information on their judgments was weak compared to its impact on the normative Bayesian solution. That is, participants were overwhelmingly conservative in their use of individuating information relative to base rates. For instance, in the bookbag-and-poker-chips task, the normative Bayesian solution is .97, whereas typical responses range from .7 to .8 (see Appendix A for a detailed description of the normative solution).

To summarize, it seems unjustified to claim that there is a genuine base-rate fallacy. Instead, base-rate use seems to vary along a continuum. Good conditions for taking base rates into account are frequentistic representations, hands-on experience of random sampling, and realistic scenarios. Even under these conditions, base rates are sometimes not used to the extent they should be. If the previously mentioned conditions are not met, then use of base rates seems to deteriorate.

IMPACT OF SAMPLE SIZE

The three models in the preceding paragraphs are straightforward to apply. Once the numbers are filled in, the solution is clear. These models are also related because the model for a conditional probability includes the definition of a conjunctive probability, and Bayes' theorem includes the definition of a conditional probability. The model for influences of sample size on probability judgments is different. Let us first look at an example of a sample-size task (Bar-Hillel, 1979):

OPINION POLL
Two pollsters are conducting a survey to estimate the proportion of voters who intend to vote YES on a certain referendum. Firm A is surveying a sample of 400 individuals. Firm B is surveying a sample of 1,000 individuals. Whose estimate would you be more confident in accepting?
Firm A's
Firm B's
About the same   (p. 249)

If you decide for Firm B, you go with 79% of Bar-Hillel's participants, which would be a reasonable decision unless you had additional information. What is the formal justification for choosing this alternative?

The Normative Model

Most of the numerous articles describing people's performances on sample-size tasks claim that the normative model that applies is the *law of large numbers*. In its most common version, the law of large numbers looks like this (e.g., Scheaffer, 1990):

$$\lim_{n \to \infty} P\left(\left| \frac{1}{n} \sum_{i=1}^{n} X_i - \mu \right| \geq \varepsilon \right) = 0.$$

What does this equation tell us? First, look at the difference inside the vertical bars (the absolute value of this difference). The left part of the difference is the empirically determined mean, and the right part, μ, is the real mean in the population. For instance, if in the opinion poll example above, YES is coded as 1 and NO as 0,[4] the mean in the whole population of voters can be calculated obtaining a value for μ, and if the same is done for only one sample, the value for the left expression of the difference is obtained. The law of large numbers states that as the sample size (n) approaches infinity (∞), the probability that the (absolute) difference between the empirical and the real mean is larger than or equal to an arbitrarily small number (ε) approaches 0.[5]

The law of large numbers does not provide a normative solution for the opinion-poll task, however. It does not state that the difference between the empirical and the real mean becomes increasingly smaller (i.e., that the empirical mean is an increasingly good estimator of the real mean) as sample size increases. It only refers to the limiting case where n approaches infinity, and therefore leaves room for the possibility that larger samples may lead to worse estimates of the mean than do smaller ones. Thus, unfortunately, the law of large numbers is not a good model for sample-size tasks.

At the risk of disappointing the reader, it must be said that one cannot categorically exclude the possibility that a larger sample leads to a worse prediction than a smaller one, although the probability that it does can be estimated given certain conditions. Appendix B shows several models in probability theory that can serve as partial justifications for why one should have more confidence in estimates of means or proportions based on large, rather than small, samples over the whole range of sample sizes. For most purposes in daily life, however, we can rely on an empirically demonstrable phenomenon, the *empirical law of large numbers*.

The Empirical Law of Large Numbers

What is the empirical law of large numbers? Before the first law of large numbers was formulated by Bernoulli, there existed a "prehistoric" version of the law. As Daston (1988) observed:

> Gerolamo Cardano, Edmund Halley, and the author of the last chapters of the Port Royal *Logique*, had appealed to the principle that there was an approximate fit between observed frequencies and 'true' probabilities which improved as the number of observations increased. (p. 234)

This intuition—that larger samples generally give more accurate estimates of population means—is commonly referred to as the empirical law of large num-

---

[4]This example shows that proportions are just a special case of means. Instead of counting all the YES responses and dividing them by the total number of responses, one can just calculate the mean of 1s and 0s and arrive at the identical result (for an extended example, see Freedman, Pisani, Purves, & Adhikari, 1991, pp. 275–277).

[5]Strictly speaking, the law of large numbers applies only to potentially infinite populations as can, for instance, be produced by sampling balls from an urn with replacement.

bers (e.g., Freudenthal, 1972) or the law of averages (e.g., Freedman et al., 1991, p. 247). The empirical law of large numbers is a commonsense intuition and not a mathematical theorem as is the (mathematical) law of large numbers. Note that the empirical law of large numbers says only that a larger sample is better than a smaller sample for estimating a population parameter.

Now we have a model for sample-size tasks that is not as clean as the other models, but is empirically observable and is partially supported by several more formal models (see Appendix B). The results in the opinion-poll task discussed previously suggest that people have an intuition conforming to the empirical law of large numbers. This intuition seems to be limited in its actual application by participants, however, to a subset of the sample-size tasks reported in the literature. Sedlmeier and Gigerenzer (1997) analyzed the published research about people's use of sample-size information and concluded that there are actually two different kinds of tasks, *frequency-distribution* and *sampling-distribution* tasks,[6] and that the intuition conforming to the empirical law of large numbers— henceforth called the *size–confidence intuition*—applies only to the former.

Easy and Not So Easy: Frequency- Versus Sampling-Distribution Tasks

Consider the following—probably most well-known—sample-size task from Kahneman and Tversky (1972):

MATERNITY WARD
A certain town is served by two hospitals. In the larger hospital about 45 babies are born each day, and in the smaller hospital about 15 babies are born each day. As you know, about 50% of all babies are boys. The exact percentage of baby boys, however, varies from day to day. Sometimes it may be higher than 50%, sometimes lower.
Sampling-distribution version
For a period of 1 year, each hospital recorded the days on which more than 60% of the babies born were boys. Which hospital do you think recorded more such days?
The larger hospital
The smaller hospital
About the same (i.e., within 5% of each other). (p. 443)

There are three choices for a response, larger hospital, smaller hospital and about the same. Now, how can the size–confidence intuition be used to solve this task? The answer is that it cannot, at least not in a straightforward way. If there are two samples, the intuition results in higher confidence for the mean calculated

---

[6]In hindsight, this nomenclature was not ideal. The distinction between frequency- and sampling-distribution tasks is not the same as that between frequency and probability formats as the labels might imply. Both frequency- and sampling-distribution tasks involve some kinds of frequencies. They differ only in the kind of distribution involved, distributions of scores versus distributions of aggregate values.

from the larger sample. However, we have many samples for each of the two hospitals, one for each of the 365 days in a year. The proportions of boys calculated from these samples form (empirical) sampling distributions. This is why we called this kind of task sampling-distribution task. One could, of course, apply the size–confidence intuition to each individual day, but this seems not to be what people commonly do. The solution rates for this kind of task (i.e., the percentage of participants who correctly chose smaller hospital) typically fall in the range from 20% to 40%, which is about what one would expect if people chose randomly among the three response alternatives.

What would happen if instead of two sampling distributions the maternity-ward task only involved two samples (like the opinion poll task), that is, the births in the larger and in the smaller hospital on one day? In that case, the second part would read like this: "Which hospital do you think is more likely to find on one day that more than 60% of the babies born were boys?" Now we have only two samples, but each sample again consists of a *frequency distribution*, which gives the frequency of persons or items falling into a particular category. From such a distribution one can calculate means and proportions. This is why we called such tasks *frequency-distribution tasks.*[7] If the size-confidence intuition helps in solving such frequency-distribution tasks, then people should be remarkably better at solving them than sampling-distribution tasks. This is what we found in the literature analysis of studies that did not directly address this issue, and in independent studies as well (Sedlmeier, 1998b). Figure 1.1 compares the solution rates for frequency- and sampling-distribution tasks reported in the literature in which the choice was among three response alternatives.

Figure 1.1 shows the percentages of participants who made the correct choices for frequency-distribution tasks (left side) and sampling-distribution tasks (right side) in the form of *a stem-and-leaf plot.* The *stem* (the central, vertical part of Fig. 1.1) represents multiples of 10 and the *leaves* represent units of the percentage of correct choices. For sampling-distribution tasks, the percentage of correct choices ranges from 7% to 59%, while for frequency-distribution tasks, the range is from 54% to 87%. The medians are 33.5% and 73%, respectively, and there is not much overlap between the two distributions. Note that the median percentage of correct answers for the sampling-distribution tasks is nearly what one would expect by chance, that is, if participants had randomly picked one of the three alternatives.

---

[7]In the maternity-ward task, we only have two categories, boys and girls. The frequency distribution is simply the number of children falling into the boy and the girl category. Again, one can easily see that proportions are just special cases of means. If boys are coded 1 and girls 0, the mean of all babies gives the proportion of boys. In many distributions, there are more categories than two, for instance, the distributions of body size.

```
              0 │ 7,8
              1 │ 3,9
              2 │ 0,1,3,7,8,9
              3 │ 0,1,1,2,3,3,4,7,9
              4 │ 1,2,2,3,3,3,5,5,8
        6,4   5 │ 4,5,8,9
          7   6 │
  9,7,5,3,3   7 │
          7   8 │
```

Frequency   Sampling
distribution   distribution
tasks   tasks

FIG. 1.1. Stem-and-leaf plot of percentages of participants taking sample size into account in multiple-choice studies. Results are shown separately for frequency-distribution
tasks (left leaves, $N = 9$ studies) and sampling-distribution tasks (right leaves, $N = 32$ studies). The stem represents multiples of ten, and the leaves represent the units place. For in-
stance, the top row of the diagram "| 0 | 7, 8" represents two studies (sampling-distribution
tasks) in which 7% and 8% of participants took sample size into account, respectively. The
studies shown are drawn from Exhibit 1 in Sedlmeier and Gigerenzer (1997) and from
Sedlmeier (1998b).

The distinction between sampling- and frequency-distribution tasks accounts
for most of the differences in studies that used multiple-choice tasks. Does it apply to other kinds of tasks?

Other Tasks

In the 1950s, Piaget and Inhelder (1951/1975) examined whether children are
sensitive to the influence of sample size on the quality of sample estimates. For
instance, in one of their studies (p. 49 ff.), they simulated raindrops (or hail-
stones) falling on square tiles by sifting small glass beads through a sieve onto a
sheet of paper with tiles drawn on it. The children were asked to predict where
the successive drops would fall and how their distribution would be affected by
an increasing number of drops. Children aged 11 or 12 years of age showed a full
understanding of the fact that the proportion of raindrops falling on two tiles
converges on the same value as the number of drops increases. In several other
tasks, Piaget and Inhelder found a similar sensitivity to sample size for the same
age group. All of these tasks were frequency-distribution tasks.

Apart from Piaget and Inhelder's studies, we identified 35 studies involving
frequency distributions, in 31 of which people were found to be sensitive to the
impact of sample size (Sedlmeier & Gigerenzer, 1997). Many of these studies

involved chance devices such as cards, poker chips, or Galton boards. Other tasks involved explicit   numerical information and more everyday questions. For instance, Levin (1974) asked college students to indicate on a rating scale how much they liked to shop at different grocery stores. Before doing this, they were presented with sets of numbers that represented the percentage increases in price over the past 2 years for randomly selected food items from a grocery store. The number of price increases (i.e., the sample size) differed among sets, as did the mean percentage increase per set. Students took account of both pieces of information. When the mean price increase was low, they preferred shops with large sets over those with small sets, and when the mean price increases were high, they did the opposite. In summary, a considerable number of studies with both children and adult participants show that people do quite well on a wide variety of frequency-distribution tasks.

Sampling-distribution tasks in most studies were formulated as choices, but occasionally, participants had to construct their own sampling distributions such as in this construction task (adapted from Kahneman & Tversky, 1972):

DISTRIBUTION OF SEXES
Imagine that in a certain country demographic properties in different regions are recorded. In one region (Region A) there are about 10 births per day and in another region (Region B) there are about 40 per day. Every day, the proportion of boys and girls is registered.
Please estimate the percentages of female births that can be expected in both regions over a period of 100 days. Just divide the 100 days over the categories, for each region.

Region A	Region B
About 10 births daily	About 40 births daily
__ Up to 5% girls	__ Up to 5% girls
__ 6% to 15% girls	__ 6% to 15% girls
__ 16% to 25% girls	__ 16% to 25% girls
__ 26% to 35% girls	__ 26% to 35% girls
__ 36% to 45% girls	__ 36% to 45% girls
__ 46% to 55% girls	__ 46% to 55% girls
__ 56% to 65% girls	__ 56% to 65% girls
__ 66% to 75% girls	__ 66% to 75% girls
__ 76% to 85% girls	__ 76% to 85% girls
__ 86% to 95% girls	__ 86% to 95% girls
__ 96% to 100% girls	__ 96% to 100% girls. (p. 437)

Usually, participants' sampling distributions involving different sample sizes (here: $N = 10$ and $N = 40$) are quite flat and do not differ from one another at all (Fischhoff, Slovic, & Lichtenstein, 1979; Kahneman & Tversky, 1972; Olson, 1976; Sedlmeier, 1992; Teigen, 1974). In fact, the sampling distributions for sample sizes of 10 and 40 births per day should differ quite markedly, as shown in Fig. 1.2.

N=10

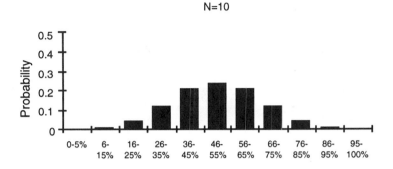

N=40

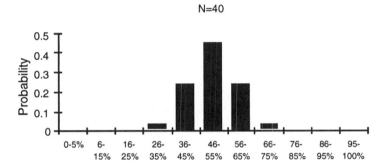

FIG. 1.2. The sampling distributions theoretically expected for binomial variables with $p=.5$ (e.g., sex of child, coin toss) for sample sizes $N = 10$ and $N = 40$. Note that the intervals for the sampling distribution with $N = 40$ include more than one possible event (e.g., in the case of coin tosses, the interval 0% to 5% included 0 and 1 heads out of 40 tosses, the interval 6% to 15% included 2, 3, 4, and 5 out of 40, etc.).

If one multiplies the probability values in Fig. 1.2 by 100, one obtains the normative values to be inserted into the distribution-of-sexes task. We cannot expect participants to calculate binomial distributions,[8] but we might expect

---

[8]Sampling distributions for binary variables, that is, variables that only can have two values and a fixed probability of occurrence (e.g., $p = .5$ like in the distribution-of-sexes task) are called binomial distributions. The chance that an event will occur exactly k times out of n is given by the binomial formula (e.g., Scheaffer, 1990):

$$p(k) = \binom{n}{k} p^k (1-p)^{n-k}, \text{ where } \binom{n}{k} = \frac{n!}{k!(n-k)!}.$$

For instance, if we want to know the probability that five out of 10 babies born are girls, we set

$p = .5$, $k = 5$, and $n = 10$ and obtain: $p(5) = \binom{10}{5} 0.5^5 (1 - 0.5)^5 = .246$.

them to insert higher values in the middle category (e.g., "46% to 55% girls") and smaller values in the end categories of the distribution for the larger sample than for the smaller sample. This was, however, not the case in any study. It seems quite difficult for untutored people to appreciate the impact of sample size when constructing sampling distributions. This lends further credence to the distinction between frequency- and sampling-distribution tasks.

Other Factors

Especially in choice tasks, other factors have been hypothesized to influence solution rates. These include hands-on experience with a simple Galton board (Jones & Harris, 1982), ratio between sample sizes (J. Murray, Iding, Farris, & Revlin, 1987), extreme cut-off percentages (e.g., "more than 90%" instead of "more than 60%"; Bar-Hillel, 1979, 1982; Evans & Dusoir, 1977), and the part of the distribution to which the question refers (e.g., Kahneman & Tversky, 1972; Reagan, 1989). Comparatively high sensitivity to sample size was observed when the question referred to the center (as opposed to the tails) of the distribution (Well, Pollatsek, & Boyce, 1990), but this variant seems to have been studied only for sampling-distribution tasks. There is also some indication that population size can influence judgments about sample size (Evans & Bradshaw, 1986). For instance, Bar-Hillel (1979) proposed that it is not absolute sample size, but sample size relative to the population size, to which people attend. However, her data only partially support this hypothesis. None of the examined factors had an influence on solution rates that was nearly as large as the distinction between frequency- and sampling-distribution tasks.

In summary, people are generally sensitive to the fact that the larger the sample, the closer the means or proportions calculated from a sample are to the population means or proportions. This sensitivity is higher when the (random) sampling is directly experienced than when the task is presented in text form only. However, this result is restricted to frequency-distribution tasks and is not found in tasks requiring judgments about the variability of sampling distributions. Such sampling-distribution tasks remain difficult regardless of the manipulations tried to date. This difficulty, as well as problems with the correct interpretation of conditional probabilities, is also found in the use of so-called significance tests.

THE RITUAL OF SIGNIFICANCE TESTING

Significance testing is an integral part of the methods courses in nearly all undergraduate and graduate programs in the social sciences (e.g., Aiken, West, Sechrest, & Reno, 1990). It has become so dominant in the field that it may be ascribed the status of a ritual (e.g., Salsburg, 1985). In fact, if the ritual is not

performed, or if it does not yield the proper results, publication of research results may be seriously hindered (Atkinson, Furlong, & Wampold, 1982; Bredenkamp, 1972; L. H. Cohen, 1979; Coursol & Wagner, 1986; Frick, 1996;
Greenwald, 1975; Melton, 1962). At least, if everybody knows and uses the procedure, one might expect that researchers generally know what the result of a
significance test means. Is this so? Unfortunately that does not generally seem to
be the case.

Before we turn to some common misinterpretations of the result of a significance test, let us examine a hypothetical example. A psychologist visiting a
remote tribe suspects that the ratio of males to females in this tribe is not the
usual 50:50. Instead, she assumes that 70% of all newborns are females. This
simple setup provides us with two competing hypotheses, usually referred to as
null hypothesis, H_0 and *alternative hypothesis*, H_1. H_0 commonly denotes the
hypothesis of no difference or no effect, whereas H_1 specifies the size of an effect
in the population.[9] The birth of a baby can be considered a binomial process
with two possible outcomes (female and male) whose probabilities of occurrence
add up to 1. Thus H_0 can be specified as p(female) = .5, and H_1 as p(female) = .7.
On a randomly selected day, the researcher visited the place where all children of
this tribe are born and found that 13 of 19 children born were females. Because
childbirth is considered a binomial process here, we can specify what the
researcher had to expect if she took an infinite number of samples, given that
either H_0 or H_1 were true.[10] The probabilities, with which the different percentages of female births may be expected, can be calculated by using binomial distributions (see Footnote 8). Figure 1.3 shows these probabilities for both H_0
(dark bars) and H_1 (light bars). For instance, the probability that 10 out of the 19
newborns (the interval ranging from 51% to 55% in Fig. 1.3) are females is p =
.18 given that H_0 is true and p = .05, given that H_1 is true.

Now we have almost everything we need to conduct a significance test, the
distributions of possible proportions given the truth of H_0, and of H_1, and empirical data, that is, the proportion found by the researcher. How do we determine
whether the test comes out significant or not significant, the two possible
results of the significance test? For this purpose, p(Data | H_0), the conditional
probability of the empirically found or more extreme data given the truth of H_0 is
compared against a theoretically fixed conditional probability, usually called

---

[9]The description of significance testing follows ongoing practice. This common practice does
not, however, strictly conform to any theoretical approach. Instead, it is a mixture of the approaches of Neyman and Pearson's theory of hypotheses testing, Fisher's theory of null hypothesis
testing, and some ingredients from a Bayesian approach (Acree, 1979; Gigerenzer, 1993; Gigerenzer & D. J. Murray, 1987; Oakes, 1986). However, the arguments made here apply regardless
of the theoretical perspective.

[10]The view that sampling distributions arise from an infinite number of repetitions of a sampling
procedure under essentially similar conditions originated from the Neyman & Pearson approach
and is presently the most widely accepted view (see Oakes, 1986, also for some criticism on that
view).

significance level or α. If p(Data | H_0) which is often referred to as the *p value*, is smaller than α, the test result is said to be significant, otherwise it is not. In Fig. 1.3, α is marked by the dotted vertical line and has an arbitrary value of α = .03. Given the above specifications, the result found by our researcher would not be significant, because p(Data | H_0) turns out to be .08, which is larger than α. There is some controversy about what exactly it means if the p value is or is not smaller than α (see Appendix C), but there are some interpretations of p values which are definitely wrong. Some of these misinterpretations hinge on the reversal of conditional probabilities and others hinge on the neglect of the impact of sample size.

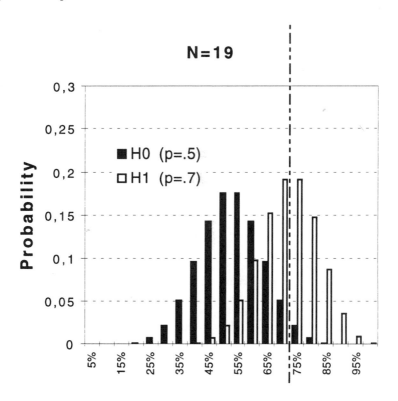

FIG. 1.3.   Two binomial (sampling) distributions with N = 19 and p = .5 (sampling distribu-tion given the truth of H_0), and p = .7 (sampling distribution given the truth of H_1). The ver-tical dotted line indicates the location of α. The percentages below the axis represent the upper bounds of the proportions that fall into particular categories. Each category only contains one possible outcome (e.g., 10 out of 19 in the category denoted 55%). See text for further explanation.

As illustrated previously, the specification of a sampling distribution given the truth of H_0 lets one calculate $p(\text{Data} \mid H_0)$. Of course, the more interesting information would be $p(\text{Data} \mid H_0)$, the probability of the null hypothesis, given the data found. Unfortunately, there is no way to derive the latter conditional probability from the result of a significance test. Despite this fact, 26 of 70 (37%) academic psychologists in a study by Oakes (1986) believed that the p value allowed them to make a probability statement about H_0, and 50 of 70 (71%) thought that a probability statement about H_1 could be made from the result of a significance test.

Forty-two of Oakes' (1986) participants (60%) also believed that the complement of the p value gives the probability that in an exact replication, the result would again be significant. Figure 1.3 shows why this cannot be true. When expressing this belief, Oakes' participants apparently believed that the alternative hypothesis was true. In this case, three factors influence the probability that a result will be significant, also called (statistical) *power*: α, effect size, and sample size. Given the setup in Fig. 1.3, the power of the test is expressed by the part of the H_1 sampling distribution (light bars) to the right of α. Here, the value of the power is .47 which is clearly different from $1 - p$. If Oakes' participants had obtained a significant result with this setup, their chances of replicating it would be 47% and not 92% (assuming that the obtained effect size is a good estimate of the effect size in the population). Other things being equal, the power increases with increasing α, increasing effect size, and increasing sample size (see J. Cohen, 1988).

The effect of sample size can be seen by comparing Fig. 1.3 and Fig. 1.4. The difference in the sampling distributions in the two figures is solely due to different sample sizes ($N = 19$ vs. $N = 39$). The implications for a significance test are dramatically different. The empirical result of our hypothetical researcher (about 70% of newborns are females) would be significant, if found in a sample of $N = 39$ babies. Moreover, given the truth of H_1, the probability that a significant result could be replicated under similar circumstances is now .74, instead of .47.[11] The influence of sample size on power is a notoriously neglected topic (e.g., J. Cohen, 1962, 1992). Given researchers' emphasis on significance tests, a mean power of less than 50%, as usually found in psychological studies (Rossi, 1990; Sedlmeier & Gigerenzer, 1989), means that the probability of achieving a significant result given that H_1 is true was on average less than if one would decide that issue by tossing a coin. In conjunction with the publication bias that favors significant results, this implies a waste of time and money. Low power is even worse if a researcher wants to find evidence for the truth of H_0 (on the use of nonsignificant test results as evidence see Blackwelder, 1982;

---

[11]Note that because of the discreteness of binomial distributions, the exact values for α in Fig. 1.3 and Fig. 1.4 are not identical, in Fig. 1.3, $\alpha = .032$, and in Fig. 1.4: $\alpha = .027$. Note also that due to the same cause, the exact values (referred to as about 70% in the text) for our hypothetical researcher differ somewhat (68%, that is, 13 out of 19 vs. 67%, that is, 26 out of 39).

Gigerenzer et al., 1989; Huntsberger & Billingsley, 1973). Low power means that the a priori chance to erroneously not detect an existing effect, that is, to find a nonsignificant result given the truth of H_1 may be quite high. For instance, with the setup shown in Fig. 1.3, the a priori chance to obtain a nonsignificant result if H_1 were true would be 53%. Apparently, researchers do not care much about this problem. In their analysis of published research, Sedlmeier and Gigerenzer (1989) found that in cases where null hypotheses corresponded to the research hypotheses, the median power was as low as .25. In none of these cases was the issue of power discussed by the respective authors. Thus, it seems that the impact of sample size on sampling distributions is a problematic topic even for statistically sophisticated professionals.

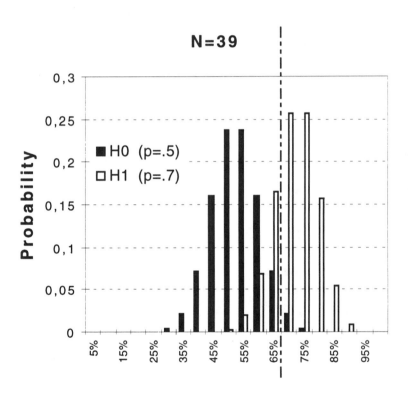

FIG. 1.4.   Two binomial (sampling) distributions with $N=39$ and $p=.5$ (sampling distribution given the truth of H_0), and $p=.7$ (sampling distribution given the truth of H_1). The vertical dotted line indicates the location of α. The percentages below the axis represent the upper bounds of the proportions that fall into particular categories. Each category includes two possible outcomes (e.g., 20 and 21 out of 39 in the category denoted "55%").   See text for further explanation.

Significance testing is a complex topic and the previous treatment was rather informal, keeping in mind that this book is not a statistics textbook (for excellent textbooks see Freedman, et al., 1991; Huntsberger & Billingsley, 1973). A more thorough discussion of issues and arguments concerning the interpretation of significance test results can be found in Appendix C and in the literature cited therein. After this excursion, which illustrated that the basic models discussed before, such as conditional probabilities and the impact of sample size, may also appear in combination, normative issues in statistical reasoning are addressed.

IS THERE A UNIQUE NORMATIVE SOLUTION FOR EVERY TASK?

Until now, we have assumed that, for every task, there is only one normative model that applies to it. That this solution is normative means that all other solutions are wrong. In many cases, experts in the field could probably agree on one model that fits the task best. Moreover, participants tend to readily concur with the experimenters when the discrepancy between their solutions and the normative model offered by the experimenters is pointed out to them (e.g., Kahneman & Tversky, 1982). Nonetheless, there are cases in which several models might be applicable and there are even cases in which the normative models proposed are arguably wrong.

Single-Event Versus Frequentist Conceptions of Probability

In probability theory there are a variety of conceptions of probability (e.g., Gigerenzer et al., 1989; Hacking, 1965), some of which even ignore the requirement of additivity (e.g., L. J. Cohen, 1981; Shafer, 1976). Here we will only be concerned with the difference between single-event probabilities and probabilities derived from relative frequencies, the latter being the focus of the dominant school of probability since about 1848 (Daston, 1988; Porter, 1986). Gigerenzer (1991, 1996b) has argued that from many experts' points of view, allowing there to be a discrepancy between the probability attached to a single event and that calculated from long-run relative frequencies, is not an error or a violation of probability theory.

For instance, in the original Linda conjunction task, participants are asked which of the two statements, (a) Linda is a bank teller, and (b) Linda is a bank teller and is active in the feminist movement, is more probable. Thus, the question is about single-event probabilities. If participants judge alternative (b) to be more probable than alternative (a), that is, they commit the conjunction fallacy, this does not have to be a violation of frequentist probability theory because for "a frequentist, this problem has nothing to do with probability theory" (Gigerenzer, 1991, p. 92). We have already seen that if the Linda task is formulated in a frequentistic manner (e.g., "How many of the women who are like Linda are both bank tellers and in the feminist movement?"), the conjunction fallacy largely disappears. This argument makes clear that before one classifies a particular solution to a statistical task as an error, one first has to check (if possible) the participants' underlying conceptions of probability. One might not agree with their conceptions, but the correctness of a response can only be evaluated on the basis of certain theoretical assumptions. If there is disagreement about this theoretical basis, the normative response is open to dispute, and as far as the conception of probability is concerned, one has to acknowledge that there are different theories (see Gigerenzer, 1991; MacDonald, 1986; for further examples, see L. J. Cohen, 1982).

Underspecified Models

In the preceding paragraph, we saw that different conceptions of probability or different probability theories may lead to contrasting conclusions concerning the correctness of a task solution. Even if we can agree on one conception of probability, some task description may not allow for complete specification of the model, leaving it open to different solutions. Two examples illustrate the issue. Consider first this apparently simple task (Bar-Hillel & Falk, 1982): "Mr. Smith is the father of two. We meet him walking along the street with a young boy whom he proudly introduces as his son. What is the probability that Mr. Smith's other child is also a boy?" (p. 109).

Bar-Hillel and Falk (1982) report that two professors of mathematics who were presented this task immediately gave their solutions, although different ones (i.e., 1/2 and 1/3). Both solutions assume that a newborn child is female (or male) with a probability of 1/2 and that the gender of each of Mr. Smith's children is independent of that of the other. If these assumptions hold, knowing the gender of one child does not affect the probability that the other child is male, and therefore the sought-for probability is 1/2. This solution depends, however, on the additional assumption that Mr. Smith chose the child at random. If, for instance, in the culture in which Mr. Smith lives, a male child is selected to go for a walk whenever possible, there would be three equally possible cases of two children of whom at least one is a boy: boy-boy, boy-girl, and girl-boy. The probability of boy-boy given that Mr. Smith was accompanied by a boy would then be 1/3.

Let us turn to another example. Kunda and Nisbett (1986a) had participants estimate the probability that a student named Johnny received a higher grade than Danny on one spelling test during a school term. Participants were then asked to estimate the probability that Johnny would get higher grades than Danny on average on all 20 tests of the term. According to Kunda and Nisbett, the probability that Johnny gets higher grades than Danny on average, given that he gets a higher grade on one test, is equal to the probability that Johnny gets a higher grade on one test, given that he gets a higher grade on average, that is, p(one | all) = p(all | one). They claim that the law of large numbers, particularly a straightforward implication thereof—the aggregation principle—is the underlying rule which justifies that solution of symmetry. According to Kunda and Nisbett, the aggregation principle states: "The confidence one may have in predictions increases with the size of the sample one is predicting from and with the size of the sample one is predicting to" (p. 340). How did Kunda and Nisbett apply the aggregation principle in their analysis of this particular task? They justified their claim about the symmetry of the two kinds of prediction as follows: "Since the magnitude of a correlation is independent of the direction of prediction, aggregation increases predictability equally whether it is performed on the predictor or on the predicted events" (p. 341). Following that assertion, they first transformed participants' probability estimates into Kendall's τ and then into Spearman's r (Kunda & Nisbett, 1986b, 199–201). A simple example demonstrates that, contrary to Kunda and Nisbett's (1986a) assumption, it in fact makes a difference whether one predicts from the single to the aggregate event or vice versa.

Imagine the following simplified two-stage, coin-tossing game. Two players, A and B, each flip a coin. A head corresponds to 1 point and a tail corresponds to 0 points. The probabilities of heads and tails are p and $1 - p$, respectively. Let us denote the points (0 or 1) that players A and B gain at the ith stage of the game by the random variables X_i and Y_i. At each stage, player A can win or lose, or there can be a draw. Assuming X_i and Y_i are independent, then the probabilities of A winning, A losing (i.e., B winning), and the probability of a draw in one stage are: $P_{\text{A-one}} = p(1 - p)$, $P_{\text{B-one}} = p(1 - p)$, and $P_{\text{D-one}} = 1 - 2p(1 - p)$, respectively. Now let us compute $P_{\text{A-average}}$, the average probability that A wins in a two-stage game, that is, that the sum of her points is larger than the sum of B's points. A wins if she wins one of the two stages and there is a draw in the other, or if she wins both stages:

$$
\begin{aligned}
P_{\text{A-average}} &= 2P_{\text{A-one}} P_{\text{D-one}} + P_{\text{A-one}}{}^2 \\
&= 2p(1 - p)(1 - 2p(1 - p)) + [p(1 - p)]^2 \\
&= p(1 - p)[2 - 3p(1 - p)]
\end{aligned}
$$

This short analysis shows that the probability of A winning in the first stage if she wins on average p(A-one | A-average) is not equal to the probability of A winning on average if she won in the first stage, p(A-average | A-one).[12] A more

---

[12]From the definition of conditional probabilities we have $p(A \mid B) = p(A \cap B) / p(B)$ and $p(B \mid A) = p(B \cap A) / p(A)$. If we now divide $p(A \mid B)$ by $p(B \mid A)$, we obtain $p(A \mid B) / p(B \mid A) = p(A) / p(B)$. This proves that if the prior probabilities $p(A)$ and $p(B)$ are equal, the conditional probabilities must also be equal. It also proves that if the prior probabilities differ, the conditional probabilities must also. In our example, if, for instance, $p = .5$, we obtain p(A-one | A-average) = (1/4 × 5/16) / (5/16) and p(A-average | A-one) = (1/4 × 5/16) / (1/4), which are clearly different.

general analysis (Sedlmeier & Eden, 1998) reveals that depending on various factors such as—to stay with the above example—differences in the skills or true values of the players, the ranges of X_i and Y_i, and the exact specification of what on average means, predictions can be better either from a single event to an aggregate event or the reverse. Only rarely can equal probabilities be attached to both predictions. In these and similar kinds of tasks, it might turn out to be very difficult, if not impossible, to fully specify a model.

The examples discussed previously do not imply that normative solutions to statistical tasks cannot be found in principle. They do imply, however, that the correct model can be hard, even for experts, to determine. Thus, for tasks that leave room for several mutually inconsistent ways to specify the appropriate model fully, it does not make sense to label participants' responses as being in error. One should, however, not overstate this point.

STATISTICAL REASONING RECONSIDERED

We have seen that people solve conjunctive and Bayesian tasks with less difficulty when they are stated in terms of natural frequencies instead of in probabilities or percentages. We have also seen that the normative models used to determine whether a task solution is right or wrong are sometimes controversial. May we conclude that there are no real problems with human competence, that tasks given in a probability format are artificial, and that if one searches long enough one can find a normative model that justifies any task response as rational? Certainly not.

Tasks stated in a probability format are commonplace in the media and in scientific publications. Not knowing how to reason about such tasks remains a widespread problem. In addition, although a frequency format helps people reach adequate solutions, the percentage of such solutions is sometimes still as low as 50% (e.g., Gigerenzer & Hoffrage, 1995). Furthermore, sample-size tasks of the sampling distribution variety are still very difficult to solve even when they are stated in terms of frequencies (e.g., in the maternity-ward task, the number of days with certain percentages of male births).

Although there are cases in which several models are applicable and in which models cannot be fully specified, in the vast majority of everyday situations in which we must deal with uncertainty, a majority of experts (or even people in general) can be expected to agree on a best one. Thus, despite all positive results and alternative explanations there remains a problem with statistical reasoning. In the next chapter, the four prominent theoretical approaches in the field explain why this problem exists and whether and how it might be remedied.

2

Are People Condemned to Remain Poor Probabilists?

SUMMARY: Four theoretical approaches provide different explanations for the occurrence of statistical reasoning errors and differ markedly in their predictions about whether and how statistical reasoning can be improved by training. The pragmatic-implications approach states that errors arise partly from people's misunderstanding of the text of tasks. The implications of this approach for training are less clear than for the other approaches. The heuristics-and-biases approach claims that stable judgmental heuristics lead to reasoning biases and are largely resistant to training. The abstract-rules approach holds that people have abstract rules for sound statistical reasoning, but only apply them when certain cues are present. According to this approach, effective training teaches people to apply these rules whenever it is appropriate to do so. Finally, the adaptive-algorithms approach asserts that the format in which tasks are presented makes the difference between poor and sound statistical reasoning. If tasks are presented in an information format that is close to a naturally occurring format (e.g., event frequencies instead of probabilities), people do not make errors. Training in this approach entails letting participants translate tasks into a natural format, rendering further training unnecessary. It is suggested that the results of training studies provide a good test of the four approaches, which have not been directly compared to date.

This chapter considers how several theoretical accounts[1] explain why people sometimes have problems processing statistical information. It also examines how these explanations suggest that training can help people to overcome these difficulties. The foci of the four explanations to be dealt with are quite different. The *pragmatic-implications* explanation examines the implications of linguistic and social context for judgment under uncertainty. The *heuristics-and-biases* explanation focuses on demonstrating people's proneness to make reasoning errors with an abundance of examples, some of which we saw in chapter 1. The *ab-*

---

[1]The explanations dealt with here are not the only ones that have been advanced to explain why people commit errors in statistical reasoning. However, all other explanations appear to be either restricted to a particular task, of an ad hoc nature, or do not suggest how effective training should be designed.

stract-rules explanation[2] is mainly concerned with the role that intuitive versions of abstract rules (which were called models in chapter 1) play in statistical reasoning, and how such rules can be used in training. Finally, the *adaptive-algorithms* explanation has mainly been used to specify conditions under which people should show sound judgment.

These four explanations are first described in detail and are then compared to one another with respect to what they say about whether, how, and how well statistical reasoning can be taught. We will use these predictions to analyze published training studies (chapter 3) and the results of training programs that were designed according to the recommendations the theoretical approaches make (chapters 5–11).

PRAGMATIC IMPLICATIONS

Imagine a headline of a major newspaper that reads, "Former President Reagan was loyal to his wife while in office." How strongly would you believe in that assertion? Gruenfeld and Wyer (1992) asked one group of participants to indicate their degree of belief in this assertion, and most doubted it to be true. Another group of participants who learned that the newspaper headline said that Reagan had not been loyal to his wife while in office, however, tended to believe more in Reagan's loyalty than the first group. How did this paradoxical effect arise? The basic answer, initially advanced by Grice (1975), is that communication is governed by both linguistic and social rules or *conversational maxims*. These maxims obey the *cooperative principle*: "Make your conversational contribution such as required, at the stage at which it occurs, by the accepted purpose or direction of the talk exchange in which you are engaged." (p. 67).

According to Grice (1975), one expects other communicators to adhere to the cooperative principle and to the conversational maxims. In particular, these maxims require that contributions be as informative as necessary (not more or less so—*maxim of quantity*), relevant (*maxim of relation*), truthful (*maxim of quality*), and finally, brief, orderly, and unambiguous (*maxim of manner*). Although communicators can be assumed to adhere to the cooperative principle, sometimes a conversational contribution seems to violate one or more of these maxims. Consider one of Grice's examples (p. 70): "A is standing by an obviously immobilized car and is approached by B; the following exchange takes place: A: I am out of petrol. B: There is a garage round the corner."

Until one realizes that B's response is intended to imply that the garage is open and has petrol to sell, one might think that B is violating the maxim of relation. In order to understand, A has to go beyond the semantic meaning of B's

---

[2]With the exception of the heuristics-and-biases approach, this nomenclature does not follow established usage, but is used here for convenience.

sentence and draw what Harris and Monaco (1978) called a *pragmatic implication*. Pragmatic implications not only help people to fill in missing information, but also help to interpret apparently strange assertions, such as the Reagan headline. If, as Gruenfeld and Wyer (1992) assumed, most people believe that Reagan was loyal to his wife, then the headline is highly redundant (why repeat common knowledge?). A pragmatic implication of this could be that there are some (justified) rumors of disloyalty that the writer of the article wants to suppress.

How does language understanding relate to judgment under uncertainty? Most research about judgment under uncertainty applies normative models with little or no regard for linguistic or social context. The phrasing of tasks can, however, invoke several kinds of pragmatic implications that are neither intended nor expected by the experimenter, but that can critically influence the results. This has been demonstrated in conjunction and probability revision tasks. Consider again the Linda task (Kahneman & Tversky, 1983):

> Linda is 31 years old, single, outspoken, and very bright. She majored in philosophy. As a student, she was deeply concerned with issues of discrimination and social justice, and also participated in anti-nuclear demonstrations.
> Please indicate which of the two following statements is more likely:
> Linda is a bank teller. (A)
> Linda is a bank teller and is active in the feminist movement. (A and B)

If the description of Linda is assumed to be relevant, then it should help the participant to decide between the two alternatives. One can think of at least four pragmatic implications that preserve the relevance of Linda's personality description in this task. First, A can be read as A and not B (Linda is a bank teller and not active in the feminist movement). In several studies, up to 53% of participants drew this pragmatic implication (Dulany & Hilton, 1991; Hertwig & Gigerenzer, in press). Judging A and B as more probable than A and not B is not a conjunction error (consider, for instance, the case where B refers to younger than 70 years). Second, probability can be understood to mean something other than mathematical probability. According to Hertwig and Gigerenzer (in press), in adhering to the maxim of relation, participants infer other meanings of probability (e.g., plausibility, possibility) to make sense of Linda's description. In their Study 1, they gave participants a list of mathematical and nonmathematical meanings of probability from respected dictionaries, and asked them to check off the one(s) that best reflected their understandings of the term in the Linda task. The vast majority of participants (72%) understood probability in a non-mathematical sense.

A third way to preserve the relevance of the personality description is to apply it to a task that precedes the probability judgment. This preceding task could, for instance, require a typicality rating (e.g., how typical Linda is of a bank teller). In this case, the maxim of relation should not prevent participants from inferring the mathematical meaning of probability and applying the conjunction rule in a later task. Hertwig and Gigerenzer (in press, Study 2) gave one group of participants a typicality task to complete before the probability judgment. Whereas only 15% of the participants who gave only probability judgments followed the conjunction rule, consistent with previous results, 57% of those who first made typicality judgments gave answers consistent with the conjunction rule. A fourth way to render Linda's description relevant is to interpret the "and" in the conjunction as an If, then statement (If she is a bank teller, then she is [at least] active in the feminist movement). The resulting conditional probability could be larger than the probability of a constituent event without violating the conjunction rule. The simplest and most effective way to override such relevance judgments is, however, to ask participants directly for frequencies instead of probabilities. When a frequency format was used, up to 100% of participants obeyed the conjunction rule (Studies 3 and 4).

Pragmatic implication effects have also been found in Bayesian inference tasks. Let us have another look at the engineer–lawyer task, which consists of a personality description constructed to be either similar to a typical engineer or to a typical lawyer, or to be uninformative with respect to the requested judgment. This description is usually followed by base-rate information (e.g., the fact that 30 out of the 100 persons involved are engineers and the other 70 are lawyers). If participants consider the order of information presentation to be relevant, then giving the base-rate information first (as compared to second) should increase the use of base rates. Krosnick, Li, and Lehman (1990) found this effect. When they told participants that the order of presentation had been randomly determined, however, they obtained no such differential effect. This result makes sense from the perspective of the pragmatic-implications approach because in the latter condition there was no one whose intentions (expressed in order of presentation) could be inferred.

Recall the (hypothetical) headline about Ronald Reagan. When Gruenfeld and Wyer (1992) told participants that it was a line from an encyclopedia instead of a newspaper, the results changed. When the source asserted Reagan's loyalty, participants believed more strongly in his loyalty than when it asserted that he had not been loyal. Thus, the paradoxical effect mentioned at the beginning of this section seems to hinge on the credibility of the information source. An experiment by Ginossar and Trope (1987, Experiment 5) mentioned in chapter 1 lends credence to this assumption. They told participants that the information source (about the information in the engineer–lawyer task) was either a trained psychologist (high credibility), a beginning psychology student (medium credibility), or a palm reader (low credibility). A pragmatic-implications explanation would predict greater reliance on the base-rate information (which was objective) given a low-credibility than a high-credibility source, which is what Ginossar and Trope found.

A special kind of pragmatic implication can be drawn when text is partly or wholly misunderstood. For instance, Cummins, Kintsch, Reusser, and Weimer (1988) found that children's apparent errors in arithmetic word tasks were often correct solutions to tasks which they had not understood as intended by the experimenters. A similar argument can be made about the results of Piaget and Inhelder's (1969) conservation experiments (Donaldson, 1982). Such global task misunderstandings are not restricted to children. For instance, Pollatsek et al. (1987) contended that details of wording might make it difficult for participants to interpret conditional-probability tasks as intended by researchers. Another example is a study about sample size tasks conducted by Well et al. (1990, Study 4). They asked participants to paraphrase a sampling distribution task in their own words and found that 52% paraphrased it as a frequency-distribution task.

Implications for Training

In a thorough review of research about pragmatic implications (which he calls *conversational inference*), Hilton (1995) proposed a two-stage model for text-task solving. In the first stage, people form hypotheses about the intended meaning and in the second stage they apply solution strategies to this task interpretation. This model could be used as a basis for a statistical training regimen. We will focus on training that deals with the first stage because the second cannot be specified using results obtained in pragmatic-implication studies. It might turn out that when people fully understand the task, training in inference strategies is unnecessary. How could people's understanding of statistical reasoning tasks be facilitated?

The simplest way to ensure that a receiver has understood a message as it was intended is to convey the information clearly, to test the receiver's understanding, and to provide additional explanation if required. In statistical tasks, such a training procedure involves explaining the meaning of connectives (such as *and* and *or*) and teaching people to translate natural language into probability language. Graphical representations could play an important role in this translation process. Of course, one would expect people's understanding to be best when they can experience the tasks they are reading, for instance, by physically sampling balls from an urn when solving tasks involving urns and balls. We will see that the same would be predicted by the adaptive-algorithms approach.

HEURISTICS AND BIASES

The *heuristics-and-biases* approach still represents the main line of thinking in research about judgment. Its view is described well by a quote from the famous initiators of that program, Kahneman and Tversky (1973):

> In making predictions and judgments under uncertainty, people do not ap-
> pear to follow the calculus of chance or the statistical theory of prediction.
> Instead they rely on a limited number of heuristics which sometimes yield
> reasonable judgments and sometimes lead to severe and systematic errors.
> (p. 237)

Note that the meaning of heuristic here is quite different from that used in Artificial Intelligence (AI) research (e.g., Lopes & Oden, 1991), in which heuristics
are considered to be an intelligent way of making computer programs solve
complex problems that cannot be solved by a clear-cut algorithm. In AI, heuristics are flexible instruments that can be readily modified if it turns out that a
problem requires another solution. In the heuristics-and-biases approach, however, heuristics are considered inflexible rules of thumb that are used to explain
why people commit biases, that is, judgment errors. These errors are identified
by comparing participants' behavior to "accepted rules of statistics" (Kahneman
& Tversky, 1982, p. 124). The models introduced in the last chapter are such
accepted rules. There, we saw several examples of biases, but here we will focus
on the heuristics assumed to underlie the biases.

By far the most important of these heuristics in terms of number of cases in
which it can be applied is the *representativeness heuristic*. If questions about the
probability of object A belonging to a class B or of event A originating from
process B are asked, then (Tversky & Kahneman, 1974):

> people typically rely on the representativeness heuristic, in which prob-
> abilities are evaluated by the degree to which A is representative of B that
> is, by the degree to which A resembles B. For example, when A is highly
> representative of B, the probability that A originates from B is judged to be
> high. On the other hand, if A is not similar to B, the probability that A
> originates from B is judged to be low. (p.1124)

Why, for instance, do people violate the conjunction rule? Consider the Linda
task again. Linda is first described as a young, bright, leftist, and intellectual
woman. Then, participants are asked whether she is more likely to be a bank
teller (A) or a bank teller and active in the feminist movement (A and B). According to Tversky and Kahneman (1983), if offered these two options, people
prefer A and B because this option is more similar to (or more representative of)
Linda's description.

The representativeness heuristic is also used to account for the fact that $p(A \mid B)$ is sometimes judged to be the same as $p(B \mid A)$ (Dawes, 1986).[3] The same
heuristic is assumed to lead people to ignore sample size and to neglect base
rates in Bayesian inference. Let us look again at the engineer–lawyer task, a

---

[3]Dawes is not very specific about how exactly representative thinking works in this case but
concludes that "representative thinking does not distinguish between P(c | S) and P(S | c) and con-
sequently introduces a symmetry in thought that does not exist in the world" (1986, p. 430),
whereby he refers to c as a characteristic and to S as a schema or category.

Bayesian task (chapter 1). According to the heuristics-and-biases approach, the representativeness heuristic induces people to base their judgments on the similarity of the personality description to a prototypical engineer or lawyer, and to ignore the base-rate information (e.g., 30% engineers and 70% lawyers; Tversky & Kahneman, 1980). The maternity-ward task (chapter 1) serves as an example of how the representativeness heuristic is said to be used in sample size tasks. In this task, people have to compare the birth rates in a larger (45 births per day) and a smaller (15 births per day) hospital during one year. Because the size of the sample does not affect the similarity of the samples to the population of all childbirths in the city (i.e., the samples are equally representative), people judge the probability of a 10% deviation from the true values of 50% boy births to be equally likely for both hospitals (Kahneman & Tversky, 1972).

Another heuristic that is often cited to determine people's judgments is the *availability heuristic*. For instance, it is hypothesized to work in some kinds of conjunction tasks. Participants in one of Tversky and Kahneman's (1983) studies were asked to estimate the number of seven-letter words of the form '-----n-' there are in four pages of text. Later in the same questionnaire, participants did the same with seven-letter words of the form '----ing'. Their estimates of the latter were consistently higher than those of the former, although '----ing' is a conjunction of '-----n-' and '---i-g'[4]. The heuristics-and-biases approach attributes this result to the availability heuristic, which leads people to "assess the frequency of a class or the probability of an event by the ease with which instances or occurrences can be brought to mind" (Tversky & Kahneman, 1974, p. 1127). Several other demonstrations of the availability heuristic involved judging relative frequencies, the basis for judgments of probability.[5] For instance, in Tversky and Kahneman's (1973) famous-names study, participants had to judge whether a list of 39 names contained more males or more females. The lists included either 19 names of famous women and 20 names of less famous men or 19 names of famous men and 20 names of less famous women. Participants generally judged the number of names belonging to the sex that was exemplified by more famous people to be larger.[6]

Many other heuristics and corresponding biases have been identified since Tversky and Kahneman's (1974) influential *Science* article. However, judging by

---

[4]It is not clear whether this study was performed between or within participants. Whereas the original report (Tversky & Kahneman, 1983) does not mention this issue, Tversky and D. J. Koehler (1994, p. 547) describe it as a between-subjects and Kahneman and Tversky (1996, p. 586) as a within-subjects design. If it is between subjects, then the result is not necessarily a violation of the conjunction rule.

[5]One could argue that probability judgments can also originate from sources other than the relative frequencies of events. However, for naturally occurring events, probabilities can always be reduced to frequencies that, at least in principle, are observable.

[6]We will see in chapter 15 that this result can be explained by a precise model that does not carry the implication that people's behaviors are irrational.

the number of articles referring to each heuristic, it seems that representativeness and availability play the most important roles in this approach.

Implications for Training

Kahneman and Tversky have repeatedly stressed the analogy between visual and cognitive illusions (Kahneman & Tversky, 1996; Tversky & Kahneman, 1974, 1983), which implies that people cannot do much to overcome their biases. Indeed, Tversky and Kahneman (1983) found that previous training in statistics did not have an effect on how well people solved conjunction tasks (see chapter 3). With respect to proper use of sample-size information, they concluded that "a strong tendency to underestimate the impact of sample size lingers on despite knowledge of the correct rule and extensive statistical training" (Kahneman & Tversky, 1972, p. 445). They even found that mathematically sophisticated colleagues had incorrect beliefs about the impact of sample size (Tversky & Kahneman, 1971).

Kahneman was involved in a training program about judgment under uncertainty that was developed at the University of Jerusalem between 1974 und 1980 (Beyth-Marom, Dekel, Gombo, & Shaked, 1985). This program was only evaluated in a preliminary way (Beyth-Marom & Dekel, 1983), was not applied afterwards (Beyth-Marom, personal communication, September 1996), and is now largely ignored in the heuristics-and-biases literature. This might be a further indication that heuristics are considered to be resistant to training, a view explicitly expressed by Dawes (1988, p. 142), "Attempts to train people not to think representatively and not to be influenced by availability or other biases have not been very successful," perhaps because "it is impossible for us to think in a way we do not think." Such a pessimistic view has been taken more recently by Piattelli-Palmarini (1994, p. 140), who asserts that cognitive illusions are inevitable, subjectively incorrigible, and independent of intelligence and education.[7]

ABSTRACT RULES

In contrast to proponents of the heuristics-and-biases approach, Nisbett, Krantz, Jepson, and Kunda (1983) claimed that people are often sensitive to the impact of sample size. They argued that evidence of this sensitivity can even be found in proverbs such as "Don't judge a book by its cover" and "All that glitters is not gold" and in expressions such as "beginner's luck." Based on their several experiments, Nisbett et al. (1983) concluded that sample size is appropriately taken

---

[7]That statistical reasoning has low chances of improvement by any training procedure does not, according to the heuristics-and-biases approach, mean that people show no insight when confronted with a normative solution (see Kahneman & Tversky, 1982). It just means that they will commit the error again and again.

into account when three facilitating features are present in tasks: (a) clarity of sample space and the sampling process, (b) recognition of the role of chance in producing events, and (c) cultural prescriptions to think statistically. There is also some indirect evidence for this conclusion from studies in which tasks were divided into probabilistic (e.g., involving randomizing devices), objective (e.g., involving sports events) and subjective (e.g., involving personality traits). The three facilitating features are most likely to be present in probabilistic, and least likely to be present in subjective tasks. This corresponded with the finding that the solution rates for the probabilistic tasks were remarkably higher than those for the other tasks, and that the solutions of subjective tasks rarely involved deliberations about sample size (Fong, Krantz, & Nisbett, 1986; Jepson, Krantz, & Nisbett, 1983). Later, Nisbett and coworkers considered other factors such as familiarity with the data and codability of the data to be essential for people to apply the law of large numbers (e.g., Kunda & Nisbett, 1986b). According to E. E. Smith, Langston, and Nisbett (1992), this law says that "sample parameters approach population parameters as a direct function of the number of cases in the sample, and as an inverse function of the degree of variability associated with the parameter" (p. 13—see appendix B for discussion of the difficulties with this definition).

The law of large numbers is one of the abstract rules of which people are assumed to have intuitive versions. Abstract rules means that the rules work fully independent of domain at a high level of abstraction. Other, nonprobabilistic abstract rules (or rule systems) presumed to be in people's repertoires are *modus ponens*, *modus tollens*, contractual rules, and causal rules (E. E. Smith et al., 1992). How do we know that people have intuitive versions of these rules? "We know this because they solve problems that require use of the rule systems, because they articulate the rule systems in justifying their solution, and because instruction in the rule systems increases the correct solution of the problems" (Nisbett, 1993, p. 6).

If people have abstract rules dictating the proper use of sample size, why do they still commit the errors reported in the literature on these tasks? Nisbett et al. (1983) seem to believe that faulty heuristics coexist with correct abstract rules. For instance, the low solution rates in the maternity-ward task (Kahneman & Tversky, 1972) indicate to them that "most subjects used the representativeness heuristic and very few subjects used the law of large numbers" (Nisbett et al., 1983, p. 341). In later work, they attribute failure to apply the law of large numbers not to the working of heuristics, but to people's difficulties in recognizing the applicability of this rule (Nisbett, Fong, Lehman, & Cheng, 1987).

Implications for Training

Nisbett and coworkers perceive their view as opposed to the prejudices of 20th century (American) psychology, which according to them assumes that the mind does not use abstract inferential rules, but only uses highly domain-specific empirical rules that enable no transfer to problems of identical formal structure (e.g., Nisbett et al., 1987)[8]. They see their approach more in agreement with the work of Piaget and of other thinkers before the 20th century who argued for formal discipline, which holds that "rules can be taught in the abstract, in the form of mathematics or logic, and they will then be applied across the concrete domains of everyday life" (Fong & Nisbett, 1991, p. 34). Nisbett et al. (1987) proposed two means of teaching abstract rules: "(i) brief formal instruction in the abstract rule system and (ii) brief instruction in the use of the rule system in a single domain" (p. 627). In their attempts to train people in statistical reasoning, this means explaining a formal model and then demonstrating its use with the help of examples.

ADAPTIVE ALGORITHMS

Based on a growing body of evidence, it has recently been claimed (e.g., Cosmides & Tooby, 1996; Gigerenzer, 1994, 1997) that the human mind is equipped with evolutionarily acquired cognitive algorithms that are able to solve even complicated statistical tasks. Whereas the abstract-rules explanation does not really explain why people should have abstract rules in their heads, proponents of this view (e.g., Cosmides & Tooby, 1994, 1996; Gigerenzer, 1994, 1997) try to explain why we have *adaptive algorithms* in terms of evolutionary theory. According to these authors, adaptive algorithms arose to help us solve adaptive problems, "An adaptive problem is a problem whose solution can affect reproduction, however distally. Avoiding predation, choosing nutritious foods, finding a mate, and communication with others are examples of adaptive problems that our hominid ancestors would have faced" (Cosmides, Tooby, & Barkow, 1992, p .9). Because of the long time it takes natural selection to shape new cognitive algorithms, the relevant adaptive problems are those that existed during the Pleistocene period (Symons, 1992). This holds for all sorts of adaptive mental algorithms, but here we will only be concerned with algorithms suitable for solving statistical tasks. To which adaptive problems could algorithms that solve statistical tasks have been an answer?[9] Here is a fictitious example (Gigerenzer & Hoffrage, 1995):

---

[8]This claim is surprising given the existence of at least two very influential attempts to formulate a comprehensive theory of cognition based on abstract production rule models, ACT theory (e.g., Anderson, 1983, 1995) and SOAR (Newell, 1990).

[9]This question drives one path of research in evolutionary psychology. It starts with a psychological mechanism and tries to find the adaptive function it fills, if any, by examining it in the context of hunter–gatherer life and known selection pressures. This is sometimes referred to as reverse engineering (e.g., Dawkins, 1995, p. 64). The other main path proceeds in the opposite direction: Knowledge about problems our ancestors faced can lead to hypotheses about the design

> Imagine an old, experienced physician in an illiterate society. She has no books or statistical surveys and therefore must rely solely on her experience. Her people have been afflicted by a previously unknown and severe disease. Fortunately, the physician has discovered a symptom that signals the disease, although not with certainty. In her lifetime she has seen 1,000 people, 10 of whom had the disease. Of those 10, 8 showed the symptom; of the 990 not afflicted, 95 did. Now a new patient appears. He has the symptom. What is the probability that he actually has the disease? (p. 686)

You may have recognized this task as a variant of the mammography task described in chapter 1. Indeed, it is formally and numerically identical to that task, if the 95 out of the 990 not afflicted who showed the symptom are replaced by 99 out of 990. We have seen that the mammography task can be solved by applying Bayes' formula but can also be solved by a much simpler algorithm: Divide the number of cases with disease and symptom ($N = 8$) by the total number of cases with symptom ($N = 8 + 95 = 103$). The result, p(disease | symptom) = .078, is the same as that found with Bayes' formula. This example illustrates a critical property of adaptive algorithms designed for solving statistical tasks: they work for frequencies but not for probabilities or percentages. Mathematical probability and percentages are, after all, comparatively recent developments in human history (Gigerenzer, et al., 1989). As already mentioned in chapter 1, studies in which the two presentation formats have been tested against each other using conjunction and Bayesian tasks showed a huge advantage for the frequency format.

More generally, because adaptive algorithms are shaped by their natural environments, they should be more effective the more faithfully the task represents that environment. In the case of statistical tasks, people should not only do better when information is represented in absolute frequencies than in probabilities, but should also be sensitive to the way in which items or events are sampled. Participants should, for instance, show higher solution rates if they experience the sampling process (or a vivid illustration thereof) themselves than if they merely read about it.

The aim of the adaptive-algorithms approach is to find out why people's mental capacities are as they are, rather than to explain why people's judgments did not conform to normative models, in a great number of studies on statistical tasks. However, the account allows one to infer the conditions in which people's judgments should be less than optimal: when the presentation of the task is not similar to a representation in the natural environment. This was the case for the vast majority of the tasks in which judgmental errors were found. Most of these tasks were presented as texts with the numerical information formulated as probabilities.

---

of psychological mechanisms that solved these problems and should be found in humans today (for examples of each kind of research, see Barkow, Cosmides, & Tooby, 1992).

Implications for Training

According to the adaptive-algorithms approach, people should have little difficulty in solving statistical tasks if they are presented in a natural format. Therefore, to improve performance it should suffice to teach people how to translate
information from the format encountered in the task (e.g., texts involving probabilities) into a natural format. Teaching the normative models and their applicability, as advocated in the abstract-rules approach, should not be as effective. The
single most effective translation strategy seems to be that going from probabilities or percentages into frequencies. Adaptive algorithms tuned to the natural
format are expected to take care of the rest.

TRAINING PROGRAMS AS EVALUATION INSTRUMENTS

To date, the four theoretical approaches have not yet been directly compared
against each other. This is probably due to their different foci and the different
sizes of the areas they cover. There have been experimental studies that compared
two approaches each, however. In recent years, the heuristics-and-biases account
has been increasingly criticized on both theoretical and empirical grounds (e.g.,
Gigerenzer, 1991; Gigerenzer, 1996b; Gigerenzer & Murray, 1987; Lopes,
1991). The critique relies substantially on arguments originating from the adaptive-algorithms approach (e.g., Gigerenzer, 1994; Gigerenzer & Hoffrage, 1995).
The abstract-rules approach has also been criticized by advocates of the adaptive-
algorithms approach, mostly on the application of logical rules such as modus
tollens (Cosmides, 1989; Gigerenzer & Hug, 1992; see also Volume 4, 1995, of
the journal *Thinking & Reasoning*). The pragmatic-implications approach has
been sporadically contrasted with the heuristics-and-biases approach (see Hilton,
1995).

In the subsequent chapters of this book, a direct comparison of the four approaches to judgment under uncertainty will be attempted. It should be apparent
by now that the approaches differ widely in their predictions about whether statistical training is possible, and if so, how such training should look. We have
developed several training programs according to the different approaches. These
programs have been used as evaluation instruments. Chapters 5 to 11 report on
the results. The predictions about whether, how, and how well statistical reasoning can be trained derived for each approach here enable a direct comparison.
Table 2.1 summarizes these predictions as well as explanations from each approach as to why people (sometimes) do not reason according to probability
theory.

TABLE 2.1

Explanations for People's Deviations From Probability Theory in Their Judgments, and Implications for Training

	Why Do People (Sometimes) Not Reason According to Probability Theory?	*Can Statistical Reasoning Be Taught? How?*
Pragmatic implications	The mind draws pragmatic implications when interpreting texts. When texts are understood differently than intended by the experimenter, judgments may not follow probability theory. (Some deviations from probability theory may be due to faulty statistical reasoning, but explaining these is beyond the approach.)	People should be trained to translate the language of probability into natural language. The training suggested by the adaptive-algorithms explanation could be one way of doing so.
Heuristics and biases	The mind has no mechanisms for making good probability judgments but rather uses rules of thumb (heuristics) that rely on similarity or ease of retrieval. Use of these heuristics leads to biases or cognitive illusions, which are as stable as visual illusions.	Effective training is not possible.
Abstract rules	The mind has rules conforming to probabilistic models, but their applicability is sometimes not clear. In such cases, heuristics may take over and lead to biased judgments.	Statistical rules should be taught in their abstract forms and their applicability should be demonstrated by examples.
Adaptive algorithms	The mind has evolved adaptive algorithms that only work on natural frequencies. If tasks are presented in a probability format, judgments may not follow probability models.	People should be taught to translate conventional statistical tasks stated in probability format into a natural frequency format.

Although the pragmatic-implications and the adaptive-reasoning approaches imply a very similar kind of training, there are some slight differences. First, the pragmatic-implications approach is open as to whether additional training in inference strategies (stage two) is needed, whereas the adaptive-algorithms approach predicts that training should teach people how to translate unnatural representational formats (e.g., probabilities) into natural ones (e.g., frequencies). Second, unlike the adaptive-algorithms approach, the pragmatic-implications approach does not specify whether a given representation should be superior to another.

On a superficial level, one might expect similar recommendations for training from the heuristics-and-biases, the abstract-rules, and the adaptive-algorithms approach because rules play a key role in each. There are fundamental differences, however, between the kinds of rules central in each approach. Heuristics are faulty rules that may lead to correct solutions, but often do not. Abstract rules and adaptive algorithms, in contrast, are bound to lead to correct solutions. The difference between the latter two is that abstract rules are assumed to be format independent, whereas adaptive algorithms are held to be highly dependent on a specific input format. In chapter 14, a model that draws on the adaptive-algorithms approach will explain more about the exact specification of rules and the role of input format.

Although the diverse theoretical perspectives on statistical reasoning have not been systematically compared before in training studies, such training studies have been performed. Chapter 3 reviews studies about training for statistical reasoning and examines (post hoc) how well the four approaches account for the results.

3

Prior Training Studies

SUMMARY: Training based on either ad hoc approaches, the pragmatic-implications approach, or the abstract-rules approach yielded little or moderate improvement in performance on statistical reasoning tasks. Training on conjunctive probabilities had a moderate beneficial effect, but after training, about half of participants were still not able to solve conjunction tasks correctly. The results of the few training studies about conditional probabilities were similar. Attempts to train Bayesian reasoning were even less successful. Training about the impact of sample size led to moderately improved performance, although training effects were not larger than item effects. Overall, the results of training studies do not support the heuristics-and-biases approach and do not allow for strong conclusions about the other three approaches.

The four approaches discussed in chapter 2 give different explanations for why people do or do not follow probability theory in their judgments. Because the approaches differ in their predictions about whether training is possible and how training about statistical reasoning should look, the results of training studies can be used to discriminate among them. This chapter analyzes all training studies about conjunctive and conditional probabilities, Bayesian inference, and the impact of sample size that could be found in the literature, and examines how their results bear on the four theoretical approaches.[1] Because the studies used different designs and dependent measures, an overall metaanalysis could not be conducted, but summaries of subsets of the results are given whenever possible.

The training curriculum developed by Beyth-Marom et al. (1985) covers several basic issues of *thinking under uncertainty* in everyday life such as listing and grouping possible answers, random sampling, and the estimation of conjunctive and conditional probabilities. It does not, however, include more advanced topics such as Bayesian inference or a thorough treatment of the impact of sample size. Designed for 14-year-old students to use in a classroom setting, the training

---

[1]In addition to training studies, there have been suggestions on how to improve judgment under uncertainty. For instance, von Winterfeldt & Edwards (1986, pp. 536–537) gave advice on how Bayesian inference could be improved, including helping the subject structure the problem, modeling prior probabilities explicitly, stressing the statistical nature of base rate information, clarifying causal chains or providing individuating information about base rates. These suggestions have not, however, been systematically evaluated.

lasted 35 to 40 hours. Unfortunately, although the approach looks very promising, it was evaluated in only a preliminary way, and therefore its effectiveness is unclear. It appears that all other previous training programs about judgment under uncertainty centered on one or another specific kind of task (e.g., conjunctive but not conditional probabilities). This chapter separately reviews prior attempts to train people on conjunctive probabilities, conditional probabilities including Bayesian inference, and the impact of sample size. For all types of tasks, the results are considered separately with respect to each of the approaches discussed in chapter 2. Training approaches that are not grounded in a larger theoretical framework, such as priming and corrective feedback, are also reported in the appropriate sections.

CONJUNCTIVE PROBABILITIES

Abstract Rules

Statistics courses can be seen as training in the abstract rules of probability theory, which are usually first introduced in their general form and then applied to examples. Extensive training in abstract rules, that is, taking a larger number of statistics courses, might be expected to yield greater improvement in statistical thinking than taking one or no course. To test for this possibility in conjunction tasks, Tversky and Kahneman (1983) examined whether statistical sophistication made a difference in solution rates in the Linda task and in other tasks. Comparing the solution rates of *naive* (no background in probability or statistics), *informed* (one or more basic courses in statistics), and *sophisticated* (several advanced courses in probability, statistics and decision theory) student participants, they found only slight differences. On average, 9.5% of naive, 12% of informed, and 16% of sophisticated participants reasoned according to the conjunction rule. In another study, Tversky and Kahneman (1983, p. 300) found that 64% of a statistically sophisticated group applied the conjunction rule in the Linda task. However, this study lacked a control group and used a probability rating scale instead of the usual response format. Comparing medical student participants who either had or had not studied decision theory, Wolford, Taylor, and Beck (1990) found similar performance in the two groups for the original Linda task, that is, 8% and 11% of solutions were in accord with the conjunction rule in the two groups, respectively. However, when they added a *prediction scenario* to the Linda task, different results emerged. In the prediction scenario, a computer was said to have randomly generated predictions about college graduates. Three of these predictions concerned what occupation (e.g., bank teller, bank teller and active in the feminist movement) Linda, a hypothetical roommate, would have in 10 years. Participants were asked to bet on the most likely prediction. In this version of the Linda task, the percentage of conjunctive solutions covaried with statistical expertise. Whereas the solution rates for statistically naive participants were 27% and 35% in Studies 2 and 3, the respective results for those who knew some statistics were 57% and 59%.

Abstract statistical rules were also taught in a more direct way than in statistics courses. Several studies examined the impact of training in the conjunction rule on reasoning in conjunction tasks. Crandall and Greenfield (1986) taught participants the conjunction rule and used Venn diagrams to illustrate the rule in specific examples. After the training, all participants were given four conjunction tasks from Tversky and Kahneman (1983). The solution rate in the training condition was modestly higher than in a placebo condition (53% vs. 27% correct solutions). In another study, Agnoli and Krantz (1989) asked participants to read an 11-page text that introduced Venn diagrams as a general thinking tool. After illustrating how to apply them to categories and subcategories (e.g., Chevrolets, cars, and vehicles), the text taught participants the conjunction rule by explicating Venn diagrams of partially overlapping categories (e.g., "women who swim regularly for exercise" and "professional women volleyball players"). The test consisted of eight conjunction tasks. Participants in the training group gave 56% and 55% correct solutions in Experiments 1 and 2, respectively, whereas those in the corresponding control groups solved only 27% and 26% of the tasks correctly in the two experiments, respectively. Benassi and Knoth (1993, Study 3) gave participants the same training regimen used by Crandall and Greenfield (1986), but asked one of the two training groups to give brief justifications for their answers and the other to indicate why their answers were correct in light of the instructions given in the training. The latter prompt should force students to consider their answers in relation to the conjunction rule. For the two tasks used (including the Linda task), the training led to 44% correct solutions in the former and 65% correct solutions in the latter group. Although this study did not include a control condition, the 33% correct solutions Benassi and Knoth (1993) found in the condition without instructional set or training in Study 2 provide a rough estimate for comparison. Finally, using Agnoli and Krantz's (1989) training procedure, Fisk and Pidgeon (1997) found 48.7% correct solutions in the control group and 58.1% in the training group (averaged across all types of tasks in their Table 2).

Taken together, the results of these abstract-rules training studies about conjunctive probabilities indicate that such training is effective. Statistics courses per se do not seem to be very successful unless hints are given, which might work as extensional cues. Teaching the conjunction rule directly is more effective, but even this training effect cannot really be seen as a big success because almost half of participants still were not able to solve conjunction tasks correctly after training.

Pragmatic Implications

Crandall and Greenfield's (1986) attempts to train also included a linguistic train-ing, which was intended to make participants sensitive to the logical meaning of conjunctions in natural language by explaining the explicit and implicit mean-ings of the conjunction "and." It also tried to make clear that in the conjunction task, A (e.g., Linda is a bank teller) does not mean A and not B (e.g., Linda is a bank teller and is not active in the feminist movement). The effect of this inter-vention was quite small (33% correct solutions compared to 27% in the placebo condition). Although the experimenters did not verify that participants under-stood the tasks after the training, they did check as to whether participants were able to recognize conjunctions in texts. Compared to a control group, the lin-guistic training group recognized only 10% more conjunctions (72% vs. 62%). Thus, it remains possible that a more thorough training might have achieved a better result.

Priming

Fiedler (1988) examined whether priming participants with particularly easy tasks, that were not expected to produce the conjunction fallacy (Study 1) or Venn diagrams (Study 3) would accomplish higher solution rates in later con-junction tasks. Neither priming manipulation had an effect, the difference be-tween priming and no-priming conditions being -3% in Study 1 and +2% in Study 3. Benassi and Knoth (1993, Study 2) also tried to prime participants with an easy conjunction task. In the group that was told that the difficult task fol-lowing the prime could be solved analogously, the correct solution rate (35% correct solutions) was only 2% higher overall than in the group that received no such instruction.

Evaluation of Training on Conjunctive Probabilities

Figure 3.1 summarizes the findings of training studies about conjunctive tasks. The data are averaged across studies and weighted by sample size. Note that the results for the different kinds of training differ in reliability because the number of studies[2] represented by each percentage varies from one for the pragmatic-im-plications training to six for the abstract-rules training. As the unshaded columns indicate, the spontaneous solution rates are generally about 30% across studies, consistent with the findings of nontraining studies about conjunctive-probability tasks. The first three pairs of columns show that neither priming nor having some general background in statistics had much impact on reasoning in conjunc-tion tasks. However, when the tasks contained hints due to a supposedly com-puter-generated scenario (Wolford et al., 1990), having statistical background

---

[2]Each comparison which used an independent group of participants was classified as a study.

improved performance (fourth pair of columns). The modest size of this training effect was comparable to that of conventional abstract-rules training (fifth pair of columns).

The results obtained with priming, pragmatic-implications training, and statistics courses seem at first to support the no-effect prediction of the heuristics-and-biases approach. This picture changes when one considers the results of studies that relied on the abstract-rules approach, whether in the form of prior statistical training plus hints (to a frequentistic view?),[3] or in a form directly dealing with conjunction tasks. Even the improvement (of about 25%) due to abstract-rules training does not look like a huge success, however, if one recalls that almost half of participants were not able to solve the tasks correctly immediately after training.

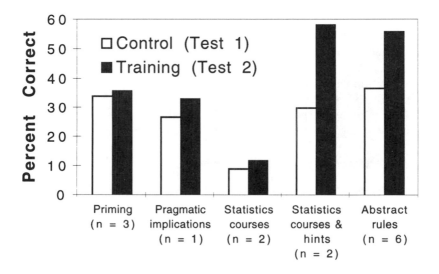

FIG. 3.1.   Percentages of solutions in accord with the conjunction rule in studies examining several kinds of training. Values are means of weighted means (by sample size per study).

---

[3]These hints might have overruled the pragmatic implications from the personality description of Linda, an explanation which might also hold for the isolated result Tversky and Kahneman (1983) found (not included in Fig. 3.1). One could suspect that the effect in the Wolford et al. (1990) study was due to some participants creating a frequentistic representation of the task by considering the many possible predictions generated by the program. As mentioned in chapter 1, Tversky and Kahneman (1983) also found that an extensional understanding greatly helped to solve conjunction tasks.

CONDITIONAL PROBABILITIES AND BAYESIAN INFERENCE

Conditional probability tasks have received much less attention in training programs than have conjunctive probability tasks. Despite the large number of studies demonstrating people's difficulties in solving Bayesian inference tasks (for overviews, see Bar-Hillel, 1980; Borgida & Brekke, 1982; Medin & Bettger, 1991), there have been only a few attempts to train Bayesian inference. Most of the few training attempts for conditional probabilities focused on Bayesian inference only. The exception is a training regimen developed by Bea and Scholz (1995) that dealt with conditional probabilities in a broad sense, including Bayesian inference. Bea and Scholz's main focus was on mathematics education, that is, they were mainly interested in assessing the effectiveness of various types of training rather than in testing a specific theoretical approach. They compared different ways of representing conditional probabilities graphically to find out which of these was most suitable to visualizing conditional probabilities. Although Bea and Scholz did not provide an explicit theoretical foundation for their training program, it can be regarded as a realization of training based on the abstract-rules approach. Rule-training programs such as Bea and Scholz's are designed to teach reasoning about conditional probabilities by first explaining the rule (e.g., Bayes' formula) in its abstract form and then explaining how to use that rule (Falk & Konold, 1992).

Abstract Rules

Bea and Scholz performed their training in an advanced statistics course. The participants were second-year business students at a German university who had completed at least one course in statistics. Most of them had received training in statistics during secondary school (the German Gymnasium) as well. During the training, the experimenter thoroughly explained the conditional probability rule (10 minutes), then introduced Bayes' formula and (except in the control condition) its connection to one of four representational formats (10 minutes), and finally demonstrated the use of the format in three conditional probability tasks, two of which were Bayesian inference tasks (about 30 minutes). The representational formats were either mathematical formulas or one of three graphical formats: the tree, the reversed tree, and the unit square. Figure 3.2 shows simple versions of the three graphical representations. There are two hypotheses, H and $\neg H$ ("$\neg$" being logical "not") and two kinds of data, D and $\neg D$. Each of the three representations allows one to derive conditional probability judgments.[4]

---

[4]For instance, the representations allow one to model Bayesian inference tasks such as the mammography task (see chapter 1). If we let H denote the hypothesis that a woman has breast cancer, and D denote that a mammography resulted in a positive result, the hypothesis that a woman who has tested positive actually has breast cancer, $p(H \mid D)$ can be solved by the three

Tree

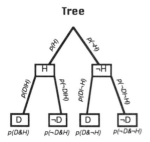

Reversed Tree

Unit Square

FIG. 3.2. Simplified versions of the three graphical representations used in Bea and Scholz's (1995) training program on conditional probabilities: the tree, reversed tree, and unit square (after Bea and Scholz, 1995, Figures 1–3).

Bea and Scholz's participants completed a baseline pretest about 1 week before the training and a test immediately after training. About one half of the participants completed a retest about 6 months after the first one. Each test consisted of five tasks that dealt with conditional probabilities in different ways. The mean improvements immediately after training and 6 months later are shown in Fig. 3.3 (immediate and long-term). The groups did not differ in their baseline performances which were 52% for all participants, including the subgroup that was tested after 6 months on the long-term effect of the training.[5] In the control group, the improvement from baseline to first test was 12% without any specific

representations as follows: From the tree, one only needs the first and the third lower nodes, $p(D \ \& \ H)$ and $p(D \ \& \ \neg H)$ to arrive at a version of Bayes' formula:

$$p(H \mid D) = p(D \ \& \ H) \ / \ [p(D \ \& \ H) + p(D \ \& \ \neg H)].$$

From the reversed tree, only the left part is needed: $p(H \mid D) = p(D \mid H)p(H) \ / \ p(D)$. The unit square finally shows the solution most directly and leads to the same version of Bayes' formula as the tree above.

[5]German second-year business students probably have had a higher amount of exposure to statistics than American college students, the typical population used in judgmental studies. This might explain the unusually high pretest results.

training. Compared to the control group, the training groups did from about 10% to 15% better on the first test (Fig. 3.3).

There was no marked difference among the four training conditions. On the 6-month retest, however, the groups who had learned to use graphical displays showed larger gains than the group trained with formulas only. The training effect was largest in the unit-square group. Unfortunately, there was no control group for the retest because all participants had received training by that time. In addition, Bea and Scholz do not report how those participants who underwent a retest after 6 months had performed on the first test after training, although the non-difference between the baseline results of that subgroup and those of the whole group supports their conclusion that there is a differential effect due to the different representations. However, the 12% improvement in the control group's performance from baseline to the first test suggests that influences other than the training (e.g., the course itself or the task repetition) had some beneficial effect.

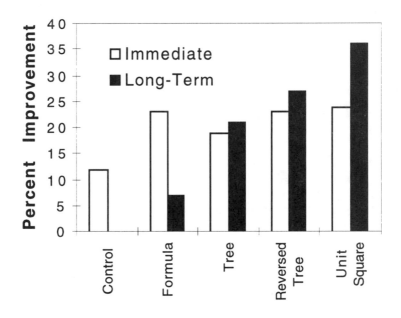

FIG. 3.3. Mean percent improvement in performance on conditional probability tasks (averaged across tasks) after Bea and Scholz's (1995) training program, both immediately after training (Immediate) and after about 6 months after the training (Long-Term) for a control group, a training group that learned formulas, and three training groups that learned tree, reversed-tree, and unit-square graphical representations, respectively (adapted from Tables 2 and 3, Bea and Scholz, 1995).

The most serious drawback of this study is that statistical training continued after the immediate retest, in the form of the advanced statistics course in which all participants were enrolled. The superior effect of the unit-square representation and the comparatively higher training effects in the conditions with graphical representations could be due to contents of the ongoing course.[6] These problems make an evaluation of this training attempt difficult.

Fong, Lurigio, and Stalans (1990, Study 2) seem to have been the only other researchers who attempted to teach Bayesian reasoning using the abstract-rules approach. They administered abstract-rules training about the (empirical) law of large numbers (see chapter 1), predicting that participants would generalize it to Bayesian inference tasks. (They did not explain why there would be such a generalization effect.) The trainees were probation officers at different stages in their careers. After the training, participants were asked to judge the likelihood of recidivism for several criminal offenders described in case descriptions. In one condition, participants received *high-risk base-rate information* stating that the cases were selected from a group of 100 offenders, of whom 80% had actually committed crimes while on probation. In the other condition, participants received *low-risk base-rate information*, with the recidivism rate stated to be only 20%. A typical case description read as follows (Fong et al., 1990):

> Offender F is a 22-year-old, black male sentenced to probation for a felony theft. Mr. F is married, has a high school diploma, and has been steadily employed as a punch press operator. Currently, he is unemployed and claims to be looking for work, which he has been able to successfully find in the past. Mr. F appears to be of average intelligence and reports no addiction, but states that he has experimented with cocaine on several occasions. His rap sheet shows five prior arrests for property offenses and one prior probation, which he completed without incident. (p. 381)

The training, although not designed for Bayesian tasks, enhanced the use of base-rate information as compared to a control group that had not received the training. However, the training effect was only found in the high-risk but not the low-risk condition. Fong et al. (1990) explain this differential effect in terms of mental effort: Because misjudging high-risk cases has more severe consequences, officers usually think harder about high-risk cases.

Corrective Feedback

In the 1960s, before the heuristics-and-biases program dominated research on judgment and decision making, it was often found that participants were conservative in revising the probability of a hypothesis (H) being correct in light of new data (D) (e.g., Phillips & Edwards, 1966; Phillips, Hays, & Edwards,

---

[6]For instance, if the course relied heavily on graphical teaching aids, this could be expected to markedly enhance the training effect of the graphical training conditions.

1966). That is, they updated $p(H \mid D)$, the probability of their hypothesis being correct given the new data, to a lesser extent than one would if one were applying Bayes' formula. Assuming that participants' probability revisions adhered to Bayes' formula, but were based on the wrong $p(D \mid H)$, Peterson, DuCharme, and Edwards (1968, Exp. 2) examined whether conservatism in revising $p(H)$ could be reduced by improving participants' judgments of the likelihood $p(D \mid H)$.

The training regimen they designed to do this proceeded as follows. In the first step, participants were asked to imagine two urns that contained different numbers of red and blue marbles or poker chips in symmetric proportions (e.g., one urn containing 60 red and 40 blue and the other 40 red and 60 blue). They were then presented with samples of red and blue marbles and were asked to estimate $p(H \mid D)$, the (a posteriori) probability that this sample came from the predominantly red urn. Participants made estimates for many combinations of r (red) out of n marbles (the varying total number of marbles) and varying values of p, the base-rate probability of drawing a red marble. In the next step, participants estimated sampling distributions for $p(D \mid H)$, that is, they indicated the probability that r out of n marbles would come out red. They responded by distributing 100 counters across $n + 1$ columns. For instance, with an n of 3, and a given p, the counters were used to indicate the probability that 0, 1, 2, and 3 marbles in the sample were red. In this way, Peterson et al. (1968) obtained standardized (because 100 counters were used each time) sampling distributions for each combination of n (3, 5, and 8) and p (.6, .7, and .8). As predicted, the values of $p(D \mid H)$ or equivalently, $p(r \mid n,p)$, they found accounted for people's initial (conservative) estimates of $p(H \mid D)$. Now the real training began. Participants were shown theoretical sampling distributions and were prompted to pay attention to the characteristics that changed as n and p varied, notably to the fact that sampling distributions become more peaked as n and p increased. In the last step, participants again judged values of $p(H \mid D)$, but were instructed to apply what they had learned during the training stage. The training effect was weak: Participants' $p(H \mid D)$ judgments still showed considerable conservatism.

Schaefer (1976) let his participants construct subjective probability distributions for prior distributions (e.g., p[female]), likelihoods (e.g., p[car owner | female]), and posterior distributions (e.g. p[female | car owner]), referring to the student population of which they were members. Participants had received considerable training in statistics and mathematics and were acquainted with the assessment technique used.[7] In each of five sessions they had to construct 66 sub-

---

[7]For constructing a subjective probability distribution, participants had to assign probabilities (or probability masses) to proportions that were partitioned into 10 equidistant classes, 1% to 10%, 10% to 20%,…, 90% to 100%. For instance, if a task was to construct a subjective probability distribution for the prior probability p(female), the probability that a member of the student population was female, each of the 10 intervals would be given a probability value ranging from 0 to 1 with a

jective probability distributions and received feedback at the beginning of sessions 2 to 5 about their overall performances. This feedback, which was also the basis for a participant's monetary payoff, rested on the probabilities he or she had assigned to the classes that contained the true values for each of the 66 distributions. Despite all these efforts, training had no noticeable effect.

Another kind of corrective feedback in Bayesian reasoning tasks was given in a study by Lindeman, van den Brink, and Hoogstraten (1988). Participants received different versions of Kahneman and Tversky's (1973) engineer–lawyer task (see chapter 1), which consists of base-rate information, $p(H)$, and a personality description that can be used to estimate $p(D \mid H)$. For each of 16 different personality descriptions, participants first had to make a judgment given a base rate of .5 (i.e., 50 engineers and 50 lawyers) and then (using the same personality description) a judgment given a different base rate. The training group received feedback about the normative Bayesian answer to the second judgment, which can be calculated from the first judgment (see appendix A). The effect of this training procedure was later evaluated using a task (from Zukier & Pepitone, 1984) that was formally equivalent to the engineer–lawyer task. The group that had received corrective feedback did as poorly as a control group on this task.

Focusing and Explanations

Fischhoff et al. (1979, Study 1) tried to increase participants' sensitivities to the impact of base rates by varying the base rates within the same individual, but without giving feedback on participants' solutions. They used two tasks which are formally equivalent to the mammography task (see chapter 1). One was the cab task (cf. Fischhoff & Bar-Hillel, 1984)[8]:

> Two cab companies, the Blue and the Green, operate in a given city. Eighty-five percent of the cabs in the city are Blue: the remaining 15% are Green. A cab was involved in a hit-and-run accident at night. A witness identified the cab as a Green cab. The court tested the witness' ability to distinguish between Blue and Green cabs under nighttime visibility conditions. It found that the witness was able to identify each color correctly about 80% of the time, but confused it with the other color about 20% of the time.

---

sum of 1 (e.g., in the case of total ignorance, a participant might assign probabilities of .1 to all 10 classes).

[8]This task has become quite famous in the literature about judgment and decision making and the wording was changed several times (e.g. from Fischhoff et al., 1979 to the cited version) because of criticisms of the proposed normative solution (see Birnbaum, 1983). The proposed solution via Bayes' formula is $p(\text{Green} \mid \text{"Green"}) = .41$, calculated as:

$$p(\text{Green} \mid \text{"Green"}) = \frac{p(\text{"Green"} \mid \text{Green})\, p(\text{Green})}{p(\text{"Green"} \mid \text{Green})\, p(\text{Green}) + p(\text{"Green"} \mid \text{Blue})\, p(\text{Blue})},$$

with the base rates $p(\text{Green}) = .15$ and $p(\text{Blue}) = .85$, and the likelihoods $p(\text{"Green"} \mid \text{Green}) = .80$ and $p(\text{"Green"} \mid \text{Blue}) = .20$.

What do you think are the chances that the errant cab was indeed Green, as
the witness claimed? (p.178)

A given participant might receive this task first with the above numbers,
then be told that actually only 2% (or 98%) of the cabs in the city are green.
This focusing manipulation had some effect on participants' repeated judgments
on the same task, but almost no generalizing effect on a second task with a similar structure. In three later experiments, Fischhoff and Bar-Hillel (1984) examined the effect of different focusing techniques[9] on performance on Bayesian inference tasks. Participants indeed took the information to which the experimenters called their attention into account. However, they did so whether the information was relevant to the probability judgment or not.

In a recent training study (Wolfe 1995, Exp. 3), the training group received
explanations about the hit rate, $p(D \mid H)$, because in prior studies participants
had been found to commit conversion errors, that is, they had confused $p(D \mid H)$
with $p(H \mid D)$. Explanations were given on a computer screen either in the form
of a text or as a pictorial representation of the hit-rate concept in a task that dealt
with balls and jars. In Wolfe's experiments, participants had to solve Bayesian
tasks by choosing from a menu of Bayesian information; some pieces were relevant for solving a given task and some were not. The training resulted in more
participants in the training group examining relevant information than participants in the control group examined. This was, however, the case only for a task
that dealt with balls and jars, and there apparently was no transfer to other tasks.
Participants in the training group were more accurate in respect to their solutions
than those in the control group in only one of five Bayesian tasks.

Evaluation of Training Attempts on Conditional Probability Tasks

Neither giving participants corrective feedback on their probability estimates
(Lindeman et al., 1988; Peterson et al., 1968; Schaefer, 1976), nor directing
their attention to relevant information (Fischhoff & Bar-Hillel, 1984; Wolfe,
1995) seem to be very helpful in teaching Bayesian inference. Whereas Peterson
et al. (1968) argued that participants' estimates of $p(H \mid D)$ originated from biased estimates of $p(D \mid H)$ and therefore attempted to improve their estimates of
$p(D \mid H)$, Lindeman et al. did not provide much theoretical justification for their
approach of giving feedback to estimates of posterior probabilities. Fong et al.
(1990) based their training on the abstract-rules approach, but did not explain

---

[9]Techniques used were *Subjective Sensitivity Analysis*, which requires participants to consider
what judgments they would make, were a given item of information to assume each of a series of
possible values; *Isolation Analysis*, which requires people to consider what judgment they would
make were each item of information the only one available; *Minimal Focusing*, which exhorts
people to think harder; and *Balanced Subjective-Sensitivity Analysis*, which is Subjective-Sensitivity Analysis applied to both usually-ignored and usually-not-ignored items (Fischhoff & Bar-Hillel,
1984).

why training on the impact of sample size should improve use of base-rate information. Moreover, their design did not allow for comparisons between participants' solutions and an exact Bayesian solution, because only base-rate information was given. Due to both this and to their inconsistent results, that is, training effects only if p(recidivism) was high but not when it was low, no strong conclusions about the abstract-rules approach can be drawn on the basis of their data. Bea and Scholz's (1995) results provide better support for the abstract-rules approach. However, their long-term result implies that not only abstract rules, but also the kind of graphical representation, play important roles in training; recall that participants trained on the unit square fared better than those trained on the tree- and reversed-tree representations. Unfortunately, methodological weaknesses (see above) make it difficult to evaluate the effectiveness of the training programs used in the study.

IMPACT OF SAMPLE SIZE

Nisbett and colleagues originated almost all regimens for teaching the impact of sample size (for an overview, see Nisbett, 1993). All of these regimens are based on the abstract-rules approach and deal exclusively with frequency-distribution tasks (see chapter 1).

Abstract Rules

Fong et al.'s (1986) training program taught participants the rule that sample parameters approach population parameters as a function of sample size and as an inverse function of sample variability. Although different versions of the training were tested, we will only consider what proved to be the most effective one: full training. In this version, the rule was explained in words, demonstrated with the help of an urn, and illustrated with written examples.[10] After the training, raters coded participants' responses on open-ended sample-size tasks as either deterministic, poor statistical, or good statistical. For instance, in one task, a young man named Keith stops at a gas station and plays two slot machines for a short time. He loses money on the left one, but wins on the right one, and concludes that the right slot machine provides a higher chance of winning. An old man who has lived nearby and played both machines for years disagrees. In the old man's judgment, the left machine gave an about even chance of winning but the one on the right was fixed so that the chance of losing was much higher than that of winning. Participants were asked to comment on Keith's conclusion that

---

[10]In the urn demonstration, the experimenter drew several samples of blue and red gumballs from an urn. One could argue that this part of the training is consistent with the adaptive-algorithms approach (see chapter 11). The urn demonstration was, however, not used in all training studies, and the translation from sampling from an urn to other tasks was not practiced. The latter is an essential part of a training according to the adaptive-algorithms approach.

the chance of winning on the right machine was higher. Fong et al. gave examples of the three kinds of responses for this task. The following one was classified as *entirely deterministic*: "Keith's reasoning was poor, provided the information given by the man was accurate. The man, however, may have been deceiving Keith." (p.258)

The next response was considered a *poor statistical* one: "I think that Keith's conclusion is wrong because the old man had better luck on the left one, so he thought it was better. Keith had better luck on the right one so he thought it was better. I don't think you could have a better chance on either one." (p. 259)

Finally, a good statistical response is this one: "Keith's conclusion is weak. He is wrong in making the assumptions against the old man. Keith is judging the machines on only a handful of trials and not with the sample number the old man has developed over the years. Therefore, Keith's margin of error is much more great than the old man's." (p. 259)

Combining poor and good statistical responses, Fong et al. obtained 64% and 77% statistical responses after full training in Experiments 1 and 2, respectively. The corresponding results for the control groups, which received no training, were 42% and 53%, respectively. The gains achieved by training were thus 22% and 24%, respectively.

When considering these results, one should realize that they are averaged across three different types of task, termed subjective, objective, and probabilistic by Fong et al., as already mentioned in chapter 2. For instance, subjective tasks dealt with whether a 3-year-old child will like sports in later life, or why some nurses are unusually warm and compassionate toward patients when they first start to work and later turn out to be not much more concerned and caring than their colleagues. Objective tasks were about, for example, college admissions decisions or choosing baseball players for a team. The slot-machine task was an example of a probabilistic task. One could argue that most of the subjective tasks, and perhaps to some degree the objective tasks as well, do not meet two criteria that have to be met in order to justify greater confidence in larger samples. First, the expected values (e.g., the proportions of wins for the slot machines) must be stable over time, and second, samples must be randomly drawn. Participants might be sensitive to whether a task meets these criteria, and treat subjective and objective tasks differently from probabilistic ones as a result. For instance, people might expect a 3-year-old's predilection for sports to change over time, and might believe college admissions samples to be biased, and therefore might not apply the empirical law of large numbers (see chapter 1). There is evidence for this conjecture in Fong et al.'s studies.

When the three types of tasks reported by Fong et al. are analyzed separately, the corresponding percentages of spontaneous statistical answers in the no-training control group differ considerably. For Experiments 1 and 2, these percentages were 66% and 84% for the probabilistic tasks, 36% and 52% for the objective tasks, and 23% and 25% for the subjective tasks (estimated from Figures 3 and

5, Fong et al., 1986). Thus, the task type seems to make a big difference, possibly indicating participants' sensitivities for whether or not expected values are stable over time, and whether samples can be considered as randomly drawn. Fong et al.'s Experiment 3 gives another example of the importance of hints about randomness. In it participants were presented with a task about restaurant quality. In the *no randomness cue* version, a traveling business woman often returns to restaurants where she had an excellent meal during her first visit and is usually disappointed because the meals are rarely as good as the first time. In the *randomness cue* version, an American businessman in Japan with no knowledge of the Japanese language chooses his restaurant meals by blindly dropping a pencil on the menu and ordering the dish closest to it. He is also usually disappointed when he returns to restaurants where he chose his meals by this method and where the food was superb the first time. Participants worked on one task each and were asked to explain in writing why the person in the scenario was disappointed. Statistically naive participants (without a college level course in statistics) gave only about 5% statistical responses in the version without random sampling as compared to about 50% in the version with random sampling.[11] Thus, participants seem to be sensitive to the stability of expected values and to randomness in applying the empirical law of large numbers.

The training regimen of Fong et al. was tested several more times (Fong & Nisbett, 1991; Kosonen & Winne, 1995). Instead of percentages of correct solutions, Kosonen and Winne reported only statistical reasoning scores. These scores were computed by assigning a value of 1 to an entirely deterministic response, a value of 2 to a poor statistical one, and a value of 3 to a good statistical one. Then they calculated the means of these scores for each participant.[12] Such scores had also been calculated in the original studies, and all studies were comparable in respect to these scores. Following the percentages of correct solutions found in the original studies, also the reasoning scores showed pronounced differences between the three types of tasks and they were high for probabilistic tasks already without any training.

---

[11]Why is this a sample-size task? In this task, a sample of one (the excellent meal at first visit) is compared to a larger sample (e.g. first and second meal). For one meal the chance of a deviation from the true quality of the meals offered in the restaurant is higher than for the average across many meals. So, the first meal might just be seen as a random deviation from the normal quality. In the problem including the businesswoman, wherein participants seldom reasoned statistically, they might, for instance, have expected that the businesswoman had some background knowledge (e.g., about the cook's specialty) that justifiably lead her to choose a certain dish.

[12]There is a problem with calculating means of such values because the calculation of means assumes an interval scale, which in the present case would suggest that a difference between a *deterministic answer* (coded as 1) and a *poor statistical one* (coded as 2) can be treated as equivalent to the difference between a poor statistical and a good statistical answer (coded as 3). This seems to be a problematic assumption. Moreover, statistical reasoning scores cannot easily be transformed into percentages of correct solutions, because for calculating the latter, scores of both 2 and 3 are considered correct. Assume, for instance, that five tasks were solved and a mean statistical reasoning score of 1.8 was obtained. This mean score could have been the result of 40% correct solutions (scores of 1, 1, 1, 3, 3) or of 80% correct solutions (scores of 1, 2, 2, 2, 2).

Fong et al. (1986) did not examine the long-term impact of their training, but this was done in a later study by Fong and Nisbett (1991, Experiment 1). In that study, training resulted in a 17% increase in statistical responses immediately after training from 37% at baseline to 54% immediately after training (averaged across all tasks). After two weeks, this difference had dropped to 12%. Tasks were either about sports training or ability testing, that is, about one of two content domains. The performance decrement was particularly large for tasks taken from a content domain (e.g., sports training) that differed from the domain used in the training tasks (e.g., ability testing).

Abstract Rules—Statistics Courses

In addition to the impact of directly applied abstract-rules training, Fong et al. (1986, Experiments 3 and 4) examined the impact of background in statistics on solving sample-size tasks. The differences found between groups of participants with differing statistical expertise were roughly comparable in size to the training effect achieved with their full training program. For instance, the difference in spontaneous solution rates between statistically naive participants and PhD-level scientists who had taken many statistics courses was about 40% for the traveling businesswoman task (estimated from Figure 7, Fong et al., 1986). In a later study, Lehman, Lempert and Nisbett (1988) argued that instruction in abstract-rule systems, which some experimental participants receive as part of graduate training, should affect reasoning about everyday-life events in tasks in which these rule systems could be of use to arrive at good judgments. To explore this idea, they employed tasks that were intended to measure four kinds of reasoning, including methodological, conditional, verbal, and statistical. The tasks to measure statistical reasoning, such as the following example, exclusively concerned the impact of sample size (Lehman et al., 1988):

> After the first two weeks of the major league baseball season, newspapers begin to print the top ten batting averages. Typically, after two weeks, the leading batter has an average of about .450. Yet no batter in major league history has ever averaged .450 at the end of a season. Why do you think this is? (p. 442)

The following exemplifies a correct response: "A player's high average at the beginning of the season may be just a lucky fluke." An example considered as an erroneous response is: "A batter who has such a hot streak at the beginning of the season is under a lot of stress to maintain his performance record. Such stress adversely affects his playing." (p. 442)

Lehman et al. gave such tasks in four different subjects: law, medicine, psychology, and chemistry to graduate students in the 1st and 3rd years of graduate study. Because only medicine and psychology required statistics courses, students of these two subjects were expected to choose statistical answers more often than law or chemistry students. This was indeed the case. A longitudinal design in which students were given the tasks twice, once in their 1st year and once in their 3rd year, produced comparable results (Lehman et al., 1988). Whereas the increase in percentage of statistical responses over the 2-year interval was less than 10% for law and chemistry students, it was about 25% and 65% for medical and psychology students, respectively.

Demonstration of Sampling Distributions

The training studies about the impact of sample size used frequency- and not sampling-distribution tasks. In what seems to have been the only attempt to teach the proper use of sample size in sampling-distribution tasks, Well et al. (1990, Study 4) showed participants how a sampling distribution arises by repeatedly drawing samples from a frequency distribution of the heights of adult males, and then computing their means. The training consisted of oral explanations, a demonstration of random sampling using slips of paper, and a simulation on a computer screen. After the training, a computer program generated a sampling distribution of the mean heights of 100 samples of men (10 men per sample). Participants were shown this distribution and asked whether it would have made a difference to the shape of the distribution if the sample means had been based on sample sizes of $n = 100$ instead of $n = 10$. In answering this question, only 24% of participants seemed to grasp how sample size affects the variability of sampling distributions.

Evaluation of Training Attempts on the Impact of Sample Size

Efforts to train people to take account of sample size using frequency-distribution tasks were moderately successful overall. The effects of nonspecific training (statistics courses) and specific training (training regimens completed in the laboratory) were comparable, although it is not entirely clear what aspects of the nonspecific training were responsible for the effect. Overall, the training effect was smaller than the differences between the spontaneous solution rates for different types of tasks. For instance, in Fong et al. (1986), the spontaneous solution rate was high in probabilistic tasks, in which sampling was random and the expected values of the population parameter were stable, whereas it was much lower in objective and especially in subjective tasks, in which sampling was not random and stability could not be taken for granted. This result may reflect participants' sensitivities to appropriate use of the empirical law of large numbers.

Whereas people seem to spontaneously appreciate the impact of sample size in frequency-distribution tasks in which the size-confidence intuition (see chapter 1) is justified, they seem to have persistent difficulties in solving sampling-distribution tasks, even when the process that generates the sampling distribution is explained to them as in Well et al.'s (1990) training regimen. The necessity of training in the case of frequency-distribution tasks is therefore questionable, although people definitely seem to need training in order to solve sampling-distribution tasks (Sedlmeier & Gigerenzer, 1997; Sedlmeier, 1998).

EVALUATION OF PRIOR TRAINING ATTEMPTS

Despite the differences between the tasks used to test effectiveness of training, some general conclusions about prior statistical training regimens can be drawn. The less successful attempts to teach statistical reasoning such as corrective feedback, priming, and pragmatic-reasoning training on conjunctive probability all failed in two respects. First, during training participants were given hints, but were not explicitly told how the tasks could be solved. Second, participants were not actively involved in the training process. The only exception to that is Well et al.'s (1990) attempt to teach the impact of sample size. Their procedure approximated the one suggested by the adaptive-algorithms approach because participants experienced the whole process that leads to the construction of sampling distributions. However, evolutionary history probably did not put selection pressures on the mind to evolve a specific algorithm for solving sampling-distribution tasks (Sedlmeier & Gigerenzer, 1997); and therefore from the adaptive-algorithms perspective one would expect the training effect in Well et al.'s (1990) study to be small, and it was.

The tests of some of the training regimens reviewed in the last paragraph could be interpreted as support for the heuristics-and-biases approach, which predicts all statistical training to be fairly ineffective. Training attempts based on the abstract-rules approach, however, speak against heuristics-and-biases as a good explanation of poor statistical reasoning. Such training procedures lead to moderate success in all applications. As Bea and Scholz's (1995) study showed, however, the long-term success of training seems to hinge on the kind of representation used, although the abstract-rules approach does not predict that different representations of the same abstract rule should lead to different performances. Overall, it is not clear how taking statistics courses, an indirect version of abstract-rules training, affects performance on statistical task. The majority of results suggests, however, that it generalizes to situations beyond those dealt with in the course; its effect is about the same size as that of direct rule training. However, the moderate effects obtained in different versions of abstract-rules training hardly constitute satisfactory results as one would expect from an efficient training procedure.

The training studies reviewed in this chapter provide insufficient data to test the pragmatic-reasoning and the adaptive-algorithms approaches, so there is no basis for drawing comparative conclusions about all four approaches. Moreover, it may be possible to improve on the results with training programs based on the abstract-rules approach. In the next chapter, results from instructional theory will be used to derive predictions about what factors should make training programs more effective. Chapter 4 will also specify how training programs based on the abstract-rules and the adaptive-algorithms approaches should differ, thus providing the basis for a comparison of the two approaches.

4

What Makes Statistical Training Effective?

SUMMARY: This chapter recapitulates prior training results on the four theoretical approaches to statistical reasoning outlined in chapter 2. It is argued that the merely modest success of prior training studies is at least partly attributable to a failure to take into account two features, which according to instructional theory should be helpful in training: learning by doing and flexible training materials. The importance of representational format in distinguishing the abstract-rules from the adaptive-reasoning approach is stressed, and a short preview of the training studies to be reported in later chapters is provided.

The results of training studies about statistical reasoning reported in the last chapter were meager to modest, but showed that training can be effective. Overall, the results speak against the view held by supporters of the heuristics-and-biases approach, which states that it is impossible to teach people statistical reasoning. The modest results found for abstract-rules training regimens might not be the last word about what can be achieved by statistical training, however. Surprisingly, previous training regimens did not yet explicitly apply important results from instructional theory. This chapter specifies two conditions which are informed by instructional theory, with which better training results should be found. The first is learning by doing, which has been proposed to be an essential ingredient of successful teaching, but which was largely neglected in prior training studies. The second is the use of flexible tutoring systems, which are implied and specified by results from research about computer-based instruction. These two conditions should boost the effectiveness of any kind of statistical training. However, tutoring programs derived from the abstract-rules approach differ from those derived from the adaptive-algorithms approach. Whereas for the abstract-rules approach, the representational format does not matter, its form is crucial for the adaptive-algorithms approach. This difference between the two approaches is decisive in the studies reported in following chapters. Although the pragmatic-implications approach does not specifically take representational formats into account, it is arguably closer to the adaptive-algorithms approach in this respect.

HOW TO IMPROVE TRAINING IN STATISTICAL REASONING

In order to fairly compare different training approaches, one should first try to optimize each approach, and only then to put them in competition. Learning by doing, and the use of flexible computer programs are proposed to improve training in statistical reasoning regardless of its specific design.

Learning by Doing

As good teachers know, students learn better when they are actively involved in the learning process. Not only is this observation intuitively obvious, but it rests on a sound theoretical foundation (e.g., Glaser & Bassok, 1989). The best-known theory in which learning by doing plays a central role is J. R. Anderson's ACT (*Adaptive Control of Thought*) theory, now known as ACT-R (e.g., J. R. Anderson, 1983, 1995). ACT is intended to be a comprehensive theory of human cognition that also spells out principles for instruction. Application of these principles has proved to be successful in extensive tests using computer-based tutoring systems (J. R. Anderson, Corbett, Koedinger, & Pelletier, 1995). ACT theory suggests that in order to acquire new procedural (how) knowledge, learners have to be actively engaged in problem solving; just understanding the solution to a problem when it is explained is often not enough. The importance of learning by doing has been pointed out by many other researchers as well (e.g., Anzai & Simon, 1979; Klahr, 1984; Neches, 1984; Zhu & Simon, 1887).

The instructional goal of systems for tutoring statistical reasoning is to impart a kind of procedural knowledge, specifically, to teach people to apply rules (in the abstract-rules approach) or to teach people how to translate numerical information into a different and more psychologically tractable representational format (in the adaptive-algorithms approach).[1] Therefore, according to ACT theory, participants need not only receive explanations of how to solve the tasks, but need to work through examples on their own. ACT tutors also require an elaborated student module, that is, a model of a student's current knowledge based on extensive analyses of that student's possible solution paths and typical errors. However, the student module does not seem to be a prerequisite in order for a tutoring system about statistical reasoning to be effective.

---

[1]The pragmatic-reasoning and heuristics-and-biases approaches are not dealt with here separately because the former is not specific about what kind of procedural knowledge should be imparted (although the recommendations of the adaptive-algorithms approach could be seen as one possible kind) and the latter does not expect any substantial training effect.

Flexible Tutoring Systems

There are good arguments for using computer programs in instruction. They allow a high degree of flexibility, rich presentation facilities, an arbitrarily large number of repeated trials, and immediate feedback (Sedlmeier & Wettler, 1998). What aspects of such programs make them effective? Based on more than 2 decades of research about computerized instruction, J. R. Anderson et al. (1995) concluded that the user interface, that is, what the user sees on the computer screen, is particularly critical to the effectiveness of tutoring systems. The interfaces of successful tutoring systems constructed by this group of researchers, such as the Lisp tutor (J. R. Anderson, Conrad, & Corbett, 1989) and the geometry tutor (J. R. Anderson, Boyle, & Yost, 1986), were built on the basis of extensive research and a thorough analysis of the relevant tasks. The structure of these interfaces largely determines the tutoring system's teaching procedures. Therefore, in the construction of tutoring systems for statistical reasoning, emphasis should be placed on building interfaces that represent probabilistic models well.

Especially in research on so-called intelligent tutoring systems, it was thought that modeling the student's learning process in order to tailor instructions to the student's current needs was crucial. Is such a student module necessary for effective tutoring? Increasing evidence suggests not. More than 25 years of research about intelligent tutoring systems has not yielded convincing student modules (Elsom-Cook, 1993; Sedlmeier & Wettler, 1998). Even if student modules could precisely diagnose a student's current knowledge state (which they cannot), they would still often lack instructional interventions that make use of the diagnosis (Self, 1990). An exact diagnosis does not seem to be necessary for individual-tailored instruction. The student modules of expert human teachers tend to be undifferentiated, incomplete, and sometimes outright wrong (McDougall, Cumming, Cropp, & Sussex, 1995; Putnam, 1987). This suggests that for practical purposes one could do without the student module altogether.[2] Therefore, the tutoring systems described and tested in the next chapters do not have elaborated student modules, but instead concentrate on the effect of various theoretically derived user interfaces and on learning by doing.

REPRESENTATIONAL FORMAT: ADAPTIVE ALGORITHMS VERSUS ABSTRACT RULES

Pictorial representations help people to solve many kinds of tasks, including mathematical and statistical tasks (Schnotz & Grzondziel, 1996; Tukey, 1977).

---

[2]This does not mean that research about student modules is superfluous—it can reveal (and has revealed) important insights about how students learn (e.g., J. R. Anderson, Farrell, & Sauers, 1984). One should, however, dispense with the expectation that such modules will help much in teaching students, at least in their current versions.

Different explanations of this fact have been advanced. For instance, the dual coding theory (e.g., Paivio, 1971, 1978) posits two independent, but interacting, cognitive subsystems, a verbal system and an imaging system, both of which are involved in the processing of visual information. With regard to processing and retaining information, the theory predicts that visual representations, which are processed by both systems simultaneously, have an advantage over text, which is processed only by the verbal system. However, neither the dual coding theory nor another account of why pictorial representations are superior to text for learning and retention (for an overview, see Molitor, Ballstaedt, & Mandl, 1989) can explain why one type of picture should be more helpful than another. The same holds for the abstract-rules approach.

In contrast, the adaptive-algorithms approach makes differential predictions for different pictorial representations. It assumes that pictorial and other external representations are the more helpful in solving statistical tasks the more closely they resemble the naturally occurring events they represent. In the case of statistical tasks, frequency representations are predicted, therefore, to be more helpful than probability representations because unlike probabilities, frequencies can be directly experienced. The adaptive-algorithms approach also leads to the prediction that participants will be better at solving tasks involving random sampling when they witness a simulation of the sampling process themselves than when they merely read about it. Therefore, for training in statistical reasoning to be effective, it must use representations that are as close to participants' realities as possible. These realities are not those that we experience today. If they were, we would be good at solving the statistical problems we encounter in modern-day newspapers and textbooks. Instead, due to the slowness of evolutionary processes, the adaptive-algorithms approach suggests that our cognitive algorithms are adapted to a Stone-Age environment, and therefore the reality that has to be dealt with is that of Stone-Age people. Admittedly, speculations about how human environments looked in the Pleistocene are problematic. In chapters 13 and 14, an associationist model of statistical reasoning will be developed that can do without such assumptions.

RECAPITULATION AND PREVIEW

Where do we stand now? In chapter 1 we saw that people sometimes have considerable difficulties in solving statistical tasks. Chapter 2 introduced four theoretical approaches that offer different explanations for this and derived their predictions (again different) about whether and how statistical reasoning can be improved. These predictions enable comparison of the theoretical merit of the four approaches, which has not explicitly been attempted to date. In chapter 3, training studies conducted to test the effectiveness of isolated training regimens were used to make this comparison post hoc. A review of the relevant studies led to the conclusion that the overall results do not support the heuristics-and-biases approach and are inconclusive with respect to the other three approaches.

The pragmatic-implications approach differs from the other approaches in that, at least in its first phase, it does not require explicit training (see chapter 2). It states that errors might be due to a misunderstanding of the text in which a task is phrased, implying that making sure that people fully understand the text should help them to solve the task. Chapter 9 reports a study testing this implication.

Most of the other studies reported are concerned with the effects of training regimens based on the abstract-rules and the adaptive-algorithms approach. Both kinds of training will involve learning by doing and flexible computer-based tutoring systems. They differ, however, in the kind of representational format used. Recall that, whereas according to the abstract-rules approach the representational format shouldn't matter, the adaptive-algorithms approach holds that cognitive algorithms perform much better when the relevant information is presented in a form analogous to that of the events to which it pertains. In the training programs about conjunctive and conditional probabilities and Bayesian inference, this means that probabilities and percentages should be replaced by absolute frequencies (chapters 5–8). The effectiveness of a dynamic frequency representation, a virtual urn, in spontaneously solving statistical tasks and in training on the impact of sample size will be explored in chapters 10 and 11.

5

Conjunctive-Probability Training

SUMMARY: Two types of training in conjunctive probabilities were used to test the abstract-rules approach against the adaptive-algorithms approach. The training regimens differed only in type of representation used. Whereas the abstract-rules training used Venn diagrams to represent probabilities, the adaptive-algorithms training included a frequency grid that enabled participants to translate the probabilities given in the tasks into more natural frequency representations. Both types of training yielded a median of 100% correct solutions in immediate and long-term evaluations. It is concluded that this result, which surpasses that of all earlier training attempts, is mostly due to learning by doing. This ceiling effect does not permit comparison of the two theoretical approaches.

The training study about conjunctive probabilities reported in this chapter was designed to address two issues. First, it examined whether training procedures that fulfill the conditions specified in chapter 4 can yield greater improvements in performance than those found in previous training studies. Second, it tested whether, and to what extent, a frequentistic pictorial representation is superior to a conventional pictorial representation. The training was implemented as a computer program with a flexible user interface, and required that participants get actively involved in solving the tasks. The basic training consisted of teaching participants how to translate numerical information into pictorial representations and how to derive conjunctive probabilities using that representation. The conventional pictorial representations were Venn diagrams and the frequentistic pictorial representations were frequency grids.

The theoretical analysis in chapter 4 predicted that both types of training would yield better results than previous attempts at training, due to the flexible computer interface, and more important, due to the fact that participants learned by doing. Based on the adaptive-algorithms approach, it was hypothesized that the frequentistic representation would be more effective than Venn diagrams, which do not include explicit cues to frequencies. Unlike previous studies, which reported only immediate training effects, this study also examined the stability of the training effects over a 5-week period as well as the degree to which they generalized to tasks not covered during training.

METHOD

Training Program

The training program was written in Macintosh Common Lisp (Apple Computer, Inc., 1992) and run on Macintosh Performas. The program had two versions, one that taught the use of Venn diagrams and another that taught the use of frequency grids. These two versions will be referred to as *Venn training* and *grid training*. In both versions, the program represented knowledge in framelike structures (Minsky, 1975; Sedlmeier & Robles de Acuña-Ponseti, 1992). Some slots of the frame were devoted to the text, the question, and the title of the task. Other slots contained the events in question and information as to whether a particular event was a conjunction. If an event was a component event of a conjunction, the corresponding slot contained a pointer to the conjunction of which it was a part. With that representation, the program could use each task for both training and testing. It was able to solve each task for the purpose of demonstration, to determine whether a task was solved correctly, and to draw a representation of the information contained in a task.

In both versions, the program had two modes of teaching, the *explanatory mode* and the *practice mode*. In the explanatory mode, the program explained the use of the appropriate representational format and demonstrated how conjunction tasks can be solved using that format, occasionally prompting the user to respond by offering several choices. The practice mode allowed participants to solve tasks on their own and provided help if they encountered difficulties. More detailed descriptions of the two versions of the program follow. In all studies, the language used was German.

Venn Training.   Similar to the training done by Agnoli and Krantz (1989), Venn diagrams were introduced as a means of thinking about categories and were used to demonstrate the relations between subordinate and overlapping categories. Participant's understanding was tested using multiple-choice questions (e.g., Which category is totally contained in the other, passenger car in BMW-Coupé or the reverse?) and giving pictorial feedback in addition to the answers. After the connection between probability and the relative areas of Venn diagrams was explained, the program used Venn diagrams to demonstrate that the probability of a conjunction of two categories can only be as large as the probability of the smaller category. In a step inspired by the linguistic training of Crandall and Greenfield (1986), the difference between single sentences and compound sentences was then explained with the help of some examples, and participants were asked to identify the component events in some tasks (by clicking with the mouse on the appropriate assertions). After identifying the component events, participants were asked to rank order the events given in a specific task (e.g., the eight events given in the Linda task) according to their probability. Up to that point, all explanations and questions had been accompanied by program-generated Venn diagrams. Next, participants were taught how to draw (and in case of error, to erase) Venn diagrams themselves (using a combination of keystrokes and mouse clicks) and were asked to do so for several tasks. The location of the diagram was determined by the position of the mouse cursor. Figure 5.1 shows a situation during the solution of the Linda task.[1] A user had just drawn the Venn diagram for the categories Bank Teller and Feminist assuming that the latter category was the larger one, and had clicked on the intersection of the two categories. In response, the area of intersection became crosshatched and was labeled Bank Teller & Feminist.

This step concluded the explanatory mode of the program. The practice mode started next. In the practice mode, a total of eight tasks, each of which included only one conjunction, were presented. Participants had to complete three steps to solve each task. First, they had to mark those events that were a component of the compound sentence or conjunction. Second, they had to draw Venn diagrams for the two component events that also appeared in the conjunction, and to make the conjunction crosshatched by clicking on it. Third, they had to rank order the events in each task according to their probabilities. The program ensured that every participant was able to finish this phase by providing several kinds of help. It helped automatically if the user gave incorrect input, and also if the user requested help by clicking on a button marked "Help--> click me!" (Fig. 5.1, lower right). Although the program used only tasks with one conjunction in the practice mode, it showed the solutions for tasks involving more than one conjunction at several points in the explanatory mode, and at the very end of training.

Grid Training. The grid training used the same tasks as the Venn training and proceeded analogously. First, the frequency grid consisting of 100 squares (see Fig. 5.2, left window) was introduced. The notion of a category was not explicitly mentioned, but as in the Venn training, participants were shown that some categories were included in others. For instance, the 100 squares in the grid were said to represent all cars in a village. Some of these squares were then shaded to represent passenger cars and some of the shaded squares were marked by an X to represent BMW-Coupés. As in the Venn training, subordinate and overlapping categories were explained interactively; that is, users were occasionally asked to make choices by clicking on buttons. Eventually, the program pointed out that the number of squares that represented two categories and therefore were marked twice (e.g., shaded blue for Bank Teller and crossed with an X for Feminist; see Fig. 5.2) could not exceed the number of squares that were marked only once (e.g., only shaded blue for "Bank Teller"). After explaining

---

[1]Here and in all other screen shots taken from training programs, different screen colors are represented as different shadings.

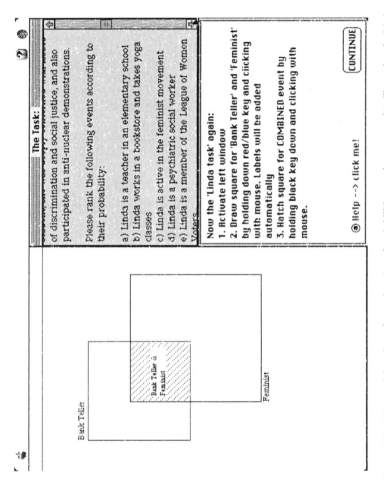

The Task:

of discrimination and social justice, and also participated in anti-nuclear demonstrations.

Please rank the following events according to their probability:

a) Linda is a teacher in an elementary school
b) Linda works in a bookstore and takes yoga classes
c) Linda is active in the feminist movement
d) Linda is a psychiatric social worker
e) Linda is a member of the League of Women Voters

Now the 'Linda task' again:
1. Activate left window
2. Draw square for 'Bank Teller' and 'Feminist' by holding down red/blue key and clicking with mouse. Labels will be added automatically
3. Hatch square for COMBINED event by holding black key down and clicking with mouse.

⊛ Help --> click me!

[CONTINUE]

Bank Teller

Bank Teller & Feminist

Feminist

FIG. 5.1. Screen during Venn training about the conjunction of probabilities (explanatory mode), illustrating the Linda task. In the left window a participant has just drawn a small square for the category Bank Teller and a larger one for the category Feminist. She has also clicked on the overlap between the two categories, whereupon the program shaded the overlapping area and labeled it Feminist & Bank Teller. The upper right window displays part of the (scrollable) text of the Linda task. In this situation, additional help in drawing could be requested by clicking on "Help --> click me!" (lower right window). Original texts were in German.

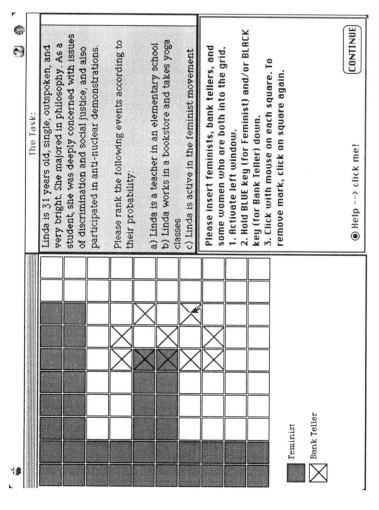

The Task:

Linda is 31 years old, single, outspoken, and very bright. She majored in philosophy. As a student, she was deeply concerned with issues of discrimination and social justice, and also participated in anti-nuclear demonstrations.

Please rank the following events according to their probability:

a) Linda is a teacher in an elementary school
b) Linda works in a bookstore and takes yoga classes
c) Linda is active in the feminist movement

Please insert feminists, bank tellers, and some women who are both into the grid.
1. Activate left window.
2. Hold BLUE key (for Feminist) and/or BLACK key (for Bank Teller) down.
3. Click with mouse on each square. To remove mark, click on square again.

⊙ Help --> click me!

CONTINUE

☐ Feminist
⊠ Bank Teller

FIG. 5.2.   Screen during grid training about the conjunction of probabilities (explanatory mode), illustrating the Linda task. In the left window a participant has just shaded 40 squares that represent feminists and X-marked 10 squares that represent bank tellers with X's. The two squares representing both feminists and bank tellers are marked by shadings and X's. The upper right window displays part of the (scrollable) text of the Linda task. In this situation, additional help in inserting and erasing the marks could be requested by clicking on "Help --> click me!" (lower right window). Original texts were in German.

the difference between conjunctive and component events, the program showed users how to mark (and unmark) a square themselves (by holding down a key and clicking on the square), and asked them to practice marking and unmarking squares. In Fig. 5.2, the user shaded 40 squares to represent feminists and crossed 10 with X's to stand for bank tellers. Altogether, two women who are like Linda were marked as both bank tellers and feminists.

The only respect in which the practice mode in the grid training differed from that in the Venn training was that participants were required to translate the problem information into different numbers of shaded or crossed squares instead of Venn diagrams of different sizes.

Participants

Forty-six students from a wide variety of fields of study at the University of Paderborn took part in the study. They were randomly divided into two groups, each of which received either the grid or the Venn training. Although the results are mixed, there is some evidence that statistical expertise leads to higher solution rates in conjunction tasks (see chapter 3). Therefore, only students with little or no knowledge of statistics—specifically, who had taken no more than one statistics course—were allowed to participate. When in doubt about the statistical expertise of a participant, the experimenter conducted a brief interview. Despite these precautions, 13 participants had to be excluded after the initial test because they solved more than two thirds of the tasks correctly, thus making an evaluation of the effectiveness of the training program impossible. Of the remaining 33 participants, 15 were assigned to the grid version and 18 to the Venn version. The average age of the group—of which 64% were female and 36% were male—was 22 years (median 21 years) with a range from 20 to 29 years.

Tasks

Most of the 38 tasks used in the study were taken directly from the literature (Agnoli & Krantz, 1989; Dawes, 1988; Gavanski & Roskos-Ewoldsen, 1991; Shaugnessy, 1992; Tversky & Kahneman, 1983), and some others were constructed to be similar to existing tasks. The full set of tasks was divided into five lists, a list for the training (10 tasks) and four lists (Lists A, B, C, and D) of 9 tasks each for the tests. Two of the tasks, the Linda and the Cindy tasks (Agnoli & Krantz, 1989), were used in all five lists to allow for a check of how well the training effect generalized to tasks not encountered during training. About one third of the tasks (12) contained more than one conjunction and were evenly distributed across the four test-lists. As a precaution against a ceiling effect at baseline, tasks that were solved correctly by more than two thirds of participants in the initial test were omitted from the rest of the study. This was the case for 7 tasks altogether: one in List A, one in List C, two in List B, and three in List D.

In addition to the conjunction tasks, each list contained two conditional-probability tasks. The reason for including these tasks was that the participants in the present study served as a control group for the experimental groups in the study described in chapter 6 (and vice versa). The initial test consisted of 11 tasks in all: 9 conjunction tasks and 2 conditional-probability tasks. The 3 following tests consisted of 6 to 8 conjunction tasks, depending on the lists used. They always included 2 conditional-probability tasks.

Procedure

Participants were told that the goal of the study was to evaluate several computer tutors regarding statistical thinking skills, and that they had been randomly chosen to receive one of the tutors. They were then informed that the study would take place during three consecutive sessions. The design of the study is shown in Table 5.1. At the beginning of the first session, participants in the two training groups were given one of the four lists of nine conjunction tasks (A, B, C, or D) and two conditional-probability tasks (see next chapter). After the initial test, participants received the training and were tested again at the end of Session 1 using a different list of tasks. Participants completed the study individually on a computer and were permitted to work at their own paces. The time needed for Session 1 varied between 60 minutes and 140 minutes, with a median of 90 minutes in the Venn training and 105 minutes in the grid training. About 1 week and 5 weeks after the first session, in Sessions 2 and 3, respectively, participants underwent a second and a third retest. Note that the removal of the seven tasks that were solved by more than two thirds of the participants at the first test could not have had any systematic influence on the results because the lists of tasks were completely counterbalanced according to a Latin square (for task sequences, see last four columns of Table 5.1).

The participants from a study that examined training on conditional probabilities (see chapter 6) served as a control group for the two training groups in the present study. This control group, which was given conditional-probability training, allowed the effect of the specific conjunctive-probability training to be disentangled from the effects of merely being exposed to the tasks and taking part in a training program on a related topic (conditional probabilities). Each participant in the control group worked on one conjunction task (and several conditional-probability tasks) per test. Four conjunction tasks from Agnoli and Krantz (1989)—the Linda, Cindy, Don, and Bill tasks—were used in the control group. The tasks were presented according to a Latin square design over the four tests (see Table 5.1).

TABLE 5.1
Design of Study

	Training Groups	Control Group	Task Lists
Session 1	Test 1	Test 1	A B C D
	Training	—	List for Training
	Test 2	Test 2	B A D C
Session 2 (one week later)	Test 3	Test 3	C D A B
Session 3 (five weeks later)	Test 4	Test 4	D C B A

RESULTS

As expected, both versions of the training yielded a substantially higher training effect than the previous training attempts discussed in chapter 3. The effect in both versions was stable over an extended time period, indicating that participants had acquired the knowledge necessary for solving conjunction tasks. Figure 5.3 shows the mean percentages of correct solutions in the training group, in the control group (one task each), and weighted (by n) mean percentages in comparable prior training studies (Agnoli and Krantz, 1989; Benassi and Knoth, 1993; Crandall and Greenfield, 1986, and Fisk and Pidgeon, 1997; see chapter 3 for more details). Immediately after training, the two training groups correctly solved a mean of 94% of tasks compared to a mean of 56% correct solutions obtained in the prior training attempts. Excluding those tasks that were solved by more than two thirds of the participants, the baseline before training was somewhat lower in the present training (27%) than the weighted average of the baselines found in prior training studies (36%). Including all tasks in Test 1, the baseline in this study was 35% correct solutions. Thus, statistical knowledge as inferred from the baseline results seems to be quite comparable between the present and prior studies.

To complement the raw effects shown in Fig. 5.3, effect sizes, rather than significance tests, were used for the statistical analysis (for good reasons for using effect sizes, see appendix C in this book, as well as J. Cohen, 1990; Loftus, 1993; Rosnow & Rosenthal, 1996; Schmidt, 1996; Sedlmeier, 1996), but the information provided in footnotes allows for making such tests by consulting tables of F- and t-distributions in any statistics textbook. Correlation coefficients

(r) were chosen as measures of effect size because they are more general than distance measures (e.g., d), and can be translated into the latter if desired (e.g., Rosenthal & Rosnow, 1991; Sedlmeier, 1996). Expressed in terms of r, which can be seen here as the correlation between the binary variable "Test" (Test 1 vs. Test 2), and the continuous variable "Improvement" (difference between mean solution rates at Tests 2 and 1), the immediate training effect in both conditions was huge. It yielded $r = .95$ for both versions of the training program combined, $r = .93$ in the grid version and $r = .97$ in the Venn version.[2]

This strong training effect held steady over a period of 5 weeks, indicating long-term stability. Although it started at the same level as the training groups, the control group did not remarkably improve with respect to solving conjunction tasks after training, and remained at a low level of performance across all tests (Fig. 5.3). This result indicates that people must be trained in conjunctive probabilities specifically to learn to solve conjunctive-probability tasks. Neither repeatedly solving conjunctive-probability tasks nor taking part in training about a related topic (conditional probabilities) had any effect on the control group's performance.

Contrary to expectation, participants who received the grid training did not outperform those who received the Venn training. However, it was not possible for the grid training to show any superiority because participants solved a median of 100% of tasks correctly in all three retests in both the Venn training and the grid training. The difference between the means (Fig. 5.3) and the medians (not shown) in Tests 2 to 4 is due to a few outlying participants who seemed not to have profited from the training at all. Another way to find out whether the nondifference is due to a ceiling effect is to check whether or not there is a difference between old tasks, that is, tasks that were used in training, and new tasks, which had not been presented before. Unless there is a ceiling effect, old tasks should have an advantage over new tasks because they can be solved both by applying the learned strategy and by remembering the solution from the training session. Comparison of the results for the old and new tasks reveals a negligible mean difference of at most 2 percentage points (in both directions), thus providing additional evidence that a ceiling effect masked any difference in the effectiveness of the grid and Venn versions of the training.

---

[2]Effect sizes were calculated as $r = (F / (F + df))^{1/2}$ (e.g., Rosenthal & Rosnow, 1991) from the results of repeated measures ANOVAs with tests (Test 1, Test 2) as the repeated factor. For the grid and Venn versions combined, the training yielded $F(1, 32) = 302.4$. Separate analyses resulted in $F(1, 14) = 87.7$ for the grid and $F(1, 17) = 302.2$ for the Venn version.

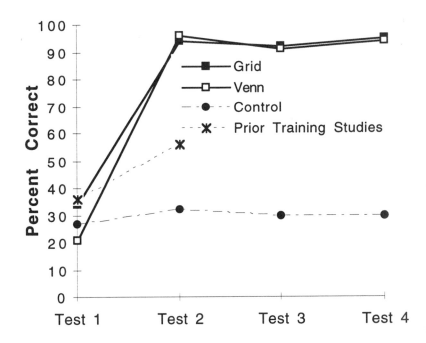

FIG. 5.3.   Mean percent correct solutions before and after training on the conjunction of probabilities compared to a control group and to results in prior training studies (means weighted by *n*). Data at baseline (Test 1) and three retests (Tests 2 to 4) are shown. For the prior training studies the values given for Test 1 and Test 2 show the results of control and training groups, respectively.

DISCUSSION

This study demonstrated that statistically naive people can be trained to obey the conjunction rule consistently over time in tasks that commonly and persistently yield a high number of conjunction violations. Although the training effect obtained in the present study, which used a within-participants design, cannot be directly compared to the results of prior training studies, which all relied on between-participants designs, a rough comparison can be made. In terms of raw percentages, the present study was about three times as effective as prior studies reported in chapter 3. Comparison of the effect sizes in prior studies (chapter 3) which amount to an *r* of about .3[3] and the average effect size *r* = .95 in the pres-

---

[3]Those studies that were based on the abstract-rules approach differed in their baseline results, ranging from 23% to 49% correct solutions. The performance gain in terms of percentage correct after training varied from 9% to 32%, with a median of 27%. One might object that the detectability

ent study reveals a similar result. The long-term impact of the present and previous types of training cannot be compared because previous studies did not include follow-up tests. However, the difference between the immediate training effect in Study 1 and previous studies seems clear. What could explain it?

Comparison With Prior Training Studies

This difference might be due to any of the ways in which the present study differed from previous ones: participant characteristics, specific tasks used, experimental design (within vs. between participants), implementation (computer vs. paper and pencil), length of training, and learning by doing (with vs. without). The possible impact of each of these factors on the results will be examined in turn.

Participants. In two of the four prior training studies, participants were undergraduate students from American universities (Benassi & Knoth, 1993; Crandall & Greenfield, 1986). In the third they were adult women (Agnoli & Krantz, 1989), and in the fourth (Fisk & Pidgeon, 1997), which was conducted in England, they were mostly grammar school students (aged 16–19) or adults engaged in higher education. Although the German university system differs somewhat from the American—for instance, German students are about 2 years older when they enter university—most participants in the current study were students at an educational stage (first or second year at university) comparable to that of American undergraduates. If the German sample tested in this study were a priori much better at solving statistical tasks than previous American samples, the baseline results should be higher than those found in prior training studies. They are not. The present baseline results were very close to the control group results found in the four earlier studies that used the abstract-rules approach (chapter 3). It therefore seems unlikely that the specific sample of participants can explain the strong training effect found in this study.

Tasks. Could the specific tasks used have led to the larger training effect observed in this study? This does not seem to be the case. Most of the 23 tasks used in all tests of the present study were taken from prior studies, and the 9 newly constructed ones were comparable to them in difficulty. At baseline, the mean rate of correct solutions (weighted by the number of participants working on each list) was 25% for the tasks taken from earlier research and 30% for the newly constructed tasks. Moreover, it is also nearly impossible that a selection

---

of differences in percentages or proportions depends on where along the scale for a proportion (between 0 and 1) that difference occurs (J. Cohen, 1988). Because the differences observed in these four studies lie in different ranges on the scale, their absolute sizes cannot be compared directly. Therefore, an effect size that takes account of their different detectabilities, h, was used to compare the results ($h = 2 \arcsin P_1^{1/2} - 2 \arcsin P_2^{1/2}$, where P_1 and P_2 are the proportions to be compared, J. Cohen, 1988, p. 181). The median effect size due to training was $h = .55$. This is slightly higher than the $h = .50$ proposed as a medium effect size by J. Cohen (1992), and if expressed as a correlation coefficient, is roughly equivalent to an r of about .30 (J. Cohen, 1988, p. 185).

effect caused the large training effects (e.g., that the tasks in Tests 2, 3, and 4 were easier than those in Test 1), because the Latin-square design (Table 5.1) ensured that every task was included in each of the four tests.

Within- Versus Between-Participants Design. All previous training studies employed a between-participants design, that is, each participant was tested only once, either without any training (control groups) or immediately after training (training groups). The present study, in contrast, tested the same participants before and after training. Participants' performances could, therefore, have profited either from completing the first test or learning between the two tests. Fortunately, this objection can be addressed using the results of the control group in the present study. This control group completed the two conjunctive-probability tests, but received training in conditional rather than conjunctive probabilities. This group showed only a very small immediate training effect of 5% (Fig. 5.3), suggesting that neither completing a prior test nor nonspecific training caused the improvement in the present training groups. Therefore, the discrepancy between the present and previous training results cannot be attributed to the use of a within- instead of a between-participants design.

Length of Training. The different types of training used in previous studies did not vary much from each other with respect to effectiveness despite large differences in amount of training time, ranging from about 5 to 20 minutes. Moreover, Agnoli and Krantz's (1989) studies, which lasted up to 60 minutes for training plus test, took about as long to complete as the present study (60–140 minutes for training plus two tests). The exact time participants spent on training in the present study was not recorded, but rough estimates would vary between 15 and 30 minutes. This length of training differs little from that in Agnoli and Krantz's (1989) studies. Therefore, time spent on training is also unlikely to explain the discrepancy between prior studies and the present one.

Implementation. Instead of training participants with a computer, prior studies used booklets, oral presentations, and blackboard demonstrations. However, the explanatory mode of the Venn version in the current study is very similar to the training used by Agnoli and Krantz (1989), and there is no reason to think that presenting Venn diagrams on a computer screen would have more impact than showing them on paper. Even intelligent tutoring systems used in the past yielded results that are generally no better than those achieved with standard group teaching (e.g., Legree & Gillis, 1991). The training program's practice mode provided options (including graphical manipulations on the screen and feedback on errors) by which participants learned to solve tasks themselves. In other words, it prompted them to learn by doing. Although a computer greatly facilitates this aspect of training, a computer is by no means necessary—learning by doing does not depend on the instructional medium. Therefore, the use of a computer alone cannot be held responsible for the strong training effect found in this study.

Learning by doing. The largest difference between prior training studies and the present studies seems to be that in the latter, participants were actively involved in the training and learned by solving examples themselves, whereas in the former, participants were passive listeners and readers. Because other possible causes for the discrepancy between prior and present studies do not seem to be very likely, the most plausible explanation for the difference is that learning by doing in the current training had a strong effect on participants' uses of the conjunction rule. This explanation is derived from theoretical accounts such as J. R. Anderson's ACT theory (see chapter 4).

This study was not, however, designed to measure the precise contributions of each of the factors just discussed. It was designed to test the effectiveness of what was expected to be an optimal tutoring system for statistical reasoning. It also aimed to find out if a frequency representation—specifically, frequency grids—yields better training results than a nonfrequency pictorial representation, Venn diagrams.

Venn Diagrams Versus Frequency Grids

Contrary to initial expectations, no difference was found between the performance of participants who received the two different kinds of representational formats, frequency grids and Venn diagrams, because of what seems to be a ceiling effect on every retest in both conditions. This uniformly high level of performance might be due to the relative simplicity of the conjunction task. In any case, the ceiling effect in this study rendered the test of the superiority of the grid representation over the Venn representation inconclusive.

The very large training effects found in this study support the hypothesis that the success of statistical training can be increased by both flexible computer programs and learning by doing. The next chapter also tests a training regimen based on the abstract-rules approach against one based on the adaptive-algorithms approach. Because it uses conditional-probability tasks, which due to their higher complexity can be expected to be more difficult than conjunction tasks, a differential training effect should be found, assuming that the low difficulty of the tasks used in this study was responsible for the nondifferential effect of the two types of training.

6

Conditional-Probability Training

SUMMARY: Two types of training in conditional probabilities were used in another attempt to test the abstract-rules against the adaptive-algorithms approach. Venn diagrams and frequency grids were used to represent probability information in the abstract-rules and adaptive-algorithms training, respectively. If the ceiling effect found in the conjunctive-probability training (chapter 5) was due to low task difficulty, then it should be easier to compare the training effects using more difficult conditional-probability tasks. Indeed, there was no ceiling effect in this study, and the adaptive-algorithms training yielded superior results, especially with regard to the long-term effects of training.

The training study reported in this chapter was designed to examine the effect of training on conditional probabilities in tasks in which participants had to decide which of two conditional probabilities was larger (or whether both were equal). To date, there seems to have been only one training program that examined this kind of task. However, this training program (Bea & Scholz, 1995) is difficult to compare to other programs because it was included in a statistics course. Disentangling the effect of the conditional-probability training itself from that of the statistics course, especially in the long term, seems nearly impossible (see chapter 3). However, it may be possible to use the results obtained in training studies about conjunctive probability as benchmarks against which to compare the effectiveness of conditional-probability training. Considering that a conditional probability is formally more complex than conjunctive probabilities, any training effect that surpasses the 20% to 30% improvement previously achieved by training on the conjunction rule could be seen as a successful result.

Apart from examining the overall effectiveness of teaching people to use representations to deal with conditional probabilities, the grid and Venn representations were compared the same way they were in the conjunctive-probability training (chapter 5). It was again expected that the grid representation would yield results superior to the Venn diagram representation. The study was designed to measure immediate and long-term training effects, as well as generalization, to a type of task not used in the training, and to different task contents.

METHOD

Training Program

As did the training about conjunctive probabilities, the conditional-probability training consisted of two versions, grid training and Venn training. The framelike structure that the program used to represent the tasks differed somewhat from that used for the conjunction tasks. There were two additional slots: one stating which of the two categories used in each task was larger (more probable) and another containing the correct solution. As in the conjunction training, both versions of the program had two modes of teaching, explanatory mode and practice mode. The first part of the explanatory mode, in which the frequency grid and the Venn diagrams were explained, was identical to that in the conjunction training. In the second part, the use of the two kinds of representations in conditional-probability tasks was demonstrated.

Venn Training. The demonstration of the use of Venn diagrams to solve conditional-probability tasks began with the Bavarian police task mentioned in chapter 1 (see Fig. 6.1). The program explained that the category of marijuana smokers is much larger than that of heroin addicts and it drew the two diagrams accordingly. It also ascertained that the area representing marijuana smokers covered 60% of the area representing heroin addicts, consistent with the information given in the task. The full text version of the task was translated into a multiple-choice version (see Fig. 6.2, upper right window). It was then shown that depending on which alternative one chooses, the common part of the two diagrams (Fig. 6.1) has to be related either to the heroin area (a heroin addict has smoked marijuana in the past) or to the marijuana area (a person who has smoked marijuana in the past is a heroin addict). The program pointed out that the conditional probabilities are rarely equal because the categories usually differ in their probabilities (and the corresponding Venn diagrams in their sizes). This inequality was again demonstrated for the green-eyes task,[1] in which the area representing men was drawn larger than that representing people with green eyes. Then participants were given a (hypothetical) example involving equally large categories —"likes vanilla ice-cream" and "likes chocolate ice-cream"—and were shown that if the two categories are equally probable, then the conditional probabilities are also equal. As in the conjunctive-probability training, participants then practiced how to insert and to delete Venn diagrams of two different sizes on the screen. In the last step in the explanatory mode, participants had to solve the choice version of the Bavarian police task again.

---

[1]Green-eyes task: Please indicate which of the two events, A or B, is more probable. If you think the events are equally probable, indicate by circling C: A) A man has green eyes. B) A green-eyed adult is a man. C) both events are equally probable. (after Pollatsek et al., 1987, p. 260)

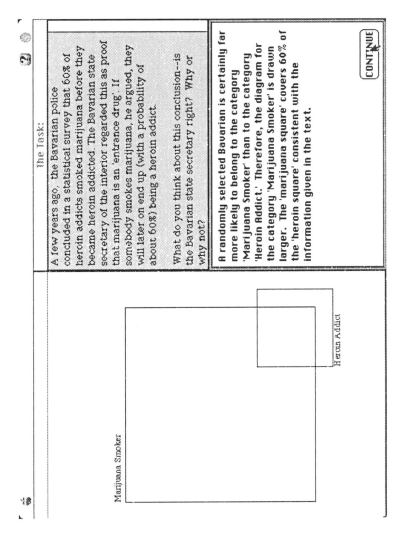

The Task:

A few years ago. the Bavarian police concluded in a statistical survey that 60% of heroin addicts smoked marijuana before they became heroin addicted. The Bavarian state secretary of the interior regarded this as proof that marijuana is an 'entrance drug'. If somebody smokes marijuana, he argued, they will later on end up (with a probability of about 60%) being a heroin addict.

What do you think about this conclusion—is the Bavarian state secretary right? Why or why not?

A randomly selected Bavarian is certainly far more likely to belong to the category 'Marijuana Smoker' than to the category 'Heroin Addict'. Therefore, the diagram for the category 'Marijuana Smoker' is drawn larger. The 'marijuana square' covers 60% of the 'heroin square' consistent with the information given in the text.

CONTINUE

Marijuana Smoker

Heroin Addict

FIG. 6.1.   Screen during Venn training about conditional probabilities (explanatory mode), illustrating the Bavarian police task. The program has just drawn a large diagram representing the category Marijuana Smoker and a smaller one for the category Heroin Addict. The diagram for Marijuana Smoker overlaps with 60% of the diagram for Heroin Addict. Original texts were in German.

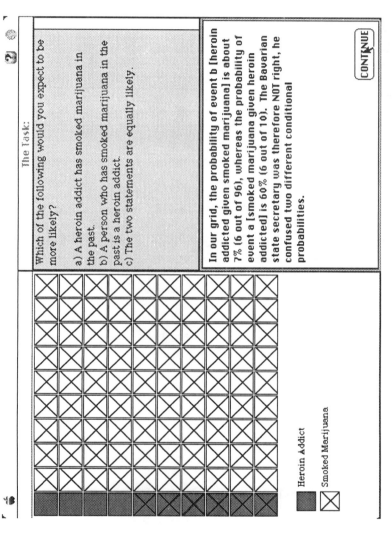

The Task:

Which of the following would you expect to be more likely?

a) A heroin addict has smoked marijuana in the past.

b) A person who has smoked marijuana in the past is a heroin addict.

c) The two statements are equally likely.

In our grid, the probability of event b [heroin addicted given smoked marijuana] is about 7% (6 out of 96), whereas the probability of event a [smoked marijuana given heroin addicted] is 60% (6 out of 10). The Bavarian state secretary was therefore NOT right, he confused two different conditional probabilities.

CONTINUE

▨ Heroin Addict

☒ Smoked Marijuana

Fig. 6.2.   Screen during grid training about conditional probabilities (explanatory mode), illustrating the Bavarian police task. The program has just shaded ten squares representing heroin addicts and marked 96 squares representing marijuana smokers with X's. Original texts were in German.

In the practice mode, six additional choice tasks were presented. Participants first had to decide which category was larger (i.e., had the higher probability) and then had to draw the diagrams accordingly. Thereafter, they were prompted to think about which of the two categories the conjunction had to be conditionalized on and to choose among the three alternatives accordingly. The program provided feedback at every step. Several help options ensured that every participant was able to solve all tasks.

Grid Training.   The grid training followed the same sequence of steps as the Venn training. Figure 6.2 shows a situation during the solution of the Bavarian police task. In this particular solution (left window in Fig. 6.2), 10 out of the 100 people who comprise a representative sample (of marijuana smokers and heroin addicts) are heroin addicts (shaded squares) and 96 out of 100 have smoked marijuana before (squares crossed by an X). The program explained that comparing the number of people who are both (shaded squares crossed by an X) to either the number of heroin addicts alone or the number of marijuana smokers alone yields vastly different conditional probabilities. A similar demonstration was given for the green-eyes task (not shown), in which the 100 squares stood for a representative sample of adults with 50 squares marked by an X representing men and 32 shaded squares representing green-eyed people. Sixteen squares were both shaded and marked by an X, thus representing green-eyed men; the 34 remaining white squares represented women with eye colors other than green.

In the practice mode, participants had to work on the same six tasks that were used in the Venn training. First, they were asked to shade and mark the grid according to their estimates of the number of people or items falling into the two categories in each task. Then, by inspecting the grid, they had to decide which of the two conditional probabilities was larger (or if they were equal) and to choose among the three response alternatives accordingly.

Participants

Participants were 50 students from the University of Paderborn, selected by the same procedure as in the conjunctive-probability training (chapter 5). Of those 50 participants, 13 were excluded because they solved more than two thirds of the choice tasks correctly at the first test. This left 37 participants, 18 in the grid condition and 19 in the Venn condition. The average age of the participants—69% of whom were females—was 22 years (median 22 years) with a range from 19 to 29 years.

Tasks

The conditional-probability tasks used were either taken or adapted from the literature (Dawes, 1988; Pollatsek et al., 1987; Shaugnessy, 1992) or were constructed to be similar to these. As in the conjunctive-probability training, the tasks were divided into four lists. Because it does not make sense to train people to solve tasks they already know how to solve, the first step was to select those tasks with which participants had difficulties. Tasks that were correctly solved by more than two thirds of participants were excluded from further analysis. This left the green-eyes and five other tasks, none of which was used in the training. The green-eyes task will be considered separately because it was used in training.

The spontaneous solution rates at Test 1 were also inspected for the free-response tasks. Participants' responses on these tasks were analyzed by two raters. These responses differed widely in how explicitly they addressed the question posed by the task. For instance, one participant (Ingo E.) answered the Bavarian police task in this way (translated from German):

> The statement is not right. The percentage used with the heroin addicts says in reality that 60% of them have smoked marijuana before. However, only because of that one cannot say that an equal proportion of marijuana smokers will take heroin later on.

This response explicitly referred to the difference in the base rates, p(heroin addict) and p(marijuana smoker), which is the reason that the conditional probabilities are also different. If a response explicitly referred to such a difference (or nondifference) between base rates, it was scored as a *lower-bound response*. The term lower-bound response refers to the correct responses conservatively defined, that is, including only those responses in which one can be sure that the participant understood the task (e.g., Ingo E.'s response above). Some responses did not qualify as lower-bound responses because they alluded to the difference between base rates without being explicit. For instance, Petra W. wrote: "This conclusion is wrong because this is a reversed conclusion." What she probably meant was that the 60% allowed one to draw conclusions about p(marijuana | heroin) and not p(heroin | marijuana). In some cases, such responses might be the result of guessing rather than of sound statistical reasoning. Therefore, responses such as Petra W.'s, as well as all lower-bound responses, were scored as *upper-bound responses*. The term upper-bound response refers to a correct response that at least indirectly refers to the difference between base rates.[2] Although the upper-bound analysis might provide a more appropri-

---

[2] All solutions were judged by two raters. In the rare cases in which there was disagreement among the raters, they discussed the ratings until they both agreed on a solution. The protagonist's conclusion in every task was considered to be wrong (e.g., that of the Bavarian secretary of state in the Bavarian police task). If participants agreed with the protagonist's conclusion, but used conditional probabilities in their arguments, their responses were considered to be correct. The following response to the Bavarian police task is an example (Inge K., before training): "In my opinion, the view of the Bavarian state secretary, that marijuana is an entrance drug, is right. He is not right, however, in how he determined the probability because it only says that 60% of the heroin addicts have smoked marijuana before, not how many of the original marijuana smokers take drugs later on. Perhaps, for instance, 1000 people took marijuana, of whom only 60 took other drugs (e.g., heroin) later on. If one then considers 100 heroin addicts, of whom 60 have smoked marijuana, one cannot infer the probability of 60% used by the state secretary."

ate picture of participants' knowledge, both lower- and upper-bound results will be reported hereafter to ensure a balanced analysis. All of the free-response tasks were included in the analysis.

Procedure

The procedure was identical to that used in the conjunctive-probability training in all important respects and the design was the same as in that study (see Table 5.1). In Session 1, participants completed a baseline test, training, and the first retest. Free to work at their own paces, participants spent from 45 to 140 minutes in Session 1, with a median of 65 minutes in the grid version and 60 minutes in the Venn version. The second and third retests were held in Sessions 2 and 3, respectively, about 1 week and 5 weeks after Session 1. Participants were encouraged to comment about every task they solved in the tests by opening a window on the computer screen and inserting text. The participants from the conjunction training study who had to solve two conditional-probability tasks, one a choice task and the other a free-response task, served as the control group. Again, the purpose of this group was to control for the effects of task repetition and for receiving a similar statistical training (on conjunctive probabilities) that was not specifically tailored for solving conditional-probability tasks.

RESULTS

The first aim of this study was to investigate whether the conditional-probability training yielded a substantial effect, both immediately after training and after several weeks. Two comparisons provided measures of generalization: one between the results in choice tasks (which were extensively used in the training) to those in free-response tasks (which were not), and one comparing the results in old tasks to those in new tasks. Its second aim was to find out whether the grid version and the Venn version differed in effectiveness; the grid version was expected to lead to greater improvements in performance. The results for choice and free-response tasks will be presented separately.

Choice Tasks

The results in the five choice tasks that fulfilled the selection criterion of less than two thirds of correct answers at the first test are shown in Fig. 6.3.[3] In both versions, the training yielded an immediate improvement of about 40% (43% in the grid and 38% in the Venn training), almost twice the effect obtained in prior

---

[3] Two of the five tasks were included in Lists C and D, one in List A, and none in List B. Because the number of participants receiving the different lists was not exactly equal, the number of solutions differed slightly across the four testing sessions. The results shown in Fig. 6.3 are means across the five tasks.

training attempts on conjunctive probabilities. The control group ($n = 33$) did not show such an effect (5% improvement). In terms of effect sizes, the overall improvement amounted to an $r = .68$, with the effect in the grid version ($r = .71$) slightly more pronounced than that in the Venn version ($r = .65$).[4] The control group did not show such an effect, performing roughly at baseline. This was true regardless of whether two tasks that were solved by more than two thirds of participants were included (not shown) or excluded (see Fig. 6.3). The effects of the two versions of the conditional-probability training differed to a greater extent with respect to their stability over time. Whereas the percentages of correct solutions monotonically decreased from Test 2 to Test 4 in the Venn version, in the grid version these values remained stable from Test 2 to Test 3, and even increased from Test 3 to Test 4. If one compares the long-term effects,

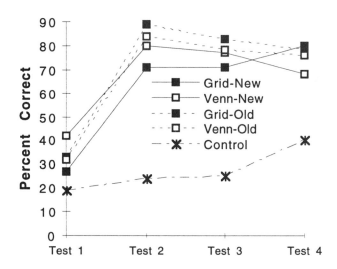

FIG. 6.3.   Mean percent correct solutions before and after training about conditional probabilities, choice tasks. Mean solution rates for five tasks not used in the training (Grid-New and Venn-New) and results for the green-eyes task (Grid-Old and Venn-Old) at baseline (Test 1) and three retests (Tests 2–4) are shown. Control group results are also shown.

---

[4]Effect sizes were calculated as $r = (F / (F + df))^{1/2}$ from the results of repeated measures ANOVAs with tests (Test 1, Test 2) as the repeated factor. Grid and Venn version combined yielded $F(1, 17) = 14.65$. Separate analyses gave $F(1, 8) = 8.25$ for the grid, and $F(1, 8) = 5.76$ for the Venn version. The low number of degrees of freedom for error is due to the fact that List B did not contain new tasks which affected both Tests 1 and 2 because of the Latin square design.

that is, the difference between Test 4 and Test 1 in the two versions of the training program, one finds an advantage of the grid over the Venn version amounting to an effect size of $r = .23$.[5]

There was also an increase in the control group's performance from Test 3 to Test 4. This is entirely attributable to those participants in Study 1 who received the grid version of the conjunctive-probability training. The immediate training effect for the green-eyes task, which was included in all four tests (see Fig. 6.3, Grid-Old and Venn-Old), was stronger than that for the new tasks. The difference between old and new tasks decreased in later tests, however, and even became slightly negative (-2%) in the grid version. An examination of participants' comments about the green-eyes task suggests that this decrease was at least partly due to participants' unsuccessful attempts to remember the solution given during training, instead of solving the task anew.

Free-Response Tasks

Figures 6.4 and 6.5 show the percentages of both the lower-bound and upper-bound responses given for the free-response tasks. Both analyses show a substantial initial training effect (Test 1 to Test 2), which in the upper-bound analysis was considerably larger for the grid training (39%) than for the Venn training (11%). In terms of effect sizes, the overall training effect was $r = .38$ for lower- and $r = .34$ for upper-bound responses. This effect was larger in the frequency grid than in the Venn version ($r = .45$ versus. $r = .32$, and $r = .55$ vs. $r = .15$, for grid vs. Venn training and lower- and upper-bound responses, respectively).[6] Whereas the results in the control group remained relatively stable across the whole period, both in the lower- and upper-bound analysis, the discrepancy between the two training conditions increased with time (see Fig. 6.4 and Fig. 6.5). After 5 weeks (Test 4), performance in the Venn version group was back to baseline, whereas the percentage of correct responses in the grid version group increased to 94% in the upper-bound analysis. If one compares the long-term training effects for the two training groups, that is, the differences between Tests

---

[5]The effect-size calculation was based on the result of a t test that compared the long-term training effects (Test 4 - Test 1) obtained in the grid version with those in the Venn version: $t(14) = .91$. The correlation coefficient r was calculated using the formula $r = (t^2 / (t^2 + df))^{1/2}$. Only participants who had not worked on List B in either Test 1 or Test 4 were included in the analysis.

[6]Effect sizes were calculated as $r = (F / (F + df))^{1/2}$ from the results of repeated measures ANOVAs with correct solutions coded as 1 and incorrect solutions as 0 and tests (Test 1, Test 2) as the repeated factor. In the lower-bound analysis, grid and Venn version combined yielded $F(1, 36) = 6.15$, and separate analyses gave $F(1, 17) = 4.21$ for the grid and $F(1, 18) = 2.12$ for the Venn version. The corresponding values for the upper-bound analysis were $F(1, 36) = 4.69$, $F(1, 17) = 7.37$, and $F(1, 18) = .39$.

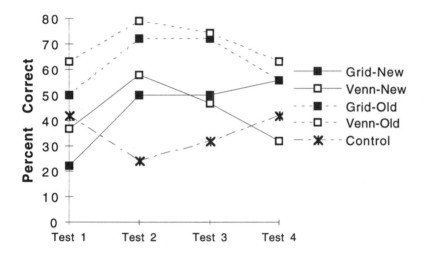

FIG. 6.4. Percentage of lower-bound correct solutions in free-response tasks before and after training about conditional probabilities. Mean solution rates for four tasks (Grid-New and Venn-New), and results for the Bavarian police task (Grid-Old and Venn-Old) at baseline (Test 1) and three retests (Tests 2– 4) for the training groups and a control group are shown.

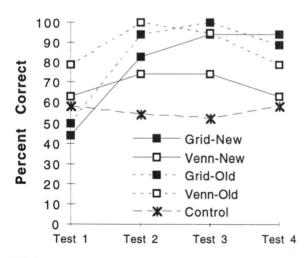

FIG. 6.5. Percentage of upper-bound correct solutions in free-response tasks before and after training about conditional probabilities. Mean solution rates for four tasks (Grid-New and Venn-New), and results for the Bavarian police task (Grid-Old and Venn-Old) at baseline (Test 1) and three retests (Tests 2– 4) for the training groups and a control group are shown.

4 and 1, one obtains an effect size of $r = .37$ whether one performs either a lower- or upper-bound analysis.[7] This effect size is medium to large according to Cohen's standards (e.g., Cohen, 1992).

The training effect in the old (Bavarian police) task was slightly stronger immediately after training in both versions than the corresponding effects in the new tasks (see Fig. 6.4 and Fig.6.5), but its rate of decrease in Tests 3 and 4 is also larger than in the new tasks. Again, participants' comments indicate that this might have been partly due to trying to remember the solution given during training. For instance, two participants explicitly referred to the percentage values given in the Venn version of the Bavarian police task in their later solutions.

DISCUSSION

This study examined two questions: whether the current approach (i.e., using a flexible interface and learning by doing) to training people to reason about conditional probabilities yields a substantial training effect, and whether the frequentistic pictorial representation is superior to the Venn pictorial representation. Both questions can be answered in the affirmative. The immediate training effect was about double the size of that obtained in prior training programs for conjunctive probabilities. Although a direct comparison between the types of training used across studies is not possible, one can argue, that in addition to the higher formal complexity (because a conjunction of probabilities is part of the calculation that leads to a conditional probability), there is also another difficulty associated with conditional-probability tasks that conjunction tasks do not have. In conjunction tasks, the sentence expressing the conjunctive event is just a combination of the two sentences expressing the component events. In conditional-probability tasks, however, sentences have first to be translated: "A man has green eyes" has to become "somebody has green eyes given that he is a man" and "a green-eyed adult is a man" has to be translated into "somebody is a man, given that he has green eyes." This translation process can be quite difficult, depending on the specific task. Considering that this process was not explicitly trained, the size of the immediate training effect obtained in the current training, especially in the grid training, is impressive.

The difference between the two kinds of training was even stronger in the free-response tasks, which were not explicitly trained. In these tasks, additional translation processes are necessary to make a comparison of conditional probabilities. Therefore, the results for the grid version indicate that generalization

---

[7]Coincidentally, the effect size was nearly identical in the lower- and upper-bound analyses. The effect-size calculations were based on the results of t tests that compared the long-term training effects (Test 4 - Test 1) obtained in the grid version with those in the Venn version: $t(35)=2.36$, for the lower-bound analysis and $t(35) = 2.32$, for the upper-bound analysis. The correlation coefficient r was calculated using the formula $r = (t^2 / (t^2 + df))^{1/2}$.

across different types of tasks successfully occurred. To judge the differential impact of Venn diagrams and frequency grids as representational formats, one should look at the whole time span used in the training. The test immediately after training (Test 2) already reveals an advantage of the grid training over the Venn training, which is slight in the choice tasks but more pronounced in the free-response tasks. For both kinds of tasks, the training effect in the Venn version was remarkably diminished (choice tasks) if not absent (free-response tasks) by the 5th week after training, whereas it continued to increase in the grid version. The grids seem to have prevented participants from forgetting the strategies they had learned. The differential impact of the two types of training was much less pronounced in the old tasks. From participants' comments about both choice and free-response tasks, it seems that at least some of them tried to remember the solution given during training, instead of solving the task anew.

A potential improvement in the training was revealed during the course of training. In the practice phase, the program did not give participants who received grid training any hint about what would be the appropriate reference class (i.e., what the squares in the grid should represent). Whereas participants in the Venn training only had to choose between two different-sized diagrams, some participants in the grid version apparently had no idea of what the 100 squares represented and how many squares they should click on, as evidenced by their comments. Incorporating instruction about how to choose an appropriate reference class might increase the effectiveness of the grid training.

Chapter 7 examines the results of training on Bayesian-inference tasks. Because this kind of task is still more complex than the conditional-probability tasks dealt with in this chapter, one should expect an even more pronounced difference between the effects of training programs based on the abstract-rules versus the adaptive-algorithms approach.

7

Bayesian-Inference Training I

SUMMARY: Efforts to train Bayesian-inference skills have been largely unsuccessful to date (see chapter 3). This study examined whether training that employs frequency representations, which the adaptive-algorithms approach implies should be most effective, yields greater improvement in Bayesian inference than training that relies on conventional representations derived from the abstract-rules approach. Although there was transfer to tasks not encountered during training across all programs, the training programs using frequency representations led to superior performance immediately and more so in the long term. This finding is taken as further support for the adaptive-algorithms approach.

This study examined the impact of teaching Bayesian reasoning by instructing people how to construct frequency representations. For this purpose two frequency representations were designed. In the *frequency grid* version, participants learned how to construct frequency representations by means of grids, and in the *frequency tree* version they learned to construct frequency representations by means of trees. A *rule-training* tutorial was designed as a control, in which participants were taught how to insert probabilities into Bayes' formula. As was the case with the preceding training programs, these three tutorials also were programmed in Macintosh Common Lisp (Apple Computer, Inc., 1992) and were implemented on Macintosh computers.

The design used allowed testing of the adaptive-algorithms approach against the abstract-rules approach. The latter predicts no difference between the effectiveness of the three tutorials, whereas the former predicts that the two frequency representations yield a higher training effect than the rule-training tutorial.

METHOD

Analogously to the training procedures about conjunctive and conditional probabilities, the Bayesian-inference training had two modes of teaching in all versions: an explanatory mode and a practice mode. The explanatory mode guided participants through two inferential tasks: the mammography task and the sepsis task (see Fig. 7.1 and Fig. 7.2). In the two tutorials that taught frequency representations, the program showed participants how to translate probability information into either a frequency grid or a frequency tree (see next sections). In the rule-training tutorial, participants were instructed how to insert probability information into Bayes' formula. After they were guided through each step in the explanatory mode, the practice mode of the training required participants to solve eight additional tasks with step-by-step feedback. The program asked them to solve each step. If participants had difficulties following the requests or made mistakes, the program provided immediate help or feedback (for a detailed description of an enhanced version of the program see Sedlmeier, 1997). The help was sufficient to ensure that all participants solved all tasks correctly and completed the training. The three tutorials are now described in more detail.

Frequency Grid. In a frequency grid each square represents one case (Cole, 1988). Figures 7.1 and 7.2 display the two training tasks used in the explanatory mode: the representation of the sepsis task by a 10×10 grid and the representation of the mammography task by a 50×20 grid (different colors in the original are represented by different degrees of shading). Both figures show screen shots taken during the explanatory mode. During training and in all three tutorials, participants saw three windows on the screen. The task window (shaded area), located in the top right part of Fig. 7.1 and in the bottom left part of Fig. 7.2, displayed the task text. The tutor window (white area) provided the explanations and instructions and asked the user to perform actions. The representation window (left half of Fig. 7.1 and top half of Fig. 7.2) displayed demonstrations and allowed the user to manipulate its contents. Participants could choose between two grid sizes (100 and 1,000 cases) and were encouraged to select the one that best represented the information given in a task. For instance, for the mammography task, the 50×20 grid is superior to the 10×10 grid because in the latter one would have to deal with rounded persons. In Fig. 7.1 and Fig. 7.2, the ratio of the number of circled pluses in the shaded squares, divided by the number of all circled pluses, gives the desired posterior probability, that is, p(sepsis I symptoms) and p(cancer I positive test), respectively.

Frequency Tree. A frequency tree (Fig. 7.3) does not represent probabilities as frequencies by means of individual cases, but instead constructs a reference class (total number of observations) that is broken down into four subclasses. The top node shows the population size (1,000 in Fig. 7.3), which can be chosen freely in the program. The two middle nodes specify the base-rate frequencies, that is, the number of cases for which the hypothesis is true (e.g., 10 women with breast cancer) and the number of cases for which the hypothesis is false (e.g., 990 women without breast cancer). The four nodes at the lowest level split up the base-rate frequencies according to the diagnostic information (the result of the mammography). The posterior probability p(cancer I positive test) is calculated by dividing the number in the left black node, the true positives, by the sum of the numbers in both black nodes, the total number of positives.

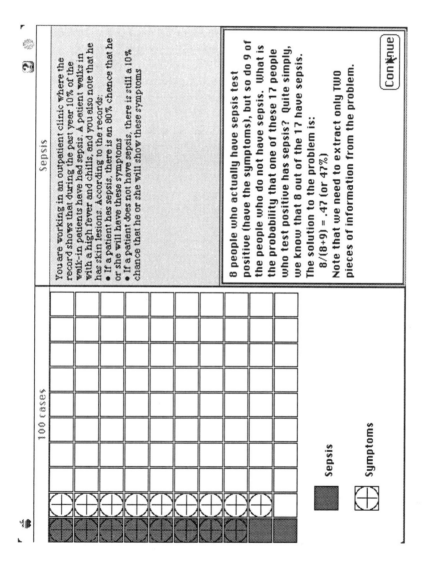

FIG. 7.1. Frequency grid: Information is represented in a 10 × 10 frequency grid. Screen shot is from explanatory mode of training (sepsis task).

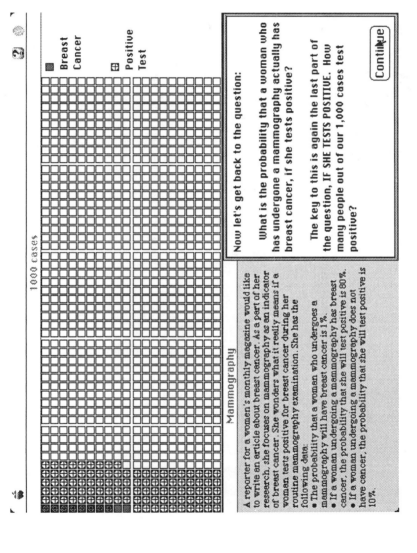

1000 cases

■ Breast Cancer

⊞ Positive Test

Mammography

A reporter for a women's monthly magazine would like to write an article about breast cancer. As a part of her research, she focuses on mammography as an indicator of breast cancer. She wonders what it really means if a woman tests positive for breast cancer during her routine mammography examination. She has the following data:

• The probability that a woman who undergoes a mammography will have breast cancer is 1%.

• If a woman undergoing a mammography has breast cancer, the probability that she will test positive is 80%.

• If a woman undergoing a mammography does not have cancer, the probability that she will test positive is 10%.

Now let's get back to the question:

What is the probability that a woman who has undergone a mammography actually has breast cancer, if she tests positive?

The key to this is again the last part of the question, IF SHE TESTS POSITIVE. How many people out of our 1,000 cases test positive?

Continue

FIG. 7.2. Frequency grid: Information is represented in a 50 × 20 frequency grid. Screen shot is from explanatory mode of training (mammography task).

95

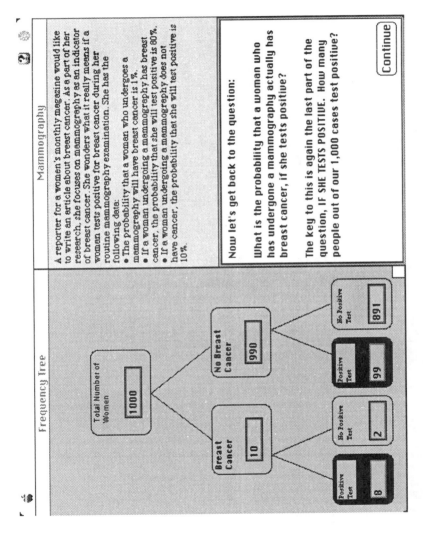

FIG. 7.3. Frequency tree: Information is represented in a frequency tree. Screen shot is from explanatory mode of training (mammography task).

Rule Training. In the rule-training tutorial, the representation window displays the probability information and Bayes' formula (Fig. 7.4). At the beginning of the first part of the training procedure, the program shows the formula (middle left) and then successively introduces $p(H)$, $p(\text{not } H)$, $p(D \mid H)$, and $p(D \mid \text{not } H)$ (upper left). H is short for hypothesis, such as breast cancer, and D stands for data, such as a positive test result. The program explains how to extract the numerical information from the task text (upper right) and how to calculate the value $p(\text{not } H)$ from the value $p(H)$. When the slots for the four pieces of information are filled, the program creates an initially empty frame for Bayes' formula (bottom left) and demonstrates how the probabilities are to be inserted into the frame. Inserting the correct numbers into that frame results in the posterior probability $p(\text{cancer} \mid \text{positive test})$. In the second part of the training procedure, the upper part of the representation window including the formula, is shown immediately. The frame for Bayes' formula appears only when all the probabilities have been correctly filled in.

Procedure

Four groups of participants took part in the study. One group worked with the frequency grid, one with the frequency tree, and one with the formula. A fourth group did not receive training and served as a control. For the three training groups, the study consisted of three sessions with four tests altogether. For the control group, there were two sessions and two tests (Table 7.1). The training and all tests were administered on the computer.

Test 1, the pretest at the beginning of the first session, provided a baseline for Bayesian inference. Participants were given 10 tasks. Throughout the study, test tasks were always given in probability format. Before participants started to work on the tasks, the use of the program was explained, and it was made sure that they understood all instructions. Figure 7.5 shows an example of a task presented to the participants in the testing phase, the cab task (Tversky & Kahneman, 1982, p. 156). Text and question of a task were always in two different windows. Participants did not have to do the calculations; they were encouraged to just type in their solution as formulas. A formula consisted of numbers, arithmetic operators, and parentheses. This answer format was used to minimize errors due to miscalculations.

After the baseline test (Test 1), participants in the three training groups received training on 10 tasks (2 in the explanatory mode and 8 in the practice mode). They then had to solve another 10 tasks (Test 2). The training took between 1 and 2 hours—the computerized tutorials allowed participants to work at their own paces. The entire first session (including Tests 1 and 2) lasted between 1 hour 45 minutes and 3 hours for the training groups, and about 15 to 30 minutes for the control group. The second session (1 week after the first session)

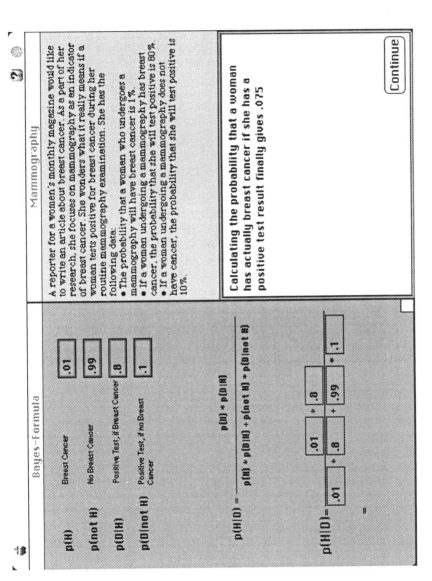

Mammography

Bayes-formula

A reporter for a women's monthly magazine would like to write an article about breast cancer. As a part of her research, she focuses on mammography as an indicator of breast cancer. She wonders what it really means if a woman tests positive for breast cancer during her routine mammography examination. She has the following data:

• The probability that a woman who undergoes a mammography will have breast cancer is 1%.
• If a woman undergoing a mammography has breast cancer, the probability that she will test positive is 80%.
• If a woman undergoing a mammography does not have cancer, the probability that she will test positive is 10%.

p(H) Breast Cancer .01

p(not H) No Breast Cancer .99

p(D|H) Positive Test, if Breast Cancer .8

p(D|not H) Positive Test, if no Breast Cancer .1

$$p(H|D) = \frac{p(H) * p(D|H)}{p(H) * p(D|H) + p(not\ H) * p(D|not\ H)}$$

$$p(H|D) = \frac{.01 * .8}{.01 * .8 + .99 * .1}$$

=

Calculating the probability that a woman has actually breast cancer if she has a positive test result finally gives .075

Continue

FIG. 7.4. Rule training: Screen shot is from explanatory mode of training (mammography task).

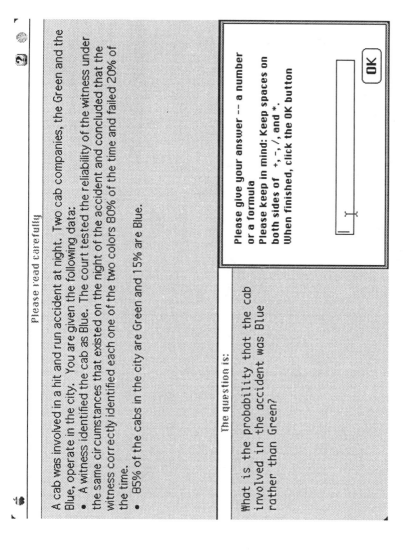

FIG. 7.5. Testing session: The text of the task (here, the cab task) is in the upper window, the question in the lower left window, and the instructions in the lower right window. Participants could type in numbers or formulas (consisting of parentheses and basic arithmetic operators).

and the third session (5 weeks after the first session) served to test transfer and stability. Participants in the control group only participated in Sessions 1 and 2, 1 week apart (Table 7.1). In all tests, participants had to solve 10 tasks each, most of them from Gigerenzer and Hoffrage (1995). Two of the tasks, the sepsis task and the mammography task (see Fig. 7.1 and Fig. 7.2), were used in all four tests and in the training. Tests 3 and 4 contained one additional old task each, that is, a task used already in the training. All the other tasks were new, that is, not used before, neither in a test nor in the training. The tasks were counterbalanced across sessions, and participants were randomly assigned to one of the four groups.

Participants

Sixty-two University of Chicago students were paid for participation. Six participants who reached 60% or more correct solutions in Test 1 (baseline) were excluded from the study. Two participants did not complete the first session. Fourteen participants were trained in the grid condition, 15 participants were trained in the tree condition, 20 participants were trained in the rule-training condition, and 5 participants took part in the control condition. There was some loss of participants over the 5-week period due to heavy study load (end of spring term). The number of participants in the second and third sessions were 12 and 7, respectively, in the grid condition, 13 and 5 in the tree condition, and 15 and 10 in the rule-training condition. Four of the five members of the control group took part in the second session.

TABLE 7.1
Design of Study

	Training Groups	Control Group
Session 1	Test 1 Training Test 2	Test 1 — —
Session 2 (one week later)	Test 3	Test 3
Session 3 (five weeks later)	Test 4	—

RESULTS

Strict criteria were used to classify an answer as a Bayesian solution: the posterior probability calculated by the participant—either in the form of a numerical value or a formula—had to match exactly the value obtained by Bayes' formula, within rounding to the next digit.[1] We measured the effect of the training in three aspects: the short-term effect of the training program (Test 1 compared to Test 2), the generalization to new tasks (transfer), and the temporal stability of learning over time (Test 2 compared to Tests 3 and 4). The median numbers of Bayesian solutions for the four groups and tests are shown in Fig. 7.6.

Immediate Effect

The baseline results (Test 1) indicate that before training, participants had little or no skills for solving the tasks by means of Bayesian inference. The median number of Bayesian solutions was 0.5 in the frequency-grid condition and zero in the other conditions. After training, there was an improvement in Bayesian reasoning in each of the three training conditions. The immediate effect of the training programs (Test 2 – Test 1), as measured by the median number of Bayesian solutions, was more than double in the two frequency-representation tutorials compared to the rule-training tutorial. In terms of effect sizes, the results were $r = .73$ for the rule-training, $r = .92$ for the frequency-grid, and $r = .93$ for the frequency-tree condition.[2] The control group showed only minimal improvement.[3]

---

[1]The data were also analyzed using a more liberal criterion, in which the posterior probability calculated by the participant had to lie within the interval of $p(H \mid D)$, plus or minus 5% with the restriction that solutions identifiably due to a non-Bayesian strategy (Gigerenzer & Hoffrage, 1995) were counted as errors. The results according to the liberal criterion were generally higher than the ones reported here in all tests, but there was no qualitative difference (Sedlmeier & Gigerenzer, 1998). Moreover, effect sizes were almost identical.

[2]The effect size was calculated as $r = (F (F + df))^{1/2}$, from the results of repeated measures ANOVAs with tests (Test 1, Test 2) as the repeated factor. The results for formula, frequency grid and frequency tree were $F(1, 19) = 21.39$, $F(1, 13) = 69.44$, and $F(1, 14) = 84.79$, respectively. The mean percentages of Bayesian solutions on which the effect size analysis is based are, for Tests 1 to 4, respectively: 3.5%, 41%, 42%, and 36% for rule training; 10%, 64%, 62%, and 63%, for the frequency grid; and 10%, 73%, 75%, and 74% for the frequency tree condition. Note that the mean values after training are higher than the median values for the rule training, but are lower for the frequency conditions. This is due to some outliers (high percentages in the rule training and low percentages in the frequency conditions) that strongly influenced the means because of the relatively small sample size.

[3]It was checked whether those subjects who participated in all four tests differed in their performance on the first three tests from the aggregated data reported in Fig. 7.6. The median percentages of Bayesian solutions for these participants were 0%, 80%, and 90% in the frequency tree condition; 0%, 70%, and 70% in the frequency grid condition; and 0%, 40%, and 40%, in the rule training. Thus, the values of those subjects who participated in all four sessions are identical or very close to the aggregate values reported in Fig. 7.6.

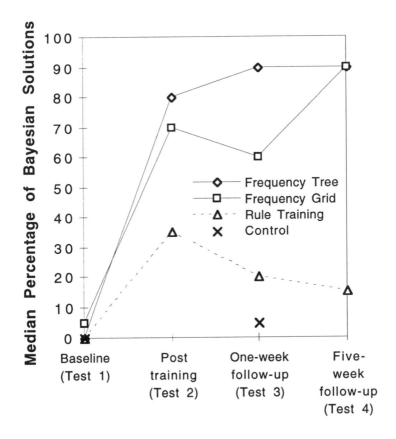

FIG. 7.6.   Median number of Bayesian solutions (out of 10 possible) for the three training conditions and the control condition.

Transfer

To what extent were participants able to generalize from the 10 tasks they solved during training (training tasks) to tasks with different contents (transfer tasks)? To test transfer, the solutions for training and transfer tasks were compared. Two of the training tasks, the mammography task and the sepsis task, were given during all four tests, and in Tests 3 and 4, participants encountered one additional training task. To the extent that a training method promotes the ability to generalize a technique—to construct frequency formats or to insert probabilities into a formula—there should be little difference between training and transfer tasks. Transfer was good for all three training methods. The mean percentage of Bayesian solutions was only a few percentage points lower in transfer tasks than in training tasks (an average of 6.3, 6.0, and 5.3 percentage points for the frequency-grid, frequency-tree, and rule-training methods, respectively). In Test 4, the two frequency-format groups even had a slightly higher percentage of Bayesian solutions for the transfer tasks than for the training tasks. To summarize, there was no difference between teaching representations and teaching rules with respect to transfer, which was in all cases nearly optimal. Note that this result relates to the difference between the number of Bayesian solutions in training and transfer tasks; the absolute number of Bayesian solutions in transfer tasks was, however, much larger for those participants who were taught to construct frequency representations.

Stability

A concern of many who teach statistics to undergraduates is that students often successfully learn for an exam, but that this is a short-term effect subject to a steep decay curve. That statistical reasoning does not turn into a habit may not be entirely the students' faults; rather, it may be due in part to the widespread use of information formats (probabilities or percentages) to which cognitive algorithms do not seem to be tuned. The theoretical argument of the adaptive-algorithms approach, that frequency representations connect cognitive algorithms with the information format to which they have been designed, if correct, lets one expect that here decay should not be as steep. For rule training, Fig. 7.6 shows a decay curve that is typical for what is commonly reported in the literature. At the final test, 5 weeks after the training, Bayesian reasoning is not entirely gone, but it is almost back to the before-training level. The two curves for the students who were taught to construct frequency representations are of a strikingly different form. Calculation of a correlational effect size that expresses the difference in the long-term training effects (Test 4 − Test 1) between the combined frequency conditions and the rule-training condition resulted in $r = .38$.[4] The higher immediate effect of training is not lost, and 5 weeks after training there is even a slight increase in the median number of Bayesian inferences.

DISCUSSION

The adaptive-algorithms approach holds that humans encode information about uncertain environments in terms of natural frequencies rather than probabilities, and if one applies this thesis to Bayesian inference, one can show that Bayesian computations are much simpler when information is represented in a frequency format. Both the frequency grid and the frequency tree are realizations of natural sampling of frequencies. The central idea is to teach people to represent informa-

---

[4]The correlation coefficient r was calculated using the formula $r = (t^2 / (t^2 + df))^{1/2}$ from $t(20) = 1.86$. This measure of effect size expresses how much higher the long-term training effect in the frequency conditions (combined) was than that in the rule-training condition.

tion in a way that is tuned to their cognitive algorithms. The adaptive-algorithms approach was contrasted with the traditional abstract-rules approach to the teaching of statistical reasoning, which emphasizes how to insert the right numbers into the right rule. The rule-training method was not without effect; it showed some short-term increase in Bayesian inference, and showed a good transfer relative to this increase. After 5 weeks, however, Bayesian reasoning had undergone the well-known decay function. When participants were taught representations instead of rules, the median initial training effect was more than twice as high as in rule training, transfer was excellent, and there was no loss of Bayesian reasoning after 5 weeks. On the contrary, the two groups that learned to construct frequency representations reached their highest median at the end of the testing period. The time needed for teaching representations was short, between 1 and 2 hours, depending on the individual speed of the participant.

Although the difference between the effectiveness of the two training programs using frequency representations and that of the training in abstract rules is impressive, this study has two weaknesses. First, it does not decisively show that the difference between probability and frequency representations accounts for all of the difference between effects because the frequency- and probability-training conditions also differed with respect to use, or lack of use of a graphical representation. The graphical representations might have been important to training success. Second, the high attrition rate toward the end of the training study demands replication. Such a replication is reported in chapter 8.

8

Bayesian-Inference Training II

SUMMARY: This second study about Bayesian-inference training tests an alternative explanation for the superiority of the training programs that used frequency representations over the one that taught Bayes' formula. The frequentistic training might have been more effective because it relied on graphics to represent information, whereas the rule training did not. The results of this study lend no support to this alternative explanation. Performance after training with the frequency tree was markedly better than that after training with the probability tree, a probabilistic graphical representation. The probability-tree training was only slightly more effective than the rule training.

The results of the study reported in chapter 7, henceforth referred to as Study B1, leave open an alternative explanation for the superiority of the frequency-grid and frequency-tree conditions over the rule-training condition. Specifically, the use of graphical representations in both types of frequency training might have been responsible for their greater effectiveness relative to the use of Bayes' formula. The primary aim of this study was to test this alternative explanation. Its secondary aim was to test the reliability of the effects found in the prior study.

A graphical-tree representation was used in both the frequency- and the probability-training conditions. If the fact that the frequency representations in the earlier study were graphical accounts for their greater success in training Bayesian inference, then there should be no systematic difference between the effectiveness of the frequency and probability training in the present study. To assess the difference in effectiveness between graphical and nongraphical representational formats, the tree conditions were compared against a rule training using Bayes' formula. Thus, this study included three types of training: frequency-tree, probability-tree, and rule training.

METHOD

The rule training and the frequency-tree training in this study were identical to those used in Study B1 (see Fig. 7.3 and Fig. 7.4) except that texts were translated into German. The probability-tree training is now described in more detail.

Probability Tree

In a probability tree (Fig. 8.1), the highest node contains the value 1, that is, the probability that the hypothesis is either true or not true. In the mammography task (see chapter 1), this is the probability that a woman who has undergone a mammography either has or does not have breast cancer. The two middle nodes show the base rate probabilities of breast cancer ($p = .01$) and its complement, no breast cancer ($p = .99$). The four nodes at the lowest level split up the base-rate probabilities according to the diagnostic information—in this case, the mammography result. Only the values in the two black nodes are needed to calculate the posterior probability, p(cancer | positive test), because this simply equals p(cancer & positive test) / p(positive test), where p(cancer & positive test) is represented by the left black node and p(positive test) by the sum of both black nodes. Thus, calculation in the probability tree is identical to that in the frequency tree, except that the value in the top node is always 1.

Procedure

Three groups of participants took part in the study. Each group received a different type of training—either the frequency-tree, the probability-tree, or the rule training—and then completed a total of three sessions. The tasks were German versions of those in Study B1. The first session included a pretest (Test 1), the training, and the first posttest (Test 2). Training and testing proceeded as in Study B1. However, as it turned out, the (German) participants in this study needed much more time than the (American) participants in Study B1.[1] To make the average completion time comparable to that in Study B1, about 2½ hours for the first session, the number of tasks was reduced to seven during each test and to six during training (2 in the explanatory and 4 in the practice mode). Each test included two old tasks, the sepsis and mammography tasks, which were also used during training, and five new tasks, which had not been used either in a test or during training. The second session (Test 3), which took place about 1 week after the first, served to assess transfer and short-term training effects. Finally, the third session (Test 4), which was held an average of 15 weeks after Session 1, measured long-term training effects. The average intervals between training and Test 4 in the frequency-tree, probability-tree, and rule-training conditions were 15.4, 14.8, and 14.8 weeks, respectively. This long delay allowed an even more stringent test of the long-term stability of training success than did Study B1.

---

[1]From observation of participants, we concluded that the Germans took the task much more seriously than their American counterparts did. When they could not solve a task the Germans did not easily switch to the next one, a behavior frequently observed with American participants.

Participants

Seventy-two students at the University of Munich in Germany were paid to participate. Twenty-four were assigned to each of the three conditions. The responses of one participant in the rule-training condition were lost due to a computer failure. There was no attrition of participants between the first two sessions. Despite the long time interval, the number of participants remaining in the third session (Test 4) was still relatively high ($n = 21$, $n = 21$, and $n = 18$ in the frequency-tree, probability-tree and rule-training conditions, respectively).

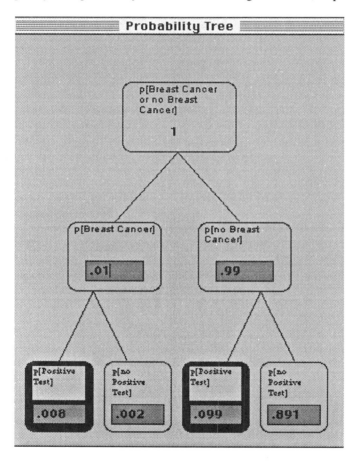

FIG. 8.1.   Probability tree. Screen shot is from the first phase of training (mammography task, original in German).

RESULTS

As in Study B1, a response was classified as a Bayesian solution if the posterior probability given by the participant matched the value obtained by Bayes' formula (allowing for rounding up or down to the next digit).[2] Again, three aspects of the data were of interest: the short-term effect (Test 1 vs. Test 2), transfer to new tasks, and temporal stability (Test 2 vs. Tests 3 and 4). As in Study B1, mean and median percentages of Bayesian solutions were calculated. Because larger sample sizes prevented means from being unduly influenced by outliers, and because the smaller maximum number of solutions (7 instead of 10) restricted the possible values for medians, Fig. 8.2 shows mean percentages of Bayesian solutions.[3]

Immediate Training Effect

As in Study B1, the results of the pretest (Test 1) indicate that participants had little or no skill in solving Bayesian tasks. Averaged across conditions, the mean percentage of Bayesian solutions before training was 7%. The immediate training effect was strong in all conditions. Expressed as correlations, the effect sizes were $r = .90$, $r = .94$, and $r = .86$ in the frequency-tree, probability-tree, and rule-training conditions, respectively.[4]

Transfer

To examine transfer, the solutions in the two old tasks, which were used in all tests as well as in the training, were compared to the results in the new tasks, which were only used once. Transfer was high in all three conditions. As would be expected, performance on the old tasks never fell short of that on the new tasks. However, the difference between old and new tasks in the percentage of correct solutions was small, ranging from 0% to 5.4%. On average, 2.1%, 3.8%, and 1.2% in the frequency-tree, probability-tree, and rule-training conditions were obtained, respectively.

---

[2]As in Study B1 (see Footnote 1 in chapter 7), an additional analysis used a more liberal criterion. There was, however, no qualitative difference between the results of the two analyses (Sedlmeier & Gigerenzer, 1998).

[3]The median percentages for Tests 1 to 4, respectively, were: 0%, 86%, 86%, and 21% for the rule training; 0%, 86%, 71%, and 57% for the probability tree; and 0%, 86%, 86%, and 86% for the frequency tree.

[4]The effect size was calculated as $r = (F / (F + df))^{1/2}$, from the results of repeated measures ANOVAs with tests (Test 1, Test 2) as the repeated factor. The results for frequency-tree, probability-tree, and rule-training conditions were $F(1, 23)=94.00$, $F(1, 23) = 187.29$, and $F(1, 22) = 63.42$, respectively.

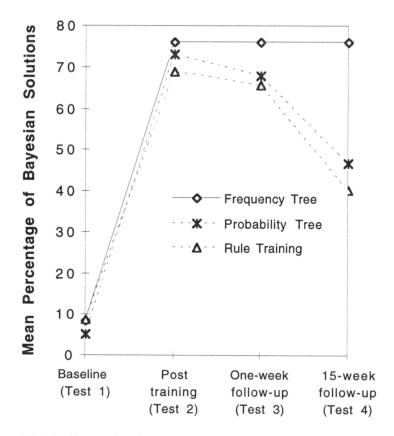

FIG. 8.2.   Mean number of Bayesian solutions in the three training conditions.

Stability

In most studies, training effects usually level out over time. In Study B1, this was true in the rule training but not in the two frequentistic training conditions. Do the results of in this study conform to the previous findings? As Fig. 8.2 shows, they do. The rule-training condition shows the familiar decay curve, de-clining to about 40% Bayesian solutions by 15 weeks. The results in the prob-ability-tree condition show a similar pattern. There is some decrement in per-formance between Test 2 and Test 3, and still more between Test 3 and Test 4. Consistent with the results of Study B1, there is no performance decrement in the frequency-tree condition. Here, the mean immediate training effect of almost 80% Bayesian solutions remains stable through 15 weeks. Comparison of the long-term training effects (Test 4 − Test 1) in the frequency-tree condition, on the one hand, and the probability-tree and rule-training conditions, on the other hand, yields effect sizes of $r = .31$ and $r = .40$, respectively.[5] Note that these values are quite similar to the $r = .38$ found in Study B1.

DISCUSSION

Study B1 left a possible alternative explanation for the superior results in the frequentistic training conditions as compared to the rule-training condition. The fact that the former used graphical representations, whereas the latter did not, might have affected the results. In the present study, the same graphical representation, a tree structure, was used in both a frequency and a probability condition. Although the immediate training results were very large in both conditions, the differences in their stability increased with time. Participants retained what they had learned in the frequency-tree training for more than three months, whereas they seemed to forget what they learned in the probability-tree training in the same period. The tree structure per se seems to have had only a small beneficial influence on performance. Although it was somewhat lower in the pretest, performance in the probability-tree condition was slightly better than that in the rule-training condition in all tests after training (see Fig. 8.2). However, at its largest, the absolute difference was only 6.5% at Test 4. Moreover, the course of decay in the two probabilistic conditions was similar. Thus, this study replicated the superior effect of frequentistic over probabilistic training regimens found in Study B1, and thereby provides additional support for the adaptive-algorithms approach.

Chapters 5, 6, 7, and 8 emphasized comparison of the abstract-rules and the adaptive-algorithms approaches. The next chapter examines the success of a training program built according to the pragmatic-implications approach.

---

[5]The correlation coefficient r was calculated using the formula $r = (t^2 / (t^2 + df))^{1/2}$. The comparison between frequency tree and probability tree resulted in a $t(40) = 2.02$, and that between frequency tree and rule training yielded a $t(37) = 2.69$.

9

Sample-Size Training I

SUMMARY: If people have difficulties solving sample-size tasks due to task misunderstanding, as the pragmatic-implications approach implies, then clarifying the task contents should increase solution rates. This should be true regardless of whether the tasks involve sampling or frequency distributions. In this study, sample-size tasks were clarified by computer simulations of random sampling and the resulting frequency and sampling distributions. Task clarification yielded a modest improvement in solution rates comparable to those of prior training studies. The improvement was about the same for frequency- and sampling-distribution tasks, that is, the difference in solution rates between these two types of tasks remained stable, consistent with Sedlmeier and Gigerenzer's (1997) theoretical analysis.

Text problems in research about judgment are notorious for being ambiguous in ways that can lead to task misunderstanding (e.g., Evans, 1972). In problems such as the maternity-ward task (see chapter 1), a statistical principle must be translated into natural language. Whereas the formal languages of mathematics and probability theory are unambiguous, translations into natural language of propositions they express can be ambiguous and can be even internally contradictory (see chapter 2). This study explored whether solution rates could be increased by making the information contained in sample-size tasks much less ambiguous. In one condition, participants received text versions of tasks, and in another they received explanations and simulations from which they extracted all of the information essential for solving the task (e.g., number of samples, size of samples, randomness of drawing procedure, method of aggregating sample means). These manipulations are consistent with the pragmatic-implications approach, but they might not be considered full-fledged training because there was no explicit instruction, only a clarification of the information. Moreover, generalization of a possible training effect to tasks not used in the demonstrations was not examined. The clarification procedure will be referred to as *disambiguation training* in following sections of this chapter.

A second goal of the study was to examine whether making the task information fully perspicuous would make the difference between frequency- and sampling-distribution tasks (chapter 1; Sedlmeier & Gigerenzer, 1997) disappear.

METHOD

Tasks

Two well-known sampling-distribution tasks invented by Kahneman and Tversky (1972) were used: the maternity-ward task and the word-length task. For each of these tasks, a corresponding frequency-distribution version was composed. Both versions of the maternity-ward task were shown in chapter 1. The original (sampling-distribution) version of the word-length task reads as follows (Kahneman & Tversky, 1972; Part headings inserted for discussion only):

> *Part 1*
> An investigator studying some properties of language selected a paperback and computed the average word-length in every page of the book (i.e., the number of letters in that page divided by the number of words). Another investigator took the first line in each page and computed the line's average word-length. The average word-length in the entire book is four. However, not every line or page has exactly that average. Some may have a higher average word-length, some lower.
> *Part 2*
> The first investigator counted the number of pages that had an average word length of 6 or more and the second investigator counted the number of lines that had an average word length of 6 or more.
> Which investigator do you think recorded a larger number of such units (pages for one, lines for the other)?
> *Part 3*
> The page investigator
> The line investigator
> About the same (i.e., within 5% of each other). (p.443)

In this task, the sampling distributions consist of as many samples as there are pages in the book. The larger samples consist of all the words on a page and the smaller samples consist of all the words in the first line of a page. The average length of all words on a given page (larger sample) is more likely to be close to the average word length in the book than the average word length of the words in the first line of that page (smaller sample). For any given page, deviations from the average word length in the book are more likely to be found in the smaller sample. Therefore, the line investigator can be expected to find more units with an average word length of six or more.

The frequency-distribution version only differs in Part 2:

> *Part 2*
> For a randomly chosen page of the book, the first investigator calculated the average length of all words on that page and the second investigator calculated the average length of all words in the first line of that page.

Which investigator do you think was more likely to find an average word-length of 6 or more?

In this version, there are only two samples, one containing the words on one page and the other the words in one line of that page. The frequency distributions consist of the frequencies of different word lengths. The page investigator can be expected to find an average word length closer to the mean length of four letters; therefore, the line investigator is more likely to find an average word length that deviates from the mean by two or more letters (i.e., mean of 6 or more, mean of 2 or less).

Participants

Sixty-eight students from a wide variety of fields at the University of Chicago were paid for participating in the study. Each participant received either the sampling-distribution ($n = 31$) version or the frequency-distribution version ($n = 37$) of both the maternity-ward and word-length tasks. Of the participants in both versions, 11 participants each received the disambiguation training and the others solved the tasks as usual. The tasks were presented one at a time in a fixed order (maternity ward followed by word length) on a Macintosh computer. Participants chose one of three responses corresponding to the larger sample, the smaller sample, and no difference by clicking with the mouse on the corresponding box. The computer program used in the disambiguation training is described in more detail in the next section.

Training Program

There were two versions of the disambiguation training, one for participants who worked on the frequency-distribution tasks and the other for those who worked on the sampling-distribution tasks. For each of the two tasks, both versions first clarified the essential pieces of task information by using explanations and simulations, and then presented the tasks, the maternity-ward task followed by the word-length task. Participants first received instructions on use of the program and were given time to familiarize themselves with it. The program then introduced the first task. The (scrollable) text appeared in the upper right window and the instructions appeared in the lower right window (see right panel of Fig. 9.1). Next, the program introduced and explained the distribution of the population from which the samples were taken (middle panel of Fig. 9.1).[1]

The frequency-distribution version allowed participants to draw random samples from that population. The left panel of Fig. 9.1 shows the screen after a

---

[1]In the word-length task, the population distribution had a mode of 4 letters and ranged from 1 letter to more than 11 letters, by increments of 1 letter. Different degrees of shading in Fig. 9.1, Fig. 9.2, and Fig. 9.3 represent different colors in the original.

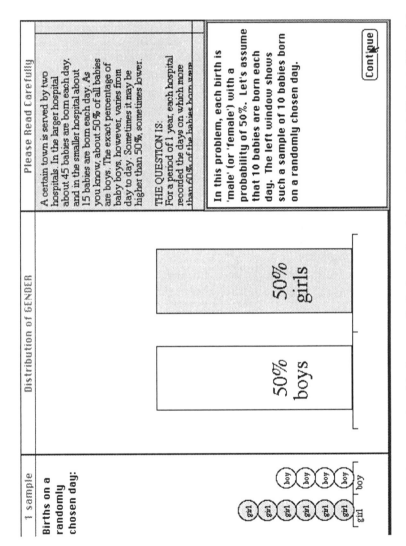

FIG. 9.1. Screen during presentation of the frequency-distribution version of the maternity-ward task. The text of the task is presented in the upper right window and the instructions are presented in the lower right window. The middle panel shows the population distribution of the variable gender. The left panel shows the result of one sample of size $n = 10$, randomly drawn from the population. In this case, 4 of the ten 10 are boys and 6 are girls.

114

simulation of the frequency-distribution version of the maternity-ward task. The sample shown contains a frequency distribution consisting of 6 girls and 4 boys. In the maternity-ward task, the size of the samples drawn was exactly the same in all trials ($n = 10$ babies), and in the word-length task, it was varied slightly and randomly (from $n = 6$ to $n = 11$ words). The latter variation was introduced to make the simulation more realistic, because nobody would expect every line in a book to have the same number of words. Participants could draw as many samples as they wished. This marked the end of the demonstration in the frequency-distribution version.

In the sampling-distribution version, participants performed two types of simulations. They had to perform each of the simulations once and were then free to repeat it as often as they wanted. In the first type, the population distribution in the middle panel was replaced by the empirical sampling distribution (e.g., of proportions of boys) after the first sampling process. The middle panel in Fig. 9.2 shows the sampling distribution of the proportion of boys after the first sample of size $n = 10$ had been drawn. The numbers on the horizontal axis indicate the upper bounds on the proportions of boys. For instance, the number 45 stands for all proportions falling between 36% and 45% (inclusive). In this simple setup, only samples including 4 boys and 6 girls fall into this range. The result of this first sampling process (40% boys, see left panel of Fig. 9.2) has just been placed above the interval marked 45. Again, participants were encouraged to draw as many samples as they wanted, limited only by the height of the panel in which sample proportions were presented.

In the second simulation in the sampling-distribution version, participants were given the opportunity to generate whole sampling distributions, each consisting of a fixed number of sample proportions (maternity-ward task), or means (word-length task). Figure 9.3 shows how the screen might look after a participant created a sampling distribution containing 50 proportions of boys, all calculated from samples of 10 babies each. As in the other simulations, participants were permitted to create as many sampling distributions as they wanted; then the demonstration for sampling-distribution tasks ended. In both versions, when the demonstration of a task ended, the program displayed the three response alternatives and asked participants to choose among them by clicking with the mouse on the appropriate box. After solving each task, participants were prompted to comment on their solutions before the demonstration for the next task began (or the program terminated).

Procedure

Prior to starting the program, the experimenter instructed participants to report any difficulties they encountered. They were allowed to work at their own paces with the experimenter nearby to answer questions. The demonstration (excluding

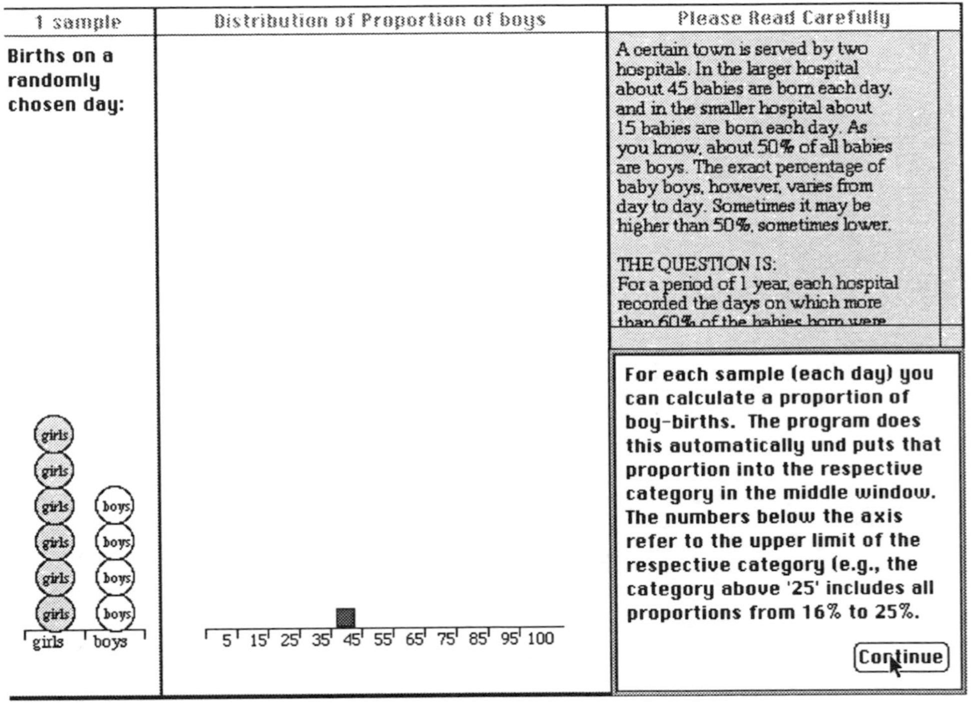

FIG. 9.2. Screen during presentation of the sampling-distribution version of the maternity-ward task. The middle panel shows the empirical sampling distribution of the proportion of boys after the first sample of size $n = 10$ was drawn from a population with 50% boys and 50% girls. This first sample, drawn in the course of constructing a sampling distribution, consists of four boys and six girls (left panel). The resulting proportion was put above the category marked with 45. The numbers below the axis in the middle panel represent the upper bounds of the proportions that fall into particular categories. For instance, the category marked 45 contains the values ranging from 36% to 45% boys (inclusive).

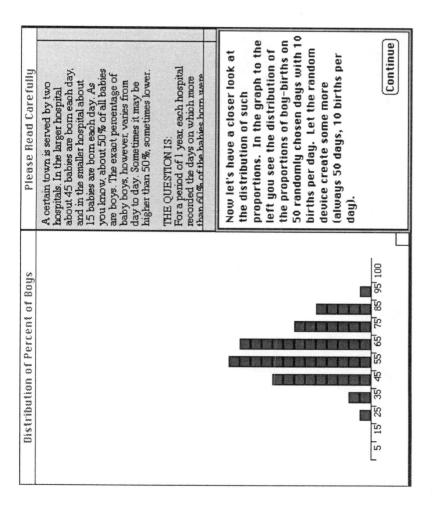

Distribution of Percent of Boys

Please Read Carefully

A certain town is served by two hospitals. In the larger hospital about 45 babies are born each day, and in the smaller hospital about 15 babies are born each day. As you know, about 50% of all babies are boys. The exact percentage of baby boys, however, varies from day to day. Sometimes it may be higher than 50%, sometimes lower.

THE QUESTION IS:
For a period of 1 year, each hospital recorded the days on which more than 60% of the babies born were

Now let's have a closer look at the distribution of such proportions. In the graph to the left you see the distribution of the proportions of boy-births on 50 randomly chosen days with 10 births per day. Let the random device create some more (always 50 days, 10 births per day).

Continue

5 15 25 35 45 55 65 75 85 95 100

FIG. 9.3. Screen during presentation of the sampling-distribution version of the maternity-ward task. A sampling distribution consisting of the proportions of boys in 50 samples of $n = 10$ each has just been generated.

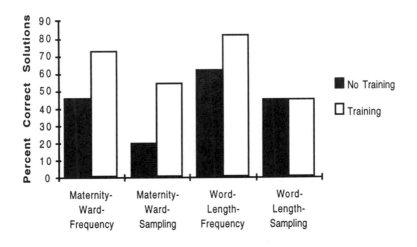

FIG. 9.4. Percentage of correct choices with and without disambiguation training. Shown are the results for frequency- and sampling-distribution versions of the maternity-ward and the word-length tasks.

the simulations) consisted of 31 steps in the frequency-distribution and 53 steps in the sampling-distribution version. Only the participants in the disambiguation-training group completed the training, which took between 15 and 45 minutes; the others solved the tasks immediately. After completing the study, participants were again asked whether they had experienced any difficulties understanding the tasks.

RESULTS

The disambiguation training clearly had an effect on solution rates, ranging from 0.5% for the sampling distribution of the word-length task to 34.6% in the sampling-distribution version of the maternity ward task (Fig. 9.4). The effect size attributable to the disambiguation training across tasks is $r = .24$, with a slightly higher effect for the frequency distribution version ($r = .26$) than for the sampling-distribution versions ($r = .21$), across the two tasks.[2] The training effect

---

[2]Effect size calculated as $r = (F / (F + df))^{1/2}$ from the results of a repeated measures ANOVA with correct solutions coded as 1 and incorrect solutions as 0, with tasks as the repeated factor, and with training as the independent variable. The F-values for all tasks combined, frequency-distribution tasks, and sampling-distribution tasks were $F(1, 64) = 3.86$, $F(1, 35) = 2.63$, and $F(1, 29) = 1.36$, respectively.

was, however, slightly less than the overall difference between frequency and sampling-distribution tasks ($r = .28$).[3]

As already mentioned, participants had the opportunity to perform as many additional simulations as they wished. The number of simulations performed could have been related to the solution rate, thus qualifying the present findings. Did this happen? Table 9.1 shows the results (without the first obligatory simulations). In the frequency-distribution version, only one kind of simulation could be performed, that is, creating samples of a specified size (Frequency in Table 9.1). In the sampling-distribution version, participants could first simulate how a proportion, mean, or median calculated from the frequency distribution provided by a specific sample was mapped to a point in the corresponding sampling distribution (Sampling A in Table 9.1). In addition, participants could create whole sampling distributions consisting of a specified number of proportions, means, or medians (Sampling B in Table 9.1). Outliers were identified according to the

TABLE 9.1

Mean Numbers of Simulations Performed (Left) and Their Correlations With Judgments (Right)

	Mean Number of Simulations		r (Number of Simulations by Judgment)	
	Maternity Ward	*Word Length*	*Maternity Ward*	*Word Length*
Frequency	1.9	1.3	−.32	−.08
Sampling A	1.0 (10)	1.5	.00 (10)	.48
Sampling B	0.6 (10)	0.91	.00 (10)	.41

Note. Before means and correlations were calculated, outliers were removed according to the method proposed by Tukey (1977). When n's deviate from total n's, they are given in parenthesis following means or correlations. Correlations are between numbers of simulations performed and judgments coded as 1 (*correct solution*) or 0 (*incorrect solution*). Simulations that showed how a proportion, or a mean, was calculated from a frequency distribution, and was mapped to one point in the sampling distribution, are termed Sampling A, and simulations that created whole sampling distributions are termed Sampling B.

---

[3]Effect size calculated as $r = (F / (F + df))^{1/2}$ from the results of a repeated measures ANOVA with correct solutions coded as 1 and incorrect solutions as 0, with tasks as the repeated factor, and with type of task as the independent variable. The F-value used was $F(1, 64) = 5.44$.

A more detailed discussion of the results reported here and results from two additional studies can be found in Sedlmeier (1998b).

method advocated by Tukey (1977) and excluded from further analysis to reduce bias, because in both conditions, a few participants performed a large number of simulations.

Based on the number of simulations performed, the sampling-distribution version of the word-length tasks was the most difficult to understand overall (left part of Table 9.1). Moreover, the substantive positive correlations between number of simulations and correctness of solutions in this task (right part of Table 9.1), might indicate a possible reason for the negligible impact the disambiguation training had on that task. Those participants who did not profit from the training might simply not have performed a sufficient number of simulations.

DISCUSSION

Training in task disambiguation based on the pragmatic-implications approach was modestly successful in getting trainees to recognize the impact of sample size on confidence in statistical estimates. This finding implies that the results reported in the literature for sample-size tasks should be treated with some caution because they might underestimate participants' true abilities. However, the effect of disambiguation training was slightly smaller than the difference between the solution rates for frequency- and sampling-distribution tasks, which remained stable even after training. This is consistent with a theoretical distinction between the two types of tasks made by Sedlmeier and Gigerenzer (1997; see also chapter 1 and appendix B).

To be flexible, a training program should employ a single statistical model that can be adapted to different tasks, rather than to a set of different models tailored to particular tasks, as, for instance, to the four tasks used in this study. Fortunately, the urn model is just such an adaptable model. Chapter 10 examines the general usefulness of urn models. Chapter 11 examines the effect of using urn models to train people to solve notoriously difficult sampling-distribution tasks. Because urn models have never before been used in statistical training of the type dealt with in this book, the next study is much more explorative in nature than were the preceding studies.

10

A Flexible Urn Model

SUMMARY: Chapter 10 examines whether urn models, which play an important role in probability theory, can aid in training people in statistical reasoning, as the adaptive-algorithms approach suggests they should. The spontaneous solution rates in conditional-probability, Bayesian-inference, and sample-size tasks explicated in terms of urn models are very high compared to corresponding previous results. It is concluded that flexible urn models should be used in training statistical reasoning.

Urn models are the most versatile devices to represent chance processes, and they have a long and successful history in statistics. In 1780, the mathematician and philosopher Condorcet claimed that, "All questions in the Calculus of Probabilities can be reduced to a single hypothesis, that of a certain quantity of balls of different colors mixed together, from which different balls are drawn by hazard in a certain order or in certain proportions" (cited after Daston, 1988, p. 230). Condorcet would be pleased to know that today's readers are guided through a well-written introductory statistics textbook with the help of a modified urn model, the box model (Freedman, et al., 1991). However, urn models are almost exclusively used by statistical experts (and those becoming statistical experts) and not by laypeople who struggle with solving statistical tasks in everyday life.

To be useful for instructional purposes, the urn model should lead to a reasonably high percentage of correct spontaneous solutions in statistical tasks based on it. The adaptive-algorithms approach would predict the urn model to lead to such positive results because it emphasizes the correspondence between task representation and task content, which coincide in urn-and-balls tasks.

In this study, several kinds of statistical tasks were modeled using an urn model, and participants were asked to give probability estimates while they experienced the sampling of balls from an urn on an animated computer screen. The tasks concerned different varieties of conditional probabilities (a priori and a posteriori, i.e., Bayesian, probabilities) and the impact of sample size on sample statistics.

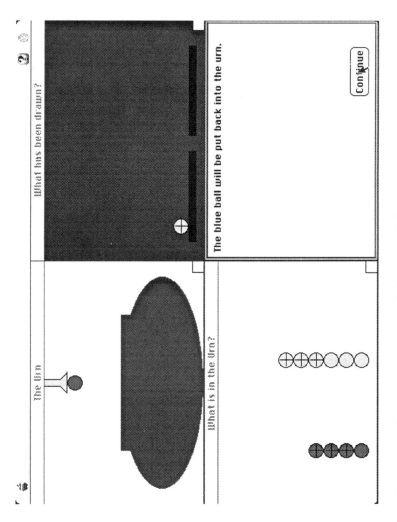

FIG. 10.1. The virtual urn has just been introduced. The lower left window shows the contents of the urn and the lower right window displays information and instructions. A blue ball has just been sampled from the urn. In the next step, this ball was put back into the urn and recorded on the right bar in the upper right window. The result of the preceding drawing, a red ball with a cross, was already recorded on the left bar. Original texts were in German.

122

METHOD

Participants and Procedure

Thirty students from different departments of the University of Paderborn were paid for their participation. They were told that this was an exploratory study whose results would be used to build a statistics tutor. Participants worked individually on Macintosh Performa machines. Before they started, the experimenter made sure that they knew how to use the computer program, which required mouse clicking, and inserting text and numbers using a keyboard. After this introductory phase, the program fully controlled the course of the study. The experimenter was available to answer participants' questions at any time.

The Virtual Urn

The program was written in Macintosh Common Lisp (Apple Computer, Inc., 1992). It started by introducing the urn (upper left window in Fig. 10.1). During sampling, a black bar with a funnel end stirred the balls (which could not be seen) with erratic movements produced by a random number generator. After a while, the stick turned yellow and became "magnetic," thus attracting the nearest ball in the urn and pulling it out. After each sample was drawn, the sampled ball was restored to the urn. Figure 10.1 displays the screen after two draws. The lower left window shows the contents of the urn. In this situation, the urn contains four blue balls and six red balls. Three of the red balls and three of the blue balls are marked by a cross. The results of the sampling processes are recorded in the upper right window (Fig. 10.1). In this case, there were two bars to hold the balls, the left bar for red balls and the right one for blue balls. The red ball with a cross that was drawn in the preceding sample appeared on the left bar. In the next step, the blue ball without a cross that had just been drawn (upper left window in Fig. 10.1), was recorded on the right bar, and the ball was put back into the urn. The lower right window displays comments (on what can be seen in the other windows) and instructions. Whereas the sampling process remained the same throughout the program, the contents of the urn, as well as the kinds of tasks to be done, changed several times.

TASKS AND RESULTS

Simple Probabilities

Referring to the situation displayed in Fig. 10.1, the program first asked participants for the probability that a blue ball would be sampled in the next draw. Eighty-three percent of participants gave the correct answer of 4/10 or 40%. The program then asked them for the probability that the next ball sampled would have a cross. This time, 93% of the participants gave the correct answer of 6/10 or 60%. Feedback was given for these two tasks only. After the first two tasks, participants were asked to comment about their solutions by typing in a comment window that popped up after they had entered and confirmed their solutions.

Conditional Probabilities

The next two questions dealt with conditional probabilities, still referring to the urn contents shown in Fig. 10.1. First, the program asked for the probability that the next ball drawn would have a cross, given that it was blue. Seventy-three percent of participants gave the correct answer of 3/4 or 75%. Next, they were asked for the probability of sampling a blue ball, given that the ball was marked by a cross. Eighty-three percent of participants correctly responded 1/2 or 50%.

Sample-size Task I

For the following task, it was stated in the lower left window that there were blue and red balls in the urn, but that the proportion of blue balls was not known. Unbeknownst to participants, the probability that a single ball would come out blue was fixed at 70%. A random sample of 10 balls was generated followed by another of 30 balls.[1] The results were shown in the upper right window. Participants were asked to estimate the true proportion of blue balls in the urn. Because the larger sample can be assumed to give a more exact estimate of the true proportion, participants' estimates should be closer to the proportion in the larger sample than to that in the smaller one. The program displayed both proportions before asking the question. Eighty-nine percent of participants correctly gave estimates closer to the proportion found in the larger sample.

Bayesian Task

The contents of the urn were still unknown, but participants were told that this time the urn also contained blue and red balls marked by a cross. The fixed prob-

---

[1]Here and in the subsequent simulations, random samples were created online by using Macintosh Common Lisp's random number generator.

ability of drawing a blue ball was 40% and of drawing a ball marked by a cross was 30%; the two events were independent of each other. The program showed one drawing and allowed participants to perform as many drawings themselves as they liked. If the number of drawings performed was less than 50 (as was the case for all participants), the program drew enough balls to bring the sample up to size 50. Figure 10.2 (upper right window) shows a representative result. At this point participants were asked to indicate the probability that the next ball would be red, given that it had a cross. Note that this task is formally equivalent to the mammography task and can be solved using Bayes' theorem.[2]

However, it can be solved more easily by dividing the number of balls that are red and have a cross ($n = 14$ in Fig. 10.2), by the number of balls that have a cross, regardless of the color ($n = 18$, in Fig. 10.2). The same task was then repeated using a sample of only 20 balls instead of 50. Observation of partici-pants as they solved these tasks, as well as their comments, indicated that many of them had great difficulty counting the number of balls on the screen exactly. Therefore, an answer was scored as correct if the numbers of red and blue balls with a cross that were used did not deviate from the actual numbers of balls pre-sented by more than one, and if the solution and written comments indicated that the participant solved the task by dividing the number of balls that were both red and marked by a cross by the number of balls that had crosses on thém.[3] This was the case for 53% of the participants in the first task and 68% in the second task.[4]

The comments suggested that four participants misunderstood the question asked in this task. Two calculated the probability that the next ball would have a cross in the first task, but later realized their mistakes and solved the second task correctly. One interpreted the conditional probabilities as conjunctive probabili-ties and gave a correct estimate of the conjunction $p(\text{red } \& +)$, and one correctly

---

[2]In the example displayed in Fig. 10.2, the base rate (red) is 37/50, the hit rate, $p(+ \mid \text{red})$, is 14/37, and the false alarm rate, $p(+ \mid \text{blue})$, is 4/13. Inserting these numbers into Bayes' formula gives:

$$p(\text{red} \mid +) = \frac{p(\text{red})p(p+ \mid \text{red})}{p(\text{red})p(p+ \mid \text{red}) + p(\text{blue})p(p+ \mid \text{blue})}$$
$$= 37/50 \times 14/37 \, / \, (36/50 \times 14/36 + 13/50 \times 4/13)$$
$$= .28 \, / \, .36$$
$$= .78$$

[3]One case (first task) was scored as correct despite an incorrect solution because the participant had committed an obvious arithmetic error. He correctly stated that the number of red balls with a cross, 12, was to be divided by the number of all balls with a cross, 19. Instead of 63%, he arrived at a value of 80%, mentioning that this was an approximate result due to not having a pocket calculator with him.

[4]A preliminary inspection of the data during the course of the study revealed an error in the program. The number of balls of each of the four kinds generated by the computer was not recorded correctly. Unfortunately, this error could only be corrected after 11 participants had already completed the study. Therefore, only the data of the remaining 19 participants were included in the analysis.

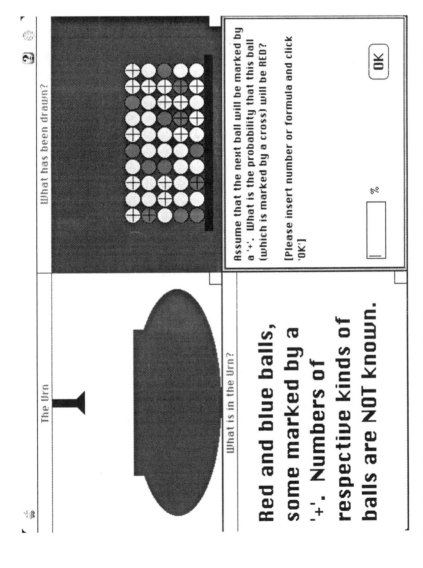

FIG. 10.2. Fifty balls have just been sampled with replacement from the urn. The results are shown in the upper right window. The lower right window displays the question and waits for the user to insert an answer. Original texts were in German.

calculated the inverse conditional probabilities, $p(+ \mid \text{red})$, in both tasks. All these solutions were scored as incorrect.

Sample-Size Task II

The last task referred to the two preceding Bayesian tasks. Participants were told that the two samples of 50 and 20 balls were taken from the same urn and were asked to estimate the probabilities again in light of this new information. They were shown their two prior estimates (which usually differed from one another) for the probability that a new ball would be red, given that it was marked by a cross. The new estimates of 84% of participants were closer to the ones given for the large sample, indicating that participants were sensitive to the impact of sample size.

DISCUSSION

This study explored the usefulness of the urn model as a tool in teaching statistical reasoning to laypeople, as indicated by the adaptive-algorithms approach. The specific question pursued was whether the use of the urn model would evoke a high percentage of spontaneously correct answers, as accounts of the superiority of frequency formats over probability formats would imply. Indeed, the percentages of correct answers given by participants using the urn model were much higher than those usually found in similar statistical tasks (see chapter 1).

Although the concept of probability was not explained to participants, the 93% correct solution rate in the second task, which asked for a simple probability, indicates that almost all participants had grasped the concept by then. In addition, the vast majority of participants were able to solve the simple conditional-probability tasks. The percentages of correct solutions obtained in the Bayesian tasks, 53% and 68%, do not at first seem to be particularly high, but they have to be compared to previous results obtained with the frequency formats. These were about three times as high as those obtained with probability formats, but still on average were a bit lower than 50% correct solutions (Gigerenzer & Hoffrage, 1995). Therefore, the spontaneous solution rates for the present Bayesian tasks can still be seen as successes. The most impressive solution rates were for the sample-size tasks, which reached almost 90% in the first task. This result is quite remarkable considering the negative conclusions researchers have drawn about how well laypeople take account of sample size (e.g., Kahneman & Tversky, 1972; Reagan, 1989).

The urn model seems to be a good way to make people sensitive to the impact of sample size. The effectiveness of the urn model in training people to solve particularly difficult sample-size tasks is examined in the next chapter.

11

Sample-Size Training II

SUMMARY: A training program that uses a flexible urn-model simulation to teach participants how to solve difficult sample-size tasks was developed and tested. The program shows participants how sample-size tasks can be mapped into an urn model and solved by analogy to that model. In an exploratory study, the program yielded a considerable immediate, and an even larger long-term effect on performance in solving sampling-distribution tasks that had previously been resistant to training attempts.

Whereas people apparently spontaneously appreciate the impact of sample size in frequency-distribution tasks, they seem to have persistent difficulties in solving sampling-distribution tasks even when the process that creates the sampling distribution is explained to them (chapters 3 and 9; Sedlmeier, 1998b). This study was conducted to find out if the urn model, which is in accord with the adaptive-algorithms approach, and which proved to be effective in frequency-distribution tasks (chapter 10), can be successfully used to teach sample-size tasks involving sampling distributions. The current study employs two versions of sampling-distribution tasks. In *choice tasks* (e.g., the maternity ward task—see chapter 1) participants have to choose among the responses larger sample, smaller sample, and does not make a difference, whereas in *construction tasks* (e.g., the distribution-of-sexes task—see chapter 1), they have to estimate the number of sample means or proportions falling within a certain category or interval. In earlier research, construction tasks usually led to even lower spontaneous solution rates than did choice tasks (Fischhoff et al., 1979; Kahneman & Tversky, 1972; Olson, 1976; Teigen, 1974).

This study not only examines the immediate effect of urn-model training, but also examines its stability over an extended time period, and the degree to which it is generalized across domains.

METHOD

Participants and Procedure

Twenty students from various departments of the University of Paderborn were paid for their participation. They were informed that the purpose of the study was to evaluate the effectiveness of different kinds of computer programs in teaching statistical reasoning. The study included three sessions. In the first session, participants completed a baseline test, received training, and finally completed the first retest. Participants were tested a third and a fourth time 1 week and 5 weeks after the first session.

Tasks

The sampling-distribution tasks used were subdivided into four lists of five tasks each. Lists were counterbalanced across the four testing sessions in the form of a Latin square, and each participant worked on one list per session (see Table 5.1). Three of the tasks in each list were choice tasks and the two others were construction tasks. An example of a construction task already mentioned is the distribution-of-sexes task in which, over a period of 100 days, the rates of female births in two regions with either 10 or 40 births per day were estimated, thus constructing an empirical sampling distribution.

The maternity-ward task and the distribution-of-sexes task were included in each list and will hereafter be referred to as the old tasks. Slightly modified versions of these two tasks were also used in the training to examine the amount of generalization across different domains. New choice tasks, which each only appeared in one list, were the word-length task (Kahneman & Tversky, 1972), the ice cream task (Swieringa, Gibbins, Larsson, & Sweeney, 1976), the weighing task (Well et al., 1990), and five additional tasks that dealt with sampling distributions of heights, proportions of white stones in the game of Go, percentages of political magazines sold in newsstands, percentages of voters in opinion polls in Bavaria, and grade-point averages of students who received stipends. The four new construction tasks were about sampling distributions of percentages of patients with appendicitis, percentages of defective products, percentages of sixes in dice rolls, and percentages of drivers' average speed falling into specified intervals.

Training Program

The program first introduced the virtual urn model (see chapter 10) and demonstrated how sample size affects sampling distributions of balls drawn from the urn. It then illustrated how other tasks, involving a binary variable such as gender and a quantitative variable such as height, can be mapped into urn models.

All samples of balls were randomly drawn using Macintosh Common Lisp's (Apple Computer, Inc., 1992) random number generator. The training is next described in more detail.

Initially, the urn was filled with 5 blue and 5 red balls, and sampling was done with replacement. The program first asked for the probability that the first ball would be blue. In the rare cases in which a participant did not respond 50%, the correct answer was thoroughly explained. Participants were next asked to imagine that two samples were taken from the urn (with replacement), one consisting of 10 balls and the other of 40 balls. They were then to decide, in which sample the proportion of blue balls would be more likely to deviate by more than 10% from the mean proportion of 50% blue balls. Participants were told that there were two ways to derive an answer to this question, one resting on a mathematical analysis and the other on an empirical law, and that they would be given an opportunity to observe a demonstration of the empirical law.

In the demonstration, the program drew random samples of 10 balls and of 40 balls and calculated the proportion of blue balls for each sample (Fig. 11.1). In the next step, these proportions were placed into distribution frames that enabled participants to watch the empirical sampling distributions arise. Participants repeated the whole process—taking samples of sizes 10 and 40, having the program calculate the proportions of blue balls, and placing these proportions into the two frames for the sampling distributions—three times. The program then filled the sampling distribution frame until the number of samples in one category reached the maximal height permissible in one of the two upper windows (see Fig. 11.2 for an example). There are two sampling distributions, one built from repeated samples of size 10 and the other from repeated samples of size 40. Figure 11.2 shows a typical result. The sampling distribution for the smaller sample size (upper left window) is flatter around the mean, having a higher variance, than that for the larger sample (upper right window). Therefore, the smaller sample is more likely to yield proportions that deviate by 10% or more from the true proportion.

Next, an extreme case, a sampling distribution based on samples of size 1000, was contrasted with one based on samples of size 10. The former sampling distribution was, of course, almost always concentrated in the middle category (46%-55% blue balls). To learn more about the impact of sample size, participants were invited to freely choose two sample sizes and let the program create sampling distributions of the proportions of blue balls, based on these sizes. Participants repeated this procedure several times. Finally, the theoretically expected sampling distributions (binomial distributions for $p = .5$) were shown for sample sizes of $n = 10$ and $n = 40$ (similar to Fig. 1.2 in chapter 1). The program emphasized that it is not necessary to have an exact mathematical model of the impact of sample size on the shape of sampling distributions in everyday

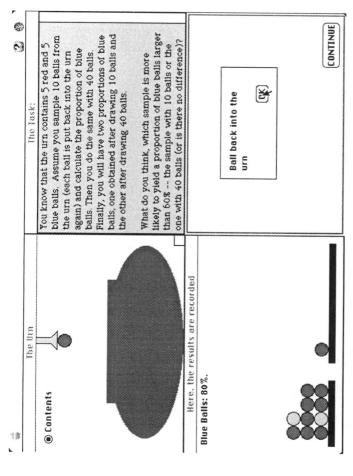

FIG. 11.1. Screen during sample-size training. The computer has already randomly drawn, with replacement, a sample of 10 balls. The results of these 10 drawings are shown in the lower left window on the left bar. The proportion of blue balls in this sample is 80%. For the other sample of 40 balls, a blue ball has already been drawn and has been placed on the right bar in the lower left window. The most recent drawing resulted in a second blue ball. In the next step, this ball is put back into the urn (see lower right window), and the result is recorded on the right bar in the lower left window. The text of the task illustrated by the urn model is shown in the upper right window. The contents of the urn (5 red and 5 blue balls) can be seen if one clicks on Contents (upper left window). Original texts were in German.

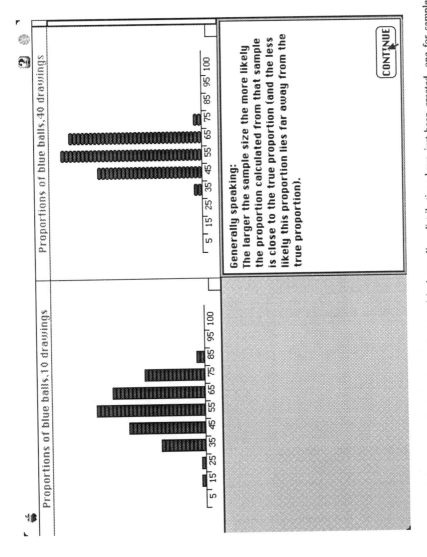

FIG. 11.2. Screen during sample-size training. Two empirical sampling distributions have just been created, one for samples of size 10 (upper left window) and one for samples of size 40 (upper right window).

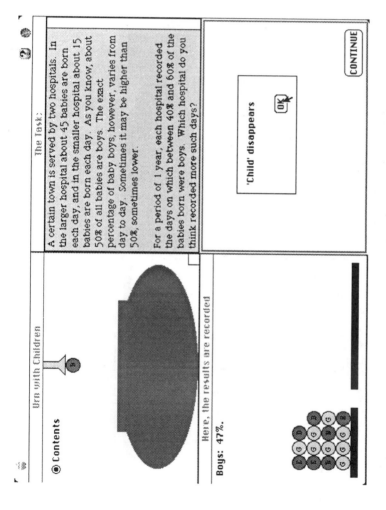

Urn with Children

⦿ Contents

The Task:

A certain town is served by two hospitals. In the larger hospital about 45 babies are born each day, and in the smaller hospital about 15 babies are born each day. As you know, about 50% of all babies are boys. The exact percentage of baby boys, however, varies from day to day. Sometimes it may be higher than 50%, sometimes lower.

For a period of 1 year, each hospital recorded the days on which between 40% and 60% of the babies born were boys. Which hospital do you think recorded more such days?

Here, the results are recorded

Boys: 47%.

'Child' disappears

OK

CONTINUE

FIG. 11.3. Screen during sample-size training. The urn contains newborn boys (B) and girls (G) in equal proportions. A sample of 15 newborns has just been drawn and has been recorded in the lower left window, on the left bar. In the most recent drawing, the first newborn of the larger sample of 45 babies has been drawn from the urn and is to be recorded in the lower left window on the right bar. The expression "Child' disappears" in the lower right window indicates that sampling is without replacement. The upper right window displays the text of the task that is currently being modeled with the urn.

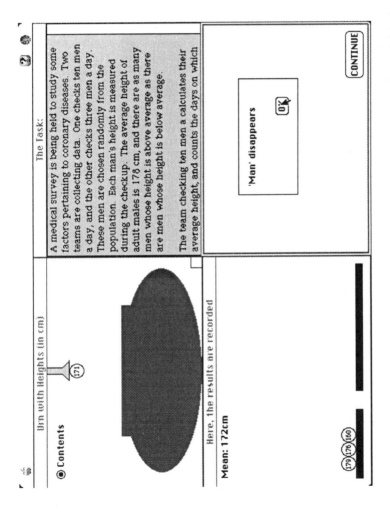

FIG. 11.4. Screen during sample-size training. The urn contains heights of adult males. A sample of three heights has already been drawn from the urn and recorded in the lower left window, on the left bar. The first height for the larger sample of 10 heights has just been drawn and will be recorded on the right bar in the same window. The upper right window displays the (scrollable) text of the task that is currently modeled with the urn. The expression ""Man' disappears" in the lower right window indicates that sampling is without replacement.

situations, but only to keep in mind that, with a larger sample size, there will be more sample proportions (or means) near the true value than with a smaller sample size.

Participants were next shown how the urn model can be applied to the maternity-ward task (previously discussed) by replacing red and blue balls by "girls" and "boys" (Fig. 11.3). The program explained that, when sampling from very large populations (e.g., unborn children), the difference between sampling with and without replacement is negligible for practical purposes. Again, sampling distributions for proportions of boys were created with sample sizes of $n = 15$ (smaller hospital) and $n = 45$ (larger hospital). This time, however, participants were asked in which hospital there would be more days on which the proportion of boys would fall between 40% and 60%, rather than outside that interval. Participants were next asked to complete a simplified construction task, the distribution-of-sexes task (previously discussed), with the numbers for most of the intervals (of days out of 100 days) already filled in except for the middle categories (46% – 55% girls). The program helped participants to fill in the missing numbers correctly before proceeding to the last task.

The urn contents in the last task represented the heights of some hypothetical male adult population ranging from 160 to 195 cm, distributed in a bell-shaped form with a mean of 178 cm. As in the two preceding tasks, the program first took samples of two different sizes, $n = 3$ and $n = 10$, and calculated the means (Fig. 11.4). It then constructed empirical sampling distributions from the means calculated from repeated samples of the two sizes step by step. After that, participants were given an opportunity to freely choose other sample sizes and to juxtapose two sampling distributions with those other sample sizes. Finally, a construction task was given in which the number of days (out of 100) on which the average height fell into a certain category (e.g., 176 – 180 cm) had to be entered. Again, most categories had already been filled in and the program ensured that all participants could solve the task. The program ended with a discussion of some issues people should keep in mind when making judgments involving the impact of sample size. The discussion included the following two points. First, samples can come from different urns (e.g., heights of men and women) and therefore might not be comparable. Second, one should always check whether the process of sampling can be considered random or whether it might be biased or even deterministic.

RESULTS

Results are reported separately for choice and construction tasks. Three measures are important in evaluating the success of the training: the size of the immediate training effect, the amount of transfer from training tasks (old tasks) to tasks not used in the training (new tasks), and the stability of the training effect.

Choice Tasks

Recall that every participant had to solve one old choice task (the maternity ward task) and two new choice tasks at every test. Whereas the old task was correctly solved by only 20% of participants before training, the corresponding mean percentage obtained in the new tasks was 52.5%. This difference may have been partly due to the difference in difficulty: Kahneman and Tversky (1972) also found solution rates of 20% versus 40% ("more" versions) for their maternity ward task and the average of their other two tasks, respectively. Closer inspection of the data suggests an additional reason for the discrepancy. Three of the tasks, the weighing task (Well et al., 1990), the height task, and the Go task[1], all asked about the *middle region* (e.g., between 40% and 60%) and not about the *tail* of a sampling distribution (e.g., 60% or more, assuming an expected value of 50%). A similar difference between what they called center and tail versions was found by Well et. al. (1990). Because it is not clear what caused the difference between the two versions, Fig. 11.5 shows the results for the maternity ward task (Old Task), the tasks not used in training (New Tasks), and the subset of the new tasks (5 out of 8) that asked about the tail portion of the distribution (Tail Tasks) separately.

Immediate Training Effect. The immediate training effect was largest for the maternity-ward task, which was not surprising given that participants could solve it in at least two ways: by applying what they learned during training or by directly retrieving the training solution given. The immediate learning effect is smaller if one includes the tasks that asked about the middle range of proportions (20%) than if one excludes them (28%). In terms of effect sizes, the immediate training effects amount to $r = .40$, a medium to large effect according to J. Cohen's (1992) conventions, already for the smaller effect (all new tasks).[2]

Transfer and Stability. Training does not make sense if it leads to immediate improvement but then loses its effect over time. The data for Test 3 and Test 4 (Fig. 11.5) reveal that training using the urn model had a lasting effect on performance. Interestingly, the solution rates for the new tasks even increased over time, reaching a high of 88% averaged across all tasks 5 weeks after training.

---

[1]GO TASK. The game of Go (a Japanese board game) involves 180 white and 180 black lens-shaped stones. These 360 stones were put into a bowl and mixed thoroughly. Two people (Person A and Person B) each drew one hundred samples (without looking) from the bowl. After each sample was drawn, the stones were put back into the bowl. Each time, Person A took 10 stones and Person B took 60 stones. Which person (A or B) do you think drew more samples in which the proportion of white stones was between 45% and 55%? [1. Person A (10 stones per sample), 2. Person B (60 stones per sample), 3. About equal].

[2]Calculated from the results of a paired t test by the formula $r = [t^2 / (t^2 + df)]^{1/2}$. The corresponding one-sided t tests which compared mean scores in Tests 1 and 2 yielded a $t(19) = 1.90$, with correct solutions coded as 1 and incorrect solutions as 0.

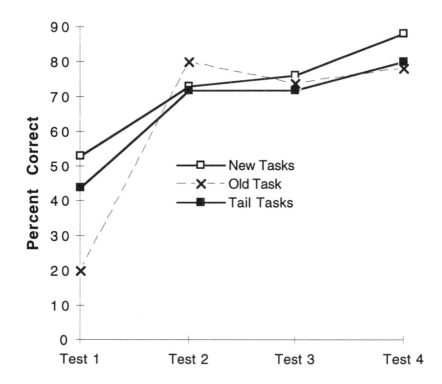

FIG. 11.5. Mean percentages of correct solutions in choice tasks. Results are shown for
the baseline test (Test 1), a test that was taken immediately (Test 2) after training, and tests
taken one (Test 3) and 5 (Test 4) weeks after training. New tasks include tail tasks.

To evaluate the amount of transfer to domains not dealt with in the training,
it is necessary to compare the results for the old tasks in Fig. 11.5 with those of
the new tasks. This comparison reveals that the transfer is not perfect immediately after training, but that it is very high later on (see Fig. 11.5).

Construction Tasks

A participant's solution to a construction task was scored as correct if the number filled in for the middle category of the sampling distribution, based on the
larger sample, was larger than for the smaller sample, and if no anomalies (e.g.,
bimodality) were observed in the distributions.

Immediate Training Effect.   The difference between the old task (distribution
of sexes) and the new tasks was not so pronounced at baseline as it was in the
choice tasks. After the training, the old task was solved correctly by all participants and the new tasks were solved by an average of 80% of participants. Thus,

the increases in performance after training were huge, 80% and 50%, respectively (Fig. 11.6). The training effect obtained for the new tasks amounted to a large $r = .60$.[3]

Transfer and Stability. There was no absolute transfer right after the training, but the difference between the old and the new tasks steadily decreased over time. After 5 weeks, the difference between the old and the new tasks was only 10%. More important, the new tasks showed remarkable long-term stability. The proportion of correct solutions increased between the second and third tests and remained at 85% correct solutions during the whole time period tested.

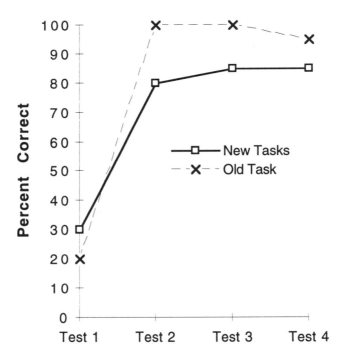

FIG. 11.6.   Mean percentages of correct solutions in construction tasks. Results are shown for the baseline test (Test 1), the test immediately after training (Test 2), and the tests 1 (Test 3) and 5 (Test 4) weeks after training.

---

[3]Calculated from a paired *t* test with correct solutions coded as 1 and incorrect solutions as 0, based on a $t(19) = 3.23$.

DISCUSSION

Did the urn help in teaching laypeople how sample size influences statistical results? An initial study (chapter 10) showed that using the urn model leads to high spontaneous solution rates in several kinds of statistical tasks, including sample-size tasks. It was, therefore, hypothesized that training people to translate other tasks into an urn model should have a strong and lasting effect on performance. The results for both the choice and the construction tasks, in which participants were tested on notoriously difficult sampling-distribution tasks, indicate that this was the case. Even looking at the results in the most unfavorable light, that is, looking at only choice tasks including the three center version tasks, one sees a gain of 20% in correct solutions (averaged across all choice tasks) approximately equal to that obtained in training with (much easier) frequency-distribution tasks (Fong et al., 1986; Fong & Nisbett, 1991).

More important than the immediate improvement in performance is the lasting effect of the urn model training. In terms of long-term effectiveness, training with the urn model was remarkably successful. For all tasks that could not be solved by retrieving old solutions, the proportion of correct responses actually increased over the period of five weeks. This result shows that the training effect generalized beyond the domains dealt with in the training. Why might the solution rate have increased over time in the absence of additional practice or training? The written comments of some participants indicated that they found the baseline test and training exhausting, which may have led them to be less attentive at the first retest than they were at later retests. In addition, some participants may have tried to solve the new tasks by analogy to the old. Solving by analogy could have caused confusion, because some questions that were posed during training related to the middle region of the sampling distribution, and others to the tail region. As participants' memories of the specific contents of training faded, the number of solutions by analogy should have decreased, thus reducing confusion about the region about which they were being asked, while increasing correct solutions accordingly.

In its present form, the training program guides the user through three task domains quite rigidly for the sake of comparability across participants' solutions. In the future, however, it could be made more flexible in order to suit the needs of individual users (e.g., by giving the user more freedom in choosing simulations). It could also be modified to cover more kinds of population distributions from which samples can be drawn (e.g., a larger variety of nonbinary variables).

This chapter concludes the reporting of results from the training studies. In the next chapter, the training results reported up to this point are recapitulated, and their practical and theoretical implications are discussed.

12

Implications of Training Results

SUMMARY: The results of the training programs described in chapters 5 to 11 have both practical and theoretical implications. They are used to derive recommendations for the construction of effective tutoring systems for statistical reasoning skills and they allow us to evaluate the four theoretical approaches dealt with in this volume. Although the results do permit a clearcut evaluation of the approaches, all four of them lack sufficient specificity, and therefore, a more elaborate model of statistical reasoning is needed.

Chapters 5 to 11 describe several training programs based on these approaches: pragmatic-implications, abstract-rules, and adaptive-algorithms. This chapter briefly summarizes the results obtained in these studies and from this derives practical and theoretical implications.

SUMMARY OF TRAINING RESULTS

The training studies described in the preceding chapters dealt with different topics in statistical reasoning and also differed in the training procedures used. The specific results are discussed in the respective chapters, but there are some general findings that deserve repeating.

Immediate Training Effect

In all studies, the immediate training effect was large. With the exception of the pragmatic-implications training about sample-size tasks (chapter 9), training results as successful as the ones reported in the preceding chapters have not yet been reported in the literature about statistical reasoning. The post hoc analysis in chapter 5 implies that learning by doing was an important factor for obtaining such large effects; another important factor was probably the use of flexible computer interfaces. Neither ingredient was part of prior attempts to train statistical reasoning skills.

Transfer

In all studies, transfer to tasks not used in the training was high. With the exception of the conjunctive-probability training, in which a ceiling effect was observed, solution rates for tasks already used in the training were slightly higher than those for tasks not used before. This result is to be expected because for the tasks used in training, an additional clue to a correct solution comes from memorizing the solution given by the tutoring system. In the conditional-probability training (chapter 6) it was shown that the training effect generalized very well to a kind of task not explicitly trained before. It seems, however, that transfer to tasks that do not use the same statistical model is limited. For instance, there was only small transfer to solving conditional-probability tasks after a conjunctive-probability training, and there was almost no transfer vice versa (see chapters 5 and 6). This issue needs further examination.

Long-Term Effectiveness

Only two prior studies examined the long-term effectiveness of their training attempts. Fong and Nisbett's (1991) sample-size training already showed a noticeable decline after 2 weeks. Bea and Scholz (1995) did not find a uniformly decreasing training effect in their different conditions, but unfortunately, they did not disentangle the effect of their training from the effect of a statistics course, which prohibits making any strong conclusion. The present training programs examined the long-term effectiveness at up to more than 3 months after the training. None of the participants attended a statistics course during that period. After this amount of time, a mechanical repetition of task solutions encountered in the training should no longer play an important role. It turned out that the long-term training effect was dependent on the complexity or difficulty of the task and, in particular, on the format used. In general, long-term stability was very high, that is, solution rates even increased as compared to immediate training effects when frequency formats, but not probability formats, were used.

Impact of Representational Format

During the conjunctive-probability training, convincing long-term stability was achieved with both a training version that used a probability representation and one that used a frequency representation. The long-term effectiveness in all other tasks was markedly different for the two types of representations, however. Thus, it seems that the representational format does not play a decisive role with relatively easy tasks such as conjunction tasks. With more difficult tasks, that is, conditional-probability tasks including Bayesian inference, the use of a frequency format yielded an advantage over probability formats even in the immediate training effect and that advantage increased with time. By the last testing session, that is, 5 to 15 weeks after training, the difference in training effects obtained with frequency versus probability formats was substantial.

In sample-size tasks, there was no comparison between different types of representational formats because of the nature of the task, which always refers to frequencies in one form or another. Although the results in this kind of training cannot be compared to prior training studies because of the difference in tasks (this study: sampling-distribution tasks, other studies: frequency-distribution tasks), the frequency format represented by a virtual urn seems to be effective, leading to a stable training effect.

PRACTICAL IMPLICATIONS

The practical implications of the current training studies for effective training for statistical reasoning are formulated in the form of do's and don'ts. Some of these recommendations follow directly from the training results and from the research reviewed; some follow only indirectly and need further empirical corroboration.

Use Computers

Probably the most salient difference between the current training programs and prior ones is that the former are implemented as computer programs and the latter were not. The present studies did not compare training procedures both with and without computers, but there is no reason to assume that the medium (i.e., computers vs. paper and pencil) has a strong impact, as long as the procedures are comparable (Sedlmeier & Wettler, 1998). There are, however, several arguments for using computers in training for statistical reasoning. Some things that are easy to do with computers are hardly imaginable to do another way. Consider, for instance, sampling a ball from an urn 1,000 times with replacement in virtually no time, as performed by the virtual urn (e.g., chapter 11). Also, paper-and-pencil material can hardly compete with a flexible computer interface, which, for example in the case of Venn diagrams and frequency grids, allows for quick manipulation of graphical interfaces and contingent feedback. Weaker students especially can benefit from the patience of computer programs, which are not bothered by showing a specific simulation 100 times. Computers also seem to have positive motivational effects on students' learning (Schofield, Eurich-Fulcer, & Britt, 1994). So, although there is no principled advantage connected to the computer, its use is highly recommended for training statistical reasoning, because it makes things easier and enables a much higher degree of flexibility than other training media.

Whereas the current research provides good reasons for using computers, but, due to a lack of direct comparison, no strong empirical support, it does provide empirical support for some other aspects of teaching statistical reasoning.

Make Sure that the Task Is Understood

This advice seems trivial, but has been frequently neglected in research about judgment under uncertainty (see chapter 2). Comparing solution rates, with and without a thorough explanation of tasks by way of demonstrations on the computer screen (chapter 9), indicates that the solution rates in the literature might be downwardly biased because of participants' task misunderstandings. Making sure that trainees understand a task and finding out what impairs task understanding might sometimes render training unnecessary.

Teach Directly

Chapter 3 reviewed several studies that attempted an indirect approach to statistical training. These training attempts tried to help participants by giving them easier tasks, with a high chance of being solved, before letting them solve more difficult tasks, giving them corrective feedback, or letting them focus on different aspects of the tasks. In all of these studies without direct instruction participants did not learn much. Somewhat higher, but still not very convincing, results were obtained when tasks were clarified by simulations, without additional instructions (chapter 9). In contrast, the more successful prior training attempts (see chapter 3), and all attempts described in chapters 5 through 8, 10, and 11 used direct instruction that told trainees exactly how to solve a task. Such direct instruction, which structures the task solution, seems to be necessary to achieve a substantial training effect.

Teach Specifically

The results in the control groups of the conjunctive- and (partially) conditional-probability training programs reveal that there was not much transfer across statistical models even for models as similar as conjunctive and conditional probabilities. This indicates that one cannot expect trainees to make generalizations on their own. It seems that if one wants trainees to generalize across models one has to teach that. One way to accomplish this would be to combine all the training programs used in the preceding chapters and show trainees the connections between the different models. The urn model (see chapter 10) would be a promising candidate representation to make the connections between the models.

Pay Attention to Model Specification

An issue sometimes neglected in research about judgment under uncertainty is the full specification of the model for a given task (chapter 1). Analyzing the specific structure of a task seems to be necessary for training, too. The example repeatedly dealt with here is the distinction needed within sample-size tasks, that is, the difference between frequency- and sampling-distributions tasks (chapter 1).

This distinction has been neglected in prior research and in prior attempts at training, in which only frequency-distribution tasks were used (chapter 3). Whereas frequency-distribution tasks do not need much training—some help in task understanding might suffice (e.g., chapter 9)—training about sampling-distribution tasks needs direct and specific instruction.

Learn by Doing

A comparison of current conjunction-training results with those of comparable prior training attempts (chapter 5) indicates that learning by doing is decisive. The importance of learning by doing is also suggested by the control group results in the conjunctive- and conditional-probability training programs. Except for the improvement between Test 3 and Test 4 in the conditional probability choice tasks (Fig. 6.3), which was comparatively small and was entirely due to the grid-version group, exposure to Venn diagrams and grids alone did not seem to have a noticeable effect on performance. Participants learned only if they worked through some examples themselves. This observation is consistent with a result reported by Hoffrage and Gigerenzer (1998), who presented physicians with Bayesian tasks stated in both frequency and probability formats. When the physicians were first given a task stated in a frequency format and then one stated in a probability format, they did well on the first, but not on the second. Thus, although they were apparently able to profit from the frequency representation, they could not spontaneously translate problems into that representation in a subsequent task that was stated in a probability format. The process of translating probability into frequency formats, and using these formats appropriately apparently requires practice; that is, it must be learned by doing.

Use Frequency Representations

In the conjunctive-probability training there was no difference between training procedures using Venn diagrams versus frequency grids. This nondifference seems, however, to be attributable to a ceiling effect, due to the relatively easy nature of the task. In the more difficult tasks about simple conditional probabilities and Bayesian inference, the frequency representations, frequency grid, and frequency tree, were superior to the probability representations, Venn diagrams, Bayes' formula, and the probability tree. The long-term training effect achieved with frequency representations is especially impressive. After all, a long-term effect is what one wants from training. The present studies do not allow the recommendation of one special frequency format over another. Although it is probably worthwhile to explore this issue further, the results in the first Bayesian training study (chapter 7) indicated that there might not be much difference.

A very general kind of (dynamic) frequency representation is the urn model (chapter 11). The usefulness of urn models has been demonstrated in training about sample-size tasks. Their effectiveness has not yet been compared to static frequency representations such as frequency grids. Even without such a comparison, the versatility of the urn recommends it for use in all sorts of statistical reasoning training. The urn model is a good candidate to provide links between different models. Its implementation on the computer seems to have been successful.

A field of instruction that seems to be notoriously plagued by missing long-term effectiveness is statistics for social scientists (e.g., Abelson, 1995; Sedlmeier & Gigerenzer, 1989). This can, for instance, be verified by reading a representative sample of German diploma theses in psychology, or by talking about statistics with advanced students who completed their statistics courses some time ago. It appears that most of these statistics courses consist of learning rules, often presented solely as formulas. The frequent use of frequency representations in these courses should increase long-term retention of the learned material substantially. In particular, the urn model could prove very helpful in helping students understand the impact of sample size on the shape of sampling distributions (see chapter 11). This would be an important achievement because the relationship between sample size and statistical power seems to be one of the most difficult topics in inferential statistics courses (see chapter 1). Some very useful kinds of frequency representations also to be used in statistics courses are suggested by exploratory data analysis (e.g., Sedlmeier, 1996; Tukey, 1977; see also appendix C).

THEORETICAL IMPLICATIONS

The main aim of the training studies was to evaluate four different approaches that make divergent predictions about whether and how success in training about statistical reasoning can be achieved (see chapter 2). These four approaches have already been discussed several times following the presentation of the results found in the respective training studies. Here, the arguments are summarized and presented in a more general form.

Pragmatic Implications

The pragmatic-implications approach implies two-stage training with only the first stage being peculiar to that approach (see chapter 2). In this first stage, trainees are guided to understand a task as intended by its originator. Although a prior pragmatic-implications training attempt about conjunctive probabilities was not very successful (Crandall and Greenfield, 1986), the pragmatic-implications training on the use of sample size described in chapter 9 increased solution rates noticeably. Overall, however, the results imply that the first stage of a pragmatic-implications training does not suffice to produce a convincing training effect.

The pragmatic-implications approach does not specify a way of representing information, and therefore, one would not expect different results for different representational formats. Such differing results have been found when comparing, for instance, Venn-diagram to frequency-grid training. It appears that pragmatic implications play an important role in statistical reasoning if text tasks are involved, as is most often the case. Making sure that people understand all information in a task does not, however, generally suffice for solving that task. People have to be taught explicitly how to use this information. In summary, the predictions with respect to training effectiveness that can be derived from the pragmatic-implications approach are too unspecified at the current state of the approach to be subjected to a strong test. One would probably have to specify different predictions for groups differing in their language use and education.

Heuristics and Biases

The heuristics-and-biases approach assumes that *cognitive illusions*, non-normative responses found in many studies about statistical reasoning (see chapter 1), are as resistant to intervening measures as are visual illusions. Therefore, it predicts no substantial training effects regardless of the type of training. Clearly, this prediction does not conform to training results. The substantial effects found in all studies indicate that people can be trained successfully to avoid reasoning errors.

The heuristics-and-biases approach has inspired researchers for more than 2 decades now, and it is remarkable that the rather crude theoretical model has not yet been elaborated (see Gigerenzer, 1996b). Recall that according to the heuristics-and-biases approach, "people replace the laws of chance by heuristics, which sometimes yield reasonable estimates and quite often do not" (Kahneman & Tversky, 1972, p. 431). Exactly how do these heuristics work, and when do they work? Surprisingly, the heuristics-and-biases literature does not provide detailed answers to these questions. Take, for instance, the availability heuristic. It says that "a person could estimate the numerosity of a class, the likelihood of an event, or the frequency of co-occurrence by assessing the ease with which the relevant mental operation of retrieval, construction, or association can be carried out" (Tversky & Kahneman, 1973, p. 207). How can the ease be assessed? Tversky and Kahneman explain that ease can be measured by actual recall: "...the availability of instances could be measured by the total number of instances retrieved or constructed in any given problem" (p. 210), but they also suggest that "it is not necessary to perform the actual operations of retrieval or construction. It suffices to assess the ease with which these operations could be performed, much as the difficulty of a puzzle or mathematical problem can be assessed without considering specific solutions" (p. 208). There seem to be many possible candidate mechanisms for ease of retrieval that could lead to widely divergent predictions (Sedlmeier, Hertwig, & Gigerenzer, 1998). This diversity of potential operationalizations makes the availability heuristic hard to falsify. A similar argument can be made in respect to the representativeness heuristic (Gigerenzer & Murray, 1987; Sedlmeier, 1992). The PASS model introduced in chapter 14 deals with the idea of availability. In contrast to the heuristics-and-biases approach it, however, fully specifies the mechanism whereby the mind arrives at judgments about probability or relative frequency.

Abstract Rules

The abstract-rules approach did well in the conjunctive-probability training (chapter 5). The immediate training effect was also convincing in training studies that used more complex tasks. The long-term effect of training regimens was, however, strongly influenced by the kind of representational format—probability representations or formulas led to increasingly poorer results than frequency representations did as task difficulty increased. The abstract-rules approach does not predict such a divergence. Therefore, it cannot be maintained as a general model of how people reason under uncertain conditions.

The abstract-rules approach specifies several conditions under which people are expected to use abstract rules, such as the four probabilistic models discussed in this book (chapter 2). These conditions are reasonable in the sense that most, if not all, researchers in the field would agree on them, but a second look shows that, similar to those describing the heuristics-and-biases approach, the concepts used to describe these conditions are not clearly defined. Take, for instance, the *codability* of events, which is seen as one of the most important factors of whether or not people apply abstract rules. Codability is defined as the "ease with which events may be unitized and given a score characterizing them in clear and readily interpretable terms," and "...familiar events are apt to be more codable" (Kunda & Nisbett, 1986b, p. 198). This characterization of codability leaves us with the question of how "ease" and "familiarity" can be measured. The idea of codability seems to convey an important aspect of objects, and once again, the PASS model (chapter 14) can be used to offer one exact way to operationalize codability.

Adaptive Algorithms

Of the four approaches, the adaptive-algorithms approach received the most support from the training studies presented in this book. The current results are in accordance with the view that the mind is able to solve statistical tasks if they are presented in a format that is close to the naturally occurring format. If people are trained to translate a nonnatural format such as probabilities into a more natural one such as frequencies, they seem to apply this translation process in tasks encountered later on, and their behavior is consistent with the view that they use preexisting cognitive algorithms that developed as a result of selection processes to solve such tasks. A strong indication for the validity of this view can be seen in the nature of the long-term training effect. Recall that performance of participants in the frequency conditions consistently remained at the high level of the initial training effect, or even surpassed it later on, without further training. If the knowledge about how to solve a statistical task was newly learned in the training session, one would expect a decay curve over time, such as that usually found in the training regimens that do not use frequency representations. The fact that this decay curve is not found in training with frequency representations indicates that participants relied on preexisting knowledge, which apparently cannot be applied to rules in general, as predicted by the abstract-rules approach, but can only be applied to cognitive algorithms that work with frequency representations.

The adaptive-algorithms approach specifies conditions for when people can be expected to solve statistical tasks. However, it does not seem plausible to assume the existence of many cognitive algorithms that are specialized for specific statistical tasks (see chapter 15). The adaptive-algorithms approach provides an interesting perspective and allows testable predictions, but, like the other approaches, it does not provide detailed mechanisms whereby cognitive algorithms work. Without such an explicit process model, its use seems to be limited. The PASS model (chapter 14) attempts to provide a process model that is at least partly consistent with the adaptive-algorithms approach.

The Need for a Detailed Model

The evaluation of the four theoretical approaches leaves us with the conclusion that the adaptive-algorithms approach came out best. The abstract-rules approach has some merit because people evidently can be trained effectively to use abstract rules to solve statistical tasks. However, this effect seems to be short lived, at least for more difficult tasks, and thus the approach is limited as a general model to describe people's statistical reasoning.[1] The issue of pragmatic implications should be paid due respect in any approach to statistical reasoning, but on its own it is too limited to account for a full-fledged model. Finally, the heuristics-and-biases approach was not supported by the training results; these results, seen in conjunction with other criticism, imply that the heuristics-and-biases approach faces severe problems when attempting to describe human statistical reasoning in general.

---

[1]Please keep in mind, that this conclusion refers to statistically naive people and not to statistical experts. Nobody would deny that abstract statistical rules can be learned and retained with sufficient effort; and, of course, advanced topics in statistics can be more effectively dealt with using abstract rules.

A drawback of all approaches, including the adaptive-algorithms approach, is their low degree of precision. One might argue that the theoretical approaches discussed in this book were precise enough to test against each other, and that such testing allows us to successfully predict the efficiency of a training regimen. This is true, but a real understanding, that is, an understanding not only of whether people can solve statistical tasks, but of how they arrive at their results, requires a more elaborate model. Apart from shedding light on how the mind processes uncertainty, such a model should eventually lead to even better advice for the practice of teaching statistical reasoning. The next two chapters are devoted to developing such a model. Chapter 13 lays the foundations and chapter 14 spells out the specifics.

13

Associationist Models of Statistical Reasoning: Architectures and Constraints

SUMMARY: This chapter elaborates on how associationist models can simulate statistical reasoning. To simulate the solution of the tasks discussed in this book, an associationist model must rely solely on the contiguity of collections of features that define the events in question, not on the contingency of events. The model should make realistic estimates of relative frequency and probability that, as empirical results show, deviate in several systematic ways from the actually encountered relative frequencies. Empirical evidence suggests that, given frequentistic input, estimates of relative frequency and probability can be treated alike.

Up to this point, this volume has dealt mostly with text tasks. This is the way statistical tasks are usually presented in experiments, and it is the way we are often confronted with statistical information in print media. However, the problem of text understanding is far beyond the scope of this book, and in an attempt to build a precise model of how the mind arrives at probability judgments, it seems appropriate to begin at a more elementary level.

This chapter lays the groundwork for the PASS (Probability ASSociator) model, which will be introduced in the next chapter. PASS is realized as a computer program that simulates how people arrive at judgments of relative frequency and probability in simple natural environments, such as when reasoning about results produced by an urn model (see chapter 10). The balls in the urn can stand for a wide variety of naturally occurring events that can be described by their features. The model is related to the adaptive-algorithms approach, whose predictions fit well with the results of the current training studies (see chapter 15, for a discussion of this relation). It does not, however, assume that evolution has shaped a separate cognitive algorithm for every facet of statistical reasoning. Instead it assumes that the mind has evolved an associationist cognitive mechanism that allows processing and evaluation of frequencies and relative frequencies of events. PASS learns about the relative frequency or probability of events and their contexts by encoding them serially. The frequency with which such events or parts of events are encoded induces a change in PASS' associative memory that represents its knowledge about relative frequency and probability.

Associationist learning uses the same kind of information that is needed to make probability judgments: frequencies with which objects or events occur and co-occur. Thus, it appears to be an ideal candidate for modeling statistical reasoning. Because of that obvious relationship between associative learning and probability judgment, one would expect that such models already exist. There are indeed associationist models of probability judgment, but these are restricted to contingency learning, that is, to the learning of action–outcome and cue–outcome relationships. Although such relationships are a very important topic in psychological research, we will not be concerned with contingency learning, because as will be argued, most kinds of probability judgments in everyday life, as well as those studied in the literature, are based on the encoding of events or objects in the absence of explicit contingencies. Thus, a model of contingency learning would not be adequate, and therefore another kind of model is called for. The issue of how such an associative model of probability judgment should look is addressed in the next section. Then we will discuss what PASS has to model, that is, the empirical constraints that a model for statistical reasoning must satisfy. Finally, the issue of the equivalence between relative frequencies and probabilities is addressed.

WHAT KIND OF ASSOCIATIONIST MODEL?

Before this chapter discusses the issue of how a suitable associationist model of frequency judgment should be constructed, a word is in order about how events or objects are represented in such models. The basic assumption of associationist learning theory is that "objects once experienced together tend to become associated in the imagination, so that when any one of them is thought of, the others are likely to be thought of also, in the same order of sequence or co-existence as before" (James, 1890, p. 561). In most of the recent computational associative approaches, "objects" are modeled by arrays of features or values on attributes or dimensions (for overview, see Estes, 1991). These attributes can be seen as independent dimensions such as color, size, height, and others in which objects in the world vary, thus placing objects on a point in multidimensional space. The set of attributes does not have to be fixed in advance, but can be learned flexibly as a consequence of categorizing and representing objects (Shyns & Rodet, 1997). Accordingly, PASS will encode objects as collections of features, which means that in James' definition, "object" is replaced by "features, or attribute values."

Most existing associationist models examine contingency judgments (e.g., Shanks, 1995; Wasserman & Miller, 1997). PASS, in contrast, will only rely on the contiguity of features. To clarify the difference between the two types of models, contingency models are described first in some detail.

Contingencies Between Events

Tasks used in examining understanding of probabilistic processes differ in many respects, but one difference is especially evident: whether or not an object or event is contingent on the occurrence of another object or event. There are several ways to express the notion of contingency formally, but all of them include the case that an outcome or response occurs in both the presence and absence of a stimulus or event. One way to formulate the contingency between a stimulus and an outcome is the following (e.g., Shanks, 1995):

Contingency = p(outcome | stimulus) − p(outcome | ¬stimulus).

In this definition, a contingency can have values from −1 to 1. The conditional probabilities are usually derived from relative frequencies. For instance, p(outcome | stimulus) is calculated by dividing the number (#) of common occurrences of outcome and stimulus by the number of occurrences of the stimulus: # (outcome & stimulus) / # stimulus. This definition of contingency implies, for instance, that if the outcome occurs often when the stimulus is present, but also when the stimulus is not (¬) present, the contingency is low. As an example, assume that we want to find out about the contingency between weather forecasts of rain and actual raining. The numbers in our hypothetical example are the following: In 100 forecasts, rain was predicted (stimulus present), and in 200 forecasts, no rain was predicted (stimulus not present). In 50 of the 100 cases in which rain was predicted it actually rained but it also did so in 100 of the 200 cases in which no rain was predicted. The contingency that expresses the causal relationship between rain forecast and actual rain is then calculated as:

$$Contingency = p(\text{rain | rain forecast}) − p(\text{rain | no rain forecast})$$
$$= 50 / 100 − 100 / 200 = 0.$$

In this example, there is no relationship between rain forecast and actual rain, and the practical consequence would be not to care about the forecast. Newer associationist models that simulate contingency judgments rely on connectionist architectures and learning procedures (e.g., Anderson, Silverstein, Ritz, & Jones 1977; Estes, Campbell, Hastsopoulos, & Hurwitz, 1989; Gluck & Bower, 1988; Shanks, 1991). The approach most often used is a simple feed-forward network that usually relies on the delta or Rescorla-Wagner rule. Figure 13.1 shows the architecture of a typical network used in modeling contingency judgments. This network uses stimuli consisting of four features each (I_1, I_2, I_3, and I_4) and two possible responses or outcomes (O_1 and O_2). In simulating contingency learning, each time a stimulus is presented to the network, a corresponding response

Outcome

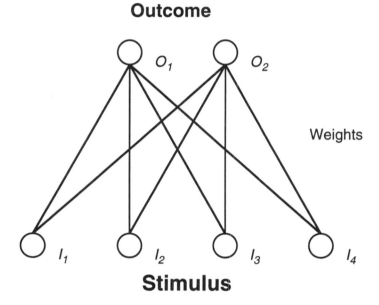

Stimulus

FIG. 13.1.   Architecture of a simple feed-forward network. Here, the stimulus consists of four features (I_1, I_2, I_3, and I_4) and there are two possible outcomes or responses (O_1 and O_2).

is paired with a certain probability.[1]

How does the network learn the contingencies? At each presentation of a stimulus and the corresponding response, the weight w_{ij} between an input node i (corresponding to a feature of the stimulus) and an output node j (corresponding to an outcome) is updated in such a way that eventually, the prediction of the outcome from knowing the stimulus is optimized; that is, the network reaches a state in which weight changes no longer improve its performance. The delta rule changes the weights according to the difference between the prespecified output and the actual output calculated by the net (see J. A. Anderson, 1995; or Rumelhart, Hinton, and Williams, 1986, for details).[2] When learning has finished, the

---

[1]A frequently used task is to let participants learn the contingency between collections of symptoms and corresponding diseases (e.g., Estes et al., 1989). For instance, in Fig. 13.1, the stimulus, consisting of I_1 to I_4, could stand for four symptoms (e.g., fever, headache, running nose, shiny eyes), and the presence or absence of the respective symptom determines the value of the corresponding feature or input node (e.g., if fever is present, I_1 has the value 1, and if it is absent it has the value 0). A given collection of symptoms is then paired with one of the two possible diseases (e.g., O_1 might stand for common cold and O_2 for gingivitis).

[2]In a simple version, the delta rule looks like this:

$$\Delta w_{ij} = \eta \delta_j a_i.$$

In words, the delta rule states: The change in the weight between input node i and output node j (Δw_{ij}) is the product of the learning parameter η, the difference between the desired output and the produced output for output node j, δ_j, and the activation of the input node i, a_i. It becomes clear from the equation that the amount of a weight change varies with the size of the difference.

probability that a certain stimulus provokes a certain outcome is calculated as follows (e.g., Estes et al., 1989): First, for a given stimulus, the output activation for each outcome is calculated. In Fig. 13.1, for every stimulus we would have two such output activations, one for O_1 (O_{O1}) and one for O_2 (O_{O2}). The probability that the stimulus used (i.e., a specific combination of features) predicts O_1 would then be $O_{O1} / (O_{O1} + O_{O2})$, and the probability that this stimulus predicts O_2 would be $O_{O2} / (O_{O1} + O_{O2})$.

Models of this type simulate participants' contingency judgments well (e.g., Estes, et al., 1989; Gluck & Bower, 1988; Shanks, 1990), and they are very useful when studying classical conditioning or causal relationships (e.g., Shanks, 1995; but see Waldmann, 1996). They do not, however, capture the way people tend to learn about probabilities in everyday life as exemplified in the examples used throughout this book.

Contiguities of Features

What are the bases for probability judgments in everyday life? Basically, we perceive contiguities between features, that is, we perceive whether features do or do not occur together. As already mentioned, features define events, including their contexts. If features often occur together, the associations among them are stronger than if they co-occur infrequently. Therefore, frequently occurring feature constellations are expected to elicit a stronger associative response than are rare feature constellations. The strength of the response can then be taken as a measure of the frequency with which a given event has occurred. To make a judgment about the relative frequency or conditional probability of an event A given a conditioning event B, the response elicited by the features defining the co-occurrence of events A and B has to be related to the response elicited by the features defining event B with and without event A (a mechanism termed CA-module will achieve this in PASS). In contrast to contingency judgments, only those cases in which the conditioning event is present are of interest.

Consider the simple example depicted in Fig. 13.2. The sample space consists of three kinds of objects which are defined by three binary valued features (red vs. not red, round vs. not round, and marked by a + vs. not marked by a +). Assume objects as defined in Fig. 13.2 are encountered in successive random drawings. To calculate p(round), the probability that a round object occurs, the number of round objects encountered (b in Fig. 13.2) is divided by the number of all objects encountered. To determine p(red | crossed) the conditional probability that an object is red given that is marked by a +, the number of objects for which both is true (a) is divided by the number of objects which are marked by a + (a and c). There are no contingencies between events involved in this type of judgment, instead, one event at a time, without a response or an outcome paired to it, constitutes the input.

Features

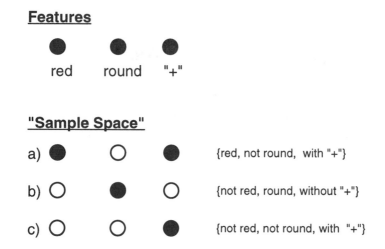

FIG. 13.2.   Sample space consisting of three possible objects that are defined by the presence or absence of the three features red, round, and marked by a +.

The same kind of reasoning holds for the tasks dealt with in this book. Consider the Linda task (chapter 1) as an example. How do we decide whether it is more likely that Linda is a bank teller or both a bank teller and a feminist? Here, we have to make a probability judgment about p(bank teller I Linda) and one about p(bank teller & feminist I Linda) and compare the two. We could arrive at our probability judgments by asking all women who are like Linda whether they are bank tellers, feminists, or both, that is, look at the number of cases in which both the features that define bank teller and bank teller & feminist co-occur with the features that define Linda, divide these two numbers by the number of women who are like Linda, and compare the two.[3] Again, no contingency is involved—it would not make sense to also consider women other than Linda, that is, p(bank teller I ¬Linda) and p(bank teller & feminist I ¬Linda). As another example, take the Bavarian police task (chapter 1). We need to compare p(marijuana smoker I heroin addict) to p(heroin addict I marijuana smoker). The former is obtained by dividing the number of people for whom the attributes heroin addict and marijuana smoker co-occur by the number of heroin addicts, and the latter is obtained by dividing the number of co-occurrences by the number of marijuana smokers. Again, we need no information about people who are neither heroin addicts nor marijuana smokers, that is, p(marijuana smoker I ¬heroin addict) and p(heroin addict I ¬marijuana smoker) are irrelevant in this

---

[3]In this case, it is not even necessary to divide by the number of times the conditioning event (Linda) occurs, because it is identical in both cases.

task. All of the tasks described in previous chapters are of the noncontingent variety.[4]

In summary, associative models for contingency judgments previously described cannot capture most kinds of judgments of probability and relative frequency in everyday life, and as we will see shortly, as examined in numerous studies. Instead, a model is needed that derives probabilities from considering only the contiguity of features that define an event. There remains the question of what exactly it must model. Do people's judgments really coincide with actual relative frequencies? Are there any systematic deviations from the encoded input?

WHAT HAS TO BE MODELED?

All statistical tasks involve estimates of conditional probabilities. Note that all probabilities can be treated as conditional probabilities by conditioning them on the disjunction of the event and its complement. For instance, p(rain) is the same as p(rain | rain or no rain). Conditional probabilities, in turn, are usually estimated from relative frequencies. The evidence for sensitivity to probabilities and relative frequencies, and apparent counterevidence is now briefly reviewed. This sensitivity does not mirror actual relative frequency exactly: Estimates of relative frequency and probability usually show several mostly small but systematic deviations from actual relative frequencies. In general, high relative frequencies are underestimated and low relative frequencies are overestimated. Moreover, if the relative frequency of an event changes with time, this is reflected in people's judgments in that the most recent relative frequency is given more weight. And finally, sample size influences probability judgments in that with increasing sample size, the judgments become more exact and are given higher confidence ratings. These points are discussed in more detail in the next sections.

Sensitivity to Relative Frequencies/Probabilities

Chapter 1 provides some examples of children's sensitivities (a) to the fact that conjunctive events are not more likely than any of the events that constitute the conjunction, and (b) to the empirical law that larger samples tend to yield proportions closer to the population values. In the developmental literature, a large number of similar results can be found. Even before the beginning of school, children show a remarkable sensitivity to relative frequencies in both choice and estimation tasks (e.g., Fischbein, 1975; Huber, 1993; Kuzmak & Gelman, 1986;

---

[4]Sample-size tasks are a bit different because with them, probability estimates are generally not made but are qualified. Sample-size tasks could be seen as second-order probability judgments, that is, as (confidence) judgments about the (first order) probability judgments. The latter are, of course, tasks of the noncontingent type.

Reyna & Brainerd, 1994). Some results that seemed inconsistent with the conclusion that children are sensitive to relative frequencies were later found to be due to their misunderstandings of the task (Hilton, 1995; Reyna & Brainerd, 1994), or to working memory limitations (Brainerd, 1981). Reliance on relative frequencies occasionally has been observed to decrease with age, dependent on the domain of tasks. There seem to be two reasons for this. First, children seem to be increasingly aware of causal connections. For instance, Jacobs and Potenza (1991) found a strong reliance on relative frequencies (e.g., relative frequency of socks of a certain kind vs. socks of another kind) when their participants made judgments about a situation in which individuation information about the agent in the story was unimportant (e.g., which socks would Mike choose using a random sampling procedure?). They found much less reliance on relative frequencies (e.g., relative frequency of girls who chose to be cheerleaders vs. band members) as well as an inverse relationship between reliance and age when additional information could be considered relevant (e.g., would *pretty* Juanita decide to become a cheerleader or band member?). Surprisingly, school is identified by Fischbein (1975) as the second reason for a diminishing reliance on relative frequencies in children's judgments. He argues that, whereas unschooled children use their valid probabilistic intuitions, these intuitions are considerably weakened or suppressed by schools' overwhelming emphasis on deterministic explanations about the world.

Evidence for the sensitivity to relative frequencies has been found in a large number of studies with adults as well (e.g., Hasher & Zacks, 1984; Hock, Malcus, & Hasher, 1986; Johnson, Peterson, Yap, & Rose, 1989; Jonides & Jones, 1992; Naveh-Benjamin & Jonides, 1986; Watkins & LeCompte, 1991; Wettler & Rapp, 1993; Wettler, Rapp, & Ferber, 1993). The findings with adults, however, have not been unanimous. For instance, Lichtenstein, Slovic, Fischhoff, Layman, & Combs (1978) found that people gave imprecise estimates of the frequency of lethal causes. For some causes such as tornadoes, cancer, and homicide, estimates were exaggerated, whereas for other causes such as diabetes, tuberculosis, and asthma, estimates were too low. Is this evidence that people are not sensitive to frequencies? It turns out that people's frequency estimates are closely tied to the frequencies with which such events are reported in the news. Whereas deaths due to a tornado are reported in every newspaper, news about the death of a diabetic are seldom published. Thus, although participants' frequency judgments did not mirror the actual state of affairs, they seem to have reflected the frequency with which these causes of death were presented to them. Such an explanation, however, does not hold for the results in the probably best known example of biased estimates of relative frequency, Tversky and Kahneman's (1973) letter study, which is cited in almost every cognitive psychology textbook as evidence of faulty estimates of relative frequency. In that study, participants had to judge whether a certain letter (e.g., the letter r) appears more often in the first or the third position in English words, and what the ratio of the letter appearing in the two positions would be. Tversky and Kahneman found that about two thirds of their participants erroneously judged the majority of the letters used (which all occurred more often in the third position) to occur more often in the first position. For many years, there seems to have been only one published, but largely ignored, replication of Tversky and Kahneman's (1973) study, a one-page article that was unable to duplicate the original result (White, 1991). Recently, Sedlmeier et al. (1998) replicated Tversky and Kahneman's (1973) study several times and consistently found that participants' estimates of the relative frequency of letters conformed well with actual relative frequencies.[5] Thus, there seems to be no convincing evidence for the view that adults are bad frequency estimators. Sometimes, people's relative-frequency estimates might, however, be more in accord with the frequencies with which descriptions of events occurred (e.g. in the news) than with actual frequencies.

PASS is designed to make probability judgments on the basis of actually presented frequencies. In respect to the Lichtenstein et al. (1978) study, this would mean that PASS' input would be the frequencies with which several causes of death are mentioned in a newspaper and not their actual frequencies, if the latter deviate from the former.

Underestimation of High and Overestimation of Low Relative Frequencies

A common phenomenon in judgments of frequency and relative frequency is the underestimation of high and the overestimation of low values (e.g., Erlick, 1964; Fiedler, 1991; Greene, 1984; Hintzman, 1969; Shanks, 1995; Varey, Mellers, & Birnbaum, 1990). This phenomenon of regression in relative frequency judgments was also found by Lichtenstein et al. (1978) and by Sedlmeier et al. (1998). In the latter study, the estimated proportions with which a certain letter appears in the first position, as compared to both first and second positions, were regressed toward 50%. For example, the letter C, which in the German language actually appears in the first position with a relative frequency of 10%, was judged to appear there with a median relative frequency of 25% to 30%, whereas for the letter S, which appears about 90% in first position, estimates were lower

---

[5]It is not entirely clear what caused participants' faulty estimates in the original study. Apart from sampling error, one possible explanation rests on a peculiarity of the experimental procedures. In the original experiment, participants' responses were checked against a corpus that used words consisting of at least three letters. The English language, however, contains many two-letter and also some one-letter words (e.g., I) and therefore, the overall frequency of letters in the first position is higher than that in the third position. If participants were not able to suppress their knowledge about one- and two-letter words, that might have led to overestimation. Sedlmeier et al. (1998), in contrast, asked for the frequency in the first and the second positions in German words. Because the German language does not have one-letter words, the overall letter frequencies in the first position and the second position are equal. Thus, participants did not have to suppress any knowledge about words shorter than two letters.

than that value (between 60% and 80%, in the median). Any model whose input is frequencies of events has to account for this regression effect.

Changing Relative Frequencies

In laboratory studies, the relative frequencies which participants estimate are usually kept constant during the course of the experiment. The assumption that relative frequencies do not change over time is, however, not very plausible in everyday life. For instance, problems experienced with personal computers (e.g., freezing of the screen) might increase over time, suggesting that the computer is going to break down soon. To use another example, the relative frequency with which the name of a celebrity is encountered in the news is normally far from stable over time. Are people sensitive to such a change of relative frequencies over time, even when they might not attend to it explicitly? If so, in which way do changing relative frequencies influence their estimates?

There is evidence that contingency judgments are strongly influenced by trial-order effects in that most recent and dense trial types have the biggest impact on judgments (Chapman, 1991; Lopez, Shanks, Almaraz, & Fernandez, 1998; Shanks, Lopez, Darby, & Dickinson, 1996). Therefore one should expect a similar effect in judgments of relative frequencies that are less complex than contingency judgments. Indeed, a recency effect for relative-frequency estimates has also been found by Sedlmeier and Hertwig (1999). These authors used pairs of visual patterns, a left and a right pattern presented together on a computer screen. Participants were seated in front of the computer screen and saw repeated presentations of pattern pairs. Five different patterns were used and each of the patterns could occur in the left and the right position of the pair. After 200 presentations of pattern pairs, participants had to estimate the relative frequencies with which each of the five patterns had occurred in the left position of the pattern pair. Unbeknownst to participants, the relative frequency with which a given pattern was presented in the left position changed after 100 presentations. Consider an example: For one of two experimental groups, Pattern 1 was presented in the left position 90% of the time in the first half of the trial, and was presented 60% of the time in the second half. For the other group, the relative frequencies were reversed, first 60% and then 90% in the left position. During the whole trial, the relative frequencies were identical in both groups, that is, 75% in the left position. If participants were insensitive to a change in relative frequencies, then their estimates should not differ. In fact, the estimates for Pattern 1, as well as for the other patterns, differed systematically in that estimates were more influenced by the second than by the first half of the pattern presentations. Thus, a suitable model should show a recency effect in its estimates of relative frequencies and probabilities.

Sensitivity to Sample Size

In tasks involving the comparison of single samples (frequency-distribution tasks) people are, in general, sensitive to the impact of sample size in that they have more confidence in the mean or proportion of a larger sample than that of a smaller one (see chapter 1). This increase in confidence is justified by the empirical law of large numbers (see appendix B). Interestingly, it is also accompanied by an increase in participants' accuracy. For instance, Erlick (1964) found that the accuracy of proportion estimates (proportion with which one of two letters occurred on a screen) increased with number of presentations. Similar results were found in contingency judgments (probability learning) with a computer-game-like scenario (Shanks, 1995).

Some studies have examined increase in confidence in more detail. For instance, Irwin, Smith, and Mayfield (1956) had participants judge whether the average of a series of numbers on cards was greater or less than zero, and then indicate their confidence in judgments. Participants were shown a pack of 500 cards and each card had a number on its back. The experimenter shuffled the first 20 cards (two identical sets of 10 cards each), and displayed them, one at a time. Participants had to indicate on a confidence scale that ranged from −100 to 100 whether the average of the whole pack was greater or less than 0 by choosing either the negative or the positive part of the scale; and they had to indicate their confidence by choosing the appropriate number between 0 and 100 (or −100). For instance, if somebody judged the average to be smaller than zero and had a medium confidence in this judgment, he or she would choose a value of −50. Irwin et al. (1956) consistently found good judgments and a greater confidence after 20 cards were presented than after 10. In another study, DuCharme and Peterson (1969) presented participants with sequences of 12 chips sampled consecutively from an urn containing unknown proportions of red and blue chips. Participants had to adjust a credible interval for the proportion of red chips by moving two markers along a scale from 0 to 1. The size of the middle interval on the scale (between the two markers) reflected participants' confidence that it included the true proportion.[6] DuCharme and Peterson found that participants monotonically decreased the size of the middle interval with increasing sample size, regardless of the true proportion, indicating that confidence grew with sample size.

---

[6]Participants had to move the markers so that the true proportion was equally likely to be in one of the three intervals. The proportion of red chips could lie anywhere between 0 and 1. Therefore, the markers were initially set to .333 and .667. In the course of the experiment, participants generally decreased the size of the middle interval, indicating an increasing confidence that the population proportion lay in this interval. In the extreme, that is, with total confidence, the interval would be concentrated on one single point. Because this task was quite demanding, participants received considerable training at the start of the experimental session.

In summary: A model of statistical reasoning must incorporate the relationship between confidence and sample size, and it must produce estimates that become more precise as sample size increases.

EQUIVALENCE BETWEEN RELATIVE FREQUENCIES AND PROBABILITIES

Until now, judgments about relative frequencies and probabilities have been treated alike. Not differentiating between the two can be justified on the grounds that, in the frequentist interpretation of probability with which we are solely concerned, the input on which such judgments are based is the same: frequencies of events. In their review of developmental studies about probability judgment, Reyna and Brainerd (1994) concluded that children indeed use frequency information to make probability judgments. The most important reason for faulty probability judgments in children appears to be a failure to retrieve frequency information due to insufficient working memory capacity (Brainerd, 1981).

Recent evidence for the equivalence of adults' judgments about relative frequencies and probabilities comes from two studies by Sedlmeier and Köhlers (1999). In these studies, participants were seated in front of a computer screen and were presented with different visual patterns such as that in Fig. 13.3, one at a time. Study 1 used three and Study 2 used four different patterns. At the end of the presentation sequence, two groups of participants were asked to make judgments about the patterns they had experienced. One group was asked for relative-frequency and the other for probability judgments. In the relative-frequency condition, participants had to estimate in what percentage of presentations each of the symbols had appeared during the whole sequence. In the probability

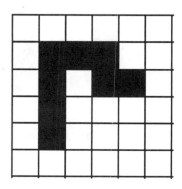

FIG. 13.3.   Example of a visual pattern as used in Sedlmeier and Köhlers (1999).

condition, the question was about the probability with which each of the symbols would occur in the immediately following presentation (participants did not know that there would be no more such presentations). Note that these two questions differed both in perspective (past vs. future) and in reference to either relative frequencies or single-event probabilities. Despite these differences, participants' responses did not differ in any systematic way. Figure 13.4 shows participants' mean judgments after 60 presentations of three patterns that were presented with proportions of 50%, 33%, and 17%. The results of Study 2, in which four patterns with proportions of 50%, 30%, 15%, and 5% were used, and in which altogether 120 patterns were presented, are shown in Fig. 13.5. Fully consistent with the results in Study 1, there is no systematic difference between relative-frequency and (single-case) probability judgments. Both studies showed the usual regression effect, that is, large proportions were underestimated and small proportions were overestimated, in both kinds of judgments. These results imply that a model for simple probability estimates does not have to differentiate between estimates of relative frequency and probability.

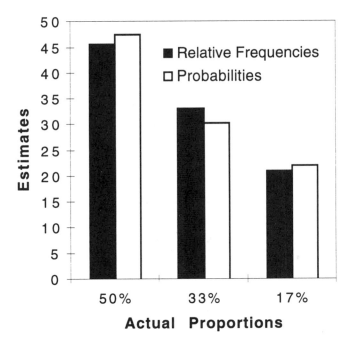

FIG. 13.4.   Probability and relative-frequency estimates after 60 presentations (mean percentages) of participants in Study 1 of Sedlmeier and Köhlers (1999) for three different proportions of patterns.

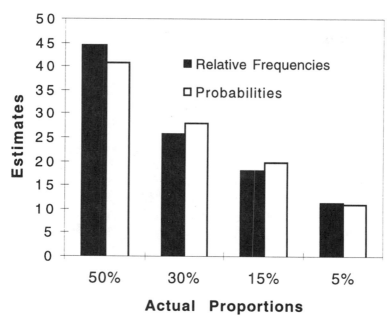

FIG. 13.5. Probability and relative-frequency estimates after 120 presentations (mean percentages) of participants in Study 2 of Sedlmeier and Köhlers (1999) for four different proportions of patterns.

At first glance, there seems to be considerable evidence which is counter to the assumption that estimates of relative frequency and probability should be treated alike. Just think about all the examples from chapter 1 in which a difference in the representational format, that is, probabilities versus frequencies, yielded remarkably different judgments. However, in these examples, the difference concerned the numerical input used in tasks. If this input was frequencies, judgments were generally much better than if it was probabilities or percentages. Consistent with that finding, the results of the training studies (chapters 5–11) showed that if participants learned how to transform input given in probabilities or percentages into frequencies, they were able to solve statistical tasks even when the response was required in the form of probabilities. Thus, a restriction applies to the equivalence between estimates of relative frequencies and probabilities: equivalence only holds in cases in which the input consists of frequencies of events whose occurrences are, at least in principle, observable, and if the estimate is based on such frequencies. PASS will be strictly applicable only in this situation.[7]

---

[7]Unlike estimates of relative frequency, probability estimates should only be made when the events in question can be regarded as the result of random sampling. The recognition of randomness,

SUMMARY: CONSTRAINTS FOR AN ASSOCIATIONIST MODEL OF STATISTICAL REASONING

An associationist model of statistical reasoning should take as input collections of features that represent one or more events, possibly including their contexts as well. The model's input should be repeatedly encountered co-occurrences (or missing co-occurrences) of features. Given this precondition, relative-frequency and probability estimates can be treated alike. The model's estimates of relative frequency or probability should not exactly follow the actually encountered relative frequencies, but should differ from them in three characteristic respects: (a) high relative frequencies should be underestimated and low ones should be overestimated, (b) changes in relative frequencies over time should lead to a stronger consideration of the recently encountered events, and (c) with increasing sample size, estimates should become more exact and should be assigned increasing confidence. The next chapter describes how the PASS model fits these constraints and models the solution of the kinds of tasks dealt with in this book.

---

and therefore the decision as to whether or not a probability estimate is adequate, should, however, pose no problem because ample evidence indicates that even children are able to differentiate between random and deterministic processes (e.g., Fischbein, 1975; Kuzmak & Gelman, 1986). Of course, if a probability estimate is influenced by important additional information (e.g., the information that situational conditions have suddenly and drastically changed), or some strong belief contrasting with the relative frequencies encountered, an equivalence between relative frequency and probability estimates may not be expected.

14

The PASS Model

SUMMARY: *PASS,* an associationist model that simulates human probability judgments, consists of two parts, *FEN,* a neural network, and the *CA-module,* which contains rules that operate on the output of the neural network. FEN, the core of PASS, encodes events, including their contexts, by their featural descriptions and builds up a representation of the frequency with which features co-occur. The CA-module consists of only two algorithms that model estimates of conditional probabilities and judgments about the impact of sample size. Possible limitations of PASS are discussed, and it is compared to competing models. Finally, PASS' relation to categorization is addressed.

The last chapter spelled out the constraints an associationist model of statistical reasoning has to obey for both theoretical and empirical reasons. Recall that such a model has to rely on the co-occurrence of features of successive events as the sole input and it has to learn without any supervision. Its estimates of conditional probabilities should roughly conform to actual relative frequencies, but the model should produce a regression effect, be responsive to a change in relative frequency over time, become more exact with increasing sample size, and put increasing confidence in judgments as sample size increases. Moreover, it should be able to simulate the results described in this book for urn-type tasks, that is, to judge $p(A \& B)$ to be at most as likely as $p(A)$ or $p(B)$, and to judge $p(A \mid B)$ as more probable than $p(B \mid A)$ if $p(A) > p(B)$ (and the reverse). The PASS model will be shown to achieve all of this.

After PASS' system architecture, as well as the way it learns and produces a response is explained, it is demonstrated how it can model all the previously mentioned results. Then, the nature of FEN is explored and some possible limitations of the model are addressed. PASS is then compared to models of a different type that have been used for judgments of relative frequency. Finally, it is argued that PASS' ability to model statistical reasoning may be seen as a by-product of its more basic ability to classify objects and events, that is, to identify categories.

ARCHITECTURE, LEARNING PROCESS, AND RESPONSES

PASS consists of two parts: FEN (Frequency Encoding Network), a simple neural network that encodes and stores frequencies of events and reacts to prompts, and the CA-module (Cognitive-Algorithms module), which contains two algorithms that work on the output of the neural network. Only FEN is used in the learning process but both components are needed to create a response, that is, some kind of probability judgment such as those previously mentioned. Figure 14.1 gives a schematic overview of PASS.

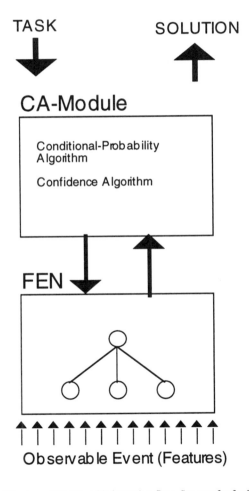

FIG. 14.1.   Architecture of PASS and information flow. See text for further explanation.

FEN

FEN should be regarded, not as a specific neural network, but as a class of net-works that work without corrective feedback (see chapter 13). Henceforth, FEN is used to denote the class of models. We will mostly deal with one instance of this class, FEN I, but later in this chapter FEN II, a different instance, will be briefly described. FEN I is a two-layered, feed-forward neural network with an input and an output layer. Input and output units are fully interconnected, that is, every output unit has weighted connections to every input unit (see Fig. 14.2). The number of input and output units is not crucial, but as networks of this type are mostly used for classification (described later), the number of output units is assumed to usually be less than that of input units. A given input consists of a pattern of 1's (feature present) and 0's (feature not present) that can be regarded as a vector (see Fig. 14.3).

FEN I learns according to the competitive learning algorithm (Grossberg, 1976; Rumelhart & Zipser, 1985), which, in contrast to the delta rule used in contingency-learning models, does not rely on corrective feedback. In a standard competitive-learning network, learning consists of adjusting the weight vector of

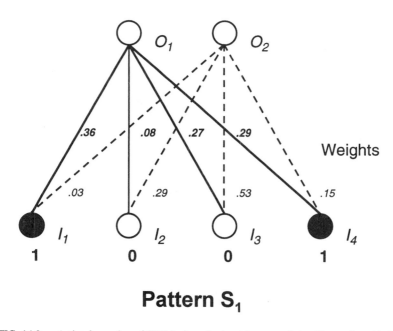

Pattern S_1

FIG. 14.2.   A simple version of FEN I where the input layer consists of four units with the first (I_1) and the fourth (I_4) units on and the other two off, and where the output layer consists of two units (O_1 and O_2). The four (randomly determined) initial weights for each output unit add up to 1.

a) Matrix

0 0 0 0 0 0 **0 1 1 1 0 0** 0 1 0 1 1 0 0 1 0 0 0 0 0 1 0 0 0 0 0 0 0 0 0

b) Vector

FIG. 14.3. An arbitrary input pattern for PASS. Shown are a matrix and an equivalent vector representation, which concatenates the rows of the matrix. White squares in the matrix are represented in the vector by 0's and black squares by 1's. Consider, for instance, the second row of the matrix (from top). It contains one 0, three consecutive 1's and two more 0's. The part of the vector representation corresponding to this second row of the matrix is in bold print.

the winning output unit. The winning output unit is that unit whose weight vector is most similar to the input vector, where similarity is measured by the scalar product (e.g., Jordan, 1986) of both vectors. (All other output units are losing units.) The learning rule that governs the change in a weight w_{ij} (all weights are positive) connecting an input unit i to an output unit j in a particular trial is:

$$\Delta w_{ij} = \begin{cases} 0 & \text{if unit } j \text{ loses on stimulus } k \\ g_w \dfrac{c_{ik}}{n_k} - g_w w_{ij} & \text{if unit } j \text{ wins on stimulus } k \end{cases}$$

(1)

where g_w stands for the learning rate for a winning unit, c_{ik} is equal to 1 if unit i is active in the input pattern S_k and 0 otherwise, and n_k is the number of active units in S_k. The (fixed) sum of the weights for any output unit j's weight vector is 1, and single weights are assigned their values randomly before learning.

Consider the hypothetical numerical example specified in Fig. 14.2. What happens when FEN I encounters the stimulus pattern S_1, in which the features represented by units I_1 and I_4 are present and those represented by units I_2 and I_3 are not? First, the winning output unit is determined. For that, the scalar product of the input vector (< 1 0 0 1 >) and each of the two weight vectors (< .36 .08

.27 .29 > for O_1, and < .03 .29 .53 .15 > for O_2) are computed. This results in a scalar product of .65 for O_1 and .18 for O_2 and thus makes O_1 the winner.[1] Only the weights of O_1 are now updated. Let us use a learning rate of $g_w = .1$. Then, by Equation 1, the new weights for O_1 are < .374 .072 .243 .311 >.[2]

Learning in FEN I consists of rearranging the weights connected to a given output unit in such a way that the active input lines, that is, the lines coming from input features that have the value 1, tend to gain weight[3] and the nonactive input lines lose weight, with the learning rate determining the amount of change. Unlike the well-known backpropagation learning procedure that, for a given input sequence always leads to the same final weights (e.g., Rumelhart, Hinton, et al., 1986), such a convergence is not guaranteed in the case of competitive learning (Rumelhart & Zipser, 1985). The remaining variations in the results are affected by the specific initial weights, the magnitude of g_w, and the number and order of presentations. However, the variation is usually quite small and can be dealt with in the same way error variance is dealt with in psychological experiments—one simply takes the mean (or median) of many individual runs. (A run involves the serial processing of a given number of inputs by the network.) The non-convergence of the competitive learning algorithm can be seen as an advantage rather than a disadvantage in respect to modeling human judgment because different runs model the error variance found in any experiment with human participants.

A response can be elicited from FEN I at any time. In this case, learning is disabled and FEN I is presented the input pattern to which it should respond. Its response to that pattern is taken to be the sum of the activation values of all output units. As we have seen, the activation for a given output unit is just the scalar product of its weight vector and the input vector. For instance, given the state of affairs in Fig. 14.2, FEN I's response to the pattern "1 0 0 1" would be .83 (.65 + .18), that is, the sum of the activations over O_1 and O_2.

---

[1]If an input vector **i** consists of n values $I_1, I_2, ..., I_n$, and a weight vector **w** consists of n weights $W_1, W_2, ..., W_n$, the scalar (or inner) product of the two vectors is calculated as:

$$\mathbf{i} \cdot \mathbf{w} = \sum_{i=1}^{i=n} I_i W_i .$$

[2]The new weights are calculated as follows:

$$w_{11\text{-new}} = w_{11\text{-old}} + \Delta w_{11} = .36 + .1(1/2) - .1 \times .36 = .374,$$
$$w_{21\text{-new}} = w_{21\text{-old}} + \Delta w_{21} = .08 + .1(0/2) - .1 \times .08 = .072,$$
$$w_{31\text{-new}} = w_{31\text{-old}} + \Delta w_{31} = .27 + .1(0/2) - .1 \times .27 = .243, \text{ and}$$
$$w_{41\text{-new}} = w_{41\text{-old}} + \Delta w_{41} = .29 + .1(1/2) - .1 \times .29 = .311.$$

[3]Strictly speaking, these weights only grow as long as $w_{ij} < 1/n_k$ (see Equation 1). If a given pattern were presented to FEN I again and again, the weight of the active lines would approach $1/n_k$, and that of the inactive lines would approach 0. In such a case, the scalar product between input vector and weight vector would approach 1. Note that because, for a given output unit j, $\Sigma w_{ij} = 1$, and because the input values are either 1 or 0 (feature present or absent), the scalar product can be regarded as a correlation coefficient that varies between 0 and 1, in this case.

CA-Module

The second component of PASS, the CA-module, enables the specific access to FEN's representation of relative frequencies that is needed to solve the statistical tasks dealt with in this book. The processes that extract and interpret the output of neural network simulations are generally referred to as *output function* and usually receive only marginal treatment (e.g., Estes, 1986; Estes et al., 1989; Gluck & Bower, 1988; see also chapter 13). Here, these processes are specified explicitly in their most general form and are termed CA-module. This is done for the sake of explicitness, especially because we will have to deal with two different output functions, which are referred to as cognitive algorithms.

The CA-module may most conveniently be described in the form of a production system (e.g., J. R. Anderson, 1995), although the exact modeling method is not crucial here.[4] For a demonstration of how the CA-module works, let us consider hypothetical objects defined by three features, red, round, and crossed (see Fig. 13.2). The patterns "1 0 1", "0 1 0", and "0 0 1", could be taken to represent red objects that aren't round but marked by a cross, nonred objects that are round but not marked by a cross, and nonred objects that aren't round but marked by a cross, respectively. Assume for the moment that the world of possible outcomes is constrained to these three events. This simple setup will serve to introduce the two algorithms of the CA-module. We will first deal with estimates of conditional probabilities, then with the influence of sample size on the confidence in probability judgments, and finally with the solution of conjunctive- and conditional-probability tasks.

Estimates of Conditional Probability. To estimate a conditional probability, the CA-module follows the definition of a conditional probability of X given Y, $p(X \mid Y) = p(X \& Y) / p(Y)$. To estimate $p(X \mid Y)$, PASS first collects FEN's summed responses to the patterns that contain X and Y but differ in important respects, and divides that value by FEN's summed responses to all different patterns that contain Y. Recall that the response to a pattern is just the sum of the activations over all of FEN's output units elicited by that pattern. Formulated as a production, this *conditional-probability algorithm* is:

IF

Task is to make an estimate of $p(X \mid Y)$

THEN

1. Determine responses to all (different) patterns that contain the conjunction of patterns X and Y and sum up these responses.

---

[4]We won't be concerned here about how exactly the CA-module is activated, that is, how it understands which kind of tasks should be solved. This would involve language understanding and other cognitive processes that clearly are beyond the scope of this book. Some ideas about whether a mechanism like the CA-module can be considered the product of evolution or learning can be found in the next chapter.

2. Determine responses to all (different) patterns that contain pattern Y as a part and sum up these responses.
3. Divide summed response from 1 by summed response from 2.
4. Use the result of step 3 as an estimate of $p(X \mid Y)$.

The conditional-probability algorithm is PASS' basic algorithm and it is needed in the solution of most statistical tasks. Let us consider an example using the setup shown in Fig. 13.2. To estimate $p(\text{red} \mid \text{crossed})$, PASS would collect FEN's response to the pattern "1 0 1" (the only pattern that contains the conjunction of red and crossed) and divide that by the sum of the responses to the patterns "1 0 1" and "0 0 1" (the two patterns that contain crossed). The same procedure applies to unconditional probabilities. Recall that simple or unconditional probabilities are just a special case of conditional probabilities that are conditioned on the sum of all events in question: $p(X) = p(X \mid X \text{ or } \neg X)$, where "X or $\neg$X" is the set of possible outcomes or the sample space with $p(X \text{ or } \neg X)$ = 1. For instance, if with the setup in Fig. 13.2, PASS was to determine $p(\text{round})$, it would first collect FEN's response to the pattern "0 1 0" and divide that by the sum of the responses to the three possible patterns, that is, by the sum of the responses to X ("0 1 0") and to $\neg$X ("0 0 1" and "1 0 1").

Note that the conditional-probability algorithm fully captures simple Bayesian tasks such as those we were dealing with in this book, in cases where the events in question are consecutively encountered. Recall, for instance, the doctor who works in a natural environment, sees her patients one by one, and wants to make an estimate of $p(\text{disease} \mid \text{symptom})$, the probability that a new patient has a severe disease given that he shows a certain symptom (Gigerenzer & Hoffrage, 1995; see also chapter 2). PASS would model this task by learning about the relative frequencies of patients who show the symptom, have the disease, or both, where symptom and disease would be assumed to be defined by a collection of features each. To make a conditional-probability estimate, PASS would elicit FEN's response to the pattern of features defining disease and symptom and then divide it by FEN's summed responses to the patterns containing the features for symptom with and without those for disease.

Confidence Judgments. PASS should show a sensitivity for the impact of sample size, that is, its conditional-probability estimates should improve in accuracy as sample size increases and it should be more confident in results from larger samples. No special algorithm is needed to model increasing accuracy in estimates; this result should become apparent from applying the conditional-probability algorithm with different sample sizes. PASS is assumed to derive its degree of confidence in an estimate about a given pattern from comparing the activities of the different output units in FEN for that pattern. The more frequently several patterns are presented to PASS, the better the weights are tuned to discriminate among them. Recall that in the beginning all weights have a randomly assigned value. Therefore, one would expect an increasing variance in the activations of output units for a given pattern with an increasing number of presentations:

$$\frac{1}{m}\sum_{i=1}^{m}(O_{i,n=N}-\overline{O}_{n=N})^2 > \frac{1}{m}\sum_{i=1}^{m}(O_{i,n<N}-\overline{O}_{n<N})^2 \qquad (2)$$

where $O_{i,n=N}$ is the activation of output unit i after $n = N$ presentations (i.e., a sample size of N), m is the number of output units and $\overline{O}$ stands for the mean activation over all output units. The inequality simply says that the variance of the output units is expected to be larger after $n = N$ than after $n < N$ presentations.[5] Larger variance is taken to correspond to higher confidence.

If, for instance, PASS were to estimate p(round) after both 20 and after 40 trials, and to decide in which estimate it is more confident, it would (given the setup in Fig. 13.2) determine the variance of the activities elicited by the pattern "0 1 0" over all output units after both 20 and 40 trials, and then choose for the estimate that is accompanied by the higher variance. The *confidence algorithm* therefore states:

IF

Task is to decide in which of two estimates of $p(X \mid Y)$ that differ only in sample size, $n_1 \neq n_2$, one should be more confident,

THEN

1. Assess variance in FEN's output units elicited by pattern X after n_1 pattern presentations.
2. Assess variance in FEN's output units elicited by pattern X after n_2 pattern presentations.
3. Be more confident in estimate that is associated with larger variance.

Conjunctive- and Conditional-Probability Tasks. How can PASS solve conjunctive-probability tasks of the Linda type, where $p(A \& B)$ is compared to $p(A)$ or $p(B)$? Or, to use our simple setup again, how would PASS arrive at a conclusion of whether p(red & crossed) is or is not larger than p(red)? It would apply the conditional-probability algorithm to the pattern "1 0 1" (red and marked by a cross) and to the sum of all patterns that contain red ("1 0 0" and "1 0 1" in our case). Comparing the two, it would find that the latter is always at least as large as the former. How would PASS find out whether, to use the same setup, p(red I crossed) is higher than p(crossed I red), that is, solve a simple conditional-probability task? Again, we do not need any additional algorithm for this—a comparison of the results yielded by the conditional-probability algorithm does the job.

---

[5]The term $1/m$ is not really necessary, but it allows us to talk about variances instead of the more awkward sums of squared deviations.

SIMULATION RESULTS

For the sake of simplicity, simulations used patterns and setups as simple as possible to illustrate a given issue. We begin with the input patterns "1 0 0", "0 1 0", and "0 0 1", where the positions one to three could be thought to correspond to red, round, and crossed, respectively. In all simulations, a 1 indicates the presence of a feature and a 0 its absence.

Estimation of Conditional Probabilities

The probability with which each of the three patterns "1 0 0", "0 1 0", and "0 0 1" occurred was $p = .5$, $p = .3$, and $p = .2$, respectively. The presentation of 100 patterns was repeated a 100 times, that is, PASS performed 100 runs. In each of the runs, pattern "1 0 0" was presented 50 times, pattern "0 1 0" 30 times, and pattern "0 0 1" 20 times, in random order.[6] FEN I had three input units and one output unit and the learning rate was set to $g_w = .1$. Of course, this setup with nonoverlapping patterns and only one output unit is highly artificial, but it has the virtue of showing PASS' behavior especially clearly. Later, more realistic setups will be used to examine the specific influence of architecture and kind of patterns on PASS' estimates.

Figure 14.4 shows PASS' relative frequency estimates (in percentages) for the three patterns used. The figure shows means and standard deviations after each of 100 presentations, calculated from 100 runs each. PASS' estimates for all three patterns started at about 33%, due to the random initialization of the weights. By about the 35th (50% Pattern, that is, pattern "1 0 0") or the 25th presentation (patterns "0 1 0" and "0 0 1") the estimates converged towards the actual relative frequencies and stayed there, although with some variation. The basic picture does not change with different learning rates. The size of the learning rate determines, however, how fast PASS' estimates converge towards the actual relative frequencies and how pronounced the variation of estimates is after reaching asymptote values: The smaller the learning rate, the longer it takes PASS' estimates to converge towards the given relative frequencies, and the less variation there is around the asymptote values. For instance, with the relatively high learning rate of $g_w = .25$, the estimates reach asymptote already after about 10 presentations, given this setup. The effect of the number of output units will be described in the next section.

---

[6]In this simulation and in all simulations reported later on, the sequence was also locally random; that is, the three patterns were chosen in such a way that each series of 10 consecutive presentations contained the respective number of patterns that corresponded to the probabilities given (e.g., five times pattern "100", three times pattern "010", and two times pattern "001" in the previous case, sampled without replacement). Without this restriction, one usually obtains somewhat more variation in the results, but the average result, that is, means or medians over many runs, remains virtually the same.

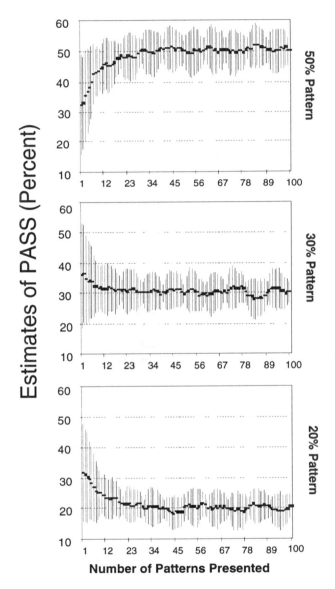

FIG. 14.4.   PASS' conditional-probability estimates (in percent) for patterns "1 0 0" (50% Pattern), "0 1 0" (30% Pattern), and "0 0 1" (20% Pattern). Shown are means and standard deviations (calculated over 100 runs) after each of 100 pattern presentations. FEN I had three input units and one output unit and the learning rate was g_w =.1.

The results of this simulation show that PASS can mimic human judgment in that estimates of relative frequency tend to approximate actual relative frequencies already after a relatively small number of presentations. In this simulation it does even better than human participants because the latter almost universally show an underestimation of high and an overestimation of low relative frequencies. PASS' overachievement is due to FEN I's simple architecture which, although unrealistic, nicely demonstrates its basic simulation results. The next paragraph shows that, with a more realistic architecture, one that includes more than one output unit and more realistic patterns exhibiting some overlap in their features, PASS, like humans, also will make regressed estimates.

Regression

How does PASS account for the empirical fact that probability estimates are generally regressed, that is, large probabilities tend to be underestimated and small probabilities overestimated? In Fig. 14.4, there is some regression in the estimates up to 20 or 30 pattern presentations, but the effect found there cannot count as a good explanation because it is dependent on the size of the learning rate, and human estimates are regressed considerably even after huge numbers of stimuli presented (e.g., Sedlmeier et al., 1998). In the PASS model, regression originates from two sources, feature overlap and interference in memory. In the simulation whose results are shown in Fig. 14.4 there was no feature overlap among the three patterns used, and there was a maximum interference between successively encountered patterns because all weights, which constitute the memory of FEN, were updated after every pattern presentation. The amount of interference decreases with an increasing number of output units because only the winner's weights will be updated after presentation of a given pattern.

Figure 14.5 illustrates the impact of the two postulated sources of regression on PASS' probability estimates. In the condition without feature overlap and maximum interference, FEN I had only one output unit and the input patterns "1 0 0 0", "0 1 0 0", and "0 0 1 0", which do not overlap. As in Fig. 14.4, there was no regression effect in this condition. Considerable regression was found if either the patterns exhibited some overlap in their features or if interference was not maximal. Regression was highest when both factors were combined. In the conditions with feature overlap, the input patterns overlapped by 25%, that is, by one feature: "1 0 0 1", "0 1 0 1", and "0 0 1 1". The decreased interference condition was created by letting FEN I have two, instead of one, output units.

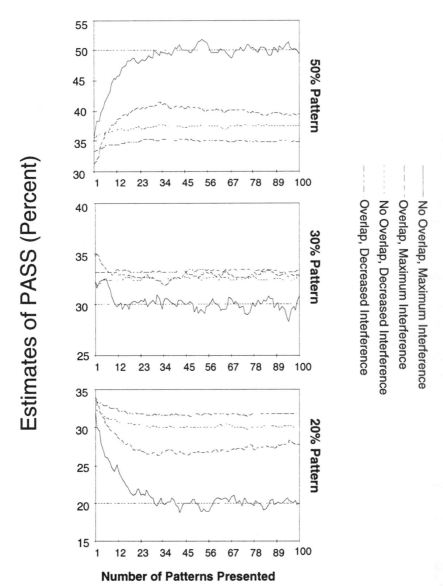

FIG. 14.5. Illustration of the impact of amount of feature overlap and strength of interference on the overestimation of low and underestimation of high probability values. Shown are mean estimates for the three patterns that were presented in 50%, 30%, and 20% of all cases (50% Pattern, 30% Pattern, and 20% Pattern, respectively) after each of 100 pattern presentations, calculated from 100 runs each. Feature overlap is realized by using the patterns "1 0 0 1", "0 1 0 1", and "0 0 1 1", which overlap in the fourth digit, and interference is decreased by allowing the distribution of responses over two output units instead of only one. The two factors have an additive effect. Note that the scales for the three patterns are not identical.

There are good reasons to postulate the existence of the two factors that cause regression in PASS, feature overlap and interference. First, in real-life situations, patterns usually have a large number of features, and only in extreme cases can they be expected not to overlap. This means that considerable regression due to overlap can usually be expected. Second, interference is commonly regarded to be the most important source of forgetting (e.g., Schwartz & Reisberg, 1991). If all weights are modified with every newly encoded object, as is the case with FEN I having only one output unit, then forgetting had almost the same impact as learning (see equation 14.1). This is clearly an unrealistic assumption (e.g., Schwartz & Reisberg, 1991). Therefore, PASS can be expected to produce regressed results because of both feature overlap and a realistic amount of interference.

Changing Relative Frequencies

Until now, we assumed that the probability with which a given pattern is presented to PASS remains constant over all the presentations. This assumption often does not hold in everyday life. We saw in chapter 13 that people are sensitive to such changes. Using two sequences of presentations with equal global, but differing local, rates with which patterns were presented on the left and right side of a computer screen, Sedlmeier and Hertwig (1999) found that more recent presentation rates influenced people's estimates more than the presentation rates at the beginning of the sequence. PASS can be used to model these specific results, but here it suffices to demonstrate the effect with simpler input patterns. Let FEN I have one output and three input units, let us use the three input patterns "1 0 0", "0 1 0", and "0 0 1", and let the learning rate be $g_w = .02$.

Figure 14.6 shows the impact of changing proportions for two conditions, termed A, (thick lines) and B (thin lines). Condition A started with proportions of $p = .7$, $p = .2$, and $p = .1$ for the 50% Pattern, the 30% Pattern and the 20% Pattern, respectively, and after 50 pattern presentations changed to proportions of $p = .3$, $p = .4$, and $p = .3$. In condition B, the proportions were used in the reverse order. Thus, the proportions over all 100 presentations were equal in both conditions, that is, $p = .5$, $p = .3$, and $p = .2$, respectively. PASS mimics the recency effect found in human judgments. For instance, the estimate for the 50% pattern in condition A where the proportion changes from 70% in the first half to 30% in the second half of the pattern sequence ends up at a value lower than 50%. In contrast, the estimate in condition B, in which the proportion changes from 30% to 70%, is higher than 50%. In both conditions, estimates respond more strongly to the proportion used in the second half of the 100 presentations. The speed with which estimates reach the asymptote values as determined by degree of feature overlap and amount of interference is influenced by the learning rate: the larger the learning rate, the more pronounced the recency effect.

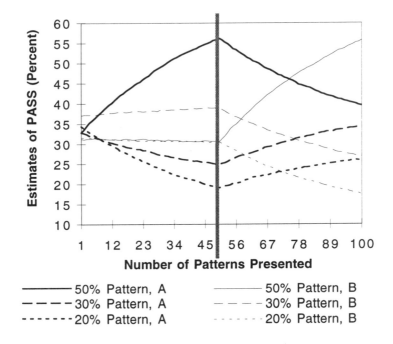

FIG. 14.6.   Percentage estimates of PASS for sets of proportions that change locally over time but are equal overall. Results are mean estimates for the three patterns that overall were presented in 50%, 30%, and 20% of all cases (50% Pattern, 30% Pattern, and 20% Pattern, respectively). In the condition termed A (thick lines) the proportions for the 50% Pattern, 30% Pattern, and 20% Pattern were $p = .7$, $p = .2$, an $p = .1$ for presentations 1 to 50 and $p = .3$, $p = .4$, an $p = .3$ for presentations 51 to 100. In condition B, patterns were presented in the reverse order. The vertical bar indicates the point where the proportions changed.

Impact of Sample Size

People's judgments usually become more exact as sample size increases. If PASS is able to simulate this increasing exactness in estimates, the deviations of its estimates from the actual proportions should decrease as the number of presentations increases. This effect can be seen in Fig. 14.4 and Fig. 14.5. The general effect is not dependent on a specific setup. However, as indicated in Fig. 14.5, amount of feature overlap and strength of interference determine the size of the minimum discrepancy between actual proportions and estimates: The more pronounced the feature overlap and the weaker the interference, the more PASS' estimates deviate from actual proportions, that is, show regression. The size of the learning rate determines the speed with which the minimum distance is reached: The smaller the learning rate, the longer it takes.

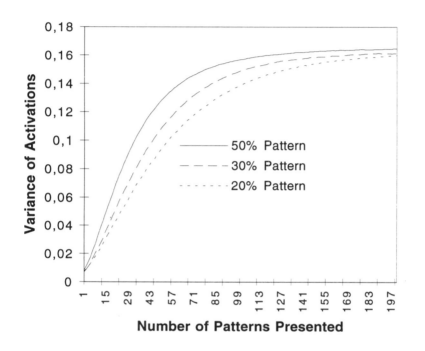

FIG. 14.7.   Impact of sample size (number of pattern presentations) on variance of output units' activations in response to a given pattern. Mean variances over 100 runs are shown. A version of FEN I with nine input and four output units was used. Patterns were presented with probabilities of 50% (50% Pattern: "100100100"), 30% (30% Pattern: "010010010"), and 20% (20% Pattern: "001001001"). The total number of patterns presented was 200 and the learning rate was set to $g_w = .1$.

How can PASS model the increase in people's confidence in their judgments as sample size increases? This is achieved by the confidence algorithm of the CA-module which examines the variances of the output units' activations. Note that there is no variance if only one output unit is used. The case with one output unit was already used several times for demonstration purposes because it has the merit of showing PASS' behavior very pronouncedly using an extreme case. It is, however, a very unlikely case. The following simulations relied on an arbitrary setup with 4 output units and 9 input units where patterns "1 0 0 1 0 0 1 0 0", "0 1 0 0 1 0 0 1 0", and "0 0 1 0 0 1 0 0 1" were presented with probabilities of $p = .5$, $p = .3$, and $p = .2$, respectively. Each run consisted of altogether 200 presentations and the resulting variances, which were calculated after every pattern presentation, were averaged over 100 runs each.

Figure 14.7 shows how the variances that represent confidence judgments increase with the number of patterns presented to FEN I. Several simulations indicated that all variances tend to converge to the same value as the number of patterns presented increases. Moreover, they revealed that the curves become steeper with fewer output units, and that the variances increase more slowly with smaller learning rates. The general picture of increasing variances is found regardless of the specific setup. As Fig. 14.7 illustrates, variances for a given pattern usually covary with the probability attached to that pattern (e.g., the variance for the 50% Pattern grows faster than that for the 30% Pattern). This can again be explained by FEN I's initial random weights. Because of these, the initial variance (before learning) can be expected to be approximately equal for all patterns. The more often a given pattern is presented to FEN I, the more it modifies the weights, that is, the more the weights for active input lines increase and those for inactive lines decrease. Therefore, usually more variance can be expected initially with patterns that have high, rather than low, presentation rates. However, this difference levels out as the number of patterns presented increases.

Solution of Conjunctive- and Conditional-Probability Tasks

How does PASS determine which of two conditional probabilities is larger? This is the kind of question asked in tasks such as the Linda and the Bavarian police tasks (see chapter 1). PASS just applies the conditional-probability algorithm twice. Let us again use some simple input patterns and one output unit in FEN. The three input patterns "1 1", "1 0", and "0 1" could be seen to represent a red object marked by a cross, a red object without a cross, and a nonred object marked by a cross, respectively. These three patterns were presented to FEN I with probabilities of $p = .5$, $p = .3$, and $p = .2$. With this setup, the actual values for $p(\text{red} \mid \text{crossed})$ and $p(\text{crossed} \mid \text{red})$ are .71, and .63.[7] This means that the probability that a ball is marked by a cross if it is red is smaller than the probability that a ball is red if it is marked by a cross.

FEN I was presented 100 patterns (fifty times pattern "1 1", thirty times pattern "1 0", and twenty times pattern "0 1") and its learning rate was set to $g_w = .1$. PASS' mean response to the three patterns in 100 runs, expressed in percentages, was 50%, 28%, and 22%. By applying the conditional-probability algorithm, PASS' average results are $p(\text{red} \mid \text{crossed}) = .69$, and $p(\text{crossed} \mid \text{red}) = .64$. In comparison to the calculated values of .71 and .63, the simulated values are regressed toward the mean of the two conditional probabilities, but they correctly yield the solution that $p(\text{red} \mid \text{crossed})$ is larger than $p(\text{crossed} \mid \text{red})$.

---

[7]For instance, $p(\text{red} \mid \text{crossed})$ is calculated by dividing $p(\text{red \& crossed})$ by $p(\text{crossed})$. Red & crossed is represented by the pattern "1 1" with the associated probability of .5, and crossed includes both the patterns "1 1" and "0 1" with a summed probability of .5 + .2 =.7. Therefore $p(\text{red} \mid \text{crossed})$ = .5 / .7 = .71.

ALTERNATIVE ASSOCIATIONIST MODELS

The contraints for an associationist model of statistical reasoning as spelled out
in Chapter 13 do not suffice to fully specify such a model. Therefore, FEN I is
not the only possible candidate. Indeed, it would be strange if other models that
also obey the outlined contraints would not be successful in modeling judgments
of relative frequency and probability. One such alternative model, FEN II, which
differs markedly from FEN I, has been examined in detail (Sedlmeier, 1999) and
is briefly described here. FEN I learns about relative frequencies by producing
indirect associations between features (via the modification of weights that connect input units to output units). In contrast, FEN II modifies its associations
directly by responding to co-occurrences or missing co-occurences of features. It
consists of only one layer with recurrent connections (Fig. 14.8) and uses a variant of Hebbian learning. The learning rule that governs the change in a weight
w_{ij} (all weights are positive) connecting two units i and j in a particular trial is
adapted from the one used in stimulus sampling theory (Estes, 1950, 1959;
Bower, 1994):

$$\Delta w_{ij} = \begin{cases} \theta_1(1-w_{ij}), & \text{if both units } i \text{ and } j \text{ are active in } Sk \\ -\theta_2 w_{ij}, & \text{if either unit } i \text{ or unit } j \text{ is active in } Sk \\ -\theta_3 w_{ij}, & \text{if neither unit } i \text{ nor unit } j \text{ is active in } Sk \end{cases} \quad (3).$$

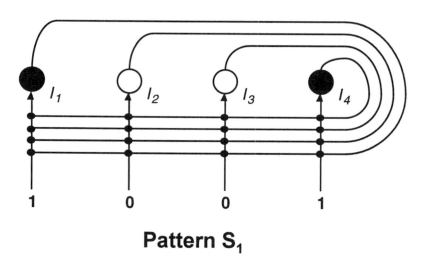

Pattern S$_1$

FIG. 14.8.   The architecture of FEN II, a simple recurrent neural network model that consists of only one layer of units and learns without corrective feedback (Sedlmeier, 1999).
Weights connecting two units (or a unit to itself) are shown as small filled circles.

In Equation 3, θ_1 stands for the learning rate and θ_2, and θ_3 stand for forgetting rates referring to interference and decay (e.g., Schwartz & Reisberg, 1991). Using that rule, weights connecting two units increase if both units are part of a stimulus pattern and decrease otherwise. This learning rule allows weights to vary between 0 and 1. As in FEN I, regression is caused in FEN II by both feature overlap and a realistic amount of interference.[8]

After learning, FEN II's response is elicited in the same way as it was with FEN I; that is, the CA-module uses the activations of all units to come up with the model's judgment. Somewhat surprisingly, the simulation results of FEN I and FEN II are nearly indistinguishable despite considerable difference in architecture and learning rule. This adds credence to the assumption that associative learning is the basis for statistical reasoning, and that the exact specification of an associative learning model is not essential as long as it obeys the constraint that learning has to take place without corrective feedback.

APPLICABILITY OF PASS

The previous simulations have shown that PASS can model basic human probability judgments. There are, however, several limitations to its applicability. One that has already been mentioned is that it strictly applies only to cases that can be modeled by a flexible urn model where objects or events are drawn one by one. Another limitation is that it does not describe situations in which people count and calculate explicitly. Furthermore, it is not clear yet whether and how PASS can deal with tasks in which the information is not directly experienced.

Counting and Exact Solutions

PASS is a model that makes estimates on the basis of activations in response to a prompt. These activations reflect the entire learning history of FEN, that is, how often and in which sequence FEN has encoded patterns. Thus, PASS is not able to reconstruct the exact number of times a given pattern was presented to FEN. Humans, however, can do that, at least for a small number of presentations. For instance, Erlick (1964) obtained more exact proportion estimates after 20 than after 40 presentations of letters, but then estimates became more exact again, with increasing sample size. Participants seem to have been able to use counting strategies for the beginning of the presentation sequence but not later. PASS does not provide for such a counting strategy, nor does it provide for a possibility to inspect the information on a frequency grid, such as those used in

---

[8]If learning and forgetting rates are equal and patterns do not overlap, FEN II does not exhibit a regression effect. However, as discussed in regard to the specification of FEN I, this is a totally unrealistic state of affairs. As is the case with FEN I, the two causes for regression act additively (Sedlmeier, 1999).

several of the training studies reported previously. In the cases in which counting and external representations can be used, one should expect more exact results than those predicted by PASS. Counting and calculating, for instance, are likely to be used in situations in which the number of encountered objects is small, and by people who have successfully finished a training program in which they learned to use static frequency representations.

Nonobservable Input

FEN, the neural network part of PASS, has to encode events or objects serially to build a representation that can be used to derive probability judgments. Thus, it can be applied to those situations where people encode repeatedly occurring events or objects. But what about statistical tasks in which only the end result of the encoding process is described? For instance, in the frequentist version of the Linda task (chapter 1), all women who fit the description of Linda are introduced at once. How could PASS deal with such a situation? It is not clear yet whether PASS can be extended to solve these kinds of tasks. A preliminary solution to this problem is the following: It is assumed that PASS can handle such situations to a limited extent by "imagining" the encoding process and solving the task by analogy (see Rumelhart, Smolensky, McClelland, & Hinton, 1986, for a related model). Clearly, this issue needs much further exploration.

Context

Unlike the experimental studies described previously, in which the wider context in which patterns occurred could be largely neglected, context might play a much more important role in everyday life situations. Context is, however, not a problem for PASS, because if patterns are encoded at the feature level, there is no real distinction between a pattern and its context—context is just part of the pattern.

TESTABILITY OF PASS

In these simulation studies, PASS was shown to be able to model empirical results in general. The model is not, however, restricted to this use, but can also make precise predictions, thereby providing a further test of its plausibility. Before considering specific predictions in more detail, we have to weed out the cases where PASS cannot make predictions. These are cases in which, similarly to the adaptive-algorithms approach (chapter 2), judgmental biases could be expected to occur.

PASS and Biases

PASS is open as to what happens when task information is not given as serially encoded events or cannot readily be translated into such events. Also, it does not make any predictions in cases where the algorithms in the CA-module do not apply. One prominent example of a type of task PASS cannot deal with is sampling-distribution tasks (see chapter 1), because of its restrictions on permissible input formats. It can only encode events and not aggregates, such as means or proportions. Neither can PASS deal with tasks in which input is given in percentages or probabilities. It can, however, give responses in terms of probabilities.

What happens if a task does not meet the requirements PASS postulates for input format and algorithms? There seems to be no clear-cut answer to this question. If other explicit ways to deal with such tasks have been learned by, for instance, statistical training, task solution should not be a problem. If, however, no such learned strategy exists, any of several factors could be influencing the solution to a given task. Mechanisms specified by the pragmatic-implications approach (chapter 2) are expected to play a prominent role in the solution process.

Predictions

If a task obeys the constraints posed by PASS, that is, events must be serially encoded and the CA-module is applicable, the model can make predictions about human judgments. PASS' only free parameters are the learning and forgetting rates. There is no a priori solution for specifying these rates and they may well be regarded as representing an individual's level of sensitivity to new events. However, the exact value of these parameters will not matter much unless the number of patterns presented is very small. Another potential difficulty PASS shares with most current approaches to information processing is the decision of what should be regarded as a feature of an event or object. PASS can be tested by comparing its prediction for an arbitrary presentation sequence of arbitrary stimuli to participants' performances on the same task. Regardless of the question of what exactly the important features are, results of both participants and PASS should covary with changes in the presentation sequence.

There are some interesting predictions that can be made without any preceding simulation. For instance, PASS would predict that the amount of regression in judgments of conditional probability or relative frequency increases with increasing feature overlap. In visual patterns, the amount of feature overlap can easily be varied (e.g., the number of common pixels in visual patterns). Another prediction not yet tested is that the increase in confidence is not equal for all patterns as sample size (i.e., the number of all patterns presented) increases. For instance, the confidence that the relative frequency of the most frequently presented pattern is correctly judged should grow faster than the respective confidence for the least frequently presented pattern (see Fig. 14.7). Other, more specific predictions for all experimental setups that follow the constraints outlined above can be derived by specifying patterns and presentation sequence, and then running a simulation.

RELATED MODELS

Both the FEN models and neural-network models that simulate contingency judgments belong to a class of models termed *prototype models* (E. E. Smith and Medin, 1981). These models do not store single events, but rather represent them by changing their weights. FEN I and FEN II seem to be the only members of this class that have been used for judgments of relative frequency and probability. However, there is another class of models, often called *exemplar models* (e.g., Estes, 1986), that store every newly presented event or exemplar. One of these models that has been used to mimic frequency estimates is MINERVA 2 (Hintzman, 1988). Another model that relies on a similar representation, but might not be strictly classifiable as an exemplar model because of its different underlying theoretical assumptions, is Fiedler's (1996) BIAS. Both will be described in more detail and related to FEN. The arguments brought forward in the next section also apply to other exemplar models.

MINERVA 2

MINERVA 2 (Hintzman, 1988) assumes that each event experienced is represented in memory by its own trace. A specific event's trace is represented as a vector of features. Experiencing new events means adding a new vector of features to an already existing and continually increasing matrix of feature vectors. Each feature is assigned either a positive value (+1), a negative value (−1), or a value of 0, which indicates that, for the present event, the feature is either irrelevant or unknown. Each individual feature of an event is stored with probability L, the learning rate. When $L < 1$, the encoding of the event into memory is imperfect. For instance, if $L = .7$, a positive feature will have the value 1 in about 70 and the value 0 in about 30 times, out of 100. In the MINERVA 2 model, frequency estimates are inferred by a function of the matrix values, called echo intensity.[9]

---

[9]The calculation of echo intensity consists of the following steps. If a probe pattern is presented to the model, it is then assumed to activate all stored memory traces in parallel. The traces respond simultaneously and produce a single, composite echo. The contribution of each memory trace to the echo depends on its similarity to the probe. The similarity of a given trace i to the probe pattern is given by:

$$S_i = \frac{\sum_{j=1}^{N} P_j T_{i,j}}{N_i}$$

MINERVA 2 can be modified to make judgments of relative frequency (Sedlmeier & Hertwig, 1999), and these could, as is done in PASS, also be interpreted as probability judgments. With slight modifications, MINERVA 2 is even able to model regression. However, PASS seems to be at an advantage over MINERVA 2 in several respects. MINERVA 2 cannot, at least in its present version, account for the fact that if relative frequencies change over time, people's estimates change, too. Moreover, it is not clear whether and how it can simulate increases of confidence in estimates with increasing sample size.

BIAS

According to Fiedler (1996), MINERVA 2 can be seen as a special case of his BIAS model. BIAS uses the same kind of matrix representation as MINERVA 2, but does not assume that the vectors of that matrix represent traces in memory. Rather, it attempts to explain several surprising judgmental phenomena described in social-psychology research as resulting from aggregation over stimuli. These stimuli are represented as column vectors of the matrix (instead of a matrix of traces) that represent multiple incomplete perceptions of distal entities. The incompleteness is thought to be due to error variance and is realized in the model as the random inversion of feature values (e.g., from a positive to a negative value). This incomplete (or erroneous) perception results in information loss, especially if a distal concept is represented by only one or a few column vectors. As the number of column vectors increases, aggregating, that is, summing up over the features of column vectors represents the distal entity with increasing accuracy.[10]

Although the emphasis of this simple and elegant model lies on explaining several judgmental phenomena, the model also can be used for frequency judgments. For instance, Fiedler (1996) used it for simulating the regression effect,

---

where P_j is the value of feature j in the probe, $T_{i,j}$ is the value of feature j in trace i, and N_i is the number of features relevant to the comparison between the probe and trace i. A feature j is irrelevant if its value both in the probe and in the trace is 0. The degree to which a trace is activated depends on its similarity to the probe and follows the activation function A_i: $A_i = S_i^3$. The simultaneous activation of all traces by a probe produces an echo, and the intensity, I, of this echo is calculated by summing the activation levels of all traces. Thus,

$$I = \sum_{i=1}^{M} A_i$$

where M is the number of traces stored in long-term memory. The greater the number of stored traces that (partly) match the probe and the larger the match, the greater the echo intensity I will be. Thus, the expected value of I elicited by a specific probe increases with observed frequency of occurrence of events which are identical or similar to the probe.

[10]If a matrix includes perceptions of more than one distal entity (or generic vector), a prompt is used to elicit judgments about a given entity. The simplest way to use the prompt, is to premultiply the matrix with a row vector that includes the prompt and use the resulting row vector of dot products (which measure the match between the prompt and all column vectors) for building a weighted aggregate over the column products. However, Fiedler (1996) does not put strong restrictions on the exact weighting scheme.

that is, the empirically demonstrable effect that low frequencies tend to be over-estimated and high frequencies tend to be underestimated. Consider, for instance, four similar but different distal entities, or generic vectors, that have been perceived different numbers of times. Now assume that in the process of perception (which results in a matrix of column vectors), error variance has produced random inversions of some of the features of these vectors. If the column vectors are recategorized into the four distal entities (e.g., by calculating the scalar product between a given column vector and each of the four entities and using the highest result for classification) classification errors occur. Misclassifications may have an equal chance to fall in any of the four categories. This would lead to inflated estimates for the more rarely perceived entities and deflated estimates for the entities with the higher perception rates. Fiedler reports a simulation that produces exactly this result.

Judged by the criterion of simplicity, BIAS has an advantage over MINERVA 2, but it is questionable whether the latter is just a more specific version of the former and nothing beyond. For instance, Fiedler seems to regard the unspecified nature of what BIAS' matrix of column vectors stands for as a virtue rather than a problem. Memory processes appear, however, to be relevant also in the kind of judgments with which BIAS is dealing (e.g., How big can the column matrix grow? How long are the items retained? Is there any change in the values of features over time?). Apart from such considerations, BIAS, like MINERVA 2, does not, at least in the present version, allow one to model people's judgments when relative frequencies change over time, nor to model their growth in confidence when sample size increases.

Thus it appears that although it cannot be excluded that future modifications of exemplar models might be able to simulate statistical reasoning as well as the FEN models, now, the latter seem to be the best solutions. Moreover, there is a firm theoretical founding for FEN: associationist learning theory.

PROBABILITY ESTIMATION AS AN EMERGENT PROPERTY OF CLASSIFICATION

PASS uses the activation values of FEN as the basis for probability judgments, but FEN is not restricted to providing the input to such judgments. In fact, probability judgments might be regarded as an emergent property of a more basic mechanism, categorization.

Before the frequency of occurrence of objects can be registered, these objects have to be classified into a category. Humans are extremely good at this task (e.g., Thorpe and Imbert, 1989). In fact, the ability to match one pattern to another might be regarded as "*the* essential component to most cognitive behavior" (Rumelhart, Smolensky et al., 1986, p. 44). Insights into how the mind categorizes events should also guide our attempts to build valid models of how it registers frequencies and relative frequencies of events. E. E. Smith and Medin (1981) summarized the vast research about the topic of categorization and offered three different views of how humans categorize events. The input used for categorizing an object in all three views is a featural description of that object, as is that used by FEN. E. E. Smith and Medin (1981) discard the classical view, which holds that a concept can be defined by singly necessary and jointly sufficient features, because of numerous theoretical and empirical problems attached to it. We have already dealt with the other two views, exemplar and prototype. Recall that whereas the exemplar view holds that all encoded events are stored in an ever-growing memory, in contrast the prototype view assumes that prior encounters with an object have led to a composite trace, or a summary description, which represents a prototype. The features of a new object entering into the summary description are probabilistically related to the latter. Recently, the latter approach to categorization has been successfully modeled with neural or connectionist networks (e.g., J. A. Anderson & Mozer, 1981; Estes et al., 1989; Gluck & Bower, 1988; Shanks, 1991).

Networks similar to FEN I, that is, networks that use the competitive learning scheme, have also been used for categorization tasks. For instance, Rumelhart & Zipser (1985) demonstrate how competitive learning networks can classify stimulus patterns into letters. Competitive learning is also a substantial part of the ART family of neural networks (e.g., Grossberg, 1987, 1988). Likewise, recurrent networks similar to FEN II have been used for categorization (e.g., McClelland & Rumelhart, 1985). Thus, the modeling of sensitivity for relative frequencies and probabilities by using a neural network is not an ad hoc endeavor, but is grounded in a greater context, which has been thoroughly researched. Probability judgments can be intimately connected to a basic human task: making classifications and categorizations.

15

Statistical Reasoning: A New Perspective

SUMMARY: The results of training studies have provided new theoretical insights into statistical reasoning. They are most consistent with the adaptive-algorithms approach and are inconsistent with the heuristics-and-biases approach, which still dominates theorizing about statistical reasoning. They are also only partly consistent with the abstract-rules approach, which has been regarded as the most successful approach to training. The newly developed PASS model is related to, but also differs from, the adaptive-algorithms approach. PASS is located at a lower level of complexity than the other approaches dealt with in this book. However, it can be used to explain empirically supported aspects of three of these approaches, and it is proposed to serve as the foundation of a more comprehensive and exact model of statistical reasoning. The chapter ends with a brief discussion of possible social impact of the present results.

To recapitulate, this book began by pointing out that people sometimes have problems when solving statistical tasks. Then, four explanations for why this is so were introduced—the pragmatic-implications, heuristics-and-biases, abstract-rules, and adaptive-algorithms approaches. These theoretical approaches allow us to predict whether and how people's problems with statistical tasks can be remedied by suitable training programs. Using the results of training programs to evaluate theories is a novel methodological procedure that enabled a direct comparison of the four approaches, an endeavor that had not yet been attempted, probably because these approaches focus on different aspects of statistical reasoning. The pragmatic-implications approach examines differences between natural language and probability language, the heuristics-and-biases approach focuses on the demonstration of judgmental errors, the abstract-rules approach concentrates on training, and the adaptive-algorithms approach explores conditions under which the mind can be expected to solve statistical tasks without problems.

The training results favor the adaptive-algorithms approach over the other approaches, and highlight the importance of representational formats in statistical reasoning. The abstract-rules approach, which has been regarded as the most effective way to teach statistical thinking (e.g., Nisbett et al., 1987), does not make any differential predictions about representational formats. However, the view that the representational format does not matter can no longer be upheld after these training studies were completed. The pessimistic outlook of the heuristics-and-biases approach cannot be maintained either. Training about statistical reasoning can be effective, and very much so, if the right representational format is used and if well-known results from instructional theory are incorporated into training programs (see chapter 12).

Despite the clear-cut results, it is not satisfactory that none of the four approaches gives a detailed explanation of how probability judgments arise. Rule-like constructs play a central role in the adaptive-algorithms, abstract-rules, and heuristics-and-biases approaches. However, although the latter offers post hoc explanations about when and how heuristics work, exact predictions seem to be quite difficult. The abstract-rules approach specifies conditions under which such abstract rules should function well, but neither this approach nor the heuristics-and-biases approach explain why the mind should be equipped with the respective kinds of rules. The adaptive-algorithms approach gives such an explanation: Cognitive algorithms are the response to adaptive problems. Moreover, the adaptive-algorithms approach is the only one to specify the input format necessary for the rules to work. Even this approach is, however, with one exception, (Gigerenzer & Hoffrage, 1995, see below), vague about how cognitive algorithms do statistical reasoning of the kind dealt with in this book. None of the approaches has anything to say about how the mind acquires knowledge about relative frequencies and probabilities.

The fully computable model introduced in chapter 14, PASS, is an attempt to create a new theoretical foundation for how the mind arrives at probability judgments. It appears to be the only model of statistical reasoning so far that includes a detailed mechanism that simulates how the mind learns about relative frequencies and probabilities. The model is quite remote from the complex tasks mostly dealt with in this book. Nonetheless, it provides a good starting point to arrive at a more satisfying account of statistical reasoning. The next section explains how PASS is related to the four theoretical approaches on statistical reasoning. Later, several issues related to a larger framework that incorporates PASS are discussed. The chapter ends with some thoughts about possible social implications of the present results.

PASS AND OTHER APPROACHES TO STATISTICAL REASONING

PASS and Pragmatic Implications

The kind of relationship between PASS and the pragmatic-implications approach is evident: There is none. PASS does not deal with processes of language understanding; its sole input is events defined by their features. This is certainly an unsatisfactory state of affairs, and future efforts should be directed at exploring the interplay between language understanding and probability estimates. For all statistical tasks that cannot be dealt with by PASS, due to inadequate input, the pragmatic-implications approach is the primary candidate to explain people's solutions.

PASS and Heuristics and Biases

PASS might be regarded as a model that captures aspects of behavior that usually are explained by the assertion that people use the availability heuristic. The availability of a given feature pattern (representing an object or event) can be operationalized by the activation value that is elicited by that pattern. FEN demonstrates that in general, a pattern is more available if it has been encoded more often. PASS could, for instance, be used to explain the results in Tversky and Kahneman's (1973) famous-names study. Recall that participants had to judge whether a list of 39 names contained more males or more females. In fact, the lists included either 19 names of famous women and 20 names of less famous men or 19 names of famous men and 20 names of less famous women. Participants generally judged the number of names of the famous sex to be more numerous in the list. PASS can explain this effect of overestimation. Famous names are read more often than other names, which is generally the reason why they are more famous. Therefore, one has to expect that PASS' weights are already tuned to these names.[1] The same can be expected for participants' memories. It just might have been difficult for them to disentangle their prior exposures to names from the exposure in the study. If participants had included prior exposures, they would not be correct in respect to the experimental questions, but they might be correct in respect to the actual frequencies encountered both prior to and during the experiment.

   Although it seems possible to redefine parts of the heuristics-and-biases approach (e.g., the availability heuristic) more precisely by using PASS, such an endeavor does not seem very promising because of this approach's many theoretical inconsistencies (e.g., Gigerenzer, 1996b; Gigerenzer & Murray, 1987; Lopes, 1991).

---

[1]If, for instance, many of the male names but only a few or none of the female names had been repeatedly encoded before (e.g., by reading magazines including the names), the sum of PASS' responses to the male names would be stronger than the sum of its responses to the female names. Thus, PASS would conclude that the males are more numerous. Note that for an exact simulation, some assumptions for the weighing of old (encoded before the experiment) and new (encoded during the experiment) information might be necessary. This problem could be studied in experiments in which the amount of old and new information is varied in a controlled way.

PASS and Abstract Rules

PASS relies on judgmental rules (the CA-module) as does the abstract-rules approach, but unlike the latter, it clearly specifies the input for these rules. The input has to be FEN's activation values, which in turn are learned by repeated exposure to collections of features that specify events. These features are encoded in a neural network and are stored in connection weights. Concepts such as codability and familiarity, which are central in the abstract-rules approach, but still lack a good definition, could be given an exact meaning in the PASS model. An event could be defined as being more codable the fewer features it shares with other events. The familiarity of an event could be defined by the amount of activation it elicits when given as a prompt to FEN. (Note that this operationalization would make familiarity and availability synonymous terms.)

PASS can make precise predictions without resorting to codability or familiarity—it suffices to specify input patterns and presentation sequences (see below). However, the most important reason why PASS cannot be used as an elaboration of the abstract-rules approach is its reliance on sequentially experienced events as the sole possible inputs.

PASS and Adaptive Algorithms

In comparison to the four theoretical approaches, PASS has the most in common with the adaptive-algorithms approach. However, the two approaches differ in respect to the nature of cognitive algorithms and to the role of learning. The common properties are addressed first.

The basic element both approaches have in common is their reliance on sequentially acquired frequencies of events. This constraint about representational formats does not apply to any other approach to statistical reasoning. The assumption that the mind is tuned to frequency and not to probability formats has found ample support from the results in the training studies reported in previous chapters. Another common element of the adaptive-algorithms approach and PASS can be seen in the way estimates of conditional probabilities are derived. Recall Gigerenzer and Hoffrage's (1995) example of the physician in an illiterate society who sees many patients, some of whom are afflicted by a previously unknown and severe disease (chapter 2). She also notices that the symptom (S) signals the disease (D), although not with certainty. To come up with an answer to $p(D \mid S)$, the probability that a patient who has the symptom will have the disease, she applies the algorithm: $p(D \mid S) = \# (D \& S) / \# S$, that is, she records the number of patients who have both the disease and the symptom, and then divides this by the number of patients who have the symptom. This procedure is very similar to PASS' conditional-probability algorithm (chapter 14). The latter, however, does not directly work on frequencies, but works on the result of frequency learning represented in FEN's connection weights. Analogously to Gigerenzer & Hoffrage's (1995) algorithm, it elicits an activation value for the pattern representing D & S, then one for the pattern representing S, and then divides the first by the second. However, despite their similarity, the two algorithms are not equivalent.

Whereas Gigerenzer and Hoffrage seem to regard their cognitive algorithm as an adaptation, that is, a solution for an adaptive problem (see chapter 2), the cognitive algorithms in the CA-module are not necessarily adaptations. They may be the direct result of evolution or a byproduct of evolution (see Gould, 1991), but more likely they are wholly or in part the products of ontogenetic learning. They just describe human behavior in a simple way, assuming the existence of a module that learns and represents relative frequencies (i.e., FEN). An argument for the innateness of these cognitive algorithms is their early occurrence in humans. Children's sensitivity to relative frequency (e.g., Fischbein, 1975) and to the impact of sample size (e.g., Piaget & Inhelder, 1951/1975) might suggest that cognitive algorithms, as described by the conditional-probability algorithm and the confidence algorithm (chapter 14) may at least in part be inborn. However, one could also argue that algorithms such as the two postulated for the CA-module might be the result of early associative-learning processes. Recent developments in connectionist computation show that neural networks have a huge potential for learning rule-like behavior (Elman at al., 1996). Also, arithmetic operations can be simulated quite well by neural networks (J. A. Anderson, 1995). Thus, it should be possible eventually to realize the CA-module as a complex neural network instead of as a collection of production rules, indicating that such rules can indeed be the products of childhood learning. One way to explore the extent to which the ability described in these algorithms is due to evolutionary selection, ontogenetic learning processes, or both might be to examine the time course of learning. If one could find arguments (possibly by studying the interplay of evolutionary and learning processes via simulation) that the time needed to learn such algorithms was unrealistically high, given what we know about human learning potential, an evolutionary explanation would gain more credence.

The most salient difference between the two approaches is in the role of learning about relative frequencies and probabilities. The adaptive-algorithms approach does not specify how events are encoded or how frequencies are represented in memory. PASS, in contrast, models this process by using a neural network architecture that enables associative learning. The choice of this type of model follows naturally from the fact that associationist learning uses the same kind of frequency and co-occurrence information that is necessary to make probability judgments. It was also motivated by the implausibility of a fully specified prewired alternative, that is, an evolved mechanism that works as a frequency counter for all kinds of input (or several counters that work for a specified input each). As illustrated by recent simulations of the interplay between evolution and learning, it may frequently be more adaptive for a genotype to stay at a level that is not sufficient to solve the task at hand and let learning do the rest (Belew,

1990; Hinton & Nowlan, 1987). Associative learning itself can be seen as the product of evolution. For instance, Todd and Miller (1991) simulated a scenario where a simple form of associative learning arises due to selective pressures.

Although associative learning as a possible explanation of how the mind learns about frequencies is not part of the adaptive-algorithms approach, such a learning mechanism does not contradict it, and may eventually lead to a synthesis of PASS and the adaptive-algorithms approach.

PASS PUT INTO PERSPECTIVE

PASS can explain people's estimates of probability and relative frequency and their confidence judgments in the case of sequentially encountered events. However, as it currently stands, it does not have implications for training beyond those of the adaptive-algorithms approach although it might be considered to provide a more satisfying explanation for the training effects reported in earlier chapters. Also, PASS cannot predict much about what happens when the input is in text form. Nonetheless, at present there seems to be no better way to describe and integrate important aspects of people's probability judgments, and it is proposed that PASS can be a starting point for building a comprehensive and fully computational framework of statistical reasoning. PASS' relation to training, its role in the solution of different kinds of statistical tasks, and reasons for implementing the model to work in a mode that can be programmed on a computer are now discussed in a bit more detail.

PASS and Training

Much of this book is about training. How can PASS be related to the results obtained in the training studies? As was the case with the four theoretical approaches discussed in chapter 2, the relationship between PASS and training is only indirect. PASS' predictions about training success would have been identical to those derived from the adaptive-algorithms approach. Because the training results were most consistent with the latter approach, they guided the direction in which a model of statistical reasoning must be developed further. What is this approach's most important ingredient for training success? Its basic tenet seems to be that adaptive algorithms are tuned to natural frequencies, that is, to frequencies of successively encoded events. This tenet also had to be a central attribute of PASS, which only works with successively encoded events as input. Training with frequency representations is assumed to be so effective (as has been shown in many of the preceding chapters) because PASS is tuned to such representations. It is assumed that PASS can provide intuitive knowledge that speeds up the training process in the event that the training relies on frequency representations. However, the exact nature of this process still awaits specification.

Different Kinds of Tasks

Statistical tasks can come either with observable frequencies, or with frequencies or probabilities described in texts. How is PASS involved in the solution of the different kinds of tasks? Let us first consider the case of observable frequencies as the input. If such tasks can be dealt with by counting and calculating, as, for instance, when only a small total number of events is encoded, or when appropriate skills have been learned (e.g., in a training program or a statistics course), an adequate probability judgment can be expected, given no calculation mistakes. Such a solution would not necessarily invoke PASS. If counting and calculation are not possible, PASS takes over and produces a probability judgment as described in chapter 14. If, however, a statistical task is expressed in text form, then PASS cannot solve it immediately. There are several possibilities that can happen in such a case. First, persons with statistical expertise might apply rules they have learned and can successfully solve the task. Second, if frequencies are spontaneously used (when the numerical information in the text is expressed in frequencies), or probabilities are spontaneously translated into usable frequencies (e.g., as a result of prior frequency training), either explicit calculations can be used to solve the task or, if that is not possible due to missing skills, PASS may be invoked to come up with an estimate. In the latter case, PASS is hypothesized to simulate the sequential encoding process in analogy to similar cases previously encountered, and to find an appropriate solution to the task. Such a simulation by analogy has not been explicitly dealt with in this book but neural network solutions to similar problems do exist (e.g., Rumelhart, Smolensky, et al., 1986). As mentioned in chapter 14, this assumption of solution by analogy certainly needs a substantial elaboration in the current model. Finally, if neither the necessary skills are available nor frequencies are spontaneously used, the outcome is not predictable yet according to the framework outlined previously. The pragmatic-implications approach might be able to offer some guidelines in this case.

Computational Model

Hypothesized pragmatic implications of language understanding in statistical tasks, as well as other hypotheses about the framework which go beyond the current version of PASS, should preferably be *computational*, that is, in principle, implementable as a computer program. Why? Because computational models have to be explicit and precise—otherwise they do not run. More than 25 years of research in the heuristics-and-biases tradition have demonstrated that imprecisely formulated theoretical models can account for almost any result, if only by explaining an inconsistent finding as an exception or a new heuristic. Computational models are not the only way to make precise models, but they allow us to make exact and testable predictions about both processes and results, and they can handle complex problems. Statistical reasoning certainly is one.

SOCIAL IMPLICATIONS

The new theoretical perspective on statistical reasoning outlined previously need not remain theoretical. In fact, the results reported here might prove to be quite useful for society. The dissemination of statistical information, beginning in the 19th century, has been intimately linked to industrialization and to the rise of democracies in Europe (Porter, 1986). Meanwhile, statistics have thoroughly permeated many aspects of society—without them there would be, for instance, no IQ testing, no industrial quality control, and no sound medical diagnoses (see Gigerenzer et al., 1989, for many other examples). Therefore, there is an increasing need to understand statistical results, not only for professional decision makers, but also for laypeople. Many reports in the popular press and on television about results of opinion polls, or about psychological, medical, or economic studies can only be satisfactorily interpreted with some understanding of statistics.

Already some 70 years ago, H. G. Wells, the author of the *Time Machine*, held that one would eventually recognize the central importance of teaching statistical reasoning for the production of an educated citizenship, with statistical reasoning being as important as reading and writing (cf. Huff, 1973, p. 6). Unfortunately, 50 years later, Nisbett and Ross (1980, p. 281) had to acknowledge that he was wrong in his prediction. This judgment has recently been supported by the results of the *Third International Mathematics and Science Study* (TIMSS). This comprehensive study has shown that in highly developed countries such as the United States and Germany, mathematical literacy, including statistical reasoning, is still at a deplorably low level among middle- and secondary-school students (Baumert, Lehman, et al, 1997; International Association for the Evaluation of Educational Achievement, 1996, 1998; B. Murray, 1997). One possible explanation for this unsatisfactory state of affairs is given by Garfield and Ahlgren (1988). In a literature review of the teaching of statistical reasoning to students at college and precollege levels, they conclude that "little seems to be known about how to teach probability and statistics effectively" (p. 45; for a similar view see Shaughnessy, 1992). Also, recommendations about how to teach statistics using computers generally seem to be based on rules of thumb rarely supported by empirical studies (Biehler, 1991).

The empirical and theoretical results reported in this book could serve as building blocks for more effective teaching of statistical reasoning.[2] They could help to improve the teaching of statistics in introductory statistics courses as well as in courses in business, politics, law, and other fields involving decision making. However, this research has implications that extend beyond the class-

---

[2]Of course, not all kinds of statistical reasoning can be subsumed under the four models dealt with in the training studies. These models, however, exemplified by the tasks described and discussed in this book, are likely to cover a substantial portion of statistical tasks encountered in daily life.

room. It concerns both the way statistical information is presented (in many contexts) and how statistical thinking is taught (see chapter 12). Statistical information in the media, for example, could be made more understandable if reporters chose appropriate frequency representations to convey it.

Consider just one (somewhat fictitious) example: The urn model could be used to teach people to deal with a problem that often arises in statistical reasoning and that has already been discussed in connection with Bayesian tasks (chapter 1): choosing the appropriate reference class. Suppose a European politician compares the crime rate among native-born citizens of his country with the crime rate among immigrants and finds that the latter rate is higher. Now he proposes to pass harsher laws against immigrant criminals (elections are coming up). Was the appropriate reference class chosen? Perhaps not. A disproportionate percentage of immigrants from the former Yugoslavia, for instance, are young male adults. It is well known that the crime rate among young males is higher than that among children or elderly people, independent of place of birth. If now a television political commentator wanted to clarify that point to the viewers, he or she could use various urns to represent different age and gender groups of native-born citizens and immigrants, with each individual represented by a ball. Comparing the contents of the urn containing young native-born citizens to the urn containing young immigrants (with some in each urn marked criminal and others noncriminal) and visualizing the results on a frequency grid might reveal that the original judgment, based on reference classes defined in terms of citizenship, but not on age and gender, was in fact unwarranted. As demonstrated in chapters 10 and 11, the urn model has the potential to teach laypeople how to solve this and many other kinds of everyday statistical tasks.

Even more important than fostering insight in some isolated issues, statistical reasoning could be taught to laypeople using optimized versions of training programs such as the ones used in this study.[3] There is no reason for people to remain statistically illiterate when we have the tools to teach them better.

---

[3]A modified version of the training program about Bayesian reasoning is publicly available (see Sedlmeier, 1997).

Appendix A

Variations of Bayesian Inference

Appendix A gives the solution to two notorious Bayesian inference tasks, the engineer-lawyer, and the bookbag-and-poker-chips tasks. Bayesian inference generally involves the revision of a hypothesis' probability, p(hypothesis), or $p(H)$ for short, when new information is acquired. One also needs the probability with which that information occurs, p(data), or $p(D)$ for short, and the probability of the information given the hypothesis, $p(D \mid H)$. In the simplest case, with which we are exclusively dealing in this book, there are only two possible hypotheses and only binary data. In this case, Bayes' formula is:

$$p(H \mid D) = \frac{p(H)p(D \mid H)}{p(D)} . \tag{1}$$

Often, the probability $p(D)$ is not given, but can be calculated as the sum of $p(D \mid H)p(H)$ and $p(D \mid \neg H)p(\neg H)$ because there are only two possibilities, either the hypothesis holds or it does not ("$\neg$" stands for "not"). Bayes' formula can be applied repeatedly, as in the bookbag-and-poker-chips task (discussed later), but often it is applied only once, as in the engineer-lawyer task.

SOLUTION OF THE ENGINEER-LAWYER TASK

In the engineer-lawyer task (Kahneman & Tversky, 1973, p. 241), only $p(H)$, also called the *base rate* is given explicitly. The text states that 30 engineers and 70 lawyers (or 70 engineers and 30 lawyers) have been interviewed and tested, which resulted in 100 respective personality descriptions. Participants are to judge the probability that one randomly drawn description is that of an engineer (or a lawyer). So participants have the first piece of information, the a priori probability that the description is about an engineer—for instance, $p(H) = p$(engineer) = .3 in the case of 30 engineers and 70 lawyers. The next piece of information given is the personality description. If that description is totally uninformative as to the chosen person's profession, then one can assume p(description | engineer) = p(description | lawyer). If, for instance, we took $p(D \mid H) = p$(description | engineer) = .5, we would arrive at (*En* stands for engineer and *PD* for personality description):

$$p(\text{En} \mid \text{PD}) = p(\text{En})p(\text{PD} \mid \text{En}) \:/\: [p(\text{En})p(\text{PD} \mid \text{En}) + p(\neg\text{En})p(\text{PD} \mid \neg\text{En})]$$
$$= .3 \times .5 \:/\: [.3 \times .5 + .7 \times .5]$$
$$= .3.$$

This solution works, however, only if $p(D \mid H)$ is known. Otherwise the only check of whether participants think Bayesian is to change $p(\text{engineer})$, the base rate of engineers, and see whether the judgments with different base rates are consistent. For that check, one needs Bayes' formula in its odds form. Divide Equation 1 by Equation 2:

$$p(\neg H \mid D) = \frac{p(\neg H)p(D \mid \neg H)}{p(D)} \tag{2}$$

and obtain Equation 3

$$\frac{p(H \mid D)}{p(\neg H \mid D)} = \frac{p(H)}{p(\neg H)} \times \frac{p(D \mid H)}{p(D \mid \neg H)}. \tag{3}$$

Now let H stand for "is an engineer" and D for a specific personality description. Then O in Equation 4 denotes the posterior odds that a particular description belongs to an engineer and not a lawyer (left part of Equation 3), Q expresses the prior odds that a randomly chosen description belongs to an engineer rather than to a lawyer (first term on right side of Equation 3), and R stands for the likelihood ratio, that is, the ratio of the probabilities that a randomly drawn engineer will be so described to the probability that a randomly drawn lawyer will be so described (second term on right side of Equation 3):

$$O = QR \tag{4}$$

The condition with 70% engineers can now be assigned the subscript H (high base rate) and the condition with 30% engineers can be assigned the subscript L (low base rate). Now, divide the two resulting odds, and obtain

$$\frac{O_H}{O_L} = \frac{Q_H R}{Q_L R}. \tag{5}$$

Note that the likelihood ratio is the same for the high- and low-base-rate conditions. Canceling the likelihood ratio and substituting Q_H, the prior odds in the high-base-rate condition, by 70/30 and Q_L, the prior odds in the low-base-rate condition by 30/70, results in a ratio of the posterior odds of 5.44. Now one can predict the Bayesian response for the high-base-rate condition if the response for the low-base-rate condition is known, and vice versa. For instance, if the response (i.e., the posterior probability in the low-base-rate condition) $p_{30}(H \mid D)$, was .4, the estimate for the high-base-rate condition of $p_{70}(H \mid D) = .78$.[1]

SOLUTION OF THE BOOKBAG-AND-POKER-CHIPS TASK

In the bookbag-and-poker-chips task (Edwards, 1982, p. 361), we have two bags, one containing 70% red and 30% blue chips and the other 30% red and 70% blue chips. We have chosen one of these bags by flipping a coin. The probability that the chosen one is the predominantly red (R-bag) or blue (B-bag) bag is therefore

$$p(\text{R-bag}) = p(\text{B-bag}) = .5.$$

Recall that in the task, 8 red and 4 blue chips are drawn with replacement (i.e., each chip drawn is put back into the bag), in 12 consecutive drawings and that the probability that the bag the samples were drawn from is the predominantly red bag must be estimated. Suppose that the first chip drawn is red. Now one needs the conditional probabilities of drawing a red chip (R) from each bag. These are

$$p(\text{R} \mid \text{R-bag}) = .7 \text{ and } p(\text{R} \mid \text{B-bag}) = .3.$$

Applying Bayes' formula results in the probability that the bag this red chip was sampled from is the predominantly red bag (R-bag).

$$p(\text{R - bag} \mid \text{R}) = \frac{p(\text{R} \mid \text{R - bag}) p(\text{R - bag})}{p(\text{R} \mid \text{R - bag}) p(\text{R - bag}) + p(\text{R} \mid \text{B - bag}) p(\text{B - bag})}$$
$$= (.7 \times .5)/(.7 \times .5 + .3 \times .5)$$
$$= .7.$$

---

[1] Substituting into Equation 5 results in:

$$\frac{p_{70}(H \mid D)/p_{70}(\neg H \mid D)}{p_{30}(H \mid D)/p_{30}(\neg H \mid D)} = \frac{70/30}{30/70} = 5.44.$$

Because there are only two hypotheses, H and $\neg H$, $p(H \mid D)$ and $p(\neg H \mid D)$ must add up to 1. Therefore, with $p_{30}(H \mid D) = .4$,

$$p_{70}(H \mid D) = 5.44 \frac{p_{30}(H \mid D)}{1 - p_{30}(H \mid D)} (1 - p_{70}(H \mid D))$$
$$= 3.63 - 3.63 \, p_{70}(H \mid D)$$
$$= .78.$$

Now suppose the chip has been put back into the bag and another red chip is drawn. How does the probability of having chosen the predominantly red bag change? The conditional probabilities of drawing a red chip from R-bag or a blue one from B-bag have not changed. What has changed is p(R-bag), the probability that the bag we chose is the predominantly red one. Therefore, p(B-bag) has also changed:

$$p(\text{R-bag}) = .7 \text{ and } p(\text{B-bag}) = 1 - p(\text{R-bag}) = .3.$$

Performing the same calculation as before one now obtains

$$p(\text{R-bag} \mid \text{R}) = (.7 \times .7) / (.7 \times .7 + .3 \times .3) = .845.$$

If this process is repeated for the remaining six red and the four blue chips, then one arrives at a probability that the chosen bag is the predominantly red one of p(R-bag) = .97, regardless of the order in which red and blue chips are sampled. Try it![2]

---

[2] Of course, if the third chip drawn were blue, p(R-bag | B) had to be calculated next, with

$$p(\text{B} \mid \text{R-bag}) = 1 - p(\text{R} \mid \text{R-bag}) \text{ and } p(\text{B} \mid \text{B-bag}) = 1 - p(\text{R} \mid \text{B-bag}).$$

In the above example, p(R-bag) would be .845 at this stage.

Appendix B

The Law of Large Numbers and Sample-Size Tasks[*]

Appendix B clarifies what the law of large numbers is, why it does not apply to the psychological research on sample size, and which mathematical results do apply.

WHAT IS THE LAW OF LARGE NUMBERS?

Simeon Denis Poisson (1837) was the first to introduce the term 'law of large numbers' for Bernoulli's theorem, which had been published posthumously in *Ars Conjectandi* (1713). In modern notation, Bernoulli's version of the theorem can be stated as follows (Stigler, 1986, p. 66). Suppose an experiment with two possible outcomes is to be repeated many times. If p is the probability of success in any single experiment, and if non-negative numbers ε and c are specified, then the number of trials n can be determined such that the number of *observed* successes m in n trials satisfies

$$P\left(\left|\frac{m}{n} - p\right| \le \varepsilon\right) > cP\left(\left|\frac{m}{n} - p\right| > \varepsilon\right). \tag{1}$$

The setup described above is known today as a 'Bernoulli process'. Bernoulli himself used an urn model with r 'fertile' and s 'sterile' equally likely cases so that $p = r / (r + s)$. He set ε equal to $1 / (r + s)$ and proposed making c large enough to ensure 'moral certainty'. Bernoulli calculated the number of trials required for the case in which $r = 30$ and $s = 20$ and, because he had high standards of moral certainty, for $c = 1,000$, $10,000$, and $100,000$ (Bernoulli, 1713, p. 238). For $c = 1000$—where the probability P of m / n falling within the interval [29/50, 31/50] is at least 1000 times larger than the probability of m / n falling outside of that interval—he calculated that he would need at least $n = 25,550$ observations. This discouragingly large number might have been one reason for the abrupt conclusion of his *Ars Conjectandi* (Stigler, 1986, p. 77).

---

[*]This appendix originally appeared in the *Journal of Behavioral Decision Making*, 1997, *10*, 47–49. Copyright © John Wiley & Sons Limited. Reprinted by permission.

A first confusion about the theorem stems from Bernoulli himself. The theorem assumes that p is known. However, Bernoulli also seems to have wanted to apply his theorem (illegitimately) to calculate the probability that the observed ratio m / n equaled an unknown p (Daston, 1988, p. 232; Pearson, 1925, p. 205).

The modern reformulation of Bernoulli's theorem (e.g., Maistrov, 1974, p. 201) considers only the limiting case. In a more general form (which applies to means as well as proportions) going beyond Bernoulli processes, the law of large numbers can be stated as follows: Assume that the X_i ($i = 1, 2, \ldots$) are independently and identically distributed random variables, each having a finite mean $E[X_i] = \mu$. Then, as n becomes arbitrarily large, the probability that the deviation of the mean of the random variables X_i from their expected value μ exceeds ε approaches 0. In formal terms (for a proof see Scheaffer, 1990, p. 282),

$$\lim_{n \to \infty} P\left(\left| \frac{1}{n} \sum_{i=1}^{n} X_i - \mu \right| \geq \varepsilon \right) = 0. \tag{2}$$

Equation 2 is a version of what is known as the 'weak law of large numbers'. The most general form of the weak law of large numbers was proven by the Russian mathematician Khintchine (Feller, 1957, p. 229). The *strong* law of large numbers is often taken as the theoretical basis for deriving probabilities from relative frequencies (Feller, 1957, pp. 189-190). For Bernoulli trials, where x_i is a 0–1 indicator variable, it can be written as

$$P\left(\lim_{n \to \infty} 1/n \sum_{i}^{n} x_i = p \right) = 1 \tag{3}$$

(Fine, 1973, p. 95). There are several versions of both the weak and strong laws of large numbers (Révész, 1968). When we refer to the 'law of large numbers' hereafter, we refer to Equation 2.

WHY DOES THE LAW OF LARGE NUMBERS NOT APPLY TO PSYCHOLOGICAL RESEARCH ON SAMPLE SIZE?

The asymptotic feature (i.e. $n \to \infty$) of the law of large numbers makes it an inappropriate model for determining how participants should solve tasks in which sample sizes are finite. As far as we know, all empirical studies on the 'law of large numbers' have used finite sample sizes. However, as we can see from the previous section, the (mathematical) law of large numbers cannot justify these claims nor can Bernoulli's formulation of the theorem, which although it can be used for finite samples, is designed for a different purpose. Bernoulli's theorem allows for the determination of a finite n, given c, but the calculation of n rests on the knowledge of p. This is not the question addressed in research on the 'law of large numbers', where n is always given, p is sometimes given, and the question typically relates to c.

If not the law of large numbers, what else could serve as a normative basis for determining when and why to consider sample sizes in judgments?

WHAT MATHEMATICAL RESULTS JUSTIFY THE IMPACT OF SAMPLE SIZE?

There are three different mathematical results that provide partial justifications. The simplest result pertains to the *variance of the sample mean*. For a sequence of independently and identically distributed random variables X_i with finite variance σ^2, the variance of the mean $\overline{X}$ (in a sample of size n) is σ^2 / n. Thus the variance of the mean decreases with increasing n (hereafter, the term 'mean' is assumed to include 'proportion' as well). This consideration provides a first partial justification for the superiority of larger samples. However, it does not allow for specification of the distribution of the mean and, consequently, is mute as to how probable it is for $\overline{X}$ to lie within a specified interval. The second result, *Chebychev's inequality*, provides information about the upper bound of the probability that the difference between mean and expectation is greater than or equal to an arbitrarily small number ε. Chebychev's inequality states that the probability of a deviation (ε or larger) of the random variable X from its expectation μ is less than or equal to the variance σ^2 of X divided by the square of that deviation (e.g., Feller, 1957, p. 219). When Chebychev's inequality is applied to the mean $\overline{X}$, it yields

$$P\left(\left|\overline{X} - \mu\right| \geq \varepsilon\right) \leq \frac{\sigma^2}{n\varepsilon^2}, \qquad (4)$$

because the variance of $\overline{X}$ is σ^2 / n. Because the right-hand side of the inequality approaches 0 as n increases, the upper bound of the probability that the sample mean deviates from the population mean by at least ε decreases as n increases.

However, because Chebychev's inequality specifies only the upper bound, it is just a partial justification for the superiority of larger samples. Indeed, as Stigler (1980) discusses, under certain distributional assumptions, exceptions in which smaller samples give better estimates can be constructed.

Is there a stronger justification for why means of larger samples vary less around the true value? A third result that can be invoked is the *central limit theorem*, which states that for large n, the term $(X - \mu) / (\sigma / \sqrt{n})$ has approximately a standard normal distribution (e.g., Huntsberger & Billingsley, 1973, p. 131). Therefore, for large n, $\overline{X}$ has (approximately) the normal distribution with mean μ and variance σ^2 / n. From the central limit theorem one can infer that the probability that $\overline{X}$ is very close to the population parameter increases monotonically with n. Thus we have a third partial justification for the superiority of larger samples. If n is very large or the population distribution is normal, then the central limit theorem provides the strongest justification because it deals with probability estimates rather than crude upper bounds on these probabilities. However, if n is small and the population distribution deviates markedly from a normal distribution, then the estimate provided by the central limit theorem may be poor, and the two previous results can provide a better justification.

These three results provide (partial) mathematical justifications for the impact of sample-size information, whereas the law of large numbers does *not*.

Appendix C

Is There a Future for Null-Hypothesis Testing in Psychology?

Null-hypothesis testing, often in its hybrid form (i.e., a mix of Fisherian, Neyman-Pearsonian, and Bayesian theories, see Acree, 1979; Gigerenzer, 1993; Gigerenzer & Murray, 1987), is the statistical procedure most widely reported in psychological journals. The ubiquity of significance tests is surprising given the devastating critiques of it that have been brought forward over a period of decades (e.g., Bakan, 1966; Dar, 1987; Meehl, 1978; Schmidt, 1992). Recently, critics have been confronted by prominent supporters of null-hypothesis testing, and the debate has intensified as a result (see special section in *Psychological Science*, January, 1997). Supporters of significance tests agree with critics that null-hypothesis testing has been misused in the past but argue that, if applied properly, it serves important purposes in psychological research. What are the arguments for using significance tests?

A strong case for using significance tests has been made by Frick (1996). He admits that null-hypothesis testing is not useful in testing quantitative claims and is insufficient in cases in which clinical or practical significance is called for, but argues that the procedure is ideally suited to examine ordinal claims. As examples of the latter, Frick cites the claims that frustration increases the tendency to behave aggressively and that smoking is positively correlated with lung cancer. According to Frick, the size of an effect (e.g., a difference or correlation) is irrelevant in cases in which one wants to test an ordinal claim, making null-hypothesis testing the statistical method of choice. Moreover, he postulates that an α of .05 should serve as a "cliff" that determines whether a particular claim enters the "corpus of psychology." Frick's position will hereafter be referred to as the *strong position*.

Several other supporters have advanced a more moderate case for null-hypothesis testing. Like Frick, Abelson (1997) advocates the use of significance tests to justify ordinal or categorical statements about experimental results, but also suggests using additional criteria to judge the quality of a research claim (e.g., magnitude of effect). He also argues that significance tests are useful in judging effect sizes by stating that they "act as a (mediocre) filter for separating effects of different magnitude" (p. 14). Some, including Abelson, see null-hypothesis testing as a guard against the possibility that "some familiar chance mechanism could have produced the results" (p. 14) and against overinterpreting "nearly random aspects of our data" (Harris, 1997, p. 11). Another supporter,

Scarr (1997), sees significance tests as one method of increasing the probability that information used in public debates (e.g., about mothers' employment) is reliable and reproducible. Finally, Estes (1997) adopts the pragmatic and flexible view that significance-test results, in conjunction with effect sizes, can be useful aids in screening manuscripts submitted for publication, but also concedes that in some cases significance tests may not be necessary at all. These arguments are hereafter referred to collectively as the *moderate position* because all the cited authors who hold it propose using at least one additional methodological tool, such as confidence intervals or effect sizes.

In this book it is argued that recent defenses notwithstanding, the continued use of null-hypothesis testing in psychological research is of little value. First, arguments against the strong position, which show that null-hypothesis testing is far from ideal even for the analysis of ordinal claims, are brought forward. Second, in contradiction to the moderate position, it is claimed that null-hypothesis testing is only a very limited means of making judgments about effect sizes, is not very helpful in deciding whether a result is due to chance, and does not on its own say much about reliability or replicability. Third, better methods for evaluating research results than null-hypothesis testing are suggested. An example is used to demonstrate some of these methods and to illustrate some of the problems with null-hypothesis testing. Finally, it is suggested that contenting ourselves with making ordinal claims, as Frick (1996) proposes, is likely to hinder progress in psychology.

PROBLEMS WITH THE STRONG POSITION

Two points speak against the strong position. First, significance test results are not sufficient to justify even ordinal claims because they do not consider the context of a study, and second, relying solely on significance tests to evaluate an ordinal claim is likely to obscure important information about the nature of the effect in question.

What does a Significant Result Tell us About an Ordinal Claim?

What do we know when a test is significant? Not much. We know, as Frick explains, that p, the probability of the observed or a larger effect given the null hypothesis, is smaller than a preset α (see chapter 1). However, as Meehl (1967) demonstrated, any test can in principle be made to yield a significant result—however small the population effect—by increasing the test's power. Should the acceptance of a researcher's ordinal claims really depend on whether he or she has resources to increase the power of his or her experiments sufficiently to make the test significant (e.g., by recruiting huge samples or searching for the best measure), even if the effect in question is tiny and practically meaningless? As well as forcing us to admit such practically irrelevant results into the corpus of psychology, putting our faith in null-hypothesis testing forces us to bar from it small but important effects that might never reach statistical significance in samples of the size generally used in social science research (e.g., Prentice & Miller, 1992; Rosenthal, 1993). Whether or not a result is significant does not necessarily tell us much about even an ordinal claim unless we consider the context, the specific research question, and the way in which the hypothesis is operationalized. In sum, a significant result alone does not provide sufficient evidence even for an ordinal claim.

Should We Deliberately Discard Important Information? The Cliff

According to Frick (1996, p. 385), "...statistical testing functions to establish sufficient evidence to support a claim, with the criterion held constant across experiments." He takes the criterion, or *cliff*, for entry into the psychological literature to be an α of .05. Apart from the question of whether the size of α should be fixed at all—it should definitely not be fixed in the Neyman–Pearson approach and as Rosnow and Rosenthal (1989) observed, "God loves the .06 nearly as much as the .05" (p. 1277)—such an inflexible criterion can lead to serious problems. If only significant results were published, as, for instance, Melton (1962) suggested, important research enterprises in psychology could be unduly abandoned after the first unsuccessful attempt to find a statistically significant effect (J. Cohen, 1990). Nonsignificant results will sometimes be found even for large population effects because of variation arising from sampling error alone (Schmidt, 1992; see also the illustrative example discussed later).

It is not clear whether Frick (1996) believes that a single significant result is sufficient to support an ordinal claim or whether multiple significant results are necessary. He does not discuss either how we should deal with tens or hundreds of (significant and nonsignificant) findings on the same research question—a state of affairs that seems to be the rule rather the exception in many areas of psychological research. Should we compare the numbers of significant and nonsignificant results across studies? Using estimates of the population effect and statistical power in a typical psychology study, Schmidt (1996) demonstrated that such a cross-study comparison could lead us to conclude that a hypothesized ordinal claim does not hold when indeed it does because test results can be nonsignificant solely due to sampling error. To explain such nonsignificant findings, we might be tempted to search for moderator variables that do not exist (Schmidt, 1996).

Even if one starts out with an ordinal hypothesis, the size of the effect and the specific data pattern found can reveal information important for revising the hypothesis or theory. For instance, closer inspection of the data might show that effect sizes are very different in subgroups not identified before the experiment, and that the significant (or nonsignificant) result is due to only one of the subgroups. Suppressing this information or, in the extreme, discarding it completely (if the test is not significant), would be a waste of useful information and a hindrance to conceptual progress.

PROBLEMS WITH THE MODERATE POSITION

If the majority of researchers used significance test results as one of many sources of evidence for judging empirical results, as proposed by Abelson (1995) and Estes (1997), for instance, there would probably be no controversy. Significance tests do no harm if correctly interpreted, but they do not help much either. Unfortunately, as they have been used up to this point, they have often led to enormous confusion. Let us consider the arguments made by moderate supporters of null-hypothesis testing (except that concerning categorical claims, which has already been discussed).

How well do p values perform as indicators of effect size? If sample size is held constant, p values generally vary with changes in effect size. Usually, however, sample sizes vary considerably across studies and p values are, therefore, difficult to interpret, even if common misinterpretations of them (see chapter 1) are avoided. Moreover, there is no need to use p values to infer effect size when effect sizes can easily be calculated directly (e.g., from raw scores or from results of significance tests; Rosenthal & Rosnow, 1991; Sedlmeier, 1996).

What do p values say about whether or not a specific result is due to chance? The usual chain of reasoning proceeds as follows. Even if there is no effect in the population, one can expect chance variation in experimental results that is entirely due to sampling error. The expected variation given that the null hypothesis of no effect is true (e.g., $\mu_A - \mu_B = 0$, $\rho = 0$, etc.), can be specified for different test statistics and degrees of freedom. If the deviation of a result from the null hypothesis is more extreme than a preset α, that is, if $p < \alpha$, then it is assumed that this result is not due to chance variation. If the deviation is less than α, one assumes that chance variation may have caused it. However, this reasoning depends heavily on the size of α, sample size, and, most especially, the size of the true effect in the population. As Hunter (1997) convincingly argues, the null hypothesis can be expected most often not to be true and not only to a negligible degree. Literature reviews estimating effect sizes in published research imply the same conclusion (e.g., Cooper & Findley, 1982; Haase, Waechter, & Solomon, 1982; Sedlmeier & Gigerenzer, 1989). Because the null hypothesis is seldom true, a p value—which is contingent on the truth of the null hypothesis—is not of much help in deciding whether an effect is due to chance. The best way to guard against chance results, that is, results that deviate from the true effect (which is rarely very close to zero) due to sampling error alone, is to replicate the study. Replication seems already to be the rule in leading journals. For instance, in the *Journals of Experimental Psychology* one seldom encounters experimental articles reporting fewer than three studies, and articles reporting more than five studies are not rare.

Finally, what do *p* values tell us about the probability that a result is reliable and reproducible? Unfortunately, the result of a significance test on its own is not very useful in judging the reliability and replicability of research results.[1] Reliability, that is, the degree to which the effect found is close to the population effect, is heavily dependent on sample size because a sample statistic (e.g., mean or proportion) of a large sample is more likely to be close to the corresponding population parameter than that of a small sample. A *p* value on its own does not reveal anything about sample size. For instance, the same *p* value could arise from either a (less reliable) large effect found in a small sample or a (more reliable) small effect found in a large sample. Likewise, a *p* value does not allow one to estimate the probability that a significant test result will be replicated because it is contingent on the truth of the null hypothesis. To estimate replicability, one needs the probability of a significant result given the truth of a specified alternative hypothesis that represents the true effect in the population. This conditional probability is the statistical power of a test and is a function of both sample size and true effect size when α is held constant (e.g., J. Cohen, 1988; Tversky & Kahneman, 1971; see also chapter 1).

In sum, *p* values are of little use in making judgments about effect sizes, about whether a result is due to chance, about whether it is reliable, and about the probability with which it will be replicated. Fortunately, there are good alternatives that are endorsed even by defenders of null-hypothesis testing. For instance, the eminent statistician Cox (1977) suggests that graphical and other descriptive analysis may render calculation of a *p* value superfluous and that effect sizes are generally essential regardless of significance-test results.

WHAT ARE THE ALTERNATIVES?

Some researchers may rely mainly on null-hypothesis testing because they are unaware of viable alternatives. This is no wonder given how quantitative methods are taught in graduate psychology programs. The vast majority of programs still teach the old standards of statistics, that is, traditional inferential statistics (Aiken, West, Sechrest, & Reno, 1990). Good alternatives, however, have existed for many years, notably, exploratory data analysis (EDA), effect size calculation, metaanalysis (e.g., J. Cohen, 1994; Loftus, 1996; Schmidt, 1992;

---

[1]When the alternatives to significance test results are anecdotes, intuitions, and sensational events, which are deplored as sources of evidence by Scarr (1997), significance tests are the more useful method for judging the reliability and replicability of information, although not in their own right, but because they are usually calculated from controlled studies based on representative samples. Members of the general public, who tend to rely on sensational or intuitively plausible events (that often have a sample size of one person) would also benefit from more and better education in statistical thinking (see chapter 15).

Sedlmeier, 1996), and methods specifically developed to address certain research questions (e.g., in the work of Piaget and Skinner).

EDA (e.g., A. F. Smith & Prentice, 1993; Tukey, 1977; Wainer, 1997) is especially useful in the early stages of analysis, but in some cases can be sufficient on its own (e.g., Sedlmeier and Gigerenzer, 1997). One can use standardized effect sizes such as d and r (e.g., J. Cohen, 1962; 1988; Rosnow & Rosenthal, 1996) to make rough judgments about the (absolute) magnitude of an effect by comparing them to conventions for what constitutes a small, medium, or large effect in representative psychological research (e.g., J. Cohen, 1992). More important, effect sizes allow for comparison of effects across studies in the same or in similar areas of research. For easy comparison, different effect-size measures can be converted into each other (Rosenthal & Rosnow, 1991; Tatsuoka, 1993). Interpretation of effect sizes, unlike significance tests, is not an automatic procedure (i.e., bigger is not necessarily better). It depends heavily on knowledge about the specific context (e.g., Yeaton & Sechrest, 1981). For instance, if a treatment can save lives, even tiny effect sizes (e.g., an $r = .04$ corresponding to 4 per 100 persons who manage to survive; see Rosenthal, 1993) are important. Finally, metaanalysis provides methods that allow one to summarize a body of research in a certain area (e.g., Bangert-Drowns, 1986; Schmidt, 1996). These methods, which rely on effect sizes, can account for sampling error and are well suited for examining the influence of moderator variables such as methodological soundness of study and specific features of the sample (e.g., Hunter & Schmidt, 1990).

Of course, there are subjective elements in the interpretation of results using these alternative methods, but the "ritual of significance testing" (Salsburg, 1985) also relies on subjective judgments. For instance, choosing values of α and β (Type II error) is highly subjective and using a fixed α of .05 in an automatic manner is even more so. There is no way to escape subjectivity in interpreting empirical data (Berger & Berry, 1988). We should simply accept that data interpretation is a matter of judgment and strive to make the process by which we interpret our data fully transparent to fellow researchers.

ILLUSTRATIVE EXAMPLE

An example illustrates some of the issues discussed previously. Let us assume that 30 studies each have been conducted to examine the effect of two similar treatments, A and B. In each study, the treatment group (A or B) has been compared to a control group, and the effect size has been calculated as r, the correlation between group membership (e.g., experimental group coded as 1 and control group coded as 0) and treatment effect. For the sake of simplicity, let us assume that the size of each control and treatment group is $n = 15$. Let us further assume that the population effects are $\rho = .20$ for Treatment A and $\rho = .40$ for Treatment

B.[2] Figure C.1 shows the results of two simulations which resulted in 30 hypothetical values each for the effects of Treatments A and B with sampling error as
the sole source of variation.[3] The results of these 60 studies are shown in the
form of a back-to-back stem-and-leaf plot, a basic EDA technique (Tukey, 1977).
The results arising from a population value of $\rho = .20$ vary from $r = -.17$ to $r =$
.55 (Fig. C.1, left leaves) with a mean of $r = .21$ and a median of $r = .22$, and
those originating from $\rho = .40$ vary between $r = .09$ and $r = .70$ (right leaves)
with a mean of $r = .38$ and a median of $r = .41$. The simulations show that although the mean value found in replications of a study may correspond closely
to the population value, the variation that can be expected from sampling error
alone is enormous.

```
                        |  7 | 0
                        |  6 | 5
            5,4,0       |  5 | 0,1,3,5,9
              3,2       |  4 | 3,3,3,3,4,6,7,8
        7,3,3,0,0       |  3 | 1,6,6,7,7,8,9
    9,9,7,3,3,1,0       |  2 | 0,4,8
      9,8,6,6,3         |  1 | 1,1,5,9
        8,5,5,4         |  0 | 9
              0         | -1 |
          7,2,0         | -1 |
```

Treatment A (ρ=.2)   Treatment B (ρ=.4)

FIG. C.1.   Back-to-back stem-and-leaf plot displaying distributions of correlations that express the results in 30 simulated treatment studies each, with population effect sizes of $\rho =$
.20 for Treatment A and $\rho = .40$ for Treatment B. The variation in results is due only to
sampling error. See text for further explanation.

---

[2]Effect sizes of $r = .20$ and $r = .40$ are typical in psychology. For instance, the global effect of
psychotherapy found in M. Smith and Glass' (1977) well-known metaanalysis lies about halfway
between these two values. Values of $r = .20$ and $r = .40$ are what J. Cohen (1992) has classified as
small ($r = .10$) to medium ($r = .30$), and medium to large ($r = .50$) effects, respectively.

[3]In each of the two simulations, 30 random samples were drawn from noncentral t-distributions
with 28 degrees of freedom, and noncentrality parameters of 1.1 for Treatment A and 2.3 for
Treatment B. The t values were converted into correlations using the formula $r = t^2 / (t^2 + df)^{1/2}$. For
instance, $t(28) = 1.1$ resulted in $r = .20$. All calculations were performed using Lisp-Stat (Tierney,
1990). For similar simulations, see Hunter and Schmidt (1990) and Schmidt (1992).

How do the simulation results pertain to the issues discussed previously? First, if a cliff of $\alpha = .05$ (two tailed) were applied to the hypothetical study outcomes, all results smaller than $r = .36$ would be inappropriately barred from the corpus of psychology. Second, if one compared the proportions of significant and nonsignificant results, then one might conclude that there is no effect for Treatment A, and one might even doubt whether there is one for Treatment B because about one third of the results for Treatment B are not significant. Third, if one concluded from each nonsignificant result in the example that it was the result of a chance deviation from the null hypothesis, one would err in each case. Fourth, it is evident from Fig. C.1 that a good estimate of the true effect size is crucial for judging the probability of a replication.

Faced with Fig. C.1, most people would probably agree that Treatment B is more effective than Treatment A, and that their effectiveness differs by about $r = .20$. What if Treatments A and B were considered equally effective prior to the analysis of the 60 studies? Could the difference between them be detected a posteriori? Indeed it could. Looking at the combined results (Fig. C.2), one might not at first think about the possibility that this distribution of effect sizes is the result of two different distributions. If, however, one compares the variation in results to the variation expected from sampling error alone, as advocated in psychometric metaanalysis (Hunter & Schmidt, 1990), it turns out that separate analyses for Treatments A and B explain the variation much better than if all studies are considered together.[4]

EDA, effect size analysis, and metaanalysis are very useful tools for analyzing psychological research results. Such tools are necessary, but are not sufficient, for making theoretical progress. Real progress depends on better theories, which generally result in research hypotheses that are more precise than categorical or ordinal claims. Because null-hypothesis testing assumes categorical or ordinal claims (however inappropriate it is for testing them), its continued use in psychology effectively discourages the formulation of more precise, quantitative hypotheses.

---

[4]Psychometric metaanalysis examines the extent to which variance of sample correlations (s_r^2) can be explained by variance due to sampling error (s_e^2). Ideally, the variance in population correlations $(s_\rho^2 = s_r^2 - s_e^2)$ is zero or very close to zero, which means that all effect sizes stem from only one population (one treatment). If the variance in population correlations is considerably reduced when subgroups are analyzed, one can conclude that the effect sizes do not arise from one, but arise from several populations (e.g., from those described by the subgroups). An analysis of the effect sizes displayed in Fig. C.1 and Fig. C.2 results in s_ρ^2 values of .0127, .0088, and .0043 for the combined effect sizes, and those for Treatments A and B, respectively. The smaller values for s_ρ^2 in the separate analyses indicate that the effect sizes cannot be regarded as originating from only one population, but are likely to stem from two different populations, Treatments A and B.

```
 7 │ 0
 6 │ 5
 5 │ 0,0,1,3,4,5,5,9
 4 │ 2,3,3,3,3,3,4,6,7,8
 3 │ 0,0,1,3,3,6,6,7,7,7,8,9
 2 │ 0,0,1,3,3,4,7,8,9,9
 1 │ 1,1,3,5,6,6,8,9,9
 0 │ 4 5,5,8,9
-0 │ 0
-1 │ 0,2,7
```

FIG. C.2.   Stem-and-leaf plot displaying the distribution of correlations based on the results of 60 simulated treatment studies with half of the results originating from a population effect size $\rho = .20$ (Treatment A) and half from one of $\rho = .40$ (Treatment B). The variation in results is due only to sampling error. Values are identical to those in Fig. C.1. See text for further explanation.

TOWARD (MORE) PRECISE HYPOTHESES

Gigerenzer (1991) showed that researchers' methodological tools (e.g., analysis of variance) can heavily influence their theorizing (see also Gigerenzer, 1998; Loftus, 1996). In a similar vein, Dar (1987) suggested that null-hypothesis testing seems to replace rather than undergird good theory building in psychology: "When passing null-hypothesis tests becomes the criterion for successful predictions, as well as for journal publications, there is no pressure on the psychology researcher to build a solid, accurate theory; all he or she is required to do, it seems, is produce 'statistically significant' results" (p. 149). Frick (1996, p. 383) claims that "the current status of psychology is that theories and laws are tested by ordinal patterns." This is probably true for a substantial portion of psychological research. It is not evident, however, why "psychology perhaps should take pride in its successes as an ordinal science" (p. 383).

Should psychology limit itself to asking ordinal questions, even if quantitative questions are more appropriate and can be realistically posed and addressed? There have always been researchers who attempt to build quantitative psychological models. Many examples can be found in research about perception (e.g., Fechner, 1860; Stevens, 1957; Swets, 1964), learning and memory (e.g., J. R. Anderson & Schooler, 1991; Ebbinghaus, 1885/1913; Estes et al., 1989), and thinking (e.g., Gigerenzer et al., 1988; Kahneman & Tversky, 1973; Sedlmeier et al., 1998). Significance tests are already of little use for examining ordinal claims, but they are even less useful when one wants to test models that make more precise predictions than static and crude group differences or correlations.[5] Instead of allowing null-hypothesis testing to hinder progress in psychology, we should instead recognize its inadequacy and turn to alternative methods. This development cannot happen without improvements in methodological education for psychologists, including teaching of the logic of null-hypothesis testing. Training procedures as described in this book could play an important part in this endeavor. If researchers fully understand significance tests and know alternative methods, there will be no need to ban null-hypothesis testing—it will naturally fade into extinction.

---

[5]Results of significance tests are sometimes reported (and are not discussed) in cases in which simple measures of deviation from a specified model would seem sufficient, suggesting that they are only included pro forma.

References

Abelson, R. P. (1995). *Statistics as principled argument*. Hillsdale, NJ: Lawrence Erlbaum Associates.

Abelson, R. P. (1997). On the surprising longevity of flogged horses: Why there is a case for the significance test. *Psychological Science, 8*, 12–15.

Acree, M. C. (1979). Theories of statistical inference in psychological research: A historico-critical study. *Dissertation Abstracts International, 39*, 5073B. (University Microfilms No. 7907000)

Agnoli, F., & Krantz, D. H. (1989). Suppressing natural heuristics by formal instruction: The case of the conjunction fallacy. *Cognitive Psychology, 21*, 515–550.

Aiken, L. S., West, S. G., Sechrest, L., & Reno, R. R. (1990). Graduate training in statistics, methodology, and measurement in psychology: A survey of Ph D programs in North America. *American Psychologist, 45*, 721–734.

Anderson, J. A. (1995). *An introduction to neural networks*. Cambridge, MA: MIT Press.

Anderson, J. A., & Mozer, M. C. (1981). Categorization and selective neurons. In G. E. Hinton & J. A. Anderson (Eds.), *Parallel models of associative memory* (pp. 251–274). Hillsdale, NJ: Lawrence Erlbaum Associates.

Anderson, J. A., Silverstein, J. W., Ritz, S. A., & Jones, R. S. (1977). Distinctive features, categorical perception, and probability learning: Some applications of a neural model. *Psychological Review, 84*, 413–451.

Anderson, J. R. (1983). *The architecture of cognition*. Cambridge, MA: Harvard University Press.

Anderson, J. R. (1995). ACT: A simple theory of complex cognition. *American Psychologist, 51*, 355–365.

Anderson, J. R., Boyle, C. F., & Yost, G. (1986). The geometry tutor. *The Journal of Mathematical Behavior, 5*, 5–19.

Anderson, J. R., Conrad, F. G., & Corbett, A. T. (1989). Skill acquisition and the LISP tutor. *Cognitive Science, 13*, 467–505.

Anderson, J. R., Corbett, A. T., Koedinger, K., & Pelletier, R. (1995). Cognitive tutors: Lessons learned. *The Journal of the Learning Sciences, 4*, 167–207.

Anderson, J. R., Farrell, R., & Sauers, R. (1984). Learning to program in LISP. *Cognitive Science, 8*, 87–130

Anderson, J. R., & Schooler, L. J. (1991). Reflections of the environment in memory. *Psychological Science, 2*, 396–408.

Anzai, Y., & Simon, H. A. (1979). The theory of learning by doing. *Psychological Review, 86*, 124–140.

Apple Computer, Inc. (1992). *Macintosh Common Lisp Reference*. Cupertino, CA.

Arkes, H. R., & Hammond, K. R. (Eds.). (1986). *Judgment and decision making: An interdisciplinary reader*. New York: Cambridge University Press.

Atkinson, D. R., Furlong, M. J., & Wampold, B. E. (1982). Statistical significance, reviewer evaluations, and the scientific process: Is there a (statistically) significant relationship? *Journal of Counseling Psychology, 29*, 189–194.

Bakan, D. (1966). The test of significance in psychological research. *Psychological Bulletin, 66*, 423–437.

Bangert-Drowns, R. L. (1986). Review of developments in meta-analytic method. *Psychological Bulletin, 99,* 388–399.

Bar-Hillel, M. (1979). The role of sample size in sample evaluation. *Organizational Behavior and Human Performance, 24,* 245–257.

Bar-Hillel, M. (1980). The base-rate fallacy in probability judgments. *Acta Psychologica, 44,* 211–233.

Bar-Hillel, M. (1982). Studies of representativeness. In D. Kahneman, P. Slovic, and A. Tversky (Eds.), *Judgment under uncertainty: Heuristics and biases* (pp. 69–98). New York: Cambridge University Press.

Bar-Hillel, M. (1983). The base rate fallacy controversy. In R. W. Scholz (Ed.). *Decision making under uncertainty* (pp. 39–61). Amsterdam: North-Holland.

Bar-Hillel, M. & Falk, R. (1982). Some teasers concerning conditional probabilities. *Cognition, 11,* 109–122.

Barkow, J. H., Cosmides, L. & Tooby, J. (1992) (Eds.), *The adapted mind: Evolutionary psychology and the generation of culture.* New York: Oxford University Press.

Baumert, J., Lehman, R., u. a. (1997). *TIMSS—Mathematisch-naturwissenschaftlicher Unterricht im internationalen Vergleich: Deskriptive Befunde* [TIMSS—An international comparison of mathematics and science education: Descriptive results]. Opladen, Germany: Leske & Budrich.

Bea, W., & Scholz, R. W. (1995). Graphische Modelle bedingter Wahrscheinlichkeiten im empirisch-didaktischen Vergleich [Graphical models of conditional probabilities compared in respect to empirical and didactical issues]. *Journal für Mathematik-Didaktik, 16,* 299–327.

Belew, R. K. (1990). Evolution, learning, and culture: Computational metaphors for adaptive algorithms. *Complex Systems, 4,* 11–49.

Benassi, V. A., & Knoth, R. L. (1993). The intractable conjunction fallacy: Statistical sophistication, instructional set, and training. *Journal of Social Behavior & Personality, 8,* 83–96.

Berger, J. O., & Berry, D. A. (1988). Statistical analysis and the illusion of objectivity. *American Scientist, 76,* 159–165.

Bernoulli, J. (1713). *Ars conjectandi.* Basilea: Thurnisius.

Betsch, T., Biel, G.-M., Eddelbüttel, C., & Mock, A. (1998). Natural sampling and base-rate neglect. *European Journal of Social Psychology, 28,* 269–273.

Beyth-Marom, R., & Dekel, S. (1983). A curriculum to improve thinking under uncertainty. *Instructional Science, 12,* 67–82.

Beyth-Marom, R., Dekel, S., Gombo, R., & Shaked, M. (1985). *An elementary approach to thinking under uncertainty.* Hillsdale, NJ: Lawrence Erlbaum Associates.

Biehler, R. (1991). Computers in probability education. In R. Kapadia, & M. Borovcnik (Eds.), *Chance encounters: Probability in education. A review of research and pedagogical perspectives.* Amsterdam: Kluwer.

Birnbaum, M. H. (1983). Base rates in Bayesian inference: Signal detection analysis of the cab problem. *American Journal of Psychology, 96,* 85–94.

Borgida, E., & Brekke, N. (1982). The base rate fallacy in attribution and prediction. In J. H. Harvey, W. Ickes, & R. F. Kidd (Eds.), *New directions in attribution research* (pp. 63–96). Hillsdale, NJ: Lawrence Erlbaum Associates.

Bower, G. H. (1994). A turning point in mathematical learning theory. *Psychological Review, 101,* 290–300.

Brainerd, C. J. (1981). Working memory and the developmental analysis of probability judgment. *Psychological Review, 88,* 463–502.

Bredenkamp, J. (1972). *Der Signifikanztest in der psychologischen Forschung* [The significance test in psychological research]. Frankfurt/Main, Germany: Akademische Verlagsgesellschaft.

Casscells, W., Schoenberger, A., & Grayboys, T. (1978). Interpretation by physicians of clinical laboratory results. *New England Journal of Medicine, 299,* 999–1000.

Chapman, G.B. (1991). Trial order affects cue interaction in contingency judgment. *Journal of Experimental Psychology: Learning, Memory and Cognition, 17,* 837–854.

Christensen-Szalanski, J. J. J., & Beach, L. R. (1984). The citation bias: Fad and fashion in the judgment and decision literature. *American Psychologist, 39,* 75–78.

Cohen, J. (1962). The statistical power of abnormal-social psychological research. *Journal of Abnormal and Social Psychology, 65,* 145–153.

Cohen, J. (1988). *Statistical power analysis for the behavioral sciences* (2nd ed.). Hillsdale, NJ: Lawrence Erlbaum Associates.

Cohen, J. (1990). Things I have learned (so far). *American Psychologist, 45,* 1304–1312.

Cohen, J. (1992). A power primer. *Psychological Bulletin, 112,* 155–159.

Cohen, J. (1994). The earth is round (p < .05). *American Psychologist, 49,* 997–1003.

Cohen, L. H. (1979). Clinical psychologists' judgments of the scientific merit and clinical relevance of psychotherapy outcome research. *Journal of Consulting and Clinical Psychology, 47,* 421–423.

Cohen, L. J. (1981). Can human irrationality be experimentally demonstrated? *Behavioral and Brain Sciences, 4,* 317–331.

Cohen, L. J. (1982). Are people programmed to commit fallacies? Further thoughts about the interpretation of experimental data on probability judgment. *Journal of the Theory of Social Behavior, 12,* 251–274.

Cole, W. G. (1988). Three graphic representations to aid Bayesian inference. *Methods of Informatics in Medicine, 27,* 125–132.

Cooper, H., & Findley, M. (1982). Expected effect sizes: Estimates for statistical power analysis in social psychology. *Personality and Social Psychology Bulletin, 8,* 168–173.

Cosmides, L. (1989). The logic of social exchange: Has natural selection shaped how humans reason? Studies with the Wason selection task. *Cognition, 31,* 187–276.

Cosmides, L., & Tooby, J. (1994). Beyond intuition and instinct blindness: Toward an evolutionarily rigorous cognitive science. *Cognition, 50,* 41–77.

Cosmides, L., & Tooby, J. (1996). Are humans good intuitive statisticians after all? Rethinking some conclusions from the literature on judgment under uncertainty. *Cognition, 58,* 1–73.

Cosmides, L., Tooby, J. & Barkow, J. H. (1992). Introduction: Evolutionary psychology and conceptual integration. In J. H. Barkow, L. Cosmides, & J. Tooby, (Eds.), *The adapted mind: Evolutionary psychology and the generation of culture* (pp. 3–15). New York: Oxford University Press.

Coursol, A., & Wagner, E. E. (1986). Effect of positive findings on submission and acceptance rates: A note on meta-analysis bias. *Professional Psychology: Research and Practice, 17,* 136–137.

Cox, D. R. (1977). The role of significance tests. *Scandinavian Journal of Statistics, 4,* 49–70.

Crandall, C. S., & Greenfield, B. (1986). Understanding the conjunction fallacy: A conjunction of effects? *Social Cognition, 4,* 408–419.

Cummins, D. D., Kintsch, W., Reusser, K., & Weimer, R. (1988). The role of understanding in solving word problems. *Cognitive Psychology, 20,* 405–438.

Dar, R. (1987). Another look at Meehl, Lakatos, and the scientific practices of psychologists. *American Psychologist, 42,* 145–151.

Daston, L. (1988). *Classical probability in the Enlightenment.* Princeton, NJ: Princeton University Press.

Dawes, R. M. (1986). Representative thinking in clinical judgment. *Clinical Psychology Review*, *6*, 425–441.

Dawes, R. M. (1988). *Rational choice in an uncertain world*. San Diego, CA: Harcourt Brace Jovanovich.

Dawkins, R. (1995, November). God's utility function. *Scientific American*, 63–67.

Donaldson, M. (1982). Conservation: What is the question? *British Journal of Psychology*, *73*, 199–207.

DuCharme, W. M., & Peterson, C. R. (1969). Proportion estimation as a function of proportion and sample size. *Journal of Experimental Psychology*, *81*, 536–541.

Dulany, D. E., & Hilton, D. J. (1991). Conversational implicature, conscious representations, and the conjunction fallacy. *Social Cognition*, *9*, 85–110.

Ebbinghaus, H. (1913). *Memory: A contribution to experimental psychology* (H. A. Ruger & C. E. Bussenues, Trans.). New York: Teachers College, Columbia University. (Original work published 1885)

Eddy, D. M. (1982). Probabilistic reasoning in clinical medicine: Problems and opportunities. In D. Kahneman, P. Slovic, & A. Tversky (Eds.), *Judgment under uncertainty: Heuristics and biases* (pp. 249–267). New York: Cambridge University Press.

Edwards, W. (1982). Conservatism in human information processing. In D. Kahneman, P. Slovic, & A. Tversky (Eds.). *Judgment under uncertainty: Heuristics and biases* (pp. 359–369). New York: Cambridge University Press.

Elman, J. L., Bates, E. A., Johnson, M. H., Karmiloff-Smith, A., Parisi, D., & Plunkett, K. (1996). *Rethinking innateness: A connectionist perspective on development*. Cambridge, MA: MIT Press.

Elsom-Cook, M. (1993). Student modelling in intelligent tutoring systems. *Artificial Intelligence Review*, *7*, 227–240.

Erlick, D. E. (1964). Absolute judgments of discrete quantities randomly distributed over time. *Journal of Experimental Psychology*, *57*, 475–482.

Estes, W. K. (1950). Toward a statistical theory of learning. *Psychological Review*, *57*, 94–107.

Estes, W. K. (1959). The statistical approach to learning theory. In S. Koch (Ed.). *Psychology: A study of a science, Vol. 2* (pp. 380–491). New York: McGraw-Hill.

Estes, W. K. (1986). Array models for category learning. *Cognitive Psychology*, *18*, 500–549.

Estes, W. K. (1991). Cognitive architectures from the standpoint of an experimental psychologist. *Annual Review of Psychology*, *42*, 1–28.

Estes, W. K. (1997). Significance testing in psychological research: Some persisting issues. *Psychological Science*, *8*, 18–20.

Estes, W. K., Campbell, J. A., Hatsopoulos, N., & Hurwitz, J. B. (1989). Base-rate effects in category learning: A comparison of parallel network and memory storage-retrieval models. *Journal of Experimental Psychology: Learning, Memory, and Cognition*, *15*, 556–571.

Evans, J. St. B. T. (1972). On the problems of interpreting reasoning data: Logical and psychological approaches. *Cognition*, *1*, 373–384.

Evans, J. St. B. T., & Bradshaw, H. (1986). Estimating sample-size requirements in research design: A study of intuitive statistical judgment. *Current Psychological Research & Reviews*, *5*, 10–19.

Evans, J. St. B. T., & Dusoir, A. E. (1977). Proportionality and sample size as factors in intuitive statistical judgement. *Acta Psychologica*, *41*, 129–137.

Falk, R., & Konold, C. (1992). The psychology of learning probability. In: F. S. Gordon & S. P. Gordon (Eds.). *Statistics for the twenty-first century* (pp. 151–164). Washington, DC: The Mathematical Association of America.

Fechner, G. T. (1860). *Elemente der Psychophysik* [Elements of psychophysics] (Vol. 1). Leipzig, Germany: Breitkopf und Härtel.

Feller, W. (1957). *An introduction to probability theory and its applications* (2nd ed., Vol. 1). New York: Wiley.

Fiedler, K. (1988). The dependence of the conjunction fallacy on subtle linguistic factors. *Psychological Research, 50*, 123–129.

Fiedler, K. (1991). The tricky nature of skewed frequency tables: An information loss account of distinctiveness-based illusory correlations. *Journal of Personality and Social Psychology, 60*, 24–36.

Fiedler, K. (1996). Explaining and simulating judgment biases as an aggregation phenomenon in probabilistic, multiple-cue environments. *Psychological Review, 103*, 193–214.

Fine, T. L. (1973). *Theories of probability: An examination of foundations.* New York: Academic Press.

Fischbein, E. (1975). *The intuitive sources of probabilistic thinking in children.* Dordrecht, The Netherlands: D. Reidel.

Fischhoff, B., & Bar-Hillel, M. (1984). Focusing techniques: A shortcut to improving probability judgments? *Organizational Behavior and Human Performance, 34*, 175–194.

Fischhoff, B., Slovic, P., & Lichtenstein, S. (1979). Subjective sensitivity analysis. *Organizational Behavior and Human Performance, 23*, 339–359.

Fisk, J. E., & Pidgeon, N. (1997). The conjunction fallacy: The case for the existence of competing heuristic strategies. *British Journal of Psychology, 88*, 1–27.

Fong, G. T., Krantz, D. H., & Nisbett, R. E. (1986). The effects of statistical training on thinking about everyday problems. *Cognitive Psychology, 18*, 253–292.

Fong, G. T., Lurigio, A. J., & Stalans, L. J. (1990). Improving probation decisions through statistical training. *Criminal Justice and Behavior, 17*, 370–388.

Fong, G. T., & Nisbett, R.E. (1991). Immediate and delayed transfer of training effects in statistical reasoning. *Journal of Experimental Psychology: General, 120*, 34–45.

Freedman, D., Pisani, R., Purves, R., & Adhikari, A. (1991). *Statistics* (2nd ed.). New York: Norton.

Freudenthal, H. (1972). The 'empirical law of large numbers' or 'the stability of frequencies'. *Educational Studies in Mathematics, 4*, 484–490.

Frick, R. W. (1996). The appropriate use of null hypothesis testing. *Psychological Methods, 1*, 379–390.

Garfield, J., & Ahlgren, A. (1988). Difficulties in learning basic concepts in probability and statistics: Implications for research. *Journal of Research in Mathematics Education, 19*, 44–63.

Gavanski, I., & Roskos-Ewoldsen, D. R. (1991). Representativeness and conjoint probability. *Journal of Personality and Social Psychology, 61*, 181–194.

Gigerenzer, G. (1991). From tools to theories: A heuristic of discovery in cognitive psychology. *Psychological Review, 98*, 254–267.

Gigerenzer, G. (1993). The superego, the ego, and the id in statistical reasoning. In G. Keren & C. Lewis (Eds.), *A handbook for data analysis in the behavioral sciences: Methodological issues* (pp. 311–339). Hillsdale, NJ: Lawrence Erlbaum Associates.

Gigerenzer, G. (1994). Why the distinction between single-event probabilities and frequencies is important for psychology (and vice versa). In G. Wright & P. Ayton (Eds.), *Subjective Probability.* New York: Wiley.

Gigerenzer, G. (1996a). The psychology of good judgment: Frequency formats and simple algorithms. *Journal of Medical Decision Making, 16*, 273–280.

Gigerenzer, G. (1996b). On narrow norms and vague heuristics: A reply to Kahneman and Tversky (1996). *Psychological Review, 103*, 592–596.

Gigerenzer, G. (1997). Ecological intelligence: An adaptation for frequencies. *Psychologische Beiträge, 39*, 107–125.

Gigerenzer, G. (1998). Surrogates for theories. *Theory & Psychology, 8*, 195–204.

Gigerenzer, G., Hell, W., & Blank, H. (1988). Presentation and content: The use of base rates as a continuous variable. *Journal of Experimental Psychology: Human Perception and Performance, 14,* 513–525.

Gigerenzer, G., & Hoffrage, U. (1995). How to improve Bayesian reasoning without instruction: Frequency formats. *Psychological Review, 102,* 684–704.

Gigerenzer, G. & Hug, K. (1992). Domain-specific reasoning: Social contracts, cheating, and perspective change. *Cognition, 43,* 127–171.

Gigerenzer, G., & Murray, D. (1987). *Cognition as intuitive statistics.* Hillsdale, NJ: Lawrence Erlbaum Associates.

Gigerenzer, G., Swijtink, Z., Porter, T., Daston, L., Beatty, J., & Krüger, L. (1989). *The empire of chance: How probability changed science and everyday life.* Cambridge, England: Cambridge University Press.

Ginossar, Z., & Trope, Y. (1980). The effects of base rates and individuating information on judgments about another person. *Journal of Experimental Social Psychology, 16,* 228–242.

Ginossar, Z., & Trope, Y. (1987). Problem solving in judgment under uncertainty. *Journal of Personality and Social Psychology, 52,* 464–474.

Glaser, R., & Bassok, M. (1989). Learning theory and the study of instruction. *Annual Review of Psychology, 40,* 631–666.

Gluck, M., & Bower, G. H. (1988). From conditioning to category learning: An adaptive network model. *Journal of Experimental Psychology: General, 117,* 227–247.

Gould, S. J. (1991). Exaptation: A crucial tool for an evolutionary psychology. *Journal of Social Issues, 47,* 43–65.

Gould, S. J. (1992). *Bully for brontosaurus: Further reflections in natural history.* New York: Penguin.

Greene, R. L. (1984). Incidental learning of event frequencies. *Memory & Cognition, 12,* 90–95.

Greenwald, A. G. (1975). Consequences of prejudice against the null hypothesis. *Psychological Bulletin, 82,* 1–20.

Grice, H. P. (1975). Logic and conversation. In D. Davidson & G. Harman (Eds.), *The logic of grammar* (pp. 64–75). Encino, CA: Dickenson.

Grossberg, S. (1976). Adaptive pattern classification and universal recoding, I: Parallel development and coding of neural feature detectors. *Biological Cybernetics, 23,* 121–134.

Grossberg, S. (1987). Competitive learning: From interactive activation to adaptive resonance. *Cognitive Science, 11,* 23–63.

Grossberg, S. (Ed.). (1988). *Neural networks and natural intelligence.* Cambridge, MA: MIT Press.

Gruenfeld, D. H., & Wyer, R. S., Jr. (1992). Semantics and pragmatics of social influence: How affirmations and denials affect beliefs in referent propositions. *Journal of Personality and Social Psychology, 62,* 38–49.

Haase, R. F., Waechter, D. M., & Solomon, G. S. (1982). How significant is a significant difference? Average effect size of research in Counseling Psychology. *Journal of Counseling Psychology, 29,* 58–65.

Hacking, I. (1965). *Logic of statistical inference.* Cambridge, England: Cambridge University Press.

Harris, R. J. (1997). Significance tests have their place. *Psychological Science, 8,* 8–11.

Harris, R. J., & Monaco, G. E. (1978). Psychology of pragmatic implication: Information processing between the lines. *Journal of Experimental Psychology: General, 107,* 1–27.

Hasher, L., & Zacks, R. T. (1984). Automatic processing of fundamental information: The case of frequency of occurrence. *American Psychologist, 39,* 1372–1388.

Hertwig, R. (1995). *Why Dr. Gould's homunculus doesn't think like Dr. Gould: The "conjunction fallacy" reconsidered.* Konstanz, Germany: Hartung-Gorre.

Hertwig. R., & Chase, V. M. (1998). Many reasons or just one: How response mode affects reasoning in the conjunction problem. *Thinking & Reasoning, 4,* 319–352.

Hertwig, R., & Gigerenzer, G. (in press). The "conjunction fallacy" revisited: How intelligent inferences look like reasoning errors. *Journal of Behavioral Decision Making*.

Hilton, D. J. (1995). The social context of reasoning: Conversational inference and rational judgment. *Psychological Bulletin, 118*, 248–271.

Hinton, G. E., & Nowlan, S. J. (1987). How learning can guide evolution. *Complex Systems, 1*, 495–502.

Hintzman, D. L. (1969). Apparent frequency as a function of frequency and the spacing of repetitions. *Journal of Experimental Psychology, 80*, 139–145.

Hintzman, D. L. (1988). Judgments of frequency and recognition memory in a multiple-trace memory model. *Psychological Review, 95*, 528–551.

Hock, H. S., Malcus, L., & Hasher, L. (1986). Frequency discrimination: Assessing global-level and element-level units in memory. *Journal of Experimental Psychology: Learning, Memory, and Cognition, 12*, 232–240.

Hoffrage, U., & Gigerenzer, G. (1998). Using natural frequencies to improve diagnostic inferences. *Academic Medicine, 73*, 538–540.

Huber, O. (1993). The development of the probability concept: Some reflections. *Archives de Psychologie, 61*, 187–195.

Huff, D. (1973). *How to lie with statistics*. Harmondsworth: Penguin.

Hunter, J. E. (1997). Needed: A ban on the significance test. *Psychological Science, 8*, 3–7.

Hunter, J. E., & Schmidt, F. L. (1990). *Methods of meta-analysis*. Newbury Park, CA: Sage.

Huntsberger, D. V., & Billingsley, P. (1973). *Elements of statistical inference* (3rd ed.). Boston: Allyn and Bacon.

Inhelder, B., & Piaget, J. (1964). *The early growth of logic in the child*. (E. A. Lunzer & D. Papert, Trans.). London: Routledge & Kegan Paul. (Original work published 1959)

International Association for the Evaluation of Educational Achievement (1996). *Mathematics achievement in the middle school years: IEA's third international mathematics and science study (TIMSS)*. Chestnut Hill, MA: Center for the Study of Testing, Evaluation, and Educational Policy, Boston College.

International Association for the Evaluation of Educational Achievement (1998). *Mathematics and science achievement in the final year of secondary school: IEA's third international mathematics and science study (TIMSS)*. Chestnut Hill, MA: Center for the Study of Testing, Evaluation, and Educational Policy, Boston College.

Irwin, F. W., Smith, W. A. S., & Mayfield, J. F. (1956). Tests of two theories of decision in an "expanded judgments" situation. *Journal of Experimental Psychology, 51*, 261–268.

Jacobs, J. E., & Potenza, M. (1991). The use of judgment heuristics to make social and object decision: A developmental perspective. *Child Development, 62*, 166–178.

James, W. (1890). *The principles of psychology*. New York: Dover.

Jepson, C., Krantz, D. H., & Nisbett, R. E. (1983). Inductive reasoning: Competence or skill? *The Behavioral and Brain Sciences, 3*, 494–501.

Johnson, M. K., Peterson, M. A., Yap, E. C., & Rose, P. M. (1989). Frequency judgments: The problem of defining a perceptual event. *Journal of Experimental Psychology: Learning, Memory, and Cognition, 15*, 126–136.

Jones, C. J., & Harris, P. L. (1982). Insight into the law of large numbers: A comparison of Piagetian and judgment theory. *Quarterly Journal of Experimental Psychology, 34A*, 479–488.

Jonides, J., & Jones, C. M. (1992). Direct coding for frequency of occurrence. *Journal of Experimental Psychology: Learning, Memory, and Cognition, 18*, 368–378.

Jordan, M. I. (1986). An introduction to linear algebra in parallel distributed processing. In R. E. Rumelhart & J. L. McClelland (Eds.), *Parallel distributed processing, Vol. 1* (pp. 365–422). Cambridge, MA: MIT Press.

Kahneman, D., Slovic, P. & Tversky, A. (Eds.). (1982). *Judgment under uncertainty: Heuristics and biases*. New York: Cambridge University Press.

Kahneman, D., & Tversky, A. (1972). Subjective probability: A judgment of representativeness. *Cognitive Psychology, 3*, 430–454.

Kahneman, D., & Tversky, A. (1973). On the psychology of prediction. *Psychological Review, 80*, 237–251.

Kahneman, D. L., & Tversky, A. (1982). On the study of statistical intuitions. *Cognition, 11*, 123–141.

Kahneman, D., & Tversky, A. (1996). On the reality of cognitive illusions. *Psychological Review, 103*, 582–591.

Klahr, D. (1984). Transition processes in quantitative development. In R. J. Sternberg (Ed.), *Mechanisms of cognitive development* (pp. 101–140). New York: W.H. Freeman.

Koehler, J. J. (1996). The base rate fallacy reconsidered: Descriptive, normative and methodological challenges. *Behavioral and Brain Sciences, 19*, 1–17.

Kosonen, P. & Winne, P. H. (1995). Effects of teaching statistical laws on reasoning about everyday problems. *Journal of Educational Psychology, 87*, 33–46.

Krantz, S. G. (1997). *Techniques of problem solving*. Providence, RI: American Mathematical Society.

Krosnick,. A., Li, F., & Lehman, D. R. (1990). Conversational conventions, order of information acquisition, and the effect of base-rates and individuating information on social judgments. *Journal of Personality and Social Psychology, 59*, 1140–1152.

Kunda, Z., & Nisbett, R. E. (1986a). Prediction and the partial understanding of the law of large numbers. *Journal of Experimental Social Psychology, 22*, 339–354.

Kunda, Z., & Nisbett, R. E. (1986b). The psychometrics of everyday life. *Cognitive Psychology, 18*, 195–224.

Kuzmak, S. D., & Gelman, R. (1986). Young children's understanding of random phenomena. *Child Development, 57*, 559–566.

Legree, P. J., & Gillis, P. D. (1991). Product effectiveness evaluation criteria for intelligent tutoring systems. *Journal of Computer-Based Instruction, 18*, 57–62.

Lehman, D. R., Lempert, R. O., & Nisbett, R. E. (1988). The effects of graduate training on reasoning: Formal discipline and thinking about everyday-life events. *American Psychologist, 43*, 431–442.

Levin, I. P. (1974). Averaging processes in ratings and choices based on numerical information. *Memory & Cognition, 2*, 786–790.

Lichtenstein, S., Slovic, P., Fischhoff, B., Layman, M., & Combs, B. (1978). Judged frequency of lethal events. *Journal of Experimental Psychology: Human Learning and Memory, 4*, 551–581.

Lindeman, S. T., van den Brink, W. P., & Hoogstraten, J. (1988). Effect of feedback on base-rate utilization. *Perceptual and Motor Skills, 67*, 343–350.

Loftus, G. R. (1993). A picture is worth a thousand p values: On the irrelevance of hypothesis testing in the microcomputer age. *Behavior Research Methods, Instruments & Computers, 25*, 250–256.

Loftus, G. R. (1996). Psychology will be a much better science when we change the way we analyze data. *Current Directions in Psychological Science, 5*, 161–171.

Lopes, L. L. (1991). The rhetoric of irrationality. *Theory & Psychology, 1*, 65–82.

Lopes, L. L., & Oden, G. D. (1991). The rationality of intelligence. In E. Eels & T. Maruszewski (Eds.), *Poznan Studies in the Philosophy of the Sciences and the Humanities, Vol. 21* (pp. 225–249). Amsterdam: Rodopi.

Lopez, F. J., Shanks, D. R., Almaraz, J., & Fernandez, P. (1998). Effects of trial order on contingency judgments: A comparison of associative and probabilistic contrast accounts. *Journal of Experimental Psychology: Learning, Memory, and Cognition, 24*, 672–694.

MacDonald, R. R. (1986). Credible conceptions and implausible probabilities. *British Journal of Mathematical Psychology, 39,* 15–27.

Maistrov, L. E. (1974). *Probability theory: A historical sketch.* New York: Academic Press.

McClelland, J. L., & Rumelhart, D. E. (1985). A distributed model of human learning and memory. *Journal of Experimental Psychology: General, 114,* 159–188.

McCormick, J. (1987, August 17). The wisdom of Solomon. *Newsweek,* 24–25.

McDougall, A., Cumming, G., Cropp, S. & Sussex, R. (1995). Learner modelling by expert teachers: Learner information space and the minimal learner model. In J. D. Tinsley & R. J. van Weert (Eds.), *Proceedings of the sixth IFIP World Conference on Computers in Education* (pp. 733–742). London: Chapman & Hall.

Medin, D. I., & Bettger, J. G. (1991). Sensitivity to changes in base-rate information. *American Journal of Psychology, 104,* 311–332.

Meehl, P. E. (1967). Theory-testing in psychology and physics: A methodological paradox. *Philosophy of Science, 34,* 103–115.

Meehl, P. E. (1978). Theoretical risks and tabular asterisks: Sir Karl, Sir Ronald, and the slow progress of soft psychology. *Journal of Consulting and Clinical Psychology, 4,* 806–834.

Melton, A. W. (1962). Editorial. *Journal of Experimental Psychology, 64,* 553–557.

Minsky, M. (1975). A framework of representing knowledge. In: P. H. Winston (Ed.), *The psychology of computer vision* (pp. 211–277). New York: McGraw-Hill.

Molitor, S., Ballstaedt, S. P., & Mandl, H. (1989). Problems in knowledge acquisition from text and pictures. In H. Mandl & J. R. Levin (Eds.), *Knowledge acquisition from text and pictures* (pp. 3–35). Amsterdam: Elsevier.

Murray, B. (1997, January). America still lags behind in mathematics test scores. *APA Monitor,* 44.

Murray, J., Iding, M., Farris, H., & Revlin, R. (1987). Sample size salience and statistical inference. *Bulletin of the Psychonomic Society, 25,* 367–369.

Naveh-Benjamin, M., & Jonides, J. (1986). On the automaticity of frequency coding: Effects of competing task load, encoding strategy, and intention. *Journal of Experimental Psychology: Learning, Memory, and Cognition, 12,* 378–386.

Neches, R. (1984). Learning through incremental refinement of procedures. In D. Klahr, P. Langley, & R. Neches (Eds.), *Production system models of learning and development.* Cambridge, MA: MIT Press/Bradford Books.

Newell, A. (1990). *Unified theories of cognition.* Cambridge, MA: Harvard University Press.

Nisbett, R. E. (1993). Reasoning, abstraction, and the prejudices of 20th-century psychology. In R. E. Nisbett (Ed.), *Rules for reasoning* (pp. 1–12). Hillsdale, NJ: Lawrence Erlbaum Associates.

Nisbett, R. E., Fong, G. T., Lehman, D. R., & Cheng, P. W. (1987). Teaching reasoning. *Science, 238,* 625–631.

Nisbett, R. E., Krantz, D. H., Jepson, C., & Kunda, Z. (1983). The use of statistical heuristics in everyday inductive reasoning. *Psychological Review, 90,* 339–363.

Nisbett, R., & Ross, L. (1980). *Human inference: strategies and shortcomings of social judgment.* Englewood Cliffs, NJ: Prentice-Hall.

Oakes, M. (1986). *Statistical inference: A commentary for the social and behavioral sciences.* New York: Wiley.

Olson, C. L. (1976). Some apparent violations of the representativeness heuristic in human judgment. *Journal of Experimental Psychology: Human Perception and Performance, 2,* 599–608.

Paivio, A. (1971). *Imagery and verbal processes.* New York: Holt, Rinehart & Winston.

Paivio, A. (1978). A dual coding approach to perception and cognition. In H. L. Pick & E. Saltzman (Eds.), *Modes of perceiving and processing information* (pp. 39–51). Hillsdale, NJ: Lawrence Erlbaum Associates.

Pearson, K. (1925). James Bernoulli's theorem. *Biometrika, 17,* 14–210.

Peterson, C. R., DuCharme, W. M., & Edwards, W. (1968). Sampling distributions and probability revision. *Journal of Experimental Psychology, 76,* 236–243.

Phillips, L. E., & Edwards, W. (1966). Conservatism in a simple probabilistic inference task. *Journal of Experimental Psychology, 72,* 346–354.

Phillips, L. E., Hays, W. L., & Edwards, W. (1966). Conservatism in complex probabilistic inference. *IEEE Transactions on Human Factors in Electronics, 7,* 7–18.

Piaget, J. & Inhelder, B. (1969). *The psychology of the child.* London: Routledge & Kegan Paul.

Piaget, J., & Inhelder, B. (1975). *The origin of the idea of chance in children* (L. Leake, Jr., P. Burrel, & H. D. Fishbein, Trans.). New York: Norton. (Original work published 1951)

Piattelli-Palmarini, M. (1994). *Inevitable illusions: How mistakes of reason rule our minds.* New York: Wiley.

Poisson, S. D. (1837). *Recherches sur la probabilité des jugements en matière criminelle et en matière civile, précédé des règles générales du calcul des probabilités.* Paris: Bachelier.

Pollatsek, A., Well, A. D., Konold, C., Hardiman, P., & Cobb, G. (1987). Understanding conditional probabilities. *Organizational Behavior and Human Decision Processes, 40,* 255–269.

Porter, T. M. (1986). *The rise of statistical thinking 1820–1900.* Princeton, NJ: Princeton University Press.

Prentice, D. A., & Miller, D. T. (1992). When small effects are impressive. *Psychological Bulletin, 112,* 160–164.

Putnam, R. T. (1987). Structuring and adjusting content for students: A study of live and simulated tutoring of addition. *American Educational Research Journal, 24,* 13–48.

Reagan, R. T. (1989). Variations on a seminal demonstration of people's insensitivity to sample size. *Organizational Behavior and Human Decision Processes, 43,* 52–57.

Révész, P. (1968). *The laws of large numbers.* New York: Academic Press.

Reyna, V. R., & Brainerd, C. J. (1994). The origins of probability judgment: A review of data and theories. In G. Wright & P. Ayton (Eds.), *Subjective probability* (pp. 239–272). Chicester, England: Wiley.

Rosenthal, R. (1993). Cumulating evidence. In G. Keren & C. Lewis (Eds.), *A handbook for data analysis in the behavioral sciences: Methodological issues* (pp. 519–559). Hillsdale, NJ: Lawrence Erlbaum Associates.

Rosenthal, R., & Rosnow, R. L. (1991). *Essentials of behavioral research: Methods and data analysis* (2nd ed.). New York: McGraw-Hill.

Rosnow, R. L., & Rosenthal, R. (1989). Statistical procedures and the justification of knowledge in psychological science. *American Psychologist, 44,* 1276–1284.

Rosnow, R. L., & Rosenthal, R. (1996). Computing contrasts, effect sizes, and counternulls on other people's published data: General procedures for research consumers. *Psychological Methods, 1,* 331–340.

Rossi, J. S. (1990). Statistical power of psychological research: What have we gained in 20 years? *Journal of Consulting and Clinical Psychology, 58,* 646–656.

Rumelhart, D. E., Hinton, G. E., & Williams, R. J. (1986). Learning internal representations by error propagation. In D. E. Rumelhart & J. L. McClelland (Eds.), *Parallel distributed processing, Vol. I.* (pp. 318–364). Cambridge, MA: MIT Press.

Rumelhart, D. E., Smolensky, P., McClelland, J. L., & Hinton, G. E. (1986). Schemata and sequential thought processes in PDP models. In J. L. McClelland & D. Rumelhart (Eds.), *Parallel distributed processing, Vol. II* (pp. 7–57). Cambridge, MA: MIT Press.

Rumelhart, D. E., & Zipser, D. (1985). Feature discovery by competitive learning. *Cognitive Science, 9,* 75–112.

Salsburg, D. S. (1985). The religion of statistics as practiced in medical journals. *The American Statistician, 39,* 220–223.

Schaefer, R. E. (1976). The evaluation of individual and aggregated subjective probability distributions. *Organizational Behavior and Human Performance, 17,* 199–210.

Scarr, S. (1997). Rules of evidence: A larger context for the statistical debate. *Psychological Science, 8,* 16–17.

Scheaffer, R. L. (1990). *Introduction to probability and its applications.* Belmont, CA: Duxbury.

Schnotz, W., & Grzondziel, H. (1996, August). *Effects of visualizations on the structure and applications of mental models.* Paper presented at the XXVI International Congress of Psychology, Montreal.

Schofield, J. W., Eurich-Fulcer, R., & Britt, C. L. (1994). Teachers, computer tutors, and teaching: The artificially intelligent tutor as an agent for classroom change. *American Educational Research Journal, 31,* 579–607.

Schmidt, F. L. (1992). What do data really mean? Research findings, meta-analysis, and cumulative knowledge in psychology. *American Psychologist, 47,* 1173–1181.

Schmidt, F. L. (1996). Statistical significance testing and cumulative knowledge in psychology: Implications for training of researchers. *Psychological Methods, 1,* 115–129.

Schwartz, B. & Reisberg, D. (1991). *Learning and Memory.* New York: Norton.

Sedlmeier, P. (1992). *Untersuchungen zu einem Lehr-Lernsystem zum Urteilen unter Unsicherheit* [Studies on a tutorial system concerning judgment under uncertainty]. Unpublished doctoral dissertation, University of Constance, Constance, Germany.

Sedlmeier, P. (1993). Training zum Denken unter Unsicherheit [Training to reason under conditions of uncertainty]. In W. Hell, K. Fiedler, & G. Gigerenzer (Eds.), *Kognitive Täuschungen* (pp. 129–160). Heidelberg, Germany: Spektrum.

Sedlmeier, P. (1996). Jenseits des Signifikanztest-Rituals: Ergänzungen und Alternativen [Beyond the ritual of significance testing: Alternative and supplementary methods]. *Methods of Psychological Research - online, 1.* [Internet: http://www.hsp.de/MPR/issue1/index.html].

Sedlmeier, P. (1997). BasicBayes: A tutor system for simple Bayesian inference. *Behavior Research Methods, Instruments, & Computers. 29,* 328–336.

Sedlmeier, P. (1998a) *How to improve statistical thinking: Choose the task representation wisely and learn by doing.* Manuscript submitted for publication.

Sedlmeier, P. (1998b). The distribution matters: Two types of sample-size tasks. *Journal of Behavioral Decision Making, 11,* 281–301.

Sedlmeier (1999). *Associationist learning as the basis for frequency judgments?* Unpublished manuscript, University of Paderborn.

Sedlmeier, P., & Eden, B. (1998). *The hazards of underspecified models: The case of symmetry in everyday predictions.* Submitted for publication.

Sedlmeier, P., & Gigerenzer, G. (1989). Do studies of statistical power have an effect on the power of studies? *Psychological Bulletin, 107,* 309–316.

Sedlmeier, P., & Gigerenzer, G. (1997). Intuitions about sample size: The empirical law of large numbers. *Journal of Behavioral Decision Making, 10,* 33–51.

Sedlmeier, P., & Gigerenzer, G. (1998). *Teaching Bayesian reasoning in less than two hours.* Submitted for publication.

Sedlmeier, P., & Hertwig, R. (1999). *Estimating relative frequencies: Comparison of an exemplar and a prototype model.* Unpublished manuscript, University of Paderborn.

Sedlmeier, P., Hertwig, R., & Gigerenzer, G. (1998). Are judgments of the positional frequencies of letters systematically biased due to availability? *Journal of Experimental Psychology: Learning, Memory, and Cognition, 24,* 754–770.

Sedlmeier, P., & Köhlers, D. (1999). [Estimates of probability and relative frequency for serially encoded events]. Unpublished raw data.

Sedlmeier, P., & Robles de Acuña-Ponseti, J. (1992). "Intelligente" Hilfe beim Lösen von alltagsnahen Wahrscheinlichkeitsproblemen: Modellierung dynamischer Wissensinhalte für ein flexibles Tutorsystem ["Intelligent" help in solution of probability problems with everyday applications: Modeling of dynamic knowledge for a flexible tutor system]. *Kognitionswissenschaft, 3,* 24–37.

Sedlmeier, P, & Wettler, M. (1998). Was muß ein Tutorsystem "wissen"? [What should a tutoring system "know"?] *Zeitschrift für Pädagogische Psychologie, 12,* 219-235.

Self, J. A. (1990). Bypassing the intractable problem of student modeling. In C. Frasson & G. Gauthier (Eds.), *Intelligent tutoring systems: At the crossroads of AI and Education* (pp. 107–123). Norwood, NJ: Ablex.

Shafer, G. (1976). *A mathematical theory of evidence.* Princeton, NJ: Princeton University Press.

Shanks, D. R. (1990). Connectionism and the learning of probabilistic concepts. *Quarterly Journal of Experimental Psychology, 42A,* 209–237.

Shanks, D. R. (1991). Categorization by a connectionist network. *Journal of Experimental Psychology: Learning, Memory, and Cognition, 17,* 433–443.

Shanks, D. R. (1995). *The psychology of associative learning.* Cambridge: Cambridge University Press.

Shanks, D. R., Lopez, F. J., Darby, R. J., & Dickinson, A. (1996). Distinguishing associative and probabilistic contrast theories of human contingency judgment. *The Psychology of Learning and Motivation, 34,* 265–311.

Shaugnessy, J. M. (1992). Research in probability and statistics: Reflections and directions. In D. A. Grouws (Ed.), *Handbook of research on mathematics teaching and learning* (pp. 465–494). New York: Macmillan.

Shyns, P. G., & Rodet, L. (1997). Categorization creates functional features. *Journal of Experimental Psychology: Learning, Memory, and Cognition, 23,* 681–696.

Smith, M., & Glass, G. (1977). Meta-analysis of psychotherapy outcome studies. *American Psychologist, 32,* 752–760.

Smith, E. E., Langston, C., & Nisbett, R. E. (1992). The case for rules in reasoning. *Cognitive Science, 16,* 99–102.

Smith, E. E., & Medin, D. L. (1981). *Categories and concepts.* Cambridge, MA: Harvard University Press.

Smith, A. F., & Prentice, D. A. (1993). Exploratory data analysis. In G. Keren & C. Lewis (Eds.), *A handbook for data analysis in the behavioral sciences: Statistical issues* (pp. 349–390). Hillsdale, NJ: Lawrence Erlbaum Associates.

Stevens, S. S. (1957). On the psychophysical law. *Psychological Review, 64,* 153–181.

Stigler, S. M. (1980). An Edgeworth curiosum. *The Annals of Statistics, 8,* 931–934.

Stigler, S. M. (1983). Who discovered Bayes's Theorem? *American Statistician, 37,* 290–296.

Stigler, S. M. (1986). *The history of statistics: The measurement of uncertainty before 1900.* Cambridge, MA: Belknap/ Harvard University Press.

Swets, J. A. (1964). *Signal detection and recognition by human observers.* New York: Wiley.

Swieringa, R., Gibbins, M., Larsson, L., & Sweeney, J. L. (1976). Experiments in the heuristics of human information processing. *Journal of Accounting Research, 4,* 159–187.

Symons, D. (1992). On the use and misuse of Darwinism in the study of human behavior. In J. H. Barkow, L. Cosmides, & J. Tooby (Eds.), *The adapted mind: Evolutionary psychology and the generation of culture* (pp. 137–159). New York: Oxford University Press.

Tatsuoka, M. (1993). Elements of the general linear model. In G. Keren & C. Lewis (Eds.), *A handbook for data analysis in the behavioral sciences: Statistical issues* (pp. 3–41). Hillsdale, NJ: Lawrence Erlbaum Associates.

Teigen, K. H. (1974). Subjective sampling distributions and the additivity of estimates. *Scandinavian Journal of Psychology, 15,* 50–55.

Thüring, M., & Jungermann, H. (1990). The conjunction fallacy: Causality vs. event probability. *Journal of Behavioral Decision Making, 3,* 61–74.

Tierney, L. (1990). *Lisp-Stat: An object-oriented environment for statistical computing and dynamic graphics.* New York: Wiley.

Todd, P., M., & Miller, G. F. (1991). Exploring adaptive agency II: Simulating the evolution of associative learning. *Proceedings of the International Conference on Simulation of Adaptive Behavior: From Animals to Animats.* Cambridge, MA: MIT Press.

Thorpe, S. J., & Imbert, M. (1989). Biological contraints on connectionist modelling. In R. Pfeifer, Z. Schreter, F. Fogelman-Soulie, & L. Steels (Eds.), *Connectionism in perspective* (pp. 63–92). Amsterdam: Elsevier.

Tukey, J. W. (1977). *Exploratory data analysis.* Reading, MA: Addison-Wesley.

Tversky, A., & Kahneman, D. (1971). Belief in the law of small numbers. *Psychological Bulletin, 73,* 105–110.

Tversky, A., & Kahneman, D. (1973). Availability: A heuristic for judging frequency and probability. *Cognitive Psychology, 4,* 207–232.

Tversky, A., & Kahneman, D. (1974). Judgment under uncertainty: Heuristics and biases. *Science, 185,* 1124–1131.

Tversky, A., & Kahneman, D. (1977). Causal thinking in judgment under uncertainty. In. R. E. Butts & J. Hintikka (Eds.), *Basic problems in methodology and linguistics* (pp. 167–190). Dordrecht, The Netherlands: D. Reidel.

Tversky, A., & Kahneman, D. (1980). Causal schemas in judgments under uncertainty. In M. Fishbein (Ed.), *Progress in social psychology: Vol. 1* (pp. 49–72). Hillsdale, NJ: Lawrence Erlbaum Associates.

Tversky, A., & Kahneman, D. (1982a). Causal schemas in judgments under uncertainty. In D. Kahneman, P. Slovic, & A. Tversky (Eds.), *Judgment under uncertainty: Heuristics and biases* (pp. 117–128). New York: Cambridge University Press.

Tversky, A., & Kahneman, D. (1982b). Evidential impact of base rates. In D. Kahneman, P. Slovic, & A. Tversky (Eds.), *Judgment under uncertainty: Heuristics and biases* (pp. 153–160). New York: Cambridge University Press.

Tversky, A., & Kahneman, D. (1983). Extensional versus intuitive reasoning: The conjunction fallacy in probability judgment. *Psychological Review, 90,* 293–315.

Tversky, A., & Koehler, D. J. (1994). Support theory: A nonextensional representation of subjective probability. *Psychological Review, 101,* 547–567.

Tukey, J. W. (1977). *Exploratory data analysis.* Reading, MA: Addison-Wesley.

Varey, C. A., Mellers, B. A., & Birnbaum, M. H. (1990). Judgments of proportions. *Journal of Experimental Psychology: Human Perception and Performance, 16,* 613–625.

von Randow, G. (1992). *Das Ziegenproblem: Denken in Wahrscheinlichkeiten* [The Monty Hall problem: Thinking in probabilities]. Reinbek, Germany: Rowohlt.

von Winterfeldt, D., & Edwards, W. (1986). *Decision analysis and behavioral research.* New York: Cambridge University Press.

Wainer, H. (1997). Some multivariate displays for NAEP results. *Psychological Methods, 2,* 34–63.

Waldmann, M. R. (1996). Knowledge-based causal induction. *The Psychology of Learning and Motivation, 34,* 47–88.

Wasserman, E. A., & Miller, R. R. (1997). What's elementary about associative learning? *Annual Review of Psychology, 48,* 573–607.

Watkins, M. J., & LeCompte, D. (1991). Inadequacy of recall as a basis for frequency knowledge. *Journal of Experimental Psychology: Learning, Memory, and Cognition, 17,* 1161–1176.

Well, A. D., Pollatsek, A., & Boyce, S. J. (1990). Understanding the effects of sample size on the variability of the mean. *Organizational Behavior and Human Decision Processes, 47,* 289–312.

Wettler, M., Rapp, R. (1993). Computation of word associations based on the co-occurences of words in large corpora. *Proceedings of the Workshop on Very Large Corpora: Academic and Industrial Perspectives* (pp. 84–93). Columbus, Ohio.

Wettler, M., Rapp, R., & Ferber, R. (1993). Freie Assoziationen und Kontiguitäten von Wörtern in Texten [Free association and contiguities between words in texts]. *Zeitschrift für Psychologie, 201*, 103–112

White, P. A. (1991). Availability heuristic and judgements of letter frequency. *Perceptual and Motor Skills, 72*, 34.

Wolfe, C. R. (1995). Information seeking on Bayesian conditional probability problems: A fuzzy-trace theory. *Journal of Behavioral Decision Making, 8*, 85–108.

Wolford, G., Taylor, H. A., & Beck, J. R. (1990). The conjunction fallacy? *Memory & Cognition, 18*, 47–53.

Yates, J. F., & Carlson, B. W. (1986). Conjunction errors: Evidence for multiple judgment procedures, including "signed summation." *Organizational Behavior and Human Decision Processes, 37*, 230–253.

Yeaton, W., & Sechrest, L. (1981). Meaningful measures of effect. *Journal of Consulting and Clinical Psychology, 49*, 766–767.

Zhu, X., & Simon, H. A. (1987). Learning mathematics from examples and by doing. *Cognition and Instruction, 4*, 137–166.

Zukier, H., & Pepitone, A. (1984). Social roles and strategies in prediction: Some determinants of the use of base-rate information. *Journal of Personality and Social Psychology, 42*, 349–360.

Author Index

Subject Index

The infancy of atomic physics:
Hercules in his cradle

The infancy of
atomic physics:
Hercules
in his cradle

ALEX KELLER
University of Leicester

CLARENDON PRESS·OXFORD
1983

Oxford University Press, Walton Street, Oxford OX2 6DP
London Glasgow New York Toronto
Delhi Bombay Calcutta Madras Karachi
Kuala Lumpur Singapore Hong Kong Tokyo
Nairobi Dar es Salaam Cape Town
Melbourne Wellington

and associate companies in
Beirut Berlin Ibadan Mexico City

Published in the United States by
Oxford University Press, New York

British Library Cataloguing in Publication Data

Keller, Alex
 The infancy of atomic physics.
 1. Nuclear research—History
 I. Title
 539.7'072   QC773

 ISBN 0-19-853904-5

Library of Congress Cataloging in Publication Data

Keller, Alex, 1932–
 The infancy of atomic physics.
 Bibliography: p.
 Includes index.
 1. Nuclear physics—History. I. Title
 QC733.K4 1982   539.7'09   82–14233
 ISBN 0-19-853904-5

Made and printed in Great Britain
by Butler & Tanner Ltd, Frome and London

The store drawn upon naturally by uranium and other heavy atoms only awaits the touch of the magic wand of science to enable the twentieth century to cast into the shade the marvels of the nineteenth.

Sir William Crookes, September 1898.

PREFACE

In the course of writing this book, I have had the benefit of conversations with friends and colleagues, who helped to guide the steps of one who rushes in where angels fear to tread. I should like to thank Bill Brock for all his good advice, Bernard Norton, and especially David Adams who read through the draft—needless to say, none of them are to be held in any way responsible for any follies I might have committed. I should also like to thank Professor Thaddeus Trenn for sharing with me some of his ideas about the work of Frederick Soddy, even if I have not quite been able to follow him in his enthusiasm. But above all, I should like to thank my wife, Hannah, who typed out two drafts, and finally mastered the atrocious handwriting of belated corrections. To her, therefore, I should like to dedicate the book.

I should like to acknowledge gratefully the assistance of the following in obtaining illustrations, and for kindly granting permission to use them: Niels Bohr Institutet, Copenhagen (Figs. 17, 21); Dr W.H. Brock (Fig. 2); Prof. L. Badash (Fig. 12); Burndy Library, Norwalk, Conn. (Fig. 6); Dartmouth College, Hanover, N.H. (Fig. 7); Deutsches Museum, Munich (Figs. 3, 4, 9, 15, 16); Leicester University library (Figs. 5, 8, 10, 11, 14, 18); History of Science Museum, Oxford (Figs. 19, 20). My thanks are also due to Audio-Visual Services, Leicester University for the diagrams (Figs. 2, 13).

Leicester   A.G.K.
July 1982

CONTENTS

INTRODUCTION

For more than half a century we have been living on the intellectual muscle built up during the twenty years that ended with the outbreak of the First World War. Our art and music, our politics—our physical science, and above all our scientific technologies are working out ideas born at the turn of the century. In a few short years old assumptions were challenged and overthrown in every field. Physics was an integral part of this revolution, no less than futurism or fauvism, the Rite of Spring or the Demoiselles d'Avignon; in science, at least, it was a time of renaissance, renewal, adventure, which it was hoped would make the twentieth century even more glorious than the nineteenth. The consequences of that scientific thrust forward have not always been as cheerful as the prophets expected. And yet, at this moment we may have to choose between nuclear energy and a simpler way of life: atomic physics underlies our science, and most hopes for a continuation of present affluence.

Why then has there been so little written in any detail about the strange birth and heroic infancy of that Hercules which is modern atomic science? Popular accounts of contemporary science do sometimes include a historical introduction to their subject, but discoveries follow in simple sequence, in regular order, as if they were so revealed to the genius of enquiry. Why trouble the reader with what have since proved to be wrong answers, however exciting they may have looked at the time, or entangle us in the personalities, and the personality conflicts, that beset them? Tell us that in 1898 Bigwig observed Bigwig's effect, perhaps show us a formal picture of Bigwig taken when he was at last elevated to a professorial chair; tell us how Bigwig's effect was useful in solving this or that problem, or raised a new one—but do not waste the innocent reader's time with the man behind the picture. That is a reasonable limit if we wish only to know what science says to us now. Historians usually go too far the other way. Economic and political histories of our busy century there have been in plenty, yet they too neglect the history of its science, and show some interest only when new technologies burst noisily upon their stage. The time has come to write about the origins of that science with the same concern for events as they were lived, as would be allowed for King Edward VII or Kaiser Wilhelm, or the politicians who made headlines in the newspapers. After all, the scientists have had more influence upon our lives. And they are often more attractive people. This book is an attempt at a history of a great upheaval, as it looked at the time to those who were guiding these expeditions into the unknown, and to those who tried hard to keep up with them.

A scientist who had a goodly share in one of the great advances of twentieth-century biology has remarked that 'science seldom proceeds in the straightforward logical manner imagined by outsiders', but rather by stages which are often 'very human events in which personalities and cultural traditions play major roles'.[1] But is it possible to write a *Double helix* of the nuclear atom? Perhaps not, but those personal and national characteristics must be brought out. The language of science changes from place to place and from generation to generation, less perhaps than the language of the street or of entertainment; but it does change, nevertheless. The science of the 1890s and the Edwardian era is now becoming remote, and some effort must be made to think ourselves back into it.

Fortunately over the past decade much fresh information has been made available to help us in that effort. There are edited collections of several of the classic papers, with commentary to steer the modern reader through them, although these have to be supplemented by other papers against which the classicism of the great ones may be judged. Historians of science have ventured at last into the twentieth century and scrutinized the work of Rutherford, Thomson, Bohr, Einstein, and the rest as carefully as they examine the writings of Darwin or Newton. In their journals, the articles of Heilbron, McCormmach, Trenn, and others give us a sense of the fine detail, the false trails as well as the fruitful, and (particularly in the journal *Historical Studies in the Physical Sciences*) suggest how contemporary philosophies and social or political attitudes may have modified the path of scientific thought. Many private letters dating from the crucial years of Rutherford, Bohr, and Moseley have now been published, so that we can glimpse how their ideas took shape as they confided in their closest friends and relatives.

Science is not just the knowledge of great men. In the pages of *Nature*, in the reports of discussions and lectures at meetings of the British Association for the Advancement of Science, say, or the Royal Institution, the contemporary picture of the physical world is articulated. Textbooks and popularizations colour in the background against which the leading actors perform; they provide an audience which may applaud—or may ignore. *Nature* may speak for the ordinary scientist, for the amateur and enthusiast. What of the general public? Something at least may be gleaned from posters and advertisements, from cartoons and comic rhymes in magazines like *Punch*; the Forsytian outlook on the world is enshrined in the columns of the *Illustrated London News*, which during those years published a column of 'Science jottings' by a Dr Andrew Wilson. They are indeed mostly on medicine and biology, perhaps suited for his readership, always worried about its health, so his comments on the more dramatic developments in the physical sciences are the more intriguing, although his judgment was shaky at times. In August

1909, *after Blériot* he could declare that 'it would still be long, very long before man can really fly, if indeed he ever really 'aviates' successfully at all ...' A more comprehensive view of the science journalism of the day, of the way scientific breakthroughs were reported to the public, may be found in the *Annual register of world events*. In 1863, the editors decided to complement their purely political record of wars and rumours of war and parliamentary debates, with sections on the major activities of the past year in literature, science, and the arts. The science section was laid out in neat disciplinary sub-sections which therefore give a very compact and well-written survey of each year's doings on the scientific frontier with the benefit of only a few months' hindsight at most.

Among the cultural peculiarities revealed by enquiry into the face that science then presented are the curiously national styles in physics at the turn of the century. New paths might be trodden in one country, while the others hung back for a while; or in some controversy the majority in one country were to be found on one side, in a neighbouring land on the other. Why should this be so? Germany and the Germans are no doubt composed of protons, neutrons, and electrons identical to those of Britain or France. Yet if nature is the same, the approach to it was different.

It was a nationalistic epoch in which the language of racial competition and the imagery of war and soldiering came easily to the tongue. Behind the internationalism of science lay a simple array of loyalties which scientists usually shared, or at least very seldom tried to question. Internationalism was certainly regarded as a birthright of science. When nations were at logger-heads, their scientists could still happily coexist. On the only occasion when the British Association for the Advancement of Science rated a full page *Punch* cartoon, for its joint meeting with the parallel French organization at Dover in 1899, when Britain and France were quarrelling over their claims to various chunks of Africa, the two scientific gatherings are depicted as two girls playing happily together collecting shells on the beach. Scientific collaboration was common and many scientists trained for a period in foreign laboratories to broaden their minds. Yet a young Hungarian colleague of Rutherford's wrote to him in 1913 on the contrast between the British Association meeting at Birmingham that September, and a similar congress held at Vienna straight after: 'altogether it was more knowledge in Vienna but far more ingenuity at Birmingham'. A few months later another young colleague, Henry Moseley, described a visit from the eminent French chemist Urbain from whom he learnt that 'the French point of view is essentially different from the English—where we try to find models or analogies, they are quite content with laws'.

At the 1909 British Association meeting when J.J. Thomson was President of the Association and Rutherford of the Physics Section, it is interesting that both make a point of stressing the value of models. Men of exceptional ability as mathematicians kept insisting that mathematics must be the servant and not the master of theory. However important mathematics might be—and Thomson was keen to get more mathematics into the training of British scientists—equations were not enough. They were somewhat platonic for most, whereas a model however grossly mechanical was easier to handle and more fruitful. Rutherford too asserted that general abstract principles would not do—what he wanted was a concrete idea of the mechanism at work. That, he added, is an attitude of mind that appeals very strongly to the Anglo-Saxon temperament. Both shared a love of improvisation, practicality, above all of simplicity—theories, and the apparatus designed to test them had to be genial, simple, homespun. All the same, did not England have her abstract philosophers too? Alfred Whitehead and Bertrand Russell were bringing out their *Principia mathematica* in 1910–13, when Rutherford and Thomson were in the thick of their debate on the nature of the atom. Russell and Thomson were both Fellows of Trinity College, Cambridge at the time—although neither Russell nor Thomson mention each other in their autobiographies.

Perhaps the difference lies not in the kind of philosophy, but in the role of philosophy within the British culture. In Britain it was regarded as something specialized, too abstruse and difficult for the adolescent mind, and suitable only for those subtle wits who enjoy telling the rest of us why we do not really know what we suppose we know. In most continental countries, philosophy had long been a school subject begun by fifteen or sixteen years of age. In Germany all the sciences apart from those strictly connected to medicine were part of the faculty of philosophy. One leading German physicist, Max von Laue, reflected on the time and thought he had devoted to Kant's *Critique of pure reason* since he had been at school; even physics he believed to derive its true dignity only from the fact that it provided an essential resource for philosophy, the centre of the sciences. Einstein was introduced to Kant at thirteen by a medical student who was visiting his family. Thomson in contrast met Kant only when a candidate for a Trinity College fellowship. He was expected to choose a non-mathematical topic for his examination; 'don't suppose I really understood Kant's work', he wrote, 'but I enjoyed reading it'.

Some in those days found a difference between the German and other schools in the requirement of a thesis, which British scientists claimed would exaggerate the value of minute and trifling questions. Since the theme of the dissertation has to be narrow enough for the student to master it completely in the time available, he becomes absorbed in the details. Accuracy becomes an end in itself instead of a means to an end—students miss the wood through counting every twig on the trees. However to some bred in the German system, like the physical chemist Ostwald, the benefits were more obvious. The Ph. D. Thesis, he wrote in 1897, 'trains the student how to master unsolved problems, how to pass from the known to the unknown'. If French science had in his view become too conservative, he considered it was mainly due to the failure of the French to use the dissertation properly. They wasted too much time on examinations. 'If one has spent the best years of one's life and most vigorous years of one's life in assimilating the thoughts of others, it requires unusual energy to give oneself to original thought in later years.'

The French in turn were convinced that their methods were best. Alfred Picard in the *Bilan d'un siècle*, a retrospect of the achievements of the nineteenth century published as a memento of the 1900 Paris exhibition, declared his pride in French science; 'Noblesse oblige!' France must keep her place in the front rank 'by conserving intact as a sacred heritage the tradition of the national genius, that is to say the spirit of synthesis, simplicity and clear precision'. These virtues the patriot could contrast either with the haphazard fact-finding sorties of the British, who wanted to turn everything into wheels within wheels, or to grandiose woolly theorizing, and niggling accumulations of useless data piled up in German theses and treatises.

Once a young research student at the Cavendish laboratory in the 1920s found the place too much concernd with apparatus and experiment for his taste. 'And what kind of physics does interest you?', asked Rutherford, then head of the laboratory. 'Theories, principles, ideas' replied the student. To which the professor suddenly asked, 'Are you by any chance Scotch?' 'Yes' 'Then go and join the continentals!' And there's an irony for you. I might rather say that when discussing the British style in physics—for British read Scottish. For physics in England from the 1870s to the end of the nineteenth century had been made in Scotland—was taught by men, who had gone through the Scottish educational system, out of textbooks written by Scots- Kelvin, Tait, Rankine. The infant English physics was guided in its first steps by Kelvin's great work on natural philosophy, Maxwell's on electricity and magnetism; Kelvin, born in Belfast, was educated in Glasgow, and Maxwell in Edinburgh, his native town. Kelvin[2] declared more than once that he could only truly understand a thing if he could produce a mechanical model; until then it remained to some extent obscure. Both he and Maxwell were very fond of introducing such models, all rods and wheels, into the most abstract realms of physics.

An even purer form of Scots operationalism may be observed in David Forbes, who taught Maxwell, and other teachers of physics of that genera- tion—Stewart, Tait, Rankine—at Edinburgh University. He protested at a natural philosophy that would be ruled by higher mathematics and stood firm by a more elementary and geometrical view of nature. Are the results of experiments and observation, he asked rhetorically, to become 'mere pegs on which to suspend festoons of algebraic drapery?'[3] To a Doric mind, all these refinements were like the swags and tassels of fashionable decoration: they but concealed and spoilt the rugged simplicity of nature. When in after years a French physicist on a visit to Britain complained that instead of a 'tranquil

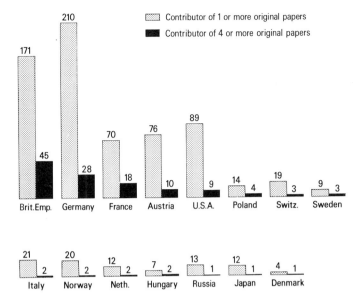

Fig. 1. Distribution of the contributors to science of radioactivity up to 1921.

and ordered temple of reason, we find ourselves in a factory', he did not realize that neither the taste for geometrical models, picturing every theory as an interaction in three-dimensional space—nor the operational approach that sprang from it—were homegrown at Cambridge. Originally, these habits of thought were no more English than tartan or porridge.

These ethnic tastes were, of course, not exclusive. Theory and experiment, models and mathematics, were everywhere expected to be in balance: it is just that the balance proved to differ a little from one country to the next. If there sometimes appeared to be a rivalry between these pairs, they were intended to complement each other like the opposed forearms of baby Hercules. Is there anyway too much Eurocentric bias in these comparisons? At that time, although individuals from around the planet were already making their contribution to the international treasury of science—resented by some, the imperial powers of Western Europe still ruled the intellectual as well as the political world. In 1921 a British scholar published a brief history of radioactivity which shows how that science was concentrated in a few countries. At the end of his article he gives data which are summarized in Fig. 1.[4] The choice of radioactivity does rather distort the comparative ratios of major to minor workers, for example:

British Empire   1:3.8
France   1:3.9

Germany 1:7.5
Austria 1:7.6
USA 1:9.9

In other expanding fields of research, such as X-radiation, relativity, and electrons, ratios more favourable to the German-speaking lands would probably have been found. But then, radioactivity had been the way into the heart of the atom and its energy, the highroad of the new physics.

The only thing we can remember of the infancy of Hercules is that tale of how he strangled twin serpents sent to kill him in his cradle. Our Hercules led a quiet life until his adult years, and nobody sought to suppress him. Yet even in his cot, enthusiastic midwives foresaw the tremendous powers he would exert one day, when he would realize 'what for the past hundred years have been the daydreams of philosophy'. For a hundred years only? No, the fantasies of all the generations have been given material form; seeing through solid barriers, speaking across the expanse of sea or empty space, changing one substance into another, a source of power and light that seems never to waste away. Hercules or Superman—the atom would fulfil the legends of all time.

The new physics had an intellectually destructive side, almost from the start. Its proponents found themselves engaged in a dispute not only with their own predecessors, but with other branches of science, whose exponents felt threatened by the dissolution of their fundamental principles. There was a curious dualism about the natural philosophy of the late nineteenth century. Nature was made of two kinds of substance: atomic, ponderable Matter, studied by chemists, and continuous, weightless, all-pervading Ether studied by physicists. Young Hercules had first to cast down this dual nature, not so much by strangulation and assault as by absorption, so the two became one, rather as Moses' rod-turned-snake swallowed up those of rival seers and took their substance into his own. For the scientist, the dream of philosophy was not mighty, magical forces, but the resolution of this difference: throughout that *belle époque* he sought in this new knowledge 'the eventual formulation of a theory embracing all phenomena accessible to our senses'.

NOTES

1. Watson, J.D. *The double helix*, Preface. Atheneum, New York (1968).
2. William Thomson was knighted in 1866 for his work on the Atlantic cable, ennobled as Lord Kelvin in 1892 for his services to physics—the first physics peer. D.S.L. Cardwell remarks that there have been many Thomsons but only one Kelvin. There are obvious possibilities of confusion with Sir Joseph Thomson, who is one of the heroes of this book. So I propose to follow Cardwell's precedent and speak of Kelvin hereafter, although it is strictly anachronistic to call him so in Chapter 1 and 2.
3. Quoted (from a review article of 1858) by G.E. Davie in *The democratic intellect*, p. 184. Edinburgh University Press (1961).

4. Lawson, R. The part played by different countries in the development of the science of radioactivity. *Scientia* **XXX** 257–70 (1921). Perhaps it is fair to count the British Empire as one unit, when so many Britons taught at colonial universities, and so many colonials worked in the home country, although his category does include Indians. Yet in that case Germany and Austria should be treated as one, since their scientific communities were no less interchangeable. Swiss too often worked in Germany. Lawson used the pre-war borders when Hungary, Czechoslovakia, and much of Poland (including Lwow, an active centre of this kind of research) were all part of the Austrian Empire.

1

MYSTERIOUS ATOM IN MYSTERIOUS ETHER

'I was brought up to look at the atom as a nice, hard fellow, red or grey in colour according to taste' said Rutherford once. In colonial New Zealand in the 1880s the atom of the schoolroom had not changed all that much since the days when Newton wrote that matter had probably been formed in the beginning 'in solid, massy, hard, impenetrable, movable particles', cannoning off one another in an endless cosmic snooker game. For they were 'incomparably harder than any porous bodies compounded of them; even so very hard as never to wear or break in pieces; no ordinary Power being able to divide what God himself made one in the first Creation'. These indivisible indestructible atoms were summoned in the seventeenth century from the oblivion in which they had lain since the decline of the Greek philosophy which had first posited them, and they were recalled for much the same purposes as those ancient Greeks had originally conceived them. They were to provide a model of the structure of matter which would enable us to reduce the multifarious qualitative changes of the world to the movements of bodies devoid of all qualities whatsoever save those which can be expressed geometrically. So all the variations and alterations of colour, temperature, texture and shape, growth and decay, action and reaction can be reduced to spatial ones. Behind this lies a problem that has troubled minds since the first Ionian philosophers began to query nature, if not before; what Plato called the opposition between the Same and the Different. What is it that survives unperturbed through all the manifold fluctuations and flickerings of nature? Is there some substrate that does *not* change, whose movements can explain the variety and instability that we see? The arguments of early atomic physics mark one stage in this ancient debate—but it is only a stage upon the road. Einstein's vain search for a unified field theory, which occupied much of the latter part of his life (to his friends' regret) is also part of this quest for an underlying unity, so too is the hunt for the elusive quark or some other sub-sub-particle, which will make sense and Sameness out of the excessive Difference of all our present particles.

Newton made old atomism more realistic by introducing the concepts of mass and force, in addition to size and shape which were all that his ancient predecessors had at their disposal. A hundred years after Newton, John Dalton gave fresh meaning to the atom: he showed how physical sense could be made of the new chemical elements, if it be supposed that these elements, by definition forms of matter that defeat analysis, are composed of Newton's indestructible atoms, each element having its own particular kind of atom. Then it should be possible to calculate atomic weights by relating the different weights of equal volumes of those elements. By the end of the nineteenth century an immense amount of successful work in chemistry seemed to rest upon this view of atoms, differing in weight alone, yet resisting absolutely any attempt to break them up.

Consider the Periodic System, which helped so wonderfully to impose a straightforward pattern on the confusion of elements. When Dalton's idea was first accepted, there were about three dozen elements. By 1860 the number had nearly doubled, and as the century drew on more continued to be discovered. Many chemists hoped to find some principle of classification that would reduce the variety. During the early 1860s, laws of octaves, zigzags, and spirals were proposed, to express the repetition of certain characters in groups of elements. Perhaps all had evolved from seven or eight original types, which would match in the organic world that evolution of organisms, whose laws were even then being demonstrated by Darwin and his friends. Among those influenced by such objectives was Dmitri Mendeleev, appointed Professor of Chemistry at Saint Petersburg in 1867. In his new post, he was impressed with the need for a logical system to teach his students about elements. In March 1869 he suddenly found his key, arranging them in order of atomic weight; at every eighth place there was a periodic return to the same chemical properties, particularly those forming compounds with other elements. When Mendeleev was able to predict three elements to fill gaps in his table, which were duly discovered, and possessed the weights and properties he said they should, the utility of his scheme was made obvious. Its reputation was confirmed by his insistence that the weights of some of the elements already known would have to be adjusted in order to fit; for fresh measurements were to prove his estimates right. But was this system merely useful—an aid to discovery, and an aid to memory? Since it depended on weights—and so on mass—it might make more sense if some of the heavier elements were compounds. Yet how could a certain increase of mass bring an element back into line with one much lighter? If chemistry depends on the indivisibility of elements, it must equally depend on the indivisibility of atoms, a *ne plus ultra* beyond which no man can pass.

Still, however convenient, the atom remained something of an *ad hoc* proposition. Its very existence was debated throughout the nineteenth century. By the standards of the day no one could produce direct evidence that there were any such things. They might help us picture the basic unities of nature to the mind's eye—but were they really there? A few were bold enough to argue that all such talk was but a name to cover our ignorance. Relative weights and proportions we know, so they claimed, but not the nature of these atoms, which as individuals we can never perceive. Some still hankered after a *prime matter*, and thought the larger atoms would turn out one day to be compounds of the smaller. At the outset of the century a London physician, William Prout, had proposed that all were aggregates of hydrogen, the lightest element, but his hopes were disappointed when more precise analysis showed that atomic weights could not be whole number multiples of hydrogen. Whatever might be chosen as the unit, every atomic weight involved a fraction. There might be a remote chance that some lighter form of matter would be discovered, of which hydrogen itself, and all the other elements, would prove to be constructed. So models of the atom were put forward which were more sophisticated than the kind of red or grey (i.e. black and white), billiard ball picture called up by Rutherford's recollection. The traditional view was certainly still accepted by most scientists, and taken for granted by ordinary educated people who thought they understood the world as science taught it. In their eyes atoms were 'infinitesimally small, but still finite units of matter impenetrable, indivisible and endowed with enormous energies ... floating like buoys in an ocean of ether'.[1] So Samuel Laing, ex-MP, ex-railway magnate described the atom, when in old age, in 1889, he sat down to expound his rationalist and agnostic philosophy of man and the universe. For such men, this atom was the sure foundation of material things in an uncertain world. True, he knew of alternatives, and in the end the real nature of the atom remained for him a 'problem for the future', still somewhat hard to comprehend.

But the great Maxwell, asked to explain the basic principles of physics for the *Encyclopaedia Britannica* in 1875, declared that in the atom 'we have something which has existed either from eternity or at least from times anterior to the existing order of nature'. Indeed the constant masses of each particular kind of atom, and their constant relationships with others, to form molecules, suggested to him the molecules too were permanent. No atoms are now being formed; none now break down. They neither come into being nor change their shape or size; 'till not only these worlds and systems, but the very order of nature itself is dissolved, we have no reason to expect' that fresh ones will be manufactured. No less constant were they in their vibrations, and their effects upon others. How could they be made up from random agglomerations of smaller parts, if all were so completely identical, 'like the nuts and screws of some locomotive or gun factory', as Laing put it. All the same, could atoms somehow have an internal structure which might explain the details of physics and chemistry? A handful of eccentrics thought so. By now, the number of elements had grown to over eighty. If each had its own atom, how were they distinguished? If an atom of gold is almost four times the weight of an atom of iron, and differs in that alone, is it not four times the size? Why then is it impossible to break down the gold, which can easily be imagined as split into four? Or, of course, assemble a gold atom out of those of iron ... No, said the great majority, let us dismiss such teasing notions as the fond dreams of alchemy, unsuited to this age of rational common sense.

On Thursday 2 September 1886, the Chemical section of the British Association for the Advancement of Science sat down to hear their President deliver his address. They could expect an exciting display of imagination and agility from William Crookes—editor of *Chemical News*, director of the Electric Light and Power Company, analyst of London's water supply, gold-mine owner, fertile inventor, speculative businessman, ardent Theosophist and leading member of the Society for Psychic Research. Always ready with ingenious ways to exploit theoretical discoveries, he was by far the most flamboyant character in British science. With the waxed points of his long moustachios perpendicular over his square grey beard, his very appearance was more showman or magician than sober scientist. His enterprises, like his hypotheses, often failed. Enough succeeded to give him a handsome livelihood, and even left him free to dash in where academics feared to tread. From such a president the audience could hope for fireworks; he always spoke in a blaze of florid metaphors and literary quotations from high romantic verse. They were not disappointed. As the orderly array of atomic elements had grown so very complicated, he began, might not most of them be modifications of some simpler nature? Otherwise confusion would continue to grow worse—or rather, as such a prosy statement was not in Crookes's style, 'they extend before us as stretched the wide Atlantic before the gaze of Columbus, mocking, taunting and murmuring strange riddles, which no man has yet been able to solve'. Lamentably he had no evidence that any of them had yet been transmuted to another, but still he felt sure that they were complex. Perhaps if no known elements could be added together to make up the remainder, there was some element of negative weight, possibly the 'etherial fluid', which could be subtracted when necessary. Or it may be helium, then known only in the solar spectrum, would turn out to have a weight only a fraction of that of hydrogen. Crookes looked with a kindly eye on these and similar fancies. But the nub, as he saw it, was to conceive this aggregation as an *evolution* on best Darwinian lines.

In the beginning, so his vision ran, some basic stuff existed—the 'protyle' or first matter—in an ultra-gaseous state. 'This vast sea of incandescent mist' would be indescribably hot; but then some process akin to cooling makes the scattered particles of the 'fire mist' come together. As their coherence requires energy, they must drain it from their neighbourhood, and so chill it down still further. So the protyle over long ages has gradually hardened, first into the lighter elements, successively into the heavier ones. Where they cooled slowly, these elements would be quite distinct. But when they did so rapidly, a group would be born with a close family resemblance, such as the iron–nickel–cobalt group, a little like Darwin's animal genera, for those that have

Fig. 2. William Crookes with Crookes tube.

numerous species resemble one another more than do the species of genera with few.

Crookes's prime example was the cluster of rare earths. Over the years since Mendeleev had published his table, several had been discovered. No other elements so upset its tidiness, for they just did not fit his columns properly: all were too alike; were to be found only in samples of a handful of rare minerals dug out of a few sites; and no one could guess how many there might be. Crookes himself had devoted much of his time to frustrated efforts to sort them out. Almost every year somebody claimed to have discovered a new one. Usually, he was wrong. Now Crookes could explain this as the curious effect of particularly rapid refrigeration, so these earths had not had time to become true species. The ores which contain them are 'the cosmical lumber room where elements in a state of arrested development ... are aggregated'—he means, like chemical Neanderthal men, surviving in odd corners like some Guyanese plateau of Conan Doyle's *Lost World*.

As well as the loss of heat, the formation of matter would also bear the impress of electric force, if you imagine that as you descend (in the cooling) you also move from side to side (as in a spiral staircase), swinging across a mean and so varying in magnetic and electric characteristics (more or less electropositive or electronegative in sequence along the horizontal line); having also chemical valency, or combining power of one, two, or three. One complete swing of the pendulum, out to each extremity and back again, would give you 'the elements of water, ammonia, carbonic acid, the atmosphere, plant and animal life, phosphorus for the brain, salt for the seas, clay for the solid earth ... nitrates, fluorides, sulphates ... sufficient for a world and inhabitants not so very different from what we enjoy at the present time. True, the human inhabitants would have to live in a state of more than Arcadian simplicity and the absence of calcic phosphate would be awkward as far as bone is concerned. But what a happy world it would be! No silver or gold coinage, no iron for machinery, no platinum for chemists, no copper wire for telegraphy, no zinc for batteries, no mercury for pumps, and alas! no rare earths to be separated.' These heavier elements were most prominent in recent invention, perhaps because relatively rare. A world could be made of the first sixteen elements—so perhaps the rest came after them, and derived from them? His evolutionary picture implied there might be 'pseudoelements' like Darwinian varieties—that have not achieved true elementary status. In the process of development, those which were chemically and electrically viable would absorb those immediately lighter or heavier than themselves. Then the atoms of each would not all be of the one weight, but an average of the whole class of particles whose weights were similar, but not identical. For this, he believed he had some very positive evidence. This lecture was Crookes at his most sparkling, and in its paragraphs are hidden many of the preposessions of the years to come, as yet still in embryo. Not that Crookes ever abandoned his offspring: he kept on at his great idea. Thirteen years later, he was still explaining how the '*vis generatrix* when full of primal vigour, as it swept to and fro in a universe of protyle and descended the irreversible spiral, segregated at suitable positions' along its way: first came hydrogen and all the lighter elements, until in the end 'at its lowest round with cooling temperature and failing energy, it could put forth nothing better than thorium and uranium'. He very quickly had to change his tune about the enfeebled character of the heavy elements—they packed in far more than the light ones.

But the idea of evolution from the simplest form remained in the background, only waiting its turn to step forward again.

To the student of physics another concept that took shape during the 1840s and 1850s was much more important than these atomic riddles, for it obliged us to adopt a basic change in the way we look at the universe and all that is in it. The conservation and transformation of energy and the increase of entropy—the laws of thermodynamics—have a long history, and their formation in acceptable terms involves a complicated story, one worse complicated by the bitter priority disputes in which several leading personalities engaged. Let others unravel what Helmholtz, Clausius, Mayer, Joule, Kelvin, Rankine, Carnot, Clapeyron contributed. But—whoever said so first—by 1870 it could be agreed that energy is conserved through all its transformations, so that in the processes of nature it is neither created nor passes away; mechanical energy may be translated into heat energy; heat has an exact mechanical equivalent; thus is made firm 'the connexion between the science of heat and the theorems of dynamics'. No less certain was the one-way movement of available energy. Heat cannot flow from a colder body into a hotter one, although there does not seem to be an obvious kinetic parallel to this irreversibility. While the second law of thermodynamics was acknowledged to be as true and as consequential as the first, there was more hesitation over its meaning. Electrical motion and chemical reactions were but other forms of energy, which must be equivalent too. Perhaps vital force was just another manifestation, subject to the same laws but different in its mode of operation, as the electromotive differs from the chemical.

Planck describes how the principle of the conservation of energy hit him like a revelation. The power of an absolute and universal law enthralled him. His teacher at school explained the relation between kinetic and potential energy by a little joke about a bricklayer, who strains to raise his hod of bricks to the roof of some high building, where the kinetic energy 'does not get lost; it remains stored perhaps for many years, undiminished and latent' in the structure, until in the course of time it is loosened, potential energy becomes kinetic again—it slips out and falls on the head of a passer-by. Some people have complained about the antique sound of 'potential energy'—it smacks too much, they say, of Aristotle's view of motion as the realization of a potentiality. J.J. Thomson found the concept troublesome when he learnt about the conservation of energy at Manchester in the early 1870s: 'I found the idea of kinetic energy being transformed into something of quite a different nature very perplexing'. Surely all energy is one, its transformation simply 'the transference of kinetic energy from one home to another, the effects it produces depending on the nature of its home'. As his friend Poynting put it, 'we see a pattern of many colours—one thread disappears, then one of a different hue under the surface of the cloth appears in its place—but is it really one thread which now exposes to us a different face?' Perhaps the energy laws have now become something to be learnt and utilized, something which literati ought to be made to know about. A hundred years ago they were novel, exciting, triumphant, a vision of those principles which underlie the multiformity of the world. As so often in science they also provided a fresh set of problems for the next generation to tackle.

If physics now had energy and chemists the periodic system to unify their respective disciplines, another achievement of those mid-Victorian years stretched out like a panhandle to join the territory of physics to the land of chemistry ... or at least to its gaseous provinces: the new kinetic model of gases, resting upon the application of statistics. Where it would be quite impossible to measure or observe the behaviour of any individual, general but precise ideas can be formulated about the average conduct of large numbers, which thus establish the probability of any particular set of events. By introducing this kind of statement in the 1860s, Maxwell opened a route to a new approach to physics. The kinetic theory of gases—then often called the dynamic or molecular theory—made it possible to subsume the gas laws in a general explanatory picture. Over the two centuries since Robert Boyle and his experiments on the springiness of the air, these laws had evolved so as to link in simple equations the volume of a gas to its pressure and temperature. If we now suppose gases to be composed of an immense crowd of molecules, buzzing like a swarm of bees in a box, 'in a state of intensely rapid motion in all directions ... very far apart in proportion to their size and continually coming into contact with each other', they will rebound without loss of motion, because perfectly elastic, explains A.R. Wallace, who saw this as one of the prime discoveries to be related in his book on *The wonderful century*. As a gas becomes hotter, its molecules move the faster, which increases the pressure of the bombardment. Through this doctrine it should be possible to understand the elasticity of gases and the process of their diffusion; to show how they will expand into as much space as they are permitted, spattering the walls of any body that encloses them with a continuous shower of molecular missiles; and see why two gases will mix so perfectly, even though they are of different density. From such a theory it should prove feasible to calculate the size of the molecules, their 'mean free path' between collisions (Wallace gives a value of two hundred times the diameter of the molecules, with eight thousand million collisions a second at room temperature, in every cubic inch), the number of them in a given volume, and above all their average velocity at a given temperature. Then the idea should also apply to liquids and solids. For if the evaporation of gases from liquids is effected by heating them, so as to intensify their motion, then in cooling, the busy racing about of the molecules must accordingly be stilled.

While matter was safely, if obscurely, corpuscular, that is made up of discrete units—smallest bits—light and energy were not. Indeed, the continuous passage of energy appeared to be a precondition for its transformation without loss. Since the 1820s an undulatory theory of light had held the field; there was no 'matter of light', no distinct particles of light, only ripples in a light-bearing ether (or 'aether', as it was often spelt in those days). Now 'we know that it is caused by waves or vibrations of an exceedingly elastic and imponderable medium or ether diffused through space'. Other researches showed that beside the light rays of the visible spectrum, solar radiation could also be analysed into infrared and ultraviolet rays, with wavelengths respectively longer and shorter than those of visible light. Early in the 1830s, Macedonio Melloni, an Italian political refugee living in Paris, and following him David Forbes, the Professor of Natural Philosophy at Edinburgh, showed that radiant heat can be polarized, refracted, and doubly refracted like light. At times, evidence was put forward to suggest that the different wavelengths of light journey through space at different speeds, blue perhaps slower than red. That proved mistaken: all these rays were travelling at the same speed. In a series of researches culminating in his *Treatise on electricity and magnetism* of 1873, Clerk Maxwell summed up the work of half a century by concluding that disturbances in electric or magnetic fields would be propagated through space at the same speed as light, and if the source of the disturbance were oscillatory, they would be propagated as waves, which would behave just like light waves.

Meanwhile, light proved to have its own chemistry, for each chemical element has its own light, its own spectrum. When incandescent, each shines only at wavelengths particular to itself, so that every one can be recognized by its own emission. In 1859, the physicist Kirchhoff and the chemist Bunsen, partners at Heidelberg, recognized these differences in spectra, while trying to identify salts by the variegated colours of the flames they give off when they burn. Methodically they went through a range of metals and published the spectral lines they found. Thus they could see into any compound which might defeat purely chemical analysis, and break it down into its components. This new method proved its worth in the customary manner, by the discovery of new elements whose presence was revealed by bright lines which could not be attached to any known: one line was bright red, so they called their find rubidium, the other sky-blue and so named caesium. Soon after, in 1861, young William Crookes made his scientific name by adding a third spectral element, which he called thallium, from its delicate green line, as *thallos* means a 'green shoot'; *caesios* really means a steely bluish grey— like the eyes of the goddess Athena: perhaps Kirchhoff and Bunsen mixed it up with *caeruleus*, which is the blue of heaven. Thus, any source of light would disclose its composition, however remote it was, whether the sun, a distant star, or the furthest galaxy. Not many years passed before, in 1868, unidentifiable yellow lines in the solar spectrum announced an element of which no trace could be found on earth at all, despite a careful search in likely environments such as the gases which volcanos belch forth in their eruption.

Since it apparently only existed in the sun, it was called helium, after the ancient Greek name for the sun. Conversely, each element has an absorption spectrum of black lines, which corresponds neatly to the bright ones which it emits, as Kirchhoff found when he realized that sodium blocks the sun's light in just those wavelengths in which it would itself give light out. But spectroscopy could be tricky. When Crookes thought that in a sample of one of his rare earths he found its characteristic citron-coloured band gone, and a double green line of a kindred earth in its stead, he concluded that perhaps there might be variations. At least in those elements which are so like one another, 'some atoms furnish some, other atoms others' of the lines and bands which the element as a whole displays. Indeed, this he claimed was the 'Rosetta stone' that enabled him to decipher the strange language of the rare earths, and uncover their peculiar place in his genesis story. Eventually, however, this proved to be one known rare earth masking the lines of another.

Clerk Maxwell himself had been very much concerned with the nature of light. If, as there was reason to believe, 'electromagnetic disturbances' travel at the speed of light, light must be just such a disturbance. But could this be proved? In 1888 Oliver Lodge reported that he had been 'endeavouring to manufacture light by direct electrical action without the intervention of heat', to see if Maxwell's theory had any practical consequences that way, but his efforts led nowhere. Maxwell's idea also caught the enthusiasm of Helmholtz, who hoped they would open the door to a real understanding of electricity; and in 1879, the year of Maxwell's death, he persuaded the Berlin Academy of Sciences to offer a prize for some satisfactory experimental test of the new doctrine. He wanted to encourage his brightest pupil at Berlin, Heinrich Hertz, to tackle the problem, for Hertz, who had begun as an engineering student, alone combined the experimental and mathematical skill that would be necessary. At first Hertz was dissatisfied with his results and dropped the matter, until after he moved to the Technical College at Karlsruhe in 1886. There he found more sensitive equipment which would let him induce sparks for relatively modest electric discharge. If electromagnetic phenomena were waves in the ether too, it ought to be possible to demonstrate their character by reproducing them, by making one oscillating electrical charge induce another. In the lecture hall of his department he set up his apparatus, generating the oscillations in a metal circuit with a spark gap. At some distance he placed a receiver—a hoop nearly a foot across with a corresponding smaller gap. Sure enough, little sparks leaped across the break in his wire—only faintly, so that the room had to be in darkness, and his eyes adjusted to it before they were visible, but then—unmistakable sparks.

Slowly over that winter of 1887-8, he came to see that he must find the speed of the waves. Direct measurement was impossible, but by moving his hoop around the hall, and knowing the frequency of the original oscillations, he could establish the wavelength—about nine metres—and so obtain a velocity that did indeed correspond to that of light. In a succession of further experiments, he reflected the waves off a zinc sheet which he leant against the wall; showed that reflected waves interfered with those advancing; focused them with concave mirrors; refracted them through a prism of hard pitch. A piece of tinfoil gave a shadow, blocking off the rays, so that no spark appeared. Nor did it, if his assistant walked in front of the apparatus. While electrically conducting substances barred the way, insulating ones did not. Put the hoop in another room and close the door—and to his astonishment the sparks still appeared. Wood might be opaque to light, but evidently not to these new rays. In fact, they passed through wood so freely that he did not bother to remove his prism from the wooden housing in which it had been mounted. This work in the dark must have laid great physical strain on Hertz, peering at sparks, squinting as he strove to estimate any slight increase in their size. But what matter ... the theories of Maxwell were triumphantly justified. The new 'Hertzian' waves, later called radio waves, behaved just as waves should; only their wavelengths were much greater than those of light, their frequency correspondingly less. As he himself once expressed it, electricity and light were like two kingdoms, close together and yet divided by a deep but narrow ravine. His experiments could serve as 'an arch stretching across an abyss of the unknown', or like a high Alpine pass that connects two broad valleys. The path would be slender at first, but would enable others to cross behind him and make a wide road to join the two territories, and so make both more intelligible. An enthusiastic Helmholtz wrote in congratulation, 'your latest feat concerns things at the possibilities of which I have nibbled for years in the hope of finding a hole where I could enter'. And all the time Hertz was a sick man, suffering from bone cancer, which had already attacked his jaw—during 1888, at the height of his research he had several teeth extracted in a vain attempt to stem the spread of the disease, the next year he had them all taken out.

Now waves must have a medium to carry them, as sound waves are carried in air and sea waves in water. The physicists of the 1880s and 1890s did not want to multiply media, to end up with as many ethers as there were different kinds of waves, all of them travelling at the same velocity. It was simpler to decide, as Maxwell said, that 'light consists of transverse undulations of the same medium which is the cause of electric and magnetic phenomena'. As little flashes jumped Hertz's gap, the electromagnetic-cum-lightbearing ether was as surely vindicated as the waves that must be crossing it. A decade later, in his book on the great deeds of *The wonderful century*, A.R. Wallace could explain that as 'ether appears to be the active, matter the passive agent in the constitution of the universe ... the recognition of the existence of the ether, together with the considerable knowledge we have acquired of its modes of action, must be held to constitute one of the most important intellectual triumphs of the Nineteenth Century'. Haeckel in his *Riddle of the universe*, published in the same year of 1899, boldly proclaims his conviction that 'the existence of ether as a real element is a *positive* fact', proved by the experiments of Hertz—ether is 'as certain as ponderable matter, as certain as my own existence'. Admittedly these two eminent men of science were both zoologists, a little out of their own territory in such questions. Still, most physicists would have agreed most wholeheartedly. In 1909, one of them declared that 'the ether is not a fantastic creation of the speculative philosopher; it is as essential to us as the air we breathe'. The genealogy of this all-pervading ether is clear enough: it descends almost in a pure line from the 'aethereal medium' of Sir Isaac Newton, which was 'exceedingly more rare and subtile than the Air, and exceedingly more elastick and active', which conveyed the vibrations of light and heat, could penetrate all bodies and was 'by its elastick force expanded through all the Heavens'.

This opposition between matter and ether did not leave everybody happy. As one physics professor, John Poynting of Birmingham, observed to the British Association (also in 1899) 'we dislike discontinuity and we think of an underlying identity'. As so many changes in character—expansion, evaporation, solution—could be made easily intelligible as the movements of the atoms of which they are composed, so perhaps this last qualitative barrier might come down one day. Then the dual pattern would merge into a single substance, the Two be replaced by the One. The most popular scheme was born in the 1860s. It was the child of Kelvin, begotten upon a piece of work by Helmholtz, and thus bore in its pedigree two of the most awesome minds in the science of the time, both of them already prominent among the parents of thermodynamics. This was the vortex atom; the idea that atoms are but 'revolving rings of a perfect fluid pervading the whole of space', rather like smoke rings which 'persist for a long time, glide before the knife so as to be indivisible and when two of them collide they rebound and vibrate'.

First, Helmholtz showed that if we suppose a perfectly incompressible fluid that offered no resistance, rotating vortex rings within it would be indestructible. Peter Tait, a pupil of David Forbes and his successor at Edinburgh, devised a pretty little experiment to make the point. To provide your smoke for the rings, take a wooden box, cut a circular hole in one side, and replace the opposite side with a thin rubber sheet, then sprinkle an ammonia solution over the bottom of the box. Now take a saucerful of ordinary salt, and pour a little sulphuric acid on to it. This will produce hydrochloric acid, and when the saucer is placed in the box, the acid and the gas will 'form a dense cloud of small crystals of sal-ammoniac in the air within the box'. In these words, instructions how to perform Tait's display are set out in *The theory of heat*, a physics textbook of 1894.[2] So these popular experiments, which now come into simple classroom chemistry, were so recently on the frontier of knowledge—imagined to show off a radical new theory about the nature of matter. For if you then tap the rubber sheet, a smoke ring floats out through the hole.

More rings can be produced in quick succession. They will pursue each other, pass through one another when they overtake, rebound and shudder when they meet. If the hole through which they escape is made oval or elliptical, they will even oscillate about the circular shape.

While watching Tait's demonstration in 1867, his friend Kelvin was suddenly struck with the thought that if such rings exist in the ether, they 'might well be called atoms'. They would be indivisible and eternal, ever of the same shape and volume; they would move forward in a straight line; and they could well vibrate like the oval smoke rings, as theory suggested. If tied or looped, they could account for all the connections and combinations of matter, whereby different elements come together to form stable molecules. No doubt that Age of Steam could take delight in a theory, which modelled the universe on little puffs of smoke—emitted at 'the first Creation' by some divine locomotive? Unfortunately, Tait's apparatus could hardly produce tied or looped rings. Besides, in the movements of air, which is far from a perfect, incompressible fluid, the rings soon break up. Yet the theory retained an appeal beyond any practical demonstration, since it raised the hope that the whole of science could one day be explained in terms of a single substance. Arthur Schuster, a young English student who worked with Kirchhoff in the early 1870s, found that 'man of cold temperament' warmed to rare enthusiasm when he talked of this idea.[3] 'It is a beautiful theory', he said, 'because it excludes all else'; because, as his English visitor wrote, 'it went to the very foundation of the edifice of nature'. For these atoms would not be material objects surrounded by an ether in which they float and swim, they would be *pieces of ether*. The known laws of hydrodynamics ought to explain all their movements and their combinations. In this way, so Tait and Kelvin hoped, they could escape from the constricting grasp of dualism. Physics stretched out a hand to free itself from the coil of the Twin Serpents, and make the cosmos One again. Instead of the material atoms of the dual world, all energy becomes energy of motion, all matter 'mere loci of particular types of motion in this frictionless fluid'. 'As we watch the weaving of the garment of Nature', declared Poynting, 'we resolve it in our imagination into threads of ether spangled over with beads of matter. We look still closer, and the beads of matter vanish; they are mere knots and loops in the threads of ether.'

There is something quaintly Cartesian about this colourful picture. The ghost of Descartes with his '*tourbillons*' and his '*matière subtile*' hovers surely over these interweaving ribbons: and as Newton said of Descartes' speculations about the fundamental order of nature, this theory too was 'pressed with difficulties'. How did the atoms acquire their weight—what kept them whirling and spinning about? But then, all ether theories had their difficulties, as the ether changed its shape to suit the logic of fashionable hypothesis. In the 1870s it was an elastic solid—by the 1880s it had to become an incompressible fluid so as to help out the vortex theory. Was it a jelly, absolutely rigid for rapid vibrations, yielding to slow ones? Or fibrous—like a haystack, say, or the threads in Poynting's image of a seamless garment, the atoms points of strain within it? By the last years of the century, after the discovery of the inert gases, it had become one of them, incomparably rare, subtle and independent of grosser matter. Was it perhaps as much lighter than helium as helium was lighter than argon? For the phantom of some element much lighter than the lightest known, still haunted the dreams of a science that longed for a weapon to banish all those maddening fractions of atomic weight. Yet, if the planets were moving through a universal medium that should resist them, the effect was so slight that nobody was able to perceive it. Two American physicists, Michelson and Morley, performed a famous experiment at Cleveland Ohio, in 1887, to measure officially the earth's motion as it swims through the ether, but they could find no trace of it. If the ether was in that case so unthinkably rare and elastic, could it also be rigid or fibrous? The nature of atoms remained a mystery—so did the nature of ether.

NOTES

1. Laing, S. *Problems of the future*, p. 46. Chapman and Hall, London (1889).
2. Preston, T. *The theory of heat*, pp. 77–8. Macmillan, London (1894).
3. Schuster, A. *The progress of physics 1875–1908*, p. 34. Cambridge University Press (1911).

2

WHY AT THAT TIME? WHY IN THOSE PLACES?

Now that the intellectual scenery has been set up, before the actors are introduced and the plot begins to unfold, we should first paint in a socio-economic backcloth. All too often, historians of science succumb to the temptation to depict their subjects as if they were playing on some bare Beckettian scene—isolated minds, cut off from the rest of humanity, arguing only with one another—thought reaching out unto thought—as they leave everything else hung up on a hook at the laboratory door. But why then should the play be confined to those places, those times? In fact, neither the labs nor the men, nor the problems were accidental. These revolutionary discoveries were made possible by the expansion of physics in the late nineteenth century; the rapid increase of jobs in physics—the opportunities for research had just not existed earlier. The growth of the physics profession was itself watered by the hopes of the whole community, which saw it blossoming into a Tree of Knowledge that would provide a new Industrial Revolution, even more fruitful than the first.

Over the fifty years from the 1860s to the 1914-18 war a new form of organization arrived in physics; the hierarchical research team. Through the first two centuries of modern science individuals usually worked independently. When institutions like the Royal Society and the French Académie des Sciences were founded in the seventeenth century their members had held to the ideal of co-operative labour. Occasionally such groups as the Florentine Accademia del Cimento in the 1650s or the comparative anatomists of Paris in the 1670s did briefly achieve it. If like them you mean to dissect an elephant, the work must needs be shared. After a while such efforts foundered, and the teams broke up. Sometimes personal rivalries forced them asunder. Usually it was just the difficulty of keeping everybody in the right place at the right time, if only for financial reasons. Unless some rich patron could be found (and some directing mind), those who wished to devote themselves to natural philosophy had to find a living elsewhere—in medicine, the church, or on their own lands. For all but a few teachers science was a spare-time activity, so that however much the scientists loved their studies, their occupations necessarily kept them physically apart from one another. Universities seldom had more than one or two teaching posts in the physical sciences. Even there the professors conducted their experiments by themselves, with only the help of a servant or assistant. In capital cities there were Societies where men could thresh out their ideas, and discuss the experiments which their friends had reported. In the anatomy schools collaboration was more common, but there too new discoveries were made by individuals. Ideas could be shared by correspondence, in the pages of a handful of scientific journals, or through meetings and visits, but not by working day in, day out in the same building.

The chemical laboratories of Germany set the pace for change. Even in 1820 or 1830 chemistry demanded more in the way of apparatus than other sciences and had closer connections with the world of industry. In 1824 the Grand Duke of Hesse was persuaded by Justus Liebig, the new Professor of Chemistry at his university of Giessen, that it would be worth while to fit out a proper laboratory in which he could teach the students of pharmacy. An old army barracks was commandeered for the purpose and there Liebig set up his benches, his stills, and his flasks. Almost from the start he attracted students, who could hope to be trained in the methods of independent enquiry in all branches of organic chemistry under his guidance. The professor showed the way from elementary analyses through ever more elaborate procedures; the students while with him undertook projects that suited his programme. He made them masters of the trade of research; they assisted him but thereafter could expect his help in the furtherance of their own careers. Once qualified, they spread across the German-speaking lands. Thus Liebig's department at Giessen became 'the mother laboratory of all those great laboratories which have secured for Germany the leadership in the domain of chemical research and technology'.[1] For the other states durst not be outdone. In 1852 Liebig was enticed to Munich by the promise of even more splendid lab facilities, while in the same year the Grand Duchy of Baden invited Robert Bunsen to Heidelberg, where at first he was installed in an ancient monastery. The refectory served as the main laboratory, the chapel as the store, and the cloisters were enclosed to provide additional rooms for his students to analyse their silicates and chlorides amid the ogive arches, and splash the tombstones of departed monks with their residues. In such unlikely surroundings he began to create a centre which would do for inorganic chemistry what Liebig had done for the organic side. In a few years indeed, the university rewarded him with a proper institute, lavishly equipped.

The rest of the world admired this system and tried to copy it, all the more so when in Germany new industries arose which all agreed were the offspring of university chemistry, the product of its training. Without impugning the sincerity of the state governments that laid out the money, when they professed devotion to *Kultur und Wissenschaft*, or an understandable desire for the honour that accrued from supporting science, experimental research on this scale demanded more solid returns. Liebig, Bunsen, and their peers could hardly have recruited so many students, or obtained such funds, were it not for a reputation with the general public that came from Liebig's work on agricultural chemistry, his fertilizers, his artificial milk, his meat extract;[2] or Bunsen's research into the manufacture of cast iron, and his discovery of the enormous waste of heat involved when he analysed the gases produced in the blast furnace. The men who built up the famous German dyestuffs and pharmaceutical industries had been instructed by Liebig: metallurgy owed as much to Bunsen. The next generation gave Germany primacy in explosives. Scientists came to trail an aura of popular enthusiasm granted in our century only to footballers and film stars. Calls to a new post were accompanied by pressure, jockeying, letters from Important Personages, and assurances of what were then held to be huge sums of money for their equipment. Bunsen embodied the image of the sociable but unassuming absent-minded professor whose theoretical research had quietly transformed an industry. When in 1869 he was badly hurt in an explosion in his laboratory, and it was feared he would be blinded, the whole town gathered in the square beneath his window. When the doctor announced from a balcony that the great chemist's sight was saved, 'the air was rent with huzzas, caps went up, men embraced each other, women wept'.[2]

From chemistry the hierarchical team spread to medicine, and infused a physiology that hoped to reduce the workings of the animal body to mechanisms which the sciences of non-living matter could explain. Physics however lagged behind. For the first sixty years of the nineteenth century great achievements in understanding the nature of heat and in optics were still made by amateurs, men outside the academic world like Joule or Mayer, men who certainly did not make a living from their research and worked essentially as their predecessors had done, by themselves and at home. Even those who were employed to make scientific discoveries were hardly less independent. Faraday laid the foundations of electromagnetic science in a converted basement kitchen with an ex-soldier as his only assistant.

True, at Göttingen Wilhem Weber had a teaching laboratory where in collaboration with the astronomer Gauss he devised the first effective electric telegraph in 1833. However, the telegraph industry did not spring from their invention, whose commercial development was only undertaken some years later in Britain and the USA. Meanwhile, after twelve years' absence from Göttingen (owing to a slight unpleasantness with the ruling house of Hanover) Weber returned in 1849 to work on the definition of electrical units. When Schuster visited him, the physics lab was a very modest affair: there was only one other research student. Admittedly that was twenty years on, and Weber was an old man, no longer a leader in science. But his establishment had never really bred physicists as Liebig and Bunsen bred chemists. At Heidelberg, Kirchhoff had a little room available for research students, but there was barely space to squeeze in two of them. If ever he had three at a time, the third was obliged to set up his apparatus in a corner of the lecture-room.

Then in the latter part of the century physics leapt forward. Historians

Fig. 3. Helmholtz, the young lion.

have conveniently dated the beginning of the upsurge from Hermann Helmholtz's move to Berlin in 1871. Is it strange that a new post for a single
professor could carry such weight? By then, Helmholtz already had a fame
which vied with Bunsen's. Now he proposed not only to transfer to a new
chair but to change to another science. He was trained as a medical man.
When he delivered his paper on 'The conservation of force' in 1847 he was
still an army surgeon attached to the Potsdam garrison, and his main objective
was to understand the bodily activities of animals within a system of energy
exchanges of purely physical character. Over the next twenty years through
his experiments he provided a 'mechanist' explanation for our aural perception of tone and our visual perception of colour. Only occasionally did he go
back to mechanics in the narrow sense, as in his mathematical investigation
of the behaviour of vortices in 1859, on which Kelvin based his theory of the
structure of matter. While still a physiologist (but now a Heidelberg professor)
in the 1860s, he became convinced that chemistry and physiology now demanded that basic science of matter and motion catch up with them. In 1871
the new German Empire was inaugurated; its rulers were determined that the
imperial capital should be the capital of science and culture too. Berlin must
dwarf all that had gone before. Although the new Reich did not put the older
centres of excellence directly under Prussian control, henceforward Berlin
was to have an unfair advantage over the rest. Talent was to be invited from

Fig. 4. Helmholtz, the *grand seigneur* of German physical science.

such places as Heidelberg and Göttingen, which suffered in consequence. The needs of Kaiser and of physics—and Helmholtz—happily coincided. Like Bunsen, Helmholtz had to wait a few years before the Institute of Physics was completed to his requirements, but he soon had more than a dozen research students and before the end of the decade he had the grandest establishment that money could buy. According to Schuster, the atmosphere was livelier in Helmholtz's first years at Berlin, before the team became a somewhat impersonal factory of physics. Yet for the next sixty years every major German physicist aimed to go there; most of them arrived sooner or later. Helmholtz even looked the part of a dignified emperor of science. All those who knew him speak of his kindly and courteous manner, but they also remark on his Olympian air: 'there was always a good deal of the *grand seigneur* in his attitude'. Once he had been a nervous young lion cub who had savaged the romantic vitalist view of living Nature (to which his own father was so deeply attached) and put in its place a mechanist model of life and of our senses, as uncompromising as it was revolutionary. Now he had himself become the lord of a pride of lions, a tolerant but unquestioned patriarch.

Many years ago a table was drawn up to show the increase of 'discoveries in heat, light, electricity and magnetism' in the nineteenth century in the three most active territories, Britain, France, and Germany.[3]

In the first five years of the century there were supposedly 74. As the years went by, the number crept up gradually, with occasional spurts. In the four periods of five years between 1850 and 1870, the average was 219, never more than five below or ten above. Then in the first quinquennium of the 1870s, it was 292, in the second 421, and so on by leaps and bounds, until in the last quinquennium of the old century the number had reached 917. And the expansion was mainly German. First passing the hundred mark in 1851–5, in 1866–70 this had stepped up to 136. The next five years present the same figure, curiously; but the next after that, 213; then 286, 419, and in 1896–1900, 525, more than five times what it had been fifty years earlier, and far more than Britain and France combined.

Of course it is not really possible to quantify discoveries like this, because the increase in the number of jobs and papers will not lead automatically to an increase in worthwhile knowledge. Some were of crucial importance, others trivial. In this present century the ratio of minor factual discoveries to those which alter our way of thinking must have grown worse: more and more discoveries, but an ever higher proportion of them of no great matter. Presumably the increase in discovery is a function of the increase in scientists—and so too the relative increase in the less important. For the hierarchical team implies a pyramid; more lecturers than professors, more research students than lecturers. Competition is intensified, and those who wish to make their way up the ladder must prove themselves by a piece of original research: it has to be original even if not very significant, since the main point is to convince the professor and his fellows of the researcher's ability to find out *something*. Early work is the masterpiece with which you earn the right to dine with your masters. But if every lecturer is to have research students as well as the professor? And if every research student is expected to end up a professor himself, or at least halfway up the ladder? So the pyramid implies continual expansion; and if one field of science becomes overcrowded, new ones will have to be opened up ... or new universities will have to be set up ... or if there are not going to be students enough to teach, special research institutes will take their place.

In fact the number of university students did grow rapidly and doubled in the first twenty years of the Second Reich. If the rate of expansion then slowed down, the original figure had still trebled by 1910. Most dramatic development was to be seen in Berlin university, which was set up in 1818 and grew throughout the century at the expense of older places. Only Vienna and Munich (as chief city of the south) were able to keep up—at Munich the university was also quite young, having been established there in 1826. New chairs were set up in physics, now split into theoretical and experimental branches. A new discipline called physical chemistry linked physics to the older laboratory science; by the turn of the century there were five departments in that too, not to mention a journal in which to publish their results.

While Liebig was preparing to start up in Giessen, the Grand Duchy of Baden created at Karlsruhe in 1826 a *Polytechnische Schule*, to teach technology at higher level, organized in imitation of the French *École Polytechnique*. Unlike centralized France, once this *Technische Hochschule* (as it was re-named) had proved a success, rivals sprang up across south Germany, in Stuttgart, Munich, and beyond. Switzerland was understandably among the first beyond the borders of the German Confederacy. In 1855 a Federal Polytechnic was opened at Zurich with Clausius as Professor of Mathematical Physics. Many other Germans of note taught or studied there, including Einstein; the language linked it to the German network, while a more liberal atmosphere prevailed than in Imperial Germany. Everywhere, especially after 1870, technical colleges were organized on German lines, as supposedly they had been the mainspring of industrial power and military success. At Paris, the city council set up in 1882 its own École de Physique et Chimie Industrielles, where Pierre Curie was to teach. The motives for these establishments were not concealed. When the British Royal Commission on Technical Education visited the trade school at Rouen in 1883, they were surprised to see a Prussian helmet prominently displayed. The headmaster explained that he had picked it up in the street after the German army marched through. Whenever his boys were slacking at their work, he laid it on his desk to remind them of what had been and might be again; 'it never fails to rouse their patriotism and their zeal for their studies'.

The German technical colleges, which already had an international reputation and a status in the public mind hardly below that of the older universities, gained in 1899 the right to grant degrees (sixty years before British colleges of advanced technology acquired that privilege). Before that, in 1887 Helmholtz and his industrialist friend and in-law, the electrical engineer Von Siemens, persuaded the government to supplement Berlin's university science with a central national laboratory for precision work in advanced physics and physical technology, known as the Physikalisch-Technische Reichsanstalt, with Helmholtz himself in command.

For Britain, it was the International Exhibition at Paris in 1867 which first alarmed a few far-sighted manufacturers and engineers. The Motherland of the Industrial Revolution was being overtaken by her daughters. Three years later the Franco-Prussian War really frightened a ruling class which had always preferred to leave industry to its own affairs and refused to waste taxpayers' money on paying people to do things (like scientific research), which they ought to be prepared to do at their own expense. However, if this newly united German Empire was to acquire not only economic but also military pre-eminence ... so there was a flurry like that in the USA after Sputnik. What the few had begged for over many years now came to them in a rush. A Royal Commission is the standard British answer to every crisis—among them in this case the Devonshire Commission on Scientific Instruction. First of all, it proposed a state laboratory—which did not come into being for more than twenty years. Still, the government did agree to grant a few thousand pounds a year to endow research. Experimental physics and chemistry became respectable subjects for higher education. Physics especially was a new territory ripe to be opened up. In response to the commission's recommendation, Cambridge University (whose cancellor was its chairman) acquired a first-rate laboratory for experimental physics, the Cavendish, officially opened in 1875 with Maxwell as professor in charge. Oxford had had a Professor of Experimental Philosophy since 1865, and with him the beginnings of the Clarendon laboratory. Still, the most enthusiastic Oxford man can hardly claim any true equality between Cavendish and Clarendon before the Great War. In fact, although the most famous, the Cavendish was the last of no less than *nine* physical laboratories founded in the UK between 1867 and 1875.

The first of England's redbrick universities in embryo, Owens College at Manchester, was born in 1851, the year of the Great Exhibition, and no less significantly in a house where Cobden the Free Trade hero had lived. But it was a sickly infant and for fifteen years had quite a struggle to keep alive. Only in the late 1860s did it pick up and was soon booming, so that in 1872 the College moved to a new site on Oxford Road where it still stands. By that year the Principal could report to the Devonshire Commission that Owens had more science students than either Oxford or Cambridge. The staff was of high calibre; such men as Osborne Reynolds, the first professor of engineering in England, and for Physics Balfour Stewart. In 1871 the Armstrong College of Science was founded at Newcastle. The next year Wales had a university college at Aberystwyth. In 1875 the Yorkshire College of Science followed at Leeds, then further south Mason's Science College at Birmingham. These last will reappear in our story only after they have at last been crowned with full university rank and status (except for boat racing purposes). All had a distinct bias toward science and technology; they were to be 'Universities of the Busy', declared a Manchester professor of chemistry, in contrast to Oxford and Cambridge which would remain 'Universities of the Wealthy'. (He was too polite to say, 'of the idle rich'.) The old Scottish universities had long been more favourable to science; Glasgow had the first physics lab in Britain set up in 1850, albeit very parsimoniously in a wine cellar converted by Kelvin; the new physics departments in England were perforce manned with Scottish teachers. When the United Kingdom leapt forward eagerly into the Industrial Revolution, only one of its seven universities was situated in one of the new boom towns; it is appropriate that two British scientists, Kelvin and Rankine, who contributed most to the new thermodynamics should have been professors at that university, with which James Watt himself had been connected when he invented the steam engine's separate condenser. Edinburgh naturally could not be left behind. The greatest of them all, James Clerk Maxwell, born and educated at Edinburgh, taught for a while at another Scots university, Aberdeen, and then at King's College London before retiring to his estate in Galloway. There he could write his *Treatise on electricity and magnetism.* From there he was lured away to Cambridge in 1871, to be its first professor of experimental physics. Kelvin himself was three times invited to take the new chair, and three times refused. The ancient English universities were unwilling to yield their intellectual primacy so easily. In their early stages all the new establishments often taught boys quite young so that the brightest among them might well go on afterwards to Oxford or Cambridge. Meanwhile, even the ablest products of Scottish universities, men like Kelvin, Maxwell, and Tait, had to go south to Cambridge to perfect themselves in mathematics. Apart from historical memories of Newton only that tradition of mathematical excellence prepared the ground there for a great physics school.

It would be wrong to limit this survey to the United Kingdom. However far away, the Old Dominions were still more of a home from home than they are today. A much higher proportion of their inhabitants were first or second generation; they were not yet so much Canadian, Australian, or New Zealander, more like colonial English Scots or Irish. An Imperial university post was a post on the British circuit, so it would be quite natural for a Bragg to take his first appointment in Adelaide, Rutherford his in Montreal. The British Association began to meet across the Ocean; in 1884 at Montreal, in 1897 at Toronto, in South Africa in 1901, then back to Canada, this time Winnipeg in 1909. As its President, J.J. Thomson proclaimed on the last of these occasions, they served not only to promote science, but also 'to strengthen the bonds which bind together the different portions of the King's Dominions'.

Silly as it would be to apply a crude reductionism to this academic expansion—the sociological pressure to create more jobs cannot explain the inner motives of scientists, still less why some were outstanding talents and others not—obviously those discoveries which required teamwork, like most radioactivity and X-ray studies, could not have been made unless there had been the employment to keep the members of the team together. In that sense the great progress made in the 1890s, and in the years before the Great War, was the first fruits of the fine trees which had been planted in the 1870s. There could have been trees without fruit, or sour fruit—but, no trees, no fruit. Why were the trees put in? Not certainly, in expectation of another scientific revolution. On the contrary, people were confident that recent knowledge was positive and decisive. The prime motives which led states to invest money in physics in the last quarter of the nineteenth century can be summed up in two words: energy and electricity.

The laws of thermodynamics had been grasped; the universality of energy, the protean forms of its interchanges, mechanical, thermal, chemical, electrical, offered vast possibilities of greater simplicity and efficiency. Smaller engines, engines burning their fuel internally, electric motors, which would be cleaner and less cumbersome than steam engines—now it became clear how much heat and energy conventional engines wasted. Even if Otto, Langen, Daimler, the inventors of the internal combustion engine, were not themselves scientists, they were advised along their route by a technical college professor, Reuleaux, an outstanding theoretician of machine design. Indeed, they would not have got very far without an appreciation of the relation between heat, pressure, and mechanical action learnt from the work of physicists during their college studies. Langen and Benz were graduates of the original Karlsruhe Technische Hochschule, while Daimler went to the one at Stuttgart nearby. The internal combustion engine was itself a child of the 1870s—Otto's four-stroke cycle was patented in 1876. Within a few years it was chugging away in the first 'horseless carriages', designed by Daimler and Benz. Soon after the turn of the century a similar engine was powering the first heavier-than-air flights. In the late 1870s Rudolf Diesel was inspired by the lectures on thermodynamics he heard at the Munich technical college to conceive a rational heat engine, based on the principle of ignition under high compression. Diesel's teacher Karl von Linde himself applied his theoretical knowledge of thermodynamics to the invention of refrigerators, and was to employ Diesel as his plant manager. Now those who set up new departments of experimental physics in the 1870s did not imagine that cars and aeroplanes would follow so soon, but they were certainly convinced that industrial might and wealth must flow from a fuller understanding of the principles of energy.

The goddess Electricity had already begun to pour even more wonderful presents from her magnificent cornucopia. Her cleanliness and speed and portability aroused great expectations that the age of steam would soon be left behind. In the 1840s the telegraph had fulfilled an ancient dream: for it offered virtually instantaneous communication across oceans and continents. In the 1850s and 1860s arc-light promised illumination brighter than a hundred candles at the flick of a switch. Meanwhile, dynamos were developed to supply enough current to carry the burden of all the new appliances. Soon in a burst of invention came the telephone in 1876 (partly derived from Helmholtz's experiments on acoustics and the electrically motivated reproduction of sound); then incandescent filament lights in 1879. Telephone and illumination gave the impetus for a real electrical industry. Scientists like Crookes were happy to do their share—he took out some patents of his own on new kinds of electric lamp bulb. In 1882 the first power-stations were erected by Edison and Swan at Pearl Street in New York and at Holborn

Viaduct in London to supply their customers. So the benefits of power on tap were spread from city to city. Nothing so beautifully embodied the aspirations of the new age. But could not the same force drive electric motors for a multitude of uses? 'The eager strife of inventors to supersede steam by electric transmission of power' excited the newspapers. The miseries of the old Industrial Revolution would soon be swept aside, since electrification did not require the concentration of machinery in factories, did not demand massive capitalization, would not pollute (except in the vicinity of power-stations), took up less space, needed no trains or trucks to move it about, but only slender wires. Early generators were steam powered, but gravity could well provide a source of energy by the agency of wind, tide, and waterfall. In the same year as Edison's light, 1879, the goddess stepped modestly into the realm of transport, when Siemens demonstrated a little electric train at the Berlin Industrial exhibition. Two years later he had a regular public tram service running on the outskirts of the city, albeit the Prussian authorities restricted his dangerous new device to 9 miles an hour.

Enthusiasm blazed like an arc-light, culminating in the first International Electrical exhibition at Paris in September 1881. There was a 'vast array of switches, fuses, cut-outs' recalled the engineer Campbell Swinton ... on his way there he found the port of Le Havre lit up by electrical Jablochkoff candles. In Paris a huge crowd marvelled at the display. Edison had a room to himself for all his inventions ... *Nature* reported on the wonders, lights that could be extinguished in a moment and re-lit in a moment ... searchlights whose 'Beams were thrown like comets' tails in all directions.' Siemens's firm ran their electric tram from the Place de la Concorde a quarter of a mile to the main gate of the exhibition hall. The favourite attraction was a telephone gallery connected to the Théâtre de l'Opéra—pick up the receiver and you could hear the arias straight from the stage, more clearly than if you were sitting in the auditorium. A model lighthouse and theatre showed what electric light could do: 'an electric boat plied on the ornamental basin, an electric balloon was propelled through the air, and machines put in motion by electric current' sawed, hammered, fanned, pumped. Exhibitors, scientists, and privileged members of the public brought the exhibition to a glorious close with a gala evening at the opera, which ended in a grand chorus that invited the world to light up on electricity. In quick succession other cities followed suit—at the Crystal Palace in London the next winter, then Munich, Vienna, St Petersburg. Each had its own special attraction—a giant candelabrum in the form of a bouquet of brilliantly coloured flowers—or a telephone which conveyed the music of a café orchestra to a loudspeaker audible to people listening in the main hall of another building. In a short while, these exhibitions proclaimed, a marvellously clean, new, equal, gleaming, well-lit world would come into being; and banish soot, and chimneys, and ancient ghosts of every kind.

But not quite yet. A range of problems had still to be answered, and not only industrial ones, such as whether direct or alternating current should be used. An international system of electrical units would have to be agreed. Since 1862 a committee of the British Association for the Advancement of Science had discussed first the appropriate unit of electrical resistance, then a complete array of units. A parallel series derived from the work of Weber was proposed in Germany. At the Paris exhibition a congress was held at which the two parties could thrash it out entirely in French, to ensure that British and German alike wasted no words. Kelvin, who had sat on the British Association committee, led the British party, Helmholtz the German. The two of them were already personal friends, and national sentiments did not prevent agreement on a modified version of the British scheme, defining ohms, volts, amps, and other familiar measures. Since Weber's time there had been question of the true relationship between the electrostatic unit of electric charge, and the electromagnetic unit. When Lord Rayleigh took over the Cavendish on Maxwell's death, in 1879, he was anxious to organize Cavendish research on a larger scale, and involve undergraduates in the use of the laboratory. Schuster was among those drawn into his plan to measure the ohm more accurately; others were appointed to establish the ratio of the units. The electromagnetic one is a current; in order to establish the ratio, the discharge of a very large number of electrostatic units through a given length must be measured. More than once, measurements had indicated that the rapidity was so great that if the time were one second, the length would be somewhat over three hundred metres. It was therefore necessary to accumulate a huge number of electrostatic units, and measure lengths, times, and electrostatic quantity with great accuracy. Now this velocity looks remarkably like the speed of light, and so, other considerations apart, may provide a convenient test for Maxwell's ideas of light as electromagnetic radiation. When in 1883 Helmholtz drew up a memorandum to outline the programme of what was later to be his Physikalisch-Technische Reichsanstalt, he stressed the importance of this ratio and its correspondence to the speed of light; 'we seem hereby to acquire a clue to the mysterious aspects of electromagnetic phenomena which probably may lead us to their deepest foundation'.

Several enquirers now began to ask themselves whether there might not be natural fundamental units of electricity, whose value would be one of the basic constants of the universe, as the velocity of light seemed to be. Faraday and Weber had both toyed with the idea of atoms of electricity, but hesitantly. A bolder advocate was Johnstone Stoney, secretary of the federal Queen's University of Ireland, and like Kelvin a member of the BA committee.[4] He was keen to find a basis for all units which would not be arbitrary. Those of length and mass we feel to be somehow primary and natural, yet our units of these are necessarily artificial, for there is no least conceivable distance, whereas in electricity there might be a smallest possible quantity. Faraday had shown that in electrolysis—the electrical decomposition of compounds—a definite amount of electricity passes, in definite proportion to the quantities of the two components thus set free. Presumably each molecule was held together by such an atom of electricity, which was released when the molecule was broken up: 'a certain quantity of electricity traverses the electrolyte which is the same in all cases', Stoney declared. These least units he named 'electrines'— those of other quantities were similarly styled, 'timine', 'lengthine', etc. Perhaps, it has been suggested, he intended the old Irish diminutive '-een' (as in colleen), so they would be electreens, but thought he had better dress his units in a more refined French costume, to avoid Anglo-Saxon smiles. Although he gave his ideas publicity at the British Association meeting at Belfast in 1874, they made little impression. Probably his audience was put off by their association with his bizarre nomenclature. 'Electreens' might well have a rakish sound to them, especially as electricity was supposed to be imponderable—could a substance without mass be composed of particles? In any case the association of the continuity of an electric fluid or two fluids, or of strain in the all-pervading ether made far more sense to most of those interested. But Stoney's idea was soon to be repeated in a much more prestigious voice.

Since his arrival in Berlin, Helmholtz had become increasingly concerned with the problems of electrodynamics—in the late 1870s it was so obviously the thing to do: utility and 'deepest foundations' of nature happily combined. In the spring of 1881, before the Paris Exhibition, he went on a tour of Britain. The Society of Telegraph Engineers received him at University College, London, where 'the large library and entrance hall will be lit up by electric light and there will be a full display of all the recent novelties in electrical science'. He was also due to lecture to the Chemical Society at the Royal Institution—their annual Faraday lecture. Since the previous autumn, he had felt that his interests were tending in a direction that could resume some of Faraday's investigations. Always very sensitive about anything that might lay him open to attack, and aware that he was about to say something radical and controversial, he was extremely worried about the reaction. His nervousness was evidently communicated to his wife, who told him at breakfast that she had felt so tense during the night that she feared she was going to die. 'It doesn't go so fast', he replied.

In the event, his speech was a triumph. He considered it appropriate before such an audience to talk about the chemical aspect of electricity. Going back to Faraday, he maintained that 'a definite quantity of either positive or negative electricity moves always with each electrically charged particle, if it be the particle of a univalent element'—one which can combine with one other—two, three, or four such quantities if the element could combine with two, three, or four. If the elements are made up of atoms, then electricity in the electrolyte, as presumably in all batteries which depend on comparable movements must likewise be made up of 'definite elementary portions, which behave like atoms of electricity'. The positive and negative atoms would attract one another, and that would explain the electronegative series which earlier generations of chemists had established. Chemical affinities could thus be brought under the heading of electrical bonding. That idea had appealed to Faraday, but he lacked the evidence Helmholtz could now marshal in its favour. Then he reminded his audience how the energy equations could be applied to the interchangeability of electrical and chemical operations, and the heat produced by them. The correspondence of 'electromotive force', the chemical action (the dissolution of each molecule), and the heat produced in consequence confirmed the association of chemical valency with electric action. The lecture was received with great applause. From then on, atoms of electricity were respectable topics of enquiry. But were they themselves atoms of 'ponderable matter'? That was another question. If they were not, they might attach pieces of solid matter to one another, but—how could they themselves be attached? Because of this uncertainty perhaps, neither Helmholtz himself nor any of his colleagues followed up his idea, which remained in the realm of ingenious, plausible but not very useful speculation. Crookes was attracted, naturally: he cites the key passages from both Stoney and Helmholtz in his 1886 Atomic Evolution extravaganza.

When the issue came to life again in the 1890s, Helmholtz was ascribed the honour of being its first progenitor. Poor Stoney then had to write and remind the world of science that he had used the same evidence of electrolysis to propose a natural least unit of electricity years before. In 1891 he returned to the fray, addressing his colleagues at the Royal Dublin Society on his electrical atoms, which might produce the lines of spectroscopy, as they turned about the ponderable atoms in elliptical orbits. Now he had a new name for his unit—he called it an 'electron'.

NOTES

1. Paulsen, Friedrich *German universities*, p. 58. Longmans Green, London (1902) [English translation 1906.]
2. Letter from T.E. Thorpe to H.E. Roscoe quoted in *The life and experiences of Sir Henry Enfield Roscoe written by himself*, p. 48. Macmillan, London (1906).
3. Rainoff, J.J. Wave-like fluctuations of creative productivity in the development of West European physics in the eighteenth and nineteenth centuries. *Isis* **XII** (1929).
4. O'Hara, J.G. George Johnstone Stoney, F.R.S. and the concept of the electron. *Notes Rec. R. Soc., Lond.* **XXIX** (1925).

3

CONTROVERSY OVER THE CATHODE

If the complacent could feel that now Hertz had confirmed Maxwell, all major problems were solved and the laws of physics covered all contingencies, practising physicists knew how many awkward manifestations of nature still refused to sit down quietly in any of the little boxes provided. One of them was the mysterious cathode ray.

Our air is not normally electrically conducting, nor are gases in general. But as gas is exhausted from a tube, until only a residue is left, it loses this inhospitable character. Then a discharge of electricity will make it glow in splendid colours, each type of gas with its own delicate shade. As the pressure drops, a dark gap first noticed by Faraday appears, and divides the glow about the positive anode from the weaker, more velvety 'negative glow' about the cathode. As it drops still further, until it is not much more than one thousandth of atmospheric pressure, another dark space intervenes between the cathode and its irradiated gas. These changes seemed promising, as well as puzzling. They might help to explore further the mysterious connections between light and electricity. For a while, however, not much was achieved. To obtain a vacuum, the only method was to pump out the air or other gas with an air pump. Many of the seventeenth-century founding fathers of classical physics and chemistry, Guericke, Boyle, Hooke, Huyghens, spent much time and energy in the development of this instrument: Francis Hauksbee, who succeeded Hooke as Curator and demonstrator of experiments to the Royal Society, so perfected their design that really there were no striking improvements for 150 years thereafter. Faraday used one—it can still be seen in the cellar he occupied at the Royal Institution—which differed only in detail from Hauksbee's.

Only when this antiquated instrument had been replaced by a revolutionary new device, could progress resume. The change began in one of the new 'physical cabinets'—a modest name for what were to become laboratories— at the young German university of Bonn. If a story must start at a particular date, perhaps it should be 1852, when Henrich Geissler, master glassblower, descended from a long line of craftsmen in glass, settled in Bonn, after the customary years of apprenticeship and wandering. There he was to develop instruments of a precision to befit new standards in university research. His thermometers were accepted as standards for heat measurement, but he invented practical devices too, such as his vaporimeters for testing the alcoholic strength of wine. During these same years another German craftsman, Daniel Ruhmkorff, who had set up shop in Paris in 1855 to supply the growing need for electrical instruments, invented first an 'electrical egg'—a bulb in which the electrical discharge through rarefied gases could be studied—and then an induction coil which gave far stronger sparks than any older machine, up to a foot long. With the aid of Ruhmkorff's coil, Geissler proposed a much more efficient device than the egg, one in which platinum electrodes would actually be fused into the glass of the tube. Only a man with the delicacy of touch he had shown with his thermometers could dare to try. But he succeeded: and 'Geissler tubes' were the favourite apparatus for many years of electrical research. And yet—if he could not exhaust the glass tubes more thoroughly than the old eggs, what advantages would there be in a better seal? For an answer Geissler went back beyond piston operation of the air-pump to the mercury column which Torricelli had used in 1644 to create an artificial vacuum even before Guericke ... With these mercury pumps he could force out far more of the residual gas, down to the merest fraction of atmospheric pressure.

With the new tubes, Julius Plücker, the local Professor of Physics at Bonn, decided in 1857 to look into what would happen if you sent an electric charge through this highly attenuated gas, while the tube was placed between the poles of a strong horseshoe magnet. What more natural than such a thought—as he explained to the Rhineland Society of Scientists, whom he hardly need remind of all that had flowed from Oersted's original observation of the reciprocal effects of magnetic field and electric current. That the stream of illuminated gas would be diverted did not surprise him. But he *was* surprised to see the 'diffuse violet light collected to a horizontal, half moon-shaped brightly lit disc ... surrounded by a beautiful bright light which followed the curvature of the glass'. This green light must be some kind of fluorescence in the wall of the tube itself. At the same time a curious flicker 'like an atmosphere' enveloped the cathode. His experiments were taken up some years later, by his former student Johann Hittorf. He concentrated on this strange patch of light on the glass, faint at first, but more brilliant as the pressure dropped. 'A beam of nearly parallel rays of glow', he decided, 'spread out from the cathode, and is the source of this fluorescence.' For a long time these two were alone in paying attention, while the rest of the scientific world saw little reason to find anything exceptional or exciting in one more side effect of electricity.

In any case, the fluorescence on the glass, like the dark space at the cathode, was hard to obtain. Even with Geissler's pumps it took hours of hard work at the lever to exhaust that far. The many coloured glories of the light inside the tube, given off by the residual gas, seemed far more important, for every gas, elementary or compound, produced a different hue; would this not prove a

Fig. 5. Induction coil and battery—a mid-nineteenth-century view of this essential electrical equipment.

new way to use electricity for illumination? Geissler expended his skill as a glassblower in making strange spirals and twists of tubes, bulbs were connected by narrow pipes to display marvellous combinations of reds, greens, mauves, yellows. He even gave his tubes the shape of letters—his English agents could offer a patriotic demonstration with 'V R' lit up in green and red.

'Mr Ladd', it was announced, 'from whom they may all be procured is constantly receiving new accessions from Germany.' Gassiot, an amateur enthusiast, designed a way of mounting three tubes on a stand so that they could be twirled round, as 'Gassiot's revolving star'. The technician delighted his public with strange and lovely luminous effects. The scientist investigated the colours given by various mixtures, as the discharge could obviously serve analysis as a new kind of spectroscope. Hittorf's own interest lay chiefly in such hopes.

In the early 1860s Geissler's method was improved by another German instrument-maker, who sought his fortune abroad. Sprengel's background was in chemistry, and he came to Oxford as a young man to introduce the lab methods of Bunsen, for whom he had worked. Eventually he turned to the more profitable trade of explosives expert. In 1865 while working in the laboratory of the Royal College of Chemistry he developed an improved Geissler pump, in which the mercury could be raised mechanically to a reservoir from which it dripped steadily drawing bubbles of gas from the tube between drops. Curiously enough his device goes still further back in history than Geissler's, for it is said to have been inspired by Sprengel's interest in the long history of entertaining devices which suck in or compress air under a water column—here replaced by a mercury column. Hard though they might be to work, such instruments did at least enable experimenters to drag out of their tubes very much more of the air or other gas than had been possible before, reducing the residue to as little as three thousandths of atmospheric pressure. Meanwhile batteries were being improved and now gave a much stronger discharge than Ruhmkorff's coil. Novel combinations of elements were tried, cells were aggregated in their hundreds. Apart from Hittorf, however, those who first exploited these technical refinements were seldom the new German professional physicists, but the last generation of the old style English amateurs, before professionalism took over here too: such as Gassiot, a wine merchant; Moulton a young lawyer; Spottiswoode and De La Rue, prominent members of the printing and stationery businesses that bear their names.

It was one of these who made the next discovery. Cromwell Fleetwood Varley—he claimed descent from Oliver Cromwell and his general Fleet-wood—was one of the new breed of telegraph engineer, and had been an active research worker in the development of submarine cables. He now found himself semi-retired, when in February 1870 the government in effect nationalized the private telegraph companies. That summer Varley, eager to break fresh ground, demonstrated a predecessor of the telephone—his 'cy-maphen', whereby a tune played in a music hall near Westminster Bridge could be heard in the Queen's Theatre in Long Acre, several hundred yards away. Did he fancy some new form of signal when he then began to investigate the discharge through rarefied gases? Or was he simply employing his time gainfully, on the principle of 'let us see what will happen'? Plücker had observed that the luminous glow inside the tube could be distorted into an arch when subjected to a magnetic field. Varley inserted in his Geissler tube 'a piece of talc bent into the form of a U', and crossed by a silk thread, on which he stuck 'a thin strip of talc, 1 inch in length, $\frac{1}{10}$ of an inch broad, weighing about $\frac{1}{10}$ of a grain'. When he got the magnet to turn the arch against his 'little talc tell-tale', it was quite clearly pushed back—if the lower part of the arch could be brought into play, by as much as 20°. And where the arch actually struck the bob of talc 'a little bright luminous cloud' appeared. From these effects he decided that the glow radiating from the cathode was 'composed of *attenuated particles of matter projected* from the negative pole by electricity in all directions'—not that the electric discharge was making the particles of gas left in the tube hit the talc but rather something, as attenuated as the gas, was actually coming off the cathode itself. When it struck the talc it presumably condensed, and the talc was thrust back as if in a wind. The same cause would make the glass fluoresce too when that something impacted against it.

These desultory attacks on the question, in which the most perceptive insights were thrown out casually, and then ignored altogether for years, gave way to intense interest from the mid-1870s on, nearly twenty years after Plücker's original observation. Everything about electricity now looked exciting. A dramatic intervention by a bold and imaginative thinker was needed to put Hittorf's 'beam of nearly parallel rays of glow' into the centre of the stage. Who could that be but William Crookes? He was never afraid to range out to the borders of knowledge, to carry out imaginative experiments, and force them on the attention of the more timorous citizens of the learned world. Yet he came to cathode rays not by way of a sudden raid on fashionable territory, but simply proceeding out of his old chemistry of the elements, step by step. Through the 1860s he had been trying to establish as accurately as possible the atomic weight of his new element, thallium. In the course of his slow and tedious investigations, he tried to compare the weights in air and in a vacuum. The results seemed to him to vary when the glass bulb containing his sample was hotter than room temperature. So long as there was air in the bulb, that could easily be explained, as his scales might well be disturbed by convection currents. But if it still happened in a vacuum, there could be no convection. Further investigation through 1873 suggested to him that a heavy metal body, or a pipe warmed by hot water flowing through it, would attract a little weight inside an exhausted tube when colder than the weight, and repel it if hotter. He tested this by suspending pithballs from balanced rods so as to register the slightest tendency to movement. It worked: when hot water was poured through a pipe close by, the ball was pushed back while ice placed next to the tube attracted the ball. In some excitement, Crookes decided he had discovered a new force—X force, he termed it. Perhaps it was the direct impact of heat radiation, a direct pressure of heat waves. But then if heat and light are comparable radiations, as Forbes, Melloni, Ampère, and others had shown forty odd years before, light too must exert such a pressure. Crookes's enthusiasm mounted: 'In that portion of the sun's radiation which is called heat we have the radial repulsive force', strong enough to explain why comets' tails point away from the sun, and how nebulae are formed. 'To compare small things with great—to argue from pieces of straw up to heavenly bodies'—and what else did Galileo and Newton? he might have asked—'it is not improbable that attraction now shown to exist between a cold and a warm body will equally prevail when for the temperature of melting ice is substituted the cold of space, for a pith ball a celestial sphere, and for an artificial vacuum the stellar void'. In this way he dared to hope that he had stumbled on the force behind gravity itself; 'that greatest and most mysterious of all natural forces, action at a distance' might prove to be the pressure of very hot and luminous bodies.

During the same years Clerk Maxwell had arrived at the conclusion that by his theory light should impart momentum to objects illuminated. But Maxwell's book was only published in 1873, the same year as Crookes was perfecting his experiment, and the two were working towards the same conclusion quite independently of each other. Crookes did not have the mathematics to follow Maxwell into the jungle of the new electromagnetic science; instead he developed his apparatus into what he called a 'Light Mill'. It was the scientific sensation of 1874. The single pith ball was replaced by a slender cross, which bears at each point a thin white disc, of pith or the like, coated with lampblack on one side. The cross is delicately pivoted or suspended so that it can rotate easily, and thus is mounted in an exhausted glass bulb. And sure enough the black sides do seem to retreat and the little windmill goes around as if it were blown by the light. Easily copied, and catching the eye by its continual movement, the light-mill was soon one of the most popular of scientific toys, as it remains to this day.

Newspapers acclaimed Crookes as the man who 'made a hole in the infinite', who had discovered the motive force of light. Scientists were not so sure. The impact of radiation supposed by Maxwell's theory was far too slight to produce an obvious effect, and in any case the lighter surface of the disc should be thrown back, not the darker. Reynolds, at Manchester, and others were convinced that the molecules of gas still in the bulb were producing this rotation. The blackened faces will absorb more heat than the light ones, so the difference in temperature between them and the surrounding residual gas will be greater accordingly; molecules of gas which hit them rebound at greater velocity than from the colder sides, so the recoil will also be greater here. To test which of these explanations was correct, Schuster, then a colleague of Reynolds at Manchester, in 1876 designed an experiment whereby the whole light-mill was suspended by a thread. If Crookes was right, the bulb should be carried round by the rotating cross, whereas if Reynolds was right, and the rotation was produced by an interaction of disc and gas, then by reaction the bulb should turn in the opposite direction. And so it was. Reynolds's student J.J. Thomson recollected his feelings of excitement when the experiment was performed, and his relief when his teachers proved right, for Crookes's theory would have had devasting consequences for physics if it had been vindicated.

One of Crookes's strengths as a scientist was that he never invested too much of himself in any one hypothesis. Unabashed by the rude collapse of one theory, he embraced his opponents' with enthusiasm. After Schuster's *experimentum crucis* he turned to new devices, lighter and more efficient, like his otheroscope and the elaunoscope, developed in the spring of 1877, 'which can be made of an infinite variety of constructions'. Indeed he had a miniature made, only half an inch in diameter, mounted as a scarf pin. It must be the ultimate in scientific display, to show off your pet experiment at your throat so all who talk to you must gaze upon it. These instruments were finally given the name of radiometer, which Crookes had coined once he saw they were not 'light-mills'. Actually radiometer is almost as much of a misnomer, because they do not directly *measure* radiation or anything else. His word elaunoscope would be a much more suitable name, for it means that they show repulsion, as indeed they do. But what's in a name—radiometer has stuck.

Now Crookes began to think of a general investigation of lines of molecular pressure in rarefied gases. If the theory of gases as molecules relatively free to charge about and collide with others were to apply when there were far fewer of them, surely it would be possible to track them down in the near empty tube. If the dark space at the cathode grew with progressive evacuation of the tube, might it not be simply the area they can traverse without a collision— the mean free path made visible. The first electric radiometers were very like the old, only the little windmill was itself the cathode, and the vanes went round once the current flowed, provided the tube was exhausted enough for the dark space to reach the wall and cause the glow on the glass. Soon he went over to a simpler form, which came to be known as Crookes's tube, although basically it is an improved and more efficient version of Geissler's. Towards the end of 1878, Crookes felt he was really making progress. With Sprengel's pump he pushed the boundary of emptiness down, down and down to a few millionths of an atmosphere.

The results were displayed with his usual flair to the Royal Institution in one of its fashionable Friday evening discourses in April 1879. Gradually the dark space expanded until it took up much of the tube; the greenish spot on the glass grew larger, at first faint, then more brilliant, although still less than a centimetre across. In tubes of different glass the phosphorescent spot had a different colour too. With his German glass it was indeed green, shading off to yellow, but with local English lead glass it would be blue, and with uranium glass a simpler green. Perhaps this method could identify fluorescent and translucent solid objects. Here would be another spectroscope, just as at milder exhaustions Geissler's tube had been a spectroscope for gases. The idea that 'a stream of airy particles' produced these effects now took hold of his imagination. As a popular science book of the day expresses it, 'the rarity of the air in the tube enables these particles to keep their line without being jostled by the other particles of air'.[1] Instead of the wild commotion in an ordinary gas, here there was a regular movement in a straight line, beating against the glass tube, or anything else that stood·in its way. One mineral might then glow crimson, another 'a rich golden yellow'. But Crookes knew the public would love to see precious stones in a display of electrical phosphorescence. 'The diamond', he explains, 'is the most sensitive substance I have yet met for a brilliant phosphorescence. Here is a very curious fluorescent diamond, green by daylight, colourless by candle light . . .' and as he darkens the room and turns on his current, it begins to shine a bright green, itself as bright as a candle. Whole heaps of diamonds from different countries were displayed, shining red, orange, yellow, green; rubies, sapphires, emerald too, emerald in crimson, the sapphire in a delicate lilac. 'In this tube', he announced to his audience, 'is a fine collection of ruby pebbles. As soon as the induction coil begins to spark you see the rubies shining with a brilliant rich red tone, as if they were glowing hot.'

Not only that: the rays could transmit energy—they were a bombardment—he set up a little wheel of vanes—this time more like a miniature watermill—and when the stream fell upon the vanes, it turned. Mount it upon rails—and it travelled the length of the tube. The streams were emitted perpendicular to the surface of the cathode, so that they could be made to converge or diverge according to whether the cathode was concave or convex, and with the concave form were brought to a focus; then they could be diverted in a magnetic field, as Plücker had first shown twenty years before . . . That they flowed straight, he demonstrated by pointing to the shadow cast by any object, such as a Maltese cross erected in their path. More curious still, as the fluorescent spot faded somewhat after a while, when you removed the object that threw the shadow . . . 'if I throw down this cross—I can easily do so by giving the apparatus a slight jerk, for it has been most ingeniously constructed with a hinge by Mr Gimingham' (his lab technician), and the black cross shadowed on the tube suddenly became much lighter than the area round it, which had been luminous all the time. And the stream transmitted heat too. Once focused against some point on the glass with his magnet, the spot became burning hot—boldly Crookes tested it with his finger, and leapt back with a blister on his finger tip. A lump of metal could be melted: to end the experiment—and the performance—he would smear wax over the place at which he meant to direct his rain of particles: first the wax would melt, 'the glass soon begins to disintegrate, and cracks are shooting starwise from the centre of heat. The glass is softening. Now atmospheric pressure forces it in, and now it melts. A hole is perforated in the middle, the air rushes in ...'

Where matter was so remarkably rarefied we should no longer think of 'gas' at all, but of a Fourth State of Matter, radiant matter, as different from the gaseous, as gas is from liquid. 'A new world', he declared, 'where the corpuscular theory of light holds good, and where light does not always move in a straight line; where we can never enter, and in which we must be content to observe and experiment from the outside.' Next morning, 'Lallah'—Alice Bird, an old friend and the muse who inspired his literary flourishes—wrote to him: 'You seemed to me like the magician of the Future from whom no secrets are hid.' Whether or not his lecture was 'discussed at a thousand breakfasts', as she claimed, he certainly created quite a stir. Even the philistine *Illustrated London News* if it found the whole thing rather abstruse, acknowledged that all was 'felicitously illustrated' by his picturesque analogies, his experiments and diagrams. In an even more triumphant lecture on his new discoveries, to the British Association that August, before an audience of nearly two thousand people, he ended with the stirring promise, that here at last we 'have within our grasp, obedient to our control, the little indivisible particles which with good warrant are supposed to constitute the physical basis of our universe ... We have actually touched the border land where Matter and Force seem to merge into one another, the shadowy realm between Known and Unknown which for me has always had peculiar temptations ... here lie Ultimate Realities, subtle, far-reaching, wonderful.'

'Nothing could exceed the beauty or brilliance of these experiments', exclaimed *Nature* in an enthusiastic account of his 'unique display of these exquisite experiments'; its reporter was specially excited by the dramatic inrush of air at the end. The applause must have been deafening. No wonder, the lovers of science and the hero-worshippers of scientists might well be cast into a rapture by such a grand finale. Some hardened professionals were less easily swayed. Crookes's revelations gave rise to a curious national controversy between a German and a British school; with William Crookes very much the captain of the English team. Not that matters were strictly on national lines. Stokes, Lucasian Professor of Mathematics at Cambridge, argued that Crookes's particles acted like tiny lamps radiating in the ultraviolet and so exciting this glow on glass just as in common forms of fluorescence.

In Germany Helmholtz himself found the particle idea quite attractive. But it was his own bright young men, his research students like Eugen Goldstein, who led the attack on it. Helmholtz was always happy to encourage them, even if he hoped for a different conclusion to emerge. Actually Goldstein could claim priority over Crookes, for if Plücker had discovered the magnetic deflection of the 'streams' and Hittorf the phenomenon of the shadow that becomes brighter than its background, Goldstein in the first paper he ever published (in 1876, when he was twenty-five) had proved before Crookes that whatever it was that poured from the cathode was identical, whatever the material of which the cathode was made; and that it flowed in straight lines perpendicular to the cathode and could therefore be concentrated by a cupped cathode. He also showed that two cathode streams diverted or repelled each other. Both these two points could well be taken to support the particle thesis. Nevertheless, the wave party were convinced that the new doctrine of Maxwellism which they were bringing over to Germany must imply that these too were waves of electromagnetic radiation. They disliked juggling with Radiant Matter: radiation was not ponderable matter, but ether. Goldstein argued that all the characteristics of cathode rays could be explained equally well by thinking of them as 'most nearly allied to light'. Deflection by magnet seemed an obstacle to such a conclusion but they felt there might be some special feature, for which there were analogies, and at all events these rays if deflected in a magnetic field were not so diverted by an electric field. All their calculations and experiments showed that the mean free path available for molecules in the most exhausted tube was barely a tenth of what Crookes's theory required. Where the expected free path was of the order of 6 mm, Crookes's space was at least 6 cm, and they could get a patch of light right down the tube—perhaps 60 or 70 cm from the cathode. The year after Crookes proclaimed his New State of Matter theory, Goldstein devised an experiment to test for a Doppler effect—a shift of wavelength in light excited by the 'torrent of particles'. None was to be found, and from this he deduced that the 'torrents' would have to flow at less than 14 miles a second, a very modest speed. Rather than 'molecular streams' or 'radiant matter', Goldstein coined a new term; if these were ethereal rays, let them be called 'cathode rays'.

Hertz took up the battle in the autumn of 1882, when he too was with Helmholtz at Berlin. He had no faithful Geissler or Gimingham; he was his own glass blower and built his own batteries, slowly and painfully. Fortunately his original training as an engineer stood him in good stead. As he wrote to his parents, he could work away like a mechanic if he needed, and he did, for there were to be a thousand cells in the battery to power his discharge, and each one was a task in itself. 'Every turn and twist has to be repeated a thousand times; so that for hours I do nothing but bore one hole and then another, bend one strip of lead after the other, and then again spend hours varnishing them one by one.' With all this electric power at his disposal, Hertz began his experiments in September. He proved that emission of the cathode rays was continuous, rather than in pulses, and felt the most elaborate experiments failed to produce any deflection of the rays in an electrostatic field. So they were not bearers of the current, indeed they had no direct connection with its path but were almost a secondary effect produced by the current in gas or glass. The cathode rays were not so much electrified stream as ether disturbance, just as Maxwell had said of light itself, so Hertz concluded, 'amongst known agents the phenomenon most nearly allied to them is light'. At last Helmholtz began to come round; 'I can not refrain from wiring to say bravo!'

In 1891 Hertz took up the thread again. In those eight intervening years little progress had been made, but in those eight years Hertz strode to the head of his profession, especially after his discovery of those electromagnetic waves which everybody was learning to call Hertzian. To show that these cathode rays were of similar character he resolved to pass them through a barrier that should be quite impervious to particles of atom size. Line the inside of the tube, where the phosphorescent patch is to appear, with pure gold leaf; at first it will throw a shadow on the glass, but at really high exhaustions the shadow will vanish—the glass will phosphoresce behind the gold leaf, which looks 'like a faint veil upon it, scarcely recognisable except by its general shape and the lines of its wrinkles'. Try other metal foils— silver, aluminium, alloys with tin or copper—the effect is the same, and equally if the silver or platinum is precipitated within the vacuum tube. Indeed aluminium seemed to work better than gold. He could prove that the cathode rays were not somehow percolating through tiny holes that must exist in metal leaf. Yet there were materials which stopped the rays getting through; a little mica plate cast a shadow through the gold leaf. Hertz was baffled at the transparence to his rays of substances like aluminium that are so opaque to ordinary light, while other things transparent to light 'offer an insuperable resistance to the passage of these rays'. A puzzle—but surely the rays he had found a few years before were also blocked by some substances that let light through, and pass through others that will not. So he felt sure that it was easier to think of these new cathode rays doing the same, than to imagine that molecules of electrified gas could carry on, still moving in their straight lines, right through his aluminium foil.

Hertz by now was extremely sick, in agony in nose, mouth, and throat. This was to be his last big experimental investigation—in the summer of 1891 he had to hand over to his new research student, Philipp Lenard, just arrived after a few months at Breslau and before that the City and Guilds Institute at London. Lenard mounted a thin aluminium foil in the glass, and found that the rays actually went right through his 'Lenard window' about a centimetre into the air. Foils of other metals could be used; the less dense the material, the more cathode rays go past. The rays made the air conductive beyond the window, spreading out as a fuzz of bluish light; they could be moved in a magnetic field; if beyond the aluminium plate there was another vacuum tube, they could certainly travel much further than a centimetre. And the window was unquestionably airtight, so none of Crookes's gas molecules would ever get through. 'Radiant Matter' implied the rarity of extreme vacuum—here were the rays passing briefly through the crowded atmosphere. For Hertz and Lenard this must clinch it. Only 'aetherial waves of very short wavelength' could possibly do this. Any particles capable of crossing such a barrier must be inconceivably smaller than molecules, smaller than atoms even—what could such particles be?

In the years between Hertz's two interventions in the cathode ray debate, Schuster had been applying his own mind to it. He held to the particle view, of course; but he held that the deflection, one of the first things that caught Plücker's attention, must prove the key. He suggested that the particles were not simply electrified molecules, but decomposed—ionized—broken up into their constituent atoms, one carrying a negative, the other the positive charge. At first he thought he could confirm this by a test with a residual mercury gas, whose vapour is composed of single atoms, and was misled into thinking he saw less glow there. The negative halves were then repelled as in Crookes's model and would carry one of Helmholtz's units of electric charge. To establish this, he sought the ratio of charge to mass of the particles which he expected could be obtained by a precise measurement of the magnetic deflection. Nobody had thought of that before, indeed. Perhaps it was a sign of the professionalization of British physics (which Schuster himself deplored) which gave him the time and the equipment for prolonged and detailed investigation rather than the discovery of dazzling effects of a qualitative kind. Schuster reasoned that if the bending of rays was produced by the magnetic 'push' it should be possible to relate the radius of curvature of their track to the intensity of the magnetic field, and their own charge and mass, such that $e/m = v/Mr$; e is the particle's charge, m its mass, v its velocity, M the intensity of the magnetic field, r the radius of the curve. This made the ratio of e/m depend on the value for v. But observing that the velocity of the cathode particle as it flew across the tube must be the result of the electric potential V through which it passed—which would give the actual kinetic energy of each particle, defined by m and v^2; then e/m would also equal $2V/M^2r^2$; and V, M, and r could all be measured. His results were subject to error in several details, and he found only very broad limits for e/m, broad enough to let him decide that he had confirmed his supposition, that the 'rays' were electrified atoms.

Three years later, in 1893, the subject was taken up by the Cambridge physicist J. J. Thomson, in connection with *Recent researches in electricity and magnetism*, an updated version of Maxwell's treatise which he had been asked to undertake. He had been a fellow-student, then a pupil of Schuster's at Manchester, but apparently did not know of Schuster's work. At all events he declared in his paper that he had not heard of any quantitative study of the magnetic deflection—much to Schuster's annoyance when he read it. He wrote off to remind Thomson, who was obliged to reply with an embarrassed apology.

Since his cheerful personality was to figure so largely in the British science of the next few years, and on till the outbreak of the war, J.J. Thomson deserves more of an introduction. Unlike most of those who have been named so far, his family were not of the professional class. His father had a rare book shop in Manchester, and there in Cheetham Hill, on 18 December 1856, Joseph Thomson was born; he was born only a few years after the basic energy laws had been threshed out; and he died in the August of the Blitz, when his son George was already chairing the 'Maud Committee' to develop an atomic weapon. For a third of a century he was Professor of Experimental Physics at Cambridge, so if there was, and perhaps still is, a Cavendish style in physics, it was a style whose fashion he set. In an appendix to his memoirs he listed nearly thirty Fellows of the Royal Society who had worked or studied under him at one time or another. His pupils held chairs in physics at every British university, and a score of foreign institutions. Five of them had already won Nobel Prizes; two more (including George Thomson) were to do so later on.

Scientific men are supposed to foreshadow their later brilliance in childhood either by building model engines or collecting bird's eggs and butterflies or wild flowers. Thomson's bent was decidedly the latter way. Perhaps surprisingly for a future physicist, he was never very good with his hands— excellent at the imaginative design of apparatus, he needed more expert help to construct it and make it work. People found in him a rather shy boy, more interested in plants than in what usually dominates the minds of schoolboys. He does give the impression that he found games a little rough, though doubtless good for the character. Many years later one of his fellows, who had since become a local bigwig, wrote a letter to the *Manchester Guardian* in which he proclaimed the virtue of practical life against mere science. 'There was a clever boy at school with me, little Joey Thomson, who took all the prizes. But what good has all his book learning done him? Whoever hears of little Joey Thomson now?' What was to be done with such a clever lad? His father decided to make him a locomotive engineer, for no doubt that profession had more prospects in mid-Victorian Manchester than the antique book trade. But he was only fourteen, there was a long waiting list for the firm Mr Thomson had in mind. Let Joey continue his education with a couple of years at Owens College. So there he went in 1871. He was then intended to be one of the new breed of science-trained engineers, but not himself a scientist. Manchester was only the second British University to have a chair of engineering: Osborne Reynolds was the professor. Thomson found Reynolds's lecturing style confusing, and he was drawn more and more to physics, through the guidance of Balfour Stewart, who taught young engineers in their second year.

Stewart's lessons were a model of clarity, but what must have made more difference was his approachability, the encouragement he gave to his pupils to test their own ideas experimentally even when those ideas might look eccentric, and the fertility of the research enquiries he himself had under way. He had been a student of David Forbes at Edinburgh, his native town; and under him took up the study of radiant heat which followed naturally on Forbes's own work. There, independently of Kirchhoff, Stewart showed that bodies will absorb radiation in precisely the same wavelengths as they themselves emit. As he had always been interested in meteorology, he then took up a post at Kew Observatory, while keeping up the connection with his old university as an examiner. From weather he was led on to sunspots; and to a study of the earth's magnetism. Perhaps his ability to keep so many pots boiling at once may have reduced the impact he made on the scientific world, for he was also one of those keen to bring science and religion together, and collaborated with Tait in a book on *The unseen universe*, which was to prove by scientific reasoning the immortality of the soul.

In 1873 the elder Thomson died. This effectively prevented his son becoming an engineer, for his widowed mother could not hope to pay the premium for his apprenticeship—sums of several hundred pounds were being demanded in the 1870s. All the same he won enough scholarships at the College to get his certificate in engineering and then two years more specializing in mathematics and physics, in the hope that he could then obtain a further scholarship to Cambridge. He would have to start again there as an undergraduate, and so depend on scholarships or on his family until he was twenty-three. It says a good deal for his mother that she had no qualms, or kept them to herself, although Joey's younger brother was only fourteen in the year her husband died and could hardly be expected to provide much support for a while. During these two extra years Thomson was closer to Stewart and helped him with his researches (and once nearly lost his eyesight when a glass vessel exploded in his face). He also made the acquaintance of two men who returned to Manchester after a spell at Cambridge: John Poynting, son of a Unitarian minister, who was to become his close friend; and Arthur Schuster. Schuster came from a German Jewish merchant family of Frankfurt-on-Main, who converted to Christianity while Arthur was a boy, like the Marxes and the Disraelis. Although five years older than Joe Thomson, he entered Owens the same year, having spent one year studying at Geneva and a couple more being dissatisfied in the family business. After one year at Manchester he went to Germany for several months, to Heidelberg, and later to Göttingen, and to Helmholtz's new institute at Berlin. With these German connections, he was better equipped than most British physicists to bring German and British science together, since he could appreciate the good points of each. But his first innovation when he began to teach at Manchester in 1875 was a course on Maxwell's treatise on *Electricity and magnetism*, then very much the latest advance on the research frontier. Only three students thought themselves capable of benefiting from it; Thomson was one.

The next spring Joey Thomson carried off his scholarship to Trinity College, where he was to remain for more than sixty years. In photographs of this time he looks the 'pallid, boney youth' one of his contemporaries recalled. In later years he softened the sharpish outlines of his angular face by growing the long hair and generous moustache which made him look more professional (and more like Lloyd George for whom he was sometimes mistaken). When Thomson arrived, Maxwell himself was still at Cambridge, but apparently he did not lecture much to the undergraduates. So Thomson only heard Maxwell once, when he gave a public lecture in the Senate House on a brand new invention, the telephone; by way of demonstration, members of the audience could listen to a tune being played in the Geological Museum down the lane. The professor's influence reached him indirectly, through the classes in mathematical physics given at Trinity by another Scot, William Niven of Aberdeen. Niven had not Stewart's gift of lucidity, so that his students saw how excited he was, and how important these new theories were, but not how all was connected, so they were forced to discuss the concepts among themselves afterwards. Thomson suggests that was better than having it all cut and dried; they had to think for themselves; perhaps that is all that is necessary if you are J.J. Thomson. His mathematical ability had already impressed his fellows. Even Niven stood a little in awe of him. He was also guided through the various theories of light and the luminiferous ether in the lectures of Sir George Stokes, Professor of Mathematics, famous for his ideas on optics, and also for being the first Cambridge professor to use a typewriter—another invention of the 1870s.

To us today the Cambridge of a hundred years ago appears a quiet place, set apart from the Industrial Revolution, keeping the railway and reform at a safe distance. None of the great scientific discoveries made earlier in the century had been made there. But to 'reading men' like Thomson, who had no intention of becoming a Blue or a swell, the university was on the move— a movement symbolized by the appearance of typewriters and telephones. To an eminence in mathematics, which had never been lost, was now joined a laboratory equal to any in the world, and a group of first-rate men to work in it. In January 1880 he took his Tripos, and came out second. He then proceded to a fellowship at Trinity which required a dissertation, undertaken on the subject that had intrigued him since he first met the concept of energy transformation—the idea that all energy is really kinetic however it may appear. Maxwell had died after a prolonged illness some weeks before, at the end of 1879, and his successor Lord Rayleigh took over in the spring. Thomson was soon drawn into Rayleigh's project of confirming the measurements and ratios of the electric units. He published his first piece of research in April 1881. Its starting-point was the experiments of Crookes and his German rival Goldstein on cathode rays. With Crookes he assumed that they were particles, and considering the distances between each one, he calculated that they must be travelling at enormous velocities. He then proceeded to show, by a mathematical treatment that would certainly have left Crookes far behind, that it follows from Maxwell's theories of electricity that an electrified sphere moving through an electric field must undergo a resistance, which amounts to an increase of its inertia—and so of its mass—as it attains greater speeds.

Meantime he also launched on an enquiry into the motion of vortex rings. The subject had been set for a mathematical prize because of its implications for the new theory of matter. He stresses how the vortex ring will never dissolve or crumble away, as its strength and volume are constant. Moreover, as they vibrate they should acquire an internal energy which might account for radiation. Above all 'if any vortex ring be knotted, or if two vortex rings be linked together in any way, they will retain for ever the same kind of be-knottedness or linking'. Since their behaviour could be interpreted within existing laws of hydrodynamics, traditional mechanics might in this manner arrive at explanations for all those characters that have to be ascribed to atoms, which had foxed all those who insisted that atoms are solid lumps of matter. The investigation goes on to work out how these little twirls of ether will behave when linked, so as to make sense not only of the gas laws, but also of chemical combination; and in particular, why elements will combine with just so many others, and no more. He decided that six is the greatest number of rings that can stay permanently knotted in a circle, for after that the assembly will be unstable, and the ring will break up. This conclusion he associated with some research on magnets done four years previously by an American scientist, Alfred Mayer. Mayer was looking for new methods to trace out lines of magnetic force. In order to establish the configurations that would be adopted by magnetized sewing needles free to move in a plane, he stuck them into corks, so they could float in water and act under the mutual repulsions of their neighbours' poles, and the attraction exerted by a large magnet hung up above them. While there were only three, four, or five needles in the bowl, if arranged at the corners of an equilateral triangle, square, or pentagon they would keep that shape. But once there were six, one would be stationed in the middle, surrounded by five forming the angles of a pentagon. The double system would hold until the number fifteen was reached, when three groups form; and so on, rings within rings. Similarities regularly recur, for example a central triangle at 3, 10, 11, then again at 20, 21, 22. With the vortices, dynamic considerations suggested that six would be the maximum in a chain. This Thomson suggested fits the laws of valency, for the union of six chlorine atoms with a single one of tungsten was the largest known association of atoms with one atom of another element.

Undoubtedly this piece of work won him much reputation; it was printed the following year, in which he was also appointed assistant lecturer. Even he however was rather surprised when he was elected professor in place of Rayleigh, who was to retire at the end of 1884. Having entered university at fourteen, Joey Thomson was now to become a full professor within a week of his twenty-eighth birthday.

Not the least of the signs of change was the appearance of women in the very male batchelor world which Cambridge had been formerly. As Thomson observed, the rush of marriages after 1882, once Fellows were allowed to wed, altered the university's style of life more noticeably than the first swallows of women students. He was a somewhat lukewarm supporter of this last innovation; in letters written in the 1880s he comments rather sardonically on their limitations, and cracks jokes about any who persist in going to his lectures for advanced pupils. However, there was one young lady who not only attended these lectures, but began a piece of research on her own, on the vibration of soap films when affected by sound, which Thomson suggested to her in October 1888. As time went on, so his biographer explains, he devoted more and more time to advising her on the progress of her work, until one day 'he came down looking highly delighted, and Miss Paget went out with a flush on her cheek' . . . two months later on 2 January 1890, J.J. became the first British professor to marry one of his research students.

In his new office, he found himself the heir to Maxwell too. It was in this capacity that in the early 1890s he was invited to prepare a new edition of Maxwell's classic work on electricity and magnetism, which gradually developed into a survey of all the great progress that had been achieved since Maxwell wrote. Some of the most important work, he decided, had been done in pursuit of the cathode ray controversy. He plunged in, eager to make his own contribution, first, by innocently repeating Schuster's attempt to measure a magnetic deflection; and seek an electrical. For a while he could not advance far beyond the point which Schuster had reached. Thomson did try a new method of measuring the velocity of the particles—or atoms as he too thought them—and came up with a value of just under 200 kilometres a second—exceedingly low as it turned out, but still above the molecular speed as estimated by Goldstein, and vastly below the velocity of light, and all other 'ethereal waves'. Later in 1895 a former student of Helmholtz, called Des Coudres, using a somewhat different technique arrived at a better figure—but still too low—of 2000 km a second.

In December, just before Christmas, Jean Perrin, a young man working on cathode rays for his doctorate at the Paris École Normale Supérieure, guided something that emanated from the cathode, presumably the rays, into a cylindrical cup linked to an electroscope, which proceeded to register a negative charge. Radiation was certainly unlikely to carry any such charge. Yet the radiation school were unconvinced. After twenty years the cathode ray question remained a question still. Then, a few short weeks after Perrin published his results, the whole scene was suddenly transformed. In the words of Munro's little *Story of electricity*, which came out early in the next year: 'The gloom of January 1896 has been relieved by a single bright spot.

Electricity has surprised the world with a new marvel, which confirms her title to be regarded as the most miraculous of all the sciences.'

NOTE

1. Munro, H. *The story of electricity*, p. 175. Newnes, London (1896).

4

LIGHT INVISIBLE

One evening in November 1895 another German professor of physics, Röntgen of Wurzburg, was in his laboratory working at his cathode ray tube like every good physicist of the 1890s 'looking for invisible rays'. He had covered the tube with a black paper mantle, possibly to check its absorptive capacity, when he noticed that a paper screen coated with barium platinocyanide, although standing on a lab bench some distance away from the tube, was glowing softly in the darkened room. When afterwards he was asked 'And what did you think of it?', Röntgen answered: 'I did not think; I investigated.' Like Hertz, Röntgen originally trained as an engineer, at the Zurich Polytechnic, but turned to 'pure' science because he found it more absorbing. Perhaps that helped to make him more skilful at the manipulation of apparatus than some of his peers. He checked to make sure that the tube really was the source of the strange fluorescence, and then began to find out what else might be transparent to rays, if such they were, which could penetrate black paper opaque to ordinary light. Wood did not block the effect, nor rubber, thin tinfoil, thick books, nor many other organic materials—nor, most startling of all, did human flesh. If he placed his hand in front of the screen, the bones cast a shadow but the flesh about them only something like a faint penumbra. During the next few weeks, Röntgen spent most of his time in a fever of activity. Above all he wanted to discover what these strange rays were. Of course, he could not first investigate—he had to think—try to conceive which among the forms of existence known to him could produce these manifestations. He had an acceptable repertoire of possibilities. But which of them could it be? It would be natural to expect that they were some new form of electromagnetic radiation. They did not seem to be cathode rays, for Lenard had not been able to lure cathode rays for more than a centimetre out of his tube, which was a mere fraction of the distance involved now. Röntgen, in common with most German physicists at the time, took cathode rays to be themselves electromagnetic. He did find some difficulty in establishing most of the standard wave characteristics derived from the study of optics; reflection, refraction, diffraction, polarization, he had some results but they seemed unsatisfactory. At all events, the material Röntgen had by late December was impressive enough. He laid his results before a local scientific society and sent off his offprints on New Year's Day 1896. In the course of his research he discovered that these X-rays, as he called them (to beg as few questions as

Fig. 6. Lord Kelvin—an X-ray portrait of his hand.

possible), would expose a photographic plate. After weeks locked each evening in his lab and locked up in himself, uncommunicative except in vague
promises that the world would think him crazy, he finally introduced his wife
Bertha to the great discovery by X-raying her hand a few days before Christmas. It was this photograph which seized the world by the collar a fortnight
after. So with copies of his articles went photographs of weights in a box,
a compass in its case—and the hand whose bones were horribly visible.
Schuster recalled how he casually dropped in at his laboratory to collect his
mail after the Christmas holidays. 'I opened a flat envelope containing photographs, which without accompanying explanation were unintelligible.
Among them was one showing the outline of a hand, with its bones clearly
marked inside ... inside an insignificant wrapper I found a thin pamphlet by

W.C. Röntgen . . .' Leaving his family waiting in the cold outside, he read the pamphlet over and over again.

A brief account then appeared in a Viennese newspaper—within a week the news had been telegraphed round the world. Later in January Röntgen himself gave a public lecture at which the X-ray photographed the hand of an anatomist colleague at the university; he was summoned to Potsdam to give a private demonstration to Kaiser Wilhelm. A Scottish doctor on a tour of the Continent records his pilgrimage to Röntgen's laboratory, where the professor, 'a tall man with dark bushy hair, a long beard, and very kindly and expressive eyes', showed him all the apparatus, including *the* screen, which the visitor thought 'should be preserved in a glass case!' Less informed journalists had already been knocking at Röntgen's door. Since Galileo looked through his telescope and found the satellites of Jupiter, no scientific discovery has created so much immediate excitement; none had ever been so quickly on everybody's lips. X-rays were the first big scientific advance since the appearance of a cheap popular press and the popular press made the most of the sensation. Much to his own annoyance, he became a public figure overnight, in a way that had never happened to Helmholtz, Kelvin, or Hertz.

The photographic aspect, to Röntgen's regret, dominated the resulting enthusiasm. Even a scientist like Wallace in his *Wonderful century* talks of X-rays in the chapter on photography, rather than in that on physics, although he was certainly hopeful that 'this new form of radiant energy will open up . . . an illimitable field of research into the properties and powers of the mysterious ether'. One of Thomson's first letters on the subject, written on 19 January describes how he was trying in vain to get photographs on plates in a wooden box *inside* the cathode tube. The *Annual register of events* speaks of Röntgen's 'electrographs of human bones, or money in a purse' primarily as evidence that 'waves produced by electric current can produce chemical reaction like light'. Similarly X-rays first appear in the 'Scientific jottings' of the *Illustrated London News* as a note on a remarkable photograph of a compass in its box. 'Invisible photography' was the catchword to indulge everyone's fancy; the cartoonists had a field day with X-rays of a flabby John Bull, to show he still had his sturdy backbone as of old, or thin actor inside a fat Falstaff.

As the basic equipment was already available in most physical laboratories, any physics department could easily switch to X-ray research and repeat Röntgen's results. As Thomson's new research student, Ernest Rutherford, put it in a letter to his fiancée on 25 January: 'The Professor of course is trying to find out the real cause and nature of the waves, and the great object is to find the theory of the matter before anyone else, for nearly every Professor in Europe is now on the warpath.' Soon Thomson, like Schuster and the rest, was busy producing Röntgen photographs for local doctors. Schuster used to travel about giving demonstrations on his children, in happy innocence of

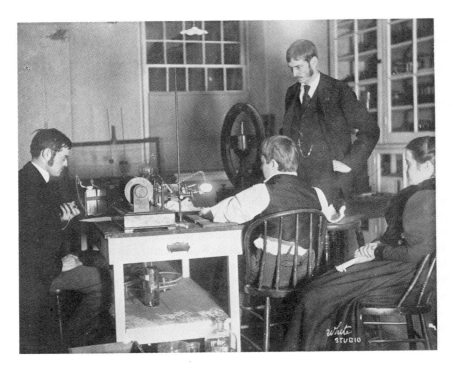

Fig. 7. X-rays in the service of medicine.

what the consequences might be—in between examination of a variety of strange objects, from a needle in the foot of a chorus girl at a local panto-mime neglected until it was deeply embedded—to a bullet lodged beneath the brain of a woman murdered by her husband.

Röntgen pointed out to his visitors a photograph taken through a pinewood door, with a band across it which had been produced by a strip of whitelead used to fasten the beading to the door. Inevitably, more excitement was generated by the medical possibilities. By the spring dentists were X-raying teeth in search of cavities; an advert has a bearded and paternal figure with flowing white locks reassuring the pretty girl who always monopolizes these scenes that Röntgen rays show all is well—because she has been using the right toothpaste, of course. Beecham's and other pharmaceutical firms were not slow to catch on; they had a cheerful little man with X-rayed skeleton, who declared; 'with this marvellous searchlight the scientists may just explore the inside of a man as he wills; Soon we shall expect our physicians to say, 'You are rather opaque, and must take Beecham's Pills''.' Perhaps there was a peepshow aspect to it as well. Journalists played on the 'skull beneath the skin' side of X-ray photography, for the notion of seeing your own skeleton appeals to a taste for the safely macabre. A poster designed for a contemporary Italian book on the wonders of science sets the mood; a woman, with the menacing look of a Belle Dame Sans Merci in the *fin de siècle* taste, looks out at us; one half of her as the eye beholds—the other half 'Röntgenized'. In London there was an X-ray exhibition at the Oxford Music Hall and Campbell Swinton set up an 'electric silhouette' studio after a demonstration to the Camera Club on 18 January. Not all those who wanted their photographs were patients with broken bones. The Prime Minister came with his wife to see their hands. So did the Prince of Wales—his only comment was, 'How disgusting!'. His son the future King George V, then Duke of York, was less squeamish. One week in July the *Illustrated London News* displayed as frontispiece the royal hands of the duke and his duchess; you can tell these are no common bones by the massive cufflinks of the duke, and the several splendid rings on the fingers of the duchess. The public were enthralled, but nervous. *Punch* summed up popular feeling in a rhyme that appeared one week which 'bids us each beware of you and of your grim and graveyard humour . . . keep them for your epitaph, these tombstone souvenirs unpleasant'. Swinton built up a picture of an entire skeleton from radiographs of various parts of the body; he pinned it on the wall, but his staff found it so disturbing that they persuaded him to take it down and destroy it.

More practical considerations applied. From the start X-rays were used to locate buckshot or needles and the like foreign objects embedded in hands or legs, and broken arms were set with their aid. The X-ray machine soon became an invaluable aid to the surgeon, and in the summer a special radiographic unit was set up in Glasgow by Macintyre, one of the first to try and take moving pictures with the new device. In February an Italian professor, Salvioni, invented a 'cryptoscope'—to see what is hidden—a fluorescent screen with shield and eyepiece that would enable you to look at what the X-rays revealed directly, rather than by means of photographs. Under the less magical name of 'fluoroscope', this handy portable instrument became a stand-by not only for medical inspection but almost for entertainment. Many of my generation saw the wonders of X-ray vision for the first time when we put our feet as children into a box with a large fluoroscope mounted on top, standard equipment in all the best shoe-shops in the 1930s. Owing to the long time needed in the early days to expose pictures so that they could be developed, it was not long before X-radiography revealed itself a two-edged sword. Blisters and reddening of the skin, loosening of the fingernails, and other nasty, but not really dangerous, symptoms soon gave way to something worse. Painful lesions appeared on the skin of those who had an overdose, and in a few years the first deaths occurred. As early as the summer of 1896, keen X-radiographers had to warn of the severe sunburn patients would suffer if too long exposed to the new rays. One of Edison's assistants died of the injuries inflicted on him while X-raying patients. Soon the first protective

Fig. 8. Edison working with a fluoroscope—at his side a vacuum pump.

clothing was designed so as to counteract these unpleasant side-effects. Natur-ally, some of the keener radiographers were anxious to dismiss the idea that X-rays themselves were doing the damage—it could only be the heat of the heavy electric current needed to produce them. Röntgen conferred powers on humanity that had once been given only by fairies to their favourite mortals: like all fairy gifts, you have to be very careful they do not have unlooked for and unwanted consequences.

It may be that was part of the fascination. Was it the discovery of X-rays which turned H.G. Wells away from the evolutionary ideas of his first two great science fictions, *The time machine* and *The island of Dr. Moreau*, towards technologies based on physics? *The invisible man*, published in 1897, maintains that the boundary between the seen and the unseen is not absolute, but may be crossed. He uses the principle that bodies are not visible in media of the same refractive index as themselves. To attain the same refractive index as the air that surrounds us, Griffin, his anti-hero, stands 'between two radiating centres of a sort of ethereal vibration ... no, not these Röntgen vibrations'—but others, even stranger, which he has discovered for himself. Meanwhile more serious physical inquiries were under way. Röntgen himself showed that a leak of electricity from a tube of gas irradiated by X-rays registered on an electrometer. So X-rays must render adjacent air conductive. Thomson and his new colleague Rutherford followed this up, since they realized that many of the problems of electrical discharge through gases could be solved if gases were made to conduct at much lower exhaustion than previously. Somehow the nature of the particles of gas was being changed. Yet this conductive character is only preserved for a short time once the gas is no longer exposed to the rays. Electric current destroys the same character, so that the passage of electricity through the gas cannot exceed a certain quantity for any given intensity of X-ray bombardment. After that, the current bears off the electrified particles as fast as the rays make them electrified, or rather ionized, on the analogy of the liquid particles in an electrolyte. In this way what they termed a 'saturation' point is reached, which varies with the gas used: besides air, they tried hydrogen, chlorine, coal gas, and mercury vapour. From the quantities measured it was possible to estimate what proportion of the gas molecules actually were ionized. It was a tiny proportion, barely a three-billionth part of the whole.

But what *were* these weird rays—or were they particles too? How did they work? The *Illustrated London News* was confident that 'in time these mysteries would be brought within the bounds of explicable science'. Professor Jackson at King's College in London proposed that the few molecules left in the tube took up so much electric charge from the cathode that they were quite swollen up; so dreadfully distended they had to explode and collapse, and this produced the radiation. Sir George Stokes developed a theory, first argued before the Manchester Literary and Philosophical Society early in 1897, according to which X-rays are thin pulses of radiation, like light in many ways, but sudden irregular bursts—like the crack of a whip when it is checked or the flash when a bullet strikes its target—and in that sense quite unlike the regular periodic waves of visible light. Attempts were made to time the duration of X-radiation at each spark. Some people interpreted Stokes's theory to mean that X-rays were a new form of matter, still smaller than cathode particles. Bottone's handbook of radiography, published in 1902, quotes a suggestion of the electrical engineer Nikola Tesla: cathode rays are indeed 'lumps of matter projected like innumerable infinitesimal bullets'. Then they are shattered into yet tinier fragments by impact with the glass wall of the Crookes

Fig. 9. Philipp Lenard.

tube and so become 'matter in a new basic form', as if they were a fifth state
of matter beyond Crookes's fourth state. So the cathode ray debate broke
out all over again. The *Annual register* for 1896 has to admit that 'the nature
of these rays still remains doubtful'; the next year X-rays were still giving
trouble 'both practically and theoretically'. One problem was Lenard, who
insisted that X-rays were simply cathode rays which had discharged their
electricity. In that case, the English school maintained, they too must be
'particulate and not ethereal'. However, in 1898 the wave phenomena of
reflection and refraction were firmly established for X-rays by Haga and Wind,
at the Dutch university of Groningen. In 1903, René Blondlot at Nancy
reported a series of measurements he had made on the velocity of X-rays, in
paraffin wax, beechwood, vaseline oil, and essence of turpentine; and in all
these media ranging from the highly viscous to the solid, the rays passed at a
speed as close as could be determined to the speed of visible light. Eventually
they could be placed on the electromagnetic spectrum, on the other side from
Hertz's radiowaves, as they had much shorter waves than visible light.

     Lenard never forgave Röntgen for having discovered X-rays first. He was convinced that he had really discovered them himself when he got the cathode rays to show their presence outside the tube. It is true that Lenard's experiment of using cathode rays to develop a photographic plate must have inspired Röntgen to do the same with his rays. Otherwise, Lenard's claim was feeble enough. He probably did *see* effects of the rays—but so probably did Thomson, Goldstein, and several others. Only Röntgen realized what he had seen, and that makes all the difference. In the summer of 1896 Glasgow university held a Jubilee celebration to honour the fifty years that Kelvin had been professor there, ending with a grand trip down the Clyde for all the visiting dignitaries. Lenard's new professor, Quincke, maintained to all about him that the whole thing was in Lenard's mind all the time. 'Ah', replied Sir George Stokes, 'Lenard may have had Röntgen rays in his own brain, but Röntgen got them into other people's bones!'.

Come September, and at the British Association meeting X-rays were all the rage. The President was a physiologist—he spoke of a halfpenny which X-rays had detected deep in a boy's gullet. At the Physics section A, there were no less than seven papers on X-rays, as against one on cathode ray effects, for cathode rays were now quite old-fashioned. J.J. Thomson was the section President. He acknowledged that Lenard had made a coated screen light up with cathode rays; had darkened a photographic plate; had discharged electrified bodies outside the cathode tube. But all these were effects produced by rays which could be bent by a magnet; and that was surely the crucial experiment which proved that cathode rays were *not* radiations in the ether, in the sense that Hertz's waves were. He was still convinced (and rightly as it proved), as he had suspected since January that this time the ether wave explanation was the right one. X-rays are 'unquestionably light', but a variety of light whose wavelength is shorter even than ultraviolet light. Lenard, who was there, held his ground. All cathode rays vary in deflectability, like colours in refractibility: these are simply cathode rays of zero deflectability ... But he did not find much comfort in his audience. His view would have won support in January, when many physicists thought the same. By September it was already ridiculous. Yet there was much sympathy for him among the British scientists. Whenever Lenard's name was mentioned in Thomson's address, he received a hearty cheer. Perhaps some felt in their hearts that it was unfair for a bright, up-and-coming young man to be pipped at the post by an obscure second-rater, who at the age of 50 had no right to dazzling new discoveries. All the same, when in November the Royal Society decided to award a medal for these great deeds, they cannily agreed to divide the glory between Röntgen and Lenard, since as they explained, both had extended the study of cathode ray effects to the space outside the tube.

Hardly was the British Association meeting over than Thomson set off for America to help Princeton commemorate a century and a half's existence by delivering a series of lectures on his recent work on electricity. Even then, he had finished with X-rays for the time being. Once his paper was safely out of the way, he could leave it to Rutherford to get it ready for publication, while he himself returned to cathode rays. He took up very much where Perrin and Hertz had left off. First he revised Perrin's experiment; where Perrin had placed his cup-receiver behind the anode of his tube, in a straight line with the cathode, Thomson placed the cup in an arm of this tube at an angle to the cathode–anode line, so that no rays would reach it *unless* diverted. As Hertz said, the electric effects recorded by the electrometer might not actually have been produced by the cathode rays, unless you gave them a chance to appear when the rays did not fall on the cup. While trying to repeat Hertz's experiment to find out if an electric field would turn the rays from their path, he thought he noticed a faint effect momentarily. It might be imagination; but perhaps the residual gas was masking any impact on the cathode rays, for if so there might be a brief period before the gas could be ionized. Then even more of the gas must be removed. After hours of pumping, and frequent discharge across the tube, he finally achieved a vacuum good enough for the rays to be deflected with a discharge of only 2 volts.

Having now managed both electric and magnetic deflection, he proceeded to trace them on a scale pasted at the far end of the tube; as the strength of electrostatic or magnetic field varied, so the luminous patch moved up or down. But how to find the centre of it—it was not nearly strong enough to look at by daylight. Thomson and his assistant Everitt had to sit in the dark, manoeuvring a needle coated with phosphorescent paint, adjustable by a screw so that the two bright points could be brought together, and the result read off the scale when the light was switched on. He reasoned that the force exerted by the electric field is the product of intensity F and of the charge e on the cathode particles: that exerted by a magnetic field is the product of the intensity of that field H, the charge e and the velocity of the particles, v. If the two deflections cancel one another, $Fe = Hev$. But then the velocity $v = F/H$; and as both F and H can be measured, you have a value for v. But as in Schuster's experiments, a curve of deflection of given radius for a given magnetic intensity equals mv/e. Now we have v, so at last we have m/e. To be on the safe side, he tried another technique, fitting a thermocouple to the inside of the cup in his revised form of Perrin's experiment. Then, if you assume that every cathode particle gives up its energy to the thermocouple— which was very simple, just very thin strips of iron and copper—a measurement of the increase in temperature of the thermocouple gives a measure of the energy imparted by the flying particles. But as that energy is defined as $\frac{1}{2}mv^2$ per particle, it is possible again to work out values for v and for m/e, in terms of the increase in temperature, the electric charge transfer registered on the electrometer, and again the curvature of deflection. For the velocity itself he arrived at a figure that was at all events more than 10 000 kilometres a second. For the ratio of mass to charge, one thing was clear; it was 770 times

Fig. 10. A contemporary photograph of the apparatus with which J.J. Thomson found the e/m ratio.

the ratio that holds with the smallest body carrying the least quantity of electricity then known, ions of hydrogen when in electrolysis. Either the charge was far greater—and he was prepared to accept it might be appreciably greater, though not a thousand times—or the mass was so much less. Indeed figures of nearly 1800 times, approaching that now held, were obtained within a few years.

He plumped for the second alternative; the cathode rays were composed of particles far smaller than anything known. His biographer, Robin Strutt, the fourth Lord Rayleigh[1], recalls that about that time Thomson stopped him in the street—Strutt was then an undergraduate—and told him that cathode rays had turned out to be particles after all, but particles quite different from atoms. Afterwards J.J. Thomson claimed that he had begun to wonder whether the particles might not be even smaller than atoms when measuring the magnetic deflection, which seemed too large unless they were smaller than molecules or even atoms of gas. In a lecture on X-rays, in the summer of 1896 he remarked that X-ray absorption depends solely on the density of the bodies through which they pass, and maintained that fact supported Prout's old notion that the basic building blocks of matter were primordial atoms of a more simple kind than those of chemistry. 'For', he said, 'if each of these primordial atoms did its share in stopping the Röntgen rays, we should have that intimate connection between density and opacity which is so marked a feature for these rays.' The ratio was virtually the same whatever the residual gas in the tube; the same whatever the material of the cathode—he reports trying six different pure metals beside sodium amalgam and silver chloride. What was the conclusion? That 'we have in the cathode rays matter in a new state, a state in which the subdivision of matter is carried very much further than in the ordinary gaseous state'—an echo of Crookes—'a state in which all matter ... is of one and the same kind; this matter being the substance from which all the chemical elements are built up'.

This revolutionary idea he put to his Cambridge colleagues on 8 February 1897, and in April proclaimed it to a wider public at the Royal Institution. As Thomson recollected much later 'there seemed no escape from the following conclusion:

(1) that atoms are not indivisible, for negatively electrified particles can be torn from them by the action of electrical forces;
(2) that these particles are all of the same mass, and carry the same charge of negative electricity from whatever kind of atom they may be derived, and are a constituent of all atoms;
(3) that the mass of these particles is less than one-thousandth part of the mass of an atom of hydrogen'.

Unavoidable as these conclusions may have looked to him, others who had tried to measure the same ratio shied away from any such astonishing implications, and he admits that he arrived at them only 'with great reluctance'. Some at least of his audience thought that whatever might be said of his experiments and his measurements, this speculation was just 'pulling their legs'. His strange opinion certainly did not carry all before him. The *Annual Register* for 1897 had not heard of it. Nearly a year later Campbell Swinton— the last person to be accused of failing to keep up with scientific discovery— and at a Friday evening lecture to the very same Royal Institution—noted that everybody was now coming round to Crookes's view of cathode rays as material particles, but we are still unsure whether 'these material particles are single atoms, single molecules or larger aggregations of matter'. He does not even mention any suggestion that they were particles far *smaller* than atoms.

There are other claimants to the discovery. A month and a day before Thomson's first Cambridge talk, Wiechert on 7 January spoke to the Mathematical and Physical Institute at his university of Königsberg. He too produced a value for the e/m ratio, derived entirely from that old favourite—the magnetic deflection, but he could only establish within limits much less exact than Thomson's that the ratio was much greater than in hydrogen ions. As he had come round to the view that cathode rays were indeed particles, he thought they must indeed be far smaller than atoms. But he supposed them independent of the atoms of ordinary chemical matter, perhaps electric bodies like those of Helmholtz. Another German scientist, Kaufmann, offered that May another comparable estimate for e/m, again based on magnetic deflection alone. He decided that his experiments showed the same result whatever the gas or material of the cathode itself, therefore they could not be particles torn from either—so he was inclined to go back to some modification of the wave theory.

Yet Thomson's hypothesis proved to account well for some other troublesome phenomena. Back in 1887 Hertz had noticed that when ultraviolet light fell on his copper rectangle, sparks jumped the gap more readily. On further investigation he learnt that some other metal would release a negative discharge into the air. Thomson (and independently Lenard, now converted) showed in 1899 that in fact negatively charged particles, which were given off from zinc, had nearly the same charge to mass ratio as those of the cathode ray. Some of the early investigators assumed the electricity was leaking away attached to quite large fragments. Perhaps ultraviolet light was raising the dust on the surface of the zinc. But Thomson was struck by the negative character of the electrified bodies thus discharged. Moreover, if they were exposed to a magnetic field on their way, they could be prevented from reaching a positive plate to which they should have been attracted. He proposed to perform the same kind of balancing feat he had tried with the cathode rays, so as to assess their e/m; he shone ultraviolet light from an arc lamp on to the zinc plate through a quartz window. Opposite the plate was a positively charged wire mesh, attached to an electrometer. Whatever carried negative electricity to the wire mesh must be turned aside by a magnetic field, through a curve ever greater as the field got stronger, until they curved right over, and failed to reach the mesh—so the electrometer stopped registering their arrival. These bodies were surely the same as cathode particles. There was now an extra benefit; the charge on the particles could be measured by a method shortly to be described, and turned out to be equal to that on hydrogen ions. So it was now certain the difference *must* be in the mass.

It was the same story with what later came to be called thermionic emission. Long since it had been observed that incandescent metals turn the air close by them into a conductor of electricity. This too could be shown to be the result of a discharge of negatively charged particles with just the same charge to mass ratio. Here Thomson was aided by the invention of an instrument that has since proved a key to unlock many of the treasure-chests of physics: the cloud chamber of C.T.R. Wilson. Although Wilson's introduction to physics was different from Thomson's there are curious parallels in their lives. The son of a progressive and successful sheep farmer in the Pentland Hills, Charles Wilson also lost his father when a boy, indeed when only four years old. His mother then took him to Manchester where her parents were living, and so he too attended Owens College, was taught by Balfour Stewart— perhaps somewhat past his best by this time—and then went on to Cambridge. He was the only student actually to take the Tripos in Physics in 1892. His family too had a struggle to support him. In his recollections, he remembered his qualms of guilt at going on to a second university with no real profession in sight. 'I felt I might be of use as an explorer as I had some knowledge of a wide range of sciences and powers of endurance tested on the Scottish hills' — so the archetypal pertinacious instrument-maker scientist had dreams of becoming an explorer ... To end his precarious condition, he took a temporary job at Bradford Grammar School for the autumn of 1894, but before that decided to combine employment, science, and a stay in the Highlands he loved by working for some weeks at the meteorological observatory which then stood on the summit of Ben Nevis. Inspired by the wonderful lighting effects produced when the sun shines on the clouds around the mountain top, the rings around the sun and the huge shadows it projects upon the heaving, swirling mass of cloud, he took it into his head to try and reconstruct these effects of light and cloud formation artificially, in order to understand them more fully.

A few months of teaching persuaded him that somehow he must get back to Cambridge; even if he had to live on part-time tuition, he must have access to a proper laboratory. Through 1895 he devoted himself to the formation of condensations. It had been known for some time that water drops have to form around dust particles. When air is saturated with water vapour and then cools, droplets will form, provided they have such a core, which enlarges them; and the larger they are, the less likely they are to evaporate. But what if all the dust is removed? Then even saturated air stays saturated—no condensation. But it was also known that sudden expansion of a volume of air will cool it, and so vapour should condense. Wilson devised an instrument for sudden expansion—simply a glass vessel, originally a glass bottle or cylindrical chamber, whose floor was a piston which could be withdrawn very rapidly by opening a cock that connected the space under the piston to an exhausted vessel. The piston then fell sharply, the volume above it expanded, and Wilson discovered to his astonishment that a few drops still formed after he had removed all the dust by frequent condensations. He could produce a precipitation like fine rain, then dense clouds, and finally a fog which when illuminated turned first a pale violet, then red. Evidently in these later stages, drops accrued round the molecules of air themselves, but at the first fine rain phase something else was at work, which 'although only present in small numbers at any given time, but as fast as they are removed they are replaced by others of the same kind'. He became excited at the thought that these few centres or nuclei were continually regenerated. Were they individual molecules—perhaps odd charged molecules, ions roaming through the empty space? These demonstrations took most of 1895. Although some photographs of his apparatus show a brass cylinder in which the piston fell, with only a hemispherical dome on top made of glass, all would be much clearer if everything, piston and cylinder, could be made of glass. The piston had to fit with perfect snugness into the cylinder, and rest smoothly on the base, for obviously all must be absolutely airtight. But the piston has to drop quite sharply: it is not surprising that he lost most of his pistons the first time he used them, after spending hour after hour of careful grinding. In those days a scientist had to be his own glassblower if he wanted anything complicated, at any rate in Cambridge. The long hours of painstaking work he put into this apparatus won him a life-long reputation, the source of many jokes.

In February 1896, when Thomson was ionizing gases with X-rays, it seemed obvious to try and see if this electrically conductive gas would pass through a connecting pipe to the cloud chamber. With delight, he discovered that although the point at which the first drops appeared was the same as before, a real heavy mist, which descended only very slowly, was to be seen well before it would manifest itself under ordinary conditions. So X-rays must produce in quantities those nuclei of condensation which were normally but a few scattered individuals.

While Wilson was working on this problem, the Cavendish team was joined by its first research student in the modern sense, John Townsend. Unlike Thomson and Wilson his family was academic—he was the son of a professor at University College, Galway, and himself educated at Trinity College Dublin. Townsend too was interested in clouds of condensation, and in the discharge of electricity through gases, in this case the gases liberated in electrolysis, bubbled through water, which then make moist air condense, even when it is not completely saturated. Using a calculation of Stokes for the speed of fall of a drop falling through a given medium, he was able to work out the dimensions, and so the mass, of each drop once he could measure the rate at which they actually fell. Absorbing the water in the condensation cloud, you can then weigh it, which gives you the mass of the whole cloud. Divide by the mass of each drop, and you have the number of drops. It is also possible to measure the electric force operating on the cloud—then divide that value by the number of drops and the electric field, and you have the charge per drop. And if each drop has at its heart an ion—you have the charge per ion, which happily turned out to be almost the same as that found on hydrogen ions in electrolysis.

The next step was to use Townsend's method to measure the X-ray-begotten ions which formed the drops in Wilson's chamber. And that proved almost the same, within the limits of error imposed by the crude nature of their apparatus. So long as results were within the right order of magnitude, the basic hypothesis was confirmed; there was a universal natural unit of least electric charge. To sum up very neatly in verses from one of the comic songs which the Cavendish people used to perform at their Christmas parties:

> and with quite a small expansion,
> 1.8 or 1.9
> You can get a cloud delightful
> Which explains both snow and rain

> Ultraviolet radiation
> From the arc or glowing lime
> Soon discharges a conductor
> If it's charged with a minus sign

At this juncture, through 1898-9, these investigations converged on a different line of enquiry altogether, one that ran in a direct line back to Maxwell via Helmholtz and the notion of electricity existing as charged particles. Hendrik Antoon Lorentz had pioneered the introduction of Maxwell's electromagnetic theory to his native Holland in the 1870s. Like Thomson, Lorentz was a man who sprang from a somewhat lower middle class background; his father was a nurseryman who worked his land near Arnhem. But he too had worked his way up through exceptional ability, and his parents' enthusiasm for learning. After the local high school, he went to study physics at Leiden University. Returning to Arnhem as a schoolteacher, he too tried to provide experimental backing for new theories with the simple apparatus he could borrow on Sunday morning from the lab at his school. In 1878 he returned to Leiden as its first professor of theoretical physics. Appointed even younger than Thomson, for he was only twenty-five, like Thomson he received this promotion more out of confidence in his promise than for anything he had yet done. The very idea of a professor specifically for *theoretical* physics must have sounded rash innovation enough, without adding to the risk by choosing a young man who had completed his doctoral thesis only a couple of years before. At Leiden Lorentz slowly elaborated his improved Maxwellism. In his version the most complete separation is made between an imponderable, immovable, and unstructured ether, and ordinary matter. In order to explain how matter can have any relations at all with such an aloof ether, he proposed that matter contains 'a multitude of small particles which bear positive or negative charge'. To these particles he gave Stoney's name, 'electrons'. These electric particles have mass, although it must be very small, presumably much less than atoms, for they do not enter into atomic weights, but they *do have* mass, and are solid bodies. An excess of positive or negative electrons in an atom or molecule makes it a charged ion; if the numbers are equal, the body is neutral. An electric current is a stream of such particles, probably separated from the atoms and molecules of matter proper; his particles create the electric and magnetic fields in the ether, which then affects other electrons elsewhere, including those somehow incorporated into matter. Light—or other radiations—makes them vibrate; and their vibrations set up waves across the ether. This theory he first put forward in 1892; but in October 1896 Pieter Zeeman, who was at the time his assistant, brought him the results of his experiments, which showed that the spectral lines of a sodium flame are broadened in a magnetic field. Lorentz proved this fitted in well with the expectations of his theory, which thus began to command much wider respect. It was no longer an ingenious speculation, but an idea which led to explanation.

At the outset this was primarily a theory of electrodynamics, not a theory of the constitution of matter. Like Hertz he was trying to link electricity to light, and did not ask himself what connections his particles might have with the atoms of chemistry. In contrast to his later life, when he enjoyed a very active old age as an international conciliator in a troubled time, during the period of his greatest scientific brilliance, Lorentz led a somewhat withdrawn life, without the constant stimulus that pervaded Berlin or Cambridge. He had little contact with scientists abroad, and did not attend any foreign scientific meetings until he had been twenty years in his chair at Leiden. In those years few visited him either; he worked in his study and communicated with the world by the reading of papers. More intimate contact with outsiders, even with his scientific peers, he disliked. Once his wife announced that she had just seen a stranger in the street, who looked like a foreign professor ... Lorentz replied—'I just hope he won't turn out to be a physicist'.

Thomson on the other hand was very much interested in the implications of his new sub-atomic particles for fundamental ideas about matter. If these corpuscles, as he called them, so much smaller than atoms and all of the same mass, could be torn off so many different substances, likely enough all atoms contained them; and large numbers at that, for he proposed that the atoms of each element had as many corpuscles as would equal that element's place in the Periodic Table of the chemists. These little bodies could be imagined to group themselves in rings, for then the particular chemical properties of each element might be derived from the number of rings, and from the number of corpuscles in each, particularly in the outer ring. For a model, he harked back to Mayer's fun with floating magnets. So a table demonstration which looks so much like those described by William Gilbert in the time of Queen Elizabeth I, that it would hardly be surprising to find it in some lost chapter of his *De Magnete*, now provided the inspiration for this outrageous new hypothesis. Naturally, Thomson did not suppose things were quite so simple within real atoms; for a start, whereas the little needles were only free to move about on the water's surface, his corpuscles could be disposed in three dimensions, throughout a spherical atom. Mayer had seen his experiment as an intriguing classroom show, to catch the imagination of children and 'illustrate the action of atomic forces, and of the atomic arrangements in molecules' for readers of 'one of my little books in the Experimental Science series'. It was Thomson's naïvety, and his boldness, that let him propose that his negative corpuscles would push each other into similar figures: and thereby convert this simple notion into a model, however crude, of what goes on *inside* an atom. The name corpuscle, which had been used so often and so vaguely in many different contexts, was soon afterwards abandoned by most people in favour of Stoney's electrons, since they were evidently not only the smallest fragments of matter but also least units of electric charge and appeared to have many of the characteristics of Lorentz electrons. And electrons they have remained.

The most hopeful feature of Thomson's theory lay in his attempt to explain the differences between the basic forms of matter in terms of the numbers and positions of a primitive underlying form, itself ever the same. Not everyone was impressed, however. Physicists and chemists alike had a feeling that the cobbler should stick to his last. The physicist should deal with forces, energy, electricity, and the ether. Chemical atoms are to be left to chemists, except in so far as they received or exchanged energy. Electrons in the ether, yes, electrons interacting with atoms, drawn to atoms like satellites to a planet— fine—but electrons *inside* atoms, flying off atoms? Nor was it strictly necessary to accept this breakdown of the atom just because you accepted electron theories. In the March 1899 number of the *Philosophical Magazine*, Thomson was annoyed to read an article from William Sutherland, a physicist, in Melbourne, on cathode, Lenard, and Röntgen rays. He agreed that electricity divided into least natural units, as Helmholtz had proposed; but did it follow, he asked, that the bearers of these least fragments of electricity were actually components of atoms? That is an idea of 'momentous importance'. Before it is to be accepted, let us try to find an alternative explanation of the experiments of Thomson, Lenard, and the rest, which will stay safely within the bounds of 'the logical development of established or widely accepted principles of electrical science'. Perhaps the cathode ray is a stream of Helmholtz– Stoney electrons, physically independent of the atoms. Then an ion is an atom with an attendant electron as its little moon. But free electrons are perfectly possible; they move through the ether, swim through gases, and thread their way through solids. In a sense electrons *are* the ether; where ether is uncharged there must be positive electrons, counterparts of the negative ones in the cathode beam. Normally the two are bound together, just as two atoms are linked to form a molecule; for such neutral doublets he first coined the word neutron. But they can be pulled apart. Since the negatives appear alone in the cathode ray, and probably in electric current, so positive ones may well be repelled from the anode. However these cathode electrons show by their effects that they have a kinetic energy, so they have inertia, size, and therefore, he holds, presumably shape. If they deform atoms on contact, they too when they strike solid matter must be set a-quiver, and then start up those waves discovered by Röntgen.

Just as Newton was furious to read how Hooke had conceived a rival interpretation of Newton's own experiments on colour, without producing any new experiments either to disprove Newton's explanation, or justify his own, so Thomson was quite rattled by an attempt to appropriate his best experiments for a rival theory, which dismissed his most promising ideas. In indignation he wrote to the *Philosophical Magazine* straight away, on 11 March. Unlike his usual lucid style, this letter is entangled in dependent

clauses and awkward expressions. He accuses Sutherland of supposing cathode rays are made up of 'disembodied electric charges, charges without
matter', rather unfairly since after all Sutherland had allowed his electrons
inertia, size, and shape—can something have those three properties, move
about and yet not be 'matter'? Perhaps the confusion involved in an ether
which was separate from matter and imponderable, although it must have
spatial dimensions, forced these contradictions on them. Certainly Thomson
insists that Sutherland's view implies that electrons are independent of matter,
and he reasonably points to the difficulties that follow ... and all this just to
save these poor atoms from being split up?

With all the evidence now at his disposal, Thomson was ready to launch
the sub-atomic vision upon a more receptive audience; the Physics section of
the British Association. As the Association was to meet in Dover that year,
and their French equivalent in Boulogne, a joint session was arranged, and
Thomson was to give the keynote paper of the day, on 'The existence of
masses smaller than atoms'. Between the excitement of welcoming their
guests, and eager discussions of the address by the section President John
Poynting, the radical implications of Thomson's thought passed over quite
quietly. For those who wanted their physics next door to philosophy, Poynting went deep into our understanding of matter and ether; he spoke in a vivid
and imaginative style, almost like Crookes, and raised disturbing questions
about the formation of scientific ideas. All the same, it is curious that Thomson's old friend from student days either had not heard of his corpuscles or
failed to see their relevance to these questions.

For those who liked their physics practical, Mr Marconi had set up a
station for wireless telegraphy by Hertzian waves in the Town Hall, where
visitors could exchange greetings with their French colleagues across the
Channel. The prospect of signalling without wires had been in view for some
years, and several inventors were trying their hand. Yet most people knew
nothing of it. When in April 1896 Tesla described his experiments in the field
and predicted that it would be possible one day to link up any place on earth,
and even the nearer planets, across the electric waves, *Punch* saw this as mere
Yankee bombast—ambitious Americans could now sing 'Rule Columbia!
rule the (electric) waves! The elements themselves shall be thy slaves.' Hertz
never won the fame of Röntgen, and Marconi had discovered no new waves.
In June 1897 *The Engineer* which had been given a preview of a talk on the
subject to the Royal Institution declared that most of what had been printed
about Marconi's new technology was 'utter nonsense'. All the same there was
something in prospect, enough indeed to 'lead us as far into the regions of
scientific romance as did the discoveries of Röntgen'. This was *The Engineer's*
first report on 'aethereal telegraphy'. There were only one or two more over
the next twenty months; and then a spate of them, fourteen in the January–
June 1899 volume. *Nature* similarly has only occasional entries through late

1896 to 1898, despite a discussion on the subject at the Physical Society led by Oliver Lodge in January 1898. The *Illustrated London News* gave a detailed, almost hour-by-hour account of how the injured Prince of Wales watched the Cowes race from his yacht, but despite its fascination with all things royal, forbore to mention that the Queen on dry land at Osborne received reports on his condition by Mr Marconi's device.

Then early in 1899, a sudden change occurred. It was the first signals across the Channel in March 1899 that did the trick. Heralded by a full-page cartoon in *Punch*, in which the fairy Electricity dismisses her two old and outdated servants the overhead telegraph wire and the submarine cable, as she waves over their heads the magic wand of wireless telegraphy—and then a run of wireless telegraphy jokes and cartoons—wireless became the talking point of the summer season. The *Illustrated London News* first mentions the 'Marconi miracle' as a scheme to join London and New York, although as the paper had heard that the height of the aerials would have to be in proportion to the distance to be covered, it was understandably doubtful. But then the magazine did show pictures of Marconi's apparatus, and of his aerial atop the crenellated battlements of Dover town hall. Letters acclaiming the Wireless Telegraphy Company's achievement appeared in *The Times* and in *Nature*.

Between the dramatic new experimental and perhaps useful hardware and Poyntings' epistemological problems, the concept of a new form of matter that should explain chemistry appeared quite modest. Much of Thomson's talk kept to the details of his experiments with his ultraviolet, photoelectric and incandescent metal corpuscles. He left his chemical speculations aside, and concentrated on the corpuscle as bearer of, perhaps identical with, the smallest natural unit of energy. The theme that this means there is 'something smaller than the atom' recurs throughout, and with it the idea that when any piece of matter is in an electrical state, a tiny part of an atom's mass has been taken from it. When a gas or a liquid is ionized, a little piece of atom—a corpuscle—breaks free and detaches itself. So an atom must contain great numbers of these 'corpuscles'; all equal in charge and size—about $3/100\,000\,000\,000\,000\,000\,000\,000\,000$ of a gram, flitting about inside a largely empty atom, like a fly in a cathedral. Now this is about thirty times as large as the currently accepted value for the mass of an electron—9.109×10^{-28} gram—a point to be borne in mind when considering Thomson's views on the number and arrangement of his corpuscles in an atom. Somehow their negative charge had to be counterbalanced by an equal positive charge spread through the area through which they move.

As *Nature* reports the discussion, he found support in plenty. As might appear from Crookes's famous speech on the evolution of elements, spectroscopists had been of all scientists the least happy with rigid unchanging atoms. Now Lockyer, one of the country's leading astronomers, got up to express his interest; he was in favour of the complex atom; and he was backed by two other speakers, including a French visitor. Oliver Lodge hoped that Thomson had founded an electrical theory of mass and inertia—an idea which was to be very popular over the next few years.

Some of the audience were much less enthusiastic. H.E. Armstrong, reformer of chemical education, was very displeased. Unrolling a black cloth which might serve as a very extended blackboard, he took the meeting through the arguments for atoms of inflexible character and unalterable mass, which could never allow morsels of themselves to be so easily chipped away. If cobblers only stuck to their shoe-leather, and physicists troubled to learn chemistry before they tried to play ducks and drakes with it, then, in his opinion they might understand how impossible it is that atoms should be made up of clouds of these new corpuscles, which wandered off under such slight provocation. Just as Aristotelian astronomers, when faced with Galileo's telescope, clung with passionate devotion to the impassivity of the celestial spheres, so did he grimly insist on the impassivity of his atoms. In far off St. Petersburg, an echo of the debate reached old Mendeleev. He too was annoyed by this new model, which threatened to shake the legs of his Periodic Table. If corpuscles can be broken off from the atoms of which they form a small part, or stuck on others to give them excess negative charge—then how easy it would be to change one element into another, as the old alchemists had dreamt. In an article 'From silver to gold' he poked fun at such nonsense.

In Cambridge that winter all this would look like obscurantist stubbornness. Thomson's students, untroubled by doubts, sang their chief's triumph at their annual feast:

> All preconceived notions he sets at defiance
> By means of some neat and ingenious appliance
> By which he discovers some new law of science
> which no-one had ever suspected before.
> All the chemists went off into fits;
> Some of them thought they were losing their wits,
>   When quite without warning
>   (Their theories scorning)
>   The atom one morning
>   He broke into bits.

Two photographs have survived from this time. One shows him as the scholar, seated (in Maxwell's old armchair) as he reads a paper; his untidy hair falls over his forehead, and he looks a little older than his years. Another, taken by Campbell Swinton in 1898, suits his character better. Standing with his hands across his waist, a billycock hat thrust jauntily forward on his head—he looks young and on top of the world, as he had good reason to feel. Rutherford described him three years earlier in a letter to his fiancée; 'dark and quite youthful still; shaves very badly, and wears his hair rather long. His face is rather long and thin; has a good head and has a couple of vertical furrows just above his nose.' This was a first impression; a year after, when

Fig. 11. J.J. Thomson on a visit to Lord Rayleigh in 1898.

Thomson had become his friend as well as his professor, he portrays his 'very-clever-looking face, and a very fine forehead and a most penetrating smile, or grin as some call it when he is scoring off anyone'.

So in less than four years' work, a basic assumption about the fundamental structure of matter, which had been generally accepted for two centuries, was quite suddenly overthrown. Instead of indivisible, impenetrable atoms, the basic units of chemistry themselves held within them still smaller components, which could be stripped from them. As for the world at large, which likes to found its view of nature and of our place in it upon the latest science—the world was baffled. Humanity had only just become used to the materialism of the atom. The American historian Henry Adams was in England in 1899, and the next year visited the Exposition Internationale at Paris. Torn between awe at the immense force of the electric dynamo and revulsion at the material ruthlessness of modern technology, he expressed his confusion in a 'Prayer to the dynamo'. Are we the masters of this vast new power—or are we its servants? Is matter itself—and that means the matter of which we too are made—but electricity, driven by electricity? 'or are we atoms whirled apace, shaped and controlled by you'—the power of electricity. Is electricity some-how squeezed out of atoms as this latest theory says?

> Seize then the Atom! Rack his joints,
> Tear out of him his secret spring!
> Grind him to nothing!
> Tho' he points to us and his life-blood anoints
> Me, the Dead Atom King

NOTE

1. Robin Strutt succeeded his father, John Strutt, the third Lord Rayleigh in 1919, and so he appears on his title page and in our bibliography as Lord Rayleigh: but it will be more convenient to call him Robin Strutt here, to distinguish father and son.

LIGHT EVERLASTING

The year 1900, last year of the Wonderful Century, which had seen discoveries and inventions beyond any former age, was a year for prophecy, a year to revel in the still greater splendours which would bedeck the twentieth century in happiness, wisdom, and wealth. At the BA that year, the President, Sir William Turner, the son of a poor cabinet maker who had risen to be President of the General Medical Council, exulted in past progress: 'Man has to a large extent overcome time and space; he has studded the ocean with steamships, tunnelled the lofty Alps, spanned the Forth with a bridge of Steel, invented machines and founded industries of all kinds for the promotion of his material welfare, elaborated systems of government fitted for the management of great communities, formulated economic principles, obtained insight into the laws of health, the cause of diseases and the means of controlling and preventing them. . . . GREAT IS SCIENCE AND IT WILL PREVAIL.'

At Paris an international exhibition was held, intended to dwarf by its splendour all the exhibitions that had gone before. A Gallery of Machines proclaimed the achievements of the era now about to be born; the huge forty-foot dynamo, and the electric travelator, and the Daimler engine, and all the bright new automobiles roaring to be off. There was an International Congress of Physicists, the first to be devoted just to them, held during August when Lorentz and Perrin spoke, and Villard discoursed of cathode rays: Thomson sent in a report on the ratio of e to m, but did not appear in person. But the star of the congress was something else. These temples of discovery were haunted by a rather disconsolate figure: Henry Adams, accompanying his friend Samuel Langley of the Smithonian Institution, who was then engaged in plans to take the automobile somehow into the air. However, as Langley explained, all was not well with physics. 'He was not responsible for the new rays, that were little short of parricidal in their wicked spirit toward science.' Ultraviolet and infrared Langley knew, and had himself devised instruments to study them. But what of these new manifestations? 'Radium denied its God—what was to Langley the same thing, denied the truths of his Science. The force was wholly new.' Bewildered, yearning for certainty in his science and his religion, disappointed in both, looking for some comprehension of a universal law of force at work, poor Adams 'wrapped himself in vibrations and rays that were new', was excited by devices that sensed radio— and X-rays—by all this 'supersensual world, in which he could measure nothing except by chance collisions of movements imperceptible to his senses, but perceptible to each other, and so to some known ray at the end of the scale'.

How could he comprehend it? 'In these seven years man had translated himself into a new universe which had no common scale of measurement with the old. He had entered a supersensual world . . .' Defeated in his aspiration—and perhaps not sorry to see the scientists confused, and uncertain how much of what they thought positive truth would survive—he confesses that after all there could be no laws of human history if there were no laws of physical force. 'And thus it happened that after ten years' pursuit, he found himself lying in the Gallery of Machines at the Great Exposition of 1900, his historical neck broken by the sudden irruption of forces totally new.' However as he remarks 'no one else showed much concern', the prospects were too exciting. What were these new rays that threatened to devour their parent science? They were the rays of radium and uranium—the force of radioactivity . . .

Whatever the furore in the 'damn newspapers' as Röntgen put it, X-rays were a wonderful new tool to put into the box of knowledge. They could be related to phenomena already understood; and was it after all so unreasonable to suppose that objects opaque to light might be transparent to rays of much shorter wavelength, just as Hertz waves passed through solid barriers? Electrons and composite atoms, however distasteful to some, had at least confirmed the expectations of a few bold spirits. But then, as a direct consequence of Röntgen's announcement, another was made just after, which was to have much more far-reaching and disturbing results.

Among the audience at the first demonstration of X-rays in Paris in that January of 1896, when Perrin showed off his skeleton pictures of a fish and a frog, sat Henri Becquerel, latest of a line of eminent scientists. He specialized in problems of fluorescence and phosphorescence. Struck with the possibility that if these new rays were produced at the fluorescent patch on the cathode ray tube, then other fluorescing substances might emit them likewise, he placed crystals of one such, uranium potassium sulphate, on photographic plates wrapped up in black paper, and then exposed them to sunlight, whose ultraviolet rays should provoke the desired effect. Indeed shadows duly appeared on the covered plates; rays had been emitted and had affected the plates through the paper, like X-rays. Fortunately Becquerel did not end his investigations at that point. By now it was the last week of February, a poor time of year for exposing anything to sunshine, and for the last four days of the month, the weather forced Becquerel to lay his experiment aside. He put away the wrapped plates in a drawer, with the crystals still in place upon them. On 1 March, he developed the plates all the same, perhaps in hope that some activity might have continued for a little while as if by phosphorescence. To his astonishment, 'the silhouettes appeared, on the contrary, with great intensity'. This radiation continued to pour out for weeks on end without any

Fig. 12. Becquerel at work.

exposure to light at all. Yet other fluorescent materials did not emit it, while any form of uranium did so, whether fluorescible or not, even as a pure metal. So uranium was the source, and the purer the better; he therefore called his discovery 'uranic rays'; others honoured him, as they did Röntgen, by naming the rays after their discoverer.

However, Becquerel's discovery aroused nothing like the same excitement as X-rays. At the meeting of the Académie des Sciences at which he delivered his paper, six of the 38 communications were on X-rays. The next meeting had as many—but no more on 'uranium rays'. *Nature* had published over a hundred and fifty X-ray items by the end of April 1896: they occupy more than half a column in the index. The next two volumes have rather less, yet it was not until well on into 1897 that the number really drops, and then only relatively: the *Annual Register* for 1898 observes that 'to the industrious physicist X-rays are a perennial delight'. But through 1896, the only references to uranium rays are the titles of Becquerel's reports, in the summary announcements of the proceedings of foreign academies. In Thomson's speech in September to the B A Section A, he takes five pages to discuss all the information on X-rays, and dismisses Becquerel's rays in as many lines. Although invisible they are 'unquestionably light', which can be polarized, they take photographs, presumably they are somewhere on the borderline of the ultraviolet. Funnily enough, Becquerel was not the only man to make the same observations of uranium rays. Sylvanus Thompson, Principal of the Finsbury Technical College, carried out an almost identical experiment also in February; he may even have observed the peculiar effect a few days earlier than Becquerel. But he did not reach the stage of publication until Becquerel had already read his account to the Académie; as Stokes regretfully advised him. Nevertheless, he did manage to read his own story at the British Association so he of all people there must have sympathized with Lenard to the full, as he talked of the relations between this type of radiation and X- and cathode rays. His own kind—independently discovered, as he reminded the audience—he thought a slow-acting phosphorescence—a hyperphosphorescence. That is all—no letters to *Nature*, no newspaper interviews, no doggerel in comic papers. Photographic feebleness has much to do with it; the photographs made with uranium rays showed only paltry shadows. So far from revealing things hidden to ordinary sight, or to photography by light in visible wavelengths, they showed very much less, little more than a fuzzy outline. The uranium rays remained a minor scientific curiosity for two years. In 1897 the industrious Elster and Geitel showed they were no phosphorescence, hyper- or otherwise. Becquerel himself found that these rays render the air conductive, and can therefore discharge electric bodies through air; this power lent itself to measurement, and to comparisons with X-rays carried out in a series of experiments by a pair of young research students at Glasgow, collaborators of Kelvin, and by Wilson at Cambridge. A story went about that some firefly had been found in the East, whose light like that of X- and uranium rays, shines through thin metal foils. Thompson was momentarily excited. But by the summer he had given the matter up. Busy in the administration of Finsbury Technical College, and always keen to apply his physics to electrical practice, he turned to more pressing matters. Only when invited to give the children's lectures at the Royal Institution, on 'Light visible and invisible' did he remember to say a few words about this new phenomenon, and recall his own share in its discovery.

After nearly two years, uranium rays were still an obscure curiosity, probably not worth the time that a thorough investigation would require. Suddenly, within a few months they moved to the centre of the scene, while mopping-up operations were still being carried out on X-rays and electrons. The person chiefly responsible was as unprecedented as the rays; the first woman in France to obtain a doctorate for scientific research, the first woman to become professor anywhere, or to win the Nobel Prize. Marie Curie was one of those thousands of students (many among them women) who escaped from the Russian prison-house to seek education and freedom in the West. Her family too was borne along in the intellectual winds that were sweeping late nineteenth-century Europe. Both her parents were teachers—her father Wladislaw Sklodowski was a teacher of science. Hampered in his career by his Polish origins after a successful Russian education, he had set up a boarding school in Warsaw, where Maria was born in 1867. Despite her own successes in high school, as a woman she could not go to university in her native land. For four years she served as a governess, trying to teach a wilful ten-year-old daughter of a Polish landowner. She suffered all the awkwardness and ambiguity that went with life as a governess, as much in Tsar Alexander's empire as in Victorian England. In Brontësque fashion, her employer's son, Casimir Zorawski fell in love with her, but, as fashionably, his parents strongly disapproved and broke up the match between their son and heir and a mere governess, although of good family. She developed a tough personality—she had to. In a society which revolved around balls, flirtations, and gossip she devoted herself to study and self-discipline. Returning to Warsaw in 1889, she took part in the 'flying university' where young people excluded from ordinary universities for one reason or another—not least by reason of their sex—could continue their studies together. It was a flying university, because the Tsarist régime not incorrectly judged that such gatherings must be hotbeds of rebellion, nationalism, and irreligion, and so frowned on them severely. There was too a Museum of Industry and Commerce, with a laboratory, where young Maria could teach herself a little chemistry. But none of this was real higher education, and that she was now resolved to have.

For a Pole, Paris was capital of that ancient friend of Poland which had given Chopin his second motherland—Paris was the obvious place to go. Her elder sister Bronia had already gone to Paris, and qualified as a doctor. In the summer of 1891 Maria set off to do the same. Leading the traditional Parisian student life in an attic, devoted to science to the exclusion of all else, with a religious fervour and strength of mind, she passed first or second in all her exams in physics and mathematics. She also met the one man whom such a woman could marry. He was Pierre Curie, director of the physical laboratory at the École Municipale de Physique et Chimie Industrielles. Son and grandson of physicians, Pierre had a brilliant youth as a science student at the Sorbonne.

Even before he graduated, he and his elder brother Jacques had distinguished themselves by their joint researches in piezoelectricity—which they discovered. Subsequently Pierre developed his own work on magnetism. The École de Physique et Chimie was only a new municipal establishment, not one of the Grandes Écoles. It lacked not only their prestige but also their funds, so that Pierre did some of his most original work in a corridor. He had a growing reputation, but not much in the way of material recompense to show for it, when he met Maria Sklodowska in the home of a mutual friend, another exiled Pole. She began to work on the magnetic properties of tempered steel—a task which seems to have begun in the spring of 1894, at almost exactly the same time as her first meetings with the master of ferromagnetism. Pierre did not have much difficulty in persuading her to share his life, 'entranced by our scientific dreams', as he wrote to her—they were married in the summer of 1895; only a few weeks after Pierre had won his doctorate for his thesis on magnetic properties of bodies at diverse temperatures.

Once she had her university course brought to a satisfactory conclusion, Marie Curie decided to follow her husband and work for a doctorate of her own. He had won his at the age of thirty-six, after nearly twenty years' continuous scientific career. For her part she had only started university six years before, and was herself thirty. What is more, she had just become a mother, after a painful and difficult pregnancy. No woman had yet achieved such an ambition; but for a young married woman, with a babe at the breast—quite unthinkable. This was the year when Cambridge decided by an overwhelming majority not to let women receive the university's degrees: they might study, attend lectures at the risk of puerile snubs; and despite the conviction of most lecturers that their pretty little heads must be incapable of taking in serious academic thoughts, they might even take examinations, and do well in them. But degrees—would that not frighten away male students, discourage them from going to Cambridge? Even *Nature* reports these declarations with a straight face, and apparently with approval. Paris, Berlin, and London might be more accommodating; yet there too, most found it easy to assume that the most suitable conclusion for a woman science student's career was to marry a male scientist; perhaps she could keep up with something light in her hours of leisure.

Marie decided she would test other substances methodically to see if Becquerel radiation was really specific to uranium. To this end she had a particularly sensitive electroscope based on a principle discovered by her husband. It may be indeed that the limitations of uranium photography prevented any real progress. Not until the electrical conductivity test made it possible to identify very small amounts of this new radiation, and measure different quantities precisely, could any real progress be made. Uranium is the heaviest of elements, so she turned to thorium, the next in weight, and had her first success there. Surprising as it may sound, for two years afterBecquerel's discovery, nobody had taken what seems an obvious step. Now two people discovered the activity of thorium at once, for Marie Curie soon learnt to her dismay that Gerhard Schmidt, lecturer at Erlangen, had forstalled her by a few weeks. He too was originally a physical chemist, interested like Becquerel in questions of phosphorescence. Schmidt, like so many at the time, satisfied himself that these new rays were but a peculiar kind of X-rays, and after his thorium finding he gave up the new subject. But Marie Curie carried on. No other element gave off this radiation. But one thing had puzzled her from quite early on. Pitchblende, an oxide of uranium, and the main European source of it, actually emitted more than the pure metal. So there must be something else in the pitchblende, so minute in comparison with the rest as to defy analysis so far. She asked the firm that mined the uranium of Joachimsthal, then used mainly in the colouring of glass and ceramics, if they could perhaps spare some of the residues of their ore, which were simply dumped in the woods. With some help from the Austrian government, the pitchblende waste was supplied—some hundreds of kilograms eventually reached Paris. All this Marie and Pierre had to crush and filter by hand, before proceeding to all the chemical procedures needed to separate one substance from another. The job would have been exhausting enough for anyone, but especially for a slightly built woman in the wretched storeroom, freezing in winter and sweltering in summer, which was all the École Municipale could spare for her laboratory. By dint of herculean efforts, they succeeded in tracing a substance like bismuth, and associated with it, which was some three hundred times stronger in radioactive powers, or rather more 'radioactive' (the word they then coined) than uranium itself. This metal they decided to call polonium after Marie's homeland. But there was more. As polonium was linked to bismuth, so too there seemed to be something else that made the electroscope shudder more violently, this time linked to the barium in their residue. They announced the existence of polonium in July 1898: as autumn drew on, it became clear to them they had now something not merely hundreds but many thousand times as radioactive as purest uranium. This they called radium— the ray element *par excellence*. By the end of the year they had obtained samples of barium with sufficient concentration of this radium to give an independent spectral line, clearly distinct from the barium lines. The accepted stamp of a true element was theirs. Two elements in five months—and such remarkable elements—quite an achievement. Not that everyone agreed they *had* found any elements. Spectral lines might be confusing—that same summer Crookes had announced his new element monium, later re-named Victorium in honour of the Diamond Jubilee. In his Presidential address to the British Association in September he modestly recalls his monium, but omits to mention polonium, which had made its bow in the *Compte Rendu* of the Académie des Sciences two months before. It must have been all the more embarrassing when eventually he had to surrender monium, since it proved to be a mixture of two known rare earths. So radium and polonium had to make their way in a jealous and suspicious world. A year later, André Debierne, a young research worker who had come to join Pierre Curie some while before, and was now going through the thorium ores as the Curies had gone through the residues of uranium, was rewarded by the discovery of yet another new element, which he named actinium, the Greek equivalent of the Latin radium.

Marie Curie was determined to prove the existence of her new elements by isolating a quantity of radium even if there might be barely a gram of it in many tons of the pitchblende ore. It took her until 1902 to obtain as much as a tenth of a gram out of all those mounds on which she had toiled, but that was enough to give its atomic weight, third in order after uranium and thorium. By this time, radioactivity had moved right into the centre of the scientific stage. But the question now was not, What things are radioactive? but What is radioactivity?—what happens when these rays are given off? Now at last this radioactivity was scientifically *à la mode*. Interest mounted through 1899. Once Becquerel had given up, because he thought he had exhausted the subject without finding anything of moment; now he returned to it. Were these truly some kind of X-ray, were they like cathode rays? Could they be deflected in a magnetic field? That proved harder to decide—when it is so easy to leave stray ions about the place, to muddle the results. Still, Dorn, professor of Physics at Halle, and then Becquerel both managed it. By the spring of 1900, it became clear that these radiations bore negative charge, and if you performed Thomson's feat of balancing the two deflections against each other, you came out with charge to mass ratios, quite close to those of cathode rays—or as the Irish physicist Fitzgerald wrote to Rutherford in May, they must be 'disembodied electrons: J.J. [Thomson] prefers to call them corpuscles'.

If these experiments helped to put the new rays back into a safe little niche, others were more troubling. It was clear that the radium stayed hotter than its surroundings. It was self-luminous, and it lit up some fluorescent materials: zinc sulphide was the favourite. It was the continuous effect which caught the imagination, and that of course took some time to reveal itself. The *Annual Register* of 1899 gave pride of place to a report that 'Uranium has disclosed possession of remarkable properties ... its peculiar radiations persist undiminished after imprisonment for three years in a wooden box encased with lead.' Where did radium get the energy? Crookes as usual bounced in, soon after the discovery of polonium. Somehow these very heavy atoms had the power of catching the faster molecules from the atmosphere around them, and using the energy of their movements as they slowly dispensed it back again. Some external source was bound to be a popular explanation in those early days. At the physicists' congress at the Paris Expo, this it was that caught everybody's imagination. *Nature*'s correspondent described the scene as he listened to the lectures of Becquerel and Curie. For most of the packed hall it was a relevation to see the glowing patch upon the screen, and marvel at 'this light which appears everlasting, radiated perpetually by radium'. Science had overflowed with ancient dreams come true in the past few years. Was it to usher in the new century with eternal light, with a burning bush that glowed but was not consumed? That would be quite against the very laws of thermodynamics, of which physics was so proud. That is why Langley was so shocked by the indecent behaviour of this radiation. Perhaps he was one of that audience so stirred by the intensity of radioactivity, which he then had to explain to a bewildered Henry Adams as they wandered through the great Hall of Machines. The mystery of radium, as the phrase went, was to be explained in due time. Although the explanation did slaughter a few sacred cows, none were quite so sacrosanct as the laws of conservation. Surprisingly the answer did not come from the Paris of the Curies, Debierne, Becquerel, Perrin; nor from Germany; but from across the Atlantic. To see how the troublesome loose ends of 1900 were tied together, it is necessary to return to Thomson's research student, Ernest Rutherford.

Ernest Rutherford's father was a millwright, whose mills sawed timber for the railways and beat flax. He married Martha Thompson, a schoolteacher, and they settled near Nelson in the South Island of New Zealand. Their son Ernest was one of ten children, brought up in the country near Nelson, in an environment of pioneering and improvisation where all the children were expected to do their bit, digging potatoes or taking the cow home. The family was not poor, yet even with the aid of scholarships they found it a struggle to give Ernest the best education that the South Island could then afford. When ten years old he was presented with a little book on physics, written by Balfour Stewart, 'to discipline the mind by bringing it into immediate contact with Nature herself', that is, teaching not by 'facts', but through a series of experiments to stimulate a child's imagination and powers of observation. James Rutherford's mills were of course water-powered, and Ernest in boyhood, like Newton, used to make model watermills. But like young Newton he was not well suited to farming life—even in childhood he showed a bent for mathematics. At fifteen he won a scholarship to Nelson College, which was organized on the lines of a public school in the old country; there he found a mathematics teacher who could really train him—the two of them used to go about the town discussing problems together, while the teacher, like Pythagoras, would draw his diagrams in the sand. Like others who have minds that way inclined he could concentrate on mathematics to the exclusion of all else. 'Some of us used to take advantage of his abstraction in various boyish ways, banging him on the head with a book, etc. and then bolting for our lives . . .' it is not recorded how young Rutherford took to these attempts to bring him into the society of his peer-group. But he was big and strong enough to avoid anything too unpleasant—anyone who played rugger for his school, as Rutherford did, was unlikely to be troubled too much.

At Canterbury College, Christchurch, a member of the infant University of New Zealand, he studied with a much stranger figure, Alexander Bickerton, the Professor of Chemistry and Electricity. His personality was too eccentric to find a university post in Britain, but in a colony at the end of the world he could make his mark, and Rutherford always expressed admiration for his teaching. Bickerton was certainly not withdrawn from the world: a graduate of the old South Kensington School of Mines, excitable and enthusiastic, he was quite a showman. He was keen to popularize science, and bring its joys and benefits to the poorest settlers. Perhaps he had not so much in the way of knowledge to impart, but he could certainly 'bring his students into immediate contact with Nature'. He had developed a cosmological theory in which almost all the main problems in astronomy were caused by the Partial Impact of two stars brushing against one another without actual collision—if both stars exploded, the result would be the conflagration we call a nova—perhaps only the side closer to the passing star would ignite, and begin to revolve, and so become a variable star—if the two were able to exert a mutual attraction strong enough to keep them together in space, they would become twins; and if they passed relatively far from one another, a tidal effect between them would later settle down into a planetary system. As Rutherford pointed out in the 1920s, his old teacher had thus at least in this part of his theory, anticipated what was for a while a very common explanation of our solar system. As time drew on, Bickerton became somewhat cranky; his chemical researches gave him the wherewithal to start inventing patent medicines, his lectures to the people became political—he turned ardent Socialist, and denounced the institution of marriage, while putting forward very 'advanced' views on Christianity. Eventually he established a kind of commune, which collapsed because he was the only member prepared to do the chores around the house. In a community determined to set up a respectable miniature of orderly British society in the furthest Antipodes, such ideas were unlikely to be approved by the authorities. Several attempts were made to rid the College of him, by charging that he neglected his students. But they were only too fond of him and his methods of education.[1]

Rutherford under his stimulus progressed as rapidly as he had done at school. A Science Society was founded at the College while he was a student there; one member proposed they discuss the hypothesis that atoms of the elements as we know them can not be the least units of matter, for there must be some more fundamental form, 'more primitive even than atoms' of which they in turn are composed. Perhaps he was thinking of Crookes's theories on the genesis of elements or of vortex rings. Rutherford led the debate on 'The evolution of the elements'; unfortunately this led on to evolution in biology and so to evolution in psychology, morality, and religion. Given Bickerton's reputation, the alarm was sure to be sounded. Instead of the science students learning useful topics they were being encouraged to dabble in subversive speculation. Ernest himself was none to keen on this line of thought, and in consequence was shy of becoming the Society's secretary. In 1894 he graduated, with a Double First of course. He had already begun a little private research in 'the old tin shed'—which was all Bickerton had for a laboratory—and then in a little cloakroom adjacent.

At first Bickerton had suggested chemical research into nitrates, but Rutherford, already a physicist at heart, launched instead on investigations of magnetism, in which he showed that iron wires could be magnetized by very rapidly alternating electric currents. Despite the primitive conditions, this research demanded very high frequency current, and very precise measurement of small amounts of time elapsed, so his success in itself shows that he was an experimenter of unusual skill. The discovery of this sensitivity by magnetization and de-magnetization to rapid electrical oscillations suggested a new field—could it not be the principle of a new kind of detector of Hertz waves? That same year 1894, Oliver Lodge delivered a lecture which we could celebrate as the birthday of radiotelegraphy, in which he surveyed the different means that could be used to detect these waves, and introduced a new one based on the principles established by Eduard Branly, science teacher at the Institut Catholique at Paris. In this 'coherer', as it was called, metal filings close together are made to stick to one another when subjected to electromagnetic radiation. Thus Hertz waves could be detected much more efficiently than in his own apparatus. Lodge was interested in the potentiality of this instrument for communications; his lecture was published, and excited a number of would-be inventors. Lodge had fired the gun; the race was on; by the next summer Popov in Russia and Tesla in the United States had some limited success. With his steel needle, magnetized with a solenoid of fine copper wire wound into a coil around it, Rutherford soon began to pick up signals right across Bickerton's lab, and realized that he had a chance to build something that would outdo the Branly–Lodge coherer. But where?

The federal University of New Zealand was allotted one of the British 1851 Exhibition Scholarships—Rutherford put in for it—and came second. Fortunately for him, the successful candidate, a chemist who was working on a new process for the separation of gold (manifestly a more useful subject than the magnetization of steel needles) decided not to take it up, and Rutherford was sent in his stead. In the meantime, he had been earning his keep by teaching at the local High School. But his interests in mathematics were way above the heads of the boys, and with his general air of abstraction, he found it impossible to keep order. To add to what must have been a miserable episode in his life, fresh attempts were afoot to oust poor Bickerton, and his senior students, in particular Rutherford, were grilled by a committee of enquiry in search of evidence that Bickerton was neglecting his laboratory.

However, there was a happier side to Ernest's life. In regular student fashion, he had fallen in love with his landlady's daughter, Mary Newton, and they were engaged to be married as soon as he had established himself. The Exhibition scholarships coincided with the creation of a new institution at Cambridge. Formerly, graduates of the university might undertake a little research, or visitors from other universities might come and visit there for the purpose, as Schuster had done. But there was no provision for a degree by research only. Now it was instituted that graduates of other universities might obtain a Cambridge BA (not a Ph.D., as now) on the strength of two years' research. Rutherford was in fact the second person to register on these terms, after Townsend. Early in August 1895, he took a ship for England. On the way he called in at Adelaide, where at the local university he met William Bragg, the professor of physics, a man only eight years older than himself, who had studied with Thomson at Cambridge, and could tell Rutherford something of what he could expect there. Bragg was in fact working on the demonstration of Hertz rays himself; he will re-appear in this story.

Ernest was not yet the ebullient and self-confident character so well remembered by those who have set down their memories of him. The student who was closest to him—they shared digs in Christchurch for a while—recalled an impression that he was 'very modest, friendly but rather shy and rather vague', and indeed an impression of diffidence appears in photographs taken at this time. But ambition he did not lack—at least for a Cambridge fellowship. When he left New Zealand he and Mary Newton seem to have hoped to marry within a year or two, and certainly not wait the five years they were obliged to. During these five years, he wrote frequently, and over the years his character can be seen acquiring confidence as he found himself in a society where his skill and enthusiasm for research were appreciated and given their head. They also reveal a frank and uncomplicated nature, little troubled by doubts or anxieties of any but the most practical kind; he was determined to make his mark, and increasingly sure that he would be able to do so. After arrival in England he stayed for a couple of weeks in London, suffering from a neuralgia that was perhaps as much due to tension as he waited to start a new life as to the clamminess of a humid London heat wave after the fresh air of a sea voyage. Once he began his research, however, there was no stopping him.

These letters also give a curious picture of Cambridge in the 1890s, as it appeared to a new student from distant New Zealand, older than other undergraduates, a little of an outsider. Most of his few friends outside the lab were fellow colonials, for instance, South African Boers who lectured him on the iniquities of the Jameson Raid. But after all, colonial or no, he felt himself as true a Briton as any public school boy, with a sturdy independence of mind that would not be hypnotized by the Cambridge aura. The celebrated Great Court of Trinity College, which he had joined as it was Thomson's College, was 'not very imposing—a narrow archway and then a big grass enclosure with college rooms all round—old and antiquated in appearance'. The dons he met at High Table were evidently learned and intelligent, but 'it is a pity so many of them fossilize as it were in Cambridge and are not that use in the world they might be'. Altogether, English society seems to have been lacking in vigour. Returning from an ethnographic excursion into wildest East Anglia to observe the old customs and measure the heads—'anthropometry' was much in fashion—he had to say that 'you can't imagine how slow-moving slow-thinking the English villager is', so very different from the enterprising and self-reliant New Zealand settler. And life was expensive, even on a scholarship of £150 a year—'the rent is so enormous' (£7.10.0 a term) and 'besides that, I pay for oil and all my own tucker, which the landlady cooks'.

It would be false to suggest that he was disgruntled or disdainful; the Cambridge to which he had travelled from the opposite side of the earth was the Cambridge of J.J. Thomson and the Cavendish Laboratory, and he was far from disappointed with either. Thomson and Rutherford took to each other immediately, and he enthused in letters home over the kindness and help of Thomson and his wife: even their son George was 'the best little kid I have seen for looks and size'. At last he was in a real laboratory, well laid out with fine equipment, perhaps then at the best moment of its existence, with a new extension just going up, no longer the almost empty place that Thomson and Schuster had found little more than a dozen years before, nor yet as crowded as it was to become by about 1910. The Demonstrators looked askance at research students at first, as if suspicious that their position as instructors was being undermined by these outsiders, but within weeks Rutherford had established himself. Indeed the Cavendish was itself developing features of an institution, with its own social life, not just a workplace. A few years earlier, in 1891, Thomson had set up the Cavendish Physical Society— Thomson's pet society, Rutherford called it—a physics colloquium after the German model, at which the latest discoveries could be discussed (Ernest found himself reporting on his magnetic detector at the beginning of December). As it was after all in England, proceedings began with tea. From the time the new rooms were completed, in the spring of 1896, the Cavendish workers gathered regularly for tea each day. Rutherford afterwards claimed he had instituted this custom, which was certainly renewed at Manchester when he went there as professor, the purpose being to discuss everything but shop-talk, about physicists yes, but not necessarily physics. Naturally, Thomson had plenty to say on everything from the conduct of the Boers to the results of the latest Test Match.

In the autumn Rutherford and his friends (in one place he refers to them as 'us researchers'), among themselves started a little seminar at which he gave the opening talk, assisted by 'coffee, biscuits, baccy and cigarettes—the usual thing in these cases'. At one such meeting, it was proposed to arrange an

annual Laboratory Christmas Dinner—the first was held in 1897. It became
the custom to sing comic songs, sung to the latest music hall tunes, in honour
of the year's discoveries. Some verses have been quoted in previous chapters.
Liam Hudson professes to find these famous ditties full of a strained jollity,
as if these dull convergent dogs were trying to prove to themselves that they
could be lighthearted after all.[2] Yet the style of them seems to me no more
forced than all the similar Christmas dinner songs, which were and perhaps
still are sung at schools and colleges around the country, poking fun in a
friendly and one might say respectful way at the teachers. These matters
might be thought very trivial; but I suspect that they contribute a great deal
to the formation of what used to be called *esprit de corps*, the sense of
belonging to a tight-knit group engaged on a common and esteemed enterprise. Breaking bread together has always been a symbol of unity; breaking
coffee, tea, and biscuits can perform a similar purpose in a more secularized
atmosphere. The sense of purpose was certainly there. From the mid-1890s
on, the innermost secrets of nature broke surface one after another. 'Us
researchers' had but to lower a bucket very skilfully into the well, and Truth
came out of it.

Meantime, Rutherford was pressing on with his magnetic detector, steadily
increasing the strength of his signals, and the range at which his detector
could pick them up, through walls across the Cavendish, to St John's tower—
then from Jesus Common up to half a mile and more; he did plan to take his
vibrator out to the Observatory, but it is not clear if this was actually tried. If
he had not realized the technological implications before, he was soon encouraged to do so. In the new year he wrote to Mary, 'the reason I am so
keen on the subject is because of its practical importance. If I could get an
appreciable effect at ten miles I should probably be able to make a great deal
of money out of it', so if the experiments succeeded, 'I see a chance of making
cash rapidly in the future'. However tentative these hopes might be, plainly
he had no intention of standing aloof from any commercial exploitation of
his research. In February the Hertzian wave apparatus was one of the high
spots of a conversazione to mark the official opening of the new extension to
the Cavendish, although it had to compete with a demonstration of X-rays.
If he did not make any fortunes in those months, at least he had the satisfaction of winning fame in Cambridge. Those who had proposed the German-
sounding innovation of full time research degrees found it useful to announce
that this rash venture had already justified itself, in the form of an invention
of great advantage to a maritime power. He was taken up by all the 'pots' of
the university: Sir Robert Ball the Professor of Astronomy; Sir George
Humphrey 'a great medical man'; Oscar Browning, the archetypal literary
don, who invited him to lunch—'a bit snobby'—and he annoyed Rutherford
by pumping him for information beforehand, and then expounding his work
to the other guests; the philosopher McTaggart who invited him to breakfast

(but not a very good one—'his philosophy doesn't count for much when brought face to face with two kidneys, a thing I abhor'). The idea was to use the apparatus to maintain contact with lighthouses and lightships, especially in time of foggy weather, perhaps as a warning signal between ships—but not for regular communication.

Despite the widespread affectation that science must be 'pure', for if work-aday it can not be part of true learning, it was precisely the utilitarian aspect, the chance that this device could become a useful instrument, which appealed to those who understood that it would be a good thing to signal lightships, even if they could not comprehend the nature of Hertzian waves. In the summer Rutherford demonstrated his apparatus to the Royal Society, quite an honour a bare year after his arrival in England, in September he read a paper to the British Association at Liverpool. This was by way of summar-izing all his work on 'electrical waves'; he wrote to Mary that he would have dedicated it to her, 'but a dedication would look rather funny in a scientific paper'. Despite a fault in the apparatus, which obliged him to ask his audience to take five minutes' break while he attended to it, the session went well. The detector is described as a compound needle—formed of a bundle of fine steel wires, abut a centimetre long and insulated from one another by shellac, magnetized and inserted through a coil of wire with a suspended magnet and mirror to reflect its motion. Rutherford's talk was followed by Chunder Bose, whose experiments like those of Lodge two years before, but more commodi-ously, as Lodge himself was prepared to admit, were intended to show the parallels in reflection, refraction, polarization, between these electromagnetic waves and those optically visible, just as Melloni Forbes and Ampère had done with heat radiation half a century before. The next day there was a short discussion of the two papers. At the end, William Preece, engineer-in-chief at the Post Office, got up and announced that 'signals have been transmitted (by Signor Marconi working with Mr Kempe) across a distance of one and a quarter miles on Salisbury Plain; further experiments are to be made on the Welsh Hills'. Rutherford can hardly have known, as his ship carried him towards England, that another young man, in an even more makeshift laboratory in the attic of his father's country house, was progressing toward the same end; and by the end of September had achieved communication across more than a kilometre, over a rise in the ground so that he had to be notified by gun shot that his signals were being received. Although he had some advice and encouragement from Righi, Professor of Physics at Bologna, Marconi was in some ways even more isolated than Rutherford, he had no colleagues, only the help of his brother and servants on the estate, who could be called on sometimes. He had no post at all, only a father who was still grumbling that Guglielmo was wasting his time and the family's money.

In after years Oliver Lodge in particular accused Marconi of stealing his thunder, and others have joined in, although Lodge did stress that he complained less of Marconi himself than of Preece and his publicity campaign. Was it Lodge perhaps who wrote a short anonymous piece for *Nature* which grumbled at the Wireless Telegraphy Company's taste for getting in the public eye; 'we have in these repeated sensational experiments a pure scientific apparatus boomed by energetic financial speculators for their own individual gain, and not for the benefit of the public—the worst feature of this money-grubbing age.' It remains the case that nobody except Marconi thought seriously how to develop the 'vibrator' and 'detectors' into a communications system. Rutherford alone saw a useful application for his apparatus; and he did not really do so until January 1896, by which time Marconi had already developed his instrument, and was preparing to come to England. In terms of distances reached, Rutherford probably outdid Marconi during February and March, while the latter was busy trying to interest someone in London in his invention. Not until June did Campbell Swinton, who had been invited to one of Marconi's parlour demonstrations at his cousin's house in Bayswater, take a few days off X-rays to put him in touch with Preece. He then gave Marconi a letter of introduction, which pointed out that his apparatus was based on the Branly–Lodge coherer but had already obtained some striking new effects. For in his early outdoor experiments in September, while still working with a spark gap like that used by Hertz, Marconi had noticed that he got better results with a vertical extension between the points. That led him to the use of poles as aerials, which proved the crucial difference that enabled him to outdistance any rivals. He saw that only if reception could be attained over long distances would wireless telegraphy compete with the established, wired variety; ever greater mileage, crossing obstacles in the terrain, transmission from ship to land, or over the Solent: all this was not a question of some scientific record, but a technological necessity. Hence there is a striking difference between Rutherford and Marconi. For all his pleasure at the thought of its potential value, Rutherford was in the end chiefly interested in his experiments as they portray for us the phenomena of nature, and help toward an understanding of these phenomena. Once the detection of electromagnetic long waves had been taken as far as it would go, he dropped it, several months before the 1896 British Association meeting, which was certainly the first inkling he had that Marconi had already gone further with the coherer. Some years later Marconi and his colleagues devised a magnetic receiver which was a technically more convenient form of Rutherford's. By then they had the field to themselves; in 1899, as we have seen, Marconi appeared at the British Association meeting at Dover to link up with the French scientists' conference across the Channel; and a mere two years after that, he had transmitted the first messages over the broad Atlantic.

Rutherford had long since abandoned research on the longest waves then known for work on the shortest. At first he was not wildly enthusiastic about X-rays, just 'the new method of photography', and by the end of February 'the air is full of the new photography, till I myself feel rather tired with it', although he did send an X-ray of a frog to amuse his parents in New Zealand. Perhaps he found all this excitement a distraction from the matter in hand—his own research. Late in March he went off with some friends, not physicists, for an early seaside holiday in Lowestoft, strolling, cycling, sailing on the Broads, swimming (a 7.30 morning dip), they ended up by cycling all the way back, some ninety miles. Three weeks of this open air life marked a complete break for him. When the new term began after Easter, he joined up with Thomson on his investigation of X-rays.

This too was still in a way 'prentice work. Thomson's was the guiding mind, even if the experimental skill which produced the data to support his hypothesis might be Rutherford's. At some point, probably at the very end of 1897, the same time as Marie Curie, Rutherford turned his attention to the radiations from uranium. Now such little work as was done on these rays in 1897 was largely concerned with their ability to render air conductive, and discharge an electrometer. After his work on the comparable effects of X-rays, it was natural for Rutherford to take this line with the uranium rays too. While still at work in the summer of 1898, almost out of the blue, he learnt that a chair in physics was going at McGill university, at Montreal. He put in for it without any great expectations, and was pleasurably surprised to learn he had been appointed. Financially, or from the point of view of intellectual contact it may not have been better than staying in Cambridge. But the great thing was 'to have a swell lab under one's control', as he wrote to Mary Newton—one of the best in the world, he thought, lavishly equipped by a tobacco millionaire, who might not spend too much money on the professors whose chairs he endowed, but had the right priorities—everything for apparatus. When Rutherford pulls ahead of his rivals, it is no discredit to his genius to look first on his swell lab and its equipment: and then on the shabby conditions where the Curies had to work, not to mention all the jobs they had to undertake in order to keep the wolf from the door.

Anxious to make sure that his supply of uranium and thorium salts would reach him at his new establishment, Rutherford wasted no time in settling down for he was keen to stake his claim to a tract of this virgin soil. His paper was not published until January 1899, but evidently completed quite early in the previous autumn. The title, 'Uranium radiation and the electrical conduction produced by it', reveals how far his mind at first continued to think along paths that were an extension of his work with Thomson. One major discovery he did make. He put his powdered uranium compounds on a zinc plate, with another above so connected that the now conductive air would complete a circuit. Then he reasoned that as some substances are opaque to X-rays and every other kind of ray, it must be possible to block the passage for these too. So on the powder he laid plates of 'Dutch metal' (a copper-zinc alloy used as a cheap substitute for gold leaf), one after another. The discharge fell off regularly at first, as if the rays were being absorbed by the layers of metal: then it continued at a steady rate without change for several layers, before it diminished anew. Different materials—aluminium, tin, silver, or even glass, so transparent to ordinary radiation—all confirmed his conclusion: that two distinct kinds of radiation were involved.

Those which could easily be stopped, he dubbed alpha rays; the more persistent, beta rays. He gave their relative powers in terms of the thickness of aluminium foil which reduced their intensity to a half: for alpha rays, one strip 0.005 mm thick would do, and four strips would reduce it to a twentieth. For the beta rays, a hundred such layers, that is 0.5 mm, would be needed to get them down to half strength. Early in 1900 Paul Villard, like Perrin a physical chemist at the École Normale Supérieure, showed that there were even more penetrating rays, which had eluded Rutherford because they were able to pass through all the screening materials he had used. These 'undeviable rays' he called after the third letter of the Greek alphabet, gamma rays. Villard had been a keen cathode ray hunter, and indeed at the Paris congress in 1900 summed up the current state of play on these, rather than discuss his gamma rays. What with actinium and the gammas, on top of all that Becquerel and the Curies were doing, the Parisian school could well feel they were comfortably in the lead. For how long however . . .?

Rutherford's paper does bear the marks of work in progress—he was keen to leap in and tell the world what he had discovered rather than wait until he was sure of everything, for fear that if he hesitated Becquerel, the Curies, or the Germans would forestall him. He had to acknowledge that most of his thorium compounds behaved rather irregularly; and he fancied that radiation might be proportionate to the surface area of uranium particles—so the finer it was ground the stronger the radiation. Perhaps, he speculated, this new polonium (he sent off his paper before he could have heard of radium), was not a 'new and powerful radiating substance', just the old one more thinly divided. But in the end he had to admit that 'the cause and origin' of this continuous radiation 'still remains a mystery'. Another of Rutherford's experiments, however, indicated a possible line of advance. He coated a sheet of paper with gum, sprinkled powdered uranium oxide over it, and once it had set folded the paper over, and then fitted it into a metal pipe so as to form a uranium tube, through which he could blow filtered air. Further down the pipe there were electrodes to test the 'after-conductivity' which might have been imparted to the air. But was the air merely conductive—or was it now radioactive?

As soon as he was in Montreal, his duty, as he wryly observed, now to supervise the research of others only a little younger than himself, he proposed to one of them that he watch over the unruly behaviour of the thorium compounds. Erratic they were—even draughts caused by open doors made the indicator tremble. Gradually Rutherford himself took over the investigation. Soon he decided that it was not so much a case of the air being affected, as that something was coming off the thorium and so floating away. Some kind of gas? To play safe, he dubbed it simply an 'emanation'. What is more, this peculiar substance had the capacity to render other materials radioactive too, even such unlikely things as paper. Rutherford was always at pains to distinguish between his emanation and a radiation, propagated in straight lines—that would be to mistake the cannon for the cannonball—because the emanation was firing particles of radiation, alphas chiefly, into everything with which it came into contact. This he called an 'excited radioactivity'. Feather, his biographer, suggests he had a boyish pleasure in giving it the same initials as his own, in preference to the term 'induced radioactivity', coined by Pierre Curie, who had noticed that even a metal plate too close to some of his radium became radioactive itself. Eventually it was realized that the affected surfaces did not actually become radioactive themselves, so Rutherford introduced the phrase 'active deposit' instead: or in the more colourful phrase of his colleague Soddy, 'a continuous snowstorm silently covering every available surface with this invisible unweighable, but intensely radioactive deposit'. The combination of emanation and active deposit allowed a popular demonstration, in which scraps of paper coated with zinc sulphide were scattered along the glass tubes through which the emanation was led, and lit up as if by magic as it wafted past. These were the discoveries of 1899: early in 1900, Dorn was able to show that Curie's radioactivity induced by radium, was equally the result of an emanation; he was rather annoyed that Rutherford seemed not to treat his discovery with sufficient respect—he wrote off to Thomson to complain of neglect. To Rutherford, this was just filling in the spaces, mopping up after the advances of Curie and himself.

The puzzling thing was that both the emanation and the induced or excited radioactivity decayed quite rapidly with time; the emanation lost half its activity in just under one minute. This decay of activity was proportionate to the quantity, and each form of radioactivity could be identified by the time it took to lose half its strength from a given level: its half life. Radioactive materials seemed to have even more evanescent features. After the new elements of the Curies and Debierne, Becquerel began to wonder whether uranium was radioactive in itself at all. In 1900, keen to produce something he could put before the international congress in the summer, he decided to extract all the active material from a sample of uranium chloride. Over several weeks he managed to get his uranium relatively quiescent, while the extract—something associated with barium— concentrated the activity. Then he was puzzled to learn that if he resumed work on his uranium after it had been left for months, in order to try and squeeze the last of its potency out of it—lo and behold, it was as active as ever, while whatever it was that radiated in his barium had now died away.

Inevitably Crookes had turned to the question of the moment; Becquerel wrote to ask his opinion. Now Crookes, working on similar lines, found that he too could isolate chemically from uranium nitrate something which produced all the photographic effects which had first caught Becquerel's eye, back in 1896. Yet it did not seem to be a new element like radium and so he called it uranium X. (X as the Unknown). This Uranium X however, like Becquerel's stuff, soon lost its power, while the original uranium nitrate recovered it. Becquerel was able to trace the period of decay, and regeneration, for somehow the radioactivity was revived, like an animal body recovering from sickness.

Thorium had proved to be like radium in giving off emanations, and in exciting activity in its neighbours, but from most points of view it would be more like uranium. Would it too have a thorium X; and would thorium's activity also decay and revive? Rutherford was sufficiently confident of his ability to solve the problem—or sufficiently frustrated at having put off his marriage so much longer than he had intended—to take five months off, so as to go home to New Zealand and get married, returning by easy stages so that he and his bride could see something of the beauties of the world on their way. While his French competitors triumphed at the Physical Congress and enjoyed the international Expo., he took a holiday from thorium and its rays, in search of more traditional pleasures. On his return late in the summer he flung himself with all the more furious energy into the fray. To establish the true character of the emanation, no less than to extract the putative thorium X, he needed the help of a trained chemist.

NOTES

1. The various vicissitudes of his life are recounted by R.M. Burdon in *Scholar errant*. Pegasus Press, Christchurch, New Zealand (1956).
2. Hudson, L.H. *Frames of mind*, p. 51. Methuen, London (1968).

6

'THESE ARE THE DAYS OF RAYS'

That summer he met his man. As Frederick Soddy recalled the occasion: 'I heard a resounding voice echoing down the corridor and a powerfully built young man strode down the passage and into the laboratory. He had all the characteristics of a Colonial and I knew it must be Rutherford ... a rather untidy moustache added to his years, and his gauche manner made me wonder how such an energetic person could possibly avoid smashing the delicate instruments which he would have to handle.' Soddy's own personality was much more subdued and in his own view more refined. Born in 1877, the son of a Sussex corn merchant, he lost his mother at the age of eighteen months; brought up by a half-sister, he had an unhappy time of it. 'This environment', he wrote, 'possibly produced in me an exaggerated deference to others more happily brought up in childhood, and to my superiors in social accomplishments.' It may also account in part for the acerbity he developed in later life, for the constant clashes when he taught at Oxford between the wars, and for the feeling which grew within his mind that his contribution to radioactivity was being ignored by a world that ascribed all to Rutherford. In his teens he toyed with the idea of becoming an electrical engineer, but the science teacher at Eastbourne College aroused his interest and enthusiasm, and indeed his loyalty, for chemistry; throughout his life he defended chemists against the detestable incursions of physicists. Before going on to Oxford, he too spent a year at a provincial university, in this case the university college of Aberystwyth. There among others he studied physics with Schott, another pupil of J.J. Thomson, although he always felt he owed more to his teacher at school than to any university lecturer. Even then, he dreamt of bringing physics and chemistry together to explain the nature of things in fundamental terms. In a prize essay on 'The relation between physical properties and the mode of linkage of their constituent atoms', he declared that 'the vast field of research on the borderland between chemistry and physics is almost virgin soil'; beyond that frontier lay territory rich in discoveries which awaited an enterprising young man. After an initial failure (in Latin!), Soddy won a scholarship to Merton College, Oxford in January 1896. That was the season of X-rays and uranium rays, but Soddy was not much stirred. He joined the Chemical Club, became chemical secretary of the Junior Scientific Club, and achieved a First in his Finals in 1898. He worked in the Balliol–Trinity laboratory, and in a private lab which a Balliol friend had installed in a cellar.

After a year of this, he took off suddenly to Canada, armed with a battery of references from Oxford. Soon he obtained a post as demonstrator at McGill in May 1900. Beside his lectures on chemistry, he gave a few on the history of his subject, tracing it back to the old alchemists. For all their aberrations, he refused to condemn the ideal they had set themselves. In a talk on 'Alchemy and chemistry', he asserted that if 'the constitution of matter is the province of chemistry, little can be known of this constitution until transmutation is accomplished. This is, as it has always been, the real goal of the chemist'. If this ambition was at the back of his mind when he met Rutherford soon after, he kept quiet about it. Their collaboration was to be strictly experimental.

First they resolved to identify the emanation. It was exposed to great heat—no change: it was powerfully chilled—passed through a metal coil inserted in a liquid air flask—and so condensed, to prove it truly was a gas. In their main apparatus, a current of air passed over their thorium compound, and then drove the emanation along with it into an ionization chamber, so that the emanation would render the air conductive, and its radiations could be measured. Soddy inserted in the passage various acids and other chemical reagents which ought to have absorbed whatever gas it was. Yet they failed completely in their task—the emanation passed on into the chamber unimpaired. Soddy was amazed. Was this a thorium gas, when somehow it had gained the essential characteristics which belong only to inert gases? But these inert gases are all elements. Can something else spontaneously turn into one of them? His excitement grew. 'I was overwhelmed with something greater than joy ... a kind of exaltation, intermingled with a certain feeling of pride that I had been chosen from all chemists of all ages to discover natural transmutation.' For him, this was the summit of their enterprise. In his state of near-religious enthusiasm, he turned to his partner and exclaimed; 'Rutherford, this is transmutation; the thorium is disintegrating and transmuting itself into an argon gas.' Rutherford was determined not to get too excited just yet—'For Mike's sake, Soddy', he replied, 'don't call it transmutation. They'll have our heads off as alchemists.' Would the ancient fantasy of the alchemists be borne out in sober truth? That is an idea more in keeping with the emotional and imaginative Soddy, whose mind was well prepared for such a concept, than with Rutherford's more common-sense and empirical approach, although in time Rutherford too came to talk of the New Alchemy. Whatever the name, the significance of the process was beyond argument.

The phrase argon gas calls for explanation, since it connects radioactivity to a series of brilliant discoveries in chemistry made but a few years before. After he retired from Cambridge and went back to his estate Lord Rayleigh had continued with physical research. In the early 1890s he was struck by a discrepancy in values for the atomic weight of nitrogen as derived from samples taken from the atmosphere and nitrogen extracted from chemical compounds. This problem aroused the interest of William Ramsay, the Professor of Chemistry at University College London, who suggested that some light unknown gas in the atmosphere might be confusing the issue. In 1894 Ramsay traced in the aerial nitrogen a tiny residue of a gas with an atomic weight some forty times that of hydrogen. On account of the new gas's refusal to react with any other substance he and Rayleigh named it 'argon'—lazy, or inert. He then decided to tackle another anomalous nitrogen, this time from a uranium ore, uraninite. The result was even more exciting; the gas he extracted, as inert as the other, had the same spectrum as helium. Nearly thirty years before, in the early days of spectral analysis, astronomers had seen in the sun's spectrum three lines that could not be associated with any element known on earth, and were a little worried that the sun and presumably other stars should possess an element our planet lacks. Ramsay by the identity of the spectra seemed to prove we do not, for there is helium here on earth, and it can be isolated.

This discovery was announced in the spring of 1895. Ramsay argued that these two formed part of a class of elements with a valency of nil; there would then be room for a whole new column on the Periodic Table. After initial hesitation Mendeleev gave the idea his blessing—very unlike his reaction to electrons. In that case there should be other such elements to fill up the Table; Ramsay set out to search for them. The liquefaction of gases made it possible to produce liquid argon; in this they found traces of new spectral lines, and separated off those parts of the fluid which were more or less volatile than the rest—these showed the different lines. So they had a new element—which they therefore called neon; two others, harder to get at, they called xenon, strange, and krypton, hidden. Neon will appear again in the story; by the end of the century Ramsay managed not only to liquefy it, but even to produce a solid form. All three were identified in the course of 1898, and the finding of no less than three new elements in a single year, coming so soon after the two previous successes, aroused quite as much enthusiasm in the chemical world as the contemporary discovery of radium. Even *Punch* hymned their success: 'New rays of light, new gases sought By a many learned *argonaut* Their eager brains expand, No mysteries their minds perplex ...'

While they were busy revealing the true nature of their emanation, Rutherford and Soddy were working just as hard to extract from their thorium its active constituent, and eventually succeeded. Once again, as with Crookes's uranium X, this thorium X began by containing all the original radioactivity, and yet lost it in a matter of four days, while the original sample recovered its powers. What is more, the decay of radioactivity in thorium X and its recovery in the thorium went together; 'the rate of increase of radioactivity due to the production of fresh material is balanced', they stressed, 'by the rate of decay of that already formed'. Both changes then proceeded in the same exponential manner. They felt bound to the conclusion that thorium was steadily changing into thorium X. Yet chemically these two are quite distinct. Uranium was soon shown to have the same relationship to uranium X. They wrote: 'The proportional amount of radioactive matter that changes in unit time is a constant', characteristic for each type of such matter. Each of these—uranium and uranium X, thorium and thorium X, radium, polonium, actinium, the emanations of radium and thorium, each had its particular rate of decay, its own particular mix of rays—even if some decayed so slowly that their decline was imperceptible, and had to be assumed. If the rate of change is proportional to the quantity changing, 'Radioactive change must be of such a kind as to involve one system only ... the chemical atom ... in radioactive change the chemical atom must suffer disintegration'. This idea was certainly in the minds of both of them by the spring of 1902. Perhaps Rutherford was prepared for it by the language of disintegrating atoms used at Cambridge about the Thomson corpuscle theory. Soddy was none too happy with that. In his recollection of the Montreal Physical Society debate on it, in March 1901 quite early in their acquaintance, he took an active part—and Rutherford was defeated. He was for a long time suspicious of electrons. This kind of disintegration, however, seemed to him a more chemical kind of behaviour. Not all his fellow chemists felt the same.

If radioactivity is a subatomic process, associated with the radioactive elements in whatever form they might be found, the one element must be decaying into the other, as it gave off something that was manufactured within. Divisible atoms were shocking enough. Now inside of five years, here comes a new doctrine to undermine the foundations of nineteenth-century science: elements that naturally changed one into another. Would it be possible one day, of course in the distant future, to excite this radioactivity artificially, and so perhaps change any element into any other? For two centuries this notion had been the prime example of those medieval fantasies which hard-headed science had long ago repudiated.

Rutherford and Soddy published their model of radioactive change in its final form in May 1903. By then Soddy and Rutherford felt that their partnership had achieved all it could for the moment. Soddy decided it would be a good idea to improve his knowledge of the inert gases, since that was what the emanations were. The best school would be with the master who had discovered all the others. So in the spring of 1903 he went off to work for a year with Ramsay at University College. As to what happened next, there is some difference of opinion. According to Rutherford, speaking twenty years later, 'I had outlined a scheme of future work before Soddy left Montreal. He was to tackle the important problem of whether he could detect the growth of radium in purified uranium salts while ... I was to examine whether helium was produced from radium.' Soddy did eventually work on the problem that Rutherford had set him. First he decided to solve the question Rutherford had chosen for himself—does radium produce helium? For his part Ramsay would have preferred Soddy to answer a query that had arisen from his own line of work: if the emanations are inert gases, are all inert gases radioactive? It did not take long to establish that they are not. Then out of the blue while going for a walk near University College, Soddy saw a sign in a shop window; 'Pure radium compounds on sale here.' He went in and learnt to his astonishment that the German physical chemist Giesel was producing them on a relatively large scale, having bought up a great quantity of the residues left in the pitchblende after uranium extraction at Joachimsthal. For the moment, radium bromide was almost cheap, eight shillings a milligram. Soddy quickly bought some 20 mg, and rushed off to tell Ramsay. After they had tested it for purity by burning a little—it should show a bright carmine flame—very pretty, but wildly extravagant to Soddy, who was hardly used to treating radium so freely—they began. For 27 April, Ramsay's lab notebook records the casual phrase, 'Trying Soddy's stuff'. Soddy meant to try and extract helium from radium relieved of any emanation, while Ramsay watched with a pocket spectroscope. Suddenly he shouted 'It's helium. That's D_3'—the bright yellow line which had first revealed the existence of helium.

Perhaps helium could have been attached to the radium some other way. So they isolated some of the radium emanation, condensed it, then let it turn to gas again—and left it pure as it was, and showing no helium lines, to recuperate from these operations. At the end of its four days' half-life, the helium lines were back, first the yellow D_3, then all the rest. There had been no helium—now there was—there could be no explanation but that the emanation was spontaneously giving off helium.

Only weeks later, before the end of May, Rutherford arrived in London on a visit, and bought some more radium for his own researches, which he loaned to Ramsay and Soddy, while he would be in Europe away from his lab. His recollections differ from Soddy's as to the price and the quantity. He implies too that he was present at the original discovery of the helium lines in the product of radium. At least both agree about how excited he was now that he had decent quantities of radium at his disposal at last; 'he was absolutely bowled over', says Soddy, 'and became as excited as a schoolboy over the coming holidays.' The two of them spent an hour watching the glow produced on an X-ray screen by the radiations of their newly obtained radium. As they blocked off the alphas, and then the betas with strips of metal foil, they saw the gamma rays go through all their foils. 'We stuck in pennies between the radium and the screen'—but the gammas could go through half a dozen pennies.

Over the next few months of 1903 and 1904 Soddy rushed about giving public lectures to engineers, military, civil, and electrical—he went to Cambridge and gave a Rede lecture—in the same series as Maxwell's on the telephone and Thomson's on X-rays. He even went off across the world and gave a series of talks on electricity and radioactivity to the gold miners of Western Australia. He developed a picturesque and attractive lecture style, full of vivid and exciting images guaranteed to provoke the imagination. When H.G. Wells wrote his science fiction on what could be done if the energies concealed within radioactive atoms were exploited, it was based on Soddy's 'Interpretation of radium', lectures he gave in 1908 in Glasgow University, where in 1904 he had been appointed lecturer in chemistry. A photograph taken soon after his arrival there depicts a slightly incongruous mixture of the elegant Edwardian gentleman and the scientific thinker in his new radiochemical laboratory. Even before his move to Glasgow, he was proposing to publish his lectures on radioactivity, so Rutherford and his friends were a little upset that he might steal some of Rutherford's thunder. Soddy's book would look like a competitor, and being in a more popular style perhaps a successful one. Rutherford was anxious to get his own book out first. In fact the two are complementary rather than rivals, since they are aimed at different audiences: Rutherford summarized in a clear and comprehensive manner all the work that had been going on over the past five years, while Soddy acknowledged straight off that his is an 'elementary treatise'. But Rutherford does seem to have felt for a time that Soddy, however good a scientist, had forestalled him in a rather underhand way. Otto Hahn, who came out to Montreal to work with Rutherford in 1905, remarks 'I noticed that Rutherford had nothing but praise for Soddy's scientific accomplishments but was reticent on the subject of his personality.' To more intimate friends, like the Yale chemist Boltwood, he could be less reticent: 'Like Soddy the results are all carefully exposed in the front window', he once wrote, and on a later occasion: 'He can never state his own results without hitting somebody else ... Soddy always reminds me of a cock crowing on his own dunghill.'

While theory strode forward, practice flitted on ahead. That same month, on 15 May, Crookes demonstrated at a soirée of the Royal Society his latest invention, the Spinthariscope, in which a tiny dab of radium bromide was mounted in front of a zincblende screen. There it could be watched through a microscope, as it bombarded the screen with alpha rays. As each alpha splashed against the zincblende wall, Crookes supposed, a glint of light shone out. They poured forth in rapid succession, like a shower of tiny meteors, 'the dancing and multitude of which', declared Vernon Boys to the physicists of the British Association, 'forcibly compel the imagination to ... realize the existence of atomic tumult'. This little instrument did as much as anything to bring radioactivity into the limelight, for it laid a demonstration of action at the atomic level on to everybody's table—and so prettily. The Royal Society's evening was quite a social event; the new Prince of Wales was there with his father-in-law, to admire exhibits which ranged from poisonous sea-snakes and pictures of Arthur Evans's excavations on Crete to the latest in equipment for wireless telegraphy. But Crookes's spinthariscope was the *pièce de résistance*.

As the radium was moved closer to the screen, the sparks fell faster and brighter. Enthusiastic metaphors flowed from the pens of journalists: 'the surface looks like a turbulent, luminous sea', or 'a multitude of bright stars twinkling brilliantly in a night sky'. L.L. Whyte recalls how his mother gave him a pocket 'scintilloscope' for his birthday, with which he could explain to his family how 'atoms in spite of their name were exploding all the time'.[1] When the assumption that the glints are splashes caused by direct impact was replaced by the explanation that what you see is actually the cleavage of the crystals of zincblende—cracking under this radioactive shellfire—the intellectual fascination and dramatic beauty of the experiment was but enhanced. In H.G. Wells's *The World set free*, Holsten, the scientist who first achieves an artificial radioactivity so to solve mankind's energy problems for ever, is first entranced by phosphorescence, like Becquerel. As a boy he looks for an answer in the anatomy of fireflies, until 'the chance present of a little scientific toy invented by Sir William Crookes, a toy called the sphinthariscope' sets him on the right track.

Stirring prospects were now in sight. Medical, first of all: as X-rays had offered diagnosis a new tool, might radioactivity do so too? Soddy himself advocated in the *British Medical Journal* that sufferers from tuberculosis would benefit from inhaling radium or, failing that, thorium. As this would excite the 'induced activity' in the patient's lungs, and so continue treatment after medication had been removed, 'if nature had designed these phenomena for the purpose proposed, it is difficult to see in what way they could be improved upon'. Despite the example of X-rays, neither he nor anyone else thought that breathing in a radioactive concentration could do you the least harm. As the years went by, radium became a panacea 'to cure surface cancers, warts, lupus and ulcers'; to relieve gout, rheumatism, and diabetes. The emanation was disssolved in mineral water; pills were exposed to radioactivity so they would be coated with 'active deposit'. In St Petersburg, it was claimed, a certain Dr London had used radiation to cure three white mice of blindness; and he hoped to do the same for human beings. Could it cure cancer? For a general cure for cancer—that will-o'-the-wisp—always attracts the scientific hunter's heart. Alexander Graham Bell, inventor of the telephone, suggested the insertion of radium compound sealed in a minute capsule right inside the cancerous area. That dream 'has stimulated the search for radium minerals over the earth and has caused neither money nor pains to be spared to bring to the doctor's hand as much of the valuable material as possible', wrote one of Rutherford's pupils a few years later.[2]

Then, radium might be a source of light too. That steady perpetual glow could be turned to good account, at least where a gentle illumination was required, for instance in luminous paint on watch dials and the like. Even the reticent Pierre Curie fancied that radium would provide the light of the future, although he had come painfully to realize the danger involved—to one journalist who asked what he would not do with a whole kilo of radium, he replied

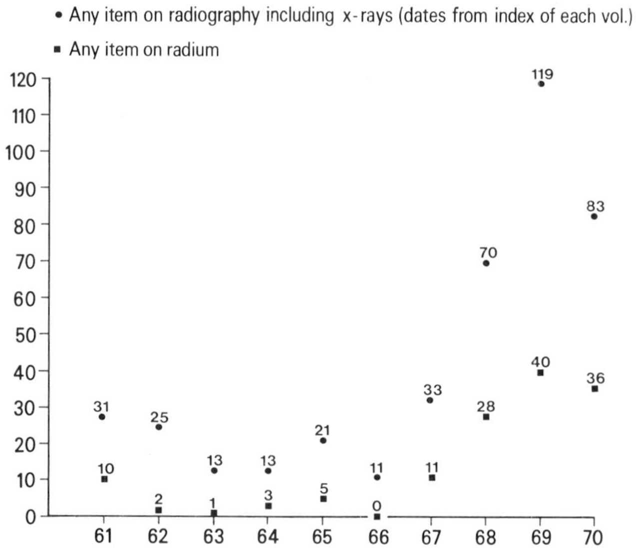

• Any item on radiography including x-rays (dates from index of each vol.)
■ Any item on radium

Fig. 13. Radiography and radium in *Nature* Vols. 61 (November 1899 to April 1900) – 70 (May 1904 to October 1904).

that it would blind you, burn the skin off your back, and most probably kill you—so, what he would do?—leave the room in a hurry. Certainly it was in the process of destroying his own health, whether or not he realized it. Rutherford recalled seeing Curie's painfully inflamed hands when he visited Paris in 1903. As early as 1901, it had been noticed that radium emanation made the skin red and sore after a while, so that eventually it peeled. Crookes suffered from 'a nasty blister in my side' after carrying radioactive samples in his fob-pockets, and learnt the hard way to enclose them in lead boxes in future. Becquerel acquired a similar scar. Some other mice exposed to the emanation went bald, then blind, and finally died in paralysis. The *Scientific American* reports on one bold fellow, who in 1903 tried tasting a solution containing some radium compound—with most unpleasant effects on the working of his heart and kidneys, and severe hallucinations. No one in the wildest frenzy of the drug culture has since tried to become not only turned on, but radioactive ... all the same, it was argued that afterwards the affected area recovers, minus any part that had previously been unhealthy. So the radiation could be used instead of the surgeon's knife.

Then Curie offered the world what princes and all other men most desire: power. That spring of 1903 Curie and his assistant inserted one end of a thermocouple into a bulb containing some barium chloride that had revealed the presence of radium within it; the other end into barium chloride free of radium. The bulb with the radium was one and a half degrees centigrade hotter than the other. They measured the production of heat involved and showed that each gram of radium must generate about 100 calories an hour. This must be due to some internal transformation. The pot seethes and seethes endlessly until at last it boils over, spattering alpha and beta particles all about it. The forces at work must be vaster than anything previously known. At one stage the Curies reckoned as much as 50 000 000 000 calories per gram. Later this was brought down to a mere one thousand million by experiments of Rutherford. Still, that is power enough—sufficient as his friend Dampier Whetham observed to heat up a hundred tons of water by one degree centigrade, or lift a weight of ten thousand tons a mile high; or five hundred tons a mile high with an ounce of radium, if you prefer the figure given by Boys. (Since there are not 20 grams to the ounce, but 28, these figures are meant to convey an impression rather than an exact value.) It would take several thousand years for this gram of radium to wear itself out by radiating away, far longer, millions of years at least for uranium or thorium to fade out. If the passage of time so little affected this outpouring of heat and radiation, temperature troubled it not at all. When Curie came to London and tried his experiment at the Royal Institution early in the summer, his radium carried on in an environment of Dewar's liquid air quite unperturbed, while in liquid hydrogen, which is colder still, it actually seemed to be *more* vigorous, and this at a temperature where ordinary chemical processes are stilled. Down to 180° C below zero, or up to 450° C above, it made no difference. No chemical reaction could release a ten thousandth of the energy per unit weight that streamed forth so freely from these radioactive bodies. The Curies were lionized—besieged by journalists—awarded a Nobel Prize (or at least Pierre was, for the Prize committee could not bring itself to acknowledge that the wife's contribution might really be equal to her husband's). When they came to England they were portrayed by the caricaturist 'Spy' as the priests of some new cult, standing guard over the sacred flame of Radium.

That was the springtime of radium. Those who before had scarcely noticed radioactivity, now went overboard. The *Illustrated London News* published pages of sketches of its wonderful works, as explained by William Crookes. The *Engineer* has one brief mention of the discovery of radium, in a summary of chemical progress in 1899, then not a word until 1903, when there are seven in the first half of the year, ten in the second half. Radium received the honour of the main editorial on 10 April: what is this stuff which gives out heat without ostensible cause? How do these strange substances fire off into space 'myriads of corpuscles smaller than the atom to an extent which the mind fails to grasp?' Perrin had worked out for a French popular journal a calculation that 1 kilo of cathode ray particles i.e. electrons, travelling at cathode ray speeds would boil a lake a thousand hectares in extent, and 5 metres deep. And these radium particles were much more powerful. According to one interpretation, based on Curie's original figures, a piece of radium would melt its own weight in ice every hour for a million years—an exaggeration, but typical of the excited language of those weeks. The enthusiasm of the scientific world at large can be gauged by this chart of the growth in items on radiography in general (including X-rays, etc.) and the number specifically devoted to some aspect of radium in the ten volumes which span 1900 to the summer of 1904.

If that was the response of sober science, the public was even more entranced. *Punch*'s frontispiece of the year was a Transformation scene, in which Harlequin Science reveals the good fairy Radium to make everybody happy with her magic powers. Other cartoons follow—a little girl at the grocer's asks 'please can I have a pennyworth of this radium everyone's talking about', a young couple dream that when they are married they will cook by radium ('but we won't have to wait for that to get married?' asks the the young lady sceptically). Or as Mr Punch sums up the year's events:

> Radium, very expensive, the source of perpetual motion,
> Take but a pinch of the same, you'll find it according to experts
> Equal for luminous ends to a couple of millions of candles
> Equal for heat to a furnace of heaven knows how many horsepower.

Already people felt the urge to speculate about the 'mystery of radium'—everybody had their pet explanation. And what does a true upper class Briton do in such circumstances? Write letters to *The Times* about it. On 26 March, Crookes wrote to revive his old 1898 theory to explain the great enigma, and so sparked off a whole series of letters through the next month between himself, old Johnstone Stoney, and characters disguised as Physicus, Spectator, and Ignoramus ('does Sir William know which of his many friends I am?' asked Ignoramus archly). Even *Nature* published a letter by S.W. (who wisely concealed himself behind initials), who asked why there was so much fuss about radium. A magnet in my drawer does not lose its powers of attraction, he declared, nor had his wife's cedarwood workbox lost its sweet fragrance over the years. Could particles be coming off the box, which had not shrunk in any way over the years—or was it radiating just like radium, all the time?

From an unknown came the first whisper of the next wonderful new insight: from W.E. Wilson of Daramona (wherever that might be), who wrote to *Nature* on 1 July to claim that radium might be the key to a great mystery which had troubled science since physics began; whence the sun's immense and apparently unlimited source of energy? If the Curie figures quoted above are to be accepted, he pointed out, a concentration of 3.6 grams in every cubic metre of sun would suffice for the sun's whole output. There is no such concentration here on earth. But then helium, so curiously linked to radium, is as rare on earth as it is abundant in the sun, so probably radium is plentiful there too. Was radium then no mere oddity, but the power that drives the sun and all the other stars? Was it the prime mover of the universe? Wilson's brief letter aroused no comment, at least for several weeks, during which every number of *Nature* contains new observations or hypotheses on radium and radioactivity. At the British Association meeting Vincent Boys very tentatively, almost apologetically proposed that comets might be radioactive, and their tails streams of alpha particles. But it was left for George Darwin, later that September, to take up Wilson's idea, aimed however in a different direction: to argue that a sun which contains a sizeable proportion of radium would last very much longer than had been estimated.

All the thrust of late nineteenth century thermodynamics and chemistry had gone to restrict that endless drawing on the bank of time, with which Charles Darwin's biology had been so spendthrift. Kelvin had insisted that neither the effect of tidal friction on the earth's rotation, nor the cooling of our planet, would allow more than at most about a hundred million years for the earth's existence. Above all, however the sun was supposed to fuel its fires, in about that period of time it must surely burn out. The longer the time we demand for the past development of the earth's surface features, and the evolution of living forms upon them, the less will be left for the human race to enjoy. That grim prospect is vividly portrayed in H.G. Wells's *The time machine* of 1895. Some claimed there simply was not time enough for evolution by natural selection to have taken place at all. So perhaps George Darwin, as Charles's son, and himself now Professor of Astronomy at Cambridge, was the right man to find some way to call in cosmology to his father's aid. Some twenty years before, in 1886, George had questioned all Kelvin's arguments, the more eagerly because the latest figures for the sun's emission implied that Kelvin's time scale was if anything too generous. Even then Darwin promised that cosmology—or 'cosmical physics'—would decide, for what goes on in our little planet can only be a particular case of universal processes, so that its history will be explained by universal principles. But Kelvin had permitted himself a line of retreat; his estimates must hold 'unless sources now unknown to us are prepared in the great store-house of creation'. And Darwin could now claim—lo and behold, here was just such a new source of energy, which allows us to put off all fears of a dead sun, and renders useless all the estimates of its past duration.

Radium had already laid low many of the best loved theories of the late nineteenth century. Was it really the secret battery of the cosmos? Not surprisingly, the old guard were unhappy at this 'indecent Curie-osity' which left nothing untouched. At the British Association meeting there was a big discussion on the matter. Rutherford set the scene with a short summary of the discoveries Soddy and he had made, and the conclusions they drew. Kelvin had sent in a rival theory, dutifully read out by Oliver Lodge, who must have been somewhat baffled, as he had already declared that the Rutherford-Soddy explanation must at the least be very near the truth. But Kelvin would have none of it. He did now accept J.J. Thomson's theory of ionization, and suggested that the beta rays were electrons (fair enough, except that he *would* call them by his own name of 'electrions'). The alpha rays however were what remained of the radium atoms after they had lost the odd electrion, and gamma rays were 'the vapour of the radioactive matter, i.e. radium'—he could not quite agree that radium is an element. Armstrong, the chemist who fought against J.J. Thomson a few years before, now rose to proclaim that there was no evidence of atomic disintegration; no doubt the radium bromide—and of course Rutherford and the others were not working with the pure element—was disintegrating. But that is just a compound, not the pure element, because that could never break up. In Kelvin's opinion, the source of radioactive energy must be external—thus saving thermodynamics from this threat of rebellion—somehow 'ethereal rays' were absorbed, retained, and eventually given off. Armstrong snatched at this straw. Soddy, Schuster, and everyone else could only repeat the arguments for believing that radio-activity works at the atomic level, so that the atoms themselves must break up; and that the source of power was internal, probably the vibrations of the atoms and their components travelling at enormous speeds, so the laws of thermodynamics are saved after all.

If the sun works on radium, is an atom of radium or thorium a little sun? In 1901, Jean Perrin put forward the theory that atoms are built as 'miniature planetary systems', in which the electrons circle the positive sun, and those furthest out in very large atoms can perhaps escape the attraction of their positive master; they would be the radiation. That might well do for the beta particles, but the alphas and gammas were obviously something else. Becquerel suggested that when such an outsize atom had lost its beta-electrons, which would fly off at a great speed, the positive parts that remained must by reaction move off at a lower velocity. They could form a gas which would settle quite soon, and render solid bodies on which it came to rest radioactive in turn, by pulling negative electrons away from them. This could make sense of emanation and excited radioactivity. The most elaborate comparison of atom to star came from another colleague of theirs, called Filippo Ré, whose theory was read before the French Académie des Sciences in June of 1903. Like Crookes, he wanted to extend the evolution of stars to the evolution of elements. At first, he imagined, the electrons and other components floated freely about, as if in a tenuous nebula; gradually they came together around 'centres of condensation', and so 'gave birth to infinitely small suns'. Most atoms are now dead, like extinct stars; but a few are still alive and kicking, not yet arrived at that final condition. As these larger atoms contract, they must give off heat. That would explain why radioactive atoms are larger than others, and why they emit energy, light, heat, ultraviolet radiation, why they discharge electric bodies, and why their powers are not dissipated in extreme cold—as Dewar and Curie had just shown—for, after all, no more are the sun's powers. Since man cannot separate by any known process the components of atoms, yet we are now convinced they do have components; what immense energies must then hold them together.

But what if we could break atoms up? If this incredible new force is at work here on earth, on our doorstep, in rain and even in the air we breathe—could we not one day control it? If atoms are made up of charged particles in a frantic whirl of vibrating or orbital motion, which sometimes sends some fragment spinning off—what if we could bend this energy to our purpose? How to tap these vast reserves? Even before the decay theory of Rutherford and Soddy, Crookes in his famous British Association address of 1898 declared that 'the store drawn upon naturally by uranium and other heavy atoms only awaits the touch of the magic wand of science to enable the twentieth century to cast into the shade the marvels of the nineteenth'. Prophetic words—and based only on Becquerel's experiments, and the Curies' earliest work! Indeed, without some such aid, the twentieth century might be a disaster, as Crookes foresaw the rapid disappearance of those virgin lands which had staved off from Europe the famines that else would have followed the expansion of her population. Unless we could exploit some of the nitrogen of the atmosphere, those lands would soon be exhausted, and starvation fall upon us. Only chemistry powered by a lavish expenditure of energy could now avert disaster; and the new rays had come in time to save us. But Crookes at that time still thought of uranium and thorium trapping some external source, whereas these new ideas presented far greater hopes. J.J. Thomson was normally a cautious character. But when that summer he crossed the Atlantic to lecture on contemporary physics, he asked whether the secondary radiation excited by X-rays might release energy on a comparable scale. If it be so, then research had already within its grasp a means to do 'by external agency what radioactive bodies can do spontaneously, i.e. liberate the energy locked within the atom . . .'

His heart stirred by the prospect, Crookes wrote to a business colleague on 20 June that one German firm 'are scooping in riches to a fabulous extent by selling radium at £12,000, and they are calling for more pitchblende, and will pay anything for it . . . were I younger I would pay all off and buy the mine myself and work up the radium and become a rival to Rothschild in wealth'. 'If it were ever possible', commented Rutherford in his book on radioactivity; 'to control at will the rate of disintegration of radio-elements an enormous quantity of energy could be obtained from a very small amount of matter.' Oliver Lodge, in a note to *Nature* also in June 1903,[3] struck like Ré by the astronomical analogies, calculated that on the electric theory of matter, all charged particles—primarily the electrons, of course—must radiate energy as they revolve about 'the much more massive rest of an atom' with its positive charge. As they do so, they lose some kinetic energy, and fall in toward the centre. But as the force that acts upon them is proportionate to the distance between electron and centre of atom and to the speed of the electron, and these two factors are in a constant relationship so as their radius of revolution diminishes, their speed increases, they radiate more and more and spin faster and faster 'until presently the speed approaches the velocity of light'. Their mass increases, and so somehow—Lodge was unsure how—they finally explode. That might explain how atoms become unstable, but hardly helps to understand why most of them are stable for such aeons of time. But it did suggest to Rutherford how radioactive decay could be an inevitable process, slowly but certainly transforming the whole of matter. It might well be dangerous to tamper with such a cosmic process. During the summer, between lectures in London, a holiday in north Wales ruined by incessant rain (some things remain constant in this unstable world), and disputation before the British Association, Rutherford naturally found time to look up his old Cambridge friends. To a young Trinity College physicist, Dampier Whetham, he remarked that one day 'some fool in a laboratory might blow up the universe unawares'. Only a joke, a 'playful suggestion' Whetham wrote. But a joke that caught his imagination, for in several articles he repeated Rutherford's fear that 'if a proper detonator be found ... a wave of disintegration might be started through matter, which would indeed make this old world vanish in smoke' or, as he put it in *The recent development of physical science*, 'would transmute the whole mass of the globe, and leave but a wrack of helium behind'. He wrote in July to apologize to Rutherford 'as I do not think you have published your views about the end of the world', and therefore offered to cut them out of his article. Still, as they appear in Whetham's book, Rutherford cannot have minded making the reader's flesh crawl with these 'nightmare dreams of the scientific imagination'. They certainly ensured that the public took radioactivity seriously. No wonder the *Punch* poem quoted above ends with a warning: 'Therefore in unskilled hands, with people addicted to arson, Likely I fancy to prove an exceedingly dangerous substance.'

Amid so many exciting rays, alpha, beta, gamma, and X, one there was which did prove a red herring. These were the N-rays of Blondlot of Nancy, who in 1903 laid before the scientific world his discovery of 'A new species of light', revealed to him while searching for a means to polarize X-rays. N-rays were given off by objects heated to incandescence, originally the Welsbach gas mantle. Like X-rays they passed through solids, disturbed electric sparks, and when they fell on faintly phosphorescent things, made them shine much brighter. Tempered steel, and such like materials in a state of strain were supposed to give off N-rays too; so did plants; and the muscles and nerves of human beings—the N-rays even made eyes see clearer. All these matters were duly reported to the Académie des Sciences through that summer and autumn, as if to rival and perhaps supersede the radioactive radiations in public interest. Toward the end of the year, interest waned, just as sharply. Outside France, few could reproduce Blondlot's experiments. Rutherford tried in vain. At the other end of the spectrum of scientists, so did the practical

Campbell Swinton, ever on the look out for knowledge that could be put to use, since these N-rays had obvious medical possibilities. But he could find nothing. Was it all a physiological effect, so that those who could see Blond-lot's effects must have abnormal sight?—at least if they were French, as J.J. Thomson mischievously remarked, seeing how hard it was to observe N-rays in any other country, despite an English translation of Blondlot's collected papers on the subject. Was it then all imagination? Blondlot insists on the need for absolute silence, no smoking, everybody to keep still—yet not to fix their eyes on the spot to be observed, but rather glance at it sideways, or even looking at something else. In such a reverent mood, they could hardly fail to see what they expected. Others were convinced that these were no new rays, but simply the effects of heat, and what could not be ascribed to heat must be the result of psychology rather than some rare gift of special vision: Blondlot was seeing things. As Whetham wrote to Rutherford in February 'is it a physiological effect—or did Blondlot dream it?'.

Eventually, in September 1904, while the effects of N-rays were being demonstrated in the dark (it had to be quite dark for the effects to be noticeable), an unbelieving spectator slipped a hand up to the prism which was supposed to refract the invisible N-rays so they would fall from a line of phosphorescent paint, on to an electric spark. He switched the prism round so the rays ought to have been bent in quite a different direction and no longer fall on the spark at all. The poor lecturer knew nothing of this, and went on talking about the effects of rays on spark—when by his own hypo-thesis they could have none. An assistant whose eyesight was sufficiently improved to see the hands of a clock, by N-rays given off by a steel file held up in a dark room, still maintained he saw them when the cunning investigator managed to replace the file by a wooden copy—which being of wood was supposedly incapable of radiating N-rays. So it was all an illusion, a 'remark-able chapter in psychological science'. Poor Blondlot! The world has forgotten that he was the first to measure the velocity of X-rays with sufficient accuracy to establish that they move at the speed of light; and recalls only his imaginary rays.

Undoubtedly, Blondlot was so entranced by the successes of the past seven years, that he was too eager to find his own. Of those who had led the triumphant search for genuine radioactivity, Soddy at least felt the excitement of discovery, knew what his findings could mean, and knew how to arouse the hopes and the enthusiasm of the people. In May 1903, as that radioactive summer began to burn, he declared in a short article, that the whole earth must be to some degree active: 'the planet on which we live is stuffed with explosives inconceivably more powerful than any we know of'. His public lectures were often tailored to the audience. To the Royal Engineers in 1904, he announced that if all heavy atoms have this power to some degree, then 'the man who put his hand on the lever by which a parsimonious Nature

Fig. 14. Soddy in his laboratory at Glasgow, about 1906.

regulates so jealously the output of this store of energy would possess a
weapon by which he could if he chose destroy the earth'. To the Institute of
Electrical Engineers, he explained more hopefully that if we could speed up
the natural processes of radioactive decay, one ton of uranium might supply
London's electricity requirements for one year. That was a modest enough
ambition, considering that London was as yet only at the dawning of the age
of electricity. For the future, Soddy held out an ever brighter prospect. In
'The interpretation of radium', the lectures he delivered at Glasgow University in 1908, he promised that 'a race which could transmute matter . . . could

transform a desert continent, thaw the frozen poles, and make the whole world one smiling Garden of Eden'. In the light of some more recent fancies, it is curious to find him then begin to speculate whether this might not have happened already in the past in some civilization which collapsed 'for some unknown reason', so plunging humanity back into savagery, 'under the undisputed sway of Nature'. Now we are again, 'at the pinnacle of one ascent of civilization, taking the first step upwards out on to the lowest plane of the next. Above us still rises indefinitely the ascent to physical power—far beyond the dreams of mortals in any previous system of philosophy.' Heady stuff, and read by a multitude who saw before them endless vistas of power, prosperity, exploration of the outer realms of space (another of Soddy's hopes). Surely the twentieth century would be a Golden Age—or rather a Radium Age . . .

One reader at least was set on fire. H.G. Wells erected on Soddy's premises the edifice of one of his most apocalyptic novels, *The world set free*. It was written in the spring of 1913, some time after 'The interpretation of radium', but he readily acknowledged that the book was inspired by Soddy, to whom it is dedicated. Indeed Soddy makes a brief appearance early in the book, thinly disguised as Rufus, a professor of physics, who 'was giving a course of afternoon lectures upon Radium and Radioactivity at Edinburgh'. The grand peroration of these lectures is reproduced over some four pages; it is a patchwork of phrases taken almost unchanged from Soddy's vatic finale; he speaks of the treasures locked up in Nature—'We can not pick that lock at present, but we will!' and ends: 'I see the desert continents transformed, the poles no longer wildernesses of ice, the whole world once more Eden. I see the power of man reach out among the stars . . .' This long speech is cleverly interwoven with the reactions of a young man, a rather stereotyped Scottish student, chuckle-headed, rawboned, and scrubhaired, 'with great sand-red hands', who is so carried away he keeps on muttering to himself; and after the lecture he rushes off, to climb Arthur's Seat and think how man will one day speed up the process of radioactive degeneration. As he watches the setting sun beyond the city and knows that now we understand the sources of its power and might bring them within our grasp: 'Ye auld thing', he said—and his eyes were shining and he made a kind of grabbing gesture with his hand, 'ye auld red thing . . . We'll have ye *yet*.'

NOTES

1. Whyte, L.L. *Focus and diversions*, pp. 15–16. Cresset Press, London (1963).
2. Russell, A. in 'The industry of radioactive substances', an appendix to S.J. Johnstone's *The rare earths industry* compiled just before the outbreak of war in 1914 and published by Crosby Lockwood, London (1915).
3. Lodge, O. Note on the probable instability of all matter. *Nature, Lond.* LXVIII, 128 (1903).

ENERGY FRAGMENTED, MATTER
DISSOLVED

Even as the old century ended, in December 1900, one more great idea was born. Its promulgation to the world, in the form of a paper read to the Physical Society of Berlin, aroused far less interest than any so far mentioned. Yet in due time this new theory was to tear down more walls in physics than X-rays, electrons, or even radioactivity. This was the quantum—the least unit of energy, the brainchild of Max Planck. In his *Scientific autobiography*, Planck describes the lonely path he plotted for himself in terms very different from the dramatic successes of the Curies or Röntgen; overcast by an anxious and uncertain mood quite unlike the ebullient, almost jolly, extrovert atmosphere in which Thomson and Rutherford worked (at least in their own recollections). Of all the leading figures of modern science, Planck at first glance is the most unlikely revolutionary. Once he called Einstein the Copernicus of the twentieth century, but the title would suit Planck himself better. In his reticent character, his withdrawal from controversy, his conservative and religious turn of mind, he much resembles the astronomer of Torun. As he said, 'by nature I am peacefully inclined and reject all doubtful adventures'. Kurt Mendelssohn, who heard Planck lecture, saw in 'the spare figure in the dark suit, starched white shirt and black tie' the look of a typical Prussian official, 'but for the penetrating eyes under the huge dome of his bald head.'[1] He comments on Planck's dry style, and his unwillingness to engage in the arguments which so enthralled his younger colleagues. But Planck was then already an old man, well into his sixties: Max von Laue, who worked with him before the Great War, and was much closer to him in background, personality, and even in appearance, speaks of a 'magic charm' that emanated from him, so perhaps if you penetrated his reserve it was easier to see the depths in his character. For there were depths, which despite that reserve gave him the intellectual courage to persevere against a lack of interest and encouragement on the part of men whose respect he most desired.

Max Karl Ernst Ludwig Planck was a contemporary of Thomson and Hertz, born only sixteen months after Thomson, in Kiel, then still a city of Danish Holstein. As a child he watched the Prussian troops march in as liberators to restore German-speaking Kiel to the Fatherland; he outlived all his contemporaries—as Von Laue remarked in his funeral oration for Planck, 'the birth and meteoric ascent of the German empire occurred during his lifetime, and so did its total eclipse and ghastly disaster'. One son was killed in action at Verdun in 1916; his elder son Erwin was put to death by the Nazis in 1944, because of his connection with the July plot. In 1945 an American Army unit was sent to rescue Planck from the ruins of the Third Reich—he had already been bombed out. As if to symbolize that the octogenarian Planck personified the 'other Germany' now to be restored, the research institutes founded by Kaiser Wilhelm just before the First World War, and named in his honour, were re-established in the Western zones, re-named the Max Planck Institute.

Planck's father taught civil law at Kiel university, and his ancestors had been lawyers or civil servants for generations. Three years after reunification, the elder Planck took up a post at Munich university, and there Max received his secondary education at the famous Maximiliens-gymnasium. He soon showed all the signs of the gifted pupil, youngest in his class, excellent at mathematics and so good at music that he toyed with the idea of a career as a pianist. 'Despite being somewhat childlike' (perhaps just because he was much younger than his intellectual equals?) 'he has a very clear, logical head' says a school report. Like some others of his type, he thought that his love for science had been inspired by his school, more than by the lectures of his university professors. Certainly he speaks very highly of his mathematics teacher at the gymnasium. From there, in 1874 he went on to Munich university, where he stayed until 1880, apart from a year in Berlin, 1877–8. There he could study with Helmholtz and Kirchhoff. But Helmholtz's lectures were badly prepared and careless; 'we had the unmistakable impression that the class bored him at least as much as it did us', so that Planck was one of the very few students who were prepared to stick his course out to the end. Kirchhoff erred to the other extreme, he was too well-prepared, and 'would sound like a memorised text, dry and monotonous'. Arthur Schuster, who spent a few months with each of them three or four years previously, gives a brighter picture, but then he came to them as a research student. Planck himself acquired a higher opinion of Helmholtz as a teacher once he came closer to him.

For a short while after graduation he taught at his old school, and at the university, until after five years in the wings he was rewarded with an assistant professorship in theoretical physics at Kiel. We can discount as too modest his suggestion that he owed this job to his family connections; and that when he won his transfer to Berlin three years later it was an accidental by-product of his support for Helmholtz in a controversy between him and the school of physics at Göttingen. Helmholtz may not have appreciated properly all that young Planck was doing, but he certainly knew how talented he was.

All his life Planck sought for the rationality of the universe; he was ruled by the idea that the cosmos works according to laws, and by use of our powers of reasoning we can understand those laws. Wherever there is something

Fig. 15. Max Planck.

absolute and permanent, there will truth be found. The search for whatever
is absolute and constant is, Planck said, 'the most sublime scientific pursuit in
life'. Such a view of the world naturally seeks for the most general application
for these laws, else they can hardly be absolutes. Somewhere it should be
possible to formulate a unified physical model, 'a single grand connection
among all the forces of nature'. With these sentiments in mind, it is hardly
surprising that he should be drawn to thermodynamics, still a new science
when he was first stirred by it as a schoolboy in the 1870s, for the inexorable
and universal character of its principles held all that must attract him. Yet the
idea that heat cannot pass from a colder body to a hotter one he found
inadequate, and wished to pursue further this concept of irreversibility, the
irrevocable one-way process that is the flow of heat energy—developing
Clausius' concept of entropy, the increasing unavailability of energy for work,
as it is dissipated. From this he was led on to Maxwell's vision of electromagnetic radiation: what was the relationship between matter, and the radiation it emitted? Unhappily his doctoral thesis, with which he hoped to recast
and reorganize the Second Law of Thermodynamics, was ignored completely.
For years he felt himself neglected and snubbed by the physicists of Germany,

who refused to allow such fundamental reformulations to be made by young fellows in their twenties. A kind of 'father-transference' is often noticeable in the relationships between professors and their research students, but seldom was it as self-abnegating and submissive as with Planck, who adored the ground that Helmholtz trod. If Helmholtz actually agreed with his theories, Planck became quite ecstatic and 'treasured the memory of those thrilling moments to the end of my days'. How much does science owe to these lonely spirits, who do not find a place in an established hierarchy? Perhaps they find it easier to abandon the hierarchy's dearest assumptions? Yet should not this yearning for recognition have made Planck all the readier to thrust aside any thoughts that his mentors might find ridiculous?

Be that as it may ... in the late 1890s, Planck set himself to tackle one problem that seemed to him of paramount importance; the problem of black body radiation, that emitted by a body which should have the property of absorbing all the radiation that falls upon it. According to current theories such radiation ought to be emitted with an intensity tending indefinitely toward the shorter wavelengths, and so concentrated in the shortest. A new concept of energy was required, to discriminate against the shorter wave-lengths and make room for the longer. Plainly there is a connection between temperature and wavelength of emission as may be observed in an ordinary iron bar, when first it is made red-hot, then at greater temperatures yellowish, and eventually it reaches white heat as if instead of one wavelength predominating a great many swarm together. As plainly, that shows the link is not a simple one. Early in 1896, Willy Wien, then one of Helmholtz's colleagues at the Physikalisch Technische Reichanstalt, worked out a formula that seemed to relate the wavelength to temperature satisfactorily. Within a few years, however, experiment proved that his law operated only at low temperatures and the shorter wavelengths. Apparatus in such an institution as the Reich-sanstalt grew more sophisticated every year, and higher temperatures were reached; it became clear that a new law would have to be established. Planck decided to tackle the problem from the thermodynamic end. Why not apply the concept of entropy to the radiation energy distribution as you would have to do with a hot gas? In order to produce a satisfactory equation, he found he had to introduce two new constants, as he explained in a lecture to the Prussian Academy of Sciences in May 1899. One of these, he decided, has 'the dimensions of energy divided by temperature', and so is not one of those universal absolutes he was always seeking. But the other was more promising.

A leading experimentalist at Berlin, Heinrich Rubens, was then carrying out experiments on radiation at very long waves and high temperatures and decided, as he explained to Planck, that intensity was governed partly by temperature of course, but also by some expression 'which remains finite with infinitely increasing temperature'. By October 1900 Planck had finally arrived at an equation which covered the varying behaviour of high and low temperatures, an equation which Rubens could assure him fitted experimental results very well. To establish its meaning, however, he felt it necessary to apply the statistical techniques of probability, which had been necessary for the understanding of entropy and the kinetic theory of gases ... In that case he would have to consider his distribution of energy not as continuous, but as a 'quantity composed of a number of finite and identical parts', just as gases are made up of molecules. These 'finite and identical parts' would be elementary units or quanta of energy. In this way he could achieve the desired equilibrium between matter and the radiation which carries energy away from it. But only if the energy is 'forced, at the outset, to remain together in certain quanta'. These would be the product of the frequency of any radiation by a particular value; in fact his second constant of the previous summer, now denoted 'h'. Now normally measured in erg seconds or joule seconds (after the thermodynamics pioneer). Planck's constant h has, he remarked, 'the dimensions of a product of energy and time', and so may be thought of as the least unit of action. In that case energy must be emitted in discrete units hf, varying as the frequency f, but never any subdivision of this unit.

Planck's quanta were therefore, as he proudly wrote in old age, 'destined to remodel basically the physical outlook and thinking of man ... founded on the assumption that all causal interactions are continuous'. Planck himself was understandably keen to reconcile his new notions with accepted theories, but in vain. Planck had made sense of black body radiation, but at the cost of saying that radiation was emitted and absorbed in separate discrete packets of Planck's constant size, and not in continuous flow. The story goes that one day that autumn he was taking his son Erwin, then only seven, for a walk through the woods, and told the boy he was on to an idea which might prove one of the greatest discoveries since Newton—or else it might be moonshine. Even then he may not have meant that the quantum would upset the most fundamental principle of continuity; he could have been thinking of the new constant simply as a constant. His two new constants, he declared in the paper that he gave at Berlin in May 1899, would help to 'establish units for length, mass, time, and temperature which are independent of specific bodies or materials, and which necessarily maintain their meaning for all civilisations, even those which are extraterrestrial and non-human'. To find such phrases, which smack almost of space fiction, in such a sober journal—and from the pen of such a sober natural philosopher! He must have been excited by the prospect, however cautious he tried to be. As the atom was disintegrating, was radiation now to be atomized?

The reaction to these ideas was distinctly muted. Those who read his paper took them in their stride without becoming too excited. His theory received honourable mention in most German studies of the subject, but nobody suggested it was more than a convenient equation. The only point of interest lay in a possible extension to the Lorentz theory of electrons. In the early years of the century, Lorentz elaborated on his ideas, making use of J.J. Thomson's 1881 paper about 'electric mass' and the e/m work of 1898–9, so as to argue that there was no other source of mass in gravitation or inertia than the electrical resistance. Besides the negative electrons, there were presumably positive ones; we know they have a charge, we know they have an effect on their environment that can be defined electrically. Is there somewhere a solid blob within? Perhaps matter is purely electromagnetic? Then mass should vary with velocity, approaching infinity as electrons approach the speed of light, which would be their absolute limit. Some experiments were carried out in 1903 at Göttingen by Walther Kaufmann, who had been one of J.J. Thomson's original rivals for priority in the measurement of the e/m ratio, and now adapted this technique to see if that ratio varied at the enormous velocities which the beta particles attain. He found that this ratio appeared to vary perceptibly in such conditions. If then the charge e is constant, the mass must be varying—and his calculations showed it did so within just over 1 per cent of what the theory would predict. Thomson took this up with enthusiasm. Dual nature was thus reconciled—not by saying that ether is matter, or that matter is ether rings, as in the vortex atom theory, but by reducing matter itself to electricity, either bunched together in atoms, or moving freely as independent electrons. As in the vortex theory, matter becomes 'a modification of the universal aethereal medium'. But is it then conserved as such? Perhaps it is not truly 'eternal and indestructible'? Even before Kaufmann had apparently produced solid experimental evidence Oliver Lodge gave a public lecture on the electron theory at Birmingham in the first week of January 1904. The *Engineer* fumed at these physicists who are now flying off into fairylands of speculation, into 'transcendental regions which are indistinguishable from metaphysics'. They tell us that electricity is particles; now they want to say that particles are all electricity. Just try 'to persuade a sailor that armour plate is electricity, an engineer that coal, steam, water and cast iron are the same'. Of course that sounded very weird to all but a few physicists. In one of the horde of popular works on radium, *Radium explained*, the author William Hampson, a chemical engineer and 'inventor of the Hampson air-liquefier', takes the opportunity to lash out at the 'electronic theory of matter', which confounds the great fundamental distinction between energy and matter. To him, electricity is energy: energy is motion. Therefore electricity cannot be matter. Matter indeed may be sub-divided; probably the electron—or rather, corpuscle—is not the last word. Ether itself must be composed of granules, one or more stages beyond Thomson's corpuscles—back to good old Descartes might have been his motto. To straightforward engineers and chemists, the electronic theory could well seem a wild flight of fancy, even to those who had now accepted electrons and atomic disintegration. Yet in the narrower confines of the physicists' world, it was now looking very attractive. Langevin, for instance, talking to the practical men assembled at the International Electrical congress held at the St Louis World Fair in 1904, tried to convey some of the fervour aroused by this new theory, 'a new America where we breathe easily, which stirs all our energies'. Beyond the new horizons of the electron hung the vision of a universal formula which would reduce to unity the multiplicity of nature. That is made very clear in the popular books on the theory, published in 1906 by Oliver Lodge and Fournier d'Albe, a friend of Crookes and later his biographer. Soddy saw this as a mirage. In a review of Lodge's book, Soddy suggested that his passion for an underlying single form is but 'a continually recurring phase of an apparently innate primitive mental aspiration', an idea deeply engrained and reflected 'in the most ancient mythologies'. Let us rather stay with our complicated world and not try too hard to simplify it. That is a sharp comment: the source of all the enthusiasm was something which went far deeper than a convenient explanation of some phenomena. But that does not mean the enthusiasts were heading in the wrong direction. Planck himself was tempted to find a link with his own idea. As he observed in a letter in 1905, 'h has the same order of magnitude as e^2/c (where e is the elementary quantity of electricity . . . and c is the speed of light)'.

There was an alternative formula to that of Planck, which was also first put forward in 1900, by Rayleigh[1] and subsequently improved by James Jeans, in England, in the course of a debate between them carried on in the correspondence column of *Nature* through the spring and summer of 1905. Jeans's theory had one great flaw: it depended on a direct relation between light intensity and temperature. All the same, it was less radical and in most people's eyes it looked more plausible than energy fragmented into 'h's. Indeed, Jeans made this aspect quite clear; for him the laws of statistical mechanics show that when Planck's theory is carried to its logical conclusion, $h = 0$. And if experiment suggests otherwise, suggests that h is a real quantity, fitting in actual measurement quite close to Planck's calculated value for it— then so much the worse for experiment. 'Of course', he wrote, 'I am aware that Planck's law is in good agreement with experiment if h is given a value different from zero, while my law, obtained by putting $h = 0$ cannot possibly agree with experiment. This does not alter my belief that the value $h = 0$ is the only value which it is possible to take'. The verdict of Lorentz, the father of electron theory, would obviously carry great weight but Lorentz temporized and would not commit himself. In the spring of 1908, Planck wrote to him to ask him to declare for the energy quantum at the international congress of mathematicians which was due to take place in Rome in a few weeks' time. In the event Lorentz had to admit that he still could not make up his mind. Planck could explain the observations better; but only by insisting on his energy elements 'whose magnitude depends on frequency', whereas any electron should be capable of radiating in all wavelengths. Sooner or later, experiment would justify some theory that could do without this kind of extravagance. So the infant quantum missed its chance to be promulgated to the world from the holy city.

Planck did not go to the congress, but Wien did, and wrote home fuming with indignation. That is what comes of listening to mathematicians, who might be good at equations but could not appreciate the significance of simple experiments. As another colleague remarked, since steel at its melting-point gives off a very intense, dazzling light, by the Rayleigh–Jeans formula, a 'black body' at room temperature, which is roughly one-sixth as hot (taken on the Kelvin scale, from absolute zero) should produce light at one-sixth the intensity, which is clearly not the case. Funnily enough, Lorentz came round to their way of thinking only a few weeks later, in June, when he wrote to Wien on similar lines; he remarked that according to Jeans's theory a silver sheet should absorb and so emit enough incident light to be perfectly visible in a dark room at only 15 °C. If that was impossible, Planck's view was the only possible alternative. Planck was very happy. At last his idea had won some international recognition. Until Lorentz's conversion in 1908, the quantum was restricted to German-speaking physicists—practically to the circle of Planck's friends and associates at Berlin. Even then, the quantum theory failed to cross the North Sea to Britain. As the *Annual Register* for 1913 comments (in its first mention of Planck's hypothesis), it was all 'so contrary to preconceived ideas that it is not surprising that veterans in physics reserved judgment on its merits'. As Rutherford wrote to his friend William Bragg, after his first real encounter with the quantum theory, 'Continental people do not seem to be in the least interested to form a physical idea of the basis of Planck's theory. They are quite content to explain everything on a certain assumption and do not worry their heads about the real cause of the thing. I must say, I think that the English point of view is much more physical and is much more to be preferred.' The electron theory could also be accused of being an attempt to explain everything on a certain assumption. But it was 'much more physical'—easier to envisage in spatial terms, and as such more credible.

However, three years before Lorentz was won over, certain ideas had been expressed in a distant corner of the German-speaking world, beyond the Empire's boundaries, which surpassed in their intellectual boldness anything Planck had said or could accept. These ideas were published in the main German physics journal, the *Annalen der Physik* and were probably refereed by Planck. However, their author, a young man of twenty-six, was not a professional scientist at all, and far from the seats of the academic mighty. He was an official at the Swiss national Patent Office; and his name was Albert Einstein. Without even a doctorate and having failed to get a university post after graduation, in 1905 he was still working as a Technical Expert Third Class at the Federal Patent office in Bern, when in a burst of intellectual energy he fired off a salvo of revolutionary new theories. A native of Ulm, a town otherwise only famous as the scene of one of Napoleon's victories, his family moved while he was small to Munich. But his gymnasium was evidently nothing like Planck's; there no physics teacher inspired him, he found only an authoritarian approach to learning against which he rebelled. By the time he was fifteen he had already thought of moving out of Germany altogether. After a stay in Italy he finally entered the Zurich Polytechnic in 1896. He was entered to study engineering—his father was a manufacturer of electrical equipment—but like Hertz, Röntgen, and Thomson, young Albert was too entranced by the ideas of physics to continue. Unlike almost every one else in this story, his student career was almost as unsatisfactory as his schooling; he kept his sceptical attitude to all authority, his unwillingness to learn what did not interest him; or else was badly taught. Even professors of the calibre of Minkowski, later advocates of Einstein's views, saw in him only a poor student who failed to turn up to lectures. Another professor who had at first befriended him complained that Einstein thought he knew everything already. In the German system, a young scholar was expected to cool his heels for a few years as a *privatdozent*, receiving no official salary, only a permit to give lectures and receive fees from those who attended them. That situation might be endurable if like Hertz you were a sparkling young lecturer who attracted students; or if like Planck you had the family support to last out for five or ten years. Einstein had neither qualification; he could not even get a job as *privatdozent*. Perhaps that very independence, that emotional unwillingness to play the university game, enabled him, almost cut off from the company of other physicists (he had a few very close friends, who knew enough mathematics to follow him, but that is not quite the same thing), to break away from the most fundamental ideas about nature.

Within the limits set for this book, Einstein's theory of relativity can be excluded. One idea, however, which he drew forth out of the well of relativity proved so potent that it must demand mention, although several years passed before its full implications became clear. Almost as an afterthought from his 1905 papers, toward the end of the year the *Annalen der Physik* published a little three-page note, which posed the question, 'Is the inertia of a body dependent on its energy content?' Most readers of the day would have seen this as yet another bright young man eager to have his say on the fashionable topic of electromagnetic mass and the electric theory of matter—and probably no more. At the same time Einstein could also appear to be making his contribution to radioactivity—to the problem, where do these heavy atoms get the energy to shoot off their alphas and their betas at such alarming speeds? He suggested that it follows from the equations used in his exposition of relativity that in radiation the accompanying loss of kinetic energy can be expressed as equal to $Lv^2/2c^2$, where L stands for light, or any other form of radiation, v the velocity of the body radiating, and c the speed of light. But, if we remember that kinetic energy is defined as $mv^2/2$ and cancel that $v^2/2$, it looks as if there will be a difference in m, the mass, as there is a difference in the amounts of kinetic energy, before and after. Indeed, there will be a loss of mass, equal to L/c^2. But, says Einstein, why limit this conclusion to radiant energy—'that evidently makes no difference'? So, change in m = change in E (for energy)/c^2. Instead of the conservation of mass by itself, and the conservation of energy by itself, they are only and always conserved together, so to speak. Einstein had given another fatal squeeze to the twin serpents of dualism. For him, that was one of the main attractions. Not very long after, in 1907, in another paper for the *Annalen der Physik* on 'the inertia of energy' as consequence of his relativity, and then in a longer one for the main radioactivity journal, Einstein developed these thoughts further. If loss of energy is equivalent to loss of mass—is not the mass which is *not being lost* also the equivalent of energy—so in effect there is mass loss just in holding things together—$m = E/c^2$—and hence, $E = mc^2$. So at last Einstein had uttered that famous equation which is now invariably linked to his name—even in the mouths of those to whom it might as well be a magic spell, calling up the spirit of nuclear explosion from the vasty deep. Everyone knows that $E = mc^2$—even if many who glibly use the phrase seem to confuse it with the equation for kinetic energy mentioned above—which is still far more relevant for the lives of creatures who move at a pace where one millionth of c, the speed of light, is pretty fast. As we hammer in nails, rub our noses, shake our heads, drive cars—even manufacture them—perhaps we do not need to worry too much about an equation that predicts effects only perceptible at very high velocities and in highly energetic activities? The author of the formula himself hoped it might explain the emissions from radium and uranium, still a nagging problem in 1907. He also hoped someone with more access to a lab and radium salts might test his idea on such 'bodies whose energy content is variable to a high degree'. But of course, nobody took any notice; no such experiments were carried out then, or for a good many years. Even in Einstein's native land there was not much notice taken except by Planck; and abroad a key journal like *Nature* simply ignored the name of Einstein in 1907, as in 1905. And yet . . . his idea does possess an essential ingredient to make sense of all the questions which so exercised the physicists of those years. There is in that equivalence an implication that was to unleash our mighty Hercules with a vengeance.

All these remarkable discoveries came crowding in on him in a short space of time while still in his middle twenties; the 'prime of his life for inventions', as Newton once said of himself. Perhaps enforced banishment from the centre of things did them both good. At any rate, another of his insights, his paper on the quantum of 1905, must have a place, although its ideas too could not really be absorbed until after the Great War. Here he asked whether perhaps the quantum idea goes to the heart of the radiation problem? Einstein remarks on the dualism implicit in the physics of the day: 'we hold that the state of a body is completely determined by the positions and velocities of a very large but finite number of atoms and electrons', whereas electromagnetic states are described in terms of continuous functions. Any body that possesses mass can be supposed to be sub-divided into its component building blocks, its atoms and *their* component electrons, whose mass and energy can also be estimated. Yet the energy of a beam of light is supposed to be continuously distributed, over an ever increasing expanse. That seems to be common ground to all wave theories of light ... All physicists try to explain how matter and ether-radiation interact. Why not try to create the desired equilibrium between matter and radiation, by treating the radiation as discontinuous too?

Atoms of light? Einstein acknowledged all the apparently watertight arguments on behalf of light-waves, and against light-particles. Was he trying to hark back to Newton and his eighteenth-century followers, who had conceived of a 'matter of light'? Not exactly—the wavelike character of light could not be disregarded. Rather, he suggested, 'optical observations refer to values averaged over time, not to instantaneous values'. Therefore, let us investigate light at the instant that it is generated or converted, when energy is interchanged. A certain definite parallel can be drawn between the expression of entropy for a volume of gas and that for radiation in a closed system. The first expression depended ultimately on the kinetic theory of gases—that they are composed of a finite number of distinct units, the gas molecules. If the formulas of Wien and Planck on the entropy of radiation and the distribution of different wavelengths are subjected to the energy equations, it makes sense to say that radiation too is composed of units, in which the ratio of energy and frequency is as Planck predicted. Then light *is* in a way particulate; it consists of 'a finite number of energy quanta, localised at points of space, which move without subdividing, and which are absorbed and emitted only as units'.

This concept might also help us to understand a troublesome feature of the photoelectric effect, in which electric charge is somehow caused to transfer itself from a metal plate, when exposed to ultraviolet light. Lenard had shown this was due to the expulsion of cathode rays, which could carry negative electricity to an opposing plate, and thence to a wire. He could then measure the current and show it was proportionate to the intensity of his source of light. In 1899, he took up the investigation where Thomson and his team had left off. By 1902 he had found a way to measure the maximum speed of what were now seen to be electrons. Greater intensity of light ought to transfer more energy to the electron, when it was ejected, and throw it faster into space. Yet his measurements did not confirm that sensible assumption. The speed and range did not alter, only the amount of electrons ejected ... Curiously enough it seemed their speed could be increased, by raising the *frequency* of the light. Lenard could only conclude that there is no direct energy exchange; the light just triggers a disturbance inside the atom, which releases an electron, which is already vibrating at the same velocity inside its atom as it will have when it flies off. What about this relationship between the frequency of the light and the electron's speed? He could only suggest that there had to be harmony between the frequency of the light wave outside, and the electron inside; so they were in tune, and the electron was stimulated to leap off. But how? And how could its vibration within the atom be measured? Einstein suggested that if Planck had been right, light must fall upon any body as quanta, which in this effect were knocking the electrons out of the metal: the stronger the light, the more light particles; the more light particles striking the metal, the more electrons—but at the same speed. But if the wavelength of the light was shortened, and so the frequency increased, so too was the energy with which the electrons were ejected.

The idea of discrete 'bits' of light had been tentatively suggested by J.J. Thomson in 1903. In the course of his American lecture tour that year, he raised a curious hare not to be taken too seriously. If a beam of X-rays is a continuous wave, they ought to ionize all the molecules of air, or other gas in their path. But they do not—far from it. How is this? He suggested going back to Faraday's tubes of force—the antedecedent of Maxwell's electro-magnetics. For Faraday radiation was a vibration of these tubes or lines. But, Thomson argues, if we think in these terms, the tubes can hardly fill the ether through which they are extended; rather, we should look on them as 'discrete threads embedded in a continuous ether', which would suit the model of an ether with a fibrous structure such as had recently been proposed. Energy moves along the tube 'as a kink runs along a stretched wire'. Then the wave of light or of X-rays must have such a structure too; the wave front will not be a continuous line of illumination, but 'a series of bright specks on a dark ground', for the bright spots will only occur where the tubes of force cut the front. Instead of an undifferentiated wave, this is one flecked with foam. In later years he was to claim that he had in this way pointed to the next stage in the story—the theory of 'photons', as the light quanta were subsequently re-named. At the same time he hardly ran to embrace Einstein for confirming his ingenious speculation. Indeed he did not take any notice of the Swiss Eruption at all. It is virtually certain that they arrived at their respective 'pieces of Light' models quite independently. J.J. Thomson did in a 1907 version use the same photoelectric result as Einstein had done, and for a few years put some of his research students at Cambridge on to experiments that might support his interpretation. None of this came to anything, although Planck used to reckon Thomson, in consequence, as one of the very few who sympathized with Einstein's bizarre suggestion. But J.J. Thomson's model was tangible and simplified: Einstein's was mathematically precise and rigor-ous. All the same, it was only when practical experimental evidence did bear out Einstein's theory, in the early 1920s, that most scientists were prepared to swallow the implications of his equations. Planck himself was none too happy with the idea. When Einstein's special theory of relativity came out a few months later, he embraced it enthusiastically. He and Max von Laue, his chief assistant at the time, got in touch with Einstein; they began to exchange letters, and even visit him in his Swiss fastness. But the light quantum—those 'darts of light'! They were too revolutionary for Planck to swallow, never mind anyone else. In 1907, he wrote to Einstein to explain that his energy quanta simply could not continue on their way in a vacuum, a view that was to be echoed in other letters that passed between him and Lorentz, and Einstein. How can the quanta keep going as separate fragments of light across the endless distances of interstellar space? Surely there must be some characteristic of free ether, which makes it necessary for bodies to take in energy in these units. They seem to have thought that an atom, or electron, or whatever, can only take in energy in measured bites, and spit it out in bites of the same size. But that does not mean radiant energy must spread across space in bite-size pieces. Lorentz and Planck patiently explained to Einstein all the evidence for a wave theory of light which just could not be squared with the propagation of radiation as separate particles. 'We should have to reject the whole of optics', Planck wrote. Should they sacrifice all that for the photo-electric effect?

Einstein commented to one of his friends that Planck, however friendly, had one weakness, an awkwardness when he tries 'to find his way into trains of thought that are strange to him'. In September 1909, Einstein, at last in a university post at Zurich, and recognized as the unknown master who had in the special theory of relativity produced an insight equal to the greatest of his contemporaries, was invited to speak to the physics section of the Versammlung Deutscher Naturforscher und Aerzte, at Salzburg, on 'The development of our views concerning the nature and composition of radiation'. He coupled his picture of the quantum with relativity; by now the latter was widely accepted. Yet Planck himself was still dissatisfied with Einstein's particles of light. Brilliant and imaginative Einstein might be, this time he had gone too far. With Planck (who chaired the meeting) in opposition, few were likely to be convinced. Only one leading scientist declared himself a supporter, Johannes Stark. There is a cruel irony here: Einstein's theory was to some extent an interpretation of the research of Lenard, and was taken up only by Stark; they became the most ardent of Nazi scientists in a later time, when the two of them led the society for the preservation of a purer Aryan science in an assault on Einstein and relativity. Indeed they were both among Hitler's earliest admirers, at least among the German intelligentsia. In the 1930s Stark delivered some of the most nauseating speeches ever uttered by a major scientist, for which he was duly rewarded with the directorship of the Reichsanstalt. However, between 1905 and 1909 Einstein corresponded with him in the most friendly way, as Stark offered what he hoped was fresh evidence in favour of quanta of light. He had a bull-at-a-gate manner in his research,

Fig. 16. Johannes Stark.

a certain aggressiveness toward received opinion—perhaps it was a defect in his character, which was to drag him into his later political aberrations. Skilled at constructing experiments and getting his practical ideas to work, he was also ready to dream up theories that accounted for one particular phenomenon, without worrying too much about their consistency with the overall picture: nor had he patience with elaborate mathematical reasoning.

Originally a product of Munich university, he also studied for a while with Goldstein and was working on positive rays, when he announced that the light they produce when they clash with the molecules of residual gas in the tube betrays a Doppler effect—a shift of the wavelength when viewed in the direction of their motion through gas. This effect, he claimed, must show there is a minimum value to exchange of energy between the oncoming positive particles and those of the gas. Having once decided to adopt the light quantum idea, he produced a rush of arguments on its behalf; it explained the apparent limit to the lower wavelengths of X-rays, and why X-rays pack so much energy some distance from their starting-point. As with the positive rays, so in general presumably atoms only emit light to a certain minimum value. The next year, 1908, he thought up some fresh arguments. With light quanta you could account for all the chemical effects of light by supposing that when these quanta strike a surface they release the outer electrons, when they can impart more energy than would be needed to bind those electrons to the main body of the atom. Unfortunately almost every argument was vitiated by some mistake or other. Stark was seldom able to produce a calculation to match his fancies to the phenomena. When criticized he became increasingly truculent. Just as Darwin complained that Chambers had queered the pitch for the theory of Evolution, by publishing a crude version full of blunders and wild surmise, so might Einstein worry that with friends like Stark the light quantum concept had no need of enemies. The friendly letters began to turn sour. By the end of 1909, another former ally, Sommerfeld, whose skill lay in precisely the opposite direction, in general theories and precise mathematical expression, was reproaching Stark for his dreadful errors. In the end he told him bluntly 'a contest between us would be unfair, for you excel in experimental ideas while I possess greater theoretical insight'. Stark's reaction can be imagined—his was not the personality to take a snub like that quietly. His readiness to rush in where angels feared to tread took Stark into fresh pastures that only a few years later were to prove exceedingly fertile. For the moment, his mistakes and his boorishness may well have deterred his colleagues from entering those green fields.

NOTES

1. Mendelsohn, K. *The world of Walter Nernst: the rise and fall of German science*, Macmillan, London. p. 118 (1973).
2. With some hesitation ('I venture to suggest'). Rayleigh, Remarks upon the law of complete radiation. *Phil. Mag.* **XLIX**, 539 (1900).

8

INTO THE CORE OF THINGS

What did happen to an atom when it went radioactive? Could the answer help to explain what prevents most atoms falling to pieces? After all, most of matter is not firing alpha particles in such a frenzy. Yet Nature out of her usual courses might explain her normal state, as Francis Bacon claimed. Atoms, apparently, contain electrons. But *how* do they contain them? What forces hold an atom together; what relation do these parts bear to the whole? Electrons are negative. Yet atoms, unless ionized, are electrically neutral, so there has to be something positive in the atom too. Except in a radioactive state, atoms are permanent, stable things, so surely they must have a definite structure which preserves them. One of the first ideas about this structure was J.J. Thomson's. He conceived of an atom as a 'sphere of uniform positive electrification' (spherical so that electric forces within would be exerted in proportion to distance from the centre) with the electrons enclosed inside it— the word 'embedded' is often used—the electrons are like pieces of plum in plum pudding, or currants in a bun, depending on your culinary tradition. But that suggests they are fixed, whereas Thomson was very clear that his 'corpuscles' would have to be in motion, whirling about at high speed around their rings, one behind the other like beads on a string. They need not be travelling in circles in the one plane either. He could envisage them as free to move in any direction just so long as they kept their distance from the centre, so that they would form spherical shells within the main enclosing sphere, a little like the planetary spheres of old Aristotle's cosmology. This was an ingenious theory, which could show how the numbers of electrons in each sphere might answer to many of the electrochemical features of various elements. Yet it seemed too fanciful, and could not offer explanations for the spectroscopic characteristics of elements, so decisive for physicists. Was there any real experimental evidence?

Soon there were other hypotheses in the field to compete. Interestingly, these speculations were much less popular among German scientists than elsewhere. A few, however, did indulge themselves. Lenard, impressed by the way electrons passed through solid metal foils, insisted that matter must be mostly empty space; he could even calculate what a tiny fraction of space was actually occupied; for instance a cubic metre of platinum would not contain above a cubic millimetre of material. For him atoms consisted of what he called dynamids, doublets in which the negative electron was attached to its positive twin—a cloud of currants without their bun, or perhaps pairs of one negative raisin and one positive sultana stuck together. Presumably in ionization one negative partner came unstuck? But this idea could find little more experimental justification than the other. The imbalance between positive and negative bothered them both. Electrically there ought to be a difference of sign only, yet it seemed that Thomson's electrons were *all* negative. The carriers of positive charge, which must exist to balance them and so preserve electrical neutrality, must possess some qualitative difference to make up— but what? James Jeans suggested that 'the outermost shell in any atom consists exclusively of negative ions'—i.e. Thomsonian electrons—to keep up the culinary metaphor, a bun coated with chocolate icing. But why the positive pastry had to keep under the negative surface he could not explain. A few years later Rayleigh proposed another version with the number of electrons in each atom so large it could be regarded as infinite, so that the 'cloud' of electrons in each atom could be treated as a fluid, with the negative floating freely through the positive, which was somehow not free. Thus the negative particles would be distributed quite uniformly through the positive sphere—perhaps we had better stop talking of buns, and think rather of chocolate sauce, the negative being the chocolate, the positive the base— being an ideal case, there are of course, no lumps . . .

Closer to the right road were models in which a central positive nucleus held electrons in orbit round it, like a miniature solar system; such was the 'nucleo-planetary' concept of Perrin. As he put it in the *Revue Scientifique* in 1901, atoms could be composed of 'one or several masses very strongly charged with positive electricity, in the manner of positive suns, whose charge will be far superior to that of a corpuscle, and on the other hand a multitude of corpuscles in the manner of small negative planets, the ensemble of their masses gravitating under the action of electrical forces'.[1] The comparison with the solar system was taken quite literally, since the same forces and the same mechanical laws ought after all to operate, so everybody assumed, in the miniature world of the atoms as in the great macrocosm. Fournier d'Albe in his book on *The electron theory* is quite carried away by the comparison: the ratios in the sizes planet:sun are curiously like those electron:atom, and if we could imagine the frequencies of revolution of the planets round the sun reduced so as to correspond to the different size of atom and electron, the frequencies too would correspond to those of the electromagnetic spectrum. To some Brobdingnagian being our sun and his planets might appear like an atom; while electrons could be so many little earths 'in which life might not very materially differ from life on our earth'—and us none the wiser. Hence the fantasies that stellar systems might be part of yet huger bodies, as we are composed of these little ones; if every pebble is a little universe, might not our visible universe be a little pebble in some still greater one? For Schott, another British physicist, each electron is an 'oblate spheroid'—flattened at the poles just like our earth, although in order to preserve both stability and the specificity of spectral lines, he did allow for electrons expanding against the pressure of the ether. Stark had his own version. Perhaps the outer electrons were but loosely attached, he thought; perhaps atoms could even share their outer electrons, and that was how they were bonded together. The different spectral lines might then be produced by a partial separation of a surface electron from its positive core, the 'archion', as this central body would have power enough to pull the electron back after it had moved away. Like a comet drawn towards the sun, it will return over a very elongated elliptical track. When quite near the centre, it has still energy enough to turn about—it is hardly clear why that should be so—as it takes the curve, it fires a burst of radiation, but will not have energy enough to carry it so far this time, before it turns back once more, with another burst, another quantum of value hf—but this time at lower frequency; and so on through a series of ever smaller ellipses until it returns to its original orbit. That means quanta are emitted at the furthest and nearest points of each revolution to the archion, the 'sun' at the centre of the atom. The different frequencies are thus related to succeeding distances of these electrons from their base line. He stood by this notion when in 1911 he wrote his major treatise on *The dynamics of the atom*.

As an alternative there was the Saturnian version of the Japanese Nagaoka. Maxwell had shown how Saturn's rings are made up of a very large number of extremely small, quite unconnected particles revolving around the planet independently but in concentric circles, which nevertheless remain stable and regular in their procession. Nagaoka endeavoured to prove that atoms are analogous. Mutually repelling (because all negative) electrons, no less than mutually attracting tiny satellites, would also preserve order, while oscillations in the rings of electrons would give rise to the emissions that produce the spectral lines that typify each element. All the phenomena of radioactivity and ionization he hoped to make clear likewise. Indeed, these crowds of tiny particles could form bands like Saturn's rings, of just such widths and distances apart as to correspond to the band spectra of each element. Unfortunately the Saturnian idea was incapable of accounting for the values of spectral lines as observed; so that too had to stay in the category of ingenious but unaccepted speculation.

Pause to consider this irruption from far outside the charmed circle. No longer was the debate confined to the universities of Western Europe and North America, almost to a handful of centres of excellence in the leading scientific countries; a non-European had stepped boldly past them all; not a colonial but a representative of the Yellow Peril on which European statesmen loved to sermonize—here was a young man, descendant indeed of a line of nobles, but certainly the first to benefit from a modern education, never mind a scientific education, one of Tokyo university's first physics graduates. After some unexciting research on magnetism under an uninspiring expatriate guide, he had been sent to study abroad in Germany; he took the opportunity to attend the 1900 international physics congress, where radioactivity was all the rage, and so found himself plunged into fundamental questions. Certainly he had no need to placate an academic establishment—there was not one yet in Japan.

Through this first decade of the century, with new atomic theories rising like pheasants every year, only to be shot down the next, Rutherford was busy with his alpha particles. The alpha particle was a harder nut to crack than the beta, but a juicier one. Several more valuable ideas came out of this investigation. Stage by stage Rutherford established that his alphas were positively charged particles, then found the ratio of their charge to their mass, and tried to compare this charge with that on electrons or hydrogen ions. Even before 1903 it had occurred to him that they might be positive atoms of helium, and he meant to pursue this line, when Soddy and Ramsay most annoyingly confirmed the association of helium with radium ahead of him. Perhaps all heavy elements would eventually break down to helium? Soddy in his 1903–4 lectures and articles usually suggested that alpha particles were basically hydrogen, the positive remainder of an atom when its negative electrons, or some of them, have been lost as beta particles. In his own 1904 book on radioactivity, Rutherford was ready to chance his arm with an outright declaration that alphas are but helium, and by 1905 he could write to his American friend Boltwood: 'I feel *sure* helium is the alpha particle of Radium and its products but it is going to be a terrible thing to prove *definitely* the truth of this statement.' As late as January 1907 he had to admit in a letter to Hahn that perhaps the alphas would turn out to be hydrogen after all and the helium came from some rayless by-product of the disintegration process. In June Norman Campbell, another fellow of Trinity, sent in to *Nature* a calculation based on Rutherford's own data, by which he concluded that alphas must be hydrogen and not helium. There was a nasty moment in July when Ramsay announced that emanation only gave off helium when dry. He had obtained neon when his emanation was dissolved in water and argon when it was in copper sulphate. So maybe all the noble gases were radioactive products after all. Boltwood in great annoyance protested to Rutherford, 'why hasn't it occurred to him that radium emanation and kerosene form lobster salad!' Had Ramsay controlled the transmutation of radium? For months there was great excitement, since Ramsay was accepted as the last word on inert gases: he had found them, now he could produce them at will. But his results were not repeated, and the whole venture proved a flop. Ramsay's hopes had carried him away.

During these middle years of the decade, a certain sour note can be heard at times, as the great explorers sailed into slack water. Now the new found land had been won, all that remained was to survey in detail; to track down each new 'metabolon'—Rutherford and Soddy's word for the temporary states of radioactive matter—and try to sort out their relationships with one another. Normal science replaced the breakthrough, and it was harder to keep ahead. Did uranium decay into radium eventually—could you prove it by growing radium in a uranium compound that was originally free of radium? Boltwood declared some of Soddy's results 'without significance'—harsh words for a respectable scientific journal. Soddy was evidently very angry, and counterattacked by challenging the purity of Boltwood's own sample. Boltwood did the same for the radium salts used in one of Soddy's experiments. It is always a blow below the belt to imply another scientist has been careless and let his materials be contaminated. Becquerel and Rutherford disputed the character of alpha rays. Rutherford began to believe that Becquerel resented the way Rutherford had taken over the lead in research into what were once 'Becquerel rays', and was determined to discredit him. Not that that frightened Ernest Rutherford; 'it will not be very long before I sail into friend B. in good style and reduce him to atomic fragments if not to electronic'. Encouraged by Boltwood ('when you go for him you will give him such a shock that he will give out gamma pulses like an X-ray tube'), Rutherford declared that 'the Lord has delivered Becquerel into my hands' (Cromwell's famous cry of pious triumph, repeated by Huxley before he pulverized bishop Wilberforce at the great Evolution debate—surely there is some psychological secret there?)

It is indeed curious that the French scientists, who were first in the field with radioactivity, largely lost their predominance after 1903. Pierre Curie was killed in a traffic accident in 1906, Becquerel died in 1908. But there is more to it than that. Was there perhaps a hesitation on the part of the powers that be in French academic life, when asked to support borderline sciences like physical chemistry and theoretical physics, still lacking in Gallic clarity and precision, for all the public excitement they generated? Was it affected by the shortage of numbers, a very small supporting cast to back up the stars? If so, any weakness there was made worse by pluralism, for sometimes two or three key posts were held by one man, which must have hindered competition, as did the concentration of talent in Paris: at one time Becquerel managed to be Professor of Physics at the Conservatoire Nationale des Arts et Métiers, at the Muséum d'Histoire Naturelle, and at the École Polytechnique—simultaneously.

In 1907 Ernest Rutherford returned to England, to Manchester. But this was a very different Manchester from the Owens College which J.J. Thomson had left thirty-odd years before. In 1900 Rayleigh formally opened a brand new physics building, the fourth largest in the world, and very much bigger than any other in the British Empire. It was even larger than Helmholtz's new establishment at Berlin. J.J. Thomson, Oliver Lodge, and all the other magnates of physics were there. Schuster, in his speech at the laying of the foundation stone in October 1898, stressed his dissatisfaction with the current trend in laboratories, where research students were largely segregated from those taking ordinary courses; sometimes they even went in by separate entrances, and then went each to his own little room. In *The progress of physics*, his very personal account of the history of these years, Schuster compared Helmholtz's previous lab in Heidelberg to the solitary splendours of the new. When his own building was constructed he made it clear that teaching and research areas were to interpenetrate in his new Mancunian stronghold. Research students would muck in together as in the good old days—no matter if they felt a little crowded occasionally, their interaction would be good for the production of new ideas. Perhaps these principles did help to promote the comradeship, the mutual aid, and the intellectual striking of sparks that distinguished the Manchester school in the years to come. Not that Schuster can have expected in 1898, or even in 1900, that his school would become a centre of radioactivity. Apart from a casual reference to the possibilities for spectroscopic and photographic work in the basement, he boasted only of the facilities for electrotechnics. That was the sort of thing which would encourage the generous but practical burghers of Manchester.

So Rutherford returned in triumph; he was welcomed back to the British scientific community at the 1907 BA meeting in Leicester, with a special discussion on 'The constitution of the atom'. To loud cheers he announced that 'the electron has come to stay'. Its existence was now proved, and so too the hypothesis that it entered into the composition of all matter. On this foundation Oliver Lodge then defended 'the electrical theory of matter', which said that the mass of the electron derives from its charge and velocity, and so all material things are in the last analysis electrical. His only problem was the number of electrons needed; to make up the mass of an atom there would have to be nearly two thousand, and yet the radiative activities of atoms imply that only a handful of electrons are there deployed. The solution was what I have called the iced bun model, in which a few relatively free electrons skim the surface, while the great majority are 'completely encased or submerged in an opposite charge'. These 'deep-seated' particles are inaccessible and unaffected by the outside; the work has to be done by the few.

But now a split appeared in the ranks. Those who saw themselves as physicists were at the least attracted. Kelvin alone stood aside. For him atoms of matter were static and unchanging things; the idea that all the differences of the elements could be accounted for by differences in the number and arrangement of identical components he abhorred; such a notion was, to say the least, 'extremely improbable'; and the transmutation of one element into another by the loss of a few of its components was quite impossible. There are 'electrions', as he would go on calling them, or 'atoms of resinous electricity' but they are loosely attached to real atoms of matter, and so intermediary between the atoms and the ether. As he put it, an atom is like 'a big gun loaded with an explosive shell' (strange how popular these military metaphors were, in that age of universal peace . . .). In reality, the gun was unimpaired when it fired; the shell was independent, not truly part of it; and the electrion, when released from the connection with its guardian atom, changed just as radically as it interacted with the ether.

Soddy now shifted his ground a little, back among the chemists—he pronounced this electrical theory of matter mere 'speculation', the rudest word in the scientific vocabulary, at least among those who think of themselves as true experimentalists. All these theories were 'little more than an ingenious mimicry of known facts'. Larmor replied that physicists were entitled to frame hypotheses even about the sacred atom. But to chemists, the constitution of atoms was a luxury, fanciful if perhaps entertaining, and only such electrons as might take part in chemical reactions could be of interest. Inevitably, as *Nature* reported, 'few decisive statements could be made'. Rutherford, more euphorically, wrote off to his mother 'It was the best discussion at the meeting'. At all events there was a star cast . . . with a peer and three knights (and a couple of future ones).

Next day, the Chemistry section held its own debate, on ionization, led by Armstrong, who was evidently determined to die in the last ditch of the old atomism. Their president, Arthur Smithells, Professor of Chemistry at Leeds, had already made known his doubts about the new radiochemistry, a 'chemistry of phantoms', which tore up the foundations of established knowledge on the basis of such tiny amounts of material that the chemist of the good old school 'is tempted to think of Falstaff's reckoning and to exclaim with Prince Henry "Oh monstrous! but one halfpennyworth of bread to this intolerable deal of sack!"' Smithells defined his ideal; a man 'not given to elaborate theories . . . nor has he usually an aptitude for mathematics'. Just as he should not know more mathematics than is good for him, so he should avoid all worries about the philosophical bases of his science; 'it is as disturbing to the proper work of a chemist for him to be constantly dwelling on the inward nature of his hypotheses as it is distracting in ordinary life to have men always talking about their emotions'. Evidently he wanted a stiff upper lip—and let us leave the inside of atoms, and our minds, severely alone. 'Could anything be more hopeless?' commented Boltwood when he read it. After that keynote address, a full airing of the subject was bound to attract those who were loooking for a fight. A good many people turned up 'with the object of combating Prof. Armstrong's views'. Phrases like 'preposterous' and 'destitute of common sense' filled the air. Lodge spoke up for the physical view, but he reassured everybody that 'chemistry was not being cold-shouldered by physics'—quite the reverse. All the same, a good many chemists of the old school disliked the idea that physics was helping them by explaining chemical phenomena in physicomathematical terms. They felt their science was reduced, their territory infringed. Recalling the Constitution of the Atom debate a couple of years later, again to the chemistry section at the BA, Armstrong declared that 'not a few of us among the audience felt that the physicists were wildly waving their hands in the air' in a desperate endeavour to find some kind of mathematical interpretation.

Luckily, in the course of 1907, and into 1908, Rutherford at last found convincing evidence of the amount of charge, using apparatus designed by Geiger (the ancestor of the famous Geiger counter), in which single alpha particles were released into a hollow brass tube, through the middle of which ran a wire with negative electric charge opposite to that of the tube. The needle of an electrometer linked to the wire could then disclose the effect of each positive alpha. Once given the charge on the alpha, and its charge to mass ratio, the mass could be found—equal to four hydrogen atoms—that is, equivalent to helium atoms, but as they carried a double positive charge, evidently lacking two electrons. Finally, he devised an experiment in which radium emanation flowed into a glass tube with very thin walls, thin enough for alphas to pass, but quite gas-tight, so no ordinary helium could get through. The alphas would penetrate the glass to an outer chamber with walls thick enough (in the end wrapped in lead) to prevent them seeping any further. The space between the inner and outer tubes had been thoroughly evacuated, so there could be no helium there before. Mercury then pushed whatever it was up into a tapered spectral chamber, where a spark was shot across—and in due course the spectrum of helium appeared. It could have only one possible source, the alphas from the radium emanation. This piece of work finally earned Rutherford his Nobel Prize in 1908 (but for chemistry!), two years after Thomson, who was also knighted as 'Sir Joseph' in 1908. The Cavendish diners that year had the right to be more than usually pleased with themselves. Rutherford was a guest: 'the boys gave me a royal reception and sang a special song on the alpha rays in my honour which went very well'.

In 1909, the British Association met at Winnipeg, the third time it had convened in Canada, but its first venture so far into new territories, 'to help strengthen the bonds which bind together the different portions of the King's dominions', as its President declared. The President, chosen to deliver that year's 'speech from the throne of science' was none other than Joey Thomson, now Sir J.J., of course, while Rutherford was the president of Section A. So their joint addresses in that last meeting of the old King's reign provide a fitting retrospect over the triumphs of the past fourteen years. They show the way the wind was blowing, when after some years without much drama, physics was in fact poised to leap forward once again. To Thomson all was going swimmingly. The revolution in physics had quite dispelled any fears that might have worried people before the discovery of X-rays that 'all the interesting things had been discovered, and all that was left was to alter a decimal or two in some physical constant'. Instead, he likened the radical new mood to the Renaissance—a 'hopeful, youthful, perhaps exuberant spirit abroad' now stirred every breast.

Not every scientist was so thrilled. The president of Section B, for Chemistry, was H.E. Armstrong; and he had not abated his hostility to the new physics in the least. That opposition must not be forgotten. Electrons and radioactivity were not greeted with universal acclaim. It was one thing to reduce the behaviour and activities of living things to chemistry. To reduce chemistry itself to physics, or rather to dynamics, to the movements and interplay of one or two unstructured and uniform bodies—that was another story. Against that threat the loyal chemist was summoned to battle, with a strange appeal to tribal loyalty. Kelvin's objections could be ascribed to the vagaries of extreme old age. But Armstrong was barely sixty, not much older than J.J. Thomson himself. He was no obscure crank, but a man honoured by his fellow chemists with all the chief offices in their society, as well as their section in the British Association. He set patterns in our chemical education which still survive today. And here he was, treating these innovations as a battleground in which concessions are torn from the enemy, if ever they accept his basic tenet that it is structure and not dynamic considerations that determine the combinations and reactions of chemistry. His world is one where the great Helmholtz must admit to being out of his depth, where physicists are 'regular excursionists into our territory' and are 'affecting almost to dictate a policy to us', while failing at bottom to understand the material or the methods of chemistry, as they gesticulate wildly to cover up their ignorance or lack of interest. While he professes to admire the experimental skill that Rutherford might display, all the new conclusions arouse in him only contempt. The electron is 'possibly but a figment of the imagination'—that 'possibly' is really just a letout. Its credentials are dubious, and probably arose from sheer inability to understand the risk of impurity or imprecision in experiment. Radium is at the least 'greatly overpainted'. Now we have high-tension electricity, why should we dream of some greater power from radium, which has certainly shown no more intense power than X-rays? At all events, disintegration of an atom is nonsensical, as Lord Kelvin had written to Armstrong: and so is any notion that elements are converted into others. If it changes or disintegrates, it is no atom, and no element. To Armstrong it was as simple as that. Not only was this stuff radium, about which there had been so much superfluous fuss, merely a compound, but quite possibly uranium is a compound too. In fact, where Kelvin had in the end come to admit that perhaps radium's energy source was *not* external, Armstrong still maintained that was the most likely explanation. Although 'at present out of favour' he would not give in.

So the argument was not quite over yet, although the election of the two chief exponents of the new science to be the year's spokesmen does imply that only an obstinate rearguard action still opposed them. Since Thomson and

Rutherford presumably did not vet each other's speeches, it is interesting to see that both speak up for the use of tangible models. Thomson discusses the ether, its possible structure, texture, and motion, or lack of motion; Rutherford discusses the current state of the atomic theory, unshaken, he insisted, by the electron or by radioactive disintegration. Atoms were indeed neither indestructible nor eternal, could surely be divided up into still smaller, more fundamental units. But what of it? Only the name of 'atom' might be affected—a subtle point of etymology, surely, since atom literally means 'uncuttable'. At one time Soddy proposed that we should henceforth speak of the 'tomic' theory. But nobody likes to think we are made up of 'toms' so his term has never caught on.

The electrical theory of matter certainly did not mean the disappearance of the ether from J.J. Thomson's universe. Indeed as long as he lived he stood by it, and claimed that Einstein's space-time continuum, or indeed the concept 'space', was but the old ether under a new name. In 1909 he had not yet had to face Einstein and relativity. But he did know of Planck, was impressed by his work, and wondered about a return to a particulate theory of light, an 'emission' theory as he calls it. In Planck's work on *The thermodynamics of radiation*, he reports, interesting evidence has been produced that 'the energy of light is made up of distinct units, the unit being the energy of one of the particles of light', which would exist if the emission model was right. All in all, he decided in the end that this tempting idea went against the Second Law of Thermodynamics, but still the energy of light waves 'is probably done up into bundles' and all those of given wavelength deliver the same amount. Thus he attempts to confront the implications of Planck's work, but that is strictly a question of the ether. Matter is quite different.

Thomson ends with a survey of the heroic story of radioactivity, from Röntgen rays and Becquerel rays to Rutherford, Soddy, and the disintegration theory—so he could congratulate his Canadian hosts, on whose territory that triumphant chapter had been composed, and introduce a few topical jokes— no doubt after that long excursion through the rarefied ether, a Manitoba audience was entitled to cracks about rays 'denoted like policemen by the letters of the alphabet', or (when he touched on the release and dispersal of the original stock of energy by stages in the transformation of radioactive matter) that 'the politician when he imposes death-duties is but imitating a process that has been going on for ages in these radioactive substances'. But why was the half life of such a substance so regular, as Rutherford had shown? Why was it a constant for each stage, so that whatever the age of a particular sample 'the expectation of life' of, for example, a radium atom is always the same. Were the source of energy external, as some had thought at first, that would be understandable, for 'in a battle the chance of being shot is the same for old and young' (another military metaphor!). But now it was clear that could not be so. One must assume that their internal energy differs, so that some are more robust than others, they have less internal energy pushing them apart. What then was the source of their tremendous energy? If it was simply the repulsion of these positive particles circling round, then given that they spend so long before they disrupt, they must be no further apart than the radius of an electron (or corpuscle as he alone still called them).

But was there a unit of positive electricity, of positively charged matter, which could complement his negative 'corpuscle'? Some plausible evidence suggested there might be, and logically it would fit the symmetry of nature. Only, most of this evidence suggested not a positive corpuscle—we should say a positron—but a body equal in mass to the smallest atom, to hydrogen. Perhaps in the beginning these positive corpuscles *were* the same size as the negative ones, but now almost all have for some reason expanded to atomic dimensions. If such a tiny body were suddenly to blow up to the usual size, that is, increase nearly two thousand times, that explosion would surely liberate energy enough to make the alpha particle shoot off as violently as it does. Of course, this calculation depends on the existence of such positive corpuscles. A few days later in fact, J.J. Thomson led off a discussion on the unit of positive electricity: is there such a thing and if so, how big is it? He repeated the evidence he had mentioned before. But *Nature*'s correspondent was not impressed. The discussion, he felt, dealt mainly with side issues and there was still a long way to go before the question could be settled.

When Rutherford gave his own account of the state of the atomic game, he too remarked on the need to know more about positive electricity. Until then, the electrical theory of matter would remain lop-sided, and so would the real structure of the atom. Like Oliver Lodge in the 1907 debate, he distinguished between the 'satellites or outliers of the atomic system', electrons that could easily be stripped off, the ones which produced all the electrical, chemical, and radiative characteristics of atoms, and those other more mysterious electrons, the 'integral constituents of the interior structure', which never left except in radioactive violence. Although from all this talk of radioactivity you might imagine that physicists see nothing through an 'atmosphere dim with the flying fragments of atoms', yet in their eyes the place of these atoms remains unaltered. They are still the least units of matter engaged in chemical composition. Indeed, radioactivity has boosted other work, like Perrin's study of the Brownian motion, which demonstrates the reality of atoms. Alpha particles can be shown to be but charged atoms of helium and *their* separate existence can be proved; presumably they stay separate when in ordinary uncharged gaseous helium. All the evidence on the number of alpha particles in a given volume confirms other evidence on the numbers of atoms in given volumes of gases. And now Crookes's spinthariscope and Geiger's counter trace the activities of individual alpha particles—that is of individual atoms. If you can discover the mass, charge, and speed of an atom or an electron, deflect them in magnetic or electric fields, calculate how many there are in any particular piece of space—how can any one again ever doubt their reality ..?

Back at Manchester, Rutherford and Geiger were still busy devising methods to count individual particles and trace their paths. The only obvious way was to look for scintillations: the beam of particles emitted by radium compounds or emanations was directed at a thin metal foil, through which they passed to strike a phosphorescent screen. As each particle struck the screen, it could be observed as a little glint. Assuming there was one scintillation per particle, they could be counted and their deflections measured in terms of the spread of scintillations. Rutherford proposed a law of single scattering of the alpha particle, each deflection the result of an encounter with a single atom, not the accumulation of many minute deviations producing one big one. This demonstrated, it remained to be seen what were the limits of an atom's powers to turn the alpha particles aside from their proper rectilinear paths. Geiger put it to Rutherford that it would be useful experience for his new research student Ernest Marsden if they could collaborate on such an investigation. In their apparatus the zinc sulphide scintillation screen was brought round in front of the metal reflector, at right angles to it, not quite in contact, and shielded by a lead plate from any direct impact of the alpha rays which streamed out of a tiny glass cone filled with the radium emanation; behind the screen was the microscope through which they observed and counted the scintillations. All this of course, had to be done in the dark, eyes glued to the instrument for long periods of time—an exhausting business.

When Rutherford first suggested that they place the screen in this position so as to see if any particles came out by that same side as in they went, he may have been faintly hopeful of getting some positive results, but certainly did not expect them. One day, Geiger came up to him to report that they had indeed managed to get some of the alpha particles coming backwards; he recalled long afterwards that 'it was quite the most incredible event that has ever happened to me in my life. It was almost as incredible as if you fired a 15-inch shell at a piece of tissue paper and it came back and hit you'. The image shows perhaps how typical it was for Rutherford to think of corpuscles as solid projectiles and their movements as bombardments. Geiger and Marsden went on to develop the basic quantitative ratios of these reflections, and found that the number that thus rebounded would vary with the atomic weight of the particular material used for the reflector and the thickness and material of the reflecting foil. For small thicknesses at least, piling one thin gold leaf upon another, the number of scintillations fell off in almost exact proportion as the number of foils was reduced. This effect applied with any material, save that the amount of scattering was related to the foil's composition, with many more scintillations produced by heavier elements like gold.

They were able to establish the ratio of particles that bounced back to the total number emitted and fired at the foil; about 1:8000.

Rutherford was immediately convinced that if these particles could be diverted through such large angles, it was the result of individual interactions; it could only be because of near collisions with extremely powerful concentrations of electric charge and mass within a radius exceedingly small by comparison with the 'sphere of influence of the atom'. Actually proving his new model took rather longer. In December 1910, he could write to his friend Boltwood, 'I think I can devise an atom much superior to J.J.'s for the explanation and stoppage of alpha and beta particles and at the same time I think it will fit in extraordinarily well with the experimental numbers ... and generally will make a fine working hypothesis.' By the beginning of February he could report that Geiger was hard at work, and so far his results 'agree well with the distribution deduced from my special atom'. In all Geiger and Marsden counted over 100 000 scintillations. They were not able to publish the outcome until 1913, taking their measurements of the variation of reflection with thickness of reflector and the atomic weight of its material to much more precise values, and adding further the ratios to the angle of incidence at which the particles struck the foil, the speed at which they were travelling, and the fraction of them scattered through any particular angle. But even their provisional findings soon confirmed Rutherford's predictions to the hilt. Instead of electrons embedded in the positive sphere, which would be far too diffuse to produce these wide angles, they circled round this minute core, whose radius it was calculated should be of the order of 1/1 000 000 000 000 of a centimetre, within an atom whose radius was about 10^4 times as great; not so much Saturn and his ring as the sun and his planets. This central core Rutherford named the nucleus. The value cited for the radius is one given by G.W.C. Kaye, *X-rays* in 1914. Rutherford, in his original paper, more cautiously speaks rather of the point at which an alpha particle 'shot directly toward the centre of the atom ... will be brought to rest ...'—at a distance of 3.4×10^{-12} cm. Currently, atomic nuclei are believed to have radii of the order of 10^{-13} cm.

At last he was ready to release his special atom to the outside world. On Tuesday 7 March 1911, he gave a talk to the Manchester Literary and Philosophical Society—that company before whom Dalton had laid his chemical atom a hundred years before—in the opinion of some of his young colleagues, however, a parcel of elderly businessmen who could never really appreciate the refinements of science, however they might be offended if they caught you talking down at them. This paper was duly reported on the Thursday, in the *Manchester Guardian*, which thus had the privilege of publishing the great news. One cannot say it was treated as a scoop like X-rays, or the wonderous powers of radium. Although headed 'The structure of the atom', the short paragraph suggests the reporter thought it was basically a paper on the scattering of alpha and beta particles; he cannot have understood the main point; 'the atom contains a strong central charge of one kind of electricity surrounded by an oppositely charged area, whose dimensions were of the same order of magnitude' ... whereas the whole idea of the new atom was the vast difference in size between the nucleus, and the atomic volume as a whole. He probably found the topic very unexciting, by comparison with a well-preserved skull of Neanderthal man, lately dug up at Gibraltar, which was displayed by the next speaker that same evening. When you think of all that has flowed from that evening's announcement it is ironic to read in the previous day's *Guardian*, an even briefer report of another talk by J.J. Thomson, on the potential of Solar Power to which I can find no other reference at all.

While this research was going on in Manchester, out of the blue Cambridge laid at Rutherford's disposal a new tool for his investigation, with a glowing future ahead of it. On his return from his summer hike through the Highlands in 1899, C.T.R. Wilson was greeted with telegrams inviting him to work for the Meteorological Council and apply his research to its original objective, studying our weather. Although he continued to improve his cloud chamber from time to time, for many years he concerned himself mainly with thunderstorms, and electricity in the atmosphere, so that basic questions were put aside. Then early in 1911, he found himself caught up in Rutherford's research, eager to keep an eye on the alpha particle. He built a new kind of cloud chamber differing from the old in the shape of piston and chamber, size and position of components. The most important improvement was his technique of photographing the motions of particles through the gas. As each droplet condenses round its ion, a vapour trail is left behind the moving particle. X-rays produce independent tracks where they hit and ionize the molecule of gas: alpha particles had a straight track, betas a trail of separate drops. If the line bent, there must be a reason why. So individual atomic particles could be followed at last, and distinguished from one another, just as we can tell where a horse has been by a trail of hoof-prints. Perhaps one day those reversing parabolas would show their traces on the plate.

Even so Rutherford's atom did not sweep its rivals from the field from then on. Geiger and Marsden's paper did not appear in the *Philosophical Magazine* until April 1913; three months later one Albert Crehore published in the same journal an attempt to show how molecules were formed from their component atoms, and compounds built up from the molecules. He started from the assumption, which he took to be generally held, that atoms were made of 'masses of positive electrification within which negative electrons are revolving', that is, Thomson's original atom. To replace Thomson's floating magnets he had made a splendid set of models, in which tiny balls of steel or aluminium were suspended by wires in castor-oil, and charged from a battery, to see whether the configurations they adopted would fit the rings and orbits of Thomson's physical chemistry. Painstaking ingenuity and no little mathematical and experimental skill were invested in this elaborate reconstruction of the currant-bun atom—but alas, he was very cleverly barking up the wrong tree.

Frankly the world of physics does not seem to have been too excited over the new model, or the 'discovery' that atoms have nuclei. In itself, the idea of an atomic nucleus was not new; Kelvin in 1905 pictured his electrions as being 'in a state of violent motion round a central nucleus'. J.J. Thomson had also used the word 'nucleus' for his positive bun. To start with, Rutherford was at least in print quite hesitant about it all. In the original version he was not even willing to commit himself as to whether this nucleus of his was positive or negative; there was not yet any 'definite evidence' though he suggested ways in which it might be obtained. The *Manchester Guardian*'s account of his original talk ends with the words, probably his own; 'we are on the threshold of an enquiry which might lead to a more definite knowledge of atomic structure'—optimistic, yes, but still very provisional. Nor did Rutherford try to pursue either the chemical or the spectroscopic implications of his model; and there lay the rub. The whole point of theories of atomic structure is that they may help to explain how atoms differ. Nineteenth-century atomic theory depended on the conviction that each element was composed of atoms which were not only indissoluble and identical; but also that the atoms of different elements likewise differ. But how did they differ? How could the characteristics of each and every chemical element be related to its structure, given only two kinds of subatomic matter: the positive charge concentrated in the nucleus and very large numbers of negative electrons circling round it? J.J. Thomson used the internal disposition of the currants in his bun to account for the most striking feature of these chemical characters, their periodicity. Could someone do the same for the solar system atom?

More than chemical differences, in the eyes of physicists the spectrographic problem blocked the path of Rutherford's theory. Nagaoka's had already failed to deliver, why should this do better? Perhaps because optics and the study of spectra were problems for physicists, part of the territory they had all had to master from their youth up, this question was more pressing for them. Chemistry was something best left to chemists, a sort of people well skilled in helping out physicists when it came to dealing with the separation of intractable substances; but their problems lacked the intellectual clarity of physics. Above all, it was the *precision* of spectrography, the clear and unambiguous answers it usually gave to experimental questions, which made the physicist feel that this witness alone could bring conviction. Rutherford did not tackle these intricate questions. Perhaps he considered the nucleus idea a useful way of looking at the behaviour of alpha particles, which might help with the issues raised by the discovery of radioactivity; but he was not yet going to try and fit the whole of physical science into his newly launched craft.

The new atom had its own problems too. Unlike Thomson's, it ought to suffer from inherent instability. Since the Saturnian atom had first been proposed, critics pointed out that unlike planets, or the fragments that make up the rings of the real Saturn, these electrons are not electrically neutral; being negatively charged, they should repel one another. Were there additional forces besides those of electromagnetism to keep the electrons in their place? Oliver Lodge includes as fifth and last of the views of the atom circulating at the time he wrote his book on electrons in 1906, 'a central "sun" of extremely concentrated positive electricity at the centre', with the electrons 'revolving in astronomical orbits like asteroids'. But in that case, they ought to travel in 'periodic times dependent on distance, which appears not to correspond with anything satisfactorily observed'. So he plumped for J.J. Thomson's atom. Besides the mechanical dangers, an even worse electromagnetic peril threatened any 'planetary' atom with imminent collapse. Most theories of radiation assumed it was produced by the electron's vibration. Lodge had made good use of this in his 1903 explanation of radioactive disintegration. If it radiated as it revolved about the centre of its orbit, the electron must be radiating, and so losing energy all the time. Now that would constantly reduce its momentum, and so it would very soon be sucked in by the nucleus, which would rapidly swallow up all its electrons—and that would be the end of that. As the electrons spiralled in on the nucleus, the frequency of their emitted radiation should increase, moving along the spectrum; so, far from having specific spectra, the elements ought all to have the same spectrum—the very opposite of the condition from which atomic theories ought to start, whereby each has its own specific one.

Despite the dramatic nature of Rutherford's experiments, the situation in 1912–13 was therefore one of uncertainty. Once again, two main tendencies can be made out, with some degree of national colouring. On the one hand, the German school slowly inched their way forward into the deep waters of the uncharted quantum sea, with many nostalgic glances at the security of the coast of classical mechanics. For they were still very loath to venture far, even the pilots of the venture, like Planck and Einstein. They were convinced the quantum would be the key to a new physics, but little concerned (except for Johannes Stark) how the new particles of the experimentalists would fit in. And the Anglo-Saxons were apparently quite happy to throw out atomic models, satisfied 'if it resembled a little, then it was so', counting scintillations in their basements, acquiring an almost intuitive feeling for the way matter works, and not overly concerned with the philosophy behind it all.

NOTE

1. Cited by M.J. Nye in *Molecular reality*, p. 84. Macdonald, London (1972).

9

NIELS BOHR

The time was ripe for someone to reconcile the two approaches: to produce a model that would be precise, mathematical, founded on experiment, and aware of its philosophical significance all at once. The man who brought the two ways together was a Dane, a citizen of a nation which somehow managed to combine the virtues of the British and the Germans, while avoiding the worst features of either. Niels Henrik David Bohr was born in Copenhagen in 1885. When first he came to England, he was a bright young post-doctoral student, a promising lad in his native country, but no more. Unlike Thomson and Rutherford, he came from the professional upper class; the son and grandson of professors, the great-grandson of a headmaster. His father was a notable physiologist, and Niels grew up in a very academic atmosphere. His mother's family were of Jewish extraction; what, if anything, remained of this in his upbringing is hard to say. As the same feature appears in the family background of so many of the German scientists of that and the next generation, from Einstein down, speculation is invited to account for this common character. In reaction against the frenzied denunciation of Jewish science by the Nazis, perhaps also in reaction against defensive historiography which lays claim to anyone of remotely Jewish descent, biographies of Bohr tend to brush this aside as do some of Einstein, on the grounds that their families, long since emancipated, followed the normal liberal-secular life style of their surroundings. Certainly, no reason has yet been found to suppose a genetic effect: still less to imagine any attraction at a distance by forms of religious thought which had been abandoned for at least a generation by Niels's mother's family, the Adlers. All the same, the connection which seems to link them to so many others—among them Hertz, Goldstein, Rubens, Schuster— deserves a mention, especially as Bohr was closer to his mother's family, for he was born and spent his early childhood in his maternal grandmother's home, his upbringing much influenced by his mother's elder sister. However his intellectual heritage came from his father's line; and this was the tradition passed on to him at his schools. The Danish educational system at the end of the nineteenth century was still irradiated by all the heat poured out of the German academic world since the great explosion of German science. After all, until 1866, the Danish king ruled over large numbers of German subjects, and Germany was the land to which Danes had always turned to complete their education. Niels's father had studied physiology at Leipzig; his brother was to pursue his mathematics at Göttingen.

The father Christian Bohr, in his own recollections of childhood, considered that his whole life as far back as he could remember had been dominated by the love of science, since as a boy he collected natural history specimens, out of a passion for what he calls 'systematic scholarship'. In later life, as a biologist, he always belonged to that school which saw its main objective as the explanation of the fundamental processes of life in physico-chemical terms. Those who see the scientific personality as 'convergent', in contrast to the literary 'diverger', might note that both Christian and his son Niels found free composition the hardest of their school subjects, although both complained of the stilted forms imposed on compositions in those days, rather than of any demand to let their imagination roam. Niels also learnt from his father a love for the poetry of Goethe, hardly the characteristic of a 'convergent' psychological structure. Another feature he had, that has often marked great scientists, a taste for handicrafts, metalwork, and woodwork, a fondness for mending things like broken bikes; and with that an ability to keep something of the boy in him throughout his life—frequently observed by friends who were amused by his fondness for throwing stones accurately. After a sound education at the Gammelholm Gymnasium, Niels Bohr in 1903 entered Copenhagen University. Given the 'German' orientation of the university, all students were naturally expected to take a course in philosophy in their first year, where in Britain it was regarded as a distraction for the serious scientist, who might well never be exposed to that way of looking at problems at all.

Despite Niels's family background, his imagination often ran ahead of his manual dexterity as a student; there is the obligatory story of an explosion in the laboratory, and of the glass instruments he managed to break. For all that, in 1905, only two years after his entry to the university, he decided to try for the annual prize essay of the Royal Danish Academy, a study of the vibration of liquid jets. Although the Academy had specified that the research 'be extended to a fairly large number of liquids', prolonged and difficult work with the apparatus Bohr had designed forced him to confine himself to water. All the same, the result was so impressive that the Academy awarded him its Gold Medal in January 1907. The next year Bohr sent off a revised version of his paper to the Royal Society. Perhaps he wished it to appear in English rather than German because his starting-point had been a theory of the English physicist Rayleigh. The paper was duly accepted; Niels was addressed by the secretary in correspondence as Professor Bohr, and had the satisfaction of pointing out that he was still only a student. Able this work may have been, and it must have given him a feel for the behaviour of matter. But it was not only his first but also the last paper he based on his own experimental work.

While this paper was being published, Bohr launched on a very different project; the most fundamental enquiry into why matter behaves as it does. For his M.Sc. dissertation, due in the summer of 1909, he was steered by his professor in the direction of the electron theory of metals. In April, while he was staying on the island of Fyn revising for his examinations, he wrote to his brother Harald, 'at the moment I am wildly enthusiastic about Lorentz's (Leiden) electron theory'. Lorentz, Drude, and others were now trying to apply the electron theory to the peculiarities of metals, supposing they contain a cloud of *free* electrons flitting about between the molecules of the metals proper. In this way Lorentz now hoped to explain not only the high electrical and thermal conductivity of metals, but also why the chemical changes that are so striking in other conductors when electricity passes through them, do not take place with metals. If this cloud of free particles were regarded as a kind of gas, their behaviour could be treated on the lines of the kinetic theory of gases; the electrons would move freely along straight paths until they bumped into a molecule. The dissertation was a foretaste of Bohr's later work, not really founded on his own experiments but a review of all existing theories in an attempt to master a fundamental problem, as he pointed out the difficulties in them all, and suggested how the assumptions on which they were based might have to be broadened or revised before that problem could be solved. When he extended his examination of the free electrons to consider what would happen if they found themselves in a piece of metal moving in a magnetic field, serious discrepancies appeared between what theory said should happen and what had been observed. What then of the unfree electrons, bound to the molecules of metal? Would they not have some influence? His concluding lines raised that question for the future.

First he had to proceed, once graduated Master, to a doctoral thesis, in November: naturally he chose to develop the problem he had now sketched out. On holiday just before Christmas he could promise hopefully that 'the investigation of my electrons can readily be carried out'; by the next June however he was murmuring to Harald about the time he had spent, 'speculating about a silly question about silly electrons, and have succeeded only in writing around fourteen more or less divergent rough drafts'. Still, finally he licked '*de dumme Elektroner*'; but there were many difficulties to be overcome, errors in calculation to be amended, the correct results to be tracked down before the task was done, and Niels could present this thesis for public examination. Before he could have the satisfaction of seeing both his sons established as scientists in their own right, Christian Bohr died, in the February of 1911.

By then, Niels had almost completed his thesis, and he was soon able to present it, and defend it publicly on 13 May according to the practice of Copenhagen university—or, as the Danish newspaper *Dagbladet* put it, 'the year after his younger brother Magister Niels Bohr follows in his footsteps'. The rival *Politiken* also gave a brief account, accompanied by caricatures of

Bohr looking more like a matinee idol than a rising young scientist—O happy land where the examinations of doctoral theses are national news! The reference to following his younger brother was perhaps a little tactless: *Politiken* too calls him 'Professor Bohr's other son'. Niels spent much of his early life in his brother's shadow. As a footballer Harald could represent his country at the Olympic Games, while Niels could only make the reserve team of their club, and Harald as *Dagbladet* observed had his doctorate a year before Niels; indeed he had already been appointed to a university post in June 1910. Happily, any emulation there may have been was very deeply submerged; the two brothers always remained extremely close. Perhaps the very fact of their intellectual companionship, quite rare with the brothers of men of Niels's calibre, helped them to overcome any sibling rivalries.

In his thesis, Bohr developed the problems he had taken up in the M.Sc. version. Faintly as yet, but definitely, he now began to suggest that a new set of laws would have to be constructed for the little world of the atom. The old mechanics would not do, whatever electrons might be, they could not be treated as 'hard elastic spheres', tiny billiard balls that bounce off one another. He starts of course with Lorentz's assumption, based on Thomson's evidence that free electrons float about in metals, all identical in every metal. Then if atoms of metal and free electrons act upon each other with the accepted mechanical forces, one can further assume a 'dynamic statistical equilibrium'—the collision will produce the same overall balance if there are no outside forces to disturb it, as gas theory would lead one to expect; so there will be a 'mechanical heat equilibrium'. Indeed, he suggests, external forces could have slight influence on the character, speed, or paths of the free electrons, or on their concentration in different parts of the metal, but only cause more of them to move in the direction imposed by the force than in the opposite direction; that would produce a flow of electrons and so a current of electricity; as they possess kinetic energy, there will also be a flow of heat through the metal.

One interesting passage compares the conduction of heat and electricity through metals, if both alike are the result of the motion of electrons. Although the conductivities of a range of metals differed widely for heat and for electricity, the ratio between the two conductivities was almost regular, and varied as the absolute temperature. 'One of the most beautiful results of the electron theory' commented Bohr, this tended to confirm the idea that electrons convey both 'flows'. But there were difficulties, so the observation did not confirm any simple answer, for all would depend on the kind of forces involved. Some alloys have conductivities lower than the metals of which they are composed. Does that mean these alloys are not physically homogeneous, but either aggregates of linked crystals of the pure metals or else 'solid solutions' of one metal in another? Bohr hoped not—he held it would be best to assume that since alloys are composed of atoms which must themselves differ in magnitude, the 'field of force in the interior (of the alloy) will be stronger than in pure metals, where the forces may be supposed to cancel one another out to a higher degree'. Not only would this hamper the flow of electrons, but it would clearly hamper the slower ones more than the fast, and so affect the heat conductivity more than the electric, just as observed. He began to wonder if the forces already known to physics could entirely account for the motion of a single electron within short intervals of time. Already in his introduction he observed that there would have to be 'forces in nature of a kind completely different from the usual mechanical sort ... there are many properties of bodies impossible to explain if one assumes that those which act inside individual molecules are operating according to the same rules as those that govern the interactions between molecules'. He instanced calculations of specific heats and radiation frequencies which show he must have read his Planck, and probably Einstein. Elsewhere he comments that electrons bound in atoms are 'apparently cut off from the influence of other atoms or electrons in a manner that does not correspond to anything known for ordinary mechanical systems'. Turning to the magnetic properties of metals, he discovered even greater difficulties in ascribing magnetic properties to the activities of either free or bound electrons, if one thought of them as elastic spheres; perhaps atoms should be regarded as tiny elementary magnets or as 'electric doublets', two halves joined together with charges of equal strength but opposite sign. In that case, their motions might not be 'free paths and separate collisions' nor the interaction a simple mechanical exchange of momentum, but operate 'through more slowly varying force fields', much as he had suggested could be true of the passage of heat and electricity. However, as the thesis concludes, 'it does not seem possible at the present stage of development of the electron theory, to explain the magnetic properties of bodies from it'.

The thesis completed, Bohr hastened to send copies to some of those he had cited, to see what they would say. All four of those whose replies he preserved wrote to him in German. Despite certain difficulties with the language, they were prepared to try and battle through a Danish thesis if the subject looked promising enough. If interest was strongest in German-speaking lands, where Planck's quantum had been born and was now beginning to flourish, one would expect that Bohr's next step would be a visit to Germany, or at least a Germanophone university. His brother had already gone to Göttingen, other Danish friends had gone before. One of them wrote to him: 'down here in Berlin, electron concepts are almost the only ones that take our interest'. Indeed, in Bohr's thesis, 46 German papers are cited, compared to 20 in English; and this represents quite well the geographical distribution of the art of electron physics at the time.

Perhaps he could have gone to Lorentz in Holland. In the event, however, he turned toward England, motivated by the tremendous reputation of the

Cavendish Laboratory and his admiration for Thomson, the father of the electron, who led the way by first proclaiming a single type of electron as the universal constituent of matter. In Bohr's M.Sc. thesis he cites Thomson's *Corpuscular theory of matter* from a German translation, but from the English original in the Ph.D. version. Thus Bohr was changing modes. At all events he made no serious attempt to have his thesis translated into German, even if some of those to whom he had sent copies did complain they found difficulties in understanding it, whereas one of his main objectives from the movement he arrived in England was to correct a rough English translation he had prepared while still in Denmark, and publish the result, so as to show English physics what could be done by pursuing the electron theory wherever it might lead. So with the aid of a convenient Carlsberg grant, Bohr arrived in Cambridge that September of 1911, full of enthusiasm: 'I found myself rejoicing this morning when I stood outside a shop and by chance happened to read the address "Cambridge" over the door.' Socially, he had a marvellous time; invitations to dinner, to tea, joining a football club, fine skating, walks across the meadows toward Grantchester, 'with the hedges flecked with red berries and with isolated windblown willows—under the most magnificent autumn sky with scurrying clouds and blustering wind . . . .' His letters home to his mother, brother, and fiancée—he had become engaged about the beginning of the year—are full of a gentle and innocent humour; there is something almost childlike about them, considering that he was now twenty-six. Like Rutherford in his letters to Mary Newton, he paints a fascinating picture of Cambridge life before the Great War, as it looked to that novel creature the foreign research student, whom Cambridge had accepted because the world wished it, but did not quite know what to do with; now treating him, and rightly, as the peer of the leading minds of the university, and now as still *in statu pupillari*, beset with weird regulations which Bohr's good nature found more entertaining than restrictive. Quite apart from all the gown-wearing and laws about where to lodge, he found it amusing that he could not invite the young ladies of Newnham to the most proper of lunch parties without a chaperone—even then the mores of Copenhagen were relatively permissive . . . In the end he seems to have remained a little outside college life, as might be expected, and dined at his flat on Eltisley Avenue in solitary state, regaled once with 'a whole duck, on which I gazed with peculiar feelings'.

In the light of the reason for his coming to Cambridge in the first place, matters were less satisfactory. Again and again, in a letter to his mother early in October, to brother Harald later in the month, to his Swedish friend Oseen in December, he complains of the lack of order in the Cavendish Laboratory; to Oseen he echoed a Scandinavian colleague's lament that 'complete molecular disorder prevails there'—'a poor foreigner who doesn't even know the names of things he can not find is very badly off'—'so little help for so many people'. Perhaps these last words provide the key. A glance at the annual photograph of the Cavendish Laboratory in 1896 when Rutherford had just arrived, and then at one taken in 1911 reveals that the establishment had grown too big for the old set-up, where everybody was left to his own devices. However powerful Thomson was as an original thinker and as a lecturer (for Bohr always writes with enthusiasm about his sparkling lecture style)—he was not too good as an organizer of research. There was no fixed time when the workers at his lab could see him about their problems or their progress. If you wanted to talk to him, he had to be disturbed, and then 'when you have talked with him for a moment he gets to think about one of his own things and then he leaves you in the midst of a sentence (they say he would walk away from the King and that means more in England than in Denmark).' Abstracted in the spinning of his own ideas, he was unready for dialogue. Bohr's own approach may not have helped. As he once ruefully acknowledged to his brother, in his early days at least new ideas had the bad habit of coming to him in the form of criticism of other people's work, so that his first approaches to men like Thomson and Jeans took the form of pointing out errors in their calculations or omissions, where they had failed to take account of something that overthrew all their argument. This procedure can hardly have enamoured him to them. Despite his assurances about how polite they were, it is hard to avoid the suspicion that he was being given the brush-off; let this foreign student earn his spurs as an experimenter first, before he starts putting his seniors right.

Bohr was in fact given the task of producing a discharge of cathode rays by means of positive rays—a line of research which was to lead Thomson himself to another major discovery, of which more later—but apparently without a proper explanation as to the function of this research in Thomson's general programme. Indeed, if Bohr learnt a little about how to handle apparatus, he got little more than that from it; in his second term at Cambridge he more or less abandoned his task and devoted his time to reading the literature and attending lectures. But he had not crossed the sea just to read the books of Jeans and Larmor. Not all the books he read impressed him so much as theirs; in one, recommended by Oseen, he comments in the margin, 'I never read anything so badly written nor such a thorough attempt at making such an easy subject difficult by thorough inaccuracy in the simplest calculations.' Thomson too disappointed him a little, however beautiful the experiments which illustrated his lectures. Clearly, a professor so rooted in the tradition of Maxwell's mechanisms would not readily entertain the idea that classical doctrine could not account for the motions of electrons. After all, Bohr was in England to put across new ideas to English physicists and to seek from them guidance where theory should go next. So far he had found neither. At this juncture, he was introduced to an alternative branch of the English school, already pulling ahead of the Cavendish.

Rutherford and Bohr first met toward the end of the year. Their meeting was to have consequences as weighty for the future of science as when Kepler set off to work with Tycho Brahe in 1600. Not that either party quite realized how important—but that was so for Kepler and Tycho too. Rutherford's paper on the atomic nucleus had come out in June, of course. But Bohr had not paid much notice. In the autumn Rutherford returned from the first Solvay Conference in Brussels. There the idea that Planck's quantum would be the key to all outstanding problems on radiation earned a thorough airing. One of the participants, Sommerfeld, observed in reply to probing by Lorentz that there must be some relation between the magnitude of Planck's constant h and the dimensions of the atom as viewed in Thomson's model. Whether the size of the atom governed the constant, or the size of the constant governed that of the atom, 'I don't see any great difference'. In general he made clear his preference for 'a general hypothesis about the constant to particular models of atoms'. Thus he brushed aside the usefulness of imagining structures for atoms, whereas to J.J. Thomson, and probably also to Rutherford at this stage, h would turn out to be derived somehow from the structure of the atom. Rutherford was coming to think that Planck's ideas might be correct. Be it said that in his letters, as in his report for *Nature*, Rutherford stressed the social side of the Conference, the value of getting everybody under one roof, and says nothing about putting Planck's constant and atomic models together. The report in *Nature* states that 'special interest was taken in ... the question of specific heats': he remarks in particular on some experiments by Nernst and 'their explanation in terms of the "quantum" theory proposed by Prof. Einstein'. But this would have been for him of secondary importance compared with the problems that directly involved radioactivity, which continued to occupy his mind. Officially, Bohr went to Manchester to study radioactivity; yet at a time very close to his first real meeting with Rutherford, Bohr wrote to his friend Oseen on 1 December, 'at the moment I am very enthusiastic about the quantum theory (I mean its experimental aspects) but I am not sure if this is not because of lack of knowledge.'

Once arrived in Manchester in March, he started work on a course to familiarize himself with what were by now standard procedures: or as Rutherford told Boltwood, 'Bohr, a Dane, has pulled out of Cambridge and turned up here to get some experience in radioactive work.' Rutherford's opinion of Bohr was soon much better than might seem from this perfunctory mention of yet another foreign student come to drink the waters of radioactive research at their purest source. Rutherford's earliest biographer remarks how one day he met for the first time 'a slight-looking boy whom Rutherford at once took into his study. Mrs. Rutherford explained to me that the visitor was a young Dane and that her husband thought very highly indeed of his work.'[1] The allusion to Cambridge suggests that Rutherford too was under the impression that Bohr had been dissatisfied there. According to what Bohr wrote to his brother at the time, the differences in personality between Rutherford and Thomson made all the difference to him. The actual research did not stretch him much, so as late as May he was complaining that he did not think it would lead anywhere very consequential. Nor was there more interest in he electron theory of metals at Manchester than there had been at Cambridge. However, where Thomson had been wrapped up in his own research, and did not seem to concern himself whether or not newcomers were progressing in theirs, Rutherford, 'comes regularly to hear how things are going and talk about every little thing'. He 'takes a real interest in the work of all the people working with him'. An atmosphere of encouragement and advice was created; that was the main thing. Whether Rutherford was a greater scientist than Thomson, was in Bohr's eyes a question of less importance—he might well be 'more able even though perhaps not so gifted'. But Rutherford was the 'leader of scientific co-operation'. In his reminiscence, Rutherford was 'almost a second father to me'.

NOTE

1. Eve, A.S. *Rutherford*, p. 218. Cambridge University Press (1939).

10

ATOM AND RADIATION RECONCILED, IN DISCONTINUITY

Early in June Bohr's ideas suddenly take on a different complexion altogether. Only then did he become fully aware of Rutherford's theory of the atom; presumably, his mind being full of other questions, it had not really sunk in before. What may have brought it to the forefront of his mind was an article by another young Manchester physicist, Charles Darwin, son of George the astronomer and grandson of 'the right Darwin' as Bohr put it. In it he set forth a theory about the absorption of alpha particles based on Rutherford's model. Niels's letters to his brother are evidence, however, that Darwin did not discuss his ideas with Bohr until they were ready for publication; his paper appeared in the June 1912 number of the *Philosophical Magazine*. When he looked at the paper, Bohr decided certain assumptions had been made which were not really acceptable. Almost at once he realized it might be possible to work out a theory as to how alpha particles react with atoms, and particularly with their component electrons, which would fit the experimental facts closely and help to disclose the true structure of atoms. He spent the rest of June and much of July in a frenzy of mental activity and excitement to which his letters bear witness. So 'a little theory' which 'may cast some light on certain things connected with the structure of atoms' gradually crystallizes in his head through long and quite painful and difficult calculations. On one point he asks Harald's advice about a certain equation which had given him some trouble, and even then it appears that he has made a slip at one stage— until he begins to feel that he has grasped 'perhaps a little bit of reality'. Little always seems his favourite word in this correspondence; those who think they can psychoanalyse great men by quantifying their stylistic tricks may try their hand at this love for the *'lille'*. A symbol of shyness, of self-deprecation? That child-like quality that has been noticed in both Bohr and Einstein? An attempt to protect his extremely revolutionary ideas about nature by suggesting they were not to be exposed to the glare of grown-up criticism; for as 'little' theories, no one would be cruel to them? At all events, by the time he left Manchester near the end of July, the main outlines of his theory were formulated. There were manifest gaps in the reasoning still, and in print he devoted himself to a discussion of the differing capacity of different atoms to slow down alpha particles, taking up exactly where Darwin had left off, with only the barest hint of the fundamental reconstruction he had in mind.

Probably he did not expect anything very novel to come out of his English experience since he had plans to get married as soon as the academic year was over, making no allowance for any chance that might hold him away from Denmark. Apart from the article, he had a rough sketch of his theory of atomic structure already, but his work was still quite incomplete when he left for Copenhagen on 23 July, and was duly wed there on 1 August—having arranged to honeymoon in Scotland so that he could leave his article with Rutherford *en route*. In this paper Bohr maintains that in order to establish a limit within which electrons produce some effect on the alpha particles' speed it will be necessary to allow for the forces which hold the atoms together and so normally keep the electrons in their proper places. These forces had so far proved a great embarrassment for the Manchester school, because 'under the influence of these forces the electrons will have a sort of vibratory motion if they are disturbed by an impulse from outside'. That phrase 'sort of', which a scientific paper should eschew, reveals how Bohr was still feeling his way in ill-charted territory. So—we must discover the frequency with which electrons vibrate while pulled both ways like this. If an atom's power to slow down alpha particles depends on this frequency—the question can be posed the other way round: if we know the stopping power of different elements, which can be measured, and know the velocity of the particles, we can discover the frequency of the electrons' vibration, and so learn something of their structure.

This article did not appear in the *Philosophical Magazine* until January of the next year and comprised only a small part of Bohr's thinking about the great question of atomic structure during these two crucial months. The closest friend he made in Manchester was, not surprisingly, a fellow foreigner called George von Hevesy, a Hungarian whose ease of social manner may have enabled him to act as intermediary between all these rather shy and introverted young men. Hevesy, who had already made quite a name for himself in work on radioactive series, at one point observed to Bohr that already more radio elements had been revealed than there was room for in the Periodic Table. Some of these extra elements, although they differed in their radioactive characteristics and in their atomic weights, had so far proved chemically inseparable from their near neighbours. In chemistry the same, in weight and radioactivity different: to Bohr this implied that if Rutherford was right, and almost all the mass of an atom was concentrated in its central nucleus, then surely the radioactivity must be a nuclear phenomenon while the other characters, optical, chemical, and so on, which identified a particular element, depended on its electrons, on the *number* of its electrons in fact. There could be elements such as George had described—they had the same number of electrons as those with which they shared a seat at the Periodic Table, but something was adding to, or subtracting from, their mass—that is, their nuclei—and what then could a radioactive transformation be, but the loss of a piece of nucleus, somehow disgorged?

For the moment these ideas were only tentative. Later he was to remember them as important, and discussed them with Hevesy, as appears from their later correspondence, but his calculations were now aimed at a different problem. He tried to consider the effects that would be produced by an atom in which one electron revolves about a centre under a force comparable to that of gravity, as if to follow the planetary model literally still; how then would it be if there were two or more electrons in a ring circling their nuclear 'sun'? In an essay he drew up to explain his ideas to Rutherford about the end of June he tried to establish the conditions under which such a ring would be stable, given a nucleus with positive charge equal to and counterbalancing the negative charge produced by the electrons in the ring; the nucleus is treated as 'point-shaped', that is, as dimensionless. He concluded that the energy possessed by each electron in the ring would be negative if there were seven electrons to a ring, or less, positive if there were more; and with this excess of energy the eighth electron would fly off. So he suggests that if each time seven is reached, a new ring forms outside, it will be possible to explain the periodicity of elements. All those with one outermost electron, those with two, with three, and so on, have common features; and if seven is indeed the limiting number a ring can hold, that explains why every eighth starts again. Although Thomson had tried to use his currant bun to explain these features, he had done so by adding extra rings inside, and was less concerned to explain an atom's power to combine with another. Unfortunately, as Heilbron and Kuhn point out, Bohr's argument here will not work. Indeed they suggest that only by a slip in his calculations could Bohr have arrived at seven as the maximum number of electrons in a ring.[1] Doubtless Bohr himself eventually realized this; and this particular argument drops out of his exposition. Anyway, it is little use talking about rings and revolutions and frequency of vibration if there is no means of fixing the radius of the electron orbits. Given their known mechanical instability, it is no use looking to classical mechanics for an answer. There must be a definite constant ratio between the kinetic energy of an electron and its frequency. For this assertion 'there will be given no attempt of a mechanical foundation; once we get down to the heart of single atoms and try to learn what holds them together, a new system will be needed, linked to concepts of the nature of radiation like the ones of Planck and Einstein'. Just what the constant might be, he was still unsure, unable as yet to insist Planck's h must be the determinant. He did try to calculate how the two-atom molecules of hydrogen and oxygen could be stable, the two electrons sharing an orbit whose axis was a line joining the two nuclei, and then for water as a combination of these two elements. But all was done in a hesitant manner.

After their Scottish honeymoon, the Bohrs returned to Copenhagen, where

Niels managed to obtain a provisional post lecturing on mechanics, while he tried to solve the outstanding problems in his theory as it stood. In the midst of his struggles, complicated by the duties involved in his first lecture course, and the business of setting up a household, Bohr through that autumn proceeded quite slowly. Just before the turn of the year, his mind was set on a new track. A postscript to the Christmas card he sent to his brother on whom he had grown accustomed to trying out his ideas, reveals that they had been discussing the theories of John Nicholson, whose work impelled Bohr to include within his model of atomic structure and activity some explanation of the spectra at least of the lightest elements. Bohr had met Nicholson in Cambridge the previous autumn; he had not been impressed. Like Bohr, Nicholson began by studying the electron theory of metals. This should have brought them together, but in October in a letter to Harald, Bohr commented that a paper on this theme, which had just appeared in the *Philosophical Magazine*, had 'not much sense' to it; this must be Nicholson's, which he later assured Oseen was 'perfectly crazy, based on inadequate calculations and using them wrongly'. Although he thought kindly of Nicholson personally (he too was then at the Cavendish—but then, of whom could Bohr not think kindly?), 'but with him I shall hardly be able to agree on very much'. Rutherford could be equally scathing: when he read Nicholson's chief work, written during 1912, he remarked on 'the awful hash he made of the alpha ray problem'—but that was a subject on which Rutherford would have high standards.

Those responsible were not deterred from appointing Nicholson Professor of Mathematics at King's College London in 1912. In the course of 1911–12, Nicholson was in the process of elaborating his own atomic theory. The main features are common to Rutherford's, in that he supposed a small massive nucleus with electrons buzzing round it. But, felt Nicholson, if radioactive decay and the changes that accompany it are a phenomenon of the nucleus, the nucleus itself must obviously be a complex assemblage of parts. Since he held that there must be more than one electron to an atom, the simplest must have two; hydrogen he suggested would have three, or possibly six if normal hydrogen was actually made up of doublets of a 'primary hydrogen'; then there would be others having four and five. Of these all the heavier elements would be built up. On earth only these compound forms would exist, but in places of tremendous activity and outpouring of energy, where there prevailed 'a state of electrical excitement', they might be found in their naked shapes. He looked: and found; in particular his five-electron element in the sun's corona—this he named 'protofluorine'; and his four-electron atom in a nebula in the constellation Orion, so he called it nebulium. The evidence was contained in certain as yet unexplained spectral lines. As every element has its own specific spectrum and radiates light, and all forms of radiation, only at its own particular wavelengths, and absorbs just those wavelengths in which it radiates, so unexpected black lines can disclose the presence of hitherto unknown elements. Nicholson claimed that the vibrations of his nebulium would account for some unexplained lines in the Orion nebula's spectrum, just as helium had been disclosed by mystery lines in solar radiation. What is more, he could predict some other nebulium lines—and sure enough, one of these was found in a plate of the Orion spectrum which had been taken back in 1908.

To arrive at such deductions, assumptions have to be made about what happens in the radiation. How are these spectral series produced? The answer he found in Planck's work. By 1911–12, claims were already being heard, if still hesitantly, that Planck's constant must have a fundamental significance derived from the dimensions of all atoms. Nicholson was struck by the observation that the ratio of the energy of his 'protofluorine' to the frequency of rotation of its electron ring would be almost exactly 25 times Planck's h. And protofluorine was to have five electrons in its ring. How to explain the appeance of h? In nebula and corona, there must be a continual coming and going, a gaining and losing of electrons. Suppose then that 'the angular momentum of an atom can only rise and fall by discrete amounts when electrons leave or return'? He adds that 'the quantum theory has not apparently been put forward as an explanation of "series" spectra consisting of a large number of related lines given by a comparatively simple atom'. All the great multiplicity of lines would not come from exactly identical atoms because in many of them their angular moments would have 'run down' in quantum jumps from the original standard for that element. With but few electrons to start with, they would radiate comparatively rapidly, and if one 'loses its energy by definite amounts, instead of in a continuous manner, it should show a series of spectrum with lines corresponding to each of the stages', as it vibrated, of course. The irony of it is that the substance which provided Nicholson with the lynch-pin of his argument—does not exist at all. There is no such element as nebulium: the spectral lines are there all right, but as it turns out they are produced by a mixture of nothing more exotic than nitrogen and oxygen. Nor are there any such underlying sub-primary elements with their own nuclei and accompanying electrons, as he supposed. However, the nebulous ghost of nebulium continued to haunt the periodic table of elements for at least a dozen years until its true identity was unmasked. This history of the discovery of the elements is indeed bedevilled with these embarrassing spirits.

For all that, Nicholson's was one of the first attempts to *use* Planck's h, instead of trying hopefully to explain it away in terms of something else that would make it possible for established mechanics to be preserved; and one of the first to suggest a new use for it, in the interpretation of the lines in atomic spectra. Thus it pointed Bohr in the right direction. To start with, he was more worried than pleased, for his own calculations of the dimensions and characteristics of *his* electron rings did not seem to square with those offered by Nicholson at all. About the end of December 1912, not long after reading Nicholson's last paper, in his Christmas card he told Harald, with some relief, that he now thought the two theories were compatible. Niels was now thinking about 'the final or classical state of the atoms'—the first time he ever spoke of this concept, so crucial for his ideas—while Nicholson was concerned with atoms as they radiate, losing energy on their way down, 'before they have occupied their final positions'. A month later he wrote in greater detail to Rutherford to explain how this new problem was going. He had decided that his own calculations related to atoms in their 'permanent (natural) state'; Nicholson's to unstable conditions in which atoms are being formed, or are radiating at appropriate wavelengths. The whole thing still refused to hang together in his mind. Like Rutherford before him, like so many scientists who feel themselves on the brink of a great discovery and cannot imagine that other minds are not heading the same way, he too feared that if he took too long he would be anticipated. On 5 February 1913, he wrote to Oseen 'I must hurry, if it is to be new when it comes'. On 7 February he wrote to Von Hevesy listing the stages he had reached so far. As yet he had not attained what was to prove his main point.

Nearly thirty years before, in 1885, a Swiss mathematician called Balmer had noticed that the lines of each element's distinctive spectrum are not at arbitrary distances apart. Working only from recent measurements of four lines which hydrogen radiates in the ultraviolet part of its spectrum, he perceived a regular pattern. The higher the frequency, the more the lines seem to converge by regular steps, looking like the rungs on a ladder stretching out into the distance, growing closer together up to a limiting point the higher the frequency. Wavelengths of these gaps could be expressed as

$$\frac{3^2}{3^2 - 2^2},$$

$$\frac{4^2}{4^2 - 2^2},$$

$$\frac{5^2}{5^2 - 2^2},$$

$$\frac{6^2}{6^2 - 2^2}$$

multiplied by h, what he called 'the basic number of hydrogen', i.e.

$$\frac{m^2}{m^2 - n^2}$$

n being 2, and m the succession of numbers following it. He seems to have assumed that each element would have its own basic number, although he foresaw considerable difficulties in establishing them, especially as only the lightest elements have single lines, for thereafter the situation becomes more complicated when on more exact analysis, the lines can be resolved into pairs or triplets of finer lines. Nevertheless Rydberg, a Swedish physicist, had produced a more general rule, translating from wavelength into its complement number of wavelengths per metre (wave number), so that the basic number—commonly called the Rydberg number R—is multiplied by $(1/n^2 - 1/m^2)$ (n and m as above). But what is R? Should it simply be given—a constant of nature, just part of the formula—or could it be resolved into the product of something more fundamental? As Bohr later wrote, the mathematical simplicity of this formulation was well known. It was all very pretty but did not seem to mean anything—like the markings on a butterfly's wing, whose regularity is so impressive. But you would hardly expect to derive the whole of biology from them. Perhaps one could compare Rydberg's rule to Bode's law which relates the distances of the planets from the sun to a numerical series; also very pretty but as yet there is no universally accepted explanation. However in Balmer's law, one factor involves the difference between two terms, so it has been suggested that this may have guided Bohr on his way, as if the frequency might be the difference between two states, 'a steplike process', as Bohr put it. As Bohr recalled, after he became interested in the optical side of atomic existence he was talking about his problems with an old friend named Hansen, who pointed out to him that there was a simple formula governing the spectral series. Thereupon Bohr went off to look up the exact formula in Johannes Stark's *Principles of the dynamics of the atom:* 'and as soon as I saw Balmer's formula, the whole thing was immediately clear to me'.

Clear to him; it had not been clear to Stark himself, that 'well-known man' who discussed the spectral formula in the context of his own model of the atom, its electrons and their distance from their 'archion'. Nor was it clear to Planck and Einstein, when they propounded the idea of radiation in discrete units. None of them had questioned the assumption that as commanded by all the laws of mechanics and electrodynamics, electrons would continue to radiate and vibrate as they revolved in their orbits. Suddenly Bohr saw that if emission could only be in quanta, then within the atom, with bodies built to the same incredible tiny scale as the quantum itself, those laws of mechanics and electrodynamics which insist on continuity would no longer apply. We could imagine it something like this. In the old belief, the electron was like a ball set rolling round a bowl. As it rolls, it loses energy in friction against the surface of the bowl. We have imparted some energy to the ball, but it will continually lose that energy in its motion, and so gravity will soon draw it down into the bottom of the bowl. The electron does not lose energy in friction, but in radiation supposedly produced by its vibration; it is electrostatic forces which are to make it fall toward the centre, rather than gravity. Still, if we hold to this rough picture, we could suppose that no bowl however well glazed is perfectly smooth, and if our ball was small enough the uneven surface will make a difference: imagine that under high magnification the glaze turns out to be stepped regularly, like an amphitheatre. Then our miniature ball will rest at each step. While it is on a step it will not move or lose energy; it will need a fresh kick to set it moving again, giving away energy only as it drops from step to step. But the quantum imposes an added qualification. As energy can only be lost or gained in definite units, that sets a limit on our 'drop' between steps, which can be so small and no smaller; and that now lets us know what height the treads have to be. If the lowest is of the right dimension, just below that minimum, the ball will never reach the bottom at all.

This image is not Bohr's: he, having made the general point of quantum-limited 'steps', then suggests that if the emission of radiation can only be in steps, the lines on the spectrum represent rungs on a ladder indeed; each emission is a drop from a higher energy level to a lower one, each absorption line a corresponding jump up. Radiation in that case is due to the reformation of an atom after it has been disturbed; the electron jerked out of its orbit returns to its place, and as it does so emits radiation appropriate to its orbit's level of energy, of necessity in whole quanta.

Balmer's formula dealt only with hydrogen: and hydrogen as the lightest element can reasonably be expected to have only one electron. If we are concerned with the binding of a single electron, and have to discover what energy will be needed to tear this electron away from its nucleus, that must be related to the frequency of the electron's revolution around the centre of its orbit, and involve Planck's constant like all exertions of energy. Since there are simple equations that describe this revolution in terms of the mass of the body in question, the force which holds it (in this case the attraction of the charge on the electron and the equal and opposite charge on the nucleus) and the ratio of the radius to the circumference of the orbit, assumed to be circular, it is possible to express the energy:

$$W = \frac{2\pi^2 m e^2 E^2}{n^2 h^2};$$

m being the mass of the electron, e its charge, and E the charge on the nucleus, and n a whole number: different values for n will thus produce different values for the energy W, and also for the orbits; 'these configurations and no others will correspond to states of the system in which there is no radiation of energy'. In these stationary states the atom will remain, as long as it is not disturbed from outside. Since the number n is in the divisor, the lower the number the greater the energy needed to tear it off. So if $n = 1$, the atom will be in its most stable state, 'in which the electron is most firmly bound and the greatest amount of energy will be needed to remove it'. The reformation of the atom, after its electron has been pulled away, will similarly correspond to the capture of an electron. And when the atom passes from one state to another, it will emit energy in quantum bursts, according to the difference between the two energy levels; only the whole number n can vary. So we can express the difference as Wn_2 (where it ends up) $-Wn_1$ (where it started from) as:

$$\frac{2\pi^2 m \, e^2 \, E^2}{h^2} \quad \left(\frac{1}{n_2{}^2} - \frac{1}{n_1{}^2}\right)$$

In view of the equivalence of e and E, in the case of hydrogen $e^2 \, E^2$ could be written as e^4. Suppose the burst is a single quantum of frequency f then hf equals

$$\frac{2\pi^2 \, me^4}{h^2} \quad \left(\frac{1}{n_2{}^2} - \frac{1}{n_1{}^2}\right)$$

slipping that first h across to the other side, the frequency $f =$

$$\frac{2\pi^2 \, me^4}{h^3} \quad \left(\frac{1}{n_2{}^2} - \frac{1}{n_1{}^2}\right)$$

That piece enclosed within the brackets is already beginning to remind us of Balmer. In fact, Bohr now suggests that if $n_2 = 3, 4, 5, \ldots$ we have the series which had been observed in the infrared, since Balmer's work had been continued beyond the visible part of the spectrum. With $n_2 = 3$, Bohr declares, 'We get the series in the ultrared observed by Paschen and previously suspected by Ritz' ... and there is more to come, as Bohr correctly predicted, for with $n_2 = 4, 5$, etc, 'we get series in the extreme ultraviolet and the extreme ultrared, which are not observed, but the existence of which may be expected'. Here we have a meaning for Rydberg's number—derived from such simple things as the mass and charge of the electron, Planck's constant, and the ratio of radius to circumference. Given those values of the first three that were then available, Bohr calculated it as 3.1×10^{15} waves per second; observation to date showed it must be 3.29×10^{15}. By late summer, he had come across some better values for the electron which let his theory estimate $R = 3.26 \times 10^{15}$, an even closer agreement with experimental measurements.

Now the diameter of the orbit can be shown to depend likewise on the same quantities, which was why the Balmer series went on so much longer in some astronomical spectra than it could ever be made to do in rarefied gases, in laboratories here on earth. For there were never more than 12 lines in gases, while some stars could produce up to 33 lines. The diameter of the orbit would vary in proportion to the squares of the number n; with $n = 12$, he worked this out as 1.6×10^{-6} centimetres; with $n = 33$, $7\frac{1}{2}$ times as much. Now the conditions for such relatively large orbits and such large numbers of spectral lines could only be found in an extremely rarefied gas; for there to be enough of it to be observed at all it must be spread over a huge amount of space.

There was one big problem; some lines in the infrared region had been ascribed to hydrogen although they did not fit the formula. One set had been observed by the astronomer Pickering in the spectrum of a star in the constellation Puppis in 1896, the other had just been noticed by Fowler in tubes containing a mixture of hydrogen and helium in late 1912, and must have caused Bohr some anxiety. They also offered a solution. For he now suggested that these mysterious lines were in fact produced by helium, which had lost its two electrons. Assume helium ought to have two electrons—so in our equation, we now need $2e$ and $2E$ for the nucleus; if $n_2 = 4$ (n_1 varying as before) we can obtain the lines from the stars; if $n_2 = 3$ those of Fowler's vacuum tube. He could even explain why these lines had not been produced in tubes with pure helium. He then proceeds to show how his theory can be generalized to cover absorption as well as emission and extended to the spectra of heavier elements. But his main purpose in the latter half of the article is to derive the angular momentum of the electron as it revolves in a circular orbit around the nucleus. He was able to find a 'universal value, independent of the charge on the nucleus' which defines stationary states of the orbits: in the stablest state $n = 1$, so we have just $h/2$. Thus we take up Nicholson's point, and derive it from general assumptions, as Bohr always sought to do. By a historic irony Bohr had to revert to circular orbits for his electrons, whereas classical mechanics had depended on breaking away from them, since Newton's system of the cosmos is built on Kepler's discovery that the planets revolve in elliptical orbits, not the age-old circles of all previous systems. Bohr then considered what would happen when several electrons on rings rotate around their common nucleus; his constant will apply there too: 'in any molecular system consisting of positive nuclei and electrons in which the nuclei are at rest relative to each other and the electrons move in circular orbits, the angular momentum of every electron round the centre of its orbit will in the permanent state of the system be equal to $h/2\pi$ where h is Planck's constant'.

Like the earlier version submitted to Rutherford, he must have written this at white heat. He had not seized on his main point until after February 7, yet by 6 March he could send off the first instalment. There would be more to come, he promised, but the whole would be too long to appear all at one time. Rutherford was most impressed but a little troubled; 'How', he wrote, 'does an electron decide what frequency it is going to vibrate at when it passes from one stationary state to another? ... Can it know beforehand where it is going to stop?' Even Rutherford had not fully digested the implications of h, as a factor defining possible orbits—forcing electrons to stop *here*, forbidding them to move on to *there*. But it is true this first instar of the Bohr atom retained much of the old mechanics for the stationary states. Although Bohr was ready to abandon the old laws, he could not yet provide new ones to account for his angular momentum equations. Worse still, Rutherford felt he had been unnecessarily long-winded. 'I do not know if you appreciate the fact that long papers have a way of frightening readers who feel that they have not time to dip into them'. It would have to be cut—Bohr in great anxiety insisted nothing could be left out, and indeed he wished to add some more. In the end there was nothing for it but for Bohr to travel to Manchester and hammer out a text for his precious article. As Rutherford later recalled, 'it impressed me how determinedly he held on to every sentence, every expression, every quotation; everything had a definite reason ... and it was impossible to change anything'. And so the article finally appeared in the July number of the *Philosophical Magazine*. The previous month Bohr visited Manchester and Cambridge again, carrying with him the second part of his paper, published in September, a third part followed in the November issue.

In the second part he starts with his universal constant of angular velocity and shows how it will determine the dimensions of the atom, the size of each electron's orbit, and the frequency it must revolve around the nucleus: and thereby we learn how many electrons there must be in each orbit, so as to form a series of rotating rings, as Thomson and Nagaoka had suggested. He assumes, too, the new concept of atomic number; that is, 'the number of electrons in the atom is equal to the number which indicates the position of the corresponding element in the series of elements arranged in order of increasing atomic weight'. This by no means goes without saying: the idea had been germinating in Bohr's mind, but only while in Manchester during June did he learn of the programme of experiments which were to demonstrate it. Bohr begins with the four lightest elements from hydrogen to beryllium, which already has for him an outer as well as an inner ring. Then he discusses the conditions for stability as you go up the scale. The rings must not only all revolve about the same axis but must do so in the same plane, so that we have a perfect little solar system with all our 'planets' orbiting in the plane of the ecliptic. Rings will normally have even numbers of electrons, up to a maximum of eight. Odd numbers will only be found in the outermost ring, naturally the least stable. On this ring will depend the valency of the atom, its capacity to combine with others, which will be odd or even as that ring is odd or even. Hence elements with odd atomic number have likewise an odd numbered valency. The exact configurations he then proposed have for the most part not survived, but the principle holds well. Just as he did for the outer ring, so too he found a role for the innermost. Thomson had argued the previous year that X-rays characteristic for each element were emitted as a result of re-formation of an atom after one of its inner electrons was knocked out of place. Bohr developed this idea on his own principles, for it suggested to him not only the energy needed—which seemed to be approximately what was known of X-rays—but the diameter of the inner ring. He arrived at a value of $1/n \times 10^{-8}$ cm—for mercury say, that would be 8×10^{-10} cm 'very small in comparison with ordinary atomic dimensions, but still very great' in

Fig. 17. Bohr and Rutherford, facing in opposite directions, but still supporting one another.

comparison with those of the nucleus. The closing section of the paper takes up another new idea, that some substances which differed in their radioactive characters and atomic weights yet seemed mechanically and in all other respects, identical. In this theory this could mean that they have the same charge on the nucleus, together with 'the configuration of the surrounding electrons', but the mass of the nucleus is different in the two cases. So radioactivity is a loss of something from the nucleus only, and did not concern the satellite electrons. He did endeavour to extend his theory from the atom to the molecule, in which there would be more than one nucleus at work. Not just in the simplest case either; he tackled quite complex situations, assuming that with several rings, the inner ones would continue to revolve round their own nucleus, while the outer could revolve round the axis which joined the two nuclei. Starting from his constant of angular momentum, perhaps the conditions of stability could be worked out. Atoms will attract one another once they have approached within a certain range, but after a certain point the repulsion of the two positive nuclei will push them away, so there could be a balance between the two forces. Water he envisaged as having an oxygen nucleus surrounded by an inner ring of four electrons, with the two hydrogen nuclei on the ring's axis of rotation, on opposite sides and equidistant from the more powerful oxygen nucleus; round each of them would go a ring with *three* electrons, two of them borrowed from the oxygen atom. With methane, in which four hydrogen atoms combine with one of carbon, there could not be a single axis of this kind, so presumably there would be a four-cornered set-up such as chemists had imagined, with the carbon nucleus at the centre, orbited by its inner ring of two electrons, while another ring of two electrons, one from the carbon and one from the hydrogen, turned round the diagonals that connect each of the four to the centre.

NOTE

1. Heilbron, J. and Kuhn, T.S. The genesis of the Bohr atom. *Hist. Stud. phys. Sci.* 1, 246 (1969) (especially note 88).

11

VERY PRETTY — BUT WILL IT WORK?

In his massive paper Bohr had successfully brought together the new theory of discontinuous radiation and the new theory of the atom's structure. In the details his glimpse within the very heart of matter has often proved inaccurate. His great achievement survives. The dualism of nineteenth-century physics was at last overthrown. Bohr opened a door into a new mansion of nature. If the furnishing proved more elaborate than appeared to his first glance, that is only to be expected.

The reaction among those who had to face these new opportunities confirms how revolutionary they were. His closest friends among the physicists of Europe, Oseen and Von Hevesy, wrote him their enthusiastic congratulations; in their eyes he had won through from theories and speculations to the facts, to a truth that should be clear to all. Most people received the paper with mixed feelings, aware that this new feast of ideas would have to be digested; and aware too that digestion might be a painful process, which could involve the loss of some very fundamental convictions about the workings of nature. In September Bohr observed in a card to Maclaren that while they agreed that much of the old mechanics would have to be jettisoned; 'but do you think such horrid assumptions as I have used are necessary? For the moment I am inclined to most radical ideas . . .'.

Horrid assumptions they were to very many of his colleagues. The view of Rayleigh must have been typical of many. When his son Robin asked him what he thought of Bohr's first paper, he replied 'I saw that it was no use to me. I do not say that discoveries may not be made in that sort of way . . . But it does not suit me.' That same curious national complementarity shows up in some of these reactions. In Germany the quantum was now intellectually respectable. But it had cost German physicists a great deal of effort to bring themselves to agree that there really were such things as atoms; to suppose one could pry inside an atom and announce on its structure sounded very fanciful to them. When Sommerfeld wrote from Munich to thank Bohr for an offprint, on 4 September, he congratulated him on his use of Planck's h to resolve the Rydberg number; and added that he himself had already been thinking on similar lines. However 'I am for the present rather sceptical about atom models in general'. Sommerfeld at least knew something of importance had been done. In conversation a little earlier, he declared that the publication of Bohr's paper would 'mark a date in theoretical physics'. At the university of Göttingen, the reception was more dubious. Harald, who was there at the time, wrote to his brother to tell him that most of those he met 'do not dare to believe that they can be objectively right; they find the assumptions too "bold" and "fantastic" '; his picture is confirmed by the recollections of another friend, Courant, who once told Bohr that 'when I reported these things at Göttingen, they laughed at me for taking such fantastic ideas seriously ... thus I became so to speak, a martyr to Bohr's model'.

When an attempt had been made previously to use Planck's *h* to find the dimensions of an atom, by Arthur Haas at Vienna, it had been much more harshly dismissed. Specifically, Haas had in mind J. J. Thomson's atom, but like Bohr he took hydrogen as the simplest case, and arrived at a value for its radius which was not bad. Haas approached the whole question from a historical standpoint. After he obtained his doctorate he applied for a post teaching the history of physics and was persuaded that in order to justify his right to do so he should first do some original work in physics himself. Presumably his teachers did not mean anything quite so revolutionary; he complained that 'the narrowness of the established leaders in physics stifled my initial attempts, which might have led to great and possibly fundamental achievements'. When in February 1910 he presented his theory to the local society for chemistry and physics, one of his professors put him down with the remark that as it was Carnival time Haas wanted to amuse them all with a seasonal prank. Another explained that the quantum is a theory in thermodynamics, while spectroscopy belongs to optics, and only someone very naïve could mix them up. By the autumn Haas's notions were taken a little more seriously. Planck mentioned them in his paper to the Solvay congress, if only to demolish them; Sommerfeld too was critical. Only Lorentz spoke up for Haas. There was something to be said for such a daring view, he felt, even if his support was very half-hearted, 'without wishing to attach too much importance to the model invented by M. Haas'. Now the new wind was blowing harder. Later, in September 1913, Von Hevesy met Einstein in Vienna: Einstein gave his opinion on Bohr's theory, very interesting if it was correct, indeed of the greatest importance; he added that 'he had very similar ideas many years ago but no pluck to develop it'. If Einstein himself had been daunted by such horrid assumptions, how bold Bohr was to venture on them.

Now Bohr had proposed an experiment which while not establishing his theory irrefutably would at least make it much more plausible, since it suggested that certain spectral lines, previously supposed to be the traces of hydrogen, were really from helium. In his first accompanying letter to Rutherford he mentioned that a friend would try to find if these lines were produced in tubes which contained a mixture of helium and chlorine, since Bohr had a reason why they had not been discovered with pure helium so far. Rutherford replied that he had put the idea to another colleague, Evans, who was interested: 'and I think it quite possible that he may try some experiments on the matter when he comes back next term'. Indeed by August Evans was able to announce in *Nature* that he had obtained one crucial line with pure helium in his tube; although he had eliminated hydrogen altogether, the line appeared. Where there was no helium but hydrogen alone, or in various combinations, the line vanished.

The publication of this *experimentum crucis* did not settle the question. Within a week of Evans's report, Fowler wrote off to *Nature* that he was by no means convinced that some residual hydrogen in Evans's tubes could not have produced the line in question; Bohr's calculations were just outside the limits of error that his apparatus would allow. Here, Bohr could object that if measurements were corrected for the motion of the centre of mass, there would be a much better fit. Nicholson chimed in, the next month. Half of his letter was devoted to a claim to priority for the idea that $h/2\pi$ was a fundamental unit of angular momentum of electrons. In his view, it increased not by whole multiples, but by their squares, although of course with hydrogen, singled out by Bohr, the number 1 and its square coincide. But, he insisted, Bohr had not dealt with the spectrum of helium in its ordinary state, only when ionized by the loss of one or both electrons. Bohr riposted to Fowler's claim in the next week's issue; Fowler accepted this, as a compromise, on the grounds that Bohr's calculations involved a modification of his theory. Indeed, he speaks quite sharply. Echoing Nicholson, he declared that 'Dr Bohr's theory has not yet been shown to be capable of explaining the ordinary series of helium lines'. This seems unfair: in fact Bohr had dealt briefly with helium lines in his paper. But Bohr simply *had* to account for these particular lines; his theory leant heavily on the Balmer formula working out, so if in this case it did not, and the lines really were produced only by hydrogen, that would be a kick on the shin for the theory. There was no further correspondence: perhaps it was all a matter of 'digestion time'. The immediate reaction to a troublesome idea is to say no—as it becomes familiar, so it becomes less disturbing, the arguments in its favour look more convincing and yet a symbolic objection is still fired as a Parthian shot—ruffled, we are not quite won over. Eminent spectroscopists were among the severest critics: such were Fowler, or Runge at Göttingen, who told Harald Bohr that any apparent conformity between his brother's predictions and observation was purely fortuitous. At heart perhaps they were rather annoyed that someone like Bohr, who had never been trained as a spectroscopist and always seemed to need someone else to do his experiments for him, should now proclaim that spectral lines, which *they* had announced were hydrogen, were really helium all along.

Lines which could not fit Bohr's theory continued to harass him for many months, because he and Evans were at work on them right through 1914. In one instance, as he wrote to Harald, an oxygen line was so close to the hydrogen that it made it look displaced. As experiment proved him right in case after case, more and more of his fellows were persuaded. As early as the end of September, Von Hevesy, talking to Einstein, assured him that Fowler's series was now established with certainty to be helium (rather jumping the gun—this was before Fowler in his second letter to *Nature* ceased to contest the point), 'When he heard this, he was extremely astonished and exclaimed "this is an enormous achievement. The theory of Bohr must then be right" ... the big eyes of Einstein looked still bigger', said Von Hevesy, 'and he told me "Then it is one of the greatest discoveries." '

'The old mechanical beliefs are past mending', Maclaren wrote back in February, while Bohr was still hard at work on Part I. That January he had published in the *Philosophical Magazine* his own 'Theory of radiation', on which he must have been working during the previous autumn, while Bohr was wrestling with his problems before he discovered Nicholson and the Balmer formula. This was Maclaren's year too, when he also was in the prime age for invention, for at the September meeting of the British Association he presented a 'Theory of magnetism' and in the October issue of the *Philosophical Magazine*, a 'Theory of gravity'. In the opening words of his first article, 'The unrest of our time has invaded even the world of Physics, where scarcely one of the principles long accepted as fundamental passes unchallenged by all.' The 'spirit of revolution' he saw as subverting all established ideas was embodied above all in the idea of a quantum (attributed to Einstein). If the continuous medium went, the ether disappeared, if continuous waves broke up into discrete parts, the resolution of all change into motions of matter would be lost with it. 'To save the classical view of radiation as a continuous wave motion ... it seems to me a small thing to sacrifice the ordinary mechanical motions of matter'—these can go—but let us not allow atoms of radiation too. So he tried to produce a new theory of radiation that should avoid this frightful dilemma. In a letter to *Nature* in October, he congratulated Bohr on making out of Planck's constant h an angular momentum. And yet— in his own theory of gravity he ventures on the most novel and imaginative ground, embracing relativity and the fourth dimension with enthusiasm. Nevertheless, he ends by urging that while the old mechanics must go, we must try to keep as much as we may of its essence. As the quantum is a notion that can not incorporate the truths of the old system, 'I suggest we ought rather to seek some system in which as much as possible of the old may be retained.'

If this was the attitude of a radical like Maclaren, more conservative thinkers were even less ready to accept the idea, unless it were first properly tamed. The papers of Maclaren, and of Rutherford and Nuttall, shared the October *Philosophical Magazine* with a new venture by J. J. Thomson, 'On the structure of the atom'. The currant bun had now become more like a landmine. In order to avoid the conclusion that the quantum signified 'that radiant energy is molecular in structure'—in order to repel this monstrous notion that energy too came in atoms — he proposed that this apparent effect was only a consequence of the dimensions of the atoms of matter, and the way they are ordered. Because the atoms are the size they are, they appear to absorb and emit radiation in lumps; but radiant energy itself must be continuous. He makes use of his old idea that light is propagated along tubes of force *à la* Faraday. Whereas some people, including Thomson himself, were to deduce as a corollary that the wave fronts of light will not be quite continuous but speckled, now he used the concept to deny the atomicity of light, and protect mechanics from these strange intrusions. It is all a question he insisted, of how radiant energy is translated into kinetic energy within the atom. One could imagine electrons held in their places by two forces, one repulsive, pushing the electrons outward from the atom's centre, and varying as the inverse cube of its distance from that centre; and the other attractive, varying according to the inverse square. The power of repulsion will be diffused right through the atom, while the attractive force is restricted to radiating tubes. All the electrons will be inside these tubes, at such distances that the two opposing forces are in equilibrium, as the one diminishes so much more rapidly than the other. The energy needed to remove an electron will be that needed to push it out of its tube; since the attractive force no longer affects it, away it goes. Then we assign the right values for these forces, so that, given the mass and charge of electrons to be removed, we can derive h from them: and all difficulties vanish. All very neat — in fact, too neat.

The stage was now set for the last round of the battle in Britain at least, at the Birmingham meeting of the British Association in September 1913. Bohr's hypothesis had brought the question of atomic structure to the forefront of the argument over energy and radiation: nuclear atom and discrete minimum units of action would stand or fall together. Madame Curie was there; Lorentz the father of the electron theory was there; Planck was invited, although in the end he could not come. Bohr was invited too. He hesitated at first, since he had been twice to England already that year, no doubt he was finding it an expensive business — and perhaps he begrudged the time, with a new academic year coming up. At the last minute he was persuaded to come. His name does not appear with those of Marie Curie and Lorentz among the distinguished foreign scholars listed at the beginning of *Nature*'s account. At least, his name does appear (last) among those who were to receive honorary degrees.

Sir Oliver Lodge was president; and it was at his home that Bohr first had a chance to put his ideas to Lorentz. In his Presidential address, Lodge set the tone — the tone of a philosophy of nature that felt itself under attack. When he announced that his theme would be 'Continuity', a rumour went about that as he was a spiritualist like Crookes, he too meant to use the British Association as a platform to proclaim his belief in the continuity of life after death. However he made it clear he was worried only to defend the continuity of the physical universe from the assault upon it; from the tide of scepticism now washing away the very foundation inherited from high Victorian science. Like Maclaren, he drew an analogy with the attacks on all accepted views of the world: ' In Education ... revolutionary ideas are promulgated concerning the advantages of freedom for infants. In Economic and Political Science or Sociology, what is there that is not under discussion? Not property alone, nor land alone, but everything—back to the Garden of Eden, and the interrelations of men and women!' In every branch of science, discontinuity was taking hold. Atomism was well enough for atoms, for chemistry or even biology—but for radiation? The whole of science had been based on the assumption that nature never leaps—now it seems she does nothing else—'her placid course ... is beginning to look like a steeplechase, with change, which had once implied a steady flow from one condition to another now to mean a series of jumps from one permitted state to another, with nothing in between'. To him that seemed to imply a discontinuity of space just as relativity implied a discontinuity of time. After seventy years, since the ether has quietly vanished away from our schoolbooks and our popular guides to the universe, it is not easy to recreate the emotions that were invested in this peculiar substance. Absolutely stationary, found everywhere yet utterly pervious, absolutely rigid yet incapable of resisting anything, suffering strain all the time and yet not reacting—so mysterious and protean was its character. Yet the greatest scientists of the day were not only convinced of its existence, but determined to convince any doubters. Bohr's theory brought the question of atomic structure into Sir Oliver's ken. He was impressed with the accuracy of its predictions, but could not believe that the quantum imposed limits on the behaviour of the atom—rather it was the other way about. Radiation is only *apparently* discontinuous; in reality it is the interior of the atom which consists of separate parts moving at a high velocity. Radiation is only emitted after some violent catastrophe has thrown a piece of the atom right out, obliging the rest to reconstitute itself—he used the analogy of a star exploding as a nova. So it is that radiation comes off in individual gushes or bursts as the atom erupts, and h as the unit of radiation is merely a consequence of the actual dimensions of atoms.

On the next day, the Physics section was to open. After a paper on X-rays, J. J. Thomson kicked off with 'The structure of the atom', the same paper that he was to publish in next month's *Philosophical Magazine*, although this was a livelier version—'it will be long before his illustration of the quantum theory by pint pots is forgotten ...' *Nature* reported. Now alas, we have to reconstruct for ourselves how pint pots illustrate the quantum theory—perhaps by fitting only a set number of times into quart pots? Then Rutherford outlined his atom. All the latest information was included, in particular some experiments he had carried out with Nuttall earlier in the summer on the scattering produced by hydrogen, helium, methane, and carbon dioxide. With the lightest of these, all was in close accord with their expectations, and he remarked on the confirmation of Bohr's assumption that a hydrogen nucleus had one unit of electric charge, a helium nucleus two. Here was 'promise of another item of support for the new model'.

On the Friday, a grand discussion was to be held on 'The theory of radiation'. The hall was packed. Although it was supposed to allow for 350 people, there was not room enough for everybody. Bohr was called on to give a brief account of his atom: Jeans, who started off the discussion, showed how Bohr's method might explain spectral series. It might be hard to justify the bold assumption on which the new model rested—but it worked, the conclusions he had drawn from them fitted the evidence. Only, as Lorentz asked, how do you account for it—ingenious it may be, but is it true? Bohr could only acknowledge that his theory was as yet incomplete. Interestingly, both of them tried to reduce the impact of h all the same. For Jeans the 'apparent atomicity of action or energy or angular momentum' (referring to the Bohr–Nicholson idea of the constant electron angular momentum) might just derive from the atomicity of electricity—h from e. But is the least unit of electric charge, the charge on the electron, universal because all electrons are equal?— or is it perhaps because electrons are 'formed out of some pervading medium?' Then all would be equal because its properties made them so—a granular ether again? Lorentz tackled the problem from a different angle. Why not solve the difficulty of the interaction of 'matter' and 'ether' by supposing an intermediate substance. Vibrating entities would oscillate each in their own frequency. Among them he would include all charged bodies, the electrons being the simplest form, exchanging energy with brute unelectric matter, and so form a general link. At least this would save us from the danger of discrete pieces of radiation flying about, against all the evidence in favour of continuous waves. This distinction between matter and radiator was firmly sat on, by Jeans as well as by Bohr. Other views were still to be heard. At least one professor got up to maintain that it was still possible to rescue the old system without any kind of quanta. For the most part, the old guard were guarded in their reactions. Rayleigh as chairman commented that when he was a young man he had believed nobody over sixty could express a useful opinion about the latest ideas in physics. Now he was over sixty himself he was not quite so sure, but in this instance he would stand by his youthful wisdom, hard as it was to imagine the new model as a picture of what really happens. Lodge 'venturing right within the electron, remarked that there at any rate, in 'a positive charge' (presumably the nucleus) accepted mechanics could not work, else the repulsive forces exerted by like charges against one another would make it fly asunder. But Thomson rejected all the probability, and the statistical arguments and the nominalism of the next generation in advance. If a calculation in probability takes up more than half a sheet of notepaper, he said, do not accept the implications without independent evidence. So much for those who try to replace the clarity and certainty of experiment with the subtlety of mathematics.

Although there were still gaps, the Birmingham meeting of the British Association marked the effective arrival of the quantum and of the new atom. In 1912, the *Annual Register* merely held out the hope that Rutherford's new work on beta particles 'would throw light on the constitution of the atom'— the same cautious phrase he had used when he talked to the Manchester Literary and Philosophical Society. In 1913, its physics report featured quite prominently Rutherford's theory that 'positive charge is not diffused throughout a sphere, but is a central point around which the electrons revolve', and explained that Bohr had strengthened this doctrine with his picture of radiation by 'contraction of electronic orbits ... in sudden steps'. Planck-sized steps. The effects could be illustrated by contrasting the first mention of Rutherford's atom in a popular work, Cox's *Beyond the atom*, of 1913, the preface being dated in February, with the exposition in Kaye's book on X-rays, of 1914. Cox makes a point of recalling 'my happy memories of those exciting times when for nine years I was privileged to witness at close quarters' the work of Rutherford, who had been a friend as well as colleague at Montreal. He claims that Rutherford had criticized the book in proof. Nevertheless, the final chapter on 'The new atom' is basically on J.J. Thomson's atom, and Cox only mentions almost in passing, in his account of Rutherford's beta ray investigation, that 'Rutherford therefore conceives the atom, like Thomson, as a positive nucleus (but of very small dimensions) surrounded by an electronic system probably rotating in rings'. But Kaye, whose preface is also dated February (1914) gives pride of place to 'Rutherford's theory of the constitution of matter', with reference to the articles by Rutherford and Bohr. J.J. Thomson only appears in a footnote, which does not even make it clear that he still stood by his own model.

A second Solvay conference was held at the end of October 1913, only six weeks after the British Association meeting. Now there were six representatives, including Thomson, who had not found the first gathering required his presence. The structure of the atom was naturally one of the main subjects on the agenda, and Thomson began the proceedings by airing his views on the subject—presumably a repetition of those he had already unfolded twice that autumn. From Rutherford's report however, it looks as if this topic was cast in the shade by the discovery of X-ray crystallography, a brand new field of research. Between sessions, the members could admire some of the technological consequences of what had once seemed a purely intellectual discovery, when they visited the 'private wireless station' which belonged to Goldschmidt, the organizer of the conference' 'one of the largest in the world, capable of transmitting messages to the Congo and to Burmah'.

At the beginning of December, Stark applied an intense electric field to an incandescent gas, and succeeded in splitting several lines of the gas's spectrum into fine lines. This was a considerable achievement, for which Stark had striven through seven years' labour; he describes his excitement when success drew near, so much so that he took his spectrographic plate while it was still being developed in the darkroom, and 'in the faint yellow light . . . I observed several lines at the position of the blue hydrogen line'. Eventually with hydrogen he was able to produce no less than five thin lines each out of two of the standard ones. The parallel to the Zeeman effect seemed obvious, and both were seen to be outstanding queries, still hanging over Bohr's atom. As Rutherford promptly wrote to Bohr, some means would have to be found to reconcile his theory with these finer lines. In December the first part of the paper of Moseley was published, of which more later; and the letter of Soddy in which he proposed the term, and concept, 'isotope': all fitted in beautifully with the nuclear atom. When Rutherford was knighted in the New Year Honours for 1914 it may not have been quite intended as a royal accolade for his new model atom—but it must have felt like that. For Bohr, the old year ended with a Christmas card from Nagaoka in Japan, where however 25 December was then celebrated—at least by scientists—as the Newton Festival, as Newton's was regarded there as a more significant birthday for that date than any other. Nagaoka thanked Bohr for offprints of his papers, and reminded him just who had first conceived of an atom built like a tiny planetary system. These ideas, he thought, seem 'to be intimately connected with the Saturnian atom, with which I was occupied about ten years ago.'

12

HOW MANY ELECTRONS?

The first theories of atomic structure after the discovery of the electron did not worry much how many electrons there might be. Some suggested vast clouds of them. If all atoms were made up of corpuscles, perhaps the relationship of 1800 to one, that is the ratio, mass of hydrogen atom: mass of electron, could mean there are 1800 electrons in the lightest of all atoms, and at least half that number if the counterbalancing positive charge was a single sphere of mass equal to that of the negative particles. If the electrons were outside the positive part of the atom, in rings like those of Saturn, there ought to be vast numbers or else the rings would lack stability. Only J.J. Thomson's plan of explaining the chemical characteristics of each element by the number of its electrons implied there must be relatively few in each atom.

As the first decade of the century drew on, the idea of few electrons made more and more sense. In 1906 Thomson tried to calculate just how many of his corpuscles an atom contained. In hydrogen gas at least the dispersion of light suggested to him that there is but one corpuscle per hydrogen atom, or at any rate 'the number ... is not much greater than unity'. That was unexpectedly few, even for him. Painfully few, for it was agreed to be a nasty blow for the electric theory of matter, which supposed everything was made up of electrons, and also for his electrons as the explanation of chemistry, which was supposed to assume a minimum of four or five electrons to the lightest atoms. Experiments by Barkla (an ex pupil of his, then teaching at Liverpool) on the scattering of X-rays in air implied 25 in every molecule of air. If the scattering in nitrogen gas is near enough the same as in air, as seemed to be the case, then there could well be 28 in each molecule of nitrogen, containing two atoms of atomic weight 14. The hint in this last result was confirmed by experiments on the absorption of beta-particles, as they are electrons too, which led him to think that the number must vary as the atomic weight of the material that absorbed them.

A quick glance at the table of the elements will immediately suggest that as you move along the line, the atomic weights go up in units roughly double that of hydrogen. Thus, carbon is 12.01, nitrogen 14.01, oxygen 16.00. This two at a time procedure does work very crudely though. If copper at 63.54 is followed by zinc at 65.38, the next in line, gadolinium, is 69.72; and while platinum 195.00 conveniently precedes gold at 196.97, mercury follows at 200.5. But the shorter and the longer gaps average out fairly well, and there are enough two unit increases to make it plausible to say that as you go up the scale, each element has one more of something (which is twice a hydrogen atom), or else two more of something (either just that atom, or something equivalent). Since the earliest days of the chemical atom, a few individuals had therefore concluded that atoms are 'manufactured articles'. The idea does have an attractive simplicity about it, and the physicist's mind adores simplicity. So if the number of electrons was in proportion to the atomic weight, that sounded hopeful. Some years after Thomson's paper, in 1911, Barkla published fresh results which corrected his earlier findings for the number of electrons to a given volume of gas and, with the aid of better values for the charge and mass of an electron, suggested that the number per atom is about half the atomic weight.

These ideas caught the attention of a Dutch teacher of mathematics called Antonis van den Broek. What first interested him was the way in which one could establish on this principle not so much how many electrons, but how many *elements* there are. The periodic table continued to excite and tease scientists from many points of view, since the roster of elements kept on growing. The discovery of the rare inert gases (also known as the noble gases owing to their snobbish refusal to form connections with the rest of matter) had been vexed by the difficulty of fitting them into the system, unless they were granted a row of their own. Elsewhere gaps remained. At the bottom, the great difference in atomic weight between hydrogen and helium suggested there might be room for one or even two elements. This was behind Nicholson's speculations, since he was tempted to think of a basic unit equal to half a hydrogen atom. After all, helium, so common in the sun, is so scarce here on earth that it took over a quarter of a century after first knowledge of it in the solar spectrum before it turned up here. Obviously there could well be other light elements which had long since drifted away from our planet, if they were ever here, but which might exist, even in great quantities, in the seething heart of a nebula.

Another problem appeared at the other end of the table, but in reverse. All the radioelements had atomic weights between lead and uranium inclusive, where there could not be nearly enough places for all the different forms through which radioactive bodies passed. A little way above the middle of the table there was another sore thumb sticking out; or rather a whole set of them appearing and disappearing, fading into one another; the rare earths. Crookes once confessed they even invaded his dreams, 'Stretching like an unknown sea before us, mocking mystifying and murmuring strange revelations and possibilities.' Just because they are rare, and tend to mask one another, several false alarms had already been given and elements 'discovered' when they really were not, for the separation was an enormously difficult job. Finally, the Table was based on a periodicity of characters if arranged in order of weights, yet there were three cases where an element if placed by weight appeared one step *after* the position, to which it ought to be allotted on the grounds of its chemical features; almost as if a pair of elements had swopped their proper places. One of the three was a pair of not uncommon metals—cobalt and nickel.

Van den Broek made his contribution to the discussion in the summer of 1911, as he was thinking over Rutherford's first atomic nucleus paper. His was the first attempt to put Rutherford's insight to wider uses. If, he claimed, the amount of charge on the nucleus corresponded to half the atomic weight, there ought to be 120 places from hydrogen to uranium; these he hoped could be arranged in a 'cubic' table, that is with relationships in a three-dimensional pattern. The differences in atomic weight should go up in even numbers, which would correspond to an increase in permanent charge, both positive and negative. To each even number there would be an element, so it would be easy to work out just how many places really remained to be filled. Early in 1913, he abandoned the 'even number' side of his pattern. Just list the elements as they appear in Mendeleev's table, and their number in the list will be the amount of charge they carry. Hence there are as many elements as possible charges. So he freed himself from having to account for their going up by twos, as was implied by talking about atomic weights. Yet he could not free himself altogether, for he still supposed the number of electrons outside the nucleus would correspond to half the atomic weight. As this would work out a little less than the number of units of charge carried by the nucleus, he felt there must be some more electrons inside it, to compensate the positive excess, and maintain a neutral atom.

Van den Broek as a private teacher had not the opportunities to follow up his imaginative suggestions experimentally. There was a young man in Manchester who had the determination and the ability to do so. Harry Moseley had already spent some two and a half years working in Rutherford's laboratory. All who knew him were struck with his immense capacity for taking pains and working impossible hours: all agreed he was the most brilliant of all the brilliant minds that clustered about their central nucleus, Ernest Rutherford. Now the time was come for him to carry out a sustained piece of research that would solve a major scientific problem and win him fame in the larger world. He was nearly Bohr's contemporary, born in 1887, like Bohr he was the son and grandson of professors—indeed, his father was also a biologist, a professor of comparative anatomy. Unlike Niels Bohr however, Moseley could not have been influenced intellectually by his father's guidance, for he lost his father when not yet four years old. It has often been remarked how many outstanding scientists were orphaned of their fathers relatively young (although at a time when the death rate in early middle age was much higher than it is today, it would not be easy to prove this was significantly above the average). To Bohr and Thomson this happened when they were already almost adult. The effects on Moseley would very likely be more severe.

Yet, by all accounts, he spent a very comfortable and secure North Oxford childhood. He seems to have been a little withdrawn from his age-group. Perhaps that came in part from his education at Eton, and then at Trinity College Oxford, a very different kind of establishment from the Cambridge Trinity, for as Moseley once joked, at his Trinity they were more interested in fox-hunting than research. Nevertheless he succeeded in fitting well enough into his background, and rowed for House and College. Only he did not form a very high opinion of his teachers. In the middle of his course he changed over from chemistry to physics, not without some misgivings, apparently justified when to his great disappointment and general surprise he failed to get a First. Fortunately, Rutherford was not deceived by this result. Despite Moseley's so-called failure, he was appointed to a lectureship in physics at Manchester in September 1910. That same autumn two other men arrived, who were to collaborate closely with Moseley during his time there: Charles Darwin, his contemporary within a few weeks, who had just graduated from Cambridge, and Kasimir Fajans, who had studied under Lenard at Heidelberg. All three came, like Bohr later, primarily to learn about radioactivity at the most fertile source. Moseley and Fajans worked on a study of various radioactive products with very short half-lives—and so, not easy to catch. At the time there seemed nothing world-shaking about his research, as such investigations were by now very much normal science. The Rutherford atom was born in the opening months of Moseley's time at Manchester. For the moment however he was not diverted from his regular path to seek out its implications. Then in the summer of 1912 a new idea broke surface. Ever since the discovery of X-rays there had been arguments whether they were really radiation or in fact particles. For all the evidence in favour of radiation, they could not produce some of the standard optical phenomena. Besides, X-rays and gamma rays pack too strong a punch not to have a mass of their own—how else could they give rise to secondary radiation, knocking electrons out of bodies they irradiate?

In a way this was a replay of the argument over the nature of cathode rays twenty years earlier. Although Barkla and Thomson were convinced that these were rays indeed, some of the most active contenders for the corpuscle theory were in Britain, notably William Bragg, while the centre of X-ray research in Germany, at Munich, where old Röntgen himself was Professor of Experimental Physics, held strongly to the ray interpretation. In Bragg's mind, these X-ray particles would travel in pairs; a negative electron 'which had assumed a cloak of darkness' wrapped in a positive charge that would neutralize it. His model seems to owe much to Lenard's theory of atomic structure. As so often, the answer to the X-ray problem came from a slightly different branch of physics; and once solved opened up a new vein of discovery just waiting to be mined.

As Röntgen's reserved character, his compulsive determination to leave no doubt unresolved, and no loophole unstopped, acted as a brake on his research students' work as well as on his own, the more dynamic young men gathered round the professor of theoretical physics, Arnold Sommerfeld. Among their company was Max von Laue, a former pupil of Planck, and already the author of a book on the theory of relativity. One day in January 1912, Paul Ewald, one of Sommerfeld's team, came to Laue to ask his advice on a problem connected with the refraction of light in a crystal. Feeling that Laue's interest in the philosophical side of physics would assure him a sympathetic hearing, he put forward the idea that the regularity of crystals must mean that the particles which compose them—perhaps but not necessarily their constituent atoms—are arrayed in the form of a regularly patterned lattice. 'And what would be the distance between these particles?' asked Laue. All Ewald could say was that it must be far less than the wavelength of visible light. Immediately Laue was set to thinking what would happen if you were to beam through a crystal a ray of very much shorter wavelength—such as an X-ray. In that case presumably the lines of atoms would serve as the closely ruled parallel lines of a grating and diffract the rays, breaking the homogeneous beam into its spectrum. That would settle the true character of X-rays once and for all. And it would settle Ewald's theory of crystal structure at the same time.

The Easter vacation arrived: Laue was due to go off on a skiing holiday in the Alps, just the right opportunity for him to put to Sommerfeld his plans for the necessary experiments. Sommerfeld was not too enthusiastic; for he feared that the internal motion of the rows of atoms would shake the diffraction of the X-rays and spoil the effect. Perhaps he did not relish diverting the assistant he had but lately acquired. On their return to Munich, Laue talked about his idea to the assistant himself, Walter Friedrich, when they met at a local café; Friedrich was quite keen, and so was one of Röntgen's assistants, Paul Knipping, who offered to join them. Between the two of them not much time would be lost, and no very elaborate apparatus would be required. The experiment worked—first with a crystal of copper sulphate, then more successfully with zincblende. Round the main mark of the rays was a ring of spots, in the first photographs blotchy and indistinct, then clear, precise, elliptical, forming a definite geometrical pattern. With great enthusiasm, the results were announced at the beginning of June. Once Laue had constructed a satisfactorily mathematical interpretation of his discovery he took little further part in its exploitation. His interest lay in basic principles. Looking at individual crystals, seeking out particular X-ray spectra was not for him. So it was in England that busy miners hurried to work the lode which Laue had uncovered: and first among them were William and Laurence Bragg. There have been several examples of sons equalling fathers in science, but the collaboration between these two on this brilliant undertaking is most unusual. Perhaps William Bragg was, at least in basic research, something of a late developer. In fact, he was only a few years younger than Thomson himself, being born in 1862. Like Thomson he seems to have been a shy and unsociable boy who felt himself separated from his fellows at school by his love of mathematics. He too entered Trinity College Cambridge on a scholarship, and his last year as an undergraduate coincided with Thomson's first year as Cavendish Professor. While on the way to one of Thomson's lectures he learnt of a chair going at a new university of Adelaide, and although he had done no work in physics at all, quickly put in an application. Thomson supported him, for he doubtless remembered how the electors for his own chair had chosen a bright young man of promise over so many senior candidates—and off Bragg went to Australia. Not for the first time, a Victorian science professor had to get up his subject in the long vacation before taking up his post; the journey round the world was long enough in those days to afford plenty of time for extra study. There Bragg had to set up a department and teach a wide range of topics. He had done no research in Cambridge, and probably did not expect to do any in Australia, but for example set up the first X-ray apparatus in South Australia, and the first Marconi radio equipment. Only in the course of talks on radioactivity did he begin to open up new territory for himself, investigating the alpha ray. His work on the alpha-stopping power of various substances won him enough repute for an invitation to come home to England in 1908, just a year after Rutherford's return from Montreal. Used as he was to treat the alpha and beta products of radioactivity as missiles, it was understandable that he might wonder if the same was true for gamma rays and so for X-rays too.

Naturally he was very excited by the new discovery of X-ray diffraction. For a while he tried to save his theory by supposing that corpuscles accompanied the X-rays in some way. Perhaps the diffraction effect was produced by pencils of particles streaming down along the vacant avenues between the atoms. A similar notion of 'shafts' through the crystal was put forward by Stark, who was the leading advocate of corpuscular X-rays in Germany. At all events, Bragg soon presciently decided it might be best to give up trying to resolve which model was right, and instead envisage a theory that would combine the advantages of both. At this time Bragg's son Laurence had just finished his first year as a research student at the Cavendish; after graduating in mathematics at Adelaide, he started all over again in England, at his father's old college, of course. Like Bohr he found the research topic Thomson set him unfruitful, and the conditions of the lab overcrowded and short of apparatus. Like Laue he had acquired more knowledge of chemistry, and particularly of crystals, than most physicists of the day. He also attended lectures on optics, in which Thomson explained his concept of X-rays as short pulses of radiation rather than a continuous undifferentiated stream. He began to think in terms of a simpler form of crystal diffraction than Laue's. Suppose the rays to be reflected off the planes formed by the rows of atoms in the three-dimensional lattice, almost like mirrors, might that not explain why the Laue spots grew more elliptical if the photographic plate was further away from the crystal? These ideas he put before the Cambridge Philosophical Society, as Bohr had done exactly a year before. In the discussion that followed, C.T.R. Wilson suggested that the external planes should reflect X-rays as well as the internal ones, provided they were sufficiently smooth. Bragg set to work with a thin strip of mica mounted on aluminium, so directing an X-ray beam upon it as to graze it at an angle of only 10°. The right trace showed up on his plate, he rushed off to tell J.J. Thomson, who was caught up in his enthusiasm. Unfortunately, in the emotion of the moment Bragg overworked his coil, and severely damaged it. Such were the stringencies of apparatus at the time that he was told he could not have another for a whole month...

The point was established all the same and William Bragg now decided to help by constructing an instrument to examine the reflected beam in proper detail, so as to do for X-rays what the spectrometer did for visible light. The crystal was to revolve so that its surface (or the sheets of crystal parallel to the surface) would reflect the rays at any desired angle into an ionization chamber where their strength could be measured. Looking at different faces it would be possible to work out the arrangement of atoms in the lattice from the angle and intensity of reflection. While the father worked in Leeds, the son continued in Cambridge; Laurence began with the structure of the most obvious crystal, common rock salt. Meanwhile his father sent off a joint paper to the Royal Society early in April 1913. His spectrometer had already disclosed two types of radiation, one analogous to white light, one type specific to each element used to produce the X-rays. In the summer vacation the two could collaborate properly at last; 'it was', Laurence recalled, 'a glorious time when we worked far into the night with new worlds unfolding before us in the silent laboratory'—he compared the new research frontier to an alluvial goldfield where the nuggets are lying about for the taking. In rapid succession, they broke down the crystal structure of calcite, fluorite, zinc-blende, and many more, culminating in a paper on the diamond. After establishing the basic point that each element had its own X-ray spectrum, and linking this with earlier attempts to break down X-radiation into different types, the Braggs left this side of the question; there were far too many nuggets to be traced in the crystal structure mine.

But over the Pennines in Manchester Harry Moseley was not going to let the matter rest there. At first he tried to keep in radioactive territory by extending Laue's work. As he wrote to his mother in October, 'Some Germans have recently got wonderful results by passing X-rays through crystals and then photographing them, and I want to see if the same results are to be found with gamma rays.' But that failed to deliver. So he decided to move over to X-rays and asked Charles Darwin to join him in an investigation of X-ray diffraction. Hastily he reassured his mother that 'there is no danger of ill effects'. By now the perils of X-ray research were widely known and the precaution of keeping the tube in a lead case generally adopted. Perhaps he already hoped this would provide the key to unlock the inner regions of the atom. Darwin was called in again to provide the mathematical skill to develop the observations of experimentalists and calculate where their assumptions would lead them. Rutherford had his misgivings because there was still plenty of radioactivity work for everybody, and he doubted whether Manchester could compete in this unfamiliar X-ray field. Indeed Darwin and Moseley had some difficulties and in the event despite all Moseley's devotion to duty into the small hours of the night using three types of crystal, salt, selenite, and potassium ferrocyanide—'a magnificent specimen'—their research did trail behind the Braggs'. William helped them with advice, pointed out where they had gone wrong, informed them of his discoveries in good time; even when they came across interesting facts independently, these did little but confirm what the Braggs had already found out. Their main theme was the distinction between the heterogeneous radiation and the monochromatic variety characteristic of each element, and the association of the latter with angles of special intensive radiation. The basic phenomenon had first been observed by the Braggs, and the Manchester team could only measure the actual wavelengths and calculate the energy involved when their research finally appeared in July 1913 in the *Philosophical Magazine* along with part of Bohr's famous trilogy.

Darwin then left this line of research, but as the Braggs turned their attention to the crystals, Moseley moved back from X-rays to the metals that emitted them. Surely their character would be revealed by the X-ray spectrum in diffraction. As has been mentioned, early in the summer Bohr called in at Manchester. There was a discussion on the significance of these new opportunities. We shall soon see, Moseley remarked, which magnitudes prove significant. Presumably he did not attend the Birmingham British Association meeting, or if he did his interventions are not recorded, but during the autumn he began the new programme with his usual assiduity. Darwin recalled that each time he looked in there was some slight change in the experimental apparatus, for Moseley's perfectionism would not let him rest until everything was just so, even if that meant altering the whole set-up for a minor improvement. In the best Manchester tradition, he ingeniously modified an experiment set up by one of Thomson's Cavendish company, G.W. Kaye, to examine the penetrating power of the X-rays excited from various elements. Kaye had the notion of putting his samples in a row on a truck in a miniature railway line inside an exhausted tube. Each in turn could then be exposed to the stream of cathode rays beamed down upon it. In Kaye's version the truck which carried the targets was advanced 'into the line of fire' by 'a magnetic device'. Moseley replaced it by an even simpler method, in the best Rutherford style: he just drew it to and fro as required 'by means of silk fishing line wound on brass bobbins', rotated by cocks above them. Originally, in fact he hung little iron counterweights at the end of the line, which floated in mercury; so the whole thing was most delicately in balance, free of the jerkiness that might be imposed by inter-screwing metal parts. As he poured mercury in, or drained some away, the weights rose and fell and the little trolley advanced.

To get the best effects, the cathode rays were concentrated on a small area of each target substance, and the X-rays thus teased out passed through a narrow slit in a platinum window, on to the face of a crystal of potassium ferrocyanide—evidently he had kept his 'magnificent specimen' from the previous enterprise—and so reflected. At first he tried turning the rays into an ionization chamber as before, but that proved unsatisfactory, and so he went right back to the original idea of a photographic plate. The effect should show up as an arc curving away from the direction of the direct beam, but the narrowness of the slit in the screen ensured that it would appear as a very slightly curved line. The position of the line gives the angle of reflection, and from this it was possible to work out the wavelength by means of an equation given by the Braggs.

By mid-November he was beginning to get results. Enthusiastically he wrote to Bohr how everything was turning out as they had expected, with two main lines given by the more penetrating radiation. One of these lines was five times as intense as the other, and there was a nearly constant relation between the frequencies of the two. And it had proved possible to find these frequencies by means of equations which linked them to our old friend the Rydberg number—and to a new number, the 'atomic number', which had been gradually moving into the limelight in the discussions of the previous months—the serial number of the element in question in the periodic table. Thus the frequency of the stronger line divided by the Rydberg number was equal to $\frac{3}{4}$ this atomic number N, minus 1. There were difficulties; assuming that X-rays were produced by the innermost ring of electrons, as most were now agreed, his calculations led him to the conclusion that there would be four in that ring, which must jump as a whole from one of Bohr's stationary states to another; or if that was unacceptable, then 'is it possible that really no inner ring exists, and that it is one electron vibrating by itself?' Yet that would involve even more radical changes in the whole theory. Bohr was nonplussed. 'For the present', he wrote back, 'I have stopped speculating about atoms.' If Moseley's discoveries did not fit the Bohr atom as it stood, let experimentation continue. Certainly Moseley's findings were encouragement enough. The next month Moseley's paper was duly published as 'The high frequency spectra of the elements', also in the *Philosophical Magazine*.

Moseley worked successfully with a sequence of nine elements from titanium to zinc—or rather brass, since pure zinc would have volatilized in the heat generated by his cathode rays—besides calcium and a couple of heavier elements. The nine include some of the most common and important metals, such as iron. Among them was an anomaly he hoped to resolve. According to its chemistry, cobalt ought to appear in the table between iron and nickel. Unfortunately its atomic weight is actually somewhat *greater* than nickel's (58.97 as against 58.68, in the figures used by Moseley) and therefore in the sequence of weights it came after it.

How beautifully all turned out may be seen from the photograph he published to illustrate his article; the two lines, one stronger, one fainter, can clearly be seen. Brass of course has copper lines as well as zinc lines, and the other extra lines could safely be put down to impurities, since he had had a hard enough job obtaining samples as pure as these, and he knew there was iron in his titanium and vanadium. That apart, the lovely regularity of the flight of steps from one element to another, the even-paced distances between the strong and the weak, and between one element and the next is plain to see. Happily cobalt behaved as he undoubtedly hoped, for it fitted in below iron according to its chemical features rather than its weight. Working out the wavelengths in detail he suggested that the difference in frequency between the strong lines could be expressed by a factor he called Q, which increased by a nearly constant amount, almost exactly unity (the gap between cobalt and nickel proved largest, 1.04). Therefore 'there is in the atom a fundamental quantity which increases by regular steps as we pass from one element to the next'. And that quantity he urged can only be the charge on Rutherford's central positive nucleus. All the evidence showed that this charge really *was* the atomic number, going up 'from atom to atom always by a single electronic unit'.

Thus his confirmation of the Rutherford atom was proclaimed. When he tried to go further and insist he was also buttressing Bohr's version, he was less popular. He would have liked to relate his factor Q to Bohr's interpretation of the ordinary hydrogen spectrum, and claimed that if the whole ring jumped from one state to the next, his findings confirmed the principle of constant angular momentum. He could point to a resemblance in the numbers, but his explanation depended on the whole ring jump and the four electrons in the inner ring, which was harder to swallow. So if Moseley's results secured the idea of atomic number, his link with Bohr was soon under attack. Before the year was out, Lindemann (the future Lord Cherwell) wrote a letter to *Nature* to claim that he could reconcile the correlation between wavelength and number of units of charge in several ways; 'if you wish to introduce the quanta' (rather disdainful)—that could be one of the factors— but it could just as well be done by substituting as a factor the distance between the nucleus and electrons, so that no model was imposed by the

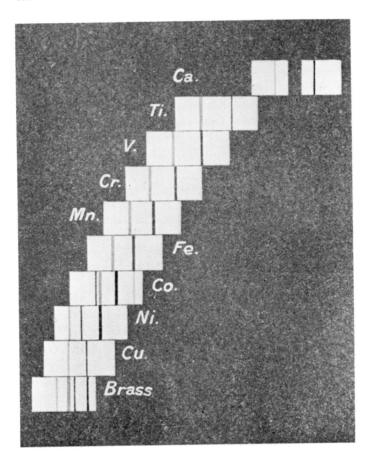

Fig. 18. X-ray spectra of the elements—illustration to Moseley's article.

succession, neither Bohr's nor any other. Bohr himself made haste to reply, complaining at the way Lindemann proposed to juggle about with factors that were not really independent of one another. Moseley wrote off too. As he explained when writing to Rutherford to ask for comments on an enclosed copy, too many people seemed to imagine that Bohr's theory just meant playing around with numbers, introducing factors as required to make the whole thing work out. 'I myself feel convinced that what I have called the "*h*" hypothesis is true.' By this he meant there are but three essential units defining the structure of atoms; the mass and charge of electrons, Planck's *h*, and nothing else. Bohr's model was the best, not just because it included '*h*' but because it needed no more than these three. Perhaps it would have been better if he had been clearer on this point in his letter to *Nature*, which stressed the value of the '*h*' hypothesis over Lindemann's use of distance *r*, on the grounds that 'no independent natural unit of length ... is known'. But the '*h*' hypothesis here means only that *h* is an essential factor which can not be left out, whereas he really believed in the more exclusive version. Not that Lindemann was prepared to accept the privilege of *h*, and throw out *r* quite as readily as all that ... and besides, some new pictures did not give lines where Moseley said there should be ... Privately, Moseley was very annoyed and wrote to Rutherford to complain that Lindemann's reply was dishonest and preposterous, but he added that as he had heard Lindemann was a pugnacious type, he would keep quiet and avoid controversy. Nor did he reply to another letter to *Nature* from Nicholson, who claimed he wanted to keep the main features of Bohr's model, but insisted that if electrostatic attraction and repulsion between the electrons was preserved, as Bohr seems to require, then there could only be *one* ring in any given place. If there was more than one ring they could be in different planes, of course, but with the same radius (rather like gimbal suspension, let us say). The assumption of coplanar rings had been made originally for mathematical convenience as much as anything, and perhaps also because the solar system or Saturn's rings had first provided an example. But our system of planets may well lie nearly in one plane for historical reasons, which would hardly apply to the atomic microcosm. However, as Nicholson pointed out, if all the rings are equidistant from their centre, there *is* no inner ring. How then could X-rays be emitted from inner rings? He proposed to give up the association between the number of units of charge and the serial number, that is, to throw out the atomic number altogether.

If Moseley replied to none of this criticism, perhaps it was less because he did not want to get into an argument than that he had better things to do. After some delay he resumed his experiments in January, and they now absorbed him completely. As soon as his first paper was safely on its way to the *Philosophical Magazine*, he left Manchester. In point of fact, his fellowship had already expired and his successor had arrived to take up his post in September, so the X-ray experiments had been done when he did not have any official position in Rutherford's laboratory at all. He did obtain a grant from Solvay to continue his work, but decided to go back to his family in Oxford. After the long hours of night work he understandably felt he needed a holiday. He was allowed to use a corner of the lab by the professor of physics there, but his letters are full of complaints about the slowness of Oxford technicians, and worse still the sluggishness of X-ray tube manufacturers, as the tube he brought with him soon broke. Like Rutherford and Bohr before him, he was very anxious that someone would make the great discovery ahead of him if he did not publish soon. And if he *was* first, it would be hard to keep in front for 'a horde of hungry Germans will be down on it directly'. When at last he resumed operations, he decided to deal with the confusion among rare earth elements, very much heavier than the metals on

Fig. 19. Harry Moseley in his Oxford laboratory.

which he had been working previously. As he had hinted in his previous paper, the new technique was a wonderful way of identifying impurities and sorting out elements, since unlike ordinary spectroscopy one element would not mask another through the multiplicity of lines.

His method could well lead to the discovery of more missing elements—every chemist's dream, not that chemists are too pleased when brash young physicists do it for them, especially when they insist how simple it all is. If nobody was quite sure whether all the rare earths were really and truly elementary, or whether there might not be a few more lurking in the shade of their neighbours, what a chance for the X-ray diffraction method to demonstrate its worth by 'weeding out the superfluous'—put each one into the right pigeon-hole and thereby indicate where there were still places for new elements. The harder 'K' radiation he could not manage past silver, so for the heavier rare earths he had to use the less penetrating 'L' radiation. In fact it would not penetrate his aluminium window, or more than an inch or so of

Fig. 20. Moseley's X-ray deflection aparatus.

air, so the spectrometer like the tube had to be evacuated, nor could it penetrate the wrapper of his plate, so that he had to work with an unprotected plate, in the dark; and exposure time had to be much longer, up to half an hour. Only the same chunk of potassium ferrocyanide still accompanied him in the new exploration. It was none too easy either to obtain samples of oxides of the earths and he had quite a time of it, but by March he had won through to increasing success. The results were made known to the atomic structure meeting at the Royal Society, and published (as Part II of *The high frequency spectra of the elements*) in April 1914. Much of this paper is taken up with a long description of his apparatus, and his samples, their purity, and the complications produced by the 'white' heterogeneous rays. For all that, he now had a complete series of strong lines right the way through the rare earths, and beyond as far as gold. He could establish which rare earths were truly elementary and which not, and revealed just three gaps between gold and aluminium. Actually there were four, and Moseley was obliged to send out emendations almost as soon as his paper was printed. Such minor discrepancies could hardly be avoided at that stage of the game, when everything was otherwise going so well they hardly mattered. Always the wavelengths basically fitted his predictions. Bohr's name and Bohr's model have quite disappeared. At least, neither is mentioned throughout. If he was convinced as ever of the main features of the Bohr atom, he must have decided to keep quiet about it until there was some positive experimental support. Only, he did claim that the differences between 'K' and 'L' lines implied they must come from 'distinct vibrating systems', which sounds like a conveniently vague way of talking about electrons in their rings. Besides, there was reason to believe that 'the 'L' system is situated so much further from the nucleus' (and so much for Nicholson, he might have added). Instead he concentrated on showing how the new findings reinforced the old. Plotting the frequencies of all the 'K' lines strong and weak from aluminum to silver, and the 'L' lines from zirconium to gold—over thirty elements in the first case and nearly forty in the second—against their atomic numbers, he found a perfect fit throughout. 'Now if either the elements were not characterized by these integers' the atomic numbers—'or any mistake had been made in the order chosen or in the number of places left for unknown elements, these regularities would at once disappear.' It has already been mentioned that one mistake was made in the last clause, but still, the numbers really do characterize the elements, one and only one number for each element, 'without using any theory of atomic structure'. Thus he quietly acknowledged that he could not prove Bohr right, only Van den Broek—but that point at least was now secure. Every element has its number, in fact 'the number of units of positive electricity contained in the atomic nucleus'. The number of electrons must be the same in a neutral atom; and each element's number could be found from its place in the order of chemical properties—that is, the ranking order of atomic weights, in all but the three inverted pairs.

13

EQUAL NUMBERS—BUT UNEQUAL WEIGHTS?

On 11 December 1913 the correspondence column of *Nature* published an indignant letter from Frederick Soddy. In a letter which had appeared the previous week, Rutherford acclaimed Moseley's work, then just out, as 'the strongest and most convincing evidence' for Bohr's ideas on the constitution of atoms, and Van den Broek's hypothesis. All very well, protested Soddy, but 'the strongest and most convincing evidence' has already appeared—he had produced it himself several months before. What was this work which Soddy claimed had clinched the question of 'atomic number' before ever Moseley's research was begun?

The concept of atomic number leaves the older view that elements are to be identified by their weights more difficult than ever, and Soddy like Rutherford and others was anxious to treat it as a secondary effect. One nagging worry about the elements was their failure to proceed in round numbers. Take what unit standard you will, virtually every element has an atomic weight which requires decimal points, and the more accurately the atomic weight is determined by more sophisticated measurements, the worse it gets. First, Prout unsuccessfully tried to render them all down to hydrogen. As evolution became the secret password that opened so many doors in science, why should it not open this one too? If there was not one prime matter, at least there might be a few basic species, seven or eight perhaps from which the others had diverged over time, just as animal species branch out from a common stock and eventually become independent types. This grand cosmic vision of atomic evolution Crookes had pictured in romantic eloquence in 1886. Rutherford and his friends were speculating along these lines when they were students. Even in 1913 an ingenious theory that leaned heavily on the analogy from natural history was propounded in the *Philosophical Magazine* along with Moseley's first study. Were atomic weights multiples of supposed ancestors, perhaps in a descent down the lines of the Periodic Table? Or were the atomic weights not so definite as people supposed? Perhaps each weight was simply the average of a cluster of weights, each of them a whole number. This idea was begotten of early spectral research, since some elements at least proved to have more than one series of lines. Crookes had then put forward the idea that each series identified a separate form of the element, chemically indistinguishable. As nobody could find any way of telling the different forms apart, and the same sets of series always appeared, his speculation miscarried. Its rebirth in 1912–13 gave physics a new word, the isotope, for bodies that occupy the same place (ancient Greek *isos*, same, equal; *topos*, place) in the Table have the same atomic number, but differ in atomic weight. So each isotope can have as its atomic weight a whole number, every sample of the element has these isotopes in the same proportions, so the atomic weight is always the same average figure. Such a concept could only be accepted if in some special circumstances the different isotopes sort themselves out naturally, and enjoy a separate existence, if only for a little while. Two lines of research revealed this. The more important was the hunt for radio-elements and their relationship.

Since Rutherford and Soddy had laid down the principles of radioactivity while still in Canada, the genealogy of the various radioactive products had grown very complicated. They were linked in an intricate minuet of half-lives, in which some stages might be so short as scarcely to be noticed at all, while long ones marked some kind of sequence. Radium's half-life, although much longer than some, was yet short enough to imply it must be produced continually out of some earlier form. But what form? Was uranium the mother of radium as Rutherford at first imagined? If not, then what? As the uranium and thorium sequences began to be worked out, the place of the actinium sequence became the more troublesome. Could uranium be the progenitor of actinium too? New elements came and went. A radiotellurium appeared uncomfortably high in the Periodic Table. Fortunately it soon disappeared from the list, when it turned out to be polonium. For a while the Curies had actually had to yield the existence of their child polonium—it must have been a wrench for them, christened as it was after Marie's native land. Happily, it quickly re-emerged. Every one of the three main lines had its emanation; each had its own uranium X, thorium X, actinium X. Then, in 1904 a 'radio-thorium' was identified; next a new thorium between it and the basic thorium, so it was called mesothorium (Greek for 'in between'). Nor can we forget 'nipponium'; the discovery of a Japanese research student at London. When so much depended on emanations and ionization it is not surprising that there should have been an 'emanium' and an 'ionium' too. Was this indeed the missing parent of radium? If a connection was to be found between uranium and radium, there must be at least one missing link. Was *that* actinium? or was it only a 'foster-parent', as Rutherford suggested? Ionium in fact is the immediate predecessor of radium, isolated from actinium by Boltwood in 1907. After Xs came As, Bs, Ds, and with radium it went as far as G. The lines of connection were beginning to look like the map of an underground railway system, although if some of the stops were very prolonged, some were extremely short. Not surprisingly it was not easy to tell how short, and there was often argument as to the exact number of minutes and seconds. If all were independent elements, the Periodic Table would look very overcrowded, particularly at the heavier end where it might be least expected, at least if you had a sneaking suspicion that the heavier elements evolved out of the lighter.

Worse still, several seemed to fit best into one tray on the Table, as when Boltwood in 1907 commented on 'the similarity in chemical behaviour' between thorium and radiothorium; and also between mesothorium and thorium X. Both pairs stuck together with a strange persistence. When in the summer of 1909 Marckwald tried to confirm the presence of Boltwood's ionium, at the Institute of Physical Chemistry at Berlin, they found that although no doubt it existed, it was remarkably similar to thorium and could not be separated from it. Whatever technique his team used to extract the one from various uranium sources invariably extracted the other. It was impossible to enrich the proportion of ionium in the sample, the ratio between them always remained the same—precipitation, crystallization, sublimation—nothing would do the trick.

The autumn of the following year, 1910, Professor Marckwald received a 'radium preparation' for analysis. He found that most of it was really 'mesothorium': since the half-life of mesothorium is only a few years, while that of radium is counted in millennia, he was worried lest some laboratory should be sent some of the wrong stuff in error, or even be tricked intentionally, and so he made haste to publish his discovery. Soddy too found the only methods that worked to separate mesothorium from its ore thorianite, as developed by Boltwood, took the radium as well, so one went with the other; 'they behave as a single substance and there is no hope of separating them'. He could show the same similiarity with thorium X. The resemblance between ionium and thorium had already been noticed, and uranium X was supposedly associated with them, and with radiothorium too; though of the former, Soddy was dubious, for it would spoil the other 'triplet'. Those who investigated radiolead found it chemically inseparable from ordinary lead, differing only in its higher atomic weight, and in its radioactivity. Presumably all lead contained some of the radioactive kind, until all had emitted away. For that reason, in his own experiments Soddy insisted that the lead to cover his electroscope be 'taken from the roof of a very old building', so that any radiolead formerly present would have had time to decay since it was extracted from its mother ore, and would not leak its own radiations into his observations.

There were then three sub-groups at least of bodies chemically identical yet radioactively diverse, and what was worse the others too probably had diverse atomic weights, so far as these could be determined. Of course, some of these atomic weights had to be based on the assumption that loss of an alpha particle means loss of a helium atom, rather than from direct measurement. The complications of rare earth sorting provided a neat analogy—it was proving hard enough to tidy them up too. Ought a chemist to indulge in such speculations? Soddy quieted these doubts by a counter-attack. Maybe the radio-elements were not alone; perhaps 'some of the common elements may ... in reality be mixtures of chemically non-separable elements in constant proportion differing step-wise by *whole units* in atomic weight. This would certainly account for the lack of regular relationships between (their) numerical values' [my italics]. Through 1911 he continued to hammer away at the problem, seeking for connections between the three main radio-lines uranium, thorium, actinium—so to speak interchange stations—or rather stations with platforms on each of the lines, for there would be no crossing between the lines. In a book on *The chemistry of the radio-elements* he pointed out the parallels between the As, Bs and Cs of each line, which had comparable lives and produced comparable radiations. The short-lived emanations too were similar. All were inert and behaved rather like inert gases. Each of his three groups was two places in the Table from its next neighbour, as if decay from one to the other meant a jump of two. Ionium, thorium, radiothorium had a valency of four; radium, thorium X, actinium X, perhaps mesothorium would seem to be like alkaline earths, with a valency of two; then you moved to the emanations with nought; and so to polonium in the next row up, valency of six; and the lead pair with four again. As for the very active As and Bs, he imagined they might be a class of substance by themselves, bridging the two ends of the table. The jump of two made good sense, if a helium atom was lost each time, having approximately mass 4, and the difference between elements roughly mass 2. So the old idea of an evolution of elements was justified at last. If you look at a photograph of a waterfall, Soddy explains, even though it looks perfectly motionless, yet you can infer that it is moving from the position of the drops, and the several sections of the sheet of water. People had long suspected from the different positions of elements along the Table that they too had been travelling along from one place to the next. Now 'Radioactivity has cinematographed these transformations', and we can trace the passage as it takes place.

Before he could go any further, it would be necessary to look into the chemical properties of all the other radioactive substances, one by one, even those of short life, so long as they lasted long enough to be examined. He gave the task to his Demonstrator at Glasgow, Alexander Fleck, who rose to be President of ICI—which just goes to show that a prolonged piece of basic scientific research is no bad training for a captain of industry. Through the remainder of 1911, 1912, 1913, Fleck toiled away at it. If Soddy's rule of movement worked, it should be possible to guess which ought to be chemically inseparable from which. The procedure was to mix two radio-elements from different sources, two of which might be expected to be tied together, and try to take them apart. If the original proportions of the two were ever altered, some of one must have been removed. But if the proportions always remained the same—then take away one, take away the other. Reporting on Fleck's labours to the Chemistry section of the British Association in September 1913, Soddy assured his audience that 'this work was purely experimental, and was done deliberately without any attempt to find the theoretical law, in order that the results might be free from all bias ... It would have been easier to speculate first and then test the speculations'. But, he claims, we did the opposite. And yet Fleck can hardly have been unaware of the 'speculations' Soddy had published already in 1911, so he must have undertaken the experiments in the expectation of results that would confirm the hypothesis which Soddy had presented. As Fleck acknowledged, his first task was always to work out what element each particular short-lived radio-product most resembled, and then try and separate out of them the two in his mixtures. Anyway, the outcome was all they could have wished. The short-lived products, like the long-lived, fell into groups so closely associated with elements already known as to be indistinguishable as well as inseparable from them. By the summer of 1912 they could show that uranium X and radioactinium were thus tied, like ionium, to thorium. Later they could add radium B and actinium B to the lead group; and attach radium A to polonium, the three Cs as well as radium E to bismuth, and so on.

Meantime, quite early in 1912, Alexander Russell, a former student of Soddy's from Glasgow but now in Rutherford's camp at Manchester, had pointed out to him that if you subtracted the equivalent of five alpha particles from the atomic weight of radium, as then established, you got 206, while the atomic weight of lead was 207.1. If you supposed that all the products of radioactive decay ended up as lead, which by now appeared more than probable, there would be a group of atomic weights all of them close to, but none of them exactly 207.1. Soddy concluded that what we know as lead is simply a mixture of these inseparable terminal stations of the various radio-elements. Russell now went back to the ionium–thorium problem, for he had decided to tackle it from the spectroscopic angle. He and a colleague, Rossi, tried to find a difference between the spectrum of what was taken to be pure thorium, and a preparation that included some ionium; but could find no difference at all. Now Bohr too was at Manchester that summer, and there is no doubt that he discussed these results, particularly with Hevesy. By the autumn Russell had a displacement law for beta ray transformations, on which he lectured, and wrote to Soddy, but it was not published until the end of January 1913. According to him if alpha ray emission meant a move two places, beta rays meant a move one place. This he thought could take place in either direction—to the right or left, so to speak, along the rows of the Periodic Table. At the same time a rival law was put forward by Hevesy. To him the beta moves were two places, not one, and always to the right, while he agreed with Soddy that alpha ray moves had to go to the left. This time neither of the Manchester proposals was quite right: the answer came from Karlsruhe—from Kasimir Fajans, a man who had indeed already spent a year at Manchester, which perhaps instilled in him the right way of thinking. The problem was, as he observed, that the loss of a beta particle made no significant difference to the atomic weight as parent and offspring apparently weighed the same, so it was only from their chemical differences that one could tell what change in character had taken place. He showed that they always became 'electrochemically nobler', that is, more negative. This law he sent off to the *Physikalische Zeitschrift* on the last day of 1912. However it did not appear until 15 February. During the first weeks of January Soddy on the basis of Russell's and Fleck's and Hevesy's work was coming to the same conclusions and working up a paper on 'The radio-elements and the periodic law', in which the same group displacement law is expressed. It is dated 18 February, and was published on the 28th. Allowing for the vagaries of journals, whose official publication day is often different from the day they actually appear, but recalling that in those days before airmail, the *Physikalische Zeitschrift* must have taken several days to reach Soddy in Glasgow, it is clear that he can not have had time for more than a hasty glance before sending off his own piece, already complete in all essentials. At most he could have satisfied himself that Fajans's theory confirmed his own, and did not upset any of his conclusions.

Not only were Soddy, Russell, and Fajans and Hevesy all thinking along parallel lines at the same time. During these same weeks Bohr's ideas and Bragg's work were coming to a climax; and Thomson too was just arriving at another revolutionary step forward. Bearing in mind that Thomson's electron and Rutherford's nuclear hypothesis were also born in the early months of the year; that Becquerel found his rays at the beginning of February, after Röntgen had found his in November; I cannot help wondering if it is more common for great discoveries to be made in the depth of winter. It would not be easy to find out, as such novel ideas might take several weeks before they finally crystallize. Would winter fertility apply to science as a whole, or just physics? Or to other fields? If it were true for scientific ideas in recent times, it might arise from the rhythm of the academic year: the long summer vacation is preceded by examinations, and followed by a period of reorientation in autumn, when we look back over the year and consider what should come next. No doubt this seasonal flow is reinforced by the habit of holding scientific conferences in summer or early autumn, as they provide a stomach to digest the previous year's work. In high summer even the most devoted of scientists is as keen as anybody to take off for country walks, sport, and excursions. As winter draws on, new ideas take shape, are tested, selected, evolve. There is less chance of diversion. The sun does not pull the scholar from his study, nor the good advice of those who reprimand him for his withdrawal from the world. So it becomes pleasanter to work into the night. Similarly with bad weather it is easier to lock oneself in a laboratory when it is pouring with rain outside. Yet I fancy this may be much more common, and by no means confined to science. It is a reflection of a human intellectual rhythm: in late winter the mind, less distracted, turns in upon itself and mulls over the products of past months' work. January and February are good months for contemplation. Does mankind's proudest activity, our rational thought about nature, have its photoperiods too, when great changes quietly pupate at the dead season, develop, and then at first light of approaching spring emerge from their chrysalis?

But to the business in hand. In his paper Soddy marshalled all the evidence from each series, and mapped out their transformations. Each member of these inseparable sets differed from the others in weight, which therefore could not be the decisive character. The uniform elements of chemistry by long standing definition are bodies which resist further dissolution—but apparently only by the methods of chemistry, since radioactivity breaks them down all the time, at least with the heaviest elements. Now they prove to be groups of similar but not identical bodies. Four days later he added an afterthought about ionium, whose spectrum Russell and Rossi had shown to be identical to that of thorium ... that indeed people might find more surprising. Yet, he remarked, in the 'modern view', the spectrum arises from the outer electrons which determine valency and other chemical characteristics; they are not the 'constitutional electrons'. And these 'constitutional electrons' are merely a name for the material atom itself, 'considered apart from its electronic satellites'. Does this mean that he had adopted Rutherford's atom, so that the 'material atom itself' is Rutherford's nucleus? His words are ambiguous, perhaps they were intentionally so.

When in September he spoke on this topic to the Chemistry section of the British Association, his theme aroused great interest, even if he had to limit his time so as to allow for 'the counter-attractions of Sir J.J. Thomson's new gas'—of which more later—indeed it seems to have been almost as popular as the radiation and quantum debate. But time was short and he 'was properly very brief'. There was little to add to the picture he had given seven months before; the position of some of the descendents of actinium was altered; he was now prepared to come out into the open and claim that his inseparables were '(probably) spectroscopically indistinguishable', besides their chemical identity. Otherwise he could reiterate that chemical elements are not ultimate, atomic weights are but averages. On 4 December, a letter from Soddy appeared in *Nature*, in which he declared that his finding supported Van den Broek's theory, albeit not in the original form. He now definitely accepted Rutherford's nucleus, although for him it was not just a concentration of positive charge but also had a small negative charge, the source of the beta particles, so the atomic number would have to be the difference between them. Fajans had felt that if the changes in chemical character produced by these moves along the rows of the Table, and indeed all chemistry follow from the arrangement of the outer electrons, so must radioactivity, rather than from the nucleus. Soddy insisted that Fleck's research proved the opposite; these beta rays really did come from the nucleus. 'There is no in- and out-going of electrons between ring and nucleus ...' Only a name now was wanting for his new elements. As they occupy the 'same place' in the Table, a friend of his wife's family proposed they be called 'isotopes'.

From the start Soddy was inclined to think that inactive elements of lower weight must surely be collections of isotopes too. In the very weeks when his ideas were taking shape a piece of evidence arrived that seemed to fit this supposition beautifully. It came from the grand old man J.J. Thomson himself. When Bohr first came to Cambridge he had been put to work on 'positive rays'—a subject for which he had little enthusiasm. Some while before Thomson had decided to take up this question as a complement to the cathode work, which he had done in days gone by. To the bright young physicist, these rays must have looked very old-fashioned. Way, way back in 1886, Thomson and Crookes's sparring partner Eugen Goldstein discovered these positive rays. The cathode in the vacuum tube will naturaly suck in any positive particles in its neighbourhood. If you drill a tiny channel in the cathode they will be swallowed up altogether, as they will have acquired sufficient velocity to pass right through and stream out the other side in a thin pencil beam. This pencil can be deflected by electric and magnetic fields just as Thomson had done with the cathode rays. In this case, the effect is to splay out the stream of particles into a cone, the slower particles being more widely deflected. There were many difficulties to be overcome, but Thomson had decided that he must investigate the smallest bearers of positive charge, no less than the bearers of the least units of negative charge, if anything was ever to be found out about the nature of the atom, whose mass is mainly associated with the positive. Perhaps these particles were equivalent to hydrogen atoms without their electrons, hydrogen nuclei in fact, although it took Thomson a long time to reconcile himself to such an interpretation. But the particles would have to be sorted out according to their different masses. A new vacuum technique evolved for research on the rare gases, using charcoal chilled by liquid air, supplemented the vacuums attainable by the old mechanical methods. Then there would be less matter in the space behind the channel for the positive rays to meet; the source of the gases became a large bulb instead of the modest tube previously used; and the channel in the cathode was replaced first by a hypodermic syringe, then by an even narrower pipe; and the fluorescent screen on which the beam scintillated as it struck was replaced once again by a photographic plate. Most of these improvements were introduced by Francis Aston, whom Thomson took on as an assistant in 1910. Aston was a Birmingham man by birth as well as by his university training; he was unique among the Cavendish men in having spent three years away from the atmosphere of pure research, as an industrial chemist in Wolverhampton. For the moment he was not officially on the Cambridge establishment, (although he too later became a fellow of Trinity) but was seconded by the Royal Institution in London, where Thomson had for some years been Professor of Physics. Like Moseley and Wilson, Aston was known for his meticulous and painstaking exactness in the construction of apparatus, something that Thomson's imaginative powers often needed to complement his fertility in hypothesizing. But this time it was Aston who adopted the novel hypothesis, and Thomson who tried to reconcile their findings with traditional assumptions.

The cone of positive particles manifests itself on the plate as a parabola, whose vertex is the spot where the undeflected rays would strike the plate; and the curvature of this parabola will depend on the charge to mass ratio, the e/m of the particles in question. The lightest particles will produce a curve tending toward the vertical line, the heavier, further down. Of course, the parabolas do not reveal only the atoms of individual elements for combinations of gases would make their own marks. Since it is not mass alone but e/m which is represented, extra charge which altered the ratios could give some baffling lines. Indeed some combinations of carbon and hydrogen were found, which being unstable had previously escaped notice. Nevertheless when all these were accounted for, it was possible to tell what elements were actually present. Thomson tried to use the apparatus to detect rare gases. And here he was struck by a curious observation. Just below the parabolic streak of neon, there was another, a little fainter but quite easy to make out. The atomic weight of neon is 20.2, and the main line streak corresponded to mass 20; but the other to mass 22. What was it? A new atom of a new element? A tempting thought. But that meant two elements right next door to one another where the Periodic Table only allowed for one. Still, the noble gases had been among the last elements to be identified, and there might well be pecularities about them yet to be discovered. Was there a clump of very similar ones, rather like some of the rare earths, or indeed the clump of metals, iron–cobalt–nickel? Then, it might be a combination of two elements: what about a hydride of neon, i.e. neon with two hydrogen atoms attached? Yet all the evidence goes to show that neon like the other inert gases will not combine with anything. J.J. Thomson thought this solution possible but unlikely; he was unsure, but fancied he had one parabola that implied a combination of helium and hydrogen. Or—the simplest explanation in a way—maybe it was just carbon dioxide with a double charge, since carbon dioxide would normally give a mass 44 streak. After all, carbon dioxide could have sneaked in, even from the grease used on the stop taps of his apparatus. But it was possible to raise the CO_2 content intentionally, produce thereby a strong 44 line, and then reduce it again to zero without the slightest effect on the 22 parabola.

All these possibilities Thomson discussed in a lecture to the Royal Institution. The only one he does not mention is that this 22 parabola might be neon indeed, but some neon with greater mass than the more common kind. And this was the suggestion now put forward by Aston. Perhaps neon was a mixture of neon 20 and neon 22? Then there could be proportionally more of the former, so that the atomic weight as found would be just a little above 20, while in reality the two forms would weigh whole numbers. First he tried to separate the two by distillation, but failed; then by diffusion through clay pipes. Inside the tube of neon he inserted a minuscule quartz balance of such delicacy that it was able to resolve even the very slight difference in density between the two neons. With that came a modest success. By the time of the British Association meeting in September he was able to announce 'A new elementary constituent of the atmosphere'. Besides neon 19.9, as he had measured it, there was also a neon 22.1. It will be seen that within the limits of his instruments, he had not arrived at whole numbers. There were no differences but weight between the two and the spectra were identical. Hevesy was excited by the idea, for to him this was proof that the same chemical properties can be shared by substances with different atomic weights. Indeed the effect, with such tiny quantities of the heavier neon involved, was not beyond the limits of error. If there was now a non-radioactive isotope, there was only one; and even that one uncertain. Lindemann in particular was suspicious. When they met during the war, he and Aston argued over this neon, for Lindemann was sure it could just as well be either CO_2 or the neon hydride NeH_2, as J.J. Thomson had thought. Lindemann had great ability at marshalling arguments against what turned out to be the right explanation.

In Thomson's own mind neon 22 was by now quite overshadowed by other discoveries he had made among the parabolas of the positive rays. Often he had been impressed by what appeared to be a 3 line—and something of atomic weight 3 would fill that uncomfortable gap between hydrogen and helium. At first it seemed to turn up in quite an arbitrary way, so he tried to match it to almost all the gases known to him or to chemistry, and only after a long and tedious search came to the conclusion that it was produced by heat from solids when bombarded by cathode rays. So, a few months before Moseley began to bombard metals to elicit their specific X-rays, Thomson did likewise, to make them cough up this mysterious gas, which apparently they were able to do quite inexhaustibly. He concentrated on metals; copper, zinc, iron (including that from a couple of meteorites) and lead. The lead which gave off the gas with the 3 line best was 'a piece from the roof of Trinity College Chapel, several hundred years old'. No doubt after thirty years as a Fellow, he thought himself entitled to chip a small piece off the college buildings when his experiments required it. At all events he observed that it produced more of the gas than a recent sample which in the course of purification must have 'been subject to severe ordeals by fire and water'. The new gas he labelled X3. Probably, he thought, it was a molecule of three atoms of hydrogen, as tightly bound as the three atoms of oxygen in ozone, and so H_3. Yet helium too seemed to be given off by the metals under attack. Could helium be a combination of the H_3 with single atoms of hydrogen; was it broken off from the metals, possibly by analogy with the alpha particles in radioactivity? In the British Association Physics section on the Tuesday three days after the radiation meeting at which Bohr's atom had been discussed, Thomson's paper created quite a stir, with the Chemistry section having to cut its own session short so that members could hear what Thomson had to say about 'X3' and the evolution of helium. Were chemists to endure 'a fresh invasion of their territory', as *Nature* remarked? Oliver Lodge was certainly convinced. To him the metal atoms were breaking down: 'it is the first case of artificial production of atomic disintegration'. Bohr was there too. He got up to suggest that perhaps X3 was not a molecule of three hydrogen atoms, but a single one, with just the single unit of charge, but a nucleus three times as heavy as ordinary hydrogen; in short what we now call tritium, a heavy isotope of hydrogen. He proposed that it would be worth trying to separate the X3, or H_3, from hydrogen by a diffusion process, through hot palladium, for the heavier X3 would pass much more slowly. Thomson understood him to mean they should try to part his H_3 molecule from ordinary free hydrogen, and that he claimed would not work since only individual atoms would diffuse. So he bluntly said the suggestion was useless. Clearly he had not grasped the idea of a hydrogen isotope at all, and poor Bohr was left looking foolish. Only Hevesy saw what he was driving at, and as he told Rutherford 'I felt bound to stick up for him'. In somewhat better English than Bohr's he explained that they could be dealing with 'a chemically non-separable element from hydrogen', although he had to admit it was not very likely. Even at that gathering, where new horizons were revealed every morning, this bold idea fell extremely flat.

A few months later, in the New Year's honours for 1914 Rutherford was awarded his knighthood. Amid the self-deprecation and teasing which traditionally accompany these marks of esteem, there was satisfaction that the world knew, appreciated and wished to honour the remarkable series of triumphs that had distinguished British physics over the past two years, culminating in the 1913 meeting of the British Association and the second Solvay conference, where British speakers had been so prominent. The 22 January 1914 issue of *Nature* includes yet another article on 'The structure of the atom', this time by Norman Campbell, who summarized the Thomson and the older planetary models, noted the inevitable difficulties, unless classical mechanics and electrostatics do not apply fully within the atom. Still, Planck and Einstein have anyway imposed limits on these laws; so he ends by recommending Bohr's atom as 'simple, plausible and easily amenable to mathematical treatment'. Certainly encouraging progress was not confined to Britain. Some experiments carried out early in the year in

Berlin, on mercury vapour bombarded with a stream of electrons, demonstrated that the atoms of the vapour would not give up energy until a definite level was reached. They then produced a single spectral line, whose frequency fitted Planck's law exactly, as if radiating in equal steps.

In March Rutherford went to London to speak at a Royal Society symposium on the structure of the atom. Announcing the news to Boltwood, he comments, 'I am speculating whether J.J.T. will turn up because he knows that I think his atom is only fitted for a museum of scientific curiosities'. He goes on to say how well the nuclear atom is working out, now fleshed out by Moseley's work, which was almost complete. Moseley himself came to the meeting. After hearing Thomson speak, he wrote, 'I was amused to hear of the amount of positive electricity in the atom, but say no word about the nuclear charge. I am glad that he is a convert, even if he still does try to disguise the fact'. Rutherford spent most of April in North America, lecturing at Washington, Yale, Princeton, Columbia, looking up old friends in Montreal—all was going swimmingly for the nuclear atom, for the evolution of radioactive elements and their existence in different isotopes, for atomic number, now Moseley and Bohr had come off best in their little clash with Nicholson and Lindemann; an era of tremendous advance was opening up before them.

On 27 June Rutherford led yet another Royal Society discussion on 'The constitution of the atom. The next day the Archduke Franz Ferdinand was assassinated at Sarajevo.

14

WAR AND DISINTEGRATION

If you glance through the pages of *Nature* in the 1930s, the shadow of the Second World War can be seen from afar. Quite soon after Hitler's accession to power, questions of racialism and academic freedom, reports of the distorted congresses of a phoney 'German Science', the urgent need to do something for refugee scientists appeared in every number; all made it clear that science could not ignore the world of public affairs. In the 1910s it was a very different story. Right up to the outbreak of war, there was no whisper of the approaching catastrophe. Scientists—but then, also musicians, artists, industrialists, men of letters—were sure that enmity between nations was obsolete. The international confraternity of science outweighed patriotic sentiment, and national styles in scientific argument were insignificant by comparison with the unity of the scientific enterprise. All sought the same heroic objective, the comprehension of nature, and all accepted the same evidence. Three of Rutherford's most able companions, Geiger, Fajans, and Hevesy were all citizens of the Central Powers. Geiger indeed had been in Manchester longer than Rutherford himself, and first worked under his predecessor Schuster, who was also born in Germany. British scientists were likewise employed in Germany and Austria-Hungary, among them James Chadwick, another of the Manchester school. We have almost forgotten how far British intellectual life, in particular scientific life, had been influenced by developments in Germany. No less was it so in relaxation. Indeed the war might have caught a sizeable proportion of Britain's scientists on walking tours through the more scenic parts of Germany or Austria, had they not been that summer on the high seas, on their way to the British Association meeting, which in those expansive imperial times was due to take place in Australia. Rutherford, Moseley, Darwin, and Nicholson were all to go, and this obliged them to leave in July. Moseley set off even earlier, in order to enjoy a holiday tour of Canada. Crossing the Pacific, he struck up a shipboard friendship with old Eugen Goldstein of the cathode and positive rays. Rutherford had been busy for some weeks before his departure with arrangements for a Radiology Congress that was to be held in Vienna in 1915. When he had occasion to write to the organizer, Stefan Meyer, the day after Franz Ferdinand's assassination, he expressed his regrets; 'the Hapsburghs have a very tragic family history'. But he wrote more out of courtesy to his Austrian colleague than because he was deeply affected, or expected any disastrous consequences.

The British Association meeting passed off quietly. In the Antipodes all concerned could take their minds off the war. Because of the war, however, no full report of the proceedings has survived. It is clear that at a discussion on the Structure of atoms and molecules the ideas of Bohr and Moseley were still thought doubtful, and Rutherford by no means absolutely convinced about Bohr's conclusions. Something at the heart of the atom baffled accepted mechanics, but Rutherford was not happy with any of the solutions so far offered. Even on isotopes he saw the difficulties the new concept would meet before it could win acceptance. In a public lecture in Australia, he commented 'there may be two pieces of lead which look exactly the same and yet their physical qualities may be quite different—that may not be believed now, but it will be later . . .'

He went on from Australia to New Zealand for more lectures and a long visit to his family. When he returned to Manchester in January 1915, he found the old world dead. In contrast to the outbreak of the Second World War, no attempt was made at the outset of the First to mobilize scientific talent in order to devise bigger and better weapons. As the same wave of patriotic enthusiasm swept the laboratories as elsewhere, by the autumn they seemed deserted. A scientific education directed men to the Royal Engineers, to Signals, or the Artillery, otherwise no distinction was made. Nobody thought that such rare skills should be husbanded. As a result, in the early years as many brilliant physicists were killed in action as brilliant poets. Moseley, a Signals Officer, fell to a Turkish bullet in the head at Gallipoli in 1915. Bohr's Birmingham friend Samuel Maclaren, now a major in the Royal Artillery, died of wounds when an ammunition lorry exploded at Abbeville in August of the following year. Hevesy was fighting on the other side, in the Austro-Hungarian army, while Geiger was an artillery officer for the Kaiser. Rutherford actually received a letter from him in March 1915, soon after his return home: four old friends (among them Reinganum, with whom Bohr had corresponded over his thesis) were already among the slain.

The war soon exposed all the weakness and flabbiness in the British political and economic system. It also exposed past unreadiness to keep technology abreast of scientific advance. Yet only in the summer of 1915 was it finally agreed to organize scientists to further the war effort, through a Board of Invention and Research under the aegis of the Admiralty, with Sir J.J. Thomson a leading member. The Board had to cope with a flood of inventions and tried to sift through them for the odd one that might prove a genuine brainwave—among their mail were plans to train cormorants to peck out the mortar from the chimneys of German factories, or to catch zeppelins with birdlime liberally smeared over the cables of barrage balloons. Various sub-committees were set up for more practical objectives. Rutherford and the elder Bragg served on one to examine the detection of submarines by sound; the younger Bragg was taken away from his battery of horse artillery, and like Darwin, worked on the kindled problem of sound-ranging for enemy guns. The Royal Aircraft establishment at Farnborough provided scope for several of the younger physicists to develop a completely new military arm. The Cavendish Laboratory was turned over to the development of a new type of radio receiver for use in field conditions. On the whole, the techniques which came out of all this work did not quite justify the brainpower invested in them, for something of the old amateurish atmosphere hung over them. In any case although useful they could hardly prove decisive. As the war dragged on, the scientists' war began to look more organized, more like the next time, with interallied committees for the sharing of information. Rutherford spent much of 1917 collaborating with French and American workers on the anti-submarine campaign. Perrin was among those involved in acoustic research on the French side.

One or two recent papers have outlined the history of this 'professionalization' of scientific war-work, and the interallied flavour it acquired. They have described the erosion of the international ideals so rudely shattered by the unexpected outbreak of war, for some slowly, for others more rapidly, until the scientists found themselves 'drifting into two hostile camps.[1] Some collaboration was maintained through Switzerland or other neutrals, sometimes through Bohr, who had been appointed to fill Darwin's place at Manchester in summer 1914, since he was able to keep up contact with German and Austrian scholars through his brother. Stefan Meyer got a letter through to Rutherford in 1915, when they should have been together on the Radiology Congress, to assure him that 'our feelings towards you and all our friends remain unchanged'. An English physicist at Vienna was still able to carry on his research, and his report had been accepted for publication by the Austrian Academy of Sciences.

But there were also nationalist reactions to the conflict. Boltwood, who had brought away from his many visits to Germany a warm sympathy for German culture and manners, assumed that Rutherford and his other English friends would be above the battle and would respect his own emotional neutrality. He was quite hurt to find a certain jolly but uncompromising patriotic pugnacity in Rutherford's comments on the war. Relations between them grew strained, and their correspondence broke off altogether in 1916. Certainly Rutherford's last letter to Boltwood suggests very much the civilian enthusiast—he had become quite out of temper with Boltwood, and must have found his 'plague on both your houses' stance very annoying. Some people, of course, took up a militant attitude from the very start. Philipp Lenard greeted the war with a pamphlet on *England und Deutschland zur Zeit des grossen Krieges*, published 'in mitte August 1914', in which he denounced the arrogance and greed of the English—and not only in commercial matters, for men like Thomson stole German scientific ideas with the same shameless effrontery as they used when robbing Germans of markets for their commerce.

In October 1914 a group of German scholars published a declaration of support for their nation, in which they struck out at the propaganda of their foes: this only had the effect of arousing greater hostility.

Civil science did not cease entirely. After the war Rutherford congratulated the Viennese school, the most severely hit by the disruption that followed the peace, on the way they had managed to keep some kind of research going right through the war. Rutherford himself published a couple of papers on X-rays, and Bohr continued to be active first at Manchester, and from 1916 back home in Copenhagen. Indeed military science occasionally inspired new ideas. In a paper which Aston and Lindemann, now converted to isotopes, produced while still at Farnborough early in 1919, they discussed possible ways of separating such isotopes. They were optimistic about separation by density, perhaps by taking samples from the stratosphere, where one would expect less of the heavier isotope, and so lower atomic weight for any particular sample, for example of neon. Why not design a balloon, which would rise to 100 000 feet and then automatically fill with air? Or fire a long range gun vertically up?—you could get samples that way from as high as 200 000 feet. The most important contributions made during the war were those of Walther Kossel and Sommerfeld at Munich. Kossel, originally a student of Lenard at Heidelberg, came to the more stimulating atmosphere of Munich in 1911. Late in 1914 he proposed a treatment of X-ray spectra which seemed to explain Moseley's data and various other observations made mainly in neutral Scandinavia, in terms of the loss of an electron from an inner ring, which then had to be replaced by one from the next outward. In 1915 Sommerfeld, using additional quantum numbers exchanged Bohr's circular orbits for ellipses. Soon this became the 'union of ellipses', as each electron in a ring had its own ellipse, but so constructed that at every moment all would be placed at the angles of a regular polygon (of as many sides as there were electrons). This polygon must then vary in size as the electrons approach and recede from the nucleus. Hence the ring itself pulsates! Truly, such a notion would have rejoiced the heart of Kepler. 'That great harmony of nature', declared Sommerfeld, 'that must prevail within the atom' embodied geometrical harmonies not unlike those Kepler first found in the solar system.

As for Rutherford, apart from X-ray work and a little on gamma rays, it was not until autumn 1917 that he could, as he explained to Bohr, 'find an odd half day to try a few of my own experiments . . .', counting and detecting the lighter atoms set in motion by alpha particles. As he observed, the results could help us understand the forces near the atomic nucleus, and indeed, 'I am trying to break up the atom by this method'. Ironically, not long before he began, in a public lecture on 'Radiations from Radium', he spoke of the immense energies involved; as yet nobody knew how to tap this immense source of power, but he hoped that no-one would succeed until man could live at peace with his neighbour . . . These experiments went back before the war, when Ernest Marsden who had played so active a part in the discovery of the nucleus was still with him and was keen to see what could happen when hydrogen was bombarded by alpha particles. Having only a quarter of the weight of the alpha they ought to be thrown forward with some strength. If the nucleus theory was right, when an alpha knocked into a hydrogen, the latter ought to move forward in the same direction with a speed 1.6 times that of the alpha which had hit it; and that should give them a correspondingly longer range. All came up to expectation. Scintillations which could only be due to the hydrogen atoms appeared on the screen up to three or four times the distance to be expected from the alphas, a few of them as far as 90 centimetres from their source. Moreover it looked as if some of the hydrogens were coming from the radioactive source itself, along with the alphas.

Then Marsden went off to New Zealand and subsequently, feeling like Moseley that he must take up the burden with everybody else, he joined up; 'the return of Professor Marsden to Europe on Active Service' states Rutherford, put an end to the investigation. Still, as he told Bohr, he could sometimes take a little time off submarines to look again into the inner recesses of nature, 'as the pressure of routine and war-work permitted'. With the help of a faithful assistant, he took up the hunt for hydrogen atoms. A few weeks after the war ended, Marsden arrived and helped out for a while too. Rutherford was struck by the sheer number of scintillations, far more than he would have expected at these greater distances. Instead of falling off, they continued to appear steadily, and nearly the same amount until about 20 cm, when the number suddenly dropped. This he could only explain if in sufficiently close contact the nuclei cease to act as point charges, minute as they are. These collisions must be almost right up against the centre of the atom. So the velocity, proportion, and dispersal of these particular atoms would tell you something of the actual size and structure of the nucleus itself. Considering how many are the hydrogens atoms through which the alphas pass, as they enter the 'sphere of action', only a tiny fraction perhaps one in a hundred thousand drove the hydrogen nucleus on in this way. It could be calculated that the collision effect only takes place when the two pass within 3/10 000 000 000 000 of a centimetre, which is one tenth of the distance needed to repel an alpha particle from an atom of some heavy metal. Now the dimensions of an electron as then estimated were very slightly greater, so it would follow that nucleus and electron were of comparable volume, though the mass of the one was nearly two thousand times that of the other.

A complex nucleus would have that same thickness, and so be disc-shaped, rather than the spherical shape which Rutherford had once assumed, perhaps as a transfer from age-old cosmological assumptions, supposing that the nucleus occupies the place of the sun in its system, as the sphere is the smallest shape that can contain a given mass in the smallest volume. For helium, for example, the disc would be made up of four hydrogen nuclei and two negative electrons. The organization of nucleus and electrons might well be deformed, and the forces at work change in unexpected ways once you penetrate so deep. When would repulsion be overcome by the attraction of the negative charge? Might it be possible to remove one of the hydrogens from the clasp of whatever forces held it to the other three? That he could not manage, but as his experiments were resumed more persistently in the autumn of 1918, he began to find evidence of something just as exciting. He was tearing away hydrogen atoms from nitrogen! He had calculated that all the lighter elements should show the knock-on effect, up to oxygen and nitrogen. Results confirmed that it was so, for about two centimetres' range. He then went back to Marsden's work on the 'natural'—that is, unprovoked—emission of hydrogen atoms from radium. As you would expect, this was most apparent when the experimental chamber was exhausted, and the number fell off rapidly if oxygen or carbon dioxide was allowed into it. But, if dried air was admitted, the number of glints on the screen actually increased. At one point there were twice as many as in the vacuum. They did look fainter than the ordinary oxygen or nitrogen scintillations. Could there be some residual water vapour? No, for no amount of drying reduced the number appreciably. Or dust? Filtering too did not affect it. If oxygen and the rarer gases were eliminated, nitrogen must be the guilty party. And indeed, pure nitrogen carefully dried produced even more glints, but feeble ones like those from hydrogen. There was, he believed, only one conclusion; these were the impacts of hydrogen atoms, coming out of nitrogen. A very few of his alphas must have literally torn a piece out of the nitrogen nucleus . . . 'Under the intense forces developed in a close collision with a swift alpha particle', it had been disrupted and one of its components shot off by itself. So he had achieved artificially something comparable with what happened in radioactivity, only with a light element instead of a heavy one. He had transmuted a handful of atoms of one element into the next down the scale, and turned them into isotopes of carbon. The old dream of the alchemists was fulfilled at last. But Rutherford, who often amused himself by talk of the New Alchemy, can hardly have imagined just how far old fantasies of a somewhat different sort would be made real by following this trail. He supposed that no such fragments were cast out of oxygen atoms, in that all elements were combinations of four basic atoms—and so presumably made up of alphas—plus singles. Oxygen on this theory would consist of four alphas, which it would be impossible to prise apart. Nitrogen would be made up of three alphas, and two single units. As there was no double unit, of mass 2, nitrogen might have two hydrogen nuclei, one of which could be detached. By the spring Rutherford had reached a satisfactory state in these enquiries; he sent up a set of four short papers to the Philosophical Magazine in April.

The previous month he was invited to take over the Cavendish from J.J. Thomson, who had been raised to the eminence of Master of Trinity in

February 1918. Originally Thomson hoped that he would keep control of his lab and of research there, when he resigned the Cavendish Professorship which he had held for so long, since the Mastership ought not to take up too much of his time, less probably than his wartime posts. The Mastership of Trinity is, at least in the eyes of the numerous tribe of Trinity men, the loftiest peak of academic wisdom; and it does allow the incumbent to feel that he is governing something. So he retired from his chair—but persuaded the university to create a new one, to which he was duly appointed. Everybody was keen to have Rutherford for the principal chair. But he had his doubts, for he sensed the likelihood of trouble with two professors of physics under one roof, especially when one of them was the old master. Would there be room in the buildings for two independent departments, or money enough? Would the new director have the power to place research students, or alter the organization of teaching or administration? 'No advantages', he wrote to Thomson, '. . . could compensate for any disturbance in cur long continued friendship, or for any possible friction'. Thomson saw the point: he agreed that Rutherford should be absolute master in his own lab. In the event, although Rutherford reassured him that any students who wished to work in Thomson's special fields would be turned over to him, few did so, except in the early years, when as Rutherford remarked, 'he is as keen as a youngster still, and is still searching for a "*bahnbrechende*". scientific event'. In Strutt's words, sooner or later it was inevitable that most of the new generation 'should elect to worship the rising sun—and the rising sun could not well help it'.

Some people at Manchester tried to play on his fears so as to retain the university's brightest star—naturally enough—and hinted that Rutherford would never have quite the independence and authority he was enjoying at Manchester, where he had won an international reputation for a young provincial school. Torn between these doubts, and the expectations promised by the Cavendish post, he could not make up his mind to apply until the very day of the election, and had to do so by telegram. So in the end Rutherford came back to Cambridge—a Cambridge to which he could attract some of his brightest Manchester planets, such as Darwin and Chadwick, besides men from the pre-war Cavendish team like Aston, and Laurence Bragg. He began by going over some of the work he had just finished, and looked again at the short range particles, supposedly atoms of nitrogen and oxygen driven forward when struck by alpha particles. It was curious that they should have the same range whether from oxygen or nitrogen. Since the oxygens are heavier they ought not to go so far. An American correspondent suggested they might be simply alpha particles themselves, perhaps forced out of the nuclei of nitrogen just like his hydrogen nuclei. At least, it was worth checking whether they too might not be 'fragments of disintegrated atoms'. A good way of finding out would be to note their deflection in a magnetic field, as they should be harder to deflect than alpha particles by a calculable amount. They could

Fig. 21. Bohrs and Rutherfords at Cambridge.

indeed be bent *much more*—about 20 per cent more—so, far from being oxygen atoms, they must be something lighter than alphas. On the other hand they could not be hydrogen nuclei, for then they ought to have a range about three times as long as the 9 cm he had observed for them. So they must have mass 3, and given the observed mass:charge ratio, two units of charge. Now there was another constituent of the atom.

On 3 June 1920 Rutherford was due to deliver a Bakerian lecture to the Royal Society, aimed not just at fellow fundamental physicists, but at a wider scientific audience. Much of it he devoted to talking about his first year's work at Cambridge. Toward the close, however, he dwelt on the implications of this research for his views on the structure of the nucleus, now the centre of his target. Might it not be possible to construct nuclei only from hydrogen clusters in units of mass 1, mass 3, and mass 4? The work of Aston, separating and measuring the various isotopes, had finally removed those decimal fractions which had plagued atomic theory since poor Prout was defeated by them. Or not quite—for there were still discrepancies. But now Einstein's $E=mc^2$ came to the rescue: the energy devoted to keeping the nucleus together involves a minuscule but measurable deficiency in mass—the whole is slightly—ever so slightly—less than the sum of its parts (which does not mean that the mass somehow turns into energy within the nucleus). But it does mean there is energy locked up there, so that exact values for the amount of this deficiency, compared with the amount that would be expected from simply totting up all the available protons and neutrons, allow you to calculate a value for the energy. Mass 1 was simply the hydrogen nucleus: but that is a long-winded phrase, and although he was still using it before the Royal Society, in September he proposed to the Physics section of the British Association that they use the term *proton*, the first, because it is the primary component of everything else—and happily puns on Prout's name. For mass 3 he used the expression X3, which Thomson had employed for his gas of mass 3. And mass 4 is our old friend, and Rutherford's faithful servant, the alpha particle. The 3s and 4s would then be stable, and would combine to form all elements heavier than helium. But how would they combine? Obviously, negative electrons could tie the positive constituents together, and would in any case be needed to produce the divergences between atomic weight and atomic number, and to explain isotopes. There must be some electrons in the nucleus too, so as to provide the beta rays. In that case, a single electron could bind the two components to make up, for example three different kinds of lithium atom, the three possible isotopes Aston had found. You could have two X3s, or two alphas, or one of each; that would add up to six, eight, or seven units of mass, but always four units of positive charge, and one negative electron to bind them, and to be subtracted from the four positive units to give a final charge, and atomic number 3. For the oxygen and nitrogen he had examined, and for carbon, he puts forward by way of illustration a more complex scheme.

The electrons are independent in these systems. But he also thought of another. If one electron binds the new mass 3 atom—could it not bind a mass 2 atom? [That would then be a positive isotope of hydrogen, in fact our deuteron, although that could not be produced until the days of the accelerator.] Or . . . could one combine an electron with one proton—an atom of mass 1 with zero nuclear charge? After all, an ordinary hydrogen atom was composed of one proton and one electron 'attached at a distance'. Why could this electron not combine with its nucleus much more tightly, coming right inside it to form a 'neutral doublet', a curious reflection of Lenard's image of the atom itself. Now such an atom as Rutherford envisaged would be hard to trace as it would have no charge: 'it should be able to pass freely through matter', and it might not be possible to contain it in a sealed vessel at all. But it could also enter easily into the nuclei of other atoms, and be swallowed up by them, or else be split into its two constituents.

At first the search for this neutral doublet seemed a minor matter, perhaps something that could be induced artificially. Rutherford set his students on to it frequently over the next few years, but in vain. In the meantime, it became clearer that if there are such pairs bonded in the tightest of conjugal embraces, they are more likely to be constituents of atomic nuclei than are free-floating electrons. Not until 1932 did Chadwick at last manage to produce some of these 'neutral doublets'. Plainly however, from the casual way in which he introduces the new word 'neutron', for them in his letter to *Nature* on the subject, the idea like the word must have been well known to the *conoscenti*. To him the neutron was not indeed a particle *sui generis*, but a complex particle, a combination. Thus atomic nuclei would consist of protons and neutrons, but the latter were really protons too, masked in a sense by their electron mates. When a beta ray is given off, the mask is thrown off and a new proton is revealed—which is why the loss of a beta *adds* one unit to the charge number. For Rutherford the electron although so much less in mass than the proton was also considerably larger. So perhaps rather than a mask, think of a voluminous but filmy robe cast aside to reveal the naked proton underneath.

Although Chadwick in his paper on 'The existence of a neutron' harks back to this 1920 Bakerian lecture, and says Rutherford there discussed the 'neutron', the word had not been used by Rutherford there. Nor had he suggested, as Chadwick now did, that neutrons with this close combination were normal components of atoms. In the Bakerian lecture, the free electron is usually not bound to any *one* proton but ties the groups of three or four together. Since Chadwick does not mention any other published exposition of 'the neutron hypothesis', as he calls it, if there be more than filial loyalty to his chief involved, that hypothesis (like the nucleus at Manchester) must have become commonplace at the Cavendish before anyone thought—or dared— to publish.

Rutherford's move to Cambridge and his Bakerian lecture mark the end of a stage, and not only in his own life. The research on the 'disintegration' of oxygen and nitrogen was the last in which he took such an active part. Even in the earlier phases of that undertaking he complained to Bohr that 'counting weak scintillations is hard on old eyes' (he was in fact forty-seven). This sense of the difficulty and wearisomeness of his task is echoed even in the published papers, whose stately progress is interrupted by his mournful comments: the strain on his eyes, the physical effort of peering down a microscope in a darkened room at glints on a little screen, so that will-power alone will not help, for after a while results become unreliable, 'It is not desirable to count for more than 1 hour per day, and preferably only a few times per week'. Thereafter he became more and more the tribal headman, less the warrior in the forefront of the struggle. The age of the big team was upon them: and also, not very much to Rutherford's liking, the age of the big machine—the expensive apparatus, which his young men kept pressing on him, for all his grumbles that 'there is no money for apparatus—we shall have to use our heads'. Thomson settled down to spend a quarter of a century of Masterhood—in appearance, manner and views, the quintessential Cambridge Don. In 1920 Bohr's government, helped by the Carlsberg Foundation, set him up in a brand-new Institute of Theoretical Physics at Copenhagen. Now he became the leader of a team in his turn.

Few of those who had already been recognised as leading scientists in the Edwardian decade stayed at the research frontier after the war. They were now in command themselves, the cause of great discoveries in others, not discoverers any more themselves. Not all of them were happy with their new situation. Of the outstanding radiochemists, Boltwood was put in charge of an enlarged chemical laboratory at Yale. The strain of the infighting which developed, brought on bouts of acute depression and breakdown, which led him to kill himself in August 1927. Soddy too moved to a chair at an ancient university—to become Professor of Chemistry at Oxford. It must be said that his record was less successful than Rutherford's. He found himself fighting too many battles over the reorganization of his laboratories; he became embittered, and those who recall his teaching found he had somehow lost the eloquence that breathes through the pages of *The interpretation of radium*. Increasingly he turned away from science to the creation of a society which should make better use of the knowledge already won. The fate of the two leading experimental physicists of Germany was much worse. Stark failed to obtain any of the scientific chairs to which he thought himself entitled. His quarrels with every faculty and scientific society to which he ever belonged grew so sharp that he gave up the lot and went into the porcelain business; and only returned to science administration in 1933, hanging on Adolf Hitler's coat-tails. Philipp Lenard sank even lower into the quagmire of racial-nationalist politics—in 1922, he was nearly lynched for refusing, in the most insulting terms, to cancel his lectures for the day of mourning in honour of the murdered Foreign Minister of the German Republic, Walther Rathenau. He too came into his own when the Nazis were in power. Planck's story is an honourable contrast. He had suffered painfully during the war, for apart from the loss of his younger son, killed in action in 1916, Planck's two daughters both perished in the aftermath, not long after their brother. Although Planck did not retire from his professorial chair until 1926, he sought the consolations of philosophy and religion in terrible times; his writings during the last third of his life were less concerned with the further advance of physics, more with its reconciliation with his deeply spiritual outlook.

The infancy of atomic physics had ended. Its lusty youth was about to begin. The twenties were dominated by the problem that Rutherford in his

Bakerian lecture said he would leave aside: 'the arrangement and modes of vibration of the external electrons'—that 'modes of vibration' already had an old-fashioned sound to it. X-ray spectroscopy looked at the inner electrons, physical chemistry at the outer. Both agreed that the flat ring atom, which had been put forward only as a provisional convenience until something better could be worked out, must now be replaced by a three-dimensional model. Early in the decade Sommerfeld and his colleagues were cracking jokes about the end of the pancake atom.

Not rings then, but shells. It was not just a question of disposition, but of the very nature of the electrons, as they proved to have the properties of wave as well as particle; a whole new mechanics, a quantum physics had to be elaborated to account for them, while the principles of Complementarity, Indeterminacy, and the Exclusion Principle provided the theoretical foundations for this fantastical new science where the electron ceased to be a blob of matter travelling at a velocity that could be established around an orbit that could be established, and possessing therefore at any instant a position that could be established: this electron was replaced by the uncatchable wave/particle—'a smear of probability'.

After the 1920s had decided 'What is an electron'—in so far as it could be decided—with the 1930s, enquiry shifted again in Rutherford's direction, toward the constitution of the nucleus. That too was a heroic age, which began when Chadwick revealed the neutron. Bohr within weeks proposed a new model for the nucleus, at first a little like his atom, a bold imaginative hypothesis full of loose ends that needed tieing. Then the neutron began to be used instead of alpha particle or proton as a missile. Within a few years bombardment was making relatively light atoms radioactive, continuing to discharge rays for some time after the bombardment had stopped. Speaking in London on his 'Liquid drop' model of a nucleus, Bohr declared that although neutron collisions might lead eventually to 'explosions of the whole nucleus', that was still far away, and anyway would bring the exploitation of nuclear energies no nearer: 'Indeed, the more our knowledge of nuclear reactions advances, the remoter this goal seems to be.' Similar remarks made by other physicists, Rutherford among them, through the early thirties are often quoted to show the innocence or the blindness of scientists, and maybe also their distrust of the technological misuse of their discoveries. But remember that since the early days, many were aware of the immense reservoirs of power in the atom, at first perhaps especially in atoms of radium, eventually in the atomic nucleus as such. Yet all these transmutations, radioactivity natural or artificial, involve only very small portions of the nucleus, the loss of one proton or two. Even when Rutherford speaks of the 'disintegration' of the nucleus of nitrogen, almost all is left behind. In any case, so much energy is needed, and so few transformations take place out of the total number of atoms in the space through which the missile particles pass. The use of neutrons reduced the amount of energy needed, but at first did not alter the fact that only one or two particles were chipped off the victim at each encounter.

Then in the summer of 1938 Otto Hahn (the discoverer of mesothorium thirty years before), and Strassmann, his colleague at Berlin, noticed some mysterious barium, after they had tried to turn uranium to radium by means of radioactivity artificially excited by neutrons. How barium—whose atomic weight and number is not much over half that of uranium? A few months later, Hahn's friend Otto Frisch saw what had happened: some of the nuclei of the uranium had been split asunder—the neutrons had caused them to break up, like cells dividing—a kind of nuclear fission . . .

NOTE

1. Kevles, D.J. Into hostile political camps: the reorganization of international science in World War I. *Isis* **LXII** (1971).

BIBLIOGRAPHY

AHES *Archive for History of Exact Sciences*
HSPS *Historical Studies in the Physical Sciences*
PM *The Philosophical Magazine*
PRS *Proceedings of the Royal Society of London*

BIOGRAPHY

The biographies of modern scientists tend to be written by former students—inevitably, admiration is the keynote, and psychologically they are rather superficial. Often we have mainly the transactions of commemorative meetings, whose purpose is not to bury their subject, but to praise him. The older style of biography did include generous quotations from personal correspondence, which made up for a stiffness in the biographer—but even that is uncommon nowadays.

E.E. Fournier d'Albe, *The life of Sir William Crookes*. Fisher Unwin, London (1923).
  Plenty of letters, and long extracts from Crookes's purpler passages.
Lord Rayleigh, *Sir J. J. Thomson*, Cambridge University Press (1942).
  Very much the official biography.
G.P. Thomson, *Sir J. J. Thomson and the Cavendish Laboratory*. Nelson London (1964).
  Straightforward and lucid—a little too straightforward, for the son of his subject, whom one might expect to have childhood memories of so many great men.
M.J. Nye, *Molecular reality*. Macdonald, London (1972).
  A study of the life and work of Perrin
E. Curie, *Madame Curie*. (English translation Heinemann, London 1938)
R. Reid, *Marie Curie*. Collins, London (1974).
G.M. Caroe, *William Henry Bragg 1862-1942 man and scientist*. Cambridge University Press (1978).
  Very readable in a somewhat old-fashioned style. By Bragg's daughter. Perhaps daughters write more percipient biographies, than sons, for she presents a far more rounded and sensitive picture than appears in the biographies of Thomson and the elder Rayleigh, by their sons.
A.S. Eve, *Rutherford*. Cambridge University Press (1939).
  Another official biography—but also plenty of letters. Eve had the advan-

tage over later biographers, that he had known Rutherford at Montreal, during his most brilliant period.

N. Feather, *Lord Rutherford*. Blackie, Glasgow (1940).

E.N. da C. Andrade, *Rutherford and the nature of the atom*. Heinemann, London (1964).

Only M. Oliphant, *Rutherford, Recollections of the Cambridge Days* Elsevier, London (1972), gets under the skin of the relationship between the young scientist and the old; and he, of course, deals with a later period than this book.

J.B. Birks (ed.), *Rutherford at Manchester*. Heywood, London (1962).

Many interesting reminiscences—but very much the commemorative volume.

L. Badash, *Rutherford and Boltwood, letters on radioactivity*. Yale University Press, New Haven Conn. (1969).

A full edition, with invaluable commentary on one of Rutherford's most interesting exchanges of correspondence.

G. de Haas-Lorentz, *H. A. Lorentz. Impressions of his life and work*. North Holland Publ. Co. Amsterdam (1957).

M.K. Howorth, *Pioneer Research on the Atom ... the life story of Frederick Soddy*. New World, London (1958).

Enthusiastic, to the point of hagiography.

P. Frank, *Einstein his life and times*. Cape, London (1948).

B. Hoffman, *Albert Einstein*. Hart Davis, McGibbon (1973).

Can best stand for the vast library of Einsteiniana.

R. Moore, *Niels Bohr, the man and the scientist*. Hodder and Stoughton, London (1967).

S. Rozental (ed.), *Niels Bohr, his life and work as seen by his friends and his colleagues*. North Holland Publ. Co. Amsterdam (1967).

B. Jaffe, *Moseley and the numbering of the Elements*. Heinemann, London (1972).

J.L. Heilbron, *H.G.J. Moseley, the life and letters of an English physicist*. University of California Press, Berkeley, Calif. (1974).

With complete correspondence.

Some of the scientists have written autobiography:

A. Schuster, *Biographical fragments*. Macmillan, London (1932).

Unfortunately, although he gives some intriguing sidelights on the great men of his youth, the fragments do not really reach our period.

J.J. Thomson, *Recollections and reflections*. G. Bell & Sons, London (1936).

Very Cambridge-y (i.e. full of College anecdotes) but very readable.

Or more briefly:

N. Bohr, Reminiscences of the Founder of Nuclear Science. *Proceedings of the Physical Society* **78** (1961).
  About his relations with Rutherford.
C.T.R. Wilson, Reminiscences of my early years. *Notes & Records of the Royal Society* **14** (1960)

German scientists have been in the practice of issuing 'scientific autobiographies'—from which anything too personal or irrational is severely excluded (although the odd academic joke might be permitted).

M. Planck, *Scientific autobiography*. (English translation Williams & Norgate, London 1950).
O. Hahn, *A scientific autobiography*. (English translation McGibbon & Kee, London 1967).
P.P. Ewald, *Fifty years of X-ray diffraction*. N.V.A. Oosthoek's Uitgeversmaatschappij, Utrecht (1962).
  Includes 'scientific autobiographies' of Max von Laue and Sir William Bragg.

Some figures on the periphery help to fill in the background:

H.E. Roscoe, *The life and experiences of Sir Henry Enfield Roscoe ... written by himself*. Macmillan, London (1906).
A.A. Campbell Swinton, *Autobiographical and other writings*. Longmans, London (1930).
L.L. Whyte, *Focus and diversions*. Cresset Press, London (1963).
G. Raverat, *Period Piece*. Faber & Faber, London (1952).
  In a fascinating evocation of a Cambridge childhood at the turn of the century, recalls what her father George Darwin, and her brother Charles Galton Darwin, were like at home. Curiously, her book is not cited in either of the articles on them in the *Dictionary of Scientific Biography*. They play a relatively minor role in our story—would that we had anything like that on some of the major personalities!

That apart, the *Dictionary of Scientific Biography* (Charles Scribner's Sons, New York 1970–80) has certainly revolutionized our understanding of scientific persons—as persons: I have frequently consulted it, especially for the numerous minor characters. For Fellows of the Royal Society, however, their obituaries published as *Obituary Notes*, and from 1955 onwards as *Biographical Memoirs*, remain prime sources. But they *are* obituaries.

Surveys of contemporary scientific advance, in chronological order:

J.J. Thomson, *Notes on recent researches in electricity and magnetism*. Clarendon Press, Oxford (1893).
W.C.D. Whetham, *The recent development of physical science*. Murray, London (1904).

E.E. Fournier d'Albe, *The electron theory*. Longmans Green, London (1906).

A. Schuster, *The progress of physics 1875–1908*. Cambridge University Press, (1911).

J. Cox, *Beyond the Atom*. Cambridge University Press (1913).

G.W.C. Kaye, *X-Rays*, Longmans Green, London (1914)

Further sources:

Several key papers are reprinted—or at least excerpted—in G.K.T. Conn and H.D. Turner, *The Evolution of the nuclear atom*. Iliffe, London (1965).

Bohr's collected works and letters are in the process of publication by North-Holland (Amsterdam) under the general editorship of L. Rosenfeld. Vol. 1, edited by J.R. Nielson, (1972) was particularly used in the composition of this book.

All Rutherford's papers have appeared in *The collected papers of Lord Rutherford of Nelson*, under the scientific direction of Sir James Chadwick, in 3 vols. Allen and Unwin, London (1962–5).

Other major sources are his book, *Radioactivity* Cambridge University Press (1904) and

J.J. Thomson, *Electricity and Matter*. Constable, London (1904).

J.J. Thomson *The Corpuscular theory of matter*. Constable, London (1907).

F. Soddy, *The Interpretation of radium*. Murray, London (1909).

F. Soddy, *Radioactivity and atomic theory* (ed. T.J. Trenn). Taylor & Francis, London (1975).

Modern Historical Studies:

D. Anderson, *The discovery of the electron*. Van Nostrand, Princeton, N.J. (1964).

M. Bunge and W.E. Shea, (eds.) *Rutherford and physics at the turn of the century*. W. Dawson, Folkestone (1977).

B. Dibner, *The New Rays of Professor Röntgen*. Burndy Library, Norwalk, Conn. (1963).

R. Harré (ed.) *Scientific thought 1900–1960*. Clarendon Press, Oxford (1969). The article on atomic physics was written by G. P. Thomson.

A. Herrmann, *The genesis of quantum theory* (*1899–1913*). (English translation MIT Press, Cambridge, Mass. 1971.)

B. Hoffmann, *The strange story of the quantum*. Harper, New York (1947).

A. Romer, *The restless atom*. Heinemann, London (1961).

T.J. Trenn, *The Self-splitting atom*. Taylor and Francis, London (1977).

Articles:

E.N. da C. Andrade, The birth of the nuclear atom. *PRS* **244A** (1956).

L. Badash, Becquerel's 'unexposed' photographic plates. *Isis* **57** (1966).

P. Forman, J. L. Heilbron, and S. Weart, Physics circa 1900: personnel, funding and productivity of the academic establishments. *HSPS* **5** (1975).

J.L. Heilbron, The Kossel–Sommerfeld theory and the ring atom, *Isis* **58** (1967).

J.L. Heilbron, The scattering of α and β particles and Rutherford's atom. *AHES* **4** (1967–8).

J.L. Heilbron and T.S. Kuhn, The genesis of the Bohr atom. *HSPS* **1** (1969).

P.M. Heimann, Moseley's interpretation of X-ray spectra. *Centaurus* **12** (1968).

R.K. de Kosky, William Crookes and the fourth state of matter. *Isis* **67** (1976).

M.J. Klein, Max Planck and the beginnings of the quantum theory. *AHES* **1** (1960–2).

R. MacCormmach, The atomic theory of John William Nicholson. *AHES* **3** (1966–7).

R. Mac Cormmach, H.A. Lorentz and the electromagnetic view of nature. *Isis* **61** (1970).

R. Mac Cormmach, J. J. Thomson and the structure of light. *British Journal for the History of Science* **3** (1967).

R. MacCormmach, Einstein, Lorentz and the electron theory. *HSPS* **2** (1970).

J.G. O'Hara, George Johnstone Stoney and the concept of the electron. *Notes and Records of the Royal Society* **29** (1975).

R. Sviedrys, The rise of physical science at Victorian cambridge. *HSPS* **2** (1970).

R. Sviedrys, The rise of physics laboratories in Britain. *HSPS* **7** (1976).

N. Schuster, Early days of Röntgen photography in Britain. *British Medical Journal* **11** (1962).

D.R. Topper, Commitment to mechanism: J.J. Thomson, the early years. *AHES* **7** (1970–1).

T.J. Trenn, The Geiger–Marsden results and Rutherford's atom, July 1912 to July 1913, the Shifting Significance of Scientific Evidence. *Isis* **65** (1974).

T.J. Trenn, Rutherford on the alpha-beta-gamma classifications of Radioactive rays. *Isis* **67** (1976).

T.J. Trenn, Rutherford and Soddy: from a search for radioactive constituents to the disintegration theory of radioactivity. *Rete* **1** (1971).

B.R. Wheaton, Philipp Lenard and the photoelectric effect, 1881–1911, *HSPS* **9** (1978).

E. Yagi, On Nagaoka's Saturnian atomic model. *Japanese Studies in the history of science* **3** (1964).

INDEX